Douglas Somerset
9th September 2004

HISTORY OF NAIRNSHIRE

HISTORY
OF
NAIRNSHIRE

BY

GEORGE BAIN, F.S.A. SCOT.

SECOND EDITION

NAIRN
"TELEGRAPH" OFFICE, 10 LEOPOLD STREET
MCMXXVIII

Facsimile edition published in 1996 by
The Nairnshire Telegraph Ltd,
10 Leopold St, Nairn.

First published in 1896

Second edition published in 1928

ISBN 0 9501714 1 7

Printed and bound by Cromwell Press Limited

PREFACE

Although Nairnshire is one of the smaller counties of Scotland, it is in many respects a most interesting part of the country. Its prehistoric remains have proved a rich field for the antiquarian, whilst the charter-chests of Cawdor, Kilravock, and Brodie have furnished materials which have enriched the history of Scotland. It has been thought that a consecutive narrative of the events which have occurred within the county, with some account of the families and persons more prominently associated with its history, may not be uninteresting to the general reader, whilst it is believed that those who by birth or residence are connected with the county or its ancient royal burgh will welcome a work relating to scenes and places with which they are more or less familiar.

The author has availed himself of the materials stored up in the family papers of the district, and has reproduced from the sheriff court books and burgh records such matters as appeared to be of interest. It was intended to have given some original documents in an appendix, but the length to which the work has extended has precluded this being done, beyond a list of the provosts of Nairn.

To the custodiers of the official records and to the gentlemen who gave him access to their books and papers, the author tenders his grateful thanks.

Nairn, *July*, 1893.

PREFACE TO SECOND EDITION

THIS new edition of the History of Nairnshire has been brought out to meet a wide public demand, the original edition having been out of print for some considerable time, and frequently asked for.

Since the first edition was published in 1893 many changes have taken place, and another generation of actors in the affairs of the county has come upon the scene. It was Mr. Bain's intention to embody these changes in a new edition of his History, and for some time before his death part of his leisure was spent in editing and bringing the work up to date. The undertaking, however, had not been finished when he died during a holiday at Newtonmore in June 1926, and it has been left to other hands to complete the task. Naturally the additions and emendations are not so full as they would have been had the author lived to finish the History himself, but the salient facts have received attention, the family histories and other progressive matters have been extended, and a chapter has been added on recent outstanding events. No attempt has been made to alter the original character of the work by " documenting " it, or otherwise. For the contemporary history of the county the author was himself the best authority; for earlier periods he has quoted his sources of information in the preface and with sufficient frequency in the text. Many of the facts—some of those connected with the Culbin Sands and Clava cairns and circles, for instance—were his own discoveries, printed for the first time; and for the details of family history he had the use of family papers and first-hand help from the representatives of the families themselves.

The " History of Nairnshire " is only one of the many services rendered to the community by its author. During all his long life Mr. Bain's whole interest was centred in Nairn, its existing institutions, and its historical associations. To his zeal and effort the town and county owe more of their present amenities and repute than they are ever likely to realize. Men and women find their pleasure in many ways. George Bain found his in his historical and antiquarian studies. For half a century he was recognised as the chief authority on all matters pertaining to the history of Nairnshire and of Nairn. Few noted personages visited Nairn without becoming indebted to the editor of " The Nairnshire Telegraph " for information regarding the district and an introduction at first hand to its interests, and he was in constant request in helping American citizens to trace their family connection with the county. No one could tell a tale of the olden days more effectively, as may be seen in his charming account of a Nairn lady of the ancient regime printed as a brochure with the title " The Last of her Race." Among countless other local services he was one of the founders of Nairn Literary Institute, and he was a Fellow of the Society of Antiquaries of Scotland. It has often, indeed, been a matter of marvel that his achievements as an antiquarian and historian were never recognised by any of the Scottish universities.

Among Mr. Bain's other literary works of permanent value, perhaps the most notable is his volume on " The River Findhorn," published in 1911, which enjoys a wide circulation, and is likely to remain a standard in its own field of literature. It was his intention to produce a companion volume on " The River Nairn," which certainly could not have failed to prove of equal value and interest.

In his personal character George Bain had the saving virtues of modesty and humour, and a fine appreciation of " the tender grace of a day that is dead," combined with an unselfish instinct to help the public good of his own day and generation.

GEORGE EYRE-TODD.

PREFACE TO THE FACSIMILE EDITION

(1996)

The second edition of the History of Nairnshire has, with time, become the standard reference work on the patch of northern Scotland that is Nairnshire. It has long since sold out and for many years second hand copies have been eagerly sought. A frequent request made to the Nairnshire Telegraph office has been for re-publication either in revised or facsimile form.

The former option has been under consideration by the publishers for some time, but in view of the continuing demand for the History of Nairnshire in its present form and the considerable task presented by a full revision of the work, it was decided to meet that demand in some way by producing this facsimile edition.

IAIN A. BAIN,
COLIN BAIN,
ALASTAIR I. R. BAIN.

CONTENTS

HISTORY OF NAIRNSHIRE

CHAPTER I

PREHISTORIC REMAINS

ABOUT three miles south of the town of Nairn, a round-shaped hill rises to the height of some 600 feet and occupies an area of several square miles. It is known as the Hill of the Ord (" Ord " in Gaelic meaning the " Round Height.") At its northerly base there is a platform of granite, but the hill itself consists mainly of a mass of gneiss, the surface of which is very much broken, while the ground is strewn with fragments of rocks and travelled boulders. Its aspect is softened to some extent by the thick firwood that crowns its heights, but it still presents conditions typical of a favourite haunt for wild animals, in its numerous rocky retreats and grassy ravines. Near the foot of one of its easterly slopes lies the small farm of Slagachorrie—a Gaelic name meaning " Hollow of the Corrie," which very accurately describes its situation. Many relics of prehistoric times have been found there. Stone axes and manufactured flints have been picked up in considerable number. Some of the axes are finely shaped and beautifully polished, and the flints, in the form of arrow-heads, saws, and scrapers, exhibit a very high degree of finish. One of these flints, now in the Nairn Museum, has a finely serrated edge of thirty teeth in the space of one inch. It is sliced on the back to enable the worker to hold it firmly between the thumb and forefinger. A hollow in the neighbourhood is known as the " Flint Pit," from the number of flint chips taken out of it. The ground in which it occurs is now planted, but it used to be a common for the adjacent properties. Until recently, remains of small cairns and circles formed of gneiss and conglomerate blocks studded the fields, and one boulder on the slope retains the name of " The Cromlech." The evidence unmistakably points to the spot having been a hunter's settlement at a time when men cut down the trees with stone axes, tipped their arrows with sharpened flints, and dressed their articles of common use with flint tools.

Slagachorrie is but an illustrative example of settlements common to the district in early times. The dwellers in the district who used stone implements were not confined to this particular spot, but roamed over hill and dale, settling on the rising ground, and leaving behind them traces of their presence in the shape of these celts and arrow-heads on almost every field and hillside. Unfortunately no collection worthy of the name has been made of these relics of the Stone Period in the district, but the specimens preserved show a considerable variety in their colour and form. One arrow-head found at Broomhill, Cawdor, is of pure white cherty rock, whilst examples have been found of almost jet black flint. A vast number —many thousands—of chipped flints in various forms have been found at the Culbin Sands, a region on the seaboard a few miles beyond the eastern boundary of the county of Nairn. They have been derived mostly from a spot to which the name of " The Armoury " has in consequence been given, and the question has been raised whether the manufactory at that locality supplied the adjacent districts. The Culbin flints have certain prevalent characteristics which render them recognisable as a class, but the specimens found on the lands to the west of that region do not appear to have been derived from that source. Each tribe in each locality probably manufactured its own flint implements. Flint cores found in the district bear the exact outline of an arrow-head on their surface, showing that the flint workers knew how to remove the flint flake from the nodule nearly in the shape required. These flint implements in their manufacture show a considerable amount of skill and taste on the part of the artificers, and in them we have probably the first and earliest examples of handicraft in prehistoric times.

A remarkable feature of the district is the abundance of cairns and stone circles. Many of these interesting memorials have been cleared away by the cultivation of the land, but examples exist, or recently existed, at Moyness, Auldearn, Urchany, Ballinrait, Dalcross, Croy, Clava, Daviot, and the upper reaches of the river Nairn. In the valley of the Nairn some thirty sites of circles are known, and the former existence of many others is preserved in the place-names.

The Moyness stone circle has been dismantled, but it was unique in one respect. One of the boulders of which the circle was composed was said to have been a rocking stone or loggan, and according to traditionary belief was used as an ordeal stone for determining the innocence or guilt of a person accused of crime. If the stone rocked when the person was placed upon it, guilt was established; if it remained unmoved, innocence was declared. Considerable sanctity, as may be supposed, attached to this tell-tale stone, with its mysterious movements, but the school children of later times, with irreverent familiarity, were wont to play upon it. A mason one night took his hammer and struck at the supports underneath, and the stone lost its poise in consequence. It was subsequently broken up. Mr. Stables, at the request of the Secretary of the Society of Antiquaries of Scotland, examined the " rocking stone " in the year 1856, after the circle had been partially dismantled, and he reported that the supposed rocking stone consisted of one of the upright pillars which had fallen over some smaller ones, leaving an end unsupported, and by jumping on this a heavy man could just move it. This prosaic explanation does not, however, accord with the traditions of the countryside. It appears that in 1825 a Mr. Aeneas Falconer, residing at Blackhills, contributed to the Northern Institution, a literary society in Inverness now defunct, an " account of a Stone Coffin, Druidical Circle, and Rocking Stone," but the MS. is not now known to exist. The centre cairn of the Moyness circle, on being opened about the year 1860, was found to contain an urn and ashes, but the pick that disclosed the urn unfortunately smashed it.

The Moyness standing stone is the only one in the district with which any popular beliefs were associated. They stand apart from the traditions and history of the country—a proof probably of their great antiquity.

The solitary pillar of the circle at Ballinrait is said to have served the purpose of a sun dial, just as a tree or post in the same neighbourhood was the clock of the clachan. The other stones of the circle were broken up about the year 1840. It is related that one old man used every morning to walk round the circle three times before beginning work, from the belief that his so doing would bring him good luck. A mound—without, however, any cairn or circle—in the neighbourhood of Clunas, Cawdor, is called " Dundeasil," preserving the memory of the same old custom of going round with the sun. But these are the only instances of these circles having been in any way connected with the ordinary life of the community within the historical period.

The highest development of these structures is attained in the group of chambered cairns and stone circles at Clava on the south bank of the river Nairn, nearly opposite Culloden moor. The river flows softly and sweetly in the valley between its favourite fringes of alders, and a hundred yards to the south, in a piece of uncultivated ground, are these remarkable memorials of remote times. They consist of three very large cairns, the hearts of which have been dug out, having been opened from the top ; also the remains of some smaller cairns ; and a number of standing stones ranged in circles more or less complete—the huge stones standing like gaunt sentinels round the iron-grey cairns.

The western cairn has in its centre the remains of a stone-built chamber of circular form, 12½ feet in diameter—the stones laid vertically for a few feet from the foundation, and then built on the concentric ring in courses inclining inwards ; that is to say, each course projects a little beyond the one below it, and thus, as the building is carried up, it assumes the form of a dome, which when complete must have given the chamber the height of an ordinary sized room, some 10 or 12 feet. The top of the dome is now removed, having been taken down when the cairn was opened in the year 1828. The builders of the chamber, of course, never intended that access should be gained to the interior by the top, for they had provided a regularly-built entrance, from 2 to 3 feet wide and 4 to 5 feet high, from the south-west. This entrance or opening was concealed by the mass of stones heaped over the chamber, and was only disclosed when the top had been demolished. Miss Campbell, of Corsica, residing at the time at Kilravock, who was at the opening of it, states that the explorers found two urns. One was smashed, but the other contained a quantity of burnt bones, and similar ashes were found about it, no doubt the contents of the broken urn. The urns were found exactly in the centre of the chamber, enclosed in a little bed of clay, whilst the remainder of the floor was strewn with gravel. The description of the vase is that of a rude cinerary urn, and there is no reason to doubt the accuracy of the details as noted by Miss Campbell at the time. The urn is figured in Sir Thomas Dick Lauder's " Moray Floods."

The next point of interest is the concentric circle of standing stones round the base of the cairn. These stones are placed close together, and are very much of the same character as the ring foundation of the chamber. The ring itself is 53 feet in diameter. The outer ring is also concentric. It is double the diameter of the intermediate ring, with two feet to spare. The exact measurement is 108 feet. The stones form a circle of twelve pillars, or eleven and a vacant space. They stand apart from each other, nearly, but not quite, at regular intervals. The height of these pillars varies from 6 to 12 feet, the tallest being on the south side, and their size gradually diminishes towards the north. The main points in the structure and form of this western circle are found almost exactly reproduced in the third or eastern circle. There is no authentic account of the opening of this third cairn—this took place somewhere about the year 1850—but it is said to have contained " a few bones "—the mere mention of that circumstance affording a presumption that the contents were similar to those of the western circle. The middle circle differs in some points from the other two. The chamber is larger, being 22 feet in diameter, but its interior is in so much disorder from the falling-in of the stones that it is difficult to arrive at any certainty as to its structure —whether it was built similarly to or differently from the others. Mr. James Fraser, C.E., who took measurements, found that its separate rings were not true concentrics; it appeared to him that the builders had slightly lost the true centre in the course of the construction. The most remarkable feature is three causeways of small stones, 7 feet in width, which lead from the pillars in the outer ring to the stones of the intermediate ring which goes round the base of the cairn. One of these points to E. 10 deg. S., another to S. 10. deg. E., and the third to W. 25 deg. N.

From these details some conclusions may be arrived at in regard to the purpose of the cairns.

In the first place, there is evidence of the burning of the bodies —proof of the practice of cremation. In the second place, there is clear evidence that the people who built these cairns were no rude barbarians. They had, it is apparent, some knowledge of the potter's art, as is shown in the manufacture of the urn. They had acquired some little skill in masonry, and could design and execute a vaulted chamber and dome roof. The concentric circle was familiar to them. Further, they were capable of taking accurate measurements—if not to mathematical exactitude, at least to remarkable precision. They knew something of the cardinal points of astronomy or of direction, as is shown by the similarity of the two built entrances and the position of the taller pillars in the outer row.

Why was there the expenditure of all this skill, labour, and knowledge ? Unquestionably, all was done in honour of the ashes enclosed in the heart of the cairn—the remains enshrined in the urn, like something very precious in a costly casket. Dr. Joseph Anderson, from this point of view, aptly describes the circles of pillars as stone-settings to the cairns. The evidence considered in detail, and the design of the structure viewed as a whole, lead to the conclusion that we have embodied here the one great idea of reverence for, and exaltation of, the dead, passing, it may be, into its higher phase of ancestral worship. These are the tombs of " the mighty dead of a past age "—the burial-places of their kings or chiefs.

But whilst burial and a species of ancestral or hero-worship was the main purpose of these circles, that statement of their primary use does not exhaust their interest or significance. It has been noticed that they are circular in form. The circle or ring has, among ancient peoples, been regarded as a sacred symbol—sometimes as an emblem of the Deity, a symbol of eternity, a sign of completeness and of unity, and a figure of the Sun, the great Ruler of Nature. It as truly and distinctively marks the pre-Christian period in any country as the cross does the Christian era.

Here we have the whole structure pervaded by the ring principle—not one ring only, but a series of rings, one of these not a mechanical ring but an ideal ring, and all of them as nearly as may be concentric circles, that is, having a common centre. It is impossible to overlook this fact in the examination of these remains, and the inference may be drawn from it that the circular form was intended to embody and express some definite idea. The intermediate ring of stones might doubtless have served to keep the stones of the cairn together, just as a row of stones placed around an earth mound keeps the soil from being scattered. But it is quite clear that the outer row of pillars, standing some distance apart, could answer no such purpose.

The whole controversy, indeed, is practically narrowed to the question, " What mean these outer standing stones ? " The description of them as the " stone-settings of the cairns " is appropriate enough in one sense, but it does not cover the whole ground. Are they to be regarded as purely ornamental, like ordinary settings ? It has been suggested that they may have served the further purpose of marking the boundary of the burial ground. But if that object had been all that was in view, the end could have been accomplished by simpler means.

There is one feature which none of these theories explains. In these three circles and in every similar circle in the district the tallest pillars are placed to the south, the range diminishing in height towards the north, where the pillars are smallest. They are put there clearly of design, and at the expenditure of much labour and care. And they never could have been placed at the different sites in such a position without some observation and knowledge of the sun's course. It must have been necessary for the men who set up these huge stones to watch and note the sun's shadow most carefully ere they could determine their position. These tall pillars do not, it is true, point due south in all the circles scattered over the district. They often vary several degrees east or west from the true point. But the amount of variation is so trifling as compared with the extent of their accuracy, that, if for no other reason, it may be due to the comparative defect of the builders' observations and not to a want of intention, which certainly appears to have been to have these tall stones pointing in a *southerly* direction. This being the case, another fact is ascertained—that, in placing these large stones to the south, the builders intended some reference to the sun's course.

The question arises—Had the other stones of the ring a similar reference to the sun's course ? Unfortunately, several of the pillars in each of the three circles are awanting, and it is doubtful whether some of those remaining are standing in their original position, while others are plainly out of position in the ring. Still, if it could be shown in any one instance that they were set up on such a principle as indicated, it may safely be concluded, from their similarity of feature, that the same idea dominated the whole group, either actively or conventionally.

Now an examination of the outer circle of the middle cairn has brought out some remarkable results. Some six or seven out of the nine stones are apparently in their original positions, and the diagram prepared by Mr. Fraser tested in this connection gives the following results :

1. The Southern Causeway.—The stone at this point marks noon each day, subject of course to ordinary equation of time. The true line strikes on the inner edge of the causeway, cutting the exact centre of the cairn, and the arc between the stone A and the causeway exactly measures the sun's variation.

2. The point E (stone restored) is as near as may be to the first point of Aries—the point at which the sun departs from the Equator towards the North, and which we call the Spring Equinox.

3. The Eastern Causeway marks the sun's entrance into Libra on 21st September.

4. A point midway between stones A and B would mark the south limit of the setting sun on December 21, the shortest day of the year, or winter solstice. There is no stone at this point, but, as the ring was evidently composed of ten or twelve stones, and only nine are shown, it may have been one of those removed. This is supported by the circumstance that stone D stands almost opposite the point where it would have stood if so placed.

5. The stone standing between G and F gives the bearing of the sun as it rises on 22nd September.

6. The Western Causeway gives the bearing of the sun as it sets on 21st April and 21st August. As these dates do not correspond to any change in the sun's course, it is probable they may stand for some division of the seasons.

These are precisely the facts which could, by mere observation of the sun's shadow alone, be observed and recorded, and it is almost beyond belief that these stones could have been set up in that order by mere accident, giving, as they do, noon time, the solstices, and the equinoxes.

The several conclusions arrived at from an examination of the Clava circles are (1) that these cairns and circles were primarily intended for, and used as, sepulchres, and were raised in honour of men of rank; (2) that, by their form they were intended to express some religious idea, probably of homage to the sun; (3) that the outer ring probably served the purpose of a sun-circle.

The next question is, " Who built them ? " They are evidently of great antiquity. There is no mark of hammer or chisel on the stones, and no particle of iron has been found connected with them. The bronze articles and the character of the pottery associated with similar structures over the country, and also the form of burial, have led to the conclusion that they belong to the Bronze Age—that is, *before* iron came into use and *after* stone implements ceased to be exclusively used.

The Clava cairns and circles have now been taken over by the Government Department concerned with the Preservation of Ancient Monuments in Scotland and are to be put into a condition favourable for further examination.

In the Kinsteary parks, at Auldearn, are several gravel ridges or kames, in which from time to time cist graves have been found. So numerous are the burial remains that the old workmen about the place when requiring gravel for the walks are said to avoid taking it from certain of the ridges, from their knowledge that they would come upon and disturb these interments, of which they have a superstitious dread. These graves were formed of three slabs, and almost invariably an urn was found at one end of the bed. In one cist opened in the year 1888, a very finely ornamented urn or vase (now at Cluny Castle) was discovered, and along with it a necklace of glass beads, or " bugles " as they are locally called from their tubular shape. The custom of burying grave goods, such as ornaments, weapons, and implements, marks off all such graves as belonging to prehistoric or pagan times.

A cairn with a " pointer " exists at Kinsteary. It was opened in the year 1894 by some members of the Nairn Literary Institute, who pierced it to the centre, but found nothing of a noteworthy character. It appeared to them that it had been opened before, but a pretty long time ago. The roots of the trees growing on the cairn had found their way down through the stones. A few weeks after the Institute's exploration Mr. Hugh W. Young of Burghead made a more thorough investigation and stated :

" There is an avenue of one row of six large standing stones proceeding from the circle round cairn ; the stones are 7 feet high and 27 feet apart, with one missing. At one time there had been very likely two rows, but in common with many other circles in Scotland the stones had been removed and broken up for building or road-making purposes. The mound has a ditch or vallum round about it. It is worth observing that the second and third stones on the line are in their original positions quite erect, and if a straight line is taken over the tops of these two stones to the cist it will strike the centre of the grave. This would seem to show that the row of standing stones served as a pointer to the place of interment. We cut right through the centre of the mound and found it to consist largely of round stones artificially thrown together, but part of the mound was a natural sandbank. It was in the sand, slightly off the centre, that we came upon the cist, 2 feet 5 inches long by 1 foot 6 inches wide. It had been a very carefully constructed grave, but unfortunately the stones were of a very brittle nature and the cover broke in two before the photograph was taken, and a small corner stone was defaced. No urn or bones were found, and the bottom was not paved, the cist being full of sand to the top. The burial could not have been a cremated one, as not a speck of charcoal or burnt bone was found. It appears to me, all things considered, to have been probably the cist of a very young person, and the absolute want of any remains could be accounted for by the eating away properties of the sand in which the cist was placed."

Mr. Young's suggestion that there had originally been two rows of stones, forming an avenue, is unsupported by any evidence, and the single row simply served the purpose of a pointer to the grave.

If the mound had been excavated before, as appearances suggested, the fact would account for the absence of any urn in the centre, and the young person's grave in the sandbank may have been of secondary importance.

In one instance, an interment was found associated with flint implements. About the year 1873, the tenants of Nairnside in the parish of Croy, in reclaiming some waste land proceeded to level down a small sand hillock. In doing so the workmen came upon a large collection of flints of various shapes and sizes, and in the heart of the hillock was found a cist grave with fragments of an urn and some black ash. The flints had been buried in the same knoll as the cist, but it is not quite certain whether any of them had been deposited in the grave.

In another instance manufactured flints were, however, found in the cist. There are several small knolls, artificial looking in appearance, known as Shian or Fairy Hills, in the district. One of these is near the Ardclach road on the farm of Mid-Fleenas. In the year 1862 an excavation was made in it, and the fragments of an urn were found, also small bits of charred bones, and two small manufactured flints.

Some of the finest examples of this ancient sepulchral pottery have been found at Cawdor. Two urns, one entire, the other broken, found in a cist grave there are in the local Museum. But a still finer specimen is preserved at Cawdor Castle. It is in perfect preservation and is beautifully ornamented.

The discovery of several cist graves was made by Sir Henry Macandrew in the year 1878 at Auchindoune, near Cawdor, of which place he was at the time the tenant. The cist graves were situated on the eastern and lower slope of the hill known as the Doune or Dunevan. The existence of the graves was discovered in the course of ploughing. Some of the graves were within a few inches of the surface, and the stones, which were marked by the ploughshare, must often have been shaken and disturbed. Owing to this, three of the four graves were filled with sand and gravel mixed with human bones, some pieces of pottery, and some black charred substance. There were no implements or ornaments of any kind. The fourth grave was at a greater depth, and had never been disturbed. The covering was formed of two large flat stones, and inside was a skeleton almost entire, lying on the left side facing the south-west, with the knees bent up to the chest. Beside it was a pottery urn quite entire, but containing no ashes or remains of food. This vessel is about nine inches in height, five inches in diameter at the top, and three at the bottom. The outside is ornamented by markings made in the clay with a sharp instrument. The only other thing found in the grave was a white pebble of irregular shape, which seemed to have been placed there.

Similarly all over the district specimens of this ancient pottery have been dug up. So far as has been ascertained, these remains do not differ in any essential respect from similar remains in other parts of the country. They merely illustrate the burial customs and practices common to the primitive race which inhabited these northern regions in prehistoric times. But two things may be noted in regard to them, namely, their extraordinary abundance, and the high degree of art manifested in the ornamentation and form of some of the urns—further proof that the district in these early times was thickly peopled, and that by tribes or communities skilled in the highest art of the time.

The number of cup-marked stones in the district of Nairn is very remarkable. At the request of Sir James Simpson, Dr. Grigor examined the Clava stone circles in the hope of discovering some examples of these cup-marks, and succeeded in finding several. Mr. Jolly subsequently made an exhaustive search in every direction for cup-marked stones, and his diligence was rewarded by the discovery of an amazing number. Mr. Romilly Allen, in tabulating the number of known examples of cup-marked stones in Great Britain according to their localities, gives the pre-eminence to Nairnshire. Nearly one-third of the whole number in Scotland occur in the valley of the river Nairn.

At Clava alone there are 22 cupped stones. In the western cairn, in the inner end of the passage on the left-hand side looking inwards, there is a stone with seven well marked cups. In the middle cairn one of the stones in the outer circle between the causeways is cup-marked; two stones standing side by side in the base ring of the cairn contain in all 13 cups, most of them very well formed. Another stone in the ring has some 20 cups grouped in clusters. The standing stone at the outer end of the western causeway of the middle circle is unique in respect that it has an immense number of apparently artificial carvings on the inner side pointing to the cairn, consisting of small shallow cups, of size sufficient to let in the point of the finger. In the eastern circle, a number of cup-marks also occur. They are also to be found on stones of dismantled cairns in the immediate neighbourhood. A stone (formerly in the fire-place of the old kitchen at Balnuran at Clava), now built into the garden wall in front of the new house, contains a number of well formed cups. Several stones dug up at Milton of Clava are cup-marked. One of these is the finest of the group. It contains thirty cups, most of them good, and several distinct evidences of being dug out by some sharp pointed instrument. Others, being first picked out in this way, have afterwards been smoothed. Several of the cups are oval in shape, and some are connected with each other by grooves or curved channels. A stone discovered in a pig-stye at the same farm of Milton has the peculiarity of being cupped on both sides—on one side there are 16 cups, on the other 11. It is a small stone, about 18 inches thick. Cup-marks are found on stones built into dykes, bridges, and cottages in the neighbourhood.

Cup-marked stones were also found at Barevan churchyard by Mr. Jolly, but some of them are now thought to have been due to weathering.

Since the discovery of cupped stones at Barevan, examples have been found in Breaklich churchyard near Fort-George Station, Daviot churchyard on the Nairn, and in other church-yards in Inverness-shire. Some of them are in all likelihood the remains of ancient circles utilised in the building of the churches. A round-shaped stone was found at Budgate of Cawdor with cup-marks in pairs connected by a gough or channel. It had the peculiarity of bearing cup-marks on the reverse side, shallow and ill-formed, and as of more recent date.

Two remarkable cup-marked stones remain still to be de-scribed.

When the old farm buildings at Little Urchany (West) fell, a stone which had been built into the wall was found to have 12 fully formed cups on it, and two or three imperfect ones. They are from 3½ to 2 inches wide and from half-an-inch to an inch deep. They are very distinct and well formed. Like the Hill of the Ord, the western spurs of the Urchany Hill bear evidence of having been the sites of early settlements, flint implements, cists, remains of cairns and stone circles being found there. The Urchany slab is now at the entrance court of Cawdor Castle.

Another stone, unique in many respects, was found at Broomtown, near Moyness. It is a yellowish sandstone, very soft, like much of the sandstone of the district, 3 feet 5 inches by 2 feet 3 or 4 inches broad. It contains, firstly, numerous cups, most of them distinct; secondly, curious grooves in various parts, some of them radiating from a centre; thirdly, a round oblong hollow basin 10 inches long by 5½ inches broad and 2 inches deep; fourthly, several cups on its sides. The surface of the stone is irregular, and full of various carvings. It was found in connection with a stone circle and cairn, which had been removed in reclaiming the land. The tenant at the time came upon several urns and other relics which he buried in a deep hole, the site of which cannot now be ascertained. The stone circle at Moyness formerly described, the large cairn on the neighbouring farm of Golford, and other remains of tumuli show that the district is rich in prehistoric relics. The Broomtown cup-marked stone is now at Cawdor Castle.

As to the origin or use of these singular cup-marks, nothing is really known, though there are numerous theories regarding them. It has been suggested (1) that they had to do with sun-worship, or astronomy; (2) that they are records of time or occurrences, of births in the family or numbers in the tribe; (3) that they are sacrificial cups; (4) that they are relics of a degraded worship of the reproductive powers of nature. Their existence in Christian places of burial is no doubt as purely accidental as their presence in the walls of modern dwellings or dykes. They have simply been utilised. Their occurrence on stones within the covered chamber at Clava shows that they are as old as the cairns. It is quite evident from the variety of positions in which they were placed that they served no definite function in any ritual connected with these remains. That they were made, many of them, with a sharp-pointed instrument is apparent from the smallness of some of the " pits," whilst, on the other hand, the larger cups generally show effects of being rubbed and smoothed by a polishing stone.

They are sometimes associated with small concentric ring-marks, sometimes connected with small channels, and in one or two instances they appear to have been gouged rather than bored. They occur singly, they occur in pairs, they occur in threes, fours, fives, and all sorts of numbers, and in groups reaching as high as 82 on a single surface at Barevan, and 69 on the Broomtown stone. No definite conclusion as to their nature or significance can be drawn from the position, form, or number of these cups. The evidence will not safely carry the investigator further than the statement that they are in all probability mystic symbols of a super-stition of a very remote antiquity.

The dwellings of prehistoric times, having been built of turf or wattles, have disappeared, and though hut-circles can still be traced on numerous hillsides where the surface is undisturbed, they do not call for any particular description.

A Lake Dwelling or Crannog was discovered in 1863 at the Loch of the Clans. This loch, which lies to the south of the great kame which stretches from Kildrummie, near Nairn, to Dalcross (nearly parallel to the railway line), has been greatly diminished by drainage operations, but at one time it must have been of considerable extent. Dr. Grigor having understood from a small farmer in the neighbourhood of the loch, that, whilst ploughing a bit of new ground some time before, he had turned up a few flints, arrow-heads, and flakes, and being anxious to possess some of them, got the farmer to accompany him to the spot. In the course of the walk Dr. Grigor came upon a cairn which differed from all he had seen before, both in situation and appearance. It was raised on the edge of a small ploughed field *within the margin of the loch*. This cairn or its situation must have formed an islet in the loch. At different places around and through the mound he observed oak beams and sticks cropping out, much charred and decayed. On a closer inspection, he found that the greater portion of the wood inclined upwards towards the summit of the cairn, and on removing a considerable number of the stones from one side, he reached a few rafters with cross sticks, which appeared to have been originally parts of an upright roof. Underneath the stones and wood, and resting on the mud bottom of the ancient loch, he found in some places from six to twelve inches of charcoal and burned vegetable matter, along with small bits of bone. These remains lay particularly at the south side, where the tenant farmer had some time before removed a part of the cairn, along with many loads of piles and half-burned wood. While he did this several stone articles of antiquity had been found, none of which were now forthcoming, with the exception of the half of a stone cup, two whetstones, and an iron axe. The Rev. Dr. Gordon of Birnie and Sir John Lubbock afterwards visited the spot, and the latter gentleman picked up a sharp-pointed piece of bone, such as are got sometimes in tumuli. Some forty years before, a canoe—described as made out of the hollowed trunk of a tree—had been dug up between the cairn and the sloping hill on the north.

In the autumn of the same year, Dr. Grigor, accompanied by Mr. Cosmo Innes and Major Rose of Kilravock, made further explorations in the island dwelling, and a minute account of the structure was furnished to the Society of Antiquaries of Scotland. Nothing of any interest was found in the work of clearance, but the remains were, in Dr. Grigor's opinion, clearly that of a primitive lake dwelling. The mound had been artificially made in the loch, an irregular square of walls about three feet high had been constructed of oak trees, piled horizontally above each other, on one side mixed with small boulders. Rafters in three tiers and having different angles of inclination were carried up, and bound down by beams crossing and re-crossing, in all directions, imparting greater strength, and the lower ones keeping out the water. The structure, when intact, would doubtless have its upright roof covered with turf.

About 150 feet in a south-easterly direction from the place above described, and in marshy ground, were found a great many pile heads covered with grass and vegetable matter—no doubt the foundations of another crannog or lake dwelling. In the neighbourhood of Loch Flemington, and in the east end of the small pond called Loch-an-Dunty, about two miles in a westerly direction from Loch Flemington, are also to be observed vestiges of piles.

The Rev. Thomas Fraser, then minister of Croy, a very able naturalist and antiquarian, refused, however, to accept the theory that this island-dwelling was an ancient crannog, and contended that it was the prison-house of Kilravock. A third theory is that the island was a leper-house. There is no tradition to account for the name Loch of the Clans, and it has been suggested that it is a corruption of *Loch-na-Cloimhean*—Loch of the Lepers. Another version gives it the name of *Loch Clamant*—the Loch of the Kite. On the whole, the evidence goes to prove that this was really an ancient lake dwelling, which, however, may have been, and probably was, used in more recent times for other purposes, such as a prison or even a leper-house. It may be noted that a small hillock in the immediate neighbourhood is known as " The Castle." The Rev. James Graves, who was familiar with the remains of lake dwellings in Ireland, considered from the description given of it that it was identical in character with those so common in the lake districts of Ireland, and Dr. Munro, who made a special study of this class of remains in Scotland, also regarded it as a lake dwelling.

Interesting remains of another class are the vitrified hill-forts of Dunevan, Dunearn, and Castle Finlay. Attention was first called to the occurrence of these singular structures in the Highlands in 1777 by John Williams, a mining engineer, sent north by the Government Commissioners to survey the Forfeited Estates in this district. Williams gave a particular description of the vitrified remains on Knockfarrel and Craig Phadrick; and the vitrified forts which occur in the Nairn district, as far as the remains of them would indicate, are of the same nature.

Dunevan, or the Doune of Cawdor, is a hill 800 feet in height, standing out distinctly and separately from the range in which it

B.H.N. B

occurs—a general characteristic of the hills on which these remains are to be found. It is not wooded, nor does it appear ever to have been so. It commands a wide view of the surrounding country and of the Moray Firth. Its sides, which are very steep and when bare would be difficult to climb, are for the most part covered with loose stones, over which the soil arising from decayed mosses and other vegetation has partially gathered. Near the top, however, the soil is of a rich black loam, due evidently to the *débris* of the food thrown out by those who occupied the fort, the soil being largely intermixed with bones of swine and other domestic animals. The contents of these deposits would indicate a late date in the prehistoric period for the occupation of these hill-forts, and point to the conclusion that they were the regular strongholds of the people who had settled on the fertile plains below, and who retired to these fortifications when danger was impending. A few special features may be noted. A cutting or track can be traced along the west and south sides of the hill. The vitrification appears to have been confined to the wall assumed to have enclosed the space on the top of the hill, but nearly all traces of vitrification have now disappeared. Some openings were made in the level space on the hill top in the hope of finding some structural remains, but the only discovery made was that of a roughly-constructed dry well, or cistern. It is on record that the Doune of Cawdor was frequently used for beacon fires for summoning the clans in feudal times, but it has all the characteristics of having been the site of an ancient vitrified hill-fort.

Dunearn, the second vitrified fort enumerated, occupies an in-land position, about 12 miles distant from the sea-board. It stands on the south bank of the river Findhorn, within a mile of Dulsie Bridge, on the verge of an extensive moor. This table-land stretches away to the south to the foot of Carn Glass (2162 feet), and is bounded on the south-east by a range of hills of which the Hill of Aitnoch (1326 feet) is the most conspicuous, separating Dunearn from Dava. Besides the expansive view to the south, the Doune from its position dominates the valley of the river Findhorn (anciently the river *Earn*, from which the Doune derives its name). The Doune is now thickly wooded with birch, pine, and alders, and the level area on top, which extends to about two acres, has in recent years been cultivated and cropped. In reclaiming the ground considerable quantities of loose rounded stones had to be removed, and, it is said, amongst them were found masses of vitrified stones. These were all cleared off. Little vitrification is now to be seen, and the Doune wears a somewhat soft, sylvan aspect, as if it had been at a subsequent time the retreat of a recluse who bestowed some care and pains in improving and beautifying the spot. That this impression may not be altogether unfounded is seen from the fact that on descending the eastern side of the hill, we come upon a piece of cleared ground which bears the name of the Chapel-field. There is an outline in the green turf of the foundation of a building of rectangular form, but there are no remains of the chapel, nor is there any record or tradition regarding it. Its name and history have alike perished. As a vitrified fort Dunearn, like its neighbour Dunevan, appears to have been in ancient times a place of safety for the dwellers in the valley to resort to when danger threatened. It was admirably suited for the purpose. It is an isolated hill, has steep sides difficult to scale, and, with a defensive wall around the top, the occupants would be perfectly secure from any ordinary assault. In later times it served as the site of a beacon fire for summoning the clans, like the Cumings and the Morays.

Castle Finlay differs in several material respects from the two previous hill-forts. Its position is less conspicuous, and its dimensions are smaller. It lies at the foot of the Geddes Hill, near its westmost corner, and has the peculiarity of being defended by ditches on both sides. A streamlet carrying a portion of the drainage of the Geddes Hill descends upon its upper end. At present the water flows past in a runlet on the south side, but the least overflow would send it down the north channel. Both water courses are distinctly marked by deep cuttings. The one separates Castle Finlay from the Geddes Hill, the other from the high ground to the west. In addition to these natural defences, the stronghold appears to have been still further protected by two ring trenches, which can be distinctly traced, the one at the natural base of the hill, the other at the foot of the mound which forms the citadel proper. On the height itself are to be found the remains of an enclosing wall, now in ruins and represented by an accumulation of loose stones, mixed with earth, and for the most part grass-grown. Amongst the *débris* on the sides of the hill, vitrified stones are to be found in considerable abundance, and the merest scratching of the surface of the old foundation brings up additional pieces completely fused together, having a skin of a brownish metallic lustre, with blisters, blotches, and blow holes, resembling iron slag from a furnace. As far as appears, the vitrification was carried round the whole enclosure, though only a certain proportion of the stones, and these the smaller ones, was fused by the heat. The accumulation of earth and stones is larger at the north and south ends than at any other part. The collapse of the wall is so complete that it is difficult to arrive at any definite conclusions as to its construction, but certain appearances suggest that after the stone-work was vitrified it may have been further protected on the outside by an earthwork. It is a curious feature that a small portion of the hilltop at the south end has been left outside the enclosing wall, but probably the morass formed by the accumulation of the water before it fell into the channels already described may have been considered sufficient protection against an assault from that quarter. The level space within the vitrified wall-foundation, extending to about a quarter of an acre, is oval-shaped, and the soil for the most part is remarkably rich. It is now a thicket of bramble and raspberry bushes, ferns, and long grass, with a few fairly grown fir trees. In digging out the roots of some older trees, the ground has been a good deal disturbed, which may account for the flattening out of portions of the hill-sides, thus rendering them less steep.

In Castle Finlay we have undoubtedly the remains of a small vitrified hill-fort, with indications of its having been protected by ditches and earth-works. How this vitrified fort came to be called Castle Finlay is unknown. In Gaelic it is *Caisteil Fhionnlaidh*, Castle of Finlay (the Fair-haired Hero). There are four saints of the name of *Finnligh* in the Irish Calendar, and Finlay was the name of Macbeth's father. Both father and son were Mormaers or Kings of Moray.

The theory that these vitrified hills were merely the sites of beacon fires will not apply to Castle Finlay on account of its inconspicuous position. It is quite evident that it was a stronghold. The circumstance that vitrified stones are to be found in every part of the foundation of the wall proves that the vitrification was done by design, and not by accident. These remains do not throw any light on the method by which the stones were fused, but there is nothing in their appearance inconsistent with the theory that the enclosing wall was built of selected stones mixed with faggots and peat and then fired, the interstices acting as powerful draughts to the flame and raising the heat to a degree sufficient to melt many of the stones and consolidate the mass.

About a mile from Castle Finlay in a south-easterly direction on the Geddes Hill there are remains of another hill-fort. But it bears no mark of vitrification. It is the highest point on the Geddes or Urchany hill. It is known as " The Cairn," and has been used in recent times as the site of a bonfire. The north and west sides are formed by the gneiss rock, rising straight up some eight feet like a wall, and the south and east sides are apparently made up with stones, many of them of larger size than is usually found in a cairn. The platform, which is quite level, is covered with greensward and an abundant crop of broom. It is quite a small place, but its situation is exceedingly bold and defiant.

A further class of remains, interesting from their associations, has to be noticed. These are a series of artificial looking mounds supposed to be Moot Hills, where justice was dispensed by the chief in association with the headmen of the tribe. Two mounds from forty to fifty feet high to the west of the church of Petty are known as *Tom mhòit*, that is, the Court-hill. A mound cut through by the railway between Culloden and Dalcross also bore the name of *Tom mhòit*. Cantraydoune, in the same district, is a hill of a similar form. At the Loch of the Clans, a round-shaped hill of the same character and formation goes by the name of " The Castle." At Auldearn a mound now known as the Doocothill was formerly called " The Castle." Similar mounds are associated with fairies and witches. The hillock at Mid-Fleenas is known as the *Shian* or Fairy Hill, and a road leading across the valley to Urchany is called the *Shian* road. This mound is the only one that appears to have been excavated. As already noticed, an opening was made in it about the year 1860, and it was previously excavated in 1845. On both occasions pagan interments were disclosed. A *Shian* hillock exists at Dulsie, and it is supposed to have given its name to that lovely spot. *Tula-Sìth* means the Fairy's Hill. In a remote corner in the southern extremity of Nairnshire, there is a small loch which bears the name of Loch-an-Tutach (the Loch of the Horn), and at one end of it there is a mound called *Shian a' Tutach*. At Moyness, the people grimly call a similar mound "The Deil's Hillock," whilst an artificial-looking knoll on the sea-bank, a little to the west of the town of Nairn, probably also a moot-hill, is called both "The Fairy Hillock" and the "Witches' Hillock." It is referred to in old writings by the latter name. Two moot-hills occur at Tearie, near Brodie.

All these mounds bear traces, more or less, of having been artificially rounded, while in some instances there is a trench round the base, and in others a cutting round the middle of the hill. The fact that interments of a pagan form have been found, in at least one instance, indicates a prehistoric origin, although they may have had later associations.

In 1925 a quarryman, in uncovering the rock at Kingsteps Quarry, came upon a stone implement of curious shape. It was new to archaeologists, and was described as a club or pestle by the Scottish National Museum authorities, to whom it was presented. The deposit cut through consisted of two feet of sand, one foot of moss, and three feet two inches of red clay. The point of the implement was embedded in blue clay. The implement was of a hard stone, 16 inches in length and tapering from $7\frac{1}{2}$ to $4\frac{1}{2}$ inches in thickness.

A few years previously a cist grave with a doubled-up skeleton was found in the same deposit.

From the foregoing account of the remains that have come down to us of prehistoric times in Nairnshire, some idea may be formed of the social conditions of the inhabitants. It is probable that the earliest settlers here, as elsewhere in these northern parts, were hunters, living on the fruits of the chase, using for all their wants the rude implements of flint and stone, examples of which have been discovered.   The conditions of life would necessarily be of the simplest character.   In their wattled huts they slept and prepared their food; in the neighbourhood of their huts they dressed the skins which clothed them, and fashioned the weapons and implements they used.   These settlements, by natural growth or by the arrival of fresh colonists, developed into tribal communities, and hunting, the occupation of the pioneers, gave place to pastoral pursuits, when cattle became their chief interest and wealth.   The land as a whole remained untilled, but, from the presence of the food-urn in some of the graves, and the occurrence of numerous querns associated with these remains, corn must have been grown.   Probably it was confined to patches on the sunny slopes of the lower district and the fertile haughs along the course of the streams.   The country for the most part must have been an uncultivated waste, differing in no essential respect from the waste ground and moorland which the modern plough has not yet broken up.   To what extent it was wooded it is impossible to say. That there were great forests of oak in primeval times there is abundant proof; thickets of alders then as now doubtless fringed the water courses, whilst the heights of the uplands were crowned with oak, fir, and ash.   There was no drainage, and large bogs occupied the place of much of the ground now under cultivation. From a general view of similar remains throughout the country, it is pretty clearly established that the early race were of Celtic or Pictish origin.   The form of burial, the weapons, the structures, and the personal ornaments are referable to only one race, the Celtic.   The old place-names, except on the coast, are intensely Celtic both in language and idea.   That there was, in these long ages, progress or development in civilisation is clearly proved. Skill and ingenuity, however, of a surprising degree are manifested in the implements fashioned in the Stone Age, no less than in the ornaments constructed after bronze came into use.   The burial places are a testimony to the attachment of the people to their honoured ancestors, and at the same time afford proof of their remarkable skill. Their selection of places well adapted for the safety of their households in time of danger, and their unique employment of the agency of fire in strengthening the stone ramparts, are characteristics of a people possessed of considerable intelligence and power. The entire absence of those abject underground dwellings—the earth-houses—to be found in some parts of the country, significant of a timid, cowed, and craven people, may be taken as an indication that the tribes settled in this district were sufficiently powerful and numerous to hold their own in the open field against their enemies. The institution of moot-hills shows the existence of an authority to administer justice between man and man. All these are indications of a people far removed from the lowest stage of barbarism. And if we try to form a picture of these early times, and localise it in the valley of the Nairn, we may imagine little communities settled here and there all along the fertile lands adjacent to the river and its tributaries, from the seaboard to the heights of Strathnairn, dwelling in huts and booths, and following primitive, pastoral pursuits ; obeying the authority of their chiefs, honouring the remains of their distinguished ancestors with rites of cremation and interment in stone-built tombs ; recognising the sun as their principal deity, but worshipping the powers of nature as their personal gods, accepting phenomenal circumstances as omens of good or evil, peopling their little world with evil spirits whose anger had to be averted and their favour conciliated according to the observances laid down by the " wise men " or priests of the time—a system of belief which after the lapse of centuries of Christian teaching has not been wholly extirpated.

CHAPTER II

EARLY HISTORY

THE first glimpse we get in history of this district is in the first century in connection with the Roman occupation of Great Britain. In the year 86 the Roman fleet was despatched from the Firth of Forth by Agricola at the close of his last campaign against the Northern Picts in the peninsula between the Forth and Tay. The fleet was sent to explore the coast and circumnavigate the island with a view to future military operations. They skirted the coast, noting the headlands, promontories, firths, rivers, and towns. The results of these observations were communicated by the sailors on their return to Ptolemy, the geographer. Whilst the work of Richard of Cirencester on the Roman progress in the north has proved to be a forgery, Ptolemy's chart may be accepted as fairly reliable. What appears certain is that the Roman fleet on entering the Moray Firth skirted the south shore. They noted the river Deveron, to which they gave the name Celnius, and proceeding came to the Spey, which they named the Tuessis. Coming to the bold promontory of Burghead, they found a native settlement upon it, which they called Alata Castra, or the Winged Camp, probably an enclosed camp with wooden palisades stretching seaward and landward on the promontory. Some of the older writers, however, make Nairn the Alata Castra, and it is very remarkable that Professor Flinders Petrie, the eminent geographer, working out the distances run by the Roman fleet along the coast by measuring the time taken, has come to the conclusion that Nairn is Ptolemy's Alata Castra, " though," he adds, " as a strategic point it would be expected to be at Inverness." This important

paper appears in vol. iv. (new series) of the Proceedings of the
Society of Antiquaries of Scotland, year 1917. Passing Burghead, the rivers Findhorn and Nairn would become visible, but
they are not noticed by Ptolemy, if the Loxa which he mentions
be the Lossie, which the similarity of the name would indicate.
In view of the undoubted existence of a numerous population on
the banks of the Nairn in prehistoric times, it is probable that a
settlement existed on the high ground known as the Castle Hill,
and it may be permissible to imagine that the appearance of the
Roman galleys with their great banks of oars as they swept along
the bay must have filled the minds of the inhabitants of these parts
with wonder and consternation. There is no record of any
previous ships having penetrated the firth. The Celts were not a
maritime people. Canoes, skiffs, and coracles or skin boats, were
doubtless in use along the shores, and an occasional Norse vessel
may have found its way or been driven into the firth, but no such
ships as the great Roman vessels of war, some of them capable of
carrying 500 men, had ever been seen there before. It is on record
that the Roman sailors occasionally landed and pillaged the native
settlements on the coast. It is reasonable to suppose that as careful
navigators they would select landing places in the sandy bays rather
than on the rock-bound coasts. There has always been a tradition—though tradition on such a point is not of much value—
of a Roman camp at Delnies near Nairn. It is recorded in
Gough's Camden's Britannia (vol. iii. p. 430) that "some years
ago was dug up in a common near Nairn an urn containing a series
of Roman silver coins of different Emperors." "At Inshoch in
the parish of Auldearn, about three miles east of Nairn, there were
found in a moss several remains of Roman coins, two heads of a
Roman hasta or spear, two heads of a Roman horseman's spear, as
described by Josephus, Lib. iii. c. 3, and a round piece of thin metal,
hollow on the underside, all of ancient Roman brass." (Chalmers'
Caledonia, vol. I. p. 179; Transactions of the Society of Antiquaries,
part II. pp. 70-136). In Roy's Military Antiquities it is stated
(vol. I. p. 88) that "Roman coins have been found at several
places along the coast of the firth, particularly at Nairn. Near to
Ardersier [Delnies] a few miles west of Nairn, were dug up about

forty years ago a very curious Roman sword and the head of a spear." These relics, if correctly described—which is open to some doubt, most of the authorities cited being strongly biased in favour of the view of a Roman occupation in the North—are interesting so far as they go, though perhaps hardly conclusive of the actual presence of the Romans in the district.

The Roman fleet appears to have sailed up the Beauly Firth, no doubt in the expectation of finding an open waterway. It is named the Varar, which name is preserved in the river Farar and Glenfarar, and later geographers have applied the name Vararis estuarium to the whole Moray Firth. Returning, they explored the Dornoch Firth. The Roman fleet then visited the Orkneys, passing round to the West Coast, and ultimately made the complete circuit of Britain, returning to their anchorage in the Firth of Forth. They described the various tribes then inhabiting Scotland. The name they gave to the people on the Moray Firth coast was *Vacomagi*, the border people, while to the north-west they placed the *Caledonii*.

Before the fleet returned, Agricola had been recalled by the Emperor Domitian, and although subsequent Roman generals attempted to carry out his plan of conquest, they failed, and in the year 410 the Roman army finally retired from Britain, and the Roman government of the province came to an end. The existence of the Roman Empire on the Continent was threatened, and every Roman soldier was needed for its defence. A vast mass of "barbarians," or Teutons, from the north of Europe had descended upon the plains, and they speedily landed upon the coasts of England, cutting off for nearly two centuries all further intercourse with Rome. South Britain was eventually over-run and conquered by these Northmen, and the light of the Christian faith kindled in the time of the later Romans was extinguished. Paganism became the dominant and almost exclusive religion throughout the whole territories formerly subjugated by the Roman army. The early British Church, even in the days of its greatest strength, had never been able to make any great progress north of the Tay, probably not beyond the Forth. Hence the Caledonian Highlands retained their original pagan faith, and these changes in the south did not affect it. Although the Romans had in view plans of subjugating Ireland, they never carried out their intentions, but some of the missionaries crossed over, and founded Christian churches in the sister isle; and whilst the light went out or became very dim in England, it burned brightly during this period of seclusion in Ireland. In the south of Scotland, one of the great missionary preachers of the first British Church, as it may be called, was St. Ninian. He was the son of a Southern Pictish chief. He travelled to Rome, visited St. Martin of Tours, and on his return from the Continent built the first stone church in Scotland at Whithorn, in Wigtonshire. His fame was great, and for centuries after his death his memory was held in the highest veneration. St. Ninian is supposed to have visited the Highlands, and traces exist of the presence of some of his missionaries, but their work had no permanent effect. The numerous St. Ninian dedications to be found are of a later date.

When the veil of obscurity is partially lifted on the introduction of Christianity by Saint Columba in the middle of the sixth century, we get our next view of these northern parts. King Brude, son of Maelchon, reigned over the kingdom of the Northern Picts, which extended from the Firth of Tay in the south to the Orkneys in the north. His residence was at Inverness, and his nobles and chiefs, his military leaders and men of rank, would doubtless be in attendance at his court or settled in the neighbourhood. The old Castle-hill of Inverness, all things considered, best answers to the description of the site of his palace, which was probably a wooden structure protected by a palisade enclosing the hill. At the gateway, Columba and his two companions demanded admittance, but on the guard refusing to open, they started to sing a psalm. Columba had a magnificent voice, and the unwonted sound of psalm-singing reaching the castle, orders were apparently given to admit the strangers. The gate was immediately flung open, and they entered and were ushered into the presence of the king. The visit of the Irish missionaries to Inverness, so picturesque and interesting in its features as an incident of missionary enterprise, really marks a turning point or epoch in the history of the Celtic nation. It was probably the year 565 in which this visit was made. Columba had come from Ireland to Iona in the year 563. King Brude, who was in the eighth year of his reign, embraced the new faith, and gave the missionaries the fullest liberty to evangelise the country. The only opposition they met with was from the Magi or Wise Men, the priests of paganism, who claimed to have power over the winds and the waves and other forces of nature through the agency of the spirits of darkness. But the influence of Broichan, the pagan priest at the court, was not sufficient to prevent the spreading of the new faith. Columba addressed large crowds in the neighbourhood of Inverness. Doubtless Inverness became a centre for missionary labour. St. Columba, having secured permission from King Brude, set sail down the Moray Firth, and is conjectured to have occasionally landed and preached to the people.

In tracing the influence of the early Celtic Church, it has to be kept in view that it was a peculiarity of the Celtic system " that the saints whose memory was held in veneration were in every instance the planters of the churches in which they were commemorated, or the founders of the monasteries from which the planters came "—a rule quite different from that of later dedications. It is in vain now to look for the remains of their places of worship. At first their cells or oratories were made of wattles, which soon decayed. Latterly they built small dry-stone chapels shaped like beehives. Few of these structures have survived the hand of time, and none is known to exist in this quarter. The sites of some of these chapels can, however, be identified by the names of the saints preserved in the dedications, or in fairs, or place-names.

There is a dedication to Saint Columba at Petty, where the saint is believed to have made his first entry. At Auldearn, the memory of Columba was preserved in St. Colm's fair. Originally observed as a Church festival in honour of the Saint, it became in course of centuries a fair. It was regarded as one of the most important markets in the north, and till quite recently the day was observed as an annual holiday throughout the district. About the year 1880, having dwindled to small dimensions, it ceased to be held.

An interesting point arises in regard to Cawdor. The old name of the parish is given as Evan. It has hitherto been assumed that it preserves the name of St. Adamnan, a successor to Columba as Abbot of Iona, and his biographer, and there is a good deal to support that theory; but Celtic scholars will not accept it, and regard it as a place-name derived from some small natural features. It is stated that a personal name would not have been given to a place embracing such prominent physical features as Barevan and Dunevan.

Whoever the saint may have been who founded the church at Cawdor, the old bell preserved at Cawdor Castle is an undoubted relic of the Celtic Church period. It is of the Celtic Church type —a square-sided, iron-hammered, loop-handled bell. All that is known of it is that it belonged to an old church in the parish, and there is no foundation for the statement that it was the bell of the private chapel at Cawdor Castle. It is vastly more ancient than the castle itself. In all likelihood, it belonged to the earliest church of Barevan, and having been blessed by the saint whose name it bore, was so venerated by the people that it was preserved when all else connected with the original church had perished. So precious were these relics considered that a special keeper of them was often appointed; he was called the *Dewar*, and his place of abode *Baile-an-deoradh*. About a mile south of Cawdor Castle, on the road leading towards Barevan church, is a small croft known as Ballindore, now generally pronounced, however, as Ballintore. It was probably there that the hereditary custodian of the old Celtic church bell dwelt. A judicial as well as a religious significance attached to these relics down to a pretty late date.

The site of a small chapel occurs near Lochloy, on the carse land, within a short distance of the western end of Lochloy. It bears marks of such extreme primitiveness that it may possibly be an early Columban chapel. The mound upon which it was built was also used as a burying place. The foundations of the wall, as far as can be seen, are built of dry-stone, and the headstones are undressed and unmarked. The well close by is known as the chapel or priest's well, but the name of the saint to which it was doubtless dedicated is lost. The circumstance that the villagers of Lochloy and the fishers of Mavistown had their burial places in more recent times at Auldearn favours its remote antiquity. Its existence had been almost forgotten until in forming the road down to the loch, fragments of human bones were disclosed, and the proprietor stopped further interference with it.

Chapels built in proximity to cairns and circles are generally of early Columban origin, and there are two instances of these—one at Urchany and another at Clava. In this latter case the dedication is to Saint Dorothy—a Greek saint—which is very remarkable, and may be a reminiscence of a very early association. At Rosemarkie there was an early Columban settlement, which was re-dedicated to a later Roman Catholic saint. The exposed promontory at Burghead was also chosen as a monastic settlement, and the saint's name is probably preserved in " Saint Ethan's Well," about a quarter of a mile to the east of the village there.

The place-names yield a few slight suggestions of probable early dedications. *Kilravock* is apparently the name of some forgotten saint. The traditionary site of the chapel is occupied by a pigeon house. *Kildrummie* is not, as might be supposed, a modern adoption of the name of the historical castle of Kildrummie in Aberdeenshire; it is one of the oldest place-names in the district. It is derived from *Cil*, church, *Druim*, a ridge, and the spot was church property. The name *Belivat*, according to tradition, preserves the memory of a saint. *Buaile Ichid* means " the enclosure of a priest called Ichid," but all that the name will yield in its present form is " Town of the Twenty." " Fichid's Fair " was held at Belivat down to the middle of the eighteenth century, when, according to common report, it was transferred to Grantown in Strathspey, where it was called " Figgit's Fair." A well at Wester Belivat is known as Ichid's Well, and a stone there used to be called Ichid's Chair. The name of one of the Abbots of Lismore was Eochaidh. His death is recorded in the year 635. The Abbots of Lismore had a not very distant connection with the neighbourhood. The Columban settlement at Rosemarkie was originally founded by Moluag of Lismore, and the church of Mortlach was also dedicated to him. A well near the village of Dyke is known as Moluag's Well to this day. He was described as " the pure, the bright, the pleasant, the sun of Lismore."

Relics of the Celtic Church have been found in another direction.

When the missionaries came from Ireland they brought with them copies of the Scriptures written on vellum, having generally the figure of a cross drawn outside, and having the cover decorated with silver-work and ornamented with designs of a peculiar character. The form of the cross is so distinct that it has been styled the Celtic cross, and the pattern is so unique that it is now known as Celtic ornamentation. From the manuscripts the peculiar form of cross and the characteristic ornaments were after a time carried on to stone-pillars and slabs. On these stones were also carved a series of peculiar symbols, confined to the period of the Celtic Church.

There are three of these Celtic Church monuments in the district. One stands on the bank above the Carse of Delnies, and an idle legend has given it the name of the Kebbock Stone. The story is that two chiefs and their clans fought a great battle for possession of a kebbock of cheese. Hence the name Kebbock Stone. The term Kebbock, however, is simply old Gaelic for Stone Black. A heap of stones, probably the ruins of an oratory, lay beside the pillar, but has been removed. The slab is very much wasted from the effects of weathering and ill-usage, but the faint outline of a Celtic cross can still be traced upon one side of it. It is a cross of the earliest form—incised and undecorated—and it would have been a most interesting memorial of early Christian times had it been better preserved.

The next example of a Celtic monument is to be found in the romantic reach of the river Findhorn, on the south side of the river below Glenferness. Legend has also been busy with it. It is known as the Princess Stone, and the story is told that a Danish prince, detained as a hostage at the court of the native king, fell in love with the king's daughter. The father refused him the hand of his daughter, on the ground that he was a son of his greatest enemy. The Dane, however, persuaded the young princess to escape with him. They were missed, pursued, and discovered in the Dulsie wood. The river was in flood, but preferring the risk of drowning to the pain of captivity, they rode on the one horse to the brink of the river, and plunged boldly into the rushing torrent. They were swept down by the foaming stream, and drowned, their bodies, locked in each other's arms, being found next morning on the sandy beach of the river below Ferness. Here, in this haugh they were interred, a cairn was raised over their grave, and this monument was erected to perpetuate their memory. The great flood of 1829, which proved so disastrous to the lands lying along the banks of the Findhorn, spared the grave of the unfortunate lovers; its waters dividing, left it an island. The river has since returned to its old bed, and the grave is now beyond its reach. Such is the story. The monument itself, whatever be the occasion of its erection, is unmistakably a sculptured stone of the Celtic Church period. It has suffered considerably from the hand of time, and is but a remnant of its former greatness, but many of the sculptures on its lichen-covered surface can still be traced. The upper part of the stone is gone, but the lower portion of a cross of the Celtic type is visible. The cross was decorated with the chain pattern, and at the corner of the arms at their intersection with the shaft are four bosses—one at each corner. With the exception of a space in the centre where the carving has become obliterated, the main portion of the slab is filled with the spiral ornament. At the foot, in a panel, are two human figures—one much stouter than the other—embracing each other. On the reverse side of the stone, the chain pattern is again visible at the top. It is much wasted, but there would seem to be a serpent in the toils of the chain ornament—an unusual subject in Celtic art. Immediately below, the figure of a man on one knee drawing the cross-bow is visible, but the object at which he aims his arrow cannot be deciphered. Behind him is what is known as the "elephant"—a creature with huge jaws, scroll-shaped feet, and a trunk springing from the back of its head. Below it occurs the symbol of the crescent and bent-rod or sceptre—both rather small in size. The main subject lower down is a magnificent bent-rod, with sceptre ends richly carved, combined with the double disc or spectacle ornament, resting upon the back of a large "elephant" figure, and apparently crushing it to the ground. The drawing is full of animation.

B.H.N.   c

The key to the meaning of these mysterious emblems and figures has been lost. They occur chiefly on slabs found in the north-eastern counties of Scotland, and illustrate one phase of the religious thought of the early Christian Church. Everything was symbolised. The very animals were taken as types of moral qualities. The goat was the type of the proud, the wild boar of the wicked, and so on. A conflict between the Christian and his spiritual enemies as represented by these animals is a constant subject. The archer in the Ferness slab is probably aiming at a wild boar, thus destroying the wicked. The figure of the "elephant" occurs upon over thirty stones in Scotland. It has been suggested that it embodies the conception of a Celtic artist who had heard of but had never seen an elephant. More probably it is a representation of an ugly, hateful beast—*i.e.* the Evil One. It is significant that in this picture the large bent-rod and double-disc are pressing the animal to the ground. The bent-rod with sceptre-like ends may be intended to represent a rod of power and a sceptre of mercy, the double disc perfect vision, the crescent shape the vault of heaven. It is noteworthy that the bosses enclosed within the disc are seven in number. The same thing occurs on several other stones in Scotland. They are probably seven stars. The interpretation of these symbols has not, however, got much beyond the region of guessing. This old weather-wasted monument, clasped together with iron rods and supported by buttresses, must have been a rich piece of sculpture in its day, fraught doubtless with lessons of interest and importance to the generations who understood its meaning.

About a mile south of the Princess Stone, occurs another of the places bearing the name of *Ballintore*—an ecclesiastical association which would indicate that a Columban chapel had existed not far from the spot. Some two miles lower down the river, the haugh has the name of Dalnaheigleish—*Dal-na-Eaglais*, "Field of the Church."

The most perfect example of these ancient Celtic cross-bearing slabs is at Brodie Castle, in the avenue near the east lodge. It formerly stood in the centre of the old village of Dyke, and is known as Rooney's Stone from the circumstance that for a time

it lay neglected in the garden of a man of that name. It is stated
that it was originally dug out of the foundations of the church
when it was altered. On the reverse side is a perfect little cross
of the Celtic type, recessed at the intersection of the arms. It is
decorated all over with the chain-pattern. On the obverse side
occur two figures with bird-like beaks. Underneath is a characteristic representation of the " elephant " symbol, the body of
which is worked in the chain-pattern. Several other Celtic symbols occur. An additional point of interest in this slab is that on
the raised border around the stone an Ogham inscription is traceable.
Several experts in Ogham writing—which consists of dashes or
strokes divided into groups to represent the alphabet—have been
at work upon it, but as yet no satisfactory reading has been arrived
at.

Similar cross-bearing slabs have been found, as might be expected,
at Rosemarkie and Burghead. One of the stones at Rosemarkie
is a beautiful specimen of fretwork, in combination with the
divergent spirals. Several small slabs with incised bulls cut on
them have been found at Burghead. They are not properly
speaking Celtic symbolic animals, and one explanation of their
origin is that they are relics of the old pagan worship, executed
within the early Christian period. At Elgin a decorated cross of
Celtic character was dug up some years ago in the High Street,
and has been placed within the Cathedral grounds.

The magnificent sculptured pillar at Forres, the crowning glory
of the school of art of the Celtic Church period, bears on one side
a very beautiful cross of the Celtic type. It is richly decorated
with the Celtic ornament, resembling the designs on the " Book
of Lindisfarne "—a manuscript of the seventh century. Beneath
the cross are two gaunt human figures, apparently in an attitude of
peace-making or reconciliation. The other side of the pillar
presents a series of representations in panels or divisions :—in the
top panel a troop of cavalry, the horses prancing proudly ; in the
second division, foot soldiers brandishing their weapons and shouting
for the battle ; in the third division, captives, naked and chained,
making their submission ; in the fourth, an executioner, with
armed attendants, at work beheading prisoners, the headless bodies

being piled up horizontally; immediately below, there appears to be a single combat going on, while an officer advances with trumpeters; in the next division, foot soldiers have put to flight a troop of cavalry; the final scene represents the horses caught, the riders beheaded, their bodies piled up or hung in chains, one head being apparently enclosed in a frame—all on front of an archway or canopy. A row of grave faces is visible below, probably representing a council or senate. The picture is one of mortal combat, and in ordinary circumstances would be accepted as a record of a battle, but from the intensely symbolic character of all similar subjects on monuments bearing the Celtic cross and ornaments, it is more probable that there is locked up in these wonderful carvings some literary conceptions of the predominating religious idea of the age—of life being a dire conflict with evil. The Forres pillar differs from other Celtic monuments only in that the Celtic emblems and typical animals are awanting, unless the top ornament, now defaced, but reproduced in a drawing of late times, be the " elephant " symbol.

Two important finds of ornaments belonging to the Early Celtic Church period were made at Croy. In the year 1875 some young people were engaged in planting potatoes in a field near the church of Croy, when in turning over the soil one of the girls found a number of curious articles and brought them home with her. They were examined by the Rev. Thomas Fraser, who at once discerned their great antiquarian value, and had them sent to the Edinburgh Antiquarian Museum. The hoard consisted of a silver brooch, two coins, some silver wire thread, part of a bronze balance beam, and a number of beads. The brooch is of penannular form—that is, has an opening in the ring. The body of the brooch is plain, 3 inches in diameter, the ends expanding in the form of circular discs, in which are amber settings surrounded by a double rope-like moulding. The ends of the circular ring or body of the brooch are finished in a way suggestive of the head of an animal holding the disc in its widely-extended jaws. The centre of the ring forming the upper part of the brooch has an oblong sunk panel with a circular amber setting and interlaced ornaments on each side. The brooch was broken, and the pin was not found. Dr.

Anderson says that while it is an undoubted Celtic brooch, it is noticeable that the art of this brooch does not possess the special characteristics of the art of the manuscripts. The inference is " that in the Croy brooch we have an example of the style of the earlier portion of the period of the type of these penannular brooches before the characteristic decoration of that period had fully developed." Only one of the coins was preserved. It is a penny of Coenwulf, King of Mercia, who reigned from 795 till 818. The time when this hoard was deposited was therefore subsequent to the close of the eighth century, and this gives an approximate indication of the period of the type of these penannular brooches. The bronze balance beam of a small pair of scales was a common equipment of the travelling merchant at a time when the country possessed no coinage of its own, and all barter was by bullion weight of the precious metal. The silver wire was of the thinness of fine thread, and the chain or band about half-an-inch in diameter and knitted with the ordinary stocking stitch. Of the four beads preserved two were of glass with spots of coloured enamels, and two of amber.

The spot where the hoard was found was at the time diligently searched, but nothing further was discovered. One day, several years later, however, the tenant of the farm came upon fragments of two similar brooches of much finer manufacture. They are decorated with the Celtic pattern. One of the brooches is of marvellously beautiful design and workmanship, and has plates of gold and filigree work. It closely resembles the fragment found at Dunbeath, of which it has been said that " if it had been entire it would have had few competitors in the world as a work of art."

That many other relics of this period may exist, though still undiscovered, is shown by the fact that in 1890 a portion of a slab was dug up at Achareidh, near Nairn, bearing carvings of the fret-work pattern similar to what appears in such perfection on the Rosemarkie stone. It is evidently the corner of a cross-bearing slab with raised border. A further search may yet reveal other portions of the ancient monument to which it belonged. It is significant that it was unearthed at the head of a small strip of land known as Allton or Allton Burn lands running down to the sea.

The old name of the land to the south was "The Grove," and was burgh land. Altein means Fire Stone.

For a century and a half, the Celtic Church held undivided sway over the Kingdom of the Northern Picts. The services of the missionaries were welcomed by the native chiefs, who gave them sites for their oratories in or near their own raths, with corn lands for their sustenance in the vicinity, and gifts of land were at subsequent times added to the original endowments. The doctrine and ritual of the church corresponded to the doctrine and ritual of the Christian Church of the fourth century. It was the Church of Augustine and Jerome, not the Church of Rome of the seventh century. Certain elements impressed upon the church in Ireland were reproduced in Celtic Scotland. The system of belief was coloured and animated by the thoughts and feelings of the period in which it took its rise. Hence it came that Christianity was introduced in the purely monastic form. In broad outline and essential features, these monastic institutions bore a striking resemblance to our modern missionary settlements in Central Africa, with, however, severer discipline and greater austerity of life. They had little or nothing in common with the mediaeval monastic cloisters. There were three orders of clergy—bishops, presbyters, and lay brethren—but the bishops had no dioceses, and exercised no special jurisdiction, their pre-eminence being confined to purely spiritual functions; whilst, on the other hand, a presbyter generally ruled as Abbot or head of the institution, to whom all the brethren, irrespective of their standing, gave obedience. The most distinguishing characteristic of this early Church was its fervent faith and burning zeal. Since Apostolic times, it has probably had no equal in the intensity of its devotion or in the self-denying spirit of its enterprise. Columba, the great central figure, was unquestionably a man of commanding genius. His biographers unfortunately have interwoven in the narrative of the events of his life, legends of marvel and miracle. Many of the incidents, freed of their exaggerated colouring, are obviously but the result and outcome of the exercise of the splendid intellectual powers and rare spiritual gifts of the man. His one absorbing idea was the overthrow of Paganism and the establishment of a higher faith and better life, and his impelling motive was his love of Christ, who, as he says in one of his poems, was to him " all in all." His brethren were of a like spirit. They were men of learning and of varied accomplishments, and commended their religion by the purity of their lives. Their settlements were centres of religious influence, seminaries of education and schools of art and industry. They practised music, painting, and engraving. They wrought in silver work, and did not despise the handicraft of the smith or the occupation of the tiller of the ground. They inspired the people with deepest reverence and affection, and everything connected with them became sacred and hallowed. No place was too obscure or remote for them to penetrate to, and no journey too arduous for them to undertake. When the new faith gained ascendancy, it stopped cremation as a form of disposing of the bodies of the dead, and introduced the Christian practice of burial, along with the Christian hope of the Resurrection ; it substituted the cross for the ring as a religious symbol ; it directed the minds of the people from the sun to the Creator of the sun ; it cast out the evil spirits, the demons, and introduced the good spirits, the angels. It delivered the people from the bondage of a crushing terrorism, placed them under the reign of peace and good will toward men, and taught them that human life was not to be governed and regulated by puerile omens and mystic signs or magic spells, but was to be placed on the sure foundations of truth, love, faith, and hope. It freed the slave, and offered a sanctuary to the oppressed. A day of rest was established on the seventh day (Saturday), and the first day of the week was observed as the Lord's Day.

The Celtic Church ended in a Disruption. Two causes are assigned for its overthrow. The Church of Southern Britain, having revived under Continental influences, came into collision with the Celtic Church about the end of the eighth century. Differences arose as to the time of keeping Easter, and the form of priestly tonsure. The matters in dispute were trivial enough, but the principle underlying them was important. The Southern Church appealed to the example of the Church of Rome as authoritative on these points. The Celtic Church refused to accept the authority of the Church of Rome, and took its stand upon the custom and practice ordained and established by Columba and its other fathers. Nectan, King of the Picts, sided with the Romanising party, and expelled from his territories the Columban brethren who would not conform. A change of dynasty for a time restored the outed Columban clergy to their former positions, but the current of events eventually proved too strong for them. In the eleventh century Queen Margaret's fostering care of the new ecclesiastical form had its effect, and the idea of a National Church founded not on a monastic but on a territorial basis took deep root. The Roman Catholic Church gradually superseded Columba's. The tendency to asceticism, early manifested in the Celtic Church, developed as time went on, and when the day of trial came proved a weak point. The recluses and hermits, good and holy men as they were, were not fit to cope with the organised ecclesiastical system of the South. They lingered on for two centuries, less or more, in different parts of the country, and were known as the Culdees, having here and there collective settlements, but these were eventually suppressed and the Church died out. "And thus," as Dr. Skene eloquently puts it, "the old Celtic Church came to an end, leaving no vestiges behind it, save here and there the roofless walls of what had been a church, and the numerous old burying grounds to the use of which the people still cling with tenacity, and where occasionally an ancient Celtic cross tells of its former state. All else has disappeared, and the only records we have of the fanes are the names of the saints by whom they were founded, preserved in old calendars, the fountains near the old churches bearing their name, the village fairs of im-memorial antiquity held on their day, and here and there a few lay families holding a small portion of land as hereditary custodiers of the pastoral staff or other relic of the reputed founder of the church, with small remains of its jurisdiction."

CHAPTER III

THE KINGDOM OF MORAY

KING BRUDE died at Inverness in the year 584. In the early years of his reign, he had waged war with the Scots, as they were called, from Ireland, who had settled on the coasts of Argyll, but after his acceptance of Christianity he lived at peace with them. They eventually formed the Kingdom of Dalriada. Saint Columba outlived his royal convert by twelve or thirteen years, and retained his influence at the royal courts both of Dalriada and Pictland. King Nectan's expulsion of the Columban monks who would not conform to the Romish Church led to frequent wars between the two kingdoms, the Irish Scots resenting the treatment received by their brethren the missionaries. In the year 844, however, a most important event happened. The two kingdoms were united under Kenneth Macalpine, who, while an Irish Scot, was of the Northern Pictish race on his mother's side. He was styled King of Alban, and his successors assumed the title of King of the Scots. Through this union of the two kingdoms the sevenfold division of the country, corresponding to the great tribal divisions described by the Romans, was destroyed, and the original name of the Picts lost.

The seat of the united kingdom being no longer Inverness but Fortrenn, the men of Moray had only a distant connection with the events transpiring. The change of dynasty probably in nowise affected them. They had their own ruler, sometimes called the Mormaer, but nearly as often Ri, or King. Moray during these early centuries was really an independent principality. For a considerable period after the Macalpine dynasty was established, almost the only references to be found in the history of those times to

41

Moray are to the effect that kings of the Scots were slain there. According to some accounts, three kings of the Scots at different periods met their death in the neighbourhood of Forres. The later chroniclers state that Donald, king of Alban, son of Constantine, was slain at Forres. Malcolm I., king of Alban, 942-54, endeavoured to push the power of his kingdom benorth the Spey, and crossed the river with an army. He slew Cellach, who was probably the native Ri, but was himself slain some few years afterwards by the people of Moray at Ullern. This place has been supposed to be Auldearn, but recent writers identify it with Blervie, near Forres, an identification supported by the occurrence of the name Ullern in a list of castles in the district of Forres at a later time. Skene doubts whether the deaths both of Donald and his son Malcolm took place so far north as the neighbourhood of Forres, but he admits that Malcolm's son Duff was probably killed at Forres, where he had fled after defeat by a rival for the throne. The story is that he was slain by the governor of the castle of Forres, and his body hidden under the bridge of Kinloss, and that the sun did not shine upon the place till the body was found and given kingly burial. The fact that an eclipse took place on 10th July, 967, may account for the tradition. Duff's body was taken to Iona for burial.

The extent of territory of the kingdom of Moray was very considerable. It varied at different periods. It first appears with the name *Moreb*, then *Murief*, or *Moravia*, signifying apparently "The Realm by the Sea." It included within its limits the whole of the counties of Elgin and Nairn, the greater part of the mainland division of Inverness, and a portion of Banff. The province of Mearn was sometimes conjoined with it, and "Moray and Ros" was also a common combination. At one time, it must have stretched across the island from sea to sea, for in one of the statutes of William the Lion, Ergadia, *i.e.*, Aregaithol, or the whole district west of the watershed between the North Sea and the Atlantic, and extending from Loch Broom on the north to Cantyre on the south, is divided into Ergadia, which belongs to Scotia, and Ergadia, which belongs to Moravia.

Counting Cellach as the first, there are nine native kings of

Moray whose names appear in history. In accordance with Celtic custom, the office was hereditary as regards the family, but elective as regards the individual. A further peculiarity, which led to frequent strife, was that the succession was held to pertain to two branches of the family, each alternately having the right to elect. A third peculiarity was that when any break occurred, the right of succession reverted to the female side of the house. The same principles ran through the whole tribal organisation of the Celtic people. Next to the King or Ri, who was the head of a mortuath or combination of tribes, came the Toshech, head of the tuath or tribe. Four of these tuaths lay between the Cawdor Burn and the Dyke Burn, namely, Calder, Moyness, Brodie, and Dyke. A fifth occupied the district from Darnaway to the Lossie. The tuath was the immediate predecessor of the thanage of a later century.

The native tribes of Moray had another enemy to contend with besides the King of the Scots.

About the year 872, Harold Fairhair having ascended the throne of Norway, sought to reduce the Norwegians from the position of freeholders of their land, to that of vassals paying *scat* or land tax. A vast number of the people, refusing to submit, left their lands and literally took to the sea. They infested the Western Islands and the Orkneys. Their winter homes were there, but their domain was the North Sea. They became a nation of vikings, " creek-men," or sea-rovers, and their long ships scoured the coasts. Some fifty years before, the Danes and Norwegians—the former called the *Dubhgaill* (or Dark-haired Strangers) and the latter the *Finngaill* (or Fair-haired Strangers) had plundered on the east and west coasts of Scotland, and this new horde of buccaneers added fresh terrors to life for the inhabitants of Moray. King Harold himself was forced to fit out a fleet of warships against these rebellious subjects of his, and he is credited with having swept the seas clear of them, burning and destroying every ship and boat he could capture. In truth, he merely made the Orkneys and Shetland a permanent settlement or colony of his kingdom, under some princeling of Norway, and organised attempts at conquest were then added to privateering by the vikings.

The Moray Firth still retains in its place-names reminiscences of those days of the vikings. The Romans had given names to the coast when their fleet visited it. A fresh set of names now appeared. The Norsemen called the Moray Firth *Breidafiord* (the Broadfirth), and *Baefiord* was applied to the Dornoch Firth, though sometimes it was used for part of the Moray Firth. The old Celtic name of Moreb or Moravia, the Norsemen made *Maerhaefui*. The bays became *wicks*, and the promontories or headlands *nesses*. Hence came *Tarbetness*, *Torfness* (Burghead), *Binsness* (at Findhorn), *Whiteness* (west of Delnies), and *Blackness* (the sand spit on which Fort-George is built, the name of the old village was Blacktown). Inverness is the mouth of the *Nessa*—a name which was in existence before the times of Norse invasion, and therefore cannot be included in the category. Delnies (*Delneish*) is probably also Celtic. Dingwall, however, is a pure Norse name, and so are Helmsdale and many others. There are also numerous *bys* and *hoys* on the north side of the Firth.

Before his return to Norway, after subjugating the vikings, King Harold Fairhair offered the Earldom of the Orkneys to Rognvald, one of his Earls, in compensation to him for the loss of his son who was killed in an affray with the sea rovers, but he passed the honour to his brother Sigurd. This Earl Sigurd, according to the Sagas, soon afterwards invaded Scotland, and obtained possession of all Caithness and " much more of Scotland —Moray and Ross "—and " he built a borg on the southern border of Maerhaefui." In another account, it is said that he carried his conquest " as far as Ekkialsbakki." The borg has been identified as Burghead, but the site of Ekkialsbakki is still in dispute. The earlier notices of it favour the opinion that it is the river Oykell in Sutherlandshire, but other references place it on the south side of the Moray Firth, near Burghead, and apparently to the west of it. Dr. Skene came to the conclusion that the river Findhorn is meant, and supposes Ekkialsbakki to be somewhere between Findhorn and Forres. The name Bakki is Icelandic, and means the bank or high bank of the river, but is sometimes used as a term for the sea-coast. Anciently the river Findhorn ran much further west than it does at present. The Old Bar within four miles of Nairn marks its channel and outflow at one time. The great sand-drift has changed the course of the river, and greatly altered this part of the coast. A deep channel extends for some distance along the inner side of the outer extremity of the Old Bar, and has still a depth of water of six or eight feet at ebb tide, when the sands all around are bare. This strype, as it is called, probably marks the old mouth of the river. With a spring tide, the water still runs easterly on the inner side of the Bar for a couple of miles, until it meets the tidal current which comes through the opening known as the E'e. That this creek was not unknown to the Norsemen is shown by the fact that in 1196 the Earl of Orkney landed at the port of Lochloy, close to this very spot. Culbin, the name of the estate overwhelmed by the sand-drift, appears to be of Norse origin. The two older villages of Findhorn have been destroyed—the site of the one is in the bed of the river, while the other is covered by the sea. If " Bakki " meant merely the side of the river, without implying a high bank, circumstances might point to a certain spot to the east of the active region of the sand-drift, close to the old channel of the river, as a possible site. It is now known as the " Armoury " (as mentioned in a former chapter), a name given to it by modern archaeologists in consequence of the vast number of arrow-heads, manufactured flints, bronze articles, rivets, cuttings and parings of bronze, coins, pins, bits of pottery, crucibles, spear heads, and various other weapons and articles indicative of a centre of population of an early time. Near it is a singular-looking mound, covered with small stones, like road metal, which appear as if they had been broken by having been first subjected to intense heat and then drenched with water. The mound, which is known as Duncan's Hillock, has been partially excavated, without, however, anything of importance being discovered. The promontory of Burghead is in full view from it, distant across the bay about a couple of miles.

While the exact site of Ekkialsbakki is thus uncertain, the finely sheltered bay of Findhorn, whether approached from its former mouth at the Old Bar or by its present short cut to the sea, would be a most advantageous resort for the ships of the Norsemen. The whole region is now extremely desolate and lonely, but at the time when the Norsemen made their summer visits to the Moray Firth, earning the nickname of Summarlidi (Summer Visitors), it must have been the scene of many a stirring event.

It was not far from Ekkialsbakki that the first recorded engagement between Malbrigda Tonn (Tooth), Mormaer of Moray, and Sigurd the Powerful, Earl of the Orkneys, took place. The story as told in the North Sagas is that Malbrigda, described as a Scottish Earl, made an arrangement with Earl Sigurd to meet at a certain place with forty horse each, in order to come to an agreement regarding their differences. On the appointed day, Sigurd, suspicious of treachery on the part of the Scots, caused eighty men to be mounted on his forty horses. When Malbrigda saw this, he said to his men, " Now we have been treacherously dealt with by Earl Sigurd, for I see two men's legs on one side of each horse, and the men, I believe, are thus twice as many as the beasts. But let us be brave, and kill each his man before we die." Then they made themselves ready. When Sigurd saw it, he also decided on his plan, and said to his men—" Now, let one half of our number dismount and attack them from behind, when the troops meet, while we shall ride at them with all our speed to break their battle array. There was hard fighting immediately, and it was not long till Earl Malbrigda fell and all his men with him. Earl Sigurd and his men fastened the heads of the slain to their saddle straps in bravado, and so they rode home triumphing in their victory. As they were proceeding, Earl Sigurd, intending to kick at his horse with his foot, struck the calf of his leg against a tooth protruding from Malbrigda's head which scratched him slightly; but it soon became swollen and he died of it. Sigurd the Powerful was buried in a mound at Ekkialsbakki."

The " borg " which Sigurd the Powerful built at Burghead was a fort of extraordinary strength. Whether he was the original builder, or merely built on foundations laid by other men, cannot now be determined. Reference has already been made to Burghead at the time of the visit of the Roman fleet, and also to its having been the site of a Columban chapel. Recent explorations among the remains of the ramparts by Mr. H. W. Young have revealed walls of the most formidable character. The rampart walls were built on a foundation of boulders laid like pavement, the sea face constructed of solid built masonry, but without lime. The land or inner face was also built of stone. Between the two walls there was a hearting of alternate layers of large stones and oak planks, joined and strengthened by log oaks, riveted to the planks with iron bolts. The wall thus constructed was twenty-two feet thick, and the fortification when intact was probably not less than twenty feet high. It is calculated by Mr. Young that it would take a thousand oak trees for every hundred yards, or an acre of oak wood for every three yards of the wall. So far as is known no similar wall exists in Britain. Strange to say, no relics of Roman, Celtic, or Norse antiquity of a sufficiently distinctive character have been found in connection with it, to throw any light upon its origin. The Norwegians were in Sigurd's time famous ship-builders, and there is no improbability in the supposition that Sigurd's men built these ramparts.

The year 976 was a memorable date in the annals of this period. Through some vagary of the seasons, the summer became winter. Snow fell in midsummer, and the weather was terrible in the extreme. There were no crops or grass that year, and the " muckle hunger," as it was called—the worst of famines—extended all over Northern Europe. In the simple language of the time, it is stated that " men ate much that was not meet for food." Old people were thrown over the cliffs into the sea to lessen the number of the hungry. Many were starved to death, and bands of men took to the waste and robbed, and were outlawed and slain therefor. A comet of fearful omen appeared in the sky all that winter, and the population seemed doomed to destruction. But relief came from an unexpected quarter. Vast shoals of herrings made their appearance on the shores. The lives of the northern nations were saved by the herrings. A northern poet of the time, who parted with all his valuables for a few herrings, calls them " the silver arrows of the sea."

A famine of another kind at this period distressed the Norsemen in Orkney. They experienced a great scarcity of fuel, but Earl Einar, who succeeded Sigurd the Powerful, made the happy dis-covery that peat would burn, and that there were plenty of peats to be had at a particular part of the Moray Firth, namely, Burghead. For this reason the promontory got the name of Torfness. Between Burghead and Findhorn, the sea has scooped out a bay, but in olden times a forest grew where the tide now rolls, and the stumps of the trees have only disappeared within the present century. Deposits of peat of immense thickness are to be found below the sand-drift now washed by the tide, and the country behind, to the south and east, abounds with peat mosses.

During the next century there was comparative rest from Norse invasion, but in the dissensions between the grandsons of Einar, the turf burning king, Malbrigda, son of Ruaidhri (Rory), Mormaer of Moray, espoused the cause of Skuli against Liot. The name of Liot is associated with a hideous picture of the social life among Norsemen of the time. Ragnhild, a beautiful but infamous woman —the daughter of a no less beautiful and infamous mother—was Liot's wife. She had married his eldest brother Arnfinn, but killed him. She then married his brother Havard, and tiring of him, got his nephew to kill him on the promise of her marrying him. This he did, but the false though fair Ragnhild hired another lover, under the same promise, to murder the nephew, and the murder was accomplished. She dealt as deceitfully with the second assassin, and married instead Liot, the brother of her first two husbands. Liot in this engagement was successful, and Skuli was slain.

On the death of Malbrigda, his brother Finlay, son of Rory, became ruler of Moray. He invaded Caithness with a large army, and challenged Sigurd the Stout, who now held Caithness, to meet him at Skida Myre. Finlay's force outnumbered Sigurd's by seven to one, and the Orkneymen were only induced to fight in such a forlorn hope by the promise of their lands being restored to them as freeholds. Sigurd is said to have consulted his mother whether he should fight, and she gave him a charmed banner with a raven worked in mysterious embroiderings, which, according to the belief of the time, obtained him the victory. He followed up his success by overrunning Moray.

Malcolm II., King of the Scots, appears to have encouraged rather than discountenanced these attacks on Moray, and he showed his regard for Sigurd by giving him his daughter in marriage—an alliance which eventually worked mischief of which Malcolm had never dreamt. His eldest daughter—he had no son—was married to Crinan, lay Abbot of Dunkeld. The office of Abbot had become secularised by this time, and was held hereditarily by some member of the family of a local chief.

In 1014, Sigurd the Stout fell at the battle of Clontarf, fighting against Brian, King of Munster—the great struggle between the Pagan and Christian faiths, between the native King and the Danish invader—and Finlay resumed his rule over Moray, and reigned until 1020, when he was slain by his two nephews, sons of his brother Malbrigda, who doubtless regarded his assumption of power as illegal. Malcolm, one of his brothers, succeeded him, and ruled till his death.

Two notices of interest occur with respect to Finlay and Malcolm. The " Ulster Annals " and Tighernac's Chronicle, in recording their deaths, designate them as Ri Alban—a title indicating that their rule extended beyond the bounds of Moravia proper. In the Book of Deer—a manuscript of the eleventh or twelfth century— it is recorded, amongst other entries of gifts of land from mormaers and toshechs, that " Malcolm, son of Malbrigda, gave the Deleric." What land is meant by the Deleric it is impossible to say, but the entry illustrates the connection between the Columban monasteries and the native chiefs of Moray at that time.

On the death of Malcolm of Moray, his brother Gilcomgan succeeded him, but his reign was cut short by an act of terrible retribution, at the instance apparently of Macbeth, in revenge for the murder of his father Finlay. Gilcomgan and fifty of his followers were burned to death in his castle. Macbeth then married Gilcomgan's widow, and took under his charge her infant son Lulach.

Macbeth, having thus cleared his path to the supreme rule in Moravia, was not long in asserting his power. His first act, however, was one of policy. King Canut the Great in 1031 invaded Scotland, and it is recorded in the Saxon Chronicle that he received the submission, not only of the King of Scotland, but also of two other Kings, Maelbathe (Macbeth), and Iemarc (of the Western

Highlands), another proof of the recognised position of independence of the Ri of Moravia.

The Macbeth of Shakespeare and the Macbeth of authentic history are very different personages. The chronicles followed by Shakespeare were to a very large extent fictitious alike as to the dates, events, places, and persons introduced. The scene of the most stirring events, however, remains, after all, in this neighbourhood. The facts of history are these. On the death of Malcolm II., Duncan, son of his eldest daughter, claimed the throne, and his claim was admitted by the Southern portion of the kingdom. Malcolm's other daughter, who had married Sigurd the Stout, had a son Thorfinn, who was now Earl of Caithness. Thorfinn refused to pay tribute to Duncan. Duncan then conferred the title of Earl of Caithness upon a kinsman named Moddan, who came north to take possession, but Thorfinn was supported by his uncle, the Earl of Orkney, and offered battle. Moddan returned to the King, who on hearing of this rebellious conduct on the part of one whom he considered his subject, organised a more formidable expedition. The plan of attack was skilfully laid. Moddan was sent by land with an army to operate in the south of Caithness. Duncan himself sailed from Berwick with a fleet of eleven warships and a numerous army to begin the attack on the north, thus cutting Thorfinn off from any reinforcements from Orkney, and placing him between two armies. Thorfinn was on the watch at Duncansbay, and on seeing the King's fleet, he set sail for Orkney to prevent communication being interrupted. He arrived off Deerness late in the evening, and despatched a messenger to his uncle to send him troops. At daybreak, the Scottish fleet closed in upon him. Although Thorfinn had but five ships against the King's eleven galleys, he determined to fight him. Not waiting for the attack, he ordered his men to row hard down upon the galleys, to fasten alongside them, and to be the first to attack. A fierce fight ensued. The Celtic king was no match for the sailor prince. The Orkneyinga Saga preserves minute details of the fighting. " The Scots in the king's ships made but a feeble resistance before the mast, whereupon Thorfinn jumped from the quarter deck and ran to the fore deck, and fought fiercely.

When he saw the crowd in the King's ships getting thinner he urged his men to board them. The King perceiving this, gave orders to his men to cut the ropes and get the ships away instantly; to take to their oars and bear away. At the same time Thorfinn and his men fastened grappling hooks in the King's ship. Thorfinn called for his banner to be borne before him, and a great number of his men followed it. The King jumped from his ship into another vessel, with those of his men who still held out, but the most part had fallen already. He then ordered them to take to their oars and the Scots took to flight—Thorfinn pursuing them south of Orkney." Duncan made off to the Moray Firth, and landed at Torfness (Burghead). He proceeded south, and gathered together from all parts of Scotland an immense army, which was augmented by forces that came over from Ireland to join Earl Moddan who had gone to Caithness. Poor Earl Moddan, waiting for the fight to begin according to the original arrangement, was surprised one night in Thurso by Thorkell (Thorfinn's uncle), who set his house on fire and slew him. His men retreated to Moray.

The coast of the Moray Firth became again the scene of warfare. The whole forces at the command of the King of Scotland were arrayed against the Norsemen of Caithness and Orkney. Duncan had on his side Macbeth, with the men of Moravia, and all the great chieftains of Scotland with their followers. Macbeth would doubtless succeed Moddan as next in command at King Duncan's side. Earl Thorfinn had taken possession of the stronghold of Burghead, the borg built by Sigurd on the promontory. Thorfinn (says the Saga) was a man of tall stature and noble spirit, though his visage was frightful and his body lean. He had been inured to hardships from his earliest years. When a lad of fifteen he had gone to sea, and joined in viking raids. His father had been converted to Christianity in a strange way. Olaf, the great King of Norway, threatened to put his boy to death unless he became a Christian. As he stood on the shore at Findhorn bay on the morning of the great battle, Thorfinn must have formed a very striking figure. He had a gold-plated helmet on his head, a coat of mail for his armour, a sword at his belt, and a spear in his hand.

His banner was the magic " Raven." We have no companion picture of the " gracious Duncan," but the account which represents him as " meek and hoary " is entirely mistaken. Both cousins were young men. Duncan was but a few years older than Thorfinn. He was equally brave, had fought a desperate battle under the walls of Durham, and had an unconquerable spirit. He had shown his pluck by his fight at sea. The Scottish monarchs as a rule were no sailors, but Duncan, brought up on the banks of the Tay, was not unaccustomed to boat sailing. Thorfinn was the author of the expression, " The unexpected frequently happens," but in going into this battle at Burghead, he could have little expectation of what did happen. His followers were greatly outnumbered by the Scots. It was on a Monday this fight began— as nearly as can be calculated it was the 12th of August of the year 1040. Thorfinn first attacked the Irish division, and so fiercely did he assail them that they were immediately routed and never regained their position. Thorfinn fought at the head of his men, using both hands in wielding his sword. King Duncan, seeing the Irish contingent giving way, ordered his standard bearer to the front, and directed his attack upon Thorfinn. A fierce struggle continued for a while, but it ended in the flight of the King. There is no record of the part taken by Macbeth in the battle. The interest centres around the two cousins as the principal figures, to the exclusion of all others. Macbeth accompanied Duncan in his flight, and it may have been in that ride through the heath, whether prompted by witches' prophecy or not, that Macbeth conceived the idea of murdering King Duncan and usurping his throne. The traditional site of the hillock where Macbeth (in Shakespeare's tragedy) met the witches lies a good many miles off the direct line from Burghead or Findhorn to Elgin, but if the story related by the later chroniclers be correct in other particulars, allowance may be made for a circuitous flight. It must stand or fall, however, with the other traditions.

The weary king, twice unsuccessful in war, sought rest in the Smith's Bothy (Bothgounan, now Pitgavenie) and during the night was treacherously slain—one contemporary account says by Macbeth, who went over immediately thereafter to Thorfinn's side, and joined with him in conquering and laying waste the country as far south as Fife. They then divided the kingdom—Macbeth taking Duncan's territory and becoming King of the Scots, and Thorfinn retaining Moray and the northern portions of the kingdom, along with his Caithness and Orkney Earldoms. For a time therefore, Moray was a Norse colony and virtually annexed to Norway.

Macbeth, the hereditary King of Moray, was now King of the Scots, and had his palace at Scone, the capital of Alban. Lady Macbeth, Gruoch, daughter of Bodhe, and widow of Gilcomgan, was of royal descent, being related to the Duff branch of the Macalpine family, and had thus some claim to the allegiance of the Scots. Macbeth in personal appearance is described as tall in stature, yellow haired, and of fair complexion. While so fierce in war as to earn the name of the " Red One," he appears to have been of a generous disposition and of pleasing manners. A Culdee monastery still held out at Loch Leven, and the record is preserved in the Register of St. Andrews of two donations of lands by Macbeth and his wife. The first entry runs—" Macbeth, son of Finlay, and Gruoch, daughter of Bodhe, King and Queen of the Scots, give to God Omnipotent and the *Keledei* (Culdees) of the said island of Loch Leven, Kyrkenes ; " and the second entry states that " Macbeth gives to God and Saint Servanus of Loch Leven and the hermits there serving God, Bolgyne." It is recorded that he visited Rome, and distributed charity to the poor of that city.

Several attempts were made to drive Macbeth from the Scottish throne. The first was led by Crinan, father of the unfortunate Duncan, but he was slain and the rebellion put down with a high hand. Duncan's infant son, Malcolm, had been removed for protection to the court of Siward, Earl of Northumbria, his maternal uncle. When the boy came of age, Siward made an attempt to place him on the throne, entering Scotland with a powerful army, accompanied by a naval force. Thorfinn's son came to Macbeth's support with the Norwegians. A great battle was fought at Scone, and Siward had to retire, after great slaughter on both sides. Three years later, young Malcolm renewed the attack, and succeeded in driving Macbeth out of Alban. Macbeth fled to Moray, his native country, but was overtaken and slain at Lumphanan. The sudden fall of Macbeth is accounted for in a measure by the absence of the Norwegian force on this occasion, Thorfinn having died about this time. Young Malcolm, who became known as Malcolm Caenmore, thus restored the crown to the Athole line. He married Ingibiorg, the widow of Thorfinn, his father's conqueror. She must have been very much his senior. She bore him a son Duncan, but died soon after. His second wife was Margaret of Northumbria—the saintly Queen Margaret—who did so much to soften and sweeten the court life of the time.

Macbeth was succeeded by his stepson Lulach. He is called " Lulach the Simple," and he met his death, four months after he came into power, at Essie, in Strathbogie, where he appears to have been betrayed or taken through stratagem of the enemy. His son Malsnechtan succeeded and assumed the title of King of Moray, but he appears to have had but a slender hold of the lowlands of Moray, and, having lost all his best men and all his treasure and his cattle, his mother also having been taken prisoner by Malcolm Caenmore, he was content to end his days in peace in the fastnesses of Lochaber. Like Malcolm, son of Malbrigda, he was a benefactor to the monastery of Deer, for it is recorded that he " gave Pett-Maldub to Drostan." Malsnechtan died in 1085. And thus came to an end the line of native Kings of Moray. The names of nine of these Kings have been preserved. They alone were powerful enough to meet and give battle to the Norsemen, and if on occasion some Norwegian Earl, more powerful than another, succeeded in planting his foot on Moray soil, his hold was but for a brief period. Except during the subsistence of the arrangement between Thorfinn and Macbeth, which was doubtless acquiesced in by the lesser chiefs, the Norsemen acquired no lengthened possession. Macbeth is the greatest figure amongst these native Kings. Ambitious he undoubtedly was. Cruel and bloody to those who stood between him and his objects of ambition he proved himself to be. The burning of his cousin in his castle may be regarded as but a due requital and punishment for the murder of his own father, and the mormaership was his of right according to Celtic law; but his slaying of the defenceless Duncan in the Smith's Bothy was an act of treachery of the deepest dye, which even the rude character of the age will not justify. His reign as King of the Scots brought prosperity to the territories over which he ruled. His benefactions to the Church and his visit to Rome were perhaps indications of contrition for the blood he had shed. His being driven from his throne by the son of the king he slew, his flight as a fugitive, and his fall at the threshold of his native country are incidents fully as dramatic as the fictitious situations presented in Shakespeare's Tragedy of Macbeth.

The tradition that Macbeth had his principal castle at Inverness is probably correct. The site of King Brude's old palace on the Crown would be a fitting abode for the native kings of Moray. It would be a stronghold difficult to attack, and a convenient centre for mustering troops for service in Ross or for expeditions into Caithness. Having no ships of any size, the mormaers would perforce have to use the ferry at Kessock, or the old Stock Ford at Beauly. The more stirring incidents of the time, however, lay in scenes more to the east. Inverness was not in the track of the Norsemen, and was too far removed for convenient attack by the Scots. The districts on the southern shore of the Moray Firth appear to have been the sphere of greatest activity, and doubtless there were strongholds or castles even thus early at Nairn, Forres, and Elgin. The name of Macbeth is associated with numerous mounds and remains, and is a common surname still in the district. His father's name Finlay occurs (as already noticed) at the vitrified fort at Geddes under circumstances of some significance. It is found again at Auchindoune, in *Tober Fionnlaidh* (Finlay's Well) at the foot of the hill-fort of Dunevan. A lofty peak of the hill range at Speyside is known as Finlay's Seat. The circumstance that local tradition appears to be quite ignorant of any historical association with the name thus preserved strengthens rather than weakens the surmise that Macbeth's father may be the Finlay of these old place-names. According to ancient Celtic custom, the king or chief of the mortuath was bound to have seven castles or residences.

The connection of the Moray family with the monastery of

Deer in Buchan is curious. It is not improbable that the explanation may be that the sons were sent there for their education, in the same way as the young nobles of Scotia and Northumbria were educated at Iona. Under the rule of its mormaers Moravia became a great and powerful province. Scottish history in later times is in a large measure the history of the South of Scotland. During the tenth and eleventh centuries Moray was the centre of greatest interest and influence in Scotland, and its mormaers were really the kings of the North.

The Norwegian connection with Scotland lasted for nearly four hundred years. Hostile invasions gave way to marriage alliances. The fair maids of Norway, half heathenish as they were, appear to have had considerable attractions for Celtic mormaers. The enormous wealth in gold and silver, the spoils of centuries of viking raids, accumulated in the possession of the principal Norse families in Orkney and the Western Isles, may have been a strong inducement. Duncan, the Celtic chief of Caithness, was the first to set the example of taking a wife from amongst the alien race, and in turn he bestowed his daughters upon viking leaders. Duncansbay (named after him), the northern portal of the entrance to the Moray Firth, thus became a friendly haunt for all the roysterers and buccaneers of the time.

As Christianity gained influence amongst the Norsemen, they settled down into steadier and more civilised ways of life, but their inborn love of the sea, with its life of danger and adventure, remained with them.

The Norsemen eventually withdrew from Moray altogether, leaving behind them a few Norwegian fishermen, who settled in villages along the coast. The surname of " Main," borne by so many fishermen's families at Nairn and neighbouring villages, is simply the Norse " Magnus," and is probably a survival from the old viking days in the Moray Firth, as also is that of " Ralph," common in Nairn. Many of the old customs and superstitions among the fishing communities are derived from the same source. Burghead, their great landing place, sank into insignificance after their withdrawal, but the strange practice of " Burning the Clavie," still an annual custom, is in all probability the Scandinavian ceremony of taking possession of territory by encircling it with fire and sword.

The Norsemen owed their power in a large degree to their skill as shipbuilders and their daring as seamen. They had several types of ships—namely, sloop, bus, scaffy, and galley. The galley or war-ship was dragon-shaped, the stem and stern springing high into the air, and resembling the head and tail of a dragon or serpent. The body or waist of the ship was the most vulnerable part, and to make boarding as difficult an enterprise as possible, rows of shields were bound together on top of the rail or bulwark. Behind these shield-rows, there was protection against the arrows and missiles of the enemy. The sailors during action wore helmets and chain armour. In a hand-to-hand encounter spears and swords were the principal weapons. Apparently by the acknowledged rules of warfare, naval engagements were fought inshore, and not on the high seas. Their ships had foresails, with which they could sail right before the wind, but they depended mainly on their oars, of which they would have sometimes as many as twenty and thirty pairs. So perfect was their rowing that it was a feat of Swein Aslifson to walk on the oars outside the ship, as they swept fore and aft in one movement like a huge fan. The favourite names for their vessels were " The Serpent," " The Snake," " The Dragon," " The Adder," and " The Bison "—" never sped more famous ship under more glorious king," is a description of the latter. The king or prince steered the ship. Every youth was sent to sea. The ceremony of launching their vessels was sometimes attended by human sacrifices, the ship receiving a baptism of blood as she slid down the ways over the bodies of serfs—doubtless the origin of the existing custom of breaking a bottle of wine on the ship's bow as she is launched. Fierce, cruel, and bloody in war, as they were, the Norsemen had many noble qualities, and the degree of civilisation to which they had attained, even long before Christianity had influenced their character and life, is surprising. They had poets to rehearse their brave deeds, and philosophers to teach them wisdom in proverb or aphorism. In personal appearance they were tall, yellow haired, fair in complexion, and had blue eyes. A Norwegian poet failed to win the affection of his lady-love because he had black curly hair !—a blemish supposed to be due to his mother having been of a Gaelic family. The " spear side " and the " spindle side " were the phrases of the time which denoted the male and female branches of the family. Ancestor worship was the common religion, and their heaven was a Valhalla where fighting, feasting, and drinking went on for ever.

CHAPTER IV

EARLY FEUDAL TIMES

MALSNECHTAN was the last of the native rulers who claimed and used the title of mormaer or ri, but the race of native chiefs was not yet extinct. Angus, who was styled Earl Angus, the son of a daughter of Lulach, threw off the yoke of the King of the Scots. Alexander I., who succeeded Malcolm Caenmore, entered Moray with a powerful army and drove Earl Angus across the Firth into hiding among the fastnesses of Ross and Sutherland. On the death of Alexander I., and the accession of David I., a fresh outbreak, headed by Angus, occurred. He carried the war as far south as Stracathro in Forfarshire, but he was met and defeated by Edward, Earl of Mercia, David's cousin, with the loss of five thousand men. Angus himself was amongst the slain. The Scots army then entered Moray, and took possession of the whole district. David himself came North, and was the first monarch of the Scottish line who personally engaged in the administration of affairs in Moray. Feudal ideas of land tenure had in a great measure taken the place of the old tribal arrangements in the southern kingdom, and David sought to introduce these into Celtic Moray, and to some extent succeeded. Brought up in England, he had become familiar with the advantages of settled industry and regular commerce, and his first step was to encourage trade in towns or communities. Markets were established, and monopolies and privileges granted to merchants for their encouragement. Laws were promulgated and enforced for the protection of life and property. Shipbuilding sprang up at

Inverness, and herring fishing became an important industry in the Moray Firth, with Inverness as the great centre. Trade was opened with the Continent and the southern ports of Scotland, and Flemish merchants frequented the northern markets. In short, a new era of commercial prosperity dawned under the beneficent rule of King David.

It is probably to David that Nairn, in common with the towns of Aberdeen, Elgin, Forres, and Inverness, owes its existence as a burgh. Possibly no formal charter was granted—that is to say, the grant was not reduced to writing. The oldest burgh charters in Scotland are only of the reign of William the Lion, but King William's charters are confirmations of rights and privileges existing in his grandfather's time. In his Aberdeen charter, William confirms to the Burgh of Aberdeen and to all his burgesses of Moray and to all his burgesses benorth the Munth their free hanse, their right of convention, to be held when they chose and where they chose, as freely and honourably as they held it in the time of his grandfather, King David. The oldest extant charter of the burgh of Nairn is dated in 1589, by James VI., but it is a deed of confirmation of a former charter "granted by our most noble ancestor the late Alexander of good memory, King of Scots, and divers others our most noble and most ancient predecessors," which erected and confirmed Nairn "into a free royal burgh and with all the liberties, privileges, and immunities pertaining to any other free burgh of this our realm." Written evidence exists that Nairn was a royal burgh in the time of William the Lion, for Alexander II. granted certain lands to the Bishop of Moray "in excambium illius terre apud Invernaren quam Dominus Rex Willelmus, pater meus, cepit de episcopo Moraviensi ad firmandum in ea Castellum et burgum de Invernaren." The old name of the town was not Nairn, but Invernarne, namely, the mouth of the river Narne, derived from the Gaelic *Uisge-Nearn*—"The River of Alders." The alder tree still forms the distinguishing badge of the stream. The Gaelic name *Arnes* for alders was applied, and is still sometimes given, to the clumps of alder trees on the right bank of the river near the town. Till comparatively recent times, there was a dense thicket of alders extending for several miles up the river, and wherever the bank of the stream remains undisturbed, both in the upper and lower valley, the alder tree makes its appearance. The name " River of Alders " was therefore singularly appropriate.

The first of a series of strong measures adopted against the independence of Moray was the forfeiture of the Earldom of Moray by David. The Earldom represented more than a title or family possession. The Earl of Moray was the hereditary ruler of a vast territory, the successor of the mormaers or kings of Moravia, and he even laid claim to the crown of Alban. The estates and revenues pertaining to the old hereditary rulers were appropriated by David, and lands were henceforward held of the Crown. David had, however, so far overcome the prejudice entertained by the men of Moray against the rival house of Athole which he represented, that when he led the Scottish army into England his force included a contingent from Moray, and the King himself commanded in person the division composed exclusively of Scots and Moravenses. But the peace thus established was not permanent. In the later years of his reign Moray men were again in insurrection. Their strong attachment to their own native ruling family was successfully worked upon by an impostor, an ex-monk, named Wymund, who gave himself out to be a son of Earl Angus of Moray. They flocked to his standard, and joined him in ravaging in the Kingdom of the Scots. Wymund is described as a man of an eloquent tongue, fine address, tall, and of athletic make. He adopted the Celtic name of Malcolm Mac Eth. He induced the King of Norway to believe in him, and Somerled, chief of Argyll, gave him his daughter in marriage. Wymund was eventually taken prisoner by David, during whose lifetime he was kept in confinement. His son was at a later time imprisoned with him. Both were liberated in the next king's reign, and Wymund was given apparently the Earldom of Ross, where he behaved so cruelly to the inhabitants that they rose against him, deprived him of both his eyes, and otherwise mutilated him. He retired to a monastery after a life of extraordinary vicissitudes and adventures, and disappears from history.

David, before his death, took all means in his power to secure to his grandson Malcolm peaceable possession of the crown, his only

son Henry of Egremont having died, to the great grief of the
nation; but the accession of Malcolm was the signal for Moray to
throw off once more its allegiance to the House of Athole.
Malcolm now took measures of an unprecedentedly strong character
against the turbulent natives of Moray.   It is stated that he transported the men of Moray and distributed them in the southern
parts of his kingdom.   The chief authority for this statement is
Fordun, and his words are that " he removed them all from the
land of their birth, and scattered them throughout the other districts of Scotland both beyond the hills and on this side thereof, so
that not even a native of that land abode there, and he installed his
own peaceful people."   The historians have sought to minimise
or explain away this extraordinary statement.   Skene says, " This
statement is probably only so far true that he may have repressed
the rebellious inhabitants of the district and followed his grandfather's policy by placing foreign settlers in the low and fertile land
on the south side of the Moray Firth extending from the Spey to
the Findhorn, and here he certainly did grant the lands of Innes
to Berowald the Fleming, by a charter granted at Perth."   " Such
a story of wholesale immigration," says Cosmo Innes, " cannot be
true to the letter."   Probably not, but it is clear that large numbers
of the leading men in the district and their followers must have
been removed, because their lands were given by David and his
immediate successors to strangers, who held them thereafter in
undisputed possession.   The Celtic chiefs of Moray holding land
were now for the most part replaced by Norman knights and
Northumberland squires serving in the army of the King of the
Scots.   Such a revolution, it is obvious, could not be effected without great violence and cruelty.   English troops would scour the
district and hunt down the natives like wild beasts.   The captives,
chained and guarded, would be formed into bands, and despatched
over the frontier in droves.   A pathetic story of enforced exile is
evidently involved in this obscure transaction.   It is probable that
the difference in language between the lowlands of Moray and the
territories to the west and south-west originated in this deportation
and planting.   Gaelic appears to have been as entirely the speech
of the Laich of Moray up to this time as of any other part of the

Highlands. The older place-names, and the names of mormaer and toshech are purely Celtic. There is no physical boundary, such as mountain or stream, to account for the difference of tongue, nor is there any subsequent event in history to which such a change can be attributed. The line of diversity of language can still be traced from the town of Nairn on the seaboard, passing between Auldearn and Ardclach, across the river Findhorn into Moray, separating Dyke from Edinkillie, and, bending round, crossing the Spey at Lower Craigellachie. Till recent times the native population west of the town of Nairn remained Celtic, while the inhabitants to the east were English-speaking.

The policy of planting Moray with southerners inaugurated by Malcolm was continued by several of his immediate successors, and the lower district of Moray in its modern or restricted sense became within the next century or two as purely English as it had previously been Celtic. The erection of King's Burghs, peopled to some extent by lowlanders, and the foundation of great Church establishments at Kinloss, Elgin, and Pluscardine, manned by southern ecclesiastics, tended still further to establish English and to supersede Gaelic as the common language of the people in the centre of the province.

Malcolm, who transported the natives of Moray from their homes, was succeeded by his brother William the Lion, in 1165. He was crowned at Scone on Christmas eve of that year, but was taken prisoner by the English at York in 1174 in attempting to take possession of Northumberland, which had been assigned him as an appanage by his father. He was liberated in the following year on what were thought to be humiliating conditions, and insurrections broke out in various parts of Scotland where the Celtic element predominated. In the year 1179, William with a large army came to the North for the purpose of putting down the insurrection in Ross, and strengthening his hold upon Moray. He was accompanied by his great earls and barons. While military operations were being conducted against the insurrection in the North, King William took up his abode at Inverness, but frequently visited Nairn, Forres, and Elgin, spending a considerable time at each of these places.

The royal castle of Nairn, which William the Lion occupied, was no doubt the castle on the high bank of the river, known as the Constabulary or Castle Hill. The tradition that there was an older castle at the shore, and that the ruins of it were seen by some fishermen during a very low ebb in the eighteenth century, rests on no good foundation. Any castle of an earlier date would have been constructed of wood; even if stones were used, the building would not have stood a winter's storm. What the fishermen saw was probably the remains of an anchorage constructed as late as the seventeenth century. The tradition that an underground passage existed between the royal fort on the hill and the castle at the seashore at the north-west corner of the links has been proved to be destitute of any truth, by the simple fact that cuttings of considerable depths have been made at various points across the track which the subterranean passage must necessarily have followed, and no such passage has been found. Shaw, the historian of Moray, states that he had never heard of any seashore castle. These traditions, however, may be accounted for by the probability that a communication between the castle and the shore at the point in question did exist at one time, but it was a water-way and not an underground passage. The river at one time ran westerly. After passing the high ground upon which the castle was built, it swept round to the west, and, flowing through the low ground now forming the links, which would be perfectly flat before the sand-drift and quarrying operations affected its surface, made its exit at the western corner of the links, where the tidal rocks appear. The name of this reef of rocks is given on the Admiralty chart as the "Fearn Rocks," but it is invariably called by the fishermen the "Fearn Head"—that is, the head of the river of alders. At a later date the river flowed in an easterly direction, but it appears to have run westerly at a much earlier period, and the name "Fearn Head" probably preserves a faint reminiscence of the fact. The name "Invernairne" given to a modern residence on the terrace nearly opposite this point thus happens to be singularly appropriate.

What William in all probability did was to substitute a stone-built fort for the wooden castle of an earlier time. The site lent itself readily to the purposes of a military stronghold. It was protected by the river on the one side, and if the palisade or wall was brought to the edge of its rocky bank, it would be unassailable from that quarter. William appears to have protected the north and west sides by ditches and ramparts, and the only entrance was by a drawbridge. The castle ground extended down as far as the present Bridge Street, probably near to the old fort at the Brochar's Brae, and was enclosed by a stout palisade and earthwork. The stronghold itself had a central keep, doubtless a square Norman tower, and its grand hall was plastered. In the Chamberlain's Accounts for 1264, credit is given to the governor for twenty-one shillings and threepence paid by him on account of repairs to the Castle of Nairn. The account sets forth that it was incurred in plastering the hall, in placing locks on the doors of the keep or tower, and in providing two cables for the drawbridge. King William and his great officers of State, with their retine of servants and their military guards, as they passed to and from the castle, must have caused no small stir among the inhabitants of the little town, which was by this time beginning to assume a corporate existence.

King William having built the castle at Nairn, erected the county into a separate sheriffdom. King David had included it in the sheriffdom of Inverness, but William appointed a sheriff to itself. The first governor of the castle and sheriff of the county was William Pratt. He had the rank of a baron, and was descended from a Northumbrian family.

When William was in the north, either on this or subsequent occasions, he superintended the erection of two other royal forts. One was on the Moray Firth near Cromarty. It stood on the brink of a ravine which intersects the high ground behind the site of the old town of Cromarty, and was called the Castle of Dunscaith. On a clear day it would be visible from the Castle of Nairn. The other fort was built on the Beauly Firth, and is now known as Redcastle. It was called " Edderdover." In each of these forts or castles a regular garrison was placed, the object being to hold the country for King William. These stone-built castles must have been a source of great wonder and awe to the native population, as their construction marked a great advance on the science of fortification as known in those times in the North. The possession of these forts, in the state of the armaments of the time, necessarily gave to their holder the key of the military position of the district.

William warmly interested himself in the burghs his grandfather had established in Moray, and many of his charters still exist. The second charter of the burgh of Inverness was written at " Eren," the old form of Auldearn. It can hardly be a mistake for Nairn, as the names of the two places were quite different in the writings of the period. The " Doocot Hill " at Auldearn still retains the name of " The Castle " (as formerly noticed), and it probably at that time had a building of sufficient accommodation for the requirements of the King and his court. If not, the church would be available. There were with him at the time the deed was executed, the Bishop of Aberdeen, Earl Duncan, Justiciar of Scotland, Richard Moreville, the High Constable, Walter Olifard, Philip de Valoniis, and Robert de Berkeley.

King William possessed lands in Auldearn, and it may have been on this occasion that he granted a part of them to endow the Bishopric of Moray. Richard, Bishop of Moray, had been his tutor, and he entertained great affection for him. He gave him a " toft at Auldearn," and also the church and benefice of Auldearn, along with similar tofts in Inverness, Forres, and Elgin. These endowments will be particularised when the history of the church is dealt with.

A third charter was granted at Elgin, which mentions the name of the first burgess of Inverness—" Geoffrey Blund, our burgess of Inverness." The earliest burgess of Elgin whose name is preserved is William Wiseman. The earliest name of a Nairn burgess is Andrew Cumming. All these names are of southern origin, a proof of English influence in burghal communities in the north. The charter to Geoffrey Blund is peculiar.

On the occasion of William the Lion's last visit to the north, he had again important business to transact. Harold, Earl of Caithness and Orkney, attempted to throw off his allegiance to the King, and William sent him an ultimatum. An English historian, Richard of Hoveden, gives the following account of the affair :—

"In the year 1196, William, King of Scots, having gathered a great army, entered Moray to drive out Harold MacMadit, who had occupied that district. But before the King could enter Caithness, Harold fled to his ships, not wishing to risk a battle with the King. Then the King of Scots sent his army to Thurso, the town of the aforesaid Harold, and destroyed his castle there. But Harold, seeing that the King would completely devastate the country, came to the King's feet and placed himself at his mercy, chiefly because of a raging tempest on the sea, and the wind being contrary, so that he could not go to the Orkneys ; and he promised the King that he would bring him all his enemies when the King should again return to Moray ; on that condition, the King permitted him to retain a half of Caithness, and the other half he gave to Harold the younger, grandson of Rognald, a former Earl of Orkney and Caithness. Then the King returned to his own land, and Harold to the Orkneys. The King returned in the autumn to Moray as far as Invernairn, in order to receive the King's enemies from Harold. But though Harold had brought them as far as the port of Lochloy, near Invernairn, he allowed them to escape, and when the King returned late from hunting Harold came to him, bringing with him two boys, his grandchildren, to deliver them to the King as hostages. Being asked by the King where were the King's enemies whom he had promised to deliver up, and where was Thorfinn his son, whom he had also promised to give as a hostage, he replied, ' I allowed them to escape, knowing that if I delivered them up to you they would not escape out of your hands. My son I could not bring, for there is no other heir to my lands.' So, because he had not kept the agreement which he had made with the King, he was adjudged to remain in the King's custody until his son should arrive and become a hostage for him. And because he had permitted the King's enemies to escape, he was also adjudged to have forfeited those lands which he held of the King. The King took Harold with him to Edinburgh Castle, and laid him in chains until his men brought his son

Thorfinn from the Orkneys; and on their delivering him up as a hostage to the King, Harold was liberated."

The " Port of Lochloy " is here mentioned for the first time. The loch at the present day is separated from the seashore by a marsh, which is now in parts planted. There is no very distinct mark as to any channel between the loch and the sea of the nature of a port or entrance, but the indications as far as they go point to the outflow of the water of the loch and the probable inflow of the sea having been at the west end of the sheet of water. The sand-hills which skirt the beach terminate when they come under lee of the point of the Old Bar, and although the sand-drift is no guide, its corner probably marked the old entrance of the Port of Lochloy. The village of Lochloy was certainly at the west end of the loch, in the ground immediately below the present public road opposite the house of Lochloy. About the year 1859, a number of hearthstones and querns and other remains of dwellings were dug up at this spot. As formerly noticed, there is the site of an old chapel a little further west. A fishing village existed about three quarters of a mile to the east, which bore, as the place still bears, the name of Mavistown—apparently a modern name, if it be not a corruption of the Norse Maestown. The fishermen may have used the port of Lochloy for their boats, while they had their houses and crofts at Mavistown. Practically, however, any vessel once under lee of the Old Bar would be safe, and a landing easily effected on the flat shore. The place might thus get the name of the port of Lochloy.

Poor Harold and his two grandsons would no doubt come to Nairn along the shore, and having crossed the river at the ford below the castle, would be taken in charge by the guard as they sought entrance to the royal fort by its drawbridge. Ushered into the great hall, they would be in the presence of Earl Duncan, the Justiciar, or Chief Justice of the Realm, and other high officers of State. The King himself was away hunting at some sporting ground in the neighbourhood, and on his return late in the evening Harold's case was adjudged by King, peers, and barons in council. The decision was adverse to him, for who would lend an ear to the incredulous tale he had to tell—that he brought the King's enemies almost to his door and then allowed them to escape ? It would add to the King's displeasure that Thorfinn, Harold's son, who had on more than one occasion headed a revolt, was not yet within his power. He had claims to much more than the Earldom of Caithness or Orkney, for his step-mother was none other than a daughter of Malcolm Mac Eth, the Impostor. During the stay of the court at Nairn, Harold and his grandsons were close prisoners in the castle, and we may fancy they cast many a wistful glance at Morven and the Ord of Caithness, visible across the firth. At a subsequent period, Harold was given the offer of half of Caithness if he would put away his wife, the daughter of Malcolm Mac Eth, and take back his first spouse, Afreka, sister of Duncan, Earl of Fife, but he refused. Thorfinn eventually fell a victim to the King's anger, for he had his eyes torn out while a hostage at the court, in retaliation for some outrage committed by his friends in Caithness.

William the Lion had to contend against another set of rivals in the north, the family of Macwilliam, who claimed the crown in virtue of their descent from Ingibiorg, Malcolm Caenmore's first wife. They were finally exterminated by Macintagart (" Son of the Priest "), the lay abbot of the old monastery of Applecross, who in recognition of his services was created Earl of Ross. William the Lion, after a reign of forty-nine years, died at Stirling in 1214, and it was to his successor, his son Alexander, shortly after his accession to the throne, that the heads of his enemies the Macwilliams were presented. Alexander vigorously and successfully put down all rebellion throughout his realms.

One effect of the policy of David and his successors, Malcolm and William, was to introduce into Moray a new set of families —foreigners they were, both as regards language and birth. The old Celtic families having been pretty well cleared out, the King of the Scots had most of the lands in his gift, and with them he liberally rewarded his knights and lords. There is a strong presumption, however, that the old thanes whose names appear were a remnant of the original Celtic people. The title of " thane " has been the subject of much discussion. On the whole, it appears to be a Saxon designation of higher importance in England applied to a minor grade in Scotland. Under Celtic rule the mormaer was chief of the confederate tribes; the toshech was chief of one tribe. The title of earl having taken the place of mormaer, it was found necessary to find an English title for the toshech, and that of thane was given him. The names of toshech, thane, and chief are practically one and the same as regards rank. The Thanes of Cawdor, Brodie, Moyness, and Dyke were, in all probability, the successors of the Gaelic chiefs of the district. This supposition is confirmed by the lands which they held being nowhere mentioned as changing hands during this transition period. Their tenure of the land appears to have been changed to that of feuars holding of the Crown in conformity with the new feudal system.

Of the Thane of Moyness we know very little. In a charter by Alexander II. to the Bishop of Moray in 1238, he grants twenty-four marks of the feu-duty of Moyness and sixteen marks of the feu-duty of Dyke and Brodie by the hands of his feodfirmii of these lands. In a valuation of the lands of Kilravock and Easter Geddes (1295) the name of William, Thane of Moyness, occurs among the jurors. The thanage of Dyke appears to have been conjoined with that of Brodie. We read of Macbeth of Dyke in 1262, who may have been toshech at that date; but in 1311 an entry runs—" Michael, son of Malcolm, thane of Dyke and Brodie." The Calders were thus at Calder and the Brodies at Brodie.

Freskinus, a Fleming like Berowald, who got the lands of Innes extending from the Lossie to the Spey, came into possession of vast territories in the north. Freskinus came to Moray from Linlithgow, and settled at Duffus in King David's reign. His family assumed the territorial name of " de Moravia "—a designation which in their case was no empty boast. They probably held the old thanage of Moray, in addition to the castle and extensive domain of Duffus, and hence their adoption of the name " de Moravia." Hugh, son of Freskinus, was Lord of Duffus when William the Lion was in Moray, and he appears to have got a grant of Sutherland on the forfeiture of Harold of Caithness, who was so sharply dealt with at the castle of Nairn. He became the founder of the House of Sutherland, and the ancestor of the Earls of Sutherland. He retained his lands in Strathspey and Moray. Out of his patrimony, he gave large estates to his relatives. Gilbert de Moravia, a cousin apparently, who was Archdeacon of Moray, received from him Skelbo in Sutherland, and the lands of Culbin in Moray. Gilbert, having devoted his life to the Church, parted with these properties, and gave Culbin to Richard de Moravia, his brother. William, the brother of Hugh of Sutherland, retained the family seat of Duffus, and added to his possessions the lands of Petty and others. He succeeded William Pratt as Sheriff of Invernairne, and held that office in 1204. His grandson, Walter, who was knighted, was Lord of Boharm, Petty, Brackley, Artrille, Croy, Daviot, and numerous other lands. A son of this Walter acquired Bothwell in the south by marriage with the Olifards, and his descendants assumed the rather curious title of Lord of Bothwell and Petty—a title which became famous in history when borne by his grandson, Andrew Moray of Bothwell, the companion in arms of Sir William Wallace.

A Norman knight, Sir Reginald Chien, made his appearance in Moray, married one of the heiresses of the house of Duffus, and succeeded to much of the family property in Moray and Nairn. He succeeded his brother-in-law as Sheriff of Nairn, whilst his son became Sheriff of Elgin.

There were Stirlings at Cantray. Alexander of Stirling married a daughter of the Morays of Petty, and got Kerdale, Cantray, and Daviot. Cantray was given as a dower by Freskyn Cantray, Sir Alexander's widow, to her daughter Isobel between 1253-98 for an annual reddendum of a pair of gloves or a penny at the Feast of Pentecost. The great family of Douglas also took its rise from association with the de Moravias.

William de la Hay, a Northumbrian lord, was a courtier of William the Lion, became one of the hostages for the payment of his ransom, was sent on a special mission to King John of England, and returned with William to the north, witnessing various deeds and charters. One of these Hays is said to have the distinction of being the first tenant farmer in Scotland—that is, one who culti-vates land he does not own. A representative of the family got the lands of Lochloy, and became in 1296 the Sheriff of Inverness. The family had large possessions at Errol and Scone.

The ancient house of St. Sauveur in Normandy had, either as branches or as vassals, families of the name of de Bosco, de Bisset, and de Rose. They came over to England with William the Conqueror, and settled there, and frequent intermarriages took place amongst them. Robert de Ros in 1227 married Isobel, daughter of King William the Lion. Representatives of the three families settled in the North—Bisset had Kilravock in Nairnshire and also the Lovat country; Bosco (or Wood) got Redcastle (King William's fort of Edderdover); and Rose first appeared at Geddes in 1230. The three names occur together in an early document —Elizabeth Bisset of Kilravock married Sir Andrew Bosco of Redcastle, and their daughter Marjory married Hugh Rose of Geddes, and got Kilravock from her mother as a dower; in 1293 Hugh Rose obtained a charter to Kilravock from the King; and in 1295, the baronies of Kilravock and Geddes at the valuation before referred to, were estimated, the first at £24, and the other at £12.

Rose of Geddes had for his neighbour Sir Gervaise de Raite. Gervaise was a Cuming—a family also of Norman origin and Northumbrian connection, which rose to great power in Scotland. The fortunes of the Cumings were made when William Cuming married Marjory, the daughter of the old Celtic mormaer of Buchan, and succeeded him in that position as Earl of Buchan. His son Walter obtained the Lordship of Badenoch, and when they were at the height of their power they could boast of four earls, the Lord of Badenoch (a mighty potentate), and thirty belted knights in the family, with lands far and near. Some doubt has been cast on the connection of Gervaise de Raite's family with the castle of Raite at Geddes, it being thought more probable that Raite Castle in Badenoch was their seat, but a receipt which appears in the State Papers puts an end to all question on the point. It bears that Thomas de Braytoft, governor of the castles of Nairn and Cromarty, received his salary by the hands of Gervaise de Raite, constable of Invernairne. It is dated at Raite, March 6, 1292, and cannot refer to any Raite but that of Nairn.

The first Grant who came into Scotland settled at Coulmony. William Pratt, the first governor of the castle of Nairn, owned the lands of Daltulich, in Ardclach, and his daughter received them as her dower when she married Sir Gilbert de Glencarnie, descended from the Earl of Strathern's second son. The Pratts also possessed Coulmony, and about the year 1258 Sir John Pratt bestowed on Sir Robert le Grant " the land of Cloumanche," now Coulmony. It would appear that a family of the name of Pratt held lands in Nottingham. The Bissets, Pratts, and Grants had thus been near neighbours in England before they came and settled together in the North of Scotland. The suggestion has been made (and Sir William Fraser thought with probable truth) that the Grants were brought to Scotland from England by John and Walter Bisset on their return from exile in 1242, the Bissets having been banished the country for their supposed complicity in the murder of the Earl of Athole.

The Chisholms, who came from the south at the same time as the Bissets and the Lovels—the latter family has long since been extinct—also possessed lands in Nairnshire.

Robert le Falconer, of Hawkerton, acquired Lethen, and John le Hunter also had a connection with the county. He was a witness at the Kilravock valuation in 1295, and a place which in old charters bears the name of Hunterbog, was probably his property. The low ground between Kinnudie and Auldearn appears to have been the Hunter's Bog of the charters.

Gilbert Durward (the hereditary Keeper of the King's Door) obtained in 1236 the lands of Both (now known as Highland Boath) and Banchor in the bailiary or shire of Invernairn. A family of the name of Durward, in humble circumstances, till recently dwelt at Highland Boath—a curious survival, like that of Macbeth in the low country of Nairn and Moray, of a great historical name. The tradition that these lands belonged to Macbeth is unsupported by any evidence.

In 1238 the Crown held the following lands in thanage in the bailiwick or shire of Nairn—" The lands of Kildrummie, Aldheren, Balnecath, Geddes, Urchany, Rait, Moyness, and Lenedycoth." The holders of these lands were practically tenants of the Crown. A large extent of land had also been gifted by the Crown to the Church.

The advent of these Norman and Anglo-Scottish families must have caused wonderful changes in the social life of the district. The only native family of any strength was that of Mackintosh (" Son of the Toshech "), but it appears to have been elbowed out of the lowlands of Nairn. The Cumings dispossessed it of Raite in Nairnshire, and the Ogilvies for a time occupied its lands in Strathnairn. Apart from some notices of the burgesses of the royal burghs, we learn little of the ordinary inhabitants of the district. They probably accepted service under these Saxon masters when their Celtic chiefs disappeared. The newcomers brought immense wealth with them, and doubtless surrounded themselves in their northern homes with Norman and English luxuries. The Moravia family built castles for themselves at Duffus, Petty, and Daviot.

The ordinary family mansion continued to be constructed of wood protected by earthworks. Orchards were planted in some instances, and the grounds embellished and beautified. The climate, fine even then, must have been an inducement to settlers accustomed to the sunny skies of the South. They still retained, many of them, their estates in England and the south of Scotland Their favourite pastime was hunting in the adjacent forests, their common amusement riding and jousting. Chivalry and knight-errantry were the fashionable ideals of the time. The style of life in Nairnshire during the reigns of Alexander II. and III., when these families were in the ascendant, would correspond to that of the leading counties of England in the same period. It was a time of comparative peace, and the districts of the country, such as Moray and Nairn, where the Norman gentry held sway, must have advanced greatly in civilisation, warranting the statement of Mr. Cosmo Innes that it reached a height not again attained till the eighteenth century was reached. They were devoted churchmen, and gave largely of their wealth to the support of the clergy, many of whom were younger sons of their own families. The great family of Freskyn was by this time connected with the Norman Court of Rouen as well as with the royal family of England. Its chiefs were familiar with the art and science of the day, with the refinement and learning prevalent in the highest circles in Europe. " They seem " (says Kingsley) " to have been, with the instinct of true Flemings, civilisers and cultivators and traders as well as conquerors ; they were in those days bringing to order and tillage the rich lands of the north-east, from the Firth of Moray to that of the Forth."

When political changes threw the kingdom into confusion and disorder, and the country was brought to the verge of ruin by contending factions, the presence of these nobles linked the district to the course of public affairs in Scotland, and many of them played a prominent part in the historical events of the time.

CHAPTER V

THE TIME OF EDWARD I.

On the death of King Alexander III., the Scottish crown devolved on a grand-daughter Margaret, the Maid of Norway. She was the only child of Eric, King of Norway, by his late consort Margaret, the daughter of Alexander, and was but three years of age at the time of her grandfather's death. A provisional Government was formed, composed of Guardians of State, viz. :—Fraser, Bishop of St. Andrews; Wishart, Bishop of Glasgow; Duncan, Earl of Fife; Alexander, Earl of Buchan; John Comyn, Lord of Badenoch; and James, the High Steward of Scotland. Bishop Fraser, the Earl of Buchan, and the Earl of Fife were entrusted with the government of the kingdom north of the Forth. They ruled the country with considerable ability for eighteen months, but, after the death of the Earl of Buchan, and the assassination of the Earl of Fife in 1288, dissensions arose between the remaining regents and other nobles, and claims were advanced by Robert de Bruce of Annandale to the Crown, which necessitated steps being taken to bring the infant Queen from her home in Norway to Scotland. Edward I. of England acted the part of friendly counsellor in the matter, but even at this early stage he appears to have set his heart upon a union of the two kingdoms, and the establishing of an absolute sovereignty over Britain. All his subsequent proceedings are traceable to this one absorbing desire. A ready means of accomplishing this purpose was to marry his eldest son Prince Edward to Margaret of Norway. They were second cousins, but the Pope's dispensation was easily procured to overcome the ecclesiastical difficulty. A State document was drawn up entitled the " Letter of the Community of Scotland," assuring Edward that the proposed alliance, which promised to be productive of so many advantages to both kingdoms, would have the unanimous and cordial assent of the signatories. It was signed by the Guardians, Bishops, Earls, Abbots, Priors, and Barons constituting the Estates of the Kingdom, and was confirmed at a meeting of Parliament at Brigham. The Chiens, de Moravias, William Hay of Lochloy, John Stirling, and Simon Frisel, were amongst the barons who signed the proclamation.

Steps were immediately taken for bringing the little Maiden Queen home to Scotland. The Abbot of Welbeck, Henry de Rye (of whom more will yet be seen), and others were dispatched by Edward to make the preliminary arrangements for her departure from Norway. They returned and reported favourable progress, and a great ship was fitted out by Edward, the victualling and decoration of which were intrusted to the chief butler of his own household. " The stores were provided with no niggard hand. They consisted, among other matters, of 31 hogsheads and 1 pipe of wine, 10 barrels of beer, 15 carcases of oxen (salted of course), 72 hams, 400 dried fish, 200 stock fish, 1 barrel of sturgeon, 5 dozen of lampreys, 50 pounds of ' whale,' along with the very necessary accompaniment of 22 gallons of mustard, with salt, pepper, vinegar, and onions in proportion. A stock of little luxuries, suited to the more delicate palate and stomach of the baby princess, was not forgotten, such as 500 walnuts, 2 loaves of sugar, grits and oatmeal, with a corresponding allowance of ginger, citron, and mace, 2 frails of figs, the same quantity of raisins, and 28 pounds of gingerbread." The good ship, gaily painted, with banners flying, and manned by a crew of forty hands, sailed for Bergen, and in due time arrived there and embarked the Maiden of Norway.

Edward, anxious that the young Queen, the moment she reached Orkney, should be well taken care of, despatched his trusted agents, the Abbot of Welbeck, Henry de Rye, and Thomas Braytoft, to meet her. These royal commissioners started from Newcastle on September 15th. They reached St. Andrews on the 19th, but were delayed there next day by a great tempest. They reached Aberdeen on the 23rd, next day they were at

Bischoprenes, the following day at Duffus, and on the 27th at Nairn. The account (in the State Papers) from which these details were taken, mentions that at Nairn they purchased a boll of wheat costing 4s. 1d. They arrived in a carriage with five horses. They left their carriage and horses at Nairn with two grooms, and proceeded by sea to Cromarty, taking a groom or attendant with them. Cromarty was reached next day, the 28th, Dornoch on the 29th, and Skelbo on the 30th. Here they appear to have received the terrible tidings that the young Queen was dead, for they record " conferring with the Scottish Envoys." The Maid of Norway, a delicate child, crossing the North Sea in tempestuous weather, fell ill, and died just on reaching the Orkney Islands. The frail life, upon which the hopes of two nations centred, had vanished. The English agents continued their journey as far as Wick, and then sorrowfully retraced their steps. They crossed over from Nigg, arrived at Nairn on October 10th, and remained for three days. Their expenses on the first day were 4s. 3d. ; the second day 3s. 9d. ; and the third day 3s. 2d. They also paid for the keep of the five horses and the two grooms' foraging at Nairn for the fifteen days during which they were absent the sum of 4s. 10d; for shoeing their horses and for iron (repairs probably) to their carriage 1s. The presence of the English envoys in Nairn would doubtless throw the quiet little town into great excitement, especially if it were intended that the infant Queen should come by the same route as that taken by her English guardians, and thence proceed southward by the carriage left in readiness at Nairn. The envoys who thus visited Nairn took their departure, but they were ere long brought on the scene again.

The death of Margaret caused the deepest sorrow to the whole nation. No provision had been made for the succession to the Crown, and now Baliol, Bruce, and several other nobles formed rival factions. The country became divided into two political parties—the one favouring Baliol and the other Bruce. Bishop Fraser of St. Andrews and John Comyn, Lord of Badenoch, assumed supreme authority, to the exclusion of the other regents, and warmly espoused the cause of Baliol. They appear to have carried matters with a high hand against their opponents, and would probably have proclaimed Baliol King of Scotland without much further delay, had not the freemen of Moray taken a bold but very unpatriotic step. They appealed to Edward, King of England, to interfere, protesting that the territory of Moray was under " the immediate government of the King of Scotland," and that the Bishop of St. Andrews and the Lord of Badenoch had usurped authority by appointing deputies. These deputies, it was stated, had destroyed and plundered the lands and towns of the freemen of the Lord, the King of Scotland, burnt the said towns and their barns full of corn, carried away with them all the property of the said men of Moray, and cruelly killed as many men, women, and little children as they could come at." This is a very dark picture of the state of the times, and the explanation of it may be that the Baliol deputies had endeavoured to oust out of their property all who adhered to Bruce. The leader of this appeal was the Earl of Mar. At first sight it is difficult to see what he had to do with Moray, but the explanation appears to be that in the preceding reign he had acted as one of the Custodiers of Moray, but had been deprived of his office by the regents. The " freemen of Moray " were the Crown tenants, who held their lands in thanage or otherwise directly from the king. They appear to have sided with Bruce, and included William de la Hay of Lochloy and John Stirling (of Cantray) who had assumed the designation of Moravia. The supporters of Baliol were the more numerous in the district, and included the clergy, the burgesses, the Chiens of Duffus, the Moravias of Petty, and the Raites and other branches of the Cumings. The " Seven Earls of Scotland," headed by the Earl of Fife, also sent an appeal to Edward. The men of Moray and the Scottish nobles thus unwittingly played into the hands of the astute English King. He wanted but a pretext for interfering in the affairs of Scotland, and it had now been given him. He held a conference with the prelates and nobles of Scotland on the 10th of May, 1291, at the church of Norham on the south bank of the Tweed, and before entering upon a discussion of the claims of the rival competitors, laid before them his claim to the title of Lord Paramount of Scotland. After some show of reluctance, one after another of the competitors and their friends acknowledged Edward as their Lord Paramount, having a right to adjudicate on their claims. Edward then demanded that the government of the country and the command of the royal fortresses be surrendered to him during the period of arbitration, and this was also agreed to. On the 11th of June the royal castles were formally handed over to him. They were twenty-three in number, including Aberdeen, Aboyne, Banff, Elgin, Forres, Nairn, Inverness, Dingwall, and Cromarty. The castle of Nairn, along with the others, was handed over to Edward's officers and garrisoned by English troops. Thomas Braytoft, who had been at Nairn the year before as an envoy to bring the Maid of Norway home, was appointed governor of the castles of Nairn and Cromarty; Henry de Rye, his companion on that occasion, was appointed governor of the castles of Elgin and Forres; William Braytoft was put in charge of the castle of Inverness; and Patrick Grant was made governor of Cluny Castle in Perthshire. All earls, barons, thanes, and burgesses were ordered to make homage to Edward by swearing an oath of fealty, and William, Earl of Sutherland (Hugh Freskyn of Moravia's grandson), administered the oath to all benorth the Spey at Inverness. The ceremony of swearing in the officers and people began on 13th July, and continued for fourteen days. At the expiration of that time, the proceedings were closed, and the peace of Edward, as Lord Paramount of Scotland, was proclaimed, as in other towns of the kingdom, at the market cross of Nairn, in due form by a herald.

Thomas Braytoft continued in command of the garrisons at Nairn and Cromarty, and drew his pay from time to time. His receipt, already mentioned as being granted to Sir Gervaise de Raite, runs thus—" To all who may see or hear of these presents, I, Thomas de Braytoft, keeper of the castles of Nairn and Cromarty, on behalf of the illustrious King, Lord Edward, by the grace of God, King of England, *constituted* Overlord of the Realm of Scotland, greeting. Know all men that I, on Thursday preceding the Feast of Pope St. Gregory, in the year of our Lord 1292, received by the hands of Sir Gervaise de Raite, Knight, constable of Nairn, as the dues and arrears of the bailieship of Invernairn, for my service and custody of the castles of Nairn and

Cromarty, £11 sterling. In witness whereof I have granted these presents to Sir G.—Given at Raite, day and year foresaid." On June 27th of the same year he received £28 17s. in payment of the "balance of his wages for the custody of the castles of Nairn and Cromarty," from the Chamberlain of Scotland.

Edward, in pursuance of his function as arbiter in the dispute as to the succession to the throne, appointed one hundred and four commissioners—forty to be nominated by Baliol, forty by Bruce, and twenty-four by himself—to discuss the claims as a preparatory step to their being submitted to him for his final decision, and the following nobles connected with the north were chosen :—By Baliol—John, Earl of Buchan ; William, Earl of Ross ; Andrew de Moravia of Petty and Bothwell ; William de Moravia of Tully-barden ; Reginald le Chien, senior ; Reginald le Chien, junior ; and Henry le Chien, Bishop of Aberdeen. By Bruce—Donald, Earl of Mar ; John, Earl of Athole ; John Stirling de Moravia ; and William de la Hay. The Commissioners gave in their report, and Edward gave his award in favour of Baliol, and immediately issued letters to the commanders of the twenty-three royal castles for the surrender of these fortresses. Thomas de Braytoft, governor of the castles of Nairn and Cromarty, received a copy of this letter dated at Berwick, 18th November, 1292, and immediately caused the colours of John Baliol to be hoisted upon the two fortresses under his charge.

Baliol was crowned at Scone twenty days later, but Edward continued to interfere in the internal affairs of the kingdom, professedly on the principle that he had to bring to completion all matters originated during his tenure of office as Lord Paramount, and on this principle he made handsome presents to his friends out of the Scottish revenues. Amongst others, Edward ordered the payment of a pension of fifty marks out of the revenues of Inverness to Reginald le Chien, junior, and Sir Robert Cameron, with two and a half years' arrears, and ordered Reginald le Chien, senior, Sheriff of Nairn, to pay to Robert Wishart, Bishop of Glasgow, as a special mark of his favour, the sum of £500, out of the arrears of Crown revenues within the counties of Nairn, Kincardine, Formartine, and Invery, and a sum of £195 19s. 4d. out of the balance of arrears in Elgin and Kintrae. The Chiens, father and son, were continued by Baliol in their sheriffdoms of Nairn and Elgin. Rose of Geddes, who had got possession of Kilravock through his wife Marjory Bosco, in the time of Alexander III., resigned the property into the hands of Baliol, in order to receive it back on the securer title of a royal charter. The deed of resignation is witnessed by Lords Andrew de Moravia (of Petty) and Reginald le Chien, and the King's charter of confirmation was duly granted. The original is now lost, having been destroyed in the burning of Elgin Cathedral in a later century, but the fact that it was sought for affords a proof that at the beginning of Baliol's reign there was a general sense of security in the country.

Baliol and the Scottish nobles having repudiated Edward's right to interfere in the affairs of Scotland, the English king crossed the Borders with an army of 30,000 infantry and 4000 cavalry. Berwick was captured, and great loss inflicted on the Scots. A still more disastrous blow fell upon the Scottish cause when Edward captured the Castle of Dunbar. In it had gathered many distinguished leaders from the north, and amongst the prisoners taken were the Earls of Ross and Athole, and John Cuming, younger of Badenoch. They were sent to the Tower of London in chains. Andrew Moray of Bothwell and his son Andrew were also taken prisoners—the former being sent to the Tower of London and the latter to Chester.

Edward's progress North was practically unopposed, and the chief men of the districts through which he passed hastened to make submission to him. One of the first of these was a laird connected with Nairnshire, Gilbert de Glencarnie, a grandson of Marjory Pratt of Daltulich, the daughter of the first governor of the castle of Nairn. Gilbert had become a great landlord by this time, possessing the estates of Fochabers, Ballindalloch, Duthil, and others on the banks of the Findhorn and Spey. He met Edward at Cluny in Perthshire, doubtless anxious to be on friendly terms with the party in power. But he was not singular. The news of Edward's triumphant progress had reached the north, and knights and barons deemed it expedient to do him homage. Accordingly we find Stirling de Moravia leaving his house at Cantray and proceeding to Aberdeen to meet the King. The Ogilvies, then great lords of Strathnairn, were there too. Reginald Chien, the Hays of Lochloy, Robert le Falconer, William de Moravia, and others, all hastened to Aberdeen and made their submission. Gervaise de Raite was not with them, but he appeared and swore fealty when the King came into Moray, and doubtless surrendered to him the royal castle of Nairn. On the 25th of July, Edward and his army crossed the Spey by the ancient ford of Bellie, situated a little above the spot on which the church of Speymouth now stands. It was a favourite crossing place for all the armies entering Moray. Following the king's highway, he entered Elgin on the 26th, and took up his residence in the castle on Ladyhill.

The Sheriff of Nairn, Sir Reginald Chien, had died, and Edward graciously reinstated his wife as heiress of the family of Ochiltree in her estates. Reports came in to Edward that the country to the north and west was quite peaceable, and he deemed it unnecessary to advance further. He despatched, however, a detachment of his troops to occupy the castles of Nairn, Inverness, Dingwall, and Cromarty. William Hay of Lochloy inspired the King with so much confidence that he gave him authority over a wide district. He was made Sheriff of Inverness, and warden of Ross-shire. After a stay of four days, Edward returned to the south. In the autumn he summoned a Scottish Parliament at Berwick, and amongst those who attended were Sir Reginald Chien, Sir Gervaise de Raite and Sir Andrew de Raite, from the county of Nairn, Alan de Moravia from Culbin, and Sir Gilbert Glencarnie. Having, as he thought, completely subjugated the kingdom, Edward proceeded to organise the government according to English ideas.

For the purposes of taxation, he divided the kingdom into two portions by the line of the Forth, placing the northern division under Henry de Rye (the companion of Braytoft at Nairn in 1292), as escheator, and appointed him keeper of the castles of Forres and Elgin. This civilian officer was immediately under and responsible only to Cressingham, the English Chancellor of the Exchequer, so that in fact Scotland had been reduced to the humiliating position of an English province or crown colony. Henry de Rye dealt with the estates of the Scottish nobles with a free hand, forfeiting those who were supposed to be unfriendly to the English interest, and imposing severe taxes, claiming escheats, levying fines and contributions, and imprisoning or outlawing every person who showed a disposition to resent this oppression.

It was in the midst of the resulting discontent that William Wallace arose and boldly attempted to throw off the English yoke, and achieve the independence of his country. One of the first to join his standard of rebellion was Andrew de Moravia or Moray of Petty and Bothwell, with his son and heir. They threw themselves heart and soul into the patriotic endeavour to deliver their country from English usurpation. At a critical stage in the fortunes of Wallace and his troops young Andrew Moray came to Moray and Nairn, and called out his own people. He made his castle of Avoch the rallying point, and large numbers joined his ranks ; but the fear of Edward's vengeance deterred others, though in warm sympathy with the patriotic movement, from doing likewise. Moray was thus once more in insurrection. David, Andrew's uncle, the Bishop of Moray, was a tower of strength for the cause. The royal castles were attacked and besieged, and many of the English soldiers slain. The castles of Forres and Elgin, which were under the special guardianship of Henry de Ryc, were burned. The castle of Duffus, the residence of the Chiens, was set on fire, and the residences of others who held office under the English king were destroyed.

Henry Chien, Bishop of Aberdeen, the Earl of Mar, and the Countess of Ross, attempted to put down the insurrection, but without avail. Sir Andrew of Raite appears to have taken an active part along with them, and he was sent south as the bearer of despatches to Edward, to give an account of the services rendered by these friends. The Bishop, in his letter of credence, mentions that, as they were " in Launoy-upon-the-Spey on the Tuesday before the feast of St. Mary Magdalene, there met us Andrew de Murray with a large body of rogues, the number of which Sir Andrew de Raite, your bachelor, can show you according to what he heard from the people of their company. And the aforesaid rogues betook themselves into a very great stronghold of bog and wood, where no horsemen could be of service." " It would be too long a business to write," says the Bishop, " but we pray you to have the goodness to give credence to Sir Andrew de Raite, your bachelor, who can tell you these affairs in all points, for he was in person at all these doings." Sir Andrew de Raite was accompanied by Bernard de Monte Alto, and they carried a letter from Euphemia, Countess of Ross, to Edward. Malise, Earl of Stratherne, also entrusted him with some business on his own account, and wrote (in Norman French) to the King—" Dear Sire, I pray you, if it please you, to have the goodness to believe Sir Andrew de Raite, the bearer of this letter, in the matter which he will tell you verbally from me." On his way south, the knight of Raite had an interview with Cressingham, the King's Chamberlain in Scotland, but did not impress him very greatly, for he wrote privately to Edward —" Sir Andrew Raite is going to you with a credence which he has shown me, and which is false in many points and obscure, as will be shown hereafter, as I fear ; and therefore, sire, if it be your pleasure, you will give little weight to it ! " The shrewd Chamberlain probably discerned that these friends were seeking important favours from Edward, namely, the estates of their rivals, by exaggerating the value of the services they had themselves rendered.

King Edward, however, at length realized that the insurrection had become a formidable affair, and he despatched an army of 40,000 troops into Scotland. It proceeded to Ayrshire, where the Scottish army under Wallace was gathered, but the nobles in the Scottish army, who were jealous of the position of Wallace, surrendered on condition of a promise of free pardon and their estates. Wallace, however, and Andrew Moray, senior, refused to sign the treaty, and proceeded with a band of patriots to the north. Whether they came to the district of Moray on this occasion is doubtful. The people were already on their side, and probably joined them in their raids in Aberdeen and Buchan in wasting the lands of the Earl of Buchan and the Chiens. Sir Andrew Moray and his son were at Wallace's side as he made his victorious journey southwards, capturing the castles of Forfar, Brechin, and Montrose, and engaging in the great battle of Stirling in which the English were completely routed. In the battle Andrew Moray, the younger, fell mortally wounded.

Sir Andrew Moray's residence was at the old Castlehill of Petty, and the family also had a house at Avoch. The title of " Bothwell," by which he is almost exclusively known in history, has been the means of concealing his identity as the Knight of Petty, Brackley, and Boharm—a descendant of the great house of Freskyn de Moravia.

In 1303, Edward, enraged at the failure of all his attempts to subdue Scotland, prepared to invade the country once more, with the deliberate design (according to Fordun) of effecting its entire and final subjugation, or of reducing it, by the total extermination of the inhabitants, to a state of utter and irrecoverable desolation. He summoned the whole strength of his dominions and invaded Scotland in two divisions. Edward himself in person commanded the right division. No resistance was offered to his advance, the inhabitants fleeing at the approach of the enemy, and the country was given up to devastation by fire and sword. Edward was at Elgin on the 10th of September, and resided in the manse of the Dean of Moray, at the north-west corner of King Street where it joins College Street. On the 13th he arrived at Kinloss Abbey, and from thence marched his army to Lochindorb, the stronghold of Sir John Cuming, who was in arms against him. The castle stands on a small island in the loch. Probably in prehistoric times it was used as a lake dwelling. Remains of piles have been found which indicate that its original construction was of this character. Its isolated position would easily recommend it as a secure retreat in times of trouble, and the Cumings had long before this fortified it. Here in this solitary abode, in the heart of a vast forest—for the country, though now bare, was at that time densely wooded for many miles around—Edward took up his abode, and enjoyed his favourite pastime of hunting. Dr. Taylor, in his exhaustive account of Edward's visits to the North, thus picturesquely describes the scene—" While the earlier part of the day was thus devoted to the pleasures of the chase, the later portion of it, no doubt, was not less agreeably spent within the walls of the royal residence. As the shades of evening set in, the battlements and watch-towers of the insular fortress, illuminated with torches on every side, sent forth a blaze of light over the surface of the lake. And while the soldiers, who either bivouacked or occupied tents and temporary huts, constructed of branches of trees, on its banks, partook around their camp fires of their evening meal before retiring to rest, the knights assembled in the banqueting hall of the castle to pass the evening in conviviality and social mirth. Here Edward presided at the festive board, dispensed his hospitality to his nobles, and listened, while the wine cup went round, to the minstrels who strung their harps and sang of love, chivalry, and war." The support of so vast an army in so inhospitable a region as the forests of Leonach and Lochindorb must have been a matter of no small difficulty, and provisions were requisitioned from the neighbouring districts. The Sheriff of Nairn was able to send up to Edward 26 cattle, 26 sheep, and 40 pigs, and similar droves were despatched from Inverness, Elgin, and Dingwall.

Edward found his position at Lochindorb convenient for despatching troops in all directions. The castles of Elgin, Forres, and Nairn were again taken possession of by English troops in their march forward. Inverness Castle was also garrisoned anew. Urquhart Castle was next besieged, and it offered a determined defence under a gallant scion of the family of Bosco or Wood of Redcastle, but after holding out for several weeks, the brave garrison was put to the sword—the only one of all the besieged who was not slain being the wife of the commander, who contrived to make her escape disguised as a servant. Having brought the north country under subjection, Edward took his departure from Lochindorb on 4th October. He had spent a fortnight there, and twenty-nine days altogether in Moray.

The English troops, however, were not allowed to have it all their own way. While they were engaged in reducing the castle of Cromarty, which used to be under the command of the governor of the castle of Nairn, the insurgents made a raid upon Nairn. Sir Climes of Ross, who figured shortly before in an attack on some English troops crossing the Stockford, was the hero of the taking of the castle of Nairn. It was an evening in autumn. The burghers were about retiring to rest, when the sound of a troop of cavalry dashing down the High Street broke the stillness of the night and drew the inhabitants to their doors. These were no belated travellers making for the ford, for on reaching the top of the Redhill, as the Brae was called, the horsemen wheeled round and fronted the castle. Each horseman dismounted, and having made his horse fast to the palisade, formed into line. Sir Climes of Ross (a Fraser, it is believed), Sir John Ramsdean, his kinsman Sir Alexander Fraser, Lord of Philorth, and a warrior named Rowan, without a moment's parley, made a dash for the draw-bridge. A trooper seized an oil lamp from the hand of a burgher who had come trembling on the scene, and declaring that they wanted a little more light, cast the burning oil rag on the thatched roof of an adjoining cottage, and in the midst of the glare and smoke of the blazing thatch, a fierce fight, with sword and spear hand-to-hand, ensued. The governor of the castle and his English soldiers made a spirited defence, but they were no match for these re-doubtable knights and their companions in arms. Sir Climes laid the governor low with a stroke from his broadsword, and his men took the castle at a rush, overpowering and killing many of the guards.

Blind Harry, in recording the episode, says that " ' the good house of Nairn ' that night was well taken, and its captain and many strong men slain." Wallace himself came north in the end of the year 1304. If the castle of Nairn remained in the hands of his followers it is possible he visited Nairn at that time. The " Wallace Butts and Crookedales " is a description of some pro-perty in the Burgh of Nairn in charters of the seventeenth century, but no tradition has come down as to the origin of the name. Wallace appears to have crossed the firth at Ardersier, and by a stratagem overcame a strong body of English troops at a hollow about four miles south of Cromarty, which retains the name of Wallace Slack or ravine. The little wooded eminence, visible from the coast at Nairn, which terminates towards the east in an abrupt cliff that overhangs the sea, and slopes away to the west in a marshy hollow, marks the spot. Hugh Miller describes the incident in his " Scenes and Legends." Wallace laid an ambuscade for a body of English troops going to join another body at Easter Ross, and completely vanquished them. He then relieved William de Monte Alto, who had held out bravely with only forty men for some time. But the tide in the fortunes of Wallace about this time turned. He is said by tradition to have had to seek refuge in one of the caves of Cromarty, within a short distance of his brilliant exploit. It was the beginning of his fugitive life, which ended in his capture and his being sent a prisoner to London, to be executed with horrible atrocities. Edward appointed new officers for the government of the North. William Wiseman was made Sheriff of Elgin; and Alexander Wiseman Sheriff of Forres and Nairn. John Stirling of Moravia was rewarded with the sheriffship of Inverness, and William de Monte Alto, having made his peace with Edward, was reinstated in the sheriffdom of Cromarty.

These arrangements were shortly overturned by Bruce taking the field as the rightful King of the Scots. Moray declared unhesitatingly for Bruce. The Knight of Petty was again on his side. He was married to Bruce's sister, and a kinsman of his, who was Bishop of Moray and had been minister of Bothwell, put himself at the head of the movement in favour of Bruce in the north. The Morays or Moravias of Culbin, Hay of Lochloy, Fenton of Beauford, William de Dollas, whose family afterwards acquired Cantray in Nairnshire, and several of the clergy of the province, warmly took up Bruce's cause. Sir Reginald le Chien, the Earl of Ross, and the Earl of Sutherland alone among the great magnates of the north remained true to Edward. Edward sent another army into Scotland, with the usual result, that many nobles made submission, and asked for the estates of their neighbours who had become fugitives, but on its withdrawal insurrection again broke out. The death of Edward on the eve of leading in person his third army into Scotland, and the overthrow of the English army by Bruce at Bannockburn a few years afterwards, brought to a close a period of internecine warfare, and re-established the Independence of Scotland.

CHAPTER VI

PERIOD OF THE ROMAN CATHOLIC CHURCH

THE Roman Catholic Church, which supplanted the old Celtic Church, attained to a position of great magnificence in Moray. Fostered by the care of William the Lion and his successors, Alexander II. and Alexander III., it had also munificent benefactors in the Anglo-Norman families who had settled in the district. The Cathedral Church at Elgin was " the mirror of the land and the glory of the Kingdom," according to one of its Bishops. The Abbey of Kinloss, founded in 1150, was on a scale of great grandeur. Its mitred Abbot had a seat in Parliament, and on three occasions entertained, with princely hospitality, within its walls the sovereign and royal court. The ruins of the Priory of Pluscarden still testify to the remarkable character of its original foundation. In addition to these three great religious establishments, there were several others of minor importance. It happens that none of these ecclesiastical institutions was situated in Nairnshire, but the greater portion of its lands was devoted to their support. The county of Nairn might really have been designated the Church's glebe, so large was the extent of the lands given over to it.

The new Church does not appear to have come into any violent collision with the older Celtic institution in Moray. On the contrary, the names of the popularly-revered patron saints of the Columban Church are mostly retained and others added. The scanty endowments of the early Church were doubtless appropriated when the native clergy were superseded. There is one instance of kindly dealing with a recluse known as "John the Hermit," probably a survivor of the Culdees. The scene of his ministrations was in the remote region of Dunlichty in Strathnairn. John the Hermit appears to have been a man of remarkable character. William the Lion on his first visit to the north heard something of him, and instructed Simon, Bishop of Moray, to give him the island which is "in the Lake of Lunnin at the east, and half-an-oxgate of land in Daldauch." On a subsequent visit King William, when Richard, his own chaplain, was Bishop of Moray, confirmed the gift by charter to John the Hermit. "Lunnin" is supposed to be Dunlichty—sometimes it is called Lunlichty— but there is no island in the loch now. The Gaelic place-name, however, supplies remarkable confirmation of the supposition of Dunlichty having been the scene of John the Hermit's insular abode. The loch is known as "The Loch of the Church." There are frequent references to a hermit's croft in Ardclach in the chartulary of Moray. It usually comes after Achagour in the list of places belonging to the Church in Ardclach, and is probably Daltra, the old form of which name is Daldarach (The Oak Wood).

The diocese of Moray included the shires of Elgin, Forres, and Nairn, and extended over a large portion of the counties of Inverness and Banff. Along the coast, it stretched from the Spey to the Beauly. The bishopric was probably founded in the reign of Alexander I., about 1122. When William the Lion came to Moray on his second visit his old friend Richard was bishop of the diocese, and he befriended his saintly instructor in many ways, enforcing his badly paid dues, granting him a tithe of the fines and escheats falling to the Crown, and giving him tofts of land in each of the burghs of Moray, excepting Nairn, in lieu of which he gave him a toft in Auldearn. Nairn was exempted on this occasion, for the reason that the Bishop had just parted with very considerable possessions in the burgh of Nairn to King William, who wanted the ground for building or enlarging the castle of Nairn. The wording of the writ of excambion seems to imply that previous to this exchange the lands of the burgh of Nairn as well as of the castle belonged to the Church.

Bishop Richard was succeeded by Bricius, a Douglas, who had been Prior of Lesmahagow. He owed his promotion to this post to the influence of the family of de Moravia, and was probably related to them. The Cathedral Church prior to this time was at Birnie, Spynie, or Kinnedor indifferently, but he had it fixed at Spynie. He gave to the Cathedral a constitution founded on the " usage of Lincoln," and instituted a chapter of eight canons. He had five brothers, whom he settled in the district, and the rise of the great house of Douglas in Scotland is attributed to this connection. Andrew de Moravia, his successor, was a son of Hugh de Moravia, Lord of Duffus, who procured from his relatives of Duffus and Petty some munificent gifts for the Church. It was he who built the Cathedral Church at Elgin, and increased the number of canons from eight to twenty-three. King Alexander II. made the Church a gift of the lands of Kildrummie, along with tithes of the feu duties paid by the Crown tenants in Nairnshire. The lands of Coulmony and Daltulich were also assigned to the Church at an early date.

The next Bishop of note was David de Moravia. He also owed his promotion to the Moravias of Petty, having been their minister at Bothwell, and probably a relative. He was both priest and warrior, and, as formerly mentioned, warmly espoused the cause of Bruce. He was accused by Edward of haranguing crowds and inciting them to throw off the English yoke and declare for Bruce. His patriotism, however, probably increased rather than diminished his popularity in Moray and Nairn.

The Bishops of Moray drew revenues from Ferness, Lethen, Daldauch, Dunlichty, and Logie (or Tullydivie in Edenkillie).

Auldearn was the most important parish from an ecclesiastical point of view. The benefice was an exceedingly rich one, probably through early benefactions of William the Lion, who possessed the lands of Auldearn. It was the benefice of the Dean of Moray. The Dean was a very great Church dignitary, and enjoyed a house with a garden of four acres in Elgin, where he resided, merely visiting Auldearn at such times as suited his convenience, and drawing the revenues of its lands. The lands of Penick, near Auldearn, were at a very early period devoted to the Church.

They appear to have belonged originally to the Priory of Urquhart, then to the Priory of Pluscardine, and latterly to the Deanery of Moray. A house of more than ordinary dimensions existed at Penick, and became the country seat of some of the later Deans. It was at one time known as the House of Penick and latterly as Penick Castle, and was ranked as one of the manor houses of the district. It is described as having been three stories high. The ruins of the old place have only recently disappeared, and an avenue of stately trees leading up to its site still exists. The present church of Auldearn no doubt occupies the original site of the ecclesiastical edifice. The Dean had a sub-dean, whose income was derived from the altarage of Auldearn, with the chapel of Nairn and the church and parish of Dallas (which latter was worth five chalders, two bolls). The value placed upon the vicarage of Auldearn in the year 1561 was £40, which would be derived from dues and gratuities. The following is given as the Dean's rental in the year 1561—Mekill Penick set for 2 chalders, 14 bolls; Little Penick 1 chalder, 14 bolls; Golford set to the Sheriff for 2 chalders, 13 bolls, 2 firlots; Moyness set to the Sheriff for 2 chalders, 10 bolls, 3 firlots; Lethenbar (1 chalder), by the rental 24 bolls, 2 firlots; Brightmony 2 chalders; Kinsteary 3 chalders; Broadland 1 chalder, 1 boll; Kinnudie 1 chalder, 1 boll; Petquhywin 8 bolls; Park (auld) 3 chalders; Easter Geddes 2 chalders, 8 bolls; Wester Geddes 14 bolls; Nairn set for 3 chalders, 11 bolls; Bothill set for 4 bolls, the sum total of the victual being 31 chalders, 5 bolls, &c. For the merts (cattle) 26s. 8d. Tiends set for money £114 13s. 4d. Temporal land rents £14 0s. 10d. Wedders, "callit kayne wedderis," five score and ten. Oats 6 bolls; capons 24. In a later return—namely, at the time of the Reformation—the lands of Foynesfield appear as part of the Deanery lands, and were let for £3 13s. 4d., a quarter mairt, 2 bolls of dry multure, 2 bolls of custom oats, and 2 horse days' work in harvest. There was at that time "ane great stone house biggit upon the lands of Bothill," which was set separately for 6s. 4d.; and there was also "a great new stone house" on the lands of Boathill, which, with "a fourth part of the town and lands of Little Penick and brewlands thereof in the barony of Penick and regality of Spynie,"

set for £5 12s. 2d.   Also " three fourth parts of the town
and lands of Penick set for £3 13s. 4d. " with various custom
gratuities.   The Dean of Moray, as things went, was thus pretty
well provided for.

The Dean was the greatest of all the clergy within the Cathedral.
Even the Bishop, though supreme in the rest of the diocese, had
to give place to him there.   The reverence due to the Dean was
thus laid down for the guidance of the clergy of Moray—All
persons, members of the choir, great and small, shall bow to him
in his stall on entering or leaving church.   None of the choir,
great or small, must be absent from the city a single night without
his leave.   When he enters or passes through the choir or chapter-
house all members of the choir are bound to rise.   Service shall
not commence before his coming or message of his not coming.
In the troublous times of the War of Independence, Walter Herok,
Dean of Moray, appears to have lost his fruitful heritage for a time,
and Edward I. on his supplication directed a writ from Berwick to
the Sheriff of Nairn ordaining him to restore to the unfortunate
Dean his lands.

The Vicarage of Auldearn was not the only place of worship
in the parish.   As formerly noticed, there are the remains of a
little chapel or oratory at Lochloy.   The castle of Moyness also
had its private chapel.   At Easter Clune the site of a Catholic
chapel is still marked, and the place is known as the Chapel-
field.

A chapel, dedicated to St. Ninian, existed at Foynesfield, and
St. Ninian's Well, just within the dyke of Bognafouran at the road
leading to the Park, enjoyed great celebrity.   The chapel was
known by the Gaelic form of St. Ninian's name, viz., St. Ringan,
and the place is called " Ringan " by the Gaelic-speaking people
to this day.   A clump of ash trees alone remains to mark the site
of the ecclesiastical settlement.   The dedication of the burgh of
Nairn is also to St. Ninian, and the burgh seal shows a figure of
the saint in proper habit holding in his right hand a cross fitchée
and in his left an open book.   There was a St. Ninian's chapel at
Culbin, and an altarage of St. Ninian at Elgin Cathedral, which
latter had an endowment of lands in Nairnshire.   The pre-

eminence of the name of the Galloway saint in this district is certainly remarkable. A possible explanation might be that the family of Moravia, who had been connected with the district which had been the scene of St. Ninian's labours, had brought with them the name and fame of the great missionary of the Southern Church, and when these free chapels were erected, they dedicated some of them to him. It is more probable, however, that the St. Ninian cult was due to the influence of the Abbey of Fearn, situate on the north side of the Moray Firth, directly opposite Nairn. An interesting notice of the founding of this Abbey is preserved by an old chronicler. It is stated that the first Earl of Ross, called Farquhar Macintagart, made a vow to God that if he overcame a famous Norman wrestler, named Dougall Duncanson, never before vanquished, " as God gave him the victory, he should found an Abbey of the first religious men that he should happen to meet after his victory, within the Earldom of Ross." The wrestling match took place in presence of Edward I. of England and Alexander III. of Scotland and their courts. The Celtic Chief of Ross obtained the victory over the Norman wrestler. Immediately afterwards " he chanced to meet with two ' white canons ' of Galloway, one called Malcolm, with another brother, having certain of St. Ninian's relics with them, which Malcolm, with his brother, the said Earl brought with him into Ross, and founded an abbey of that order and religion at Farne, beside Kincardin in Stracharrin, where the situation thereof yet does appear—whereof the said Malcolm was Abbot fifteen years, and there he deceased and was buried there, who was holden after his death among the people as a saint." This story is quite consistent with historical facts. Farquhar Macintagart, who fought so bravely for William the Lion in Easter Ross, and brought the head of Macwilliam, the Celtic claimant, to Alexander II., was employed by the King in his wars in Galloway, and accompanied him to London. The " Calendar of Fearn " is preserved at Dunrobin, and is a folio of vellum consisting of six leaves written on both sides. It bears no date, but Dr. Joass thinks it belongs probably to the close of the fifteenth century. It is in some parts written over by a later hand with various entries and memoranda of a local and personal character.   At the foot of page 1 the following weather prophecy occurs—

> " Giff Sanct Paul's day be fair and clear,
> Then shall be ane happy year,
> Giff it chances to snaw or rain
> Then shall dew all kind of grain,
> And giff the wind do fly on loft
> Than war shall vex your country aft,
> And giff the clouds make dark the sky
> Baithe nowte and fowl that year shall die."

Saint Paul's day is the 30th of June, and the rhyming prophecy of the old monk was no doubt well known in the district.

Keith in his " Scottish Bishops " states that the Abbey of Fearn was founded by Ferquhard, the first Earl of Ross, in the reign of Alexander II.   Forbes in his " Calendar of Scottish Saints," says the Abbey was founded about 1230 A.D. in the parish of Edder-town as daughter-house of the Praemonstratensian establishment at Whithorn, Malcolm of Galloway being the first Abbot.   In the presidency of his successor, Malcolm of Nigg, in consequence of the ferocity of its inhabitants, it was moved to another site 12 miles S.E. from the first, when it came to be called Nova Farina or Nova Fernia.   Twenty-one abbots presided over it whose names are still known, of whom the most remarkable were Finlay M'Fead, who died in 1485, and Donald Dunoon, a man of great learning, who succeeded to Patrick Hamilton, and died in 1540.   The noble youth Patrick Hamilton was Abbot of Fearn, and was the first Scottish martyr at the dawn of the Reformation—he was burnt at the gate of St. Salvator's College in St. Andrews in the year 1527.   Part of the ruins of the Abbey are still standing.   It was the scene of a terrible catastrophe.   The Abbey Church after the Reformation was used for service until Sunday, the 10th October, 1742, when the roof fell down upon the congregation.   The gentry, it appears, had seats in the niches and so were saved, and the minister David Ross, was protected by the sounding board, but vast numbers, it is recorded, " were wounded, and forty were dug out whose bodies were so smashed and disfigured that they could hardly be known, so that they were buried promiscuously without ceremony."   The influence of the Abbey is clearly traceable in the dedications to

St. Ninian at Fortrose, Kiltearn, Rosskeen, Urquhart, and Navidale in Sutherland, besides those already mentioned in Nairn and its neighbourhood. The lands of Delnies and Ardersier belonged to the Bishop of Ross, and the town and county of Nairn formed part of the Earldom of Ross for a considerable period of time. There is thus very strong probability that the St. Ninian dedications in Nairn are due to the old Abbey of Fearn.

An example of how lands came to be the Church's property is afforded in the case of Brightmony and Kinsteary. These lands were the property of Robert de Lauder of Quarrelwood (now Quarrywood), near Elgin, and he by deed assigned an endowment out of Brightmony and Kinsteary, with the mills and brewhouse of Auldearn, to the chapel and altar of St. Peter in Elgin Cathedral. Sir Robert Lauder was a son of Lauder, Justiciary of the Lothians, and came north on military service to King David Bruce. A daughter brought this little property in Nairnshire as her marriage portion to the Chisholms, from whom it descended in like manner to the Sutherlands. The priest was enjoined to perform perpetually masses for the soul of the donor himself, the souls of his ancestors and successors, and in particular for the soul of his dear friend Hugh, Earl of Ross. The charter is dated 1362.

John Hay of Tullybothil founded a chapel at Kincraggie out of his lands of Lochloy, the house of Wester Raite, and certain lands and pasturage. The charter is dated at Raite in 1374. There is no " Kincraggie " in Nairnshire, but Craggie was a well-known possession which lay adjacent to and was generally included in the estates of Knockoudie and Park, which belonged to the Hays of Lochloy and Tullybothil from a very early date. The name still occurs in the Valuation Roll, though these places have been united into one farm. The site of the chapel was in all probability at the high ground where the streamlet known as the Craggie Burn takes its rise. The chapel was dedicated to St. Mary, and the priest's duty was to say masses for the soul of Sir John himself, and the souls of his ancestors and successors. Sir John Hay was Sheriff of Inverness when he made this grant. He granted an annuity of four pounds usual money out of the lands of Lochloy, the one half to be paid at the Feast of Pentecost and the other at

Martinmas, with two acres of land and the mansion in the town of Wester Rait, and also pasture in the same town for twelve cows and a bull, sixty sheep, and liberty of pasturing horses on the common pasturage—no doubt the common on the Hill of the Ord adjacent.

This was not the only connection Raite had with the church of Moray. In a charter by William the Lion to his beloved Richard—in which he granted him, among other subjects, the church of Auldearn with the chapel of Nairn—the chapel of Raite is included, and it is mentioned in a subsequent charter of William's, along with the chapel of Moyness. King Alexander II. confirmed to Andrew, Bishop of Moray, in 1226, his right to various subjects in Rothiemurchus, Darnaway, Logie, and other places on the Findhorn, and to thirty acres " in Whitefield at Rathe." A doubt may exist whether in this instance the chapel of Raite in Badenoch may not be intended, but in the canonical statute a few years later assigning the benefices, it is stated that the Dean of Moray is to have the lands and church of Auldearn and Nairn, excepting the half-davach of land at Raite which belongs to the Episcopate of Moray as a table pertinent. A davach was equal to what could be ploughed by a pair of oxen, and half-a-davach of land appears to have been the extent usually assigned to the brethren of the old Celtic Church. It is incidentally mentioned in a Kilravock charter that the chapel of Raite was called the Hermit's Chapel, though re-dedicated to the Virgin.

Within a short distance of Raite was the chapel of Geddes, said to have been built in 1220 by Rose of Kilravock, whose first possession was Easter Geddes. It was dedicated to the Holy Virgin. The oldest extant charter of the chapel bears the date 1473, and was granted to Hugh Rose. The chapel had an endowment of five pounds, together with a small croft or glebe on which to erect a manse. In return for the profits of his office, the priest was bound to offer prayers as usual for the soul of the founder, and the souls of his predecessors and successors. For some time previous to this endowment, service was performed by the vicar of the neighbouring parish of Dalcross, which was a living depending on the Priory of Urquhart, and a regular agreement was entered into in 1343 between the Prior of Urquhart and the Baron of Kil-ravock that the vicar should officiate on certain conditions specified. This economical arrangement does not appear to have been suc-cessful, as the Papal interest had to be enlisted on behalf of the chapel, and Pope Sixtus IV. in the year 1475 issued a bull granting a discharge of one hundred days' penance to all who visited the chapel on specified festival days, and gave donations of a certain amount for the good of the chapel.

The name of Geddes is supposed to have been derived from Gildas, a British saint, who lived in the sixth century. The name is very ancient, as it is found in deeds early in the thirteenth century, and had then lost its original association, as is shown by its com-monplace division into " Easter " and " Wester " Geddes. The indications point rather to there having been an early Columban cell either here or at Raite, and the Celtic name of the hermit has become unrecognisable in its form of " Geddes." A fair was held at Geddes on or about the 5th April. Like St. Colm's market at Auldearn, it was frequented from far and near, and retained one trace of its origin as a church festival in respect that it was held within the precincts of the church. The churchyard till recent years was actually the site of the market. The vendors of mis-cellaneous wares used the tombstones for tables, and the whisky sellers handed round glasses to their customers as they sat on the headstones of the graves of their forefathers. This desecration was stopped only a few years ago. A memorandum is preserved at Cawdor Castle of purchases made at the " fair at the kirk of Geddes," about the year 1590, by the Thane of Cawdor's steward. It includes purchases of eggs and cakes, ticking at 4s. 6d. the ell, a salmon for 7s., a comb price 1s., butter, tallow, black and white thread, needles, a pair of cards, and two black bridles. The name of the fair does not throw any light on its origin. It is sometimes called by Gaelic-speaking people " Lady Fair," but more generally Geddes market. As it was held within the parish of Nairn, the authorities of the burgh of Nairn, according to entries in their records of the seventeenth century, used to exercise police super-vision of it—which appears to have been much needed, as it had a bad reputation for disorderliness. The market was confined to the village green and its approaches, but it has now declined. Bands of gipsies, in whose calendar it was from time immemorial a gathering place, regularly resorted to it.

The surname Geddes appears in Peeblesshire at an early date. The Geddeses of Rachan, alleged to be the chiefs of the name, came into notice as proprietors there in the beginning of the fifteenth century. They endowed a chapel or altar in St. Andrew's Church, Peebles, which they designated the " Chapel of St. Mary del Geddes."

At Little Urchany, about a mile distant from Geddes, are the remains of another churchyard and site of a chapel. Nothing is known of its history, save that in 1421, Henry, Bishop of Moray, gave (for a feu-duty of 13s. 6d.) to that " noble man, Henry Calder, Thane of that Ilk, our whole land of Little Urchany with its pertinents, lying in the Barony of Ferness," in consideration " of his advantage and support to us and our beloved Church."

The most interesting chapel of the Catholic period in Nairnshire is that of St. Ewen (or Adamnan) at Barevan. The old fabric, though a roofless ruin, forms a very striking object on a platform of the high ground two miles behind Cawdor. The walls of the old church are, for the most part, still intact. They enclose a space of about 70 feet by 20 feet. There is a piscina under an arch at the south side, where the altar stood. The architecture of the windows and design generally " is that of a Gothic chapel of the first pointed style without cusp, but there are apparently later and older portions." Some of the windows bear a close resemblance to those at Rait Castle. One window on the south of the choir is formed from the top of the arches and mullion of a single stone. It has been a double lancet outside and semicircular arch inside. A good many of the dressed stones have been taken away. The occurrence of numerous cup-markings on the stones within the chapel and its precincts, particularly on the curious row of slabs across the church where the choir and nave joined, has been already adverted to. Outside the chapel, on the north side of the church-yard, there is a stone coffin cut out of a block of the yellowish sandstone of the district, 6 feet long and 2 feet 8 inches in breadth at the top, tapering to 18 inches at the foot, with a circular space for the head contracted at the neck. It is said to have been used as a place of penance for ecclesiastical offenders. A rounded ball of reddish granite, 19 inches by 17 inches in diameter, and weighing 18 imperial stones, lies near the entrance to the chapel. According to tradition it was the " putting stone " of the neighbouring clachan, but it takes a strong man of the present day to lift it.

Service ceased to be observed at Barevan after 1619, when the parish church of Cawdor was built. The prebend of Cawdor was applied to the common expenses of the Cathedral at Elgin, such as providing wax candles, &c. Hence the designation of Common Church. A portion of the land was, however, reserved for the support of the deacon or vicar who ministered in the church of Ewen, when it was feued to Walter de Moravia in 1239, along with the lands of Budgate. In 1541, the church lands of Ewen and Dalquharne, with the brewhouse thereof, were feued to Rose of Holme for £9 11s. 4d. The latter place is still retained by Holme Rose, while the other lands now form part of the Cawdor possessions. The hill to the south-west is known as Drumournie, or the " Hill of Prayer "—an appropriate background for a religious edifice.

To the south, at Daless in the Streens, on the Findhorn, was a Chapel of Ease, as it was called, which had a small glebe. The site of the chapel is still marked. It was disused after the Reformation.

The churches and parishes of Croy and Dunlichty were assigned to the bishop's vicar. The parsonage tithes of Petty and Bracholy were given to one of Bishop Andrew's canons, who employed a deacon. Daviot and Dyke, like Cawdor, were mensal or common churches. Private chapels existed at Cawdor and Kilravock Castles and for permission to establish them a payment had to be made to the bishop. St. Dorothy's Chapel at Clava, and the ecclesiastical site at Chapeltown of Kilravock have been already referred to. There appear to have been many other small places of worship of which no notice has been preserved, an instance of which was the chapel at Galcantray discovered a few years ago by the farmer in reclaiming some land.

Ardclach was not erected into a parish till a pretty late date, but the lands now comprised in the parish were included in the barony either of Ferness or Ardclach. A chapel existed at Lethen, and there were chapels at Logie, Altyre, and other places on the south side of the Findhorn. The Church's lands included Fleenasmore; the lands of Ferness with fishing on the Findhorn; the croft of Ferness; the lands of Coulmony and Aitnoch; Belivat, with the wood of Killinglair; Torlocht; Auchagour with forest and fishing of the Findhorn; the lands of Ardclach, with the fishing on the Findhorn, and the wood of Dalvening, and mill and brewhouse of Ardclach; the Hermit's Croft, and Daldareth. Among the lands on the south side of the Findhorn were Dallasbroughty, Cullernie, Logie, and Airdrie. In the low country, Kildrummie, Croy, Little Budgate, and Little Urchany also belonged to the Church. The lands of Mid-Fleenas were devoted by some pious churchman to the chaplainries of St. James and St. Ninian, yielding £12 a year for that purpose. Many of these lands were feued out in perpetuity, or sold for a substantial sum with a small reddendo. At the Reformation the Bishop's lands were valued at £98 12s. 3d. with certain payments in kind, having been diminished to this extent by the land transactions of successive Bishops. In addition to the vast estates which belonged to the Church, the produce of the whole land was tithed. Every tenth sheaf of corn was taken up by the Bishop's servants before the crop was removed from the harvest field, and was stored in granges. The vicar claimed tithes of the stock, lambs, calves, and dairy and garden produce. As a rule, he was but the collector of these for his canonical brethren in the cathedral church, he himself having merely a small salary. When a death occurred, the vicar took the best cow. When a baby was born, he took the coverlet of the bed. When the child was baptised, or the young man or maiden confirmed, he was entitled to make further demands for payments in kind or cash.

The Episcopate of Moray was not the only ecclesiastical body which drew support from Nairnshire. The Abbey of Kinloss had a small endowment, namely, six roods of land at Newton lying beside the burgh of Nairn, called "our Ladyland of Kinloss." The Priory of Pluscardine held the "town and lands of Fornighty with the brewhouse thereof," set to Falconer of Hawkerton for £6 13s. 4d., with the carriage of four horse and their leaders for leading peats, failing which, 6s. 8d. for each horse.   Another condition of the set of Fornighty was—" And furnishing to the King's wars ane horseman."

The hospital of St. Nicholas, which had its house at the Boat of Bridge on the bank of the Spey, drew four marks yearly from the mill of Invernairn—a gift from King Alexander II.   This hospital was one of the earliest organised forms of charity.   When some poor wayfarer arrived at the ford or ferry at Spey he was received into the friendly hospice, and lodged and fed for a day or two.   The master of the hospital, who drew the four merks from the mill of Nairn, sold the endowment in 1471 to the Thane of Cawdor for an annual reddendo of 40s.

The Knights Templar had considerable possessions in the county of Nairn in 1296.   There is a writ extant granted in their favour at Berwick, addressed to the Sheriff of Invernairn, to put them in possession of their lands, they having made submission to Edward I.   This was no doubt done.   From the deed of conveyance of the Temple lands in the north from Lord Torpichen, the last Master of the Order, it appears that the following were the lands held here—" Those two roods of arable land lying within the territory of the burgh of Nairn, in that part thereof called [left blank, provokingly !] possessed by John Rose, burgess of Nairn, and his sub-tenants ;—those two roods of arable temple land and house lying within the said territory of Nairn, possessed by Hew Rose of Kilravock and his sub-tenants ;—all and haill those our temple lands called the lands of Pitfundie lying in the said Sheriffdom of Nairn, betwixt the strype that comes from the lands of Brodie on the east, the fludder or myre upon the south side of the common muir called the Hardmuir on the south side, the lands of Penick and wood of Lochloy on the west, and the Ruchcarse of Culbyn on the north, for the most part possessed by the lairds of Brodie, and their sub-tenants."   They had also lands at Ardersier, which are designated in old charters as Temple Land, Temple Cruik, Temple Bank, Bogschand.   They lay partly in the vicinity of the town of Ardersier, between Connage and the sea, and between Flemington and the sea.   A charter granted at Nairn refers to the *locus trialis* at Ardersier, doubtless an ancient place of trial by

" wager of battle." The Temple lands of Ardersier were held by Davidsons and Mackays as portioners. They were acquired by Cawdor in 1626. The Temple lands at Brodie and elsewhere appear to have been disposed of about the same time, as in a Brodie charter of date 1626 the lands of Pitfundie are included in the Brodie estate. The Templars were a religious and military order of knights who escorted pilgrims to Jerusalem at a time when such pilgrimages were attended by dangers from robbers. They wore a white robe with a red Maltese cross on the breast, and at first were all of noble birth. The Knights of St. John of Jerusalem also had lands in Nairnshire. It is impossible now to identify them. When the Knights Templar were suppressed by Edward II. their property was given to the Knights of St. John.

What had not been assigned of the lands of Ardersier to the Templars, belonged to the Bishop of Ross. He also had the lands of Delnies to increase his revenues. The See of Moray disputed the right of jurisdiction by the See of Ross over these lands, but in 1226 the dispute was settled by the Bishop of Ross agreeing to give an annual donation of a stone of wax to Elgin Cathedral as an acknowledgment of its superiority. The Bishop of Ross's lands in Ardersier were acquired by Cawdor in 1574, and a small sum is still paid by Lord Cawdor to the Crown as Bishop's rent.

The Abbey of Arbroath drew revenues from the burghs of Nairn and Inverness. The Nairn endowment consisted of lands lying to the west of Millbank, between the Kildrummie road and the river. The revenues from Inverness were of considerable amount. The payments were frequently in dispute between the Abbot of Arbroath and the magistrates of Inverness, backed by the Bishop of Moray. On one occasion at least, the Inverness burgh paid its dues to Arbroath in the form of barrels of salt herrings. The Abbey of Arbroath was founded in honour of Saint Thomas A'Beckett, the fashionable saint of the days of William the Lion, and had some thirty parishes given to it for its support. The church at Nairn was dedicated to St. Thomas.

The Holy Rood kirk of Nairn, which stood near the Constabulary garden, had an altarage to St. Modan, with a small endowment.

The golden period of the Church's history was during the reigns of Alexanders II. and III. The presence of so large a body of ecclesiastics in the Province of Moray—educated men who had seen the world and were abreast of the highest culture and learning of the time in this country and on the Continent—must have had a considerable influence on the social life and manners of the time. During the earlier years they were devoted to their church, and appear to have been zealous and diligent in the discharge of their functions. In the testing time of the War of Independence, Robert Wishart, Bishop of Glasgow, and Bishop Andrew of Moray stood true to Scotland, when many of its lay sons succumbed to the temptation of English gold and English estates. They inspired and led the patriotism of the people. When the beautiful cathedral of Elgin was burned, the canons showed a praiseworthy example in adopting a self-denying ordinance to devote two-thirds of their income to the re-building of the church whoever of them should be chosen bishop. They were powerful enough to befriend the poor against the tyranny of the barons, and to bring the proudest noble in the district to his knees for wrong-doing. The great Earl of Ross, for some mischievous act at the church of Petty, had humbly to sue for the Bishop's pardon, and in compensation to make a grant of the estate of Cadboll. The Baron of Kilravock in 1596 was sent to Dunbarton prison for several years for waylaying the Abbot of Kinloss and detaining him at Kilravock. Even the Wolf of Badenoch had eventually to succumb to the power of the Church.

Sometimes the Church crossed the line, and claimed independence in civil as well as spiritual matters. The extensive possessions of the Church being scattered up and down the province, the bishop was led to have them formed into a Regality of Spynie, and the Lord of Spynie administered the law among the tenants of the Church lands as if he were a lay baron, supreme within his own jurisdiction. But one bishop went much further. He attempted to enforce civil decrees by church censure and force. A dispute arose between the See of Moray and the Baron of Kilravock as to their boundary at Croy and Kildrummie. The case was referred to a jury of arbiters, twenty-two in number, " evenly chosen " between the Bishop of Moray and the Baron of Kilravock. On one side were the canons, chantor, and vicars; on the other the neighbouring lairds and leading burgesses of Nairn. They sat in the parish church of Nairn. The year was 1492. After several meetings and much debate, the arbiters gave their award, ordering that "the houses biggit betwixt the kirk and the wood of Croy be cast down, the corn that grows in the ground pertaining to the said houses to be given to the poor men of the samen for this crop, and thereafter to be common pasture along with the wood of Croy to be evenly kept by a forester to be chosen by both parties." And, as touching the march betwixt Kilravock and Kildrummie, it was ordained that "the march stone which was castin in the loch should be set up where it stood before, and be in time coming for even march between the two properties." The bishop sought to enforce the decreet arbitral in the ecclesiastical court, but the baron appealed to the King, and the King ordered the bishop to desist—an order which had to be repeated ere it was complied with. The ground of objection to the bishop's proceedings was that Kilravock held his lands of the King, and nothing must be done to affect the interest of the Crown.

The religious activity and life of the time centred in the cathedral city of Elgin, while the intellectual and spiritual revivals which from time to time arose within the Church found expression in varied forms within it and the abbeys and priories. But it would be a mistake to suppose that the ordinances of religion in the prevailing form of the time were awanting to the country districts. From Auldearn to Barevan—a distance of eight miles—there was a line of chapels within sight of each other, and if Barevan chapel be a fair example of the architectural style of the others, they must have formed a very picturesque feature in the valley. The picture of the times is a singular one. At Auldearn on St. Colm's Day the people held high festival, the maidens of the district trooping to the village gathering in white dresses—a custom kept up till the end of the eighteenth century, and apparently a remnant of baptismal or confirmation rites. On the crest of the Craggie hill a solitary priest chanted masses night and day for the soul of Sir John Hay of Lochloy. Then in the midst of the hamlets which clustered on the patches of greensward among the obtruding gneiss knobs and boulders at Foynesfield, a priest kept alive the hallowed memory of the great founder of the Celtic Church of the south, and the people resorted to the cool spring dedicated to St. Ringan. The light of the Hermit's Chapel at Rait, an ideal site for the abode of a recluse, shone the clearer because of the gloomy background of the Hill of the Ord against which it was placed ; while at Geddes, the penitent, albeit weary of his penance, sought by generous gifts to shorten the period of his probation. The Cawdor valley opens up, and here we have a chapel on one of the spurs of Urchany, another in the valley below at Old Calder, and a third crowning the height of Barevan.

And yet, with all its seeming attractiveness, the Church had its weakness and defects. While the canonical dignitaries lived in affluent circumstances at Elgin, the parish clergy who did the work in the country starved on a pittance. The lands on every side of them belonged to the Church, but the fruits were not for them but for their superiors. The most frequent aspect which the Bishop or Dean or other dignitary presented to the people was that of rent gatherer or produce collector. The Prelate was to them but a great landowner, though possibly not a very hard landlord. The exactions also of the lower ecclesiastics became very grievous. A spirit of worldliness appears latterly to have infected the clergy, with, it must be added, licentious and immoral conduct on the part of not a few. Patrick Hepburn, the last bishop, professing to live a life of celibacy and purity, had a numerous family of sons and daughters, provision for whom he made by parting right and left with the Church lands. When the Reformation came, the Roman Catholic Church in Moray and Nairn went down before the storm almost without a struggle and without a friend.

CHAPTER VII

THE TIMES OF THE BRUCES

THE death of Edward I. led to important changes in the north. Many who had supported his interests now espoused the side of Bruce and the cause of Scottish nationality. A remarkable meeting at Auldearn a few months after Edward's death illustrates this. William, Earl of Ross, and his two sons presented themselves at the church of Auldearn on 8th October, 1308, to make their submission to King Robert Bruce. There were few enemies whom the King could have had more difficulty in forgiving than the Earl of Ross. The Earl had been Edward's leader in the north, holding the office of Guardian north of Spey. That could have been overlooked, for men changed sides rapidly in those days, but Bruce could not forget that in the darkest hour of his life the Earl of Ross had treated the Queen with insult and contumely. While Bruce wandered as a fugitive on the shores of Kintyre, the Queen was forced to fly from Kildrummie Castle in Aberdeenshire, and with a small escort made her way to the shores of the Moray Firth, and crossing over by boat to Tain, took refuge in the chapel of St. Duthac, a recognised sanctuary. Contrary to the custom of the time, the Earl of Ross with his men forcibly entered the church, dragged the Queen out, put to death her attendants before her eyes, and sent herself and her step-daughter Marjory prisoners to England, where they remained at the time of this meeting, not having been liberated till after the battle of Bannockburn. But Bruce now accepted the Earl's services. He became a great favourite, and fought at Bruce's side on the field of Bannockburn.

At the meeting at Auldearn at which the Earl of Ross made his submission appeared Bruce's old and faithful friend, David, Bishop of Moray, who first set the Province of Moray on fire with enthusiasm for the Scottish King. A price had been set on his head by Edward, and the venerable bishop had, like Bruce himself, many devious wanderings. Edward believed that David had made his escape to Norway, and demanded of the King of Norway instantly to seize him, but David during the evil days found secure concealment in Orkney, and now appeared to witness the submission of the Earl of Ross and his sons. He lived for some seventeen years later, and spent some years in France, on his death leaving money to build and endow a college in Paris for the education of his young countrymen. The institution became the well-known Scots College, and old David's name as the founder is still to be seen in an inscription on the walls. The building, though no longer used as a seminary, remains the property of the Roman Catholic Church of Scotland. Another witness on the occasion was Walter Herock, the Dean of Moray, who, although under some obligations to Edward, followed his bishop, as likewise did Cresswell, the sub-chantor. Wiseman, the Sheriff of Moray, was also present.

The family which suffered most in the great struggle of the War of Independence was that of the Cumings. They emerged shorn entirely of their greatness. From being the most powerful of Scottish nobles, they sank into comparative insignificance, and never regained their former prestige. The vast estates they possessed were given to others. One branch of the family—the descendants of the fourth son of the Earl of Buchan, Sir Robert Cuming, who had been absent from the country during the troublous times—settling chiefly on small properties on the banks of the Findhorn—is represented at the present day by the Cumings of Altyre and Dunphail. In the latter case, singularly enough, they united with Bruce.

The other families in the north were for the time overshadowed by a new family—that of Randolph. Thomas Randolph, Bruce's nephew, was created Earl of Moray about the year 1312, the old earldom, which had been in abeyance since the days of William the Lion, being revived in his favour as one of the rewards for the services he had rendered to Bruce. It was no empty title, for the charter conferring it gave him the lands extending from the mouth of the Spey to the borders of Argyle and the marches of Ross—in fact, from sea to sea—and invested him with supreme authority in all matters whatsoever. Thomas Randolph was to all intents and purposes King of Moray. The burghs of Nairn, Forres, and Elgin, which had formerly held of the King, were deprived of that privilege and were handed over to be ruled by the new Earl of Moray. It was an unconstitutional proceeding to change the burghal tenure from holding of the King to holding of a vassal. The proviso of the charter to this effect is as follows—" We also will and grant that the burghs and their burgesses of Elgin, Forres, and Invernairne have and exercise the same liberties which they had in the time of Lord Alexander, King of Scots, foresaid, and in ours, reserving only this that they held of us without mediate, and now they hold of the said Earl (Thomas Randolph) with said liberties." The burgh of Inverness was alone exempted. According to all accounts, the Earl of Moray ruled wisely and well, protecting the innocent and bringing the wrongdoers to judgment. He dispensed justice in his own court at Inverness, and when not leading the Scottish army in the field, or engaged in his public functions in the south, abode for the most part in Moray. It was he who built the first great castle at Darnaway, but antiquarians have doubted whether the great hall known as Randolph's Hall can possibly be of so early a date.

King Robert Bruce granted a charter (which still exists at Cawdor Castle) to William, Thane of Cawdor, of his thanedom in the year 1310. The charter confirms him in the thanedom of Cawdor in the sheriffdom of Invernairn, in feu-farm for payment of twelve merks sterling as was wont to be paid in the time of King Alexander III., and on condition of the thane performing the service which used to be rendered therefor in the time of the said King Alexander.

King Robert Bruce also gave a charter to Michael, Thane of Brodie, about the years 1307-11, confirming him in his possessions as heir of his father, who (according to Shaw) was Malcolm, Thane of Brodie, in the reign of Alexander III. (which ended in 1285). This Malcolm is the first of the thanes of Brodie whose name is recorded.

About this time also, Robert Bruce knighted the Baron of Kilravock.   Knighthood in those days was never conferred except for deeds of bravery, and Sir William Rose must have won his belt and spurs by meritorious conduct on the field of battle.   The page of history does not record the part taken in the War of Independence by Cawdor, Brodie, or Kilravock, but as military service was one of the conditions of the ancient thaneage, and knighthood the recognition of personal valour, it is unlikely that they remained idle at home when a national struggle so intense was going on. The dates of the two charters are a few years prior to the battle of Bannockburn (1314).   Bruce, it may be imagined, did not bestow his favours for nothing, and when so many of the Highland chiefs were present at Bannockburn it would be strange indeed if Bruce's friends in Nairnshire did not go to his assistance.

The peace established by the overthrow of the English army at Bannockburn was not long maintained.   On the death of King Robert Bruce, Randolph, Earl of Moray, became Regent of Scotland, King David, who succeeded his father, being in his minority. While Randolph lived, affairs were administered with a firm hand, but he died suddenly, just as Edward Baliol in July, 1330, at the instigation of the nobles who had lost their estates in Scotland, invaded the country with an army.   The Scottish Parliament in a panic appointed Donald, Earl of Mar, as Regent, but he possessed no military ability, and in a great battle at Dupplin he was slain and his forces utterly defeated.   Scotland was once more ruled by a Baliol, who was crowned at Scone in the autumn of the same year. But his triumph was short-lived, for before the year was out he was driven across the Border.

In the spring of the following year, however, Edward Baliol re-entered Scotland, this time with the approval and support of the English King, Edward III.   On the 20th July, 1333, the two armies met at Halidon Hill, and the Scots sustained a crushing defeat.   The flower of the Scottish nobility perished in this disastrous engagement.   The list of the slain included the names of the Earls of Ross, Athole, Lennox, and Sutherland.   It is extremely probable that Sir William Rose, Baron of Kilravock, accompanied Hugh, Earl of Ross, to the fatal field, and as his name disappears from writs after the date of this battle, the Baron, it is supposed, must have shared the fate of the Earl.   In the gravity of the national circumstances, it was deemed expedient to send the young King and Queen to France for safety.

At this critical juncture Sir Andrew Moray, or Murray, of Petty and Bothwell, whose father and grandfather, both named Andrew, had been associated with Wallace thirty years before, came on the scene and rallied the patriotism of Scotland when at its lowest ebb.   John, Earl of Moray, second son of Thomas Randolph—the eldest son had fallen at the battle of Dupplin—joined him, but unfortunately he was captured by the English and detained a prisoner for six years.   With a handful of brave knights, Sir Andrew set out to relieve Kildrummie Castle, which was at the time besieged by the Earl of Athole, who had just bargained away the independence of Scotland to Edward for his own personal enrichment and aggrandisement.   The success of the expedition was a matter of intense personal concern to Sir Andrew, because his wife, Christian Bruce, the King's sister, had taken refuge in the castle, and was now defending it.   A desperate fight, which took place between the rival forces in a wood close by, ended in Athole's men being defeated, and himself with five knights being slain in the wood.   Sir Andrew had the joy of entering the grand old Snow Tower—still magnificent in its ruins—to receive the congratulations of his wife on her timely rescue.   Shortly afterwards he was elected by the Parliament Regent of Scotland.

One of the Regent's first military operations was to besiege Lochindorb Castle.   The old island fortress appears to have been greatly strengthened, if not entirely rebuilt, during the time of Edward I.   The ruins which still exist show the remains of a castle of the same type as Bothwell and Kildrummie—both of which, it may be here recalled, were originally founded by the family De Moravia, represented by Sir Andrew.   Athole had besieged Kildrummie Castle in which Moray's wife had taken up her abode—Moray was now besieging the castle of Lochindorb in which the wife (now the widow) of Athole had taken refuge with her infant. She was an English lady, daughter of Henry Beaumont, who figured rather discreditably in the annals of the time. The place could not be easily taken, and the siege was prolonged. It can readily be imagined that the young Countess of Athole must have felt her position very gruesome in the castle of Lochindorb. Its form was a quadrilateral enclosure, with a round tower at each of the four corners, with curtain walls running down to the edge of the water, if not indeed extending into it, on the south and part of the east sides. When the Countess looked from her iron-stanchioned chamber-window, she could see Moray's fierce men with their siege engines and catapults lining the shore, and she could see the stones and missiles, hurled across the narrower part of the lake, striking the walls and plunging into the dark water in their rebound. But further she could descry no human habitation—nothing but a vast forest backed by bare rugged hilltops. And when the shades of evening fell, the gloom and solitude of the island castle must have been intense in the extreme. It is not to be wondered at in these circumstances that the Countess wrote the most despairing letters to King Edward and to her father, imploring them to come to the help of herself and her infant in their dire distress. And we have next the singular spectacle of a great English army with its sovereign at its head rapidly marching furth the kingdom of England into Scotland, and making its way in all haste to the relief of the lady in distress at Lochindorb.

Sir Andrew Moray had failed to get a footing on the island. His engines of destruction were too feeble to break down the thick walls of the castle at the long distance from which they were directed, and, hearing of the advance of Edward and his army of relief, he prudently retired to the shelter of the woods. Edward advanced with his army, wasting by fire and sword the districts through which he marched. As he approached the region of Lochindorb, word was brought to him that Sir Andrew Moray was encamped in the wood of Stronk-altere (supposed to be Stroniviach, near the march between Altyre and Logie). Edward's army had thus cut off flight by the south or east, and the Findhorn river rushing between iron-bound walls appeared to present an

impassable barrier to an escape by the north or west.   Edward
became aware of his advantage, and immediately ordered an attack.
The outposts of the Scots were driven in, and made haste to inform
Moray.   The general was at prayers, and although the danger was
imminent, none dared to interrupt him till the service was concluded.
On being told that Edward and his army were at hand in the forest,
he observed there was no need of haste ; and when the squires
brought him his horse, began quietly to adjust its furniture, and to
see that the girths were tight and secure.   When this was going
on, the English every moment came nearer, and the Scottish knights
around Moray showed many signs of impatience.   One of the
straps which braced his thigh armour snapped as he buckled it, and
the Regent, turning to an attendant, bade him bring a coffer from
his baggage.   From this he took a skin of leather, and sitting down
leisurely on the bank, cut off a broad strip, with which he mended
the fracture.   He then returned the box to its place, mounted his
horse, arrayed his men in close column, and commenced his retreat
in such order that the English did not think it safe to attack him,
and, having at last gained a narrow defile, he disappeared from their
view without losing a man.   " I have heard," says Wyntoun,
" from knights who were then present that in all their life they
never found time to go so slow as when their old commander sat
cutting his leather skin in the wood of Stronkaltere."

The " Strait Road " or narrow defile is commonly supposed to
be the spot known as Randolph's Leap—a gorge where the rocks
on both sides come so close together as to leave but six feet of a free
passage for the water to rush through.   Local tradition seems,
however, to be at fault in this identification, for it is obviously
impossible for horsemen to cross here.   Foot soldiers by bridging
the gap with trees might have succeeded in doing so, and even the
feat performed by young Alastair Cuming of Dunphail, according
to the legend of the " Battle of the Standard "—that of leaping
from bank to bank—could have been anticipated by Moray's men
on foot, as it has been repeated in later times.   But the boldest rider
would shrink from spurring his horse to a leap from a slippery rock
to a sloping ledge, with a foaming torrent rushing through the
chasm.   Sir Andrew and his horsemen, led by their guide, no

doubt followed some path along the riverside, until they came to Sluie, where it is not entirely impossible to ford the river. Once across to the Darnaway side, they were in their own country. Edward, finding that Moray had eluded him, and probably fancying that he still lurked in the forest, as the river was supposed to be unfordable so high up, came down to Blairs of Altyre and lay there, with the view of intercepting him. He at length relieved the beleagured castle of Lochindorb, and carried the distressed countess away with him in his train. Before returning south, Edward devastated the district of Moray, Nairn, and Inverness, burning the towns and villages. He sought in vain to draw Moray into an engagement in the open field, but no sooner was he gone than the Regent reappeared and retook many of the garrisons which Edward had fortified. He even sent foraging expeditions into England, being compelled to do so in order to avert a grievous famine that had followed upon the desolation of war.

In 1337 Sir Andrew Moray appears to have retired from active service, though still only in his fortieth year. He came north to his own paternal property. The family castle, which stood on the Hallhill of Petty, having doubtless been destroyed by the English in their raids, he crossed over to Avoch, and spent his closing days in the old castle on Ormond Hill. He died there in the year 1338, and was buried at the church of Rosemarkie. Fordun states that his body was raised and carried to Dunfermline, where it now mingles with the heroic dust of Bruce and Randolph. However that may be, his son John ordered perpetual masses to be said for his soul at Elgin Cathedral, and for that purpose made a deed of gift of money, which was confirmed by his brother Thomas two years afterwards. The terms of the directions issued by John of Inverness (formerly quoted) as to the four wax candles to be lighted on his tomb on his anniversary seem to imply that he was buried at Elgin Cathedral. Monteith, writing in 1704, mentions that Sir Andrew Moray's monument at Elgin was very handsome and was upon the south pillar of the Cathedral, but even in his time it was in ruins. The practice of celebrating rites over the tomb in a church while the body is buried elsewhere is, however, not uncommon in the Roman Catholic Church. There is some doubt therefore whether it is at Rosemarkie, Dunfermline, or Elgin that the dust of the Scottish hero, Sir Andrew Moray, lies. Wyntoun, who had been a companion of some of the soldiers who served under Moray, extols him highly as a noble patriot and warrior of great renown. Christian Bruce, by his death thrice a widow, lived to a great age. Occupying Kildrummie, she had the pleasure of welcoming young King David II. and his Queen back to Scotland, and entertaining them more than once within the castle. Sir Andrew was succeeded by his son John, who got possession of the vast estates of Bothwell, Boharm, Petty, Ardmenach, and others. He died without issue and was succeeded by his brother Thomas, who held the office of Pantler of Scotland, and died in 1361 while in England as one of the hostages for King David, who was taken prisoner at the battle of Durham. He left an only child, a daughter Joan, and she married Archibald, third Earl of Douglas, known as Archibald the Grim, who succeeded to the estates of Bothwell and Petty. Archibald appears to have merited the sobriquet of " Grim," for his oppressions were excessive even in a lawless age. It was said of him that his cord at Bothwell " seldom wanted a tassel "—hanging was his favourite pastime.

The old family of Moray of Petty is represented at the present day in the male line by the Morays of Abercairny. Sir Andrew had a brother John, who was their ancestor. The Morays of Athole are descended from a branch of the same family, and the Duke of Sutherland is in the female line the descendant of Hugo Freskyn, a brother of William, founder of the family of Duffus and Petty.

The family of Chien, which held the Sheriffships of Nairn and Inverness, also ended in the direct line. Unlike their kinsmen of Petty, the house of Duffus chose to attach itself to the English cause, and not till the death of Edward I. did it return to allegiance to the Scottish King. Its fortunes were diminished by losses in the wars, but the cause of the disappearance of the family name was the failure of male issue. It ended in two heiresses. Mary Chien married the second son of the third Earl of Sutherland, who got with her a portion of the Chien estates in Caithness and Moray, and became the founder of the house of the Sutherlands of Duffus.

Morella Chien, the second daughter, married Keith of Inverugie, from whom descended the Keiths, Earls Marischal.

An offshoot of the Moray family outlasted the main line for several generations, but it too ended in an heiress. The good Bishop Gilbert Moray of Caithness, sprung from the family of Duffus, gave the lands of Skelbo to his brother Richard de Moravia of Culbin before 1235, and both properties remained in possession of the family till a late period. On 16th October, 1449, Thomas Tarrel renounced certain lands in the lordship of Skibo in favour of "the honourable lady Egidia Moray of Culbin." Egidia, heiress of Culbin, married Sir Thomas Kinnaird of Kinnaird, the estate descending to Walter Kinnaird their second son, in whose family it remained until its destruction by the great sand-drift of 1695.

A change also took place in the destination of the Earldom of Moray. Thomas, the first Earl of Moray of the Randolph family, usually designated Randolph, left by his wife, Isabel Stewart of Bonkill, two sons, Thomas and John, and a daughter Agnes. Thomas succeeded his father, but he enjoyed the title only twenty-three days, falling (as already stated) at the battle of Dupplin when Edward Baliol first entered Scotland. John, the third Earl of Moray, was one of the young patriots who rallied to the call of Sir Andrew Moray when the fruits of the thirty years War of Independence seemed trampled under foot. Previous to this he had, along with the Earl of Ross, led a division of the Scottish army at the disastrous battle of Halidon Hill, but was more fortunate than most of his compeers, having succeeded in making his escape to France. Returning to Scotland in 1334, he was appointed along with the High Steward co-Regent of Scotland. In the following year, in performing an act of chivalry—escorting some English nobles across the Border—he was captured, and was detained as a prisoner in England till 1341. The Earldom of Moray was held by the Crown during his imprisonment. No sooner did he regain his liberty than he was once more in the field. He was with the army of King David which invaded England in 1342, and he commanded the right wing at the battle of Durham on 17th October, 1349. "It was nine in the morning," says Tytler, "and the whole English force had come up. A large crucifix was carried in the

front of the line.   Around it waved innumerable banners and
pennons, gorgeously embroidered, belonging chiefly to the Church,
and the close battle immediately began, under circumstances dis-
couraging to the Scots.   The discharge of the archers had already
greatly galled and distressed them, the division commanded by the
Earl of Moray was fiercely attacked by the English men-at-arms ;
the ditches and hedges which intersected the ground broke his array
and impeded his movements, and the English cavalry charged
through the gaps in the line, making a dreadful havoc.   At last
Moray fell and his division was entirely routed."   The King was
taken prisoner, and the Scots lost fifteen thousand men—an appalling defeat.

It is with this Earl John that the legendary tales of the Findhorn
are associated.   In a short life crowded with events of greatest
moment, it is somewhat difficult to conceive of him engaging in a
petty warfare with his neighbours in Moray and Nairn.

The Earl of Moray having left no issue, the Earldom, according
to the original charter to Randolph, should have reverted to the
Crown, but Agnes, his sister, claimed it, and her claim was con-
ceded, as well it might, for she had at a critical time rendered important services to the State.   She had married the Earl of March,
and in her lord's absence, undertook the defence of their castle of
Dunbar against the English.   For five months it was subjected to
a fierce siege, with all the munitions of war known to the besiegers,
but Agnes successfully repelled every assault.   She would walk round
the ramparts deriding the English artillerymen, and whenever any
peril arose, she rushed to the point of danger, animating and direct-
ing her soldiers in person.   Agnes's heroic conduct extorted the
admiration of even her enemies.   " Agnes's love-shafts go straight
to the heart," exclaimed the Earl of Salisbury, as an English knight
was struck dead at his side by an arrow from the walls.   The
Countess was of a dark complexion, and hence was playfully called
" Black Agnes."   The English had ultimately to raise the siege,
having been completely foiled by the brave woman.   Her second
son, John Dunbar, on her death, and that of her husband, succeeded
to the Earldom of Moray, and thus a new line was inaugurated.

Once again, in David II.'s reign, Lochindorb Castle is mentioned in history. It was used or converted into a State prison, and in the later part of the reign it received at least one distinguished prisoner. William Bulloch, an ecclesiastic of obscure birth but of great military talent, had been John Baliol's chamberlain, and was greatly trusted by the English party; but for an adequate consideration he was induced to sell himself to the Scots, and deliver up the castle of Cupar, which he commanded. Bulloch's zeal and efficiency raised him so high in the good graces of the Regent that on a vacancy occurring he appointed him Chamberlain of Scotland. But confidence in a traitor is easily shaken. Suspicions arose that he had entered into a correspondence with England, and he was suddenly deposed from his office and thrown into a squalid dungeon in Lochindorb Castle, where he died of cold and hunger.

The state of the country during the later part of the reign of David II. was melancholy in the extreme. To the desolating effects of the long continued war were superadded the horrors of famine and pestilence. Much of the land ceased to be cultivated, and many of the more enterprising spirits left their native country for military service on the Continent. Heavy taxation paralysed commerce and crushed industry. David, when restored to his country, which had made so many sacrifices on his behalf in blood and treasure, turned out to be a mere lover of pleasure, selfish, indolent, and spiteful. Only once did he arouse himself to action. The Highlands were in a state of rebellion under the leadership of John of the Isles, and David came north with a considerable force, and effectually suppressed it, receiving the submission of the Lord of the Isles and his wild chieftains at Inverness in November 1369. Three months later the King died at Edinburgh, in the forty-seventh year of his reign, and his death was regarded as a national deliverance, so unworthy a son of King Robert Bruce did he prove himself to be. He was succeeded by the son of Walter Stewart and Marjory Bruce, who assumed the title of King Robert II.

CHAPTER VIII

NAIRNSHIRE UNDER THE EARLS OF ROSS

For a considerable period the history of the town and county of Nairn is linked to the fortunes of the Earls of Ross.

The sons of the Earl of Ross who made their submission at Auldearn were received into high favour by King Robert Bruce, and Hugh, succeeding to the Earldom of Ross on the death of his father, was confirmed in his lands in the north, and received the superiority of the town and county of Nairn, with the offices of Sheriff of the shire and Constable of the royal castle of Nairn. This grant has greatly perplexed legal antiquarians. It is in direct conflict with the great charter to Thomas Randolph, first Earl of Moray, in whose possession these subjects and offices were at the time. The two charters cannot easily be reconciled. The charter of the Earl of Ross was, however, the effective one. An acre of land could not be sold, feued, or alienated in any way without the consent of the Earl of Ross, the Lord Superior of Nairn. Sir John Hay of Tullybothil, when he granted the endowment out of the lands of Lochloy and Wester Raite to found the chapel of Kincraggie, had to obtain the consent of the Earl of Ross; and when Sir Robert Lauder made a similar gift out of the lands of Brightmony and Kinsteary, he had also to procure the permission of William, Earl of Ross. The lands of Cawdor, Kilravock, and all the other properties within the county ceased to be Crown holdings and became holdings under the Earl of Ross. Hugh, Earl of Ross, married Bruce's daughter Maud, and as the King's son-in-law, increased his importance and influence. The Earl of Ross was undoubtedly the greatest chief in the Highlands in the days of the

Bruces, and he had an enormous following of clansmen. The Mackenzies, Macleans, and Macraes followed his banner. He went to battle in the magic chain shirt of St. Duthac, and was acknowledged to be a mighty warrior. When he fell, leading the reserves at the disastrous battle of Halidon Hill in 1333, the mail shirt was found upon him, and was returned by the English to Tain. He was succeeded by his son William, whose daring exploit at the siege of Perth, in cutting a subterranean passage under the walls of the fortress, which led to its surrender, is set forth in Scottish history.

This William, Earl of Ross, appeared at Nairn in the year 1338 (22nd November), when he signed a charter in favour of Malmoran of Glencairney (Duthil) of certain lands in Badenoch, the lordship of which was in his possession. A few years later he signed a charter at Urquhart Castle in favour of Reginald, son of Roderick of the Isles, of lands in Kintail, and exchanged his lands of Argyll with his brother Hugh for Hugh's lands in Buchan, forfeited by the Cumings. There was much formality and state connected with the Kintail charter, and an august assemblage of prelates and nobles met on the occasion. The Earls of Ross claimed the lordship of the Isles and West Highlands, but this claim was frequently disputed, and the granting of the charter to Roderick may have been some pacific arrangement of old quarrels. If so, the peace did not last long, for a dispute between these two chiefs led indirectly to a great national disaster. On the eve of the Scottish army setting out from Perth for England in 1346, William, Earl of Ross, assassinated Ranald of the Isles in the monastery of Elcho, and, dreading the King's vengeance, led his men back to the mountains. The Islesmen, whose leader had been thus murdered, also deserted, whilst many of the lesser Highland chiefs also forsook the Scottish army. Before the battle of Durham was fought the Highland host had vanished.

Later on, the Earl of Ross proudly absented himself from Parliament, and ruled his dominions as if he were an independent monarch. The rebellion of John of the Isles, however, overthrew the power of the Earl, at least in his Western possessions. When Robert II. came to Inverness early in his reign, the Earl in a

document of date 24th June, 1371, states that " when my Lord
the King came to the town of Inverness, he found me without any
land or lordship, my whole Earldom of Ross seized and recog-
nosced." His official appointments in Nairn alone seem to have
been retained by him, and he appears to have resided at the place.
He had a daughter Euphemia who became a very notorious person.
She married as her first husband Sir Walter Leslie of Rothes, and
between them they greatly oppressed the old Earl, stripping him
of his possessions, as set forth in the above complaint to the King.
He died in 1372, and was the last of the old Celtic line of the Earls
of Ross. A canonical obstacle to the marriage of Euphemia,
Countess of Ross, and Walter Leslie existed, but the couple married
first and got the Pope's dispensation two years afterwards.

Of this marriage there was a son Alexander and a daughter
Margaret. Lady Margaret married Donald, Lord of the Isles.
On the death of her husband Walter Leslie, the Countess of Ross
married Alexander Stewart, Earl of Buchan, better known as the
Wolf of Badenoch, fourth son of Robert II. The Earldom of
Ross, with the offices of Sheriff and Constable of Nairn, was
bestowed upon the Earl in life-rent in right of his wife. No noble
was ever better endowed, for the King's charter granted to him
and his wife " the baronies or lordships of Skye and Lewes, all the
lands in Caithness and Sutherland, all the lands within the Sheriffdoms of Nairn and Inverness, all the lands within the bounds of
Athole and Sheriffdom of Perth, the barony of Fythkill, with the
pertinents within the Sheriffdom of Fife, all lands within Galloway,
the lands of Forgrundtheny, and Kinfawnys within the Sheriffdom
of Perth, and the thaneage of Glendorachy, and the lands of
Deskford within the Sheriffdom of Banff, which belonged to the
said Euphemia by heritable right." And this charter did not
exhaust the list of his possessions. The Earl speedily quarrelled
with the Bishop of Moray. As Lord of Badenoch, the Earl insisted that the lands of the Bishop of Moray in Badenoch were
held of him. The Bishop maintained the contrary. The Wolf
summoned the Bishop to a court he was holding at the Standing
Stones of Easter Kingussie. A document drawn up at the time
gives a vivid description of the scene. The Bishop, " accompanied

by a becoming retinue, directed his steps to the court, and standing without the court, after silence had been obtained, modestly offered " various protestations, one of which was that he refused to recognise the earl as Lord Superior of the lands belonging to the Church of Moray in Badenoch, and disclaimed him and his court. As a compromise he was willing to recognise him, so far, as Sheriff of Inverness, but this offer was not accepted. The Bishop then withdrew, the court went on, and the process was brought to an end. The Bishop returned and threatened with ecclesiastical censure any one who should dare to carry out the decreet of the court. Next day the Wolf and the Bishop met in the castle of Ruthven, and the controversy was renewed. There was a large company of the notables of the district, among whom were Andrew Falconer of Lethenvar, Hugh Rose of Kilravock, Barons John de Brodie, and Gilbert de Glencharny, the Lords Patrick Crawford and Alexander Man, with Martin de Calder, Archdeacon and Chancellor of the Church of Ross, " and many others, cleric and laic." It was no doubt through the persuasion of these friends that the Wolf was induced to hand over to the notary, one William of Spynie, the whole process, which he placed with his own hands " in a large fire kindled in said chamber, to be burnt and devoured and consumed in presence of the persons assembled, in token that the Lord of Badenoch cannot ask then or in future anything of the Bishop or Church in respect of the aforesaid lands."

The Wolf of Badenoch was soon in trouble with his domestic affairs. He ill-treated his wife, the Countess of Ross, and she left him. He had taken up with a woman named Marion, daughter of Athyn, and the powers of the Church were invoked against him. It was eventually agreed that the Countess should go back, on condition that she was to be treated honourably with matrimonial affection, and that Marion should be sent away. Further, since Euphemia, the Countess, alleged fear of death, the Earl was to find security for £200 " that he shall treat the lady becomingly, without the fear of death, and shall not in any way surround her with his followers, slaves, nobles, and others, contrary to law." The Earl of Sutherland, the Laird of Culbin, and Thomas Chisholm became sureties for his better behaviour. In spite of his promises, however, the Wolf seized the Bishop's lands in Badenoch. The Bishop in turn excommunicated him. In retaliation he burned the town of Forres, with the choir of the church and the manse of the Archdeacon, and a month later, emerged out of his retreat of Lochindorb, with a band of followers, and burnt the whole town of Elgin, the church of St. Giles, the Maisondieu, and the grand Cathedral, with eighteen noble and beautiful mansions belonging to the canons and chaplains, with all the books, charters, and other valuable records of the country therein kept. The deed was that of a madman. He was ultimately seized and imprisoned. He died at Dunkeld in 1394, and a monument still exists there to his " good memory." He left five illegitimate sons, all of them as ferocious and lawless as their father, though one of them, Alexander, who became Earl of Mar, redeemed his character in after years.

Euphemia, Countess of Ross, bore no children to the Earl of Buchan, Lord of Badenoch, and the earldom on her death went to Alexander her son by her first marriage. He married a daughter of Robert, Duke of Albany (brother of King Robert III.), and dying comparatively young, left a daughter Euphemia. In the midst of the wild crew at Lochindorb, it is singular to meet with a maiden of pious feelings and aspirations. But so it was, and Euphemia (bearing the ill-famed name of her grandmother, the old Countess of Ross), on whom the succession to the vast estates of the Earldom of Ross devolved, sought refuge in the cloister, and took the veil. In these circumstances, she being a nun and therefore dead to the world and incapable of holding property, the succession ought by right to have reverted to her aunt, Lady Margaret, wife of Donald of the Isles. The Duke of Albany, however, refused to acknowledge Donald's claim. In 1411, the Lord of the Isles landed with an army of 10,000 men in Ross, and the people submitted to him as their rightful lord. The Chief of the Mackintoshes and other leaders of clansmen joined him. Donald had a fleet in the Moray Firth, and was carrying on negotiations with England for the assistance of the English fleet. It is extremely probable that Donald had designs on the Crown. His mother was a sister of Albany, and daughter of King Robert II. He captured the town of Inverness, and partly burned it. Here he assembled his forces. A combined movement on the part of the Highlanders was then made for the south. As Sheriff and Constable of Nairn in hereditary right of the Earl of Ross, Donald summoned the men of Nairn to follow him. He proceeded eastwards, over-running Moray, Banff, and Strathbogie. In his victorious march, he approached Aberdeen, and threatened to sack and destroy the city if it did not surrender. Alexander, Earl of Mar (illegitimate son of the Wolf of Badenoch and cousin of Donald himself), took the field against him, and without waiting for the Duke of Albany, who was coming to his support, offered battle to Donald on the moor of Harlaw, near Inverurie. On the one side were arrayed the hordes of fighting men of the Highlands and Islands, on the other the less numerous but more disciplined troops of Lowlanders from Buchan, Mar, Kincardine, and Angus, with a body of citizens from Aberdeen headed by their provost. It was a struggle between cousins for the richest earldom of the north, and its echoes have come down to us in heroic song and martial music. The fight continued with awful carnage till the sun went down and with undecided result. The southerners were decimated to a mere handful, whilst a vast number of Highlanders lay slain on the field, among them being the Chiefs of the Mackintoshes and the Macleans. Donald drew off his men during the night, and retreated to the north. The Duke of Albany, in pursuit of Donald, came north with a great army in the autumn, took the castle of Dingwall, and appointed the Earl of Mar to administer the affairs of the region. Mar had for his companion Brodie of Brodie. Donald betook himself to the fastnesses of the Isles, where he was secure during the winter, but in the following summer Albany penetrated to every corner of his dominions, forcing him to make his submission, and renounce his claims to Ross.

The Duke of Albany got his granddaughter Euphemia reestablished in the Earldom, and in the year 1415 she surrendered it to the Duke and received back from him a charter of the Earldom (with the shire and castle of Nairn and all pertaining) for herself and the heirs of her body. In event of her dying without heirs (which was to be expected of a nun), the Duke's sons, John Stuart, Earl of Buchan, and his brother, were declared to be heirs in succession.   On Euphemia's death the Earl of Buchan became also Earl of Ross and Sheriff and Constable of Nairn.   The new Earl was mostly engaged in the wars in France, and died at the battle of Verneuil in 1424.

Donald's son, Alexander, now Lord of the Isles, immediately seized upon the Earldom of Ross.   The state of the Highlands was exceedingly turbulent at the time, and King James I., who was now upon the throne, came north to Inverness.   There he held a Parliament, to which he summoned the Highland chieftains. They came, never doubting; perhaps dreaming of riches and honours; but as each chief entered the hall alone, he was seized, bound, and cast into a separate prison.   In this way James captured Alexander, Lord of the Isles, and his mother Margaret, the rightful Countess of Ross.   Contemporary historians, in mentioning the names of the chiefs, record the number of men they could bring into the field, which varied from four to one thousand men each.   James Campbell was tried for the murder of John of the Isles, and hanged.   John Macarthur and Alexander Mackeiny, chiefs of a thousand men, were beheaded.   After a year's confinement, Alexander, Lord of the Isles, and his mother received the clemency of the King, and were liberated on parole, but soon afterwards the Lord of the Isles gathered an army of ten thousand men, and burnt the town of Inverness.   The King coming against him next year, he was forced to seek for pardon in the most abject manner.

After the death of King James I., Alexander, Lord of the Isles, took possession once more of the Earldom of Ross, and was allowed to retain it undisturbed.   His power was acknowledged by the Estates appointing him Guardian of the North, and for many years he discharged his duties in the most exemplary manner.   We find him granting charters to Cawdor, Kilravock, and others, and as superior of the lands in Nairnshire, exercising agreeably the rights of overlordship.   The Earl had a bailie or factor in Nairn, one William Fleming, who is styled burgess of Nairn.   One of his transactions was to convey absolutely to the Thane of Cawdor the lands of Belmakeith, from which he formerly drew a fixed annual rent of six merks.   The Earl of Ross married Elizabeth Seton, a sister of the first Earl of Huntly, and his family formed matrimonial connexions with families in the district. His son married a daughter of Livingston of Callendar, one of the Scottish statesmen of the time.

The Douglas Rebellion brought this happy state of matters to an end. The Earl of Douglas, the Earl of Crawford, and the Earl of Ross, entered into a treasonable confederacy against James II., which shook the throne to its foundations. The three conspirators were connected with the district. The Douglas family, which was exceedingly powerful in the south, was represented in the north by Archibald Douglas, who had become Earl of Moray. The line of the Dunbars as Earls of Moray had ended in two heiresses. The elder daughter was married to James, Lord Crichton, the younger to Archibald, third son of the Earl of Douglas. The nearest male heir was Sir Alexander Dunbar of Westfield. The Earl of Douglas, however, set the claims both of Lord Crichton and Sir Alexander Dunbar aside, and obtained from the Crown a charter of the Earldom of Moray in favour of Archibald Douglas, his brother. When the rebellion took place, Archibald, Earl of Moray, and his brother the Earl of Ormond, became involved in it. The Earl of Crawford possessed the lands of Strathnairn, with the castle of Daviot—the marriage portion of King Robert II. to his daughter Elizabeth, who married David, first Earl of Crawford. The county of Nairn, as already seen, formed a portion of the Earldom of Ross, and John of the Isles, Earl of Ross, who had inherited the treason of his father Alexander along with the title, breaking out into rebellion, seized the royal castles of Inverness, Urquhart, and Ruthven, in Badenoch.

Archibald Douglas, who had begun extensive additions to Darnaway Castle, proceeded to fortify Lochindorb Castle against the King. He, along with his brother the Earl of Ormond, joined the Earl of Douglas, and took part in the battle of Arkinholme. In that battle the Douglas troops were routed. The Earl of Moray was slain on the field, and his bleeding and mangled head was brought as a ghastly present to King James. The Earl of Ormond was taken prisoner. The Earldom of Moray was forfeited to the Crown, and its wide domains became Crown

property.   The earldom of Ormond, with the old Moray estates
of Petty, Bracklie, and Ardmenache, was annexed to the Crown.
The Earl of Crawford, known as the " Tiger " from his ferocity
and his wearing an abnormally long beard, was defeated by Huntly,
and his property in Straithnairn was confiscated.   Crawford, however, made his peace with the King and had his great possessions
restored to him, but he lived only for six months after his restoration to the King's favour, and the estates were held in ward for
his son, a minor.   The Earl of Ross escaped for the time, but
proofs of his treason coming to light a year or two afterwards, he
was summoned to Parliament to answer for his conduct, a summons
to that effect being sent to the Sheriff-Depute at Nairn.   He did
not obey the summons, but on the 10th of July, 1477, he made
his submission to the King, who pardoned him, and he received a
new charter to his lands and possessions, with the exception of the
Earldom of Ross, the Lordship of Kintyre, and the offices of
Sheriff of Inverness and Nairn, which were stated to be reserved
in memory of his offence.   Thus came to an end the connection
of the great Earls of Ross with Nairnshire.   The Prince of Wales
has as one of his titles that of Earl of Ross, and he is also Earl of
Ormond.

CHAPTER IX

EARLY FAMILY HISTORY

THE Douglas Rebellion produced considerable changes in Nairn-shire. It brought an accession of wealth to the houses of Cawdor and Kilravock, and while it occasioned the downfall of the Earl of Ross and the Douglases, it led to the rise to great power and influence of the family of Gordon in the north. Alexander Seton married the heiress of the Gordons, and assumed the name of his wife. His son, Alexander, who was styled Lord Gordon, was rewarded with large estates and important offices for the part he took in overthrowing the tiger Earl of Crawford, or, as the King said, " for haudin' the Croun on our head." He was created Earl of Huntly, and his son, George, who succeeded him, virtually ruled the north.

A transaction of Alexander, Lord Gordon, a few years before the Douglas Rebellion, led indirectly to the extinction of the family of Raite of Raite.

The history of Raite, though involved in some obscurity, can be pretty accurately traced from existing writs. The earliest pos-sessors of Raite were the Mackintoshes. Shaw Mackintosh, the fourth chief of the clan, before 1265 obtained a grant of Rothie-murcus and the lands of Meikle Geddes and Raite. He is said to have married Helen, daughter of the second recorded Thane of Cawdor. Ferquhard his son succeeded him, and dying in 1274, left an only child Angus. During the minority of Angus, the Cumings took possession of Raite and Meikle Geddes and other lands which belonged to Mackintosh. As Norman knights, they dropped their surname and appear in the records of the period

simply with the territorial title " De Rathe."   In the deed executed
in the latter part of the reign of Alexander III. by Elizabeth Bisset,
conveying the lands of Kilravock to Mary her daughter and Hugh
Rose of Geddes, her son-in-law, " Gervaise de Rate " is one of the
witnesses.   When Edward I. of England came north in the year
1296, one of the knights who made submission during the King's
stay at Elgin was Sir Gervaise de Raite.   His letter tendering his
loyalty and obedience on the occasion is published in Palgrave's
" Documents illustrating the History of Scotland."   It is written
in Norman-French.   In the roll of the Parliament held at Berwick
by Edward on his return south, the names of Sir Gervaise de Raite
and Sir Andrew de Raite, father and son, appear.   When the War
of Independence broke out, Sir Andrew de Raite took the side of
Edward against Bruce, and his mission to London in connection
with Sir Andrew Moray's doings in the province of Moray has
been already narrated.   The downfall of the powerful family of
Cuming, of which they were a branch, and the overthrow of the
political party to which they had attached themselves, could not
have left the knights of Raite unaffected.   Sir Andrew, as has been
shown, filled the office of Constable of the castle of Nairn when
Thomas Braytoft held it for Edward.   Soon after the close of the
War of Independence the Thane of Cawdor held that office.
The Mackintoshes, who greatly assisted Bruce at Bannockburn,
revived the claim to Raite, but Angus, the chief, for some reason,
was not restored to his paternal estates, but was recompensed with
other lands.   The Mackintoshes, however, still remembered that
Raite rightfully belonged to them—they also pretended some claim
to Kilravock—and Alexander Lord Gordon, on 5th October,
1442, granted a charter to Mackintosh of the lands of Raite and
Meikle Geddes, which charter (says Mr. Fraser Mackintosh) is
still extant.   A tradition exists that the name of Knocknagillean
(now Skenepark) was given in consequence of the Cumings having
hanged five young men of the Mackintosh clan on the trees on a
little height—Knock-na-gillean meaning the " Hill of the Lads."
In the statistical account of the parish of Croy and Dalcross, the
tragic incident which led to the abandonment of Raite Castle was
first related, and the traditionary account in the locality differs from

it only in giving fuller details. The story is to the effect that Cuming of Raite, under the guise of a desire to bury former animosities and establish friendly relations, invited the Mackintosh and his followers to a grand banquet at Raite. The invitation was accepted, and the Mackintoshes, never doubting, prepared to attend. They were, however, timely warned that the Cumings had planned a foul plot, and that at a given signal each Cuming would rise and slay his defenceless guest. Old Cuming had put all his household under a solemn oath that they would not reveal the plot to any person ; but his daughter, anxious for the safety of young Mackintosh, who was her lover, found a way to disclose the plot. She went to a large boulder some distance from the castle, and told the whole story to the stone, but she knew her lover was behind it, as it was their usual trysting place, and he would hear every word. The stone to this day is called " The Stone of the Maiden." The Mackintoshes, notwithstanding the warning, resolved to attend the feast. When the night of the banquet came, each Mackintosh hid his dirk in his plaid, but gaily took his seat at the festive board of Cuming of Raite. The revelry ran high, and the walls of the old castle resounded with the mirthful shouts of the carousers. At length the toast was given " The Memory of the Dead." This was the signal agreed upon for the slaughter of the guests. The Cumings rose and were about to draw their swords, but the Mackintoshes, being forewarned, were forearmed, and with a yell of derision sprang to their feet, drew their daggers and thrust them into the hearts of the Cumings. Among the few who escaped death, it is said, was the chief of the Cumings, who rushed to an upper chamber where his daughter was, whom he believed to have given the information, as he knew the girl and the young Mackintosh were lovers. Seeing the maddened state of her father, the young lady sought to escape from him by leaping out of the window, but before she could do so, he cut off both her hands with a broadsword. From the night on which the tragedy was enacted, the blood-stained walls of Raite have been tenantless. So runs the tradition.

Historically there is no improbability in the story, and the only difficulty is in reconciling it with the statement of Shaw that " about the year 1404," in consequence of Raite having killed Andrew, Thane of Cawdor, he was banished the county of Nairn, and settled in the Mearns, where he founded the family of Raite of Halgreen. There is a difference of forty years between the date given by Shaw and that of the charter to Mackintosh. The explanation may probably be that while the father was banished, a son may have remained who became the actor in the tragedy. The " half-lands of Rait " appear in the Cawdor titles for the first time in 1442, the very year of the tragic occurrence. The Mackintoshes never took possession of the lands. While Cawdor obtained one half with the mill, the Setons retained the other half with the castle and the lands of Meikle Geddes—these latter properties some time afterwards passing into the hands of the Ogilvies of Durn and Carnoussie, and ultimately to the Cawdor family, in whose possession they now are.

The ruins of Raite Castle, which still remain, are situated at the foot of the Hill of the Ord. The building, though roofless and completely gutted, exhibits several features of detail which have greatly perplexed antiquarians. It is in some respects almost unique in Scotland. The shape of the building is that of a simple oblong, 64 by 33 feet, with a round tower, 21 feet in diameter, at the south-west angle. Viewed from the outside, the building has a decidedly ecclesiastical appearance. The windows are not mere slits in the walls, but are three feet wide, with Gothic arches and mullions. M'Gibbon and Ross, who give a minute description of the architectural details, say that the windows are of a form and design very uncommon in Scotland. This aspect of the exterior has led some writers to conclude that the building was an ecclesiastical edifice. An examination of the interior, however, does not support this view. The entrance, which is at the east end of the south wall, still shows the grooves of the portcullis by which it was protected. The doorway, which is in the form of an arch, was further protected by a wooden door, as is evidenced by the jambs still remaining. "The form of the arch," say the architectural authorities already quoted, " is very unusual, and the workmanship is superior to that of ordinary castles." The building is divided into two floors. The ground floor is provided with several small square windows, varying from 12 inches to 18 inches in width. The one nearest the north-east angle is a loop with a pointed arch There is no fireplace in the basement. The doorway led by a passage or guard-room, not to the ground floor, but to the hall above, which is lighted with the handsome windows already described. These windows are furnished with stone seats and the hall is provided with a large fire-place. From the hall, the round tower is entered, and is found to contain a private room. The remains of the tower rise a few feet higher than the existing walls, which are about 20 feet in height, and when entire doubtless terminated in battlements. The object of the tower is plainly to defend the building from attack from the mass of rock rising to the south—the most easily assailable point. The tower bears a close resemblance to the round towers of the Edwardian period. There are no mouldings or ornaments to give a clue to the age of its erection. The walls are $5\frac{1}{2}$ feet thick, built mostly of fragments of the adjacent rocks, except where freestone is used for the door and window finishings, and all strongly cemented together. The general aspect of the building unites features of elegance and comfort with the severest plainness in the materials used. The castle appears to have been protected with an enclosing wall on three sides, the rocks on the south side forming a natural defence. The corners of the enclosing wall were probably furnished with protecting angle turrets. Within the courtyard, the retainers would find accommodation. That the building was not a church is abundantly evidenced by the character of the remains of the structure, and there are frequent references in the sixteenth century to " Rait with its fortalice," and to the " Castletown of Rait "— proof that at that early period its castellated character was recognised. It is exceedingly probable that in these picturesque ruins we have the actual hall in which the tragic scene occurred between the Cumings and the Mackintoshes. A castle like this must have been built before the War of Independence. It is entirely different in style from the keeps which were built during the immediately succeeding centuries.

Cordiner mentions in his " Antiquities " that a burying ground near the castle was visible when he visited the place in 1776, and that some stones placed to mark the graves bore the figure of a bow and arrow; but the green spot has been ploughed up and the stones have been broken.

The original patrimony of the Thanes of Cawdor appears to have been limited to the fertile valley lying between Brackla and Barevan. The surrounding lands were in other hands, as appears from the charters of the period. The first addition to the early heritage was the lands of Highland Boath and Banchor—a desirable summer pasturage, which at one time was held by charter from Alexander II. by the illustrious family of Durward. "The Thanes of Cawdor," says Shaw, the historian of Moray, "as constables of the King's house resided in the castle of Nairn, and had a country seat at what is now called Old Cawdor, a half-mile north from the present seat. There they had a house on a small moat, with a dry ditch and a drawbridge, the vestiges whereof are to be seen," Shaw wrote in 1720. The earliest documentary notice by name of the Thane of Cawdor occurs in the extent or valuation of the lands of Kilravock and Easter Geddes at Nairn on the feast of St. Lawrence, 1295, when Donald, Thane of Kaledor, is one of the assize. The name is variously spelled in old writs. The earliest form is *Kaledor*, but in a deed only fifteen years later, it is written *Caldor*; in the fifteenth century it is generally written *Caudor* or *Calder*, and in some instances it is strangely corrupted into *Caddell*.

The Cawdor genealogical tree gives (1) Donald, Thane of Cawdor, 1295; (2) William, Thane of Cawdor, who got a charter of the thanage from Robert I., 1310; (3) William, Thane of Cawdor, about 1350; (4) Andrew, Thane of Cawdor, who was infeft in the Sheriffship and Constabulary of Nairn and half of Dunmaglass, and died about 1405. He is said to have been murdered by Sir Alexander Raite of Raite; (5) Donald, served heir to his father in 1405, acquired the other half of Dunmaglass, Moy near Forres, and Little Urchany. For the first time a marriage connexion is mentioned in the genealogy, when a daughter of Thane Donald married John Hay of Lochloy. According to tradition, Shaw Mackintosh was married to Helen, daughter of

the second Thane.   It is extremely probable that the first half of
Dunmaglass may have come as a wife's dower.   Urchanybeg was
purchased from the Bishop of Moray in 1421.   The office of
Sheriff of the shire and Constable of the castle of Nairn carried
with it considerable emoluments, as well as local influence.   Calder
at a very early date had considerable lands in and around the burgh
of Nairn, including Balmakeith, Millbank, the Gallowslands, and
the Skateraw, and as constable of the castle he had a right to tithes
of fish and ale.   He had a charter also to the lands which belonged
to Fergus the Dempster, which probably lay within the territories
of the burgh.

During the period of the superiority of the Earls of Ross the
position of the Thane of Cawdor was that of deputy sheriff.   The
thanage itself was held of the Earl, and during a temporary forfeiture of the earldom it was renewed by King James I. as Earl of
Ross.   About the time of the ascension of James II. to the throne,
the young Calders appear to have sought public service in the south.
A tradition exists that a younger son of Donald, fifth Thane,
joined the Earl of Huntly in his attack on the Earl of Crawford at
Brechin, and in recompense for his exploit of penetrating to the
camp of the Earl, and carrying off the Tiger's drinking cup as a
trophy before the battle commenced, he received the lands of
Aussanly, and became the founder of the Calders of Aussanly.
Another son was founder of the Calders of Muirtoun.

William, who succeeded his father Donald, and who was Thane
when the Douglas Rebellion occurred, also appears to have been
when a youth an attendant at the court of James II., for the King
in a charter extant designates him his beloved familiar squire
(*dilectus familiaris scutifer noster*).   When King James came to the
north, he took up his residence chiefly at Darnaway Castle, and
summoned William, Thane of Cawdor, to his side.   The King,
after viewing the work begun but not completed at Darnaway by
the unfortunate Archibald Douglas, Earl of Moray, ordered the
additions to be carried out, but granted a commission to the Thane
of Cawdor to demolish the island fortress of Lochindorb, the forti-
fying of which and Darnaway against the King was the special
charge on which Earl Archibald's estates were forfeited.   The

Thane was allowed a sum of £24 for performing this work. Lochindorb was dismantled but not entirely destroyed, and one of the gates at Cawdor Castle is said to have been brought from Lochindorb on the occasion of the dismantling. The Thane appears to have been an excellent scholar and man of business, and the King appointed him his Chamberlain north of the Spey, jointly with Thomas Carmichael, a canon of Elgin Cathedral. The administration of the lands and revenues of the Earldom of Moray, the Crawford estates in Strathnairn, and the Petty and Ormond possessions, with the Sheriffdoms of Elgin, Forres, Nairn, and Inverness, and the maintenance and upkeep of the King's castles situated therein, was a work of no inconsiderable character. The accounts kept by the Thane are still preserved at Cawdor Castle, and extracts of them have been published in " The Book of the Thanes of Cawdor," edited by Cosmo Innes for the Bannatyne Club. Deductions were made in the accounts to the King from the rents of Glencharny (Duthil), Knok (the forest at Lochindorb), Aitenach, and a part of Strathnairn, which had been proclaimed waste by royal mandate for the purposes of sport.

In the year 1454 the Thane received letters from King James II., granting him licence to build his castle of Cawdor, to fortify it " with walls, moats, and iron portcullis, to furnish it with turrets and other defensive armaments and apparatus, and to appoint constables, janitors, and jailors to his castle, provided always that the King and his successors shall have free ingress and egress to and from the castle." Local legend tells that the Thane was much perplexed as to where he should build the stronghold, but was admonished in a dream to bind the coffer containing the treasure he had collected for the purpose on an ass, to set the animal free, to mark the spot where the ass stopped, and there to build his tower. The ass came to a hawthorn tree, and looked at it, but passed on. It came to a second hawthorn tree, and rubbed itself against it, but again passed on. When it came to the third hawthorn tree on the bank of the burn, it stopped and lay down with its burden. And around this tree the Thane built his castle. " Be this as it will," says old Lachlan Shaw, " there is in the lowest vault of the tower, the trunk of a hawthorn tree, firm and sound, growing out of the rock and reaching to the top of the vault.   Strangers are brought to stand round it, each one to take a chip of it, and then to drink to the hawthorn tree, *i.e.*, ' Prosperity to the family of Calder.' "

The old tree still remains firmly rooted in the donjon, but it is now a sapless trunk, and the ceremony of chipping has been forbidden.   The treasure chest of the legend lies beside it in the vault.   The " first " and " second " hawthorn trees, which stood within a hundred yards of the castle, have disappeared—one about the beginning of the nineteenth century and the other in the year 1836.

The castle which Thane William built was a grim square keep, three storeys in height above the dungeon, terminating in battlements, with a turret at each corner.   It was 45 feet in length by 34 feet in width, and was surrounded with a wall built on the edge of the rock on the south side next the burn, and close to the ditch on the other sides.   The gateway and drawbridge then as now gave entrance to a small courtyard shut off from the northern and southern courtyards by walls of defence, and commanded by the keep and battlements.   The entrance doorway was in the north side and is on the ground floor—an unusual circumstance in castles of the time, but the level of the ground may have been altered. Right above the door, near the top of the wall, there was a corbelled projection with a recess in the adjoining wall where stones and other projectiles were kept to hurl down upon the heads of hostile visitors who approached the door.   Each of the three storeys consisted of but one main apartment, though small rooms or recesses were cut out of the walls (which are seven feet thick), affording sleeping accommodation, garde-robes, &c.   From the entrance doorway, a straight staircase in the thickness of the wall leads to the first floor, whence a wheel stair in the angle of the north and east walls conducts to the upper floors, and finally by another straight flight to the battlements.   The top storey, like the dungeon, was vaulted, the arch being high and pointed, and it was probably covered with a flat stone roof.   Such, as distinguished from the more recent additions, are the features of the original building described by the authors of " Castellated and Domestic

Architecture in Scotland." The enclosing wall next to the burn appears to have been utilised for foundations for subsequent additions. In the castle of Old Calder there was a St. Mary's Chapel, and in the castle built by Thane William, he founded a new chapel, also dedicated to the Virgin, which was endowed out of the rents of Auchindoune and Barevan. It was probably situated within the south court, but was removed when additions came to be made in later times.

Thane William, the builder of the castle, looked out for a good match for William, his son. At this time there lived a very wealthy though untitled chieftain, Alexander Sutherland, at the old castle of Dunbeath on the Caithness coast on the Moray Firth. He had great estates in land, and much gear in corn and cattle. His wife was a daughter of Donald, Lord of the Isles, and he had several sons and daughters. The hand of his youngest daughter was sought by the young Thane of Cawdor, and about the year 1458 they were married. The old laird of Dunbeath, after making ample provision for the other members of his family, made Mariot, the young Thane's wife, his residuary legatee. " I give and assign to my douchter Mariot all the lave of my lands that I have undisponyt upon." These lands were very considerable, including large possessions in the neighbouring districts. The young Thane was in truth " a prosperous gentleman." He made on his own account numerous purchases of land in the neighbourhood. The estate of the family of Cawdor at this period was undoubtedly one of the most valuable, if not the most extensive, in the north, and the house of Cawdor was correspondingly influential. It seems, however, that for a brief time a cloud overshadowed the thanage. On the forfeiture of the Earl of Ross in 1475, the Thane felt it incumbent on him to make a fresh submission to the King, and in one of the two copies of his act of submission the Thane craves remission for past crimes. His wife, Mariot Sutherland, being a sister of John of the Isles, Earl of Ross, may have been mixed up with some of the Earl's treasonable designs which had just come to light. However that may be, he was freely forgiven, and a year later was gratified by having his thanage restored to its ancient tenure as a direct vassalage of the Crown and not of the Earls of

Ross.   A charter under the Great Seal dated at Edinburgh, 29th May, 1476, was granted to him of his whole lands and baronies united and incorporated into one thanage, to be called the thanage of Cawdor, and to be held of the King and his successors in fee and heritage for ever, with the privilege of pit and gallows, etc. Further, the offices of Sheriff and Keeper of the King's castle of Nairn were henceforward to be held hereditarily by him as principal officer and not as deputy.

We get a glimpse or two of the social and domestic life at Cawdor Castle in the arrangements this Thane made for settling his daughters in the world.   The eldest daughter Marjory was disposed of in this way.   Her father purchased from " ane noble and mychty lorde " William, Earl of Errol, Lord Hay, and Constable of Scotland, who (along with Sir Gilbert Keith of Inverugie) had bought the " haill marriage and ward " of Alexander Fraser of Philorth, his part of the wardship for certain sums of money.   Young Fraser became bound to espouse Calder's daughter, but because they were " god brother and god sister," a licence or dispensation from the Pope had to be procured before they could be married, and the Thane undertook to pay the cost in the first instance, which was to be repaid when young Philorth came into possession of his lands. The intended bridegroom was taken bound to " byde and remain daily in household " at Cawdor Castle until the dispensation came home and he be lawfully married to Marjory.   It is quaintly said in the contract that, " because the said Alexander Fraser has na seal present of his awne, he has procurit the seal of ane honourable lord, Hew, Lord Fraser of Lovat."   The marriage of Philorth and Marjory Calder was duly celebrated.   It was followed three years later by the marriage of the second daughter Marion with a young Mackintosh, designated Hugh Allanson.   The contract was made in his case by the Thane with Duncan Mackintosh, " captain of the Clancattane," Farquhar Mackintosh, son and heir apparent, and Hugh Allanson himself.   The same ecclesiastical formalities had to be gone through, as Marion and Mackintosh are stated to be two-fourths kin, but on the Pope's dispensation arriving they were happily married.   Calder's son-in-law entered into a bond of friendship with his father-in-law against all men, except his

Sovereign Lord the King and his chief, Mackintosh. Clanship took precedence even of sonship. A third daughter, Margaret, married a near neighbour, William Dallas, heir to Budgate.

The Thane was not, however, without his troubles. His neighbour, the Baron of Kilravock, and he were frequently at strife about their marches. They had exchanged "the kiss of peace and friendship" more than once, only to be at deadly feud shortly afterwards. One day matters came to a crisis. The Thane seized Kilravock's eldest son, and put him in ward in the castle dungeon. The Baron, his father, complained to the Earl of Huntly, the King's Lieutenant in the north, but the wrathful Thane defied both Earl and Baron. Kilravock sought redress from the King, and a royal warrant was issued to the Earl of Huntly to command the Thane to set young Kilravock at liberty, which he eventually did.

The Thane's mind had often been occupied with projects of putting an end to the strife between the two houses by a marriage alliance, and some curious covenants are in existence between the parties, one contract being to the effect that he should have the choice for his son of all the daughters of Kilravock, from the eldest to the youngest. The state of health of his eldest son and heir was a further cause of anxiety to Calder. That eldest son William was lame and weak of body. The Thane could not contemplate with satisfaction the Cawdor possessions passing into his hands at a time when the state of the country required firm administration. The young laird did not himself desire the succession. His mind lay in another direction than towards worldly wealth and position. He resigned his birthright that he might the more entirely devote himself to the service of God. His father accordingly procured a mandate under the Privy Seal dated 1488, settling the succession on his second son John and his lawful heirs male, whom failing, on his other sons—Andrew, Alexander, and Hugh, and their heirs male successively; all of whom failing, to the said Thane William's nearest and lawful heirs male. It would appear that the hereditary Sheriffship of Nairn could not be so easily diverted, and William, while he prepared for the Church, retained his right to that office and received a pension of £20 a year from the estate, until such times as he should get a church benefice. He ultimately became the Vicar of Barevan. The fact that Mariot, his mother, was dead by this time may have rendered it the easier to carry out these arrangements for disinheriting the rightful heir. John, a natural brother of the Thane (afterwards legitimised), kept a watchful eye on these proceedings. He was a churchman, but had acquired considerable property in Nairn and elsewhere. He was first Rector of Duthil and afterwards Precentor of Ross, and a leading man in the district. The Thane, however, was a resolute man, and no friendly counsel would turn him from his object. A matrimonial alliance was arranged on 10th May, 1492, between his son John, now the fiar or heir apparent to the Thanage, and Isabella Rose, daughter of the Baron of Kilravock. She brought as her marriage portion 900 merks secured on the reversion of the lands of Kinsteary and a quarter of Easter Geddes, and her husband was infeft in the lands of Cawdor as heir, " as sicker as men's wits can devise." About this time the Thane acquired in feu the other half of Raite and the adjoining lands of Meikle Geddes. The Thane married a second time, and with his second wife, Janet Keith of Inverugie, the widow of Alan Kinnaird of Culbin, he got the two Tullyglens, now part of Dunphail.

An event happened about this time which would not have been expected to befall a shrewd, worldly, cautious man like the Thane of Cawdor, one too who held the official position of Sheriff of the shire. It was a time, however, of extreme violence. Clan raids or herships, as they were called, had come to be very common, and the Thane appears to have become involved in a serious affray. In the year 1492 King James IV. came north to Inverness, and amongst the charges he had to dispose of was one against the Thane of Cawdor and certain accomplices, for the slaughter of Patrick Wiseman, Duncan M'Angus, William Blacklaw, and John Rede. No particulars are given of the occurrence, but it appears to have taken place at Inverness. Possibly a band of lawless men had stolen some of Calder's cattle, and he had taken the law into his own hands. The other parties involved with Calder were Thomas Hay, William Calder, John Nicolson, John Belgeam, Thomas Grant, and James Maliach. The King in the plentitude of his mercy granted them a remission, "provided that to the parents and friends of the said slaughtered individuals they make amends and satisfaction, and likewise satisfy others who have endured losses, so that regarding this matter we shall for the future hear of no just complaint." The Thane was no sooner well out of this scrape than he was into another. Along with his neighbours, William Dallas of Cantray and William Dallas of Budgate, he came within the scope of the law again. Matters looked very serious. On 26th April, 1494, Calder and his two kinsmen, the Dallases, were tried at the circuit court at Aberdeen, accused of certain criminal actions alleged to have been committed by them. They were found guilty, and sentenced to be beheaded. The King's interest was sought on their behalf when he came to Inverness in the autumn, and on the 25th of October the King "moved to pity, considering and understanding they were ever our true lieges and obedient to our laws, and never found guilty of before, granted them their lives, heritages, and goods, to live and remain in time to come our true lieges, like as they did of before the giving of the said doom upon them."

Midway between these two events, in the year 1493, the old Thane resigned his lands and thanage personally in the King's hands, in favour of his son John, reserving his own liferent, and a royal charter was granted in the following year to John and his heirs without limitation.

The marriage which the old Thane had set his heart so much upon did not, however, turn out to his satisfaction. Two daughters were born of the marriage—Jonet and Muriel; but the father died some months before Muriel was born. There is some obscurity as to Jonet, and all that is known for certain is that Muriel alone survived to claim the succession. The Thane now exerted all his craft and skill in legal forms to get the child set aside and one of his other sons placed in the succession, but he had outwitted himself. Had the entail of 1488 stood, the estates would have reverted to the nearest male heir of the Calders, but in his desire to "mak sicker" the entail on John as against his eldest son William, he had by royal charter secured the succession to John's issue, male or female. A long legal fight ensued, and the old

Thane had the mortification of seeing Muriel's right as heiress established at law in 1502. In the following year he departed this life, leaving his sons to carry on the family quarrel for a time. The heiress Muriel, a few years before this, was carried off under romantic circumstances as narrated by Shaw. " Argyle and Kilravock obtained a gift of tutors dative, and the ward of her marriage was granted to Argyll by the King's gift, of date 16th January, 1495. The child was kept in the house of Kilravock; and Argyll granted Kilravock a bond of maintenance and friendship dated 1st February, 1499, and in harvest thereafter sent Campbell of Inverliver with sixty men, to receive the child to bring her to Inveraray. The lady Kilravock, grandmother of the child, being told that she should soon be restored to her, that she might not be changed, seared or marked her hip with the key of her trunk or coffer. As Inverliver was near to Daltulich [in Strathnairn] on his way with little Muriel, he found himself closely pursued by Alexander and Hugh Calder (the child's uncles) with a superior party. Having sent off the child with an escort of six men, Inverliver faced about to stop the Calders; and to deceive them a sheaf of corn was dressed in some of the child's clothes and kept by one in the rear. The conflict was sharp, and several were killed, among whom were eight of Inverliver's sons. When Inverliver thought that the child was out of the reach of her uncles, he retreated, leaving the fictitious child to the pursuers. Inverliver was rewarded with the 20-pound land of Inverliver. 'Tis said that in the heat of the skirmish with the Calders, Inverliver had cried—'*S fhada glaodh o Lochow* ! '*S fhada cobhair o chlonn dhoaine* !—which has become a proverb signifying imminent danger and distant relief."

John Calder, the uncle, the Precentor of Ross, came to the assistance of the Calders, with the intention evidently of maintaining the old line. William, vicar of Barevan, the eldest son, claimed the lands of Little Urchany, and in a deed repudiating some transactions of David Dunbar on his behalf, a curious custom is alluded to. In token of his revoking and annulling the " state " taken wrongfully by Dunbar " at the Broomhill between Meikle and Little Urchany," the vicar, in presence of his uncle and others,

" breaks on the ground a dish with fire with his own foot, as custom is." On one occasion, a few years before this, the old Thane in token of his " breaking the sasine " taken of the lands of Meikle Geddes and half Rait by the Ogilvies, in violation, as he alleged, of his feu-charter from the Setons of Tullybody, employed the symbol of breaking a plate and throwing it into the fire in the hall of Meikle Geddes.

John the Precentor also secured the lands belonging to the Calders in the burgh of Nairn for his nephew the vicar. The sympathies of the burgesses were evidently with the Calders. As the record of the proceedings is one of the earliest minutes of the Nairn Burgh Court extant, it is given in full, the spelling being partially modernised—

" Jhesus Maria."

" The court of Nairn holden at Nairn by John the Ros and John Merchand, bailies of the sammyn burgh of Nairn, the 16th day of August in the year of God one thousand five hundred and six years—the sammyn day the judges sitting, the suits called, and the court lawfully affirmed.

" Nomina Assize.

John Merchand, John Buchane, Manne Clarke, Brande Fide, Thome Sandesoune, William Alexanderson, Willie Crestesone, Sande Fyndlesone, John Clark, John M'Crowun, Robe Thomson, William Caulder, John Caulder.

" The same day Master John Caulder, Chantor of Ross, presented an attorney in the name and behalf of Sir William Caulder, Vicar of Evan, and the said Master John asked the said Sir William to be known and entered to the said rents and lands that his father William Caulder died last vest and seissit of as of fee, within the bounds of the said burgh, the which judges understanding that desire righteous, caused the said Master John to remove the court, and took inquisition of the freemen of the town by their oaths as the manner is in burghs, the which judges found by the assize of the hail town that the said William, thayne of Caulder, died vest and seissit of the crofts beside Belmakeithe, beyond the water of Nairn, forgayne the castle of the sammyn ; also, of six roods lying within the galois, two roods in the Millbank, and two roods in the Skaytrawe, and also of 30d of annual of Cristane Flemyng's land, and of Criste Cummyng's bigging 2s of annual, and of Henry Dallas's land of Cantray 2s. of annual, the which inquest foresaid found the said Sir William lawful heir of all the said lands and annuals, and passed in incontinent and entered the said Master John attorney for the said Sir William by the deliverance of earth and stane, hesp and staple, as the manner of burghs is." The document is certified to be a true copy extracted from the burgh books by Dominus Thomas Strathauchin, notary public.

The Precentor looked next to the interests of Hugh, the next eldest surviving son, whom he destined for his heir. Hugh had married a daughter of the Laird of Culbin, getting a third of that property as dower, and the Precentor induced William, the vicar, to resign the sheriffship in his favour. Accordingly in 1510 a Crown charter was granted to Hugh of the office of Sheriff of Nairn, with the Constabulary of the King's Castle, and the assize of ale and fish. Argyll permitted this to pass, but he took care that the interests of Muriel and his son did not suffer prejudice therefrom. He got himself appointed the King's crowner within the shire of Nairn, thus securing his right to intervene if necessary, his powers being co-ordinate with that of the Sheriff.

Andrew Calder was dead. A tradition states that he had become very ferocious, was outlawed, and defied capture for a time, but was shot in the forehead as he lay concealed behind a boulder at the water dam near Raite. This tale is exceedingly doubtful.

The youngest son, Alexander, remained to be provided for, and the thoughtful uncle first found him a wife. A contract of marriage was drawn up at Auldearn on the 6th of May, 1515, by Hugh Rose of Kilravock, and Mr. John Calder, Chantor of Ross, in terms of which Alexander Calder was to marry Elizabeth Rose, her father giving " six score of merks of marriage gear and eight oxen to plenish a tack," while the uncle gave to his nephew the west half of Easter Bracklie, which he had recently purchased from Sir William Ogilvy, and also a hundred merks of ready money to lay upon land. This he did, he states in the settlement, of his free will " for kindness of blood and helping of the said Alexander."

By this time Muriel had completed her twelfth year, and she was then married to Sir John Campbell, son of the Earl of Argyll. Of Muriel's residence in her west-country home nothing is known. From a gossiping remark it appears she was a red-haired lassie. No doubt she was tenderly brought up, and as later history shows, she had in Sir John Campbell a good husband. Except that she was an exile from her native home, the connexion was everything that could be desired. She could have found no better protection than in the noble house of Argyll, now risen to great power in the land.

The marriage took place in 1510. The mantelpiece in one of the rooms of Cawdor Castle appears to have been executed in commemoration of the event. It bears the arms of the Campbells and the Calders quartered, with the date 1510, and has the initials " S.J.C." (Sir John Campbell), and " M.C." (Muriel Calder), but from the style of the carvings with which it is adorned (one of which is a fox smoking a pipe) it is supposed to have been the work of a later generation. It bears a Latin inscription—*Ceri mani memoneris mane*—" Remember in the morning the good Creator." A year later, proclamation that Muriel's brieve was to be served at Edinburgh on a particular day was made at the cross of the burghs of Nairn, Forres, and Inverness. A Crown charter followed, uniting all the possessions of Cawdor, with the castle and fortalice, into one thanage and free barony in favour of Sir John Campbell and Muriel Calder. And thus the old line of succession was changed, and continues to this day with the Campbells.

The new Thane of Cawdor was cast in quite a different mould from the old Calders. They had been content to occupy a position, respectable and influential enough in its own district, but of comparatively little prominence in the country. Not so Sir John Campbell of Cawdor. Come of a race distinguished for its capacity to rule, the new Thane of Cawdor was aggressive, ambitious, and masterful. The proudest chiefs in the Western Highlands and Isles sought his friendship and protection. The bundles of " bonds of friendship and manrent " in the charter-room of Cawdor testify to his power and influence. It was a turbulent age which needed men of strong character to meet force with force. The chiefs of the M'Leans, Camerons, M'Leods, M'Dougalls, and M'Neills, did not, as the family historian remarks, disdain to take service with him. When Sir John came to the north, the Chief of Clanchattan, the Baron of Kilravock, Munro of Foulis, Mac-Donald of the Isles and Sleat, all pressed their service upon him.

Sir John appears to have been in Nairnshire in the autumn of 1521, as Lachlan Mackintosh, the Captain of Clanchattan, signed his bond at Banchor on 10th August of that year, but it was not till 1524 that Lady Muriel and he took up their residence at Cawdor Castle. The home-coming of Lady Muriel must have been an interesting event in the county, but no scrap of information has been preserved regarding it. Her mother, Isabel Rose of Kilravock, was probably dead by that time. She resided for a time at Balivat—the village of Bellivat, it is called—of which the Roses were hereditary tenants. Her uncle Hugh was still Sheriff of Nairn, and her uncle Alexander was at Clunas. On her mother's side, her relatives at Kilravock were all in a flourishing condition, but the grandmother who had taken care that no red-haired changeling from Argyll should inherit Cawdor was not there to identify her marks.

In truth, however, the new Thane of Cawdor came north under a cloud. A dark tragedy, in which he was concerned, had been enacted but a few months before on the shores of Argyll. M'Lean of Duart, an inhuman wretch, had married Lady Elizabeth Campbell, the Thane of Cawdor's sister. Through some mad freak of temper, M'Lean took the lady out to sea in a boat and placed her on a bare rock in the ocean, covered at high tide, and there left her to perish. The story has been dramatised by Joanna Baillie in her "Family Legend," and the island is known to this day as "The Lady's Rock." The Lady Elizabeth when at the point of death was rescued from her perilous position by a passing boat. Sir John's indignation at this foul deed led him to revenge the insult. He laid waste the lands of Colonsay which belonged to M'Lean, and then followed him to Edinburgh, and, coming in the silence of night to his lodging, slew the wretched man in his bed. Remission for the "slaughter" committed in circumstances of such exceptional provocation was granted by King

James V., and in December of the year Sir John and Lady Muriel took up residence at Cawdor. They thereafter made it their home, merely visiting on occasions their possessions in Argyll.

Sir John's dealings with the old Calders were perhaps not over-generous. The old Precentor was dead, and on the plea of illegitimacy, though the writ of legitimation existed, his property went to the Crown. This property Sir John got by paying to the Crown a small composition. The Vicar of Barevan had died some years before, and the old line was represented by Hugh the Sheriff and Alexander Calder of Clunas. The Sheriff was induced to resign his office in favour of Sir John in exchange for the eight merks of land of Balmakeith, to be held in blanche ferm for a red rose annually if desired. While stripping Hugh Calder of his office, however, Sir John continued to him the whole dues and profits of the town for his lifetime, which was not very long. He died in the following year, leaving no son but five daughters, who inherited a portion of the old Calder properties in the burgh of Nairn. One daughter, Muriel, married John Bayne, burgess of Elgin, and another, Janet, married Morrison, burgess of Nairn. They were served heirs in the Burgh Court and their properties touch upon King's Steps and Househill on the one side, and Millbank, Grieship, etc., on the other.

Sir John acquired from the Ogilvies the lands of Meikle Geddes and half Raite for 1300 merks—his lands of Moy, near Forres, to count for 700 merks. Meikle Geddes and half Raite were previously held in feu-farm of the Setons, for an annual of £20. Sir John coveted the rich corn lands of Strathnairn, belonging to the Ogilvies, and being unable apparently to acquire them by purchase, sought to obtain them by force. He led an expedition against Daviot Castle, slew certain of the keepers, burned the castle, spoiled the lands, and carried away the cattle and horses belonging to James Ogilvie. For this lawless act, the Thane of Cawdor, Sheriff-Principal of Nairn, stood his trial at Inverness circuit court. His near kinsman, Sir John Campbell of Lundy, was judge (acting as depute for the Earl of Argyll), and almost as a matter of course Sir John Campbell of Cawdor was acquitted. Soon afterwards Sir John purchased the superiority of the barony of Strathnairn, with the fortalice of Daviot, from David, Earl of Crawford, for £1000 usual money.

It may have been this transaction which brought the Earl of Crawford into a closer relationship with the house of Cawdor. Sir John and Lady Muriel had five sons and three daughters. Archibald, the eldest son, married Isabel, daughter of James Grant, of Freuchie; John, the second son, was put to fosterage in Argyll, and became Commendator of Ardchattan and Bishop of the Isles; Donald, the third son, was also settled in Argyll; Duncan got Highland Boath as his portion; and Alexander, the youngest, was settled at Fleenasmore and Raite. The youngest daughter married Ross of Balnagown, and Duncan of Boath married a daughter of Balnagown. Janet was engaged to marry young Lochiel, but instead married Alexander, Lord Lovat. The eldest daughter, Katherine, had married young Alexander Dallas, the heir to Cantray, and he infeft his wife in Galcantray. He died early, however, and the young widow made another match—she married the Earl of Crawford, and as the premier countess of Scotland, it may perhaps hardly be wondered at if she is found putting on somewhat patronising airs towards some of her poorer relations. The church half-lands of Fleenasmore, which had been let on tack to Cawdor, were finally granted to Sir John by the Bishop of Moray, and he settled them on his son Alexander along with the lands of Raite. Some few years afterwards the Countess of Crawford, who was devotedly attached to her brothers, paid to Alexander £1000 for the reversion of Raite. The property came into her hands, and she granted to " her beloved David Hay of the Castletown of Raite, all and haill the two plough lands of the Castletown of Raite with the alehouse and alecroft thereof," for a period of five years, at an annual rent of six merks. One of the clauses of the lease is interesting. While David may assign his lease to his heirs, assignees, and sub-tenants, it is expressly stipulated that they must be " of no higher degree nor himself." The descendants of Alexander Calder of Clunas occupied as kindly tenants the " Hilltown of Raite," and they were proving themselves rather troublesome neighbours to Duncan Campbell, brother of the Countess. The Countess wrote from Edinburgh to the Baron of Kilravock to use his good offices with Janet Calder and her family so as to secure that her brother Duncan be not further molested, and the postscript of her ladyship's letter is delightful. "If Janet be reasonable," she writes, "I will do her and her bairns sik pleasure as I can. Otherwise she may be assured that I will show no kyndness neither to her nor her bairns gif she continues in so obstinate ane mynd as I am informit she is presentlie!" These lands were redeemed by the Thane of Calder from David, the sixth Earl of Crawford, after his mother's death.

Among other possessions Sir John acquired a tack of the lands of Stratherne, and also a tack of the Crown lands of Petty and Bracklie. Although spending most of his time at Cawdor, Sir John did not cease to take part in the public affairs of the nation. He was apparently a devout Catholic, and had no sympathy with the Reformation principles then beginning to spread. His nephew the Earl of Argyll being unwell, Sir John represented him at a meeting of Catholic earls and barons, bishops and abbots, who had met at Perth in March of the year 1542, to take measures for repressing the new movement, and he is chosen to accompany Robert Reid, the Bishop of Orkney, to submit certain proposals to the Parliament. It is easy to understand why the Bishop of Orkney was selected for this duty—his personal character placed him above all the other prelates of the time. It may have been for a similar reason that the knight of Cawdor was appointed to accompany him. One of these proposals was that Cardinal Beaton should be liberated, and another that the New Testament should not be read in the vulgar tongue. The Parliament, however, refused both requests. Two years later the Thane of Cawdor offered his sword to the Queen-mother, Mary of Guise, and signed a bond along with other nobles to support her against the Earl of Arran, who was at the head of the Government at the time. In several parliaments he was one of the committee known as the Lords of the Articles. But Sir John's course had run. In the spring of the year 1546 he died, "leaving vast possessions in his paternal country as well as in that of his adoption."

Sir John was succeeded by his son Archibald, of whom little is known. He married, in the year before his father's death, a daughter of James Grant of Freuchy, and died in 1551, leaving a son John, who succeeded him, and a daughter Beatrix, who married Patrick Grant of Glenmorriston. Dame Muriel outlived both her husband and her son. In the year 1573 the old lady deemed it expedient to settle her affairs, which she did by resigning the thanedom and baronies of Cawdor in favour of her grandson, John Campbell, who had just come of age. He married Mary Keith, daughter of the Earl Marischal, and sister of Annas Keith, Countess of Moray, and afterwards Countess of Argyll. Through this marriage connexion, John Campbell of Cawdor was drawn away from Cawdor to the shores of Argyll, and the story of his tragic end will fall to be related in the history of the Cawdor family in connection with their western possessions.

The Roses were early settled in Nairnshire. The date 1230 is given by the family chroniclers, but while some doubt exists as to whether the document—a charter of Beauly Priory—in which the name occurs was genuine (it is now lost), there is documentary evidence of Rose being in possession of Geddes in the latter part of the reign of Alexander III., who died in 1286. Marrying Mary Bosco, a grandchild of Sir John Bisset, and getting the lands of Kilravock and Culcowie with her, Hugh Rose was then styled of Kilravock.

" From their first settlement," says Cosmo Innes, " the family used for arms the water bougets of ' De Roos,' a very definite and peculiar cognizance used by all that name in England and Normandy. At a very early period, even before we have evidence of their lands being erected into a feudal barony, they took and were allowed the style of *Baron* in a manner unusual in Scotland, and in the fifteenth century the family arms appear in the seals of successive lairds of Kilravock, circumscribed—*Sigillum Hugonis Rois Baronis*—the only instance of the kind I have met with in Scotland." A Norman family first settled in England, the Roses of Geddes probably came north about the same time as the Bissets, and like them hailed from Northumbria. A peculiarity of the family has been that, with very few exceptions, the eldest son has been named Hugh, and to distinguish the one baron from the other, the family historian has to designate them as "Kilravock the First," "Kilravock the Second," and so on down the long line of barons. The second baron bore the title of knighthood, and is supposed to have fallen at the battle of Halidon Hill. He left two sons—Hugh, who succeeded him, and Andrew, who received from his mother her part of the lands of Killayne and Pitfour, within the barony of Avoch, with consent of John de Moravia of Bothwell and Avoch, son of Sir Andrew Moray, the Scottish patriot. From Andrew, the second son, are descended the Roses of Auchlossin, who had lands on both sides of the river Nairn near the town, but sold them to Calder in 1457. Hugh, dying about the year 1363, was succeeded by his son Hugh, who increased the family possessions by his marriage with Janet Chisholm, daughter of Sir Robert Chisholm of Urquhart Castle, who had inherited through his mother the lands of Quarrelwood at Elgin, Kinsteary and Brightmony at Auldearn, and lands in Strathnairn. Kilravock's portion with his wife was taken from the lands in Strathnairn—namely, Cantraybruich, Little Cantray, and Ochter Urchills (near Clava). The destruction of the Kilravock title deeds and charters at the burning of Elgin Cathedral in 1390 compelled John, the sixth baron, to make up fresh titles. Hugh, Lord Lovat, as Sheriff of Inverness, held an inquest on 2nd February, 1431. Alexander Stewart, Earl of Mar, the victor of Harlaw, as King's Lieutenant in the north, attended the inquest, and cognosced two witnesses, William Mykill and Hugh Adamson, apparently from Nairn, who deponed that they saw the King's confirmation upon the lands of Kilravock and Geddes shown to Alexander, Earl of Buchan (the Wolf of Badenoch) *in area ecclesia de Nairn*. In April following the baron got himself served heir to his father at Nairn, before Donald, Thane of Calder and Sheriff of Nairn. He then resigned his whole lands into the hands of the King (James I.), and was confirmed in them as holding of the Earl of Ross, and finally he resigned them into the hands of Alexander, Lord of the Isles, Earl of Ross, and, reserving his own liferent, got a charter of them to his second son Hugh from the said Earl. The eldest son Lachlan became a priest, retaining the Strathnairn properties, but on his death they reverted to Hugh. From this John sprang the Roses of Dunearn, from whom were descended the Roses of Broadley, known as the " Provost of Nairn " family.

Hugh, the seventh baron, formed a twofold alliance with the Mackintoshes. He married Moir Mackintosh, daughter of Malcolm Begg Mackintosh, captain of Clan Chattan, and he entered into a bond or league with Mackintosh. A previous bond had been entered into between Lord Forbes and his kinsmen on the one part and Kilravock and Mackintosh on the other. They were to defend each other against all and sundry in all causes and quarrels, saving their allegiance to the Sovereign, and on the part of Kilravock and Mackintosh, keeping their allegiance to the Earl of Ross. This indenture is dated 1467. Seven years before this, in the year 1460, the baron got a licence from the Earl of Ross, who is designated " Johne of Yle, Erle of Ross, and Lord of the Isles," to build a tower at Kilravock. The licence runs that he has full power to " found, big, and upmake a toure of fens, with barmkin, and bataling, upon which place of strength him best likis, within the barony of Kylravock, without ony contradiction or demand, question or ony objection to put in contrar of him or his heirs for the said toure and barmkin-making, with the bataling, now or in tyme to cum." The building of Cawdor Castle had been authorised just two years before, and the baron had doubtless some feelings of emulation and resolved not to be thrown into the shade by his neighbour on the opposite side of the water of Nairn. The baron chose a high rocky bank by the river side—a picturesque spot—and there built his tower. Tradition states that the masons when finished with Cawdor Castle carried their tools across the river to Kilravock, and set to work to build the baron's tower. Kilravock Castle, like its contemporary Cawdor, was simply a square keep, surrounded with high walls. The other buildings are subsequent additions.

On the downfall of the Earl of Ross, the Earl of Huntly, as King's Lieutenant, became the potent lord in the north. Kilravock and he were fast friends, and the Earl granted Kilravock the extensive territory of Urquhart and Glenmorriston, which formed part of the great lordship of Badenoch, now held by Huntly. Kilravock had some troubles with the Mackintoshes on this account. The Chief and his son swore amity, but the lesser leaders entertained feelings of deadly hostility to Kilravock, probably because they, being kindly tenants on these lands, apprehended that they were to be dispossessed by the Roses. However that may be, Lachlan Mackintosh of Galovy entered into a compact with a freebooter of the clan, Donald Angusson Mackintosh, to capture the castle of Kilravock and deliver it over to him. The reason assigned was that it was known by "the oldest in the country" that Hugh the Rose, Baron of Kilravock, had no title of right to the castle nor to the ground it stood on. The terms of the contract were extraordinary. Lachlan was to come to receive the castle when it was taken. Then Donald was to be made constable and keeper of the castle under him, and was to have as his fee all the lands lying betwixt the new mill and the town of Holme, on the water side of Nairn, and all the lands betwixt the said castle and the kirk of Croy, together with the said mill as long as the castle remained in their hands, with ten merks of land free for his lifetime, either in Petty or Strathnairn. In the event of such a contingency arising as that Lachlan should voluntarily give up the castle to Kilravock or any others, he was to make Donald "sicker" forthwith, without any longer delay, of ten pounds worth of land free in his fee for all the days of his life in such places as above mentioned, without fraud or guile. But a still more singular reward for the capture of the castle was stipulated for. Donald was to marry Margaret, daughter of Lachlan—the father to bring the dispensation out of Rome at his own expense. As soon, however, as the castle was taken Donald was to have the young lady, and the marriage would be celebrated when the dispensation came home. It is further stipulated that Lachlan was to give a marriage portion of forty merks with her, to be paid in half-yearly instalments of ten merks "that the said Lachlan shall clothe his daughter honestly as effeirs and the costs thereof nocht to be comptit in the said forty merks, and he shall had and sustain his said daughter honestly in his own house two years, should it please the said Donald that she should remain so long with her father." The agreement was ratified by swearing—"the great oath and the holy evangelist touched, all fraud, guile, cavillacione, and perwill exceptions being excluded and by put." Lachlan affixed his seal, and because Donald had no seal proper of his own, he procured the seal of ane honourable man, William, Thane of Calder, to be affixed for him at day and place before written. The Thane of Cawdor was on very bad terms with Kilravock at the time, otherwise it would be difficult to believe that he would give his seal to so base a transaction if he were aware of its nature. The date corresponds within twenty-four hours with the time when Calder seized and imprisoned a son of Kilravock.

Donald's assault on the castle was successful. A night attack was made. The constable and watchmen were slain and the baron taken in his bed. The head house of the tower was destroyed and the great hall, with the kitchen, bakehouse, brewhouse, and other office houses damaged by fire to the extent of a hundred pounds. Kilravock was treated as a prisoner, and his clothes, victuals, and other necessary comforts withheld from him. How long the castle was in the possession of the enemy, or whether Donald got his bride and the other rewards under the agreement, cannot be positively stated. The only written information regarding the occurrence is that Donald and his accomplices were summoned a few years afterwards by warrant of the King to answer for their misdeeds above narrated. Probably the castle was in the hands of the Mackintoshes only till such times as the Earl of Huntly could send a force to relieve his friend. The presumption is that Donald had to go without his bride, for Lachlan Mackintosh's six daughters had all husbands whose names are known, and Donald's name is not one of them.

In the year 1482 the baron of Kilravock was appointed Keeper or Captain of Redcastle (the old fortress of Edderdour, built by William the Lion). This appointment he received from George, second Earl of Huntly and Lord of Badenoch. Two years later the baron married Huntly's sister, and received as tocher 380 merks. As Captain of Redcastle and tacksman of the King's lands in Ardmenache, Kilravock became involved in many and grievous troubles. His authority was disputed. In vain did Huntly assure him of his support. The baron made over the difficult post to his son and heir, Hugh of Geddes, but he was not more successful.

Redcastle was besieged by the Mackenzies of Kintail, and the Roses were for the time driven out of the Black Isle. A few years later the third Earl of Huntly granted a commission to Kilravock, the Mackintoshes, and the Grants to invade the country of the Mackenzies. Their army numbered three thousand fighting men, and they were authorised to " burn, harry, and slay " the Mackenzies in the King's name, in retaliation for the raids of the Mackenzies on the King's tenants of Ardmenache.

A raid was made into Cromarty by certain of the Mackintosh clan, who carried off an enormous booty, consisting of " 600 cows and oxen, four score horses, fifty score sheep, 200 swine, with plenishing of the farms, twenty-five score bolls of victual, and £300 of the maills." Whether Kilravock and the Captain of Clan Chattan were cognisant of the raid or not, they became joint sureties to Urquhart of Cromarty for 800 merks for the raiders. Kilravock could get no satisfaction from Mackintosh for his part, and after many years of litigation the claim of Urquhart of Cromarty was settled, but in a peculiar way—Kilravock paid one-half the sum in money, and for the remainder he accepted Urquhart's daughter Agnes (a child at the time), as wife to his son. Thus young Hugh, who was alleged to have had a hand in the raid, was married to Agnes in the year 1501. Agnes is stated by the family historian to have been a pious lady, much given to charity and alms, and it was with the view of convenience of her devotions at the chapel of Geddes that the house of Geddes was built on its present site. It formerly stood near the water of Nairn, probably at Alnaha. The Roses were now spreading their wings far and near. Hugh, the governor of Redcastle had, by his first wife, Isabel Sutherland, but one child, Isabel of Kilravock, who married the last Thane of Calder under the circumstances already related. By his second wife, Margaret Gordon, sister of the Earl of Huntly, the line of barons was carried on. Their second son John was founder of the branch of Roses of Belivat, and their third son Alexander was first of the family of Roses of Insch. In the next generation there were four sons and nine daughters, and Agnes of Cromarty, their mother, had the satisfaction of seeing her sons thriving and her daughters all well settled in life by alliances with northern families of good repute. It was her husband who was taken prisoner and detained for several years in the prison of Dunbarton for capturing the Abbot of Kinloss. When he was liberated, he brought north with him Thomas Davidson, a gardener from Paisley, who introduced the art of gardening, and planted an orchard at Kilravock.

Several offshoots of the Roses took root in Nairnshire before the period of the Reformation.

The oldest of these is the family of Rose of Holme (now designated Holme-Rose) who have had a residence at a sweet spot on the left bank of the Nairn, about a mile above Kilravock, since about the year 1460. The family was founded by Alexander Rose, second son of Hugh, the seventh baron, by his wife Moir Mackintosh. The next Rose of Holme was Walter, who was succeeded by his son Alexander, who flourished about the time of the Reformation, and came in for a share of the Church lands when they were parcelled out. He and his wife Joneta Dunbar in 1546 got a feu of the ecclesiastical lands of Daldaucht in Ardclach for an annual of £10 13s. 8d., and of Ewing and Dalquharne for £9 11s. 4d. with certain personal services. They also got the lands of Drumournie. They had no doubt been kindly tenants of the pasture of these places, and the tenure of tenancy was converted into that of a feu holding. The succession was carried on by John, the second son, who married Helen Rose, daughter of Kilravock the Eighth, and widow of Innes of Drynie.

The Roses of Belivat are a generation later than their cousins of Holme. John Rose of Belivat was the second son of the eighth baron, by his wife Lady Margaret Gordon, daughter of the Earl of Huntly. John was tacksman of Belivat, and on his marriage with Marjory Dunbar, daughter of James Dunbar of Cunzie, he got a liferent tack of the old heritage of the Frasers, then of the Dunbars, consisting of Glenernie, Dallasbrachtie, Craigroy, Logiegown, the Ardrie. He purchased the church lands of Mid-Fleenas from the holders of the chaplainries of St. James and St. Ninian at Elgin in 1534. Shortly afterwards he acquired from the Bishop the lands of Belivat and others in Ardclach. The subsequent history of this turbulent sept of the Roses will afterwards be related.

The arms of the Roses are—Or, a boar's head, couped gules, betwixt three water bougets, sable.   Crest—A harp.   Motto— Constant and true.

The early history of the Brodies, as regards personal details, is singularly meagre in consequence of the destruction of their family papers.   The grounds for believing that the Brodies are of Celtic origin and were possessed of the lands of Brodie before the advent of the Anglo-Norman families in the north, have already been stated.   The following is the correct genealogy of the early Thanes whose names are recorded—(1) Malcolm, Thane of Brodie, before 1285; (2) Michael, Thane of Brodie and Dyke, who had a charter of the thanage from Robert Bruce in 1311; (3) John de Brodie, who attended the Earl of Mar when he came north after the battle of Harlaw, and was one of the party present at the castle of Ruthven when the Wolf of Badenoch and the Bishop of Moray were reconciled in 1380; (4) Thomas de Brodie, who had two sons, the younger, Alexander, becoming vicar of Dyke.   The elder son (5) John succeeded his father as laird of Brodie.   On the margin of a tombstone in the church of Dyke is recorded the name of (6) Richard Brodie and his wife, the date being 16th September, 1446. He was succeeded by (7) John Brodie of that Ilk, who granted in 1446 a right of thirlage of his thanage and estate of Brodie to the mill of Grangegreen, owned by the Prior of Pluscardine, " for some rash act done by him."   Of his gallantry and bravery a story is preserved which rests on good authority.

The Mackenzies of Kintail had received a grant of part of the property belonging to the old Earldom of Ross.   The Macdonalds of the Isles entertained a grudge against the Mackenzies on account of this, and an insult given by Kenneth of Kintail to Lady Margaret, his wife, who was a cousin of Macdonald's, brought the strife to a head.   Lady Margaret, it appears, was blind of an eye, and to insult her cousin to the highest pitch, Kenneth sent her home on a one-eyed horse, accompanied by a one-eyed servant, followed by a one-eyed dog.   To revenge this insult, Macdonald collected his friends, and, at the head of a large body of West Highlanders and other adherents, marched through Strathconan and wasted it.   He arrived at Contin on a Sunday morning and, setting fire to the church in which the aged people, the women, and the children had taken refuge, burnt the whole to ashes. At Kinellan, not far from Contin, the Mackenzies and the Macdonalds met in battle on a moor known as Blar-na-Pairc. The Mackenzies had only 600 men, whilst the Macdonalds had three times that number, but the Mackenzies won the fight, the Macdonalds being completely routed and most of them killed. The night before the battle (according to the Earl of Cromartie's narrative) young Brodie of Brodie, accompanied by the accustomed train of retainers, was on a visit to Mackenzie at Kinellan, and as he was preparing to leave next morning, he noticed Mackenzie's men in arms, whereupon he asked if the enemy were known to be so near that for a certainty they would fight before night. Being informed that they were close at hand, he determined to wait and take part in the battle in spite of Kenneth's persuasion that he should not, Brodie saying " that he was an ill fellow and worse neighbour that would leave his friend at such a time." He took a distinguished part in the battle, and behaved to the advantage of his friend and notable loss of the enemy. Immediately after the battle he went on his journey, but his conduct (says the chronicler) produced a friendship between the Mackenzies and the family of Brodie which continued between their posterity, being more sacredly observed than family ties amongst others.

The Brodie of the battle of Park was succeeded by (8) Alexander Brodie, who was chief of the jury who served William Sutherland of Duffus, heir to that estate, and was ordered to be summoned before the Lords of Council to answer for his verdict. His successor (9) John, Thane of Brodie, was one of the arbiters who sat in the Nairn parish church in 1492, to adjudicate between the Bishop of Moray and the Baron of Kilravock. He was also a signatory to the marriage contract of the last Thane of Calder of the old line with Isabella Rose of Kilravock. He was succeeded by his son (10) Alexander, whose name is mentioned on inquests serving Elizabeth, Countess of Sutherland, as heir to her brother in 1514, and Hugh, Lord Lovat, as heir to his father in 1524. He died previous to 1540, when he was succeeded by (11) Thomas

Brodie, who was at Nairn on 10th February, 1546, serving Archibald Campbell of Calder, heir to Sir John in the office of Sheriff of Nairn. He will be met with again at a later period. The old castle of Brodie was destroyed in subsequent wars. It was probably of the keep plan. The arms of the Brodies are—Argent, a chevron, gules, between three mullets, azure ; Crest, a right hand holding a bunch of three arrows ; supporters—Two savages wreathed about head and middle with laurel, each holding a club resting against right shoulder ; Motto—Be mindful to unite.

The old knightly family of Hay of Lochloy, the near neighbour of the Brodies, acquired at a very early date lands in Nairnshire. It was one of the oldest branches of the Hays of Errol. At what period the Hays acquired Lochloy it is perhaps impossible to determine. The first mention of Lochloy is in connection with the landing of Harald, Earl of Caithness, at the port of Lochloy to make his submission to King William the Lion at the castle of Nairn, as already related. Amongst the great nobles at the royal court when King William was in Moray was William de Hay. He is a signatory to some five different charters granted by the King and recorded in the Chartulary of Moray. The King had in his gift the lands of Auldearn, and it is extremely probable that the Sir William de Hay so frequently mentioned in the charters of the period received a grant of the lands of Lochloy in addition to his possessions elsewhere. When the crisis arose in regard to the succession to the Scottish throne, William de la Hay adhibited his seal to the " Letter of the Community of Scotland," 1289. During the time the Guardians of Scotland administered the affairs of the nation Sir John de Hay figured in history. When the claims of Bruce and Baliol to the throne were submitted to Edward I., Bruce nominated William de la Hay as one of his commissioners, and Dr. Taylor, in his " History of Edward I. in the North of Scotland," states that this William was the representative of the family of Hay of Lochloy in the county of Nairn. In support of Robert Bruce, he joined the Scottish nobles at Dunbar, and was taken prisoner and sent to the castle of Berkhampstead. He was soon liberated, however, and on August 28th, 1296, he swore fealty to

Edward and came north with him. He was then appointed Sheriff of Inverness, and in that capacity he took the oaths of fealty of the principal officers in the north, amongst others that of William de Monte Alto, Sheriff of Dingwall. Sir William Hay was also appointed Warden of Ross, and was practically governor of the north. So valiant a knight was too valuable a soldier to be left in civil employment, and Edward summoned him to accompany him on his expedition to Flanders. He responded, and the payments made to him for service in Flanders are recorded in the Exchequer Rolls. We learn no more of Sir William, but his son joined the patriotic party and adhered to Bruce. In 1304, one Oliver Avenal petitioned Edward to give him the lands of John de la Hay in the county of Inverness, promised him in the late war. After the War of Independence the Hays were reinstated in their lands in Inverness and Nairn. In the year 1334, Thomas Hay of Urchany in the county of Nairn, founded a chaplainry in the church of Rathven, for the weal of the soul of the founder and his wife, and Christian Cruickshank and others, the chaplain to receive five merks annually from the lands of Urchany in the county of Nairn. The deed is in the Register of the Bishopric of Aberdeen. The Hays of Rannoch were a branch of the Errol family, and have a tomb in Rathven Church. In 1364 John de Hay, Lord of Tully-bothil, was Sheriff of Inverness, and with the consent of his son John, granted out of his lands of Lochloy and Wester Raite, an endowment for the Chapel of Kincraggie. He also possessed the lands of Awn (the Enzie) and others. Mention is made of David II. having given in 1362 a grant of all the land lying between the Spey and the rivulet called the Tynot in the forest of Awne, to John de Hay of Lochloy and Tullybothil, for the purpose of being cultivated. Out of these lands in 1374 he gave a donation of four pounds for the support of a chaplain in the Chapel of Geth. Sir John married a niece of King Robert II. and had three sons. His second son William succeeded to the lands of Lochloy in Nairnshire and married Janet Mackintosh. His monument is still to be seen at Elgin Cathedral—the oldest tomb but one of a layman within the sacred precincts. The Hays were great benefactors of the Church, which may account for the place of honour given them.

The monument is in the south transept. It consists of a stone chest or sarcophagus, with the colossal figure of a knight in complete armour, with dirk and spurs still visible. The feet rest upon a lion couchant, and the stone bears the following inscription— " Hic jacet Wills. de la Hay, quonda dns. de Lochloy, qui obiit viiio die mensis Decembris anno Dom. MCCCCXXI." Mention is made of this old knight at a great gathering of northern gentry at the kirkyard of Chanonry of Rosemarkie on 16th August, 1420. Amongst those present were John, Bishop of Ross; Dame Mary of the Isles, Lady of the Isles and of Ross; Hugh Fraser, Lord Lovat; John M'Leod, Lord of Glenelg; Angus Gothrason of the Isles; Sir William Fraser, Dean of Ross; Walter Douglas, Sheriff of Elgin; Walter Innes, lord of that ilk; Urquhart of Cromarty; Donald of Kaledor, thane of that ilk; Sinclair of Deskford; John the Rose, Lord of Kilravocke; John of Nairn, Lord of Ardmuthach, "with mony others." The object of the meeting was to witness the resignation of the lands of Kerdale, Inverness-shire, by " William the Grame," into the hands of " a noble lord and a michty, Thomas, Earl of Murray," over-lord of the barony of Kerdale. The Earl conveyed back the said lands to Graham and his heirs male, failing which, to William Hay, his good-father, Lord of Lochloy, and his male heirs. The Grahams, like the Roses of Kilravock, had got part of the vast possessions of the Bissets through marriage. The proceedings at Rosemarkie meant more than appears on the face of the deed, which is simply a regulation of succession. There was match-making in the business. The Earl of Moray had at this time a particular interest in the Hays of Lochloy, for John, younger of Lochloy, was engaged to marry the Earl's daughter. But John proved very fickle. He fell in love with a daughter of the Thane of Cawdor, and wished to be off with the old love. He received a communication from the Earl of Moray on the subject, and never did a disappointed father-in-law write a more tender, dignified, and generous letter in such delicate circumstances. The letter is among the Cawdor papers, and runs as follows : " Thomas, Earl of Murray, to our right well beloved squire, John the Hay, lord of Lochloye, greeting : —It is in fresh memory with you, as we understand, that through

certain tailzie made betwixt us and your father, you are obliged to
spouse a daughter of ours, for the which thing to be done we confirmed to your father a tailzie betwixt him and the lord of Dallas
upon the Lordship of Dallas and forgave him forty pounds, the
which should have been paid to us for the relief of that land ; and
also for that same marriage we confirmed to your father a tailzie
of half the barony of Kerdale, and received you to the same lands
upon the said tailzie ; and now of new we have heard by certain
relation of our loved cousin Donald, thane of Cawdor, that you
would be released of your obligation to us of the said marriage and
have our licence, freedom, and goodwill to spouse a daughter of
the said Donald, thane of Cawdor, with such commands, freedoms,
and rewards as are forespoken, and as we granted to you before time.
Wherefore, by the tenour of these our letters, of your obligation
made to us of beforetime both by your father and by yourself, for
the marriage of our daughter, we release you, discharge you, and
quit claims you for ever, giving and granting to you our counsel,
our licence, freedom, and goodwill, to spouse and have to your wife
the daughter of the said Donald, thane of Caldor, with such freedoms, profits, and rewards, as were forespoken in our first commands,
together with our help, support, and maintenance in all our lawful
and leaveful errands in all time to come : thereto we have granted
and given, and by these our letters grants and gives, the said Donald,
Thane of Cawdor, forty merks of the relief of your lands of the
half of the barony of Kerdale, which William the Hay, your father,
was obliged to pay to us, of the which we quit claim you for ever
by the tenor of these letters, to the which our seal we have gert be
put at Elgin the 15th day of February, the year of our Lord, 1422."
     The Hays of Lochloy in the course of a generation or two
became extensive landowners.   Besides Lochloy, they had Inshoch,
Park, Kinnudie, Meikle Urchany, Wester Raite, Foynesfield,
Dallas, and other possessions in the north and south.   They were
at the height of their prosperity about the close of the sixteenth
century.   David Hay of Lochloy married Mary Rose of Kilravock
in 1605.   She lived to see her eighty-eighth year, and when she
died it is stated that there were descended of her no fewer than one
hundred and ten persons then in life !

The Hays originally had a residence at Lochloy, on the site now occupied by the house of the Baillies of Lochloy—a position on the coast commanding a wide view of the Moray Firth. At a very early period, however, a second castle was built more inland, namely, at Inshoch, and remains of it still exist. It was protected on one side by an impassable peat moss, and as the name would indicate, *Insh-ach*, the island field, was surrounded with ditches formed by the overflow of the bog.. The castle had its entrance on the ground floor, and a narrow staircase in one of the towers led to the hall on the first floor. On the landing of the stair adjoining the hall, a stone basin in a pretty little Gothic arch was provided for washing the hands, with a drain for carrying off the water. The hall itself was a handsome, well-lighted apartment, 30 feet by 17 feet, with plastered walls, a large fireplace with moulded jambs, above which is a shield displaying the armorial bearings of the Hays of Lochloy—the insignia that had floated on many a field of battle. The oldest part of the building shows a simple keep with round towers placed diagonally so as to command the four sides of the main building, and turrets in the angles. The original building appears to have been altered, and to have had additions made to it, doubtless to meet the requirements of a more advanced civilization. The ground floor was vaulted throughout, and contained a kitchen with a very large fireplace, and numerous cellars. Except the kitchen window, which may have been enlarged, the basement was lighted with narrow loops. A stone sink is fitted into the kitchen window, with a drain to the outside. In the larger turret to the south-west, there is a very pretty little private room, commanding a charming view and provided with stone seats—doubtless my lady's boudoir. The ruins are in a very dilapidated state, and a considerable portion fell in the great storm of 1879 (the night of the Tay Bridge disaster). Practical builders say that the masonry is bad work. Curiously enough, the larger courses of freestone bear the masons' private marks, some sixteen or seventeen different symbols being visible. The family rapidly declined in the middle of the seventeenth century, and the lands are now possessed by Brodie of Brodie.

The Dallases played a considerable part in early times in the county of Nairn. The first person of the name in the records is Sir William de Dollas, Lord of Dollas, who was a witness to charters in 1280 and 1286. His successor, William de Doleys, took the field for King Robert Bruce, along with the Knight of Petty, and other patriots in the north, and had the honour of being declared a rebel by Edward I. When the English King came north in 1306 the Earl of Sutherland petitioned him for the estate of Dallas forfeited by Doleys' siding with Bruce. A person of the name of Alian petitioned the King for the lands of Thomas de Doles in Moray, no doubt a cadet of the family. His lands were stated to be worth only ten pounds a year. The family line of Dallas of Dallas was carried on until Archibald de Doles executed in 1398 a deed of tailzie of the lordship of Dallas in favour of William Hay of Lochlòy, which was confirmed to his son John Hay, Lord of Lochloy, by Thomas, Earl of Moray, in 1422. Archibald left an only child, Elizabeth, who married Duncan Fraser, son of Hugh Fraser of Lovat, an ancestor of the Frasers in Moray. Elizabeth disponed, with her husband's consent, any right she might have in the lordship of Dallas, to her uncle John, and he took some steps to get back the property, but the old heritage of Dallas was never recovered. John Dallas is mentioned as Thane of Cromdale and Lord of Cromdale as witness of some Lovat writs with the Bishop of Moray. John Dallas of Easterford became a very considerable landowner, acquiring lands in the shires of Kincardine, Haddington, and Forfar. His heart, however, appeared to be in the Highlands, and he entered into an excambion with David, Earl of Crawford, in the year 1440, whereby, in exchange for lands in the south, he got Budgate in Nairnshire, and shortly afterwards a family of the same name appears in possession of Cantray. Dallas of Cantray and Dallas of Budgate appear in various transactions in the fifteenth century. The Dallases both of Cantray and Budgate stood their trial and received their doom at Aberdeen as accomplices of the Thane of Calder " in certain criminal actions," and shared in King James III.'s pardon.

Though of small estate, the family of Dallas intermarried with the principal families in the north. A remarkable characteristic was its singular devotion to the house of Cawdor. Generation after generation, a Dallas is found performing offices of friendship and kinship to the Thane of Cawdor.

It is not quite clear which was the older line, the Budgate or the Cantray Dallases. Budgate had annexed to it, through purchase from the Ogilvies, the quarter lands of Dallaschyle, Milton of Cantraymore, and Galcantray. The property became heavily mortgaged to Cawdor in the beginning of the seventeenth century, and the family decayed thereafter, though its representatives may still exist. The armorial bearings indicate rather that Budgate was the chief. In 1410 Dallas of Budgate has the boar's-head in his coat-of-arms, probably from having married a Chisholm heiress. Cantray-Dallas was, however, the more potent house. One or two incidents in the history of the family may be recalled. Henry Dallas of Cantray, whose lands paid an annual of two shillings to William Calder, vicar of Barevan, in 1506, had a brother Archibald who was murdered by Robert Stewart of Clava. This Robert was a son of Robert Stewart of Abernethy, and purchased Clava in 1495. What led to the crime is not stated, but in 1513 Henry Dallas of Cantray and John Dallas, brothers-germane to the deceased Archibald, with Walter Rose of Kinsteary, mother's-brother, Hugh Rose of Kilravock, and others, the kin and friends, granted letters of assythment remitting the crime. Henry Dallas and his kinsmen joined the Mackintoshes and the Roses in the second hership of Petty, harrying and burning the Halhill of the Ogilvies, and carrying away an enormous quantity of household stuff, the inventory of which shows that the Ogilvies had surrounded themselves with comforts and luxuries very unusual at the time.

Another tragedy occurred towards the close of the sixteenth century. Alan Shaw murdered Dallas of Cantray, and the atrocious character of the crime was heightened by the relation of the parties—Dallas being Shaw's stepfather. The family continued in comparative affluence, however, and his successor, having married a daughter of the Laird of Calder, built a new house at Cantray, and placed a stone in front bearing the initials of himself and his wife—" W.D. I.C."—(William Dallas—Janet Campbell), and bearing the date " 1641." In an after age, when the house had outlived its day, it was taken down. The mason brought the tablet to Nairn, and presented it to the representative of the family who lived in Church Street. It was built into the humble dwelling, and in 1891, after the decease of Elizabeth Dallas, the last of the race, it was taken down and sent to Mr. Dallas-Yorke of Wallinsgate. Casts of it and of another stone bearing the three mullets were sent to Colonel Dallas, the representative of a branch of the family settled in America.

The Frasers of Lovat had in early times some property in Nairnshire. In the year 1416 Hugh Fraser married Janet, sister of William de Fenton, Lord of Beaufort, who granted to them and their heirs Guisachan and other estates in Strathglass. Hugh Fraser for dowry was to give £20 lands of the lordship of Golford, in the sheriffdom of Nairn, and in case of any deficiency, it was to be made up by him out of his lands of Dalcross. Their eldest son Hugh married a daughter of the Earl of Moray, and was made a lord of Parliament. The first document which styles him a lord is a contract with the burgh of Nairn in 1472, which shows that he had considerable property in the neighbourhood of the town. The Frasers had also the " detached portion " of Nairnshire known as Glenernie in Edenkillie, and they were long the wadsetters of the lands of Daltulich in Strathnairn.

The Mackintoshes, if not in the county of Nairn, were very near and somewhat troublesome neighbours. Clan Chattan, with Mackintosh as its captain or chief, was really a confederation of some sixteen different clans, including the Mackintoshes, Camerons, Macphersons, Robertsons (or Clan Donachie), Macbeans, Macgillivrays, Macphails, Farquharsons, Shaws, Smiths, Macqueens, Gillanders, etc. Their raids into the lowlands of Moray and Nairn were of constant occurrence. They greatly oppressed the Ogilvies of Strathnairn, and were the means of driving them out of the country. In the year 1531 they attacked the Halhill of Petty, a new tower erected on the site of the old castle of Sir Andrew Moray of Petty, by Sir William Ogilvie. They burned the castle and killed young Ogilvie and eighteen of the garrison. Soon after-

wards Hector Mackintosh, who was displeased with the Earl of
Moray for having entrusted the care of Lachlan, the young heir
of the Mackintoshes, to the Ogilvies of Findlater, made a raid
upon Dyke, and wasted the lands and burned the whole houses in
that parish. They had the audacity to besiege Darnaway Castle,
but not being able to take it, they contented themselves with the
rich booty of cattle and corn which the fertile lands of Moray
afforded. The Earl of Moray in punishment apprehended eighteen of the leaders concerned, and put them to death. According
to another account, the Earl captured 200 of the Mackintoshes
along with William, the brother of Hector. William he immediately hanged and quartered, his head was affixed to the cross at
Dyke, and his four quarters were exhibited at Elgin, Forres,
Auldearn, and Inverness. The two hundred who were taken
were brought out, man by man, and offered life on condition that
they revealed the hiding place of Hector their chief, but every man
refused the proffered conditions, and was put to death. The policy
of successive Earls of Huntly had been to break up the confederacy
and thus weaken its power. Huntly ultimately succeeded in gaining over the Macphersons by giving them charters to their lands.
The Mackintoshes made an effort to re-unite Clan Chattan, and in
1609 a great meeting of the " haill clan " was held at Termet (now
known as Morayston) in Petty. The object of the gathering was
to organize a bond of unity and to acknowledge and support William
Mackintosh of Benchar as principal captain of the " haill kin of
Clan Chattan," as having the full place thereof during the minority
of Lachlan Mackintosh of Dunachton, his brother's son. The
bond was signed or subscribed by the leading men of the septs,
including Cluny Macpherson. The provost of Inverness, the
minister of Petty (Donald Macqueen), and the town clerk of
Inverness, were there to add weight and authority to the solemn
compact. In the deed drawn up at Termet, it is claimed that the
chiefship was a gift of old from the King of Scotland, viz. :—from
David II. to Lachlan Mackintosh about the year 1330. Clan
Chattan in their bond recognised the authority of the King and
the Earls of Huntly and Moray—loyalty and obedience to their
chief coming next. But the League of Termet did not last long.

Half a century later it had completely broken up. The Mackintoshes adhered to Moray as against Huntly.

The Ogilvies were not alone in their desire to get rid of their property in the neighbourhood of such turbulent neighbours as the Mackintoshes. The church lands of Ardersier and Delnies had passed into the hands of the Leslies of Ardersier, and they sold them to Cawdor in the year 1574, " having consideration of the great and intolerable damage, injury, and skaith done to them by Lachlan Mackintosh and others of the Clan Chattan, in harrying, destroying, and making herships upon the said hail lands of Ardersier and fishings thereof," and having no apparent hope of reparation for the " customary enormities of the said Clan Chattan." It is charged against the Mackintoshes that they pauperised the tenants, debarred them from fishing at the stell of Ardersier, breaking their boats and cutting their nets. The Laird of Cawdor was not allowed to have peaceable possession, and he raised an action against Lachlan Mackintosh and his clansmen for the slaughter of several of his servants and tenants. In 1581 Lachlan renounced all claim to the Ardersier lands and to Wester and Easter Delnies, and the legal proceedings were dropped.

For over three hundred years the Falconers of Hawkerton, the ancestors of the Earls of Kintore, possessed the lands of Lethen, and they appear to have resided there pretty continuously during the period, judging from the frequent occasions on which Falconer of Hawkerton is a witness to transactions in the county of Nairn. They also formed several marriage connexions with the Roses and others. When the Reformation came they still sat on, but in the beginning of the seventeenth century they parted with their property to John Grant of Freuchie. leaving two branches—one at Kincorth and the other at Downduff on the banks of the Findhorn—to carry on the family name in this district.

There were Woods at Dunphail, and Mongumries at Budgate, and a family of the name of " Nairne " flits across the pages of the old Chartulary of Moray between the town of Nairn and a possession in Cromdale, but personal details are awanting. John Belgeam, probably some English trooper who had settled in the district, had a considerable croft at Auldearn, known as Belgeam's Croft.   It lay near the church and was in later times known as the Smith's Croft.   John Belgeam was associated with the Thane of Calder in his slaughter of Patrick Wiseman at Inverness, and stood his trial along with him.   The lands, as previously stated, formed part of the inheritance designed by Precentor John to his nephew Hugh Calder, and they appear ultimately to have fallen to Sir John Campbell of Cawdor.   The Dunbars possessed Moyness, and Dunbars and Inneses were to be found at Penick and Boathill.

From the enumeration thus given of the lands and landowners in Nairnshire prior to the Reformation, it appears that the district was divided into a variety of small properties, some held in fee, and a considerable number in feu or in tack from the Church. Broadly speaking, what are now large farms were then separate properties.   The keen desire for possession of lands in Strathnairn manifested by southern families is accounted for by the scarcity of good corn land at that time.   The belt along the coast, widening out as the hills recede, was early brought under cultivation, and when but a small proportion of the county was under crop, the value of the corn lands of upper and lower Strathnairn was relatively very considerable.

CHAPTER X

THE REFORMATION

No materials exist to show to what extent the principles of the Reformation as promulgated by the early Scottish Reformers permeated the province of Moray.

Once in the earlier Reformation period, the fighting men of Moray and Nairn were drawn to the south. In the year 1547, when Mary Queen of Scots was an infant of five years of age, the English army crossed the border with the object of seizing the infant Queen and carrying her to London. The Earl of Arran sent the fiery cross throughout the north. It was carried by one Mungo Stratherne through Moray and Nairn. Lowlander and Highlander responded to the summons. The Earl of Huntly marshalled the troops from the north. Alexander, the eleventh Laird of Brodie, went south with his retinue. His neighbours the Hays of Lochloy are not mentioned, but they were doubtless not awanting, seeing that fighting was to be done. The Black Baron of Kilravock, who had but recently married the daughter of Falconer of Lethen, led his kinsmen to the field, and was accompanied by his relatives the Cuthberts of Inverness. The English and the Scots met on the field of Pinkie, near Musselburgh, on 10th September. The English cavalry hurled themselves on the solid square of steel presented by the vanguard of the Scottish army, only to be speared, spiked, or unhorsed. The brilliant charge failed, and the Scottish troops cheered for victory. But they cheered too soon. The English infantry observing that their formation had become disorganised in the moment of success, made another assault and turned the victory into defeat. The

Scots were routed. Fourteen thousand were cut down in their flight. The Laird of Brodie was slain. The Cuthberts of Castle-hill met the same fate. The Earl of Huntly and the Baron of Kilravock were taken prisoners. The fate of their humble followers is not recorded. Kilravock was carried a prisoner to England, but was ransomed on 23rd October by the Pringles of Torwoodlee, who paid 100 nobles to his captors, John Ker of Wark and two Johnstons. On his return, the baron raised the money and discharged the debt to his good friends the Pringles, who ever afterwards kept up a very close connection with Nairnshire. The Pringles were among the first families in Scotland who declared for the Reformation. The Earl of Huntly, after a year's confinement, escaped from his English prison, and on his return to Scotland was rewarded for his services by a grant of the Earldom of Moray.

Kilravock, after the battle of Pinkie, settled down to the peaceful avocations of country life, so far as these were possible, and though enjoying the confidence and friendship of the rival leaders in the stirring events of the time, he preserved an absolute impartiality and neutrality. Finding the accommodation of his ancient keep inadequate for his household—he had, between sisters and daughters, fourteen ladies in the establishment—he employed John Anderson, the mason, to build him a manor house alongside the old tower. The contract is to the effect that John Anderson shall have 20s. and his five masons 18s. of weekly wages, with £10 of bounty to the master, and forty shillings to the men over and above. They are to sleep at Kilravock, bedding being provided for them, and are to be supplied with meal at 2s. per boll. The three barrow-men employed have for wages 8s. per week.

At the memorable Convention of 1560, which sealed the fate of the Catholic Church and established the Protestant religion, the only representatives from this district who appear to have been present were John Grant of Freuchie and the lairds of Innes and Duffus. The Earl of Argyll, who had cast in his influence with the Reformers, would probably bring his kinsman John of Calder along with him. Huntly was strongly opposed to the Reformation, and was the recognised head of the Catholic party in the north. The fact that the youthful Abbot of the St. Ninian Priory of Fearn had been the first Protestant martyr in Scotland may have awakened an early interest in the doctrines and tenets he preached, but Patrick Hamilton himself does not appear ever to have laboured personally in the north. He was a non-resident titular, and but a boy when he was appointed Commendator-Abbot. The head of the Abbey at the time of the Reformation was Nicholas Ross, and he sat in the Parliament of 1560. He resigned his office in 1566, and his successor, Thomas Ross of Alness, accommodated himself to the changed times, and married Isabel Kinnaird. The abbot of Kinloss was Walter Reid, a nephew of the distinguished prelate Robert Reid. He threw in his lot with the Reformers, and was at the framing of the Act of 1560 forbidding the celebration of the mass. His name appears high in the list appended to the Solemn League and Covenant. While retaining the office of prior, he took to himself a wife, marrying Margaret Collace of Balnamoon. The abbot of Pluscardine, Robert Dunbar, made haste to provide for his family of illegitimate children by portioning off the abbey lands among them before his expulsion. The Bishop of Moray, the notorious Patrick Hepburn, continued to reside in Spynie Castle, and defied the Reformation alike as to his estate and his morals. As late as the year 1567 Hugh Rose, baron of Kilravock (described as feuar and heritor of the town and lands of Ferness and Aitnoch), came under an obligation to the Bishop " to grant pasture to twenty-four kye and ane bull, with their followers, pertaining to the Bishop, for the time of the said reverend father's lifetime, upon the best and most commodious girss within the said bounds." Bishop Patrick Hepburn died in the year 1573.

The process of disendowment was made easy for the existing incumbents. They were allowed to retain their emoluments, whether or not they changed from the old to the new religion. The general principle of dealing with the Church lands was that the Crown should appropriate one-third of the entire ecclesiastical revenues, and the return made under the Act of 1561 shows the following valuations of lands in Nairnshire—The Dean of Moray for Auldearn, Nairn, and lands, £130, equal to 650 bolls of grain at 4s. per boll ; the vicar of Nairn £6, equal to 200 bolls ; the subchantor for Rafford and Ardclach £263 0s. 8d., equal to 1316 bolls; the vicar of Ardclach £10, equal to 40 bolls. Several causes account for the diminished value of the ecclesiastical revenues as compared with what they were a century before. The rent of land had fallen over Scotland nearly one half. The currency had become debased. The church lands let to tenants at the earlier period had been feued out for a small annual payment and a considerable sum paid down. This latter proceeding was extensively practised in the county of Nairn.

In May, 1545, a feu charter was granted to John Rose of Belivat and Marjory Dunbar, his spouse, of the lands of Belivat, with the woods of Killinglaer, Torlocht, Auchingour, with the fishings on the Findhorn, Ardclach with the fishing on the Findhorn, the woods of Daldevening, and the mill and brewhouse of Ardclach, the Hermit's Croft and Daldareth. The annual payment to be £26 8s. 8d. This charter was confirmed to him and his heir-apparent John Rose, at Nairn, 12th October, 1566. One of the witnesses was John Young, minister of Nairn.

In 1527 a tack was given to Thomas Chisholm of the lands of Bothill, with the mills and a fourth part of Little Penick. Thomas Gaderar, vicar of Nairn, was one of the witnesses.

In 1566 a feu charter was granted to John Mongumrie of the lands of Little Budzett for £100 and an annual payment of £2 17s. 4d.

In 1568 Mr. Alexander Campbell of Fleenas succeeded to John Mongumrie, and in 1570 Duncan Campbell of Boath got a precept of *clare constat* from Bishop Patrick Hepburn as heir to his brother, Alexander.

A feu of the church lands of Croy was granted to Alexander Dallas of Cantray for £9 18s. 8d., and was confirmed to his nephew, Henry Dallas, in 1567, and renewed at Spynie in 1571.

In 1546 the church lands of Duldawacht, in the barony of Ardclauch, were granted on feu charter to Alexander Rose of Holme and Joneta Dunbar, his spouse, and to their heirs.

In 1566 Brodie got the Stable Acre and other lands at Dyke from the Bishop.

In 1541 Ewan and Dalcharne were feued to Alexander Rose and his spouse Joneta Dunbar, for £9 11s. 4d.

In 1564 John Wood of Tullydivies got a feu of the lands of Ferness and Aitnoch, with fishing on the Findhorn, by payment of 500 merks and £9 annually; and in 1567 these subjects were conveyed by John Wood to Hugh Rose of Kilravock and Katherine Falconer, his spouse, who continued to pay £9 annually to the Episcopate.

The Baron of Kilravock gave the Bishop in 1545 a bond for 595 merks for infeftment in Kildrummie with the fishings on the Nairn, and in Culmony and Daltulich with fishings on the Findhorn.

John Knox's complaint against the nobles and gentry that they had " greedily grippit the possessions of the kirk " was well founded. Besides its pecuniary embarrassments, the Church of the Reformation at its start found it difficult to obtain a sufficient number of persons qualified to become Protestant clergymen, and, accordingly, in John Knox's own words, " to the kirks where no ministers can be had presently must be appointed the most apt men that distinctly can read the Common Prayers and the Scriptures, to exercise both themselves and the kirk till they grow to greater perfection." In the year 1570 Mr. William Brown was appointed as reader in Ardclach. The third of the vicarage, amounting to £3 6s. 8d., was allowed him, and the Dean of Moray was ordered to pay the rest of his stipend. Ardclach remained joined with Edenkillie up till 1638. Mr. James Vaux was reader in Croy and Moy. The first Protestant minister in Nairn was Mr. John Young. He was minister or exhorter at Nairn in 1568, and £40 is charged in the Books of Assignation as paid to him. In the same year Mr. Allan Mackintosh was exhorter at Cawdor, and is styled parson in 1581 and 1586. In 1570, Mr. William Reoch was employed as exhorter at Auldearn and Nairn, and £26 13s. 4d. is charged on his account. An endowment of £5 in connection with the chapel of Nairn disappears in the general seizure of church revenues. The Dean of Moray, Alexander Dunbar, retained the parish of Auldearn, and sat on at Penick. He was Dean of Moray in 1560, 1574, and 1586.

In the year 1562 an event occurred which must have excited great interest in this district. Mary Queen of Scots, now in her twentieth year, made a royal progress to Inverness. Her mother, the Queen Regent, had been in the north in 1555, but this was the first time the young Queen had visited her northern dominions. She set out, accompanied by her natural brother James Stewart, then Earl of Mar, and the principal nobility of Scotland. Her route can be traced from the book of the Queen's Master of the House-hold, who kept a diary written in French, a summary of which has been preserved. The royal party left Edinburgh on the 11th of August, and after spending a few days at Stirling, set out thence for the north. The Queen was at Aberdeen on 1st September, arrived at Elgin on the evening of the 6th, and remained there till the 8th. After dinner on that day she journeyed to Kinloss, and abode two days at the abbey, where there was good accommodation for her court. On the 10th, after dining at Kinloss, she set out for Darnaway, where she supped and slept that night and held a State Council next morning.

The castle appears to have been in bad repair, the " house " or hall—Randolph's Hall no doubt—alone being reported to be in good order. A high-backed chair with needle-work cover, said to have been wrought by the Queen, is preserved in the hall to this day as a memento of the visit. Darnaway was left on the morning of the 11th, and (says the journal) " she dined at ' Mernes.' " This can only refer to Moyness. The corruption of the name is easily accounted for, its old pronunciation being " Meynes." The ruins of the old castle of Moyness have now all but disappeared, but it seems to have been a place of considerable strength—a keep with round towers and surrounding walls. It adds to the interest of the spot that Queen Mary dined there. The old castle stood on a ridge commanding a wide view, both of the country inland and of the coast seaward. Dinner at that time was a mid-day meal, and the sun was hardly in the zenith when Queen Mary was once more in the saddle and riding down the brae of Moyness towards Auldearn. Her host at Moyness was John Dunbar, of the family of Westfield, hereditary Sheriffs of Moray, and if the Dean of Moray was in his own parish at the time, the Queen would make the acquaintance of another Dunbar, whose stately mansion, rising three storeys in height, and surrounded by fine trees, must have attracted her attention.   The old kirk of Auldearn, standing out on the high ground which the present edifice occupies, must have been a prominent object at the time. The village itself was a hamlet of detached houses and gardens on the slope, with the mill and brewhouse on the low ground in front. Kinnudie would be visible from the high road, and on the slope further to the south were the homesteads of Knockaudie, Ballachraggan, and Park, with numerous cottar houses belonging to the Hays and their sub-tenants.   Auchnacloich was possessed at that time by a family of Roses.   A house of some repute—Balmaceardach—" the town of the smithy "—was then standing near the highway as it approached within a quarter of a mile of Belmakeith.   The castle of Nairn on the high bank of the river, still retaining some of the formidable features which caused it to be ranked as one of the great royal forts of Scotland, would probably excite some meed of admiration.   But a matter of more practical moment must very soon have engaged the Queen's attention. How was she to enter the town ?   There was as yet no bridge— the first bridge was not erected till nearly a century later—so there was nothing for it but to ford the river, which would be easy or difficult according to the character of the season.   As Queen Mary rode up the High Street of Nairn, was she saluted by the burghers ?   Did the provost and magistrates come out to meet her ?   Curiosity on these points cannot be gratified.   Neither history nor the particular journal quoted has preserved any details of the civic pageantry on the occasion.   The provost at the time was John Rose of Broadley, and Angus and Andrew Rose were prominent burgesses.   The provost is described as " a bold, resolute man."   There was but one street in the town, and the tolbooth —a low straw-thatched building—projected itself into the middle of the highway.   The beautiful young Queen, with her gay cavalcade, riding through the town, must have been the topic of conversation for many a day after.

Before nightfall Queen Mary had reached Inverness.   She demanded admittance to the castle, but was refused, and she was compelled to lodge for the night in a private house—according to universal tradition the house at the foot of Bridge Street, long

you as ane of our speciall friends that best may serve for that purpose, being assurit that ye ar of sufficient power gif ye will employ yourself that way, to do us service," etc.   The letter then proceeds to request the baron to concur with others in repressing malefactors and rebels in the district.

A further proof of the estimation in which the baron was held is afforded by the appointments conferred upon him.   He was made Sheriff Principal of Inverness and Captain of the castle of Inverness.   He was entrusted by the Earl of Moray with the administration of his estates in Strathnairn and Kerdale, and was employed by the Earl of Argyll to look after the Cawdor property and to act as interim sheriff of the county of Nairn during the minority of the thane.   The baron heard of Queen Mary's engagement to Darnley, and of her creating him Earl of Ross and Ardmenache on their betrothal, and probably wondered how the revival of these old earldoms would affect local interests.   Her marriage with Darnley took place, and the King and Queen sent Kilravock a letter in which they referred to the " defection of the Earl of Moray so unnaturally against us."   The baron was sorely distressed by the daily cutting down and destroying of trees on his property of Coulmony and other lands on the banks of the Findhorn, as well as pasturing of cattle and burning of moorland.   He accordingly represented the matter to the Crown, and Mary Queen of Scots issued a proclamation to be made at the market cross of Nairn forbidding the same.   A cautious note from the Earl of Huntly making an appointment suggests some plotting on the part of the ambitious Gordon.   The Regent Moray came into power, and a request was made by him that the baron fail not to be at Inverness at a convention of the loyally affected on the first day of June of that year (1569) " substantially accompanied by his haill kin, friends, servants, tenants, and all that will do for him."

The Regent presently met his death, and his widow, Annas Keith, confirmed to her traist friend, the baron of Kilravock, his appointment in connection with the Moray estates, and carried on with him an extensive business correspondence.   The Earl of Mar became Regent in Moray's place, and addressed to the baron a sympathetic letter, counselling him and his friends to take comfort and remain steadfast. The Earl of Morton was his next correspondent; and amidst the exciting cares of State wrote a very pathetic little note—" I am advertised of the slaughter of my kinsman and servant Hutchon Ros of Logy, whereof I am sorry, and since he is so taken away by the pleasure of God, I will request you maist heartily to stand guid friend to his wife and bairns, and not to suffer them to receive wrang by ony, but that they may live peaceably and quiet upon the little roumes that is provided unto them, and as you will do me pleasure suffer no man to do them harm."

Annas Keith, the widowed Countess of Moray, was a prominent figure in the district. A kindly, shrewd, practical lady, she entered into the work of administering the Moray estates with great vigour and much good sense. On one occasion she acted as " overs-woman " in the settlement of marches between Delnies and Kilravock, and her award was accepted by both parties. The countess married the Earl of Argyll, but continued her management of the estates of the Earldom of Moray.

Argyll also corresponded with Kilravock, and his letters form a link in the chain of historic events then taking place. The Countess of Crawford and her husband occasionally wrote to the baron for counsel; and the Earl of Huntly, in all the vicissitudes of the fortunes of his house, never failed to fall back upon Kilravock for friendly service. The Earl of Lennox was at Elgin in 1594. His favourite charger fell sick and died, and he wrote Kilravock to send him another horse, his " black halknay nag," and he can have the choice of his stable some day to make up for it.

Change followed upon change among the actors in the national drama, but the Black Baron of Kilravock lived on undisturbed; and when James VI. made a royal progress to the north in the year 1598 the venerable baron was at Kilravock to welcome him. The family chronicler records that when the King asked him how he could live amongst such turbulent neighbours, he replied that they were the best neighbours he could have, for they made him thrice a day to go to God upon his knees, when perhaps otherwise he would not have gone once. The King addressed him as " Father," evincing a kindly interest in the aged baron. " He was of a venerable grave aspect ; his beard white and long in his old age, and he died full of days, not so much of sickness as nature being worn out." He was nearly ninety years of age when he died, having outlived all his family except his youngest son William, who succeeded him.

The designation of " Black " Baron was given to him solely on account of his swarthy complexion. He was a genial, kindly man, with a dash of native humour, as witness his signing his name in a formal deed adjusting a dispute between two neighbours— " Hugheon Rose, ane honest man, ill guided between you baith ! " He forms a striking figure of steadfastness and constancy in a shifting scene of national trouble and disorder.

CHAPTER XI

CLAN RAIDS AND PRIVATE FEUDS

ABOUT the beginning of the seventeenth century the county of Nairn was in a most turbulent condition. The chief disturbers of the peace were the Roses of Belivat. John Rose, fourth of Belivat, had in 1588 to stand his trial for the murder of Hugh Rose in Auldearn. He was also accused of the slaughter of Robert Rose, who had come to his house with twenty-five others to compel him to give up a removal notice he had obtained. His father some years before appeared at Inverness, according to the family historian, with " fifty-five proper personal men, all descended of his own branch and all cousins-german, twice or at most thrice only removed from him." Two years later he quarrelled with Falconer of Lethen and Hawkerton. John Rose's mother was a daughter of Lethen, but Lethen and he were too near neighbours to be good friends. On May 27, 1596, Alexander Falconer of Hawkerton and Hugh Falconer of Fleenas complained to the Lords of Council against John Rose of Belivat, Alaster Rose in Clune, Walter Rose in Coulmony, Lachlan Rose in Levrattich (spelt Leauwriddich), David Rose in Lyne, Hugh in Reurple, and others, for sorning, harrying, and wracking of their tenants, and in particular for having violently reft from Robert Falconer in Lethenbar certain horse and cattle. The Roses did not appear, and no immediate action having been taken against them, they came in a band one night in September, armed with bows, swords, hagbuts, and pistols to Falconer of Lethen's lands of Meikle Dulsie, where his tenants were taking their night's rest, and broke open the doors of the houses and carried away their corn and goods with

carts and sledges which they had brought with them.   The Lords
of Council denounced Belivat rebel.   About the same time his
kinsmen had a feud with the Tullochs of Tannachie, and it took
several years before the peace between them was restored.   The
laird of Belivat was also complained against by William Sutherland
of Duffus.   Belivat had in tack from Sutherland a ploughgate of
the lands of Brightmony, and the tack having expired Duffus sent
an officer—a relative of his own—to warn out Belivat.   The
Roses seized the officer and his assistants, beat them, and threatened
to hang them.   Belivat was again denounced rebel.   The historian
of Moray, Lachlan Shaw, says " the Roses of Belivat were a bold,
daring, and headstrong people, who put up with no injuries or
affronts, but warmly resented any wrong, real or supposed."   An
instance of this occurred about this time.

One David Rose, known as Macwilliam, was in the Clune.
He was a descendant of a natural son, who had been legitimised by
the Queen's letters, of the first Rose of Belivat.   The Dunbars of
Moyness claimed the Clune as theirs, but David Rose Macwilliam
said he had a better right to it than any Dunbar, as his forebears had
occupied the holding long before him.   He put his fact of possession
before and above their written title.   His grandfather had certainly
a charter to the Clune, but, curiously enough, it is not pled.   Perhaps
the Dunbars had acquired it.   Legal processes were beginning to
come into use at this time as between owners and occupiers, and
David was ignominiously ejected by the sheriff officer from Nairn,
and two new tenants, George Dunbar and Robert Falconer, were
placed in possession.   The hot blood of the Roses was roused at
this unusual proceeding, and David found ready associates among
his clan to resent the wrong done him.   They came, a party two
hundred strong, including many broken Highlandmen, to the Clune
one night in the autumn of 1598, and a scene of great violence
ensued.   They drove out the new tenants and their wives to the
hill, gathered together all the corn, victual, and goods, and having
set fire to the houses, made off with their plunder to the banks of
the Findhorn.

The Dunbars raised a criminal prosecution against David and
his associates, but they disregarded their summonses, feeling quite

safe in their retreats in upper Ardclach. They were outlawed
and officers sent to apprehend them. This greatly enraged them.
They set the law at defiance and sought their revenge on the
Dunbars whenever they got the chance. David, the evicted
tenant of the Clune, associated with him a bold and desperate gang
of his own name, particularly the M'Williams, M'Watties, and
M'Conachies, and, acting as outlaws, burned and spoiled the lands
of Moyness, Dunphail, and Mundole, and lived upon plunder and
rapine. Finding the law unable to cope with the Roses, three of
the leading families of the Dunbars, namely Moyness, Tarbet, and
Burgie, with their followers, made war upon them. They laid
waste the lands of Belivat, came down and burned Kilravock's
house of Geddes, and destroyed the lands and even threatened the
baron's life. The town of Nairn was in considerable danger, on
account of its connection with the Roses, and Provost John Rose
of Broadley thought it prudent to remove the papers and valuables
in his family chest for safe keeping to the castle of Kilravock.
Rose of Belivat had a house in Nairn situated near Millbank.

The feud nearly came to a head one market-day in Nairn.
The Dunbars came into the town in considerable numbers and
challenged the Roses in the place to fight. The latter, though
inferior in numbers, prepared for the combat, when the baron of
Kilravock (the peaceful William) and the laird of Mackintosh
" cam' with a great companie," and put an end to what might
have turned out to be a bloody and disastrous fight. The evil day,
however, was but postponed.

For years the feud went on, increasing in violence. The
Dunbars, unable to cope with the Roses, called in a party of the
Clanranald, from Lochaber, to their assistance. The Roses
strengthened their ranks by getting the assistance of a band of the
M'Gregors from Strathspey, as violent and savage as the others.
These robbers or reivers were paid by what they could spoil the
enemy of. One of the M'Gregors, bribed by Dunbar, at length
betrayed his leader, and poor David Rose was immediately hanged.
The Belivat Roses could not stand this. They had hitherto confined their hostilities to injury to property, but they now attacked
the Dunbars with serious intent and killed Dunbar, the laird of

Tarbet, who was also laird of Dunphail and resided there.   The Government had now its attention called to the " Wars of the Roses " in Ardclach, and an Act of Privy Council was passed to put down the " rebels."   Kilravock was called upon to apprehend his outlawed kinsmen, but he declared that that was beyond his power, as they had now become a roving band in the wilds of Ardclach without fixed residence or abode.   He was held responsible, however, and failing to give satisfaction, was imprisoned, both he and his son, in Edinburgh, and heavily fined.   On 23rd August, 1603, Kilravock was liberated by King James " to go home to his ain house and do his lawful affairs and business," having doubtless given ample assurance that he would take no part with his kinsmen.   The Roses now betook themselves to the Mackintosh country, coming down from time to time from the heights of Strathdearn to make a raid upon the lands of Moyness and carry away booty.   Mackintosh was pretty sharply told by the Government that unless he cleared his lands of the Belivat Roses he would be held responsible, and an Act was passed in 1611 ordaining him to do his duty.   He was thus compelled to take action and drive them away.   They, however, had by this time got quite used to the life of the bold outlaw, and continued harassing the Dunbars of Moray and Nairn.

The Sheriff of Moray—a Dunbar—dealt very severely with the laird of Belivat, who appears to have taken no direct part with his kinsmen in regard to the Clune.   He obtained a commission from the Government to pursue and take Belivat on the old charges formerly narrated.   He found him living peaceably in his house at Fleenas, took him prisoner, and sent him in irons to Edinburgh. He then proceeded to Belivat and burned down the house, with all its contents of goods, gear, and writs.   He took the eldest son a prisoner, and also succeeded in capturing Rose of Levrattich and young Alaster of the Clune, who were thrown into prison at Forres.   The young laird was liberated on caution, and his father, after an exciting trial in Edinburgh, was sent down to be tried before the Sheriff of Moray and a jury on certain charges.   The result of the trial was that Rose of Levrattich was executed. Alaster Rose shared the same fate.   The young laird appears to have been acquitted, but his father was sent back to Edinburgh, and was finally liberated only after suffering imprisonment for some considerable time. He resumed possession of his lands of Belivat, but soon after parted with them to Lethen, and removed to Banffshire. His roving clansmen, though they had wellnigh ruined the Dunbars of Moyness, finally made peace with them, and were allowed to settle on their old lands. Belivat's second son returned and settled at Blackhills, marrying a daughter of Sutherland of Kinsteary. A son in a later generation erected a monument in Geddes churchyard to the memory of the Roses of Belivat and Blackhills.

John Rose, the provost of Nairn, was also the hero of a raid in the country of the Munroes—in defence of a lady. He was a son of Rose of Dunearn, and his father had been provost of Nairn. The first glimpse we get of the provost is in 1537, when his grandfather conveyed to him while yet a boy certain lands in the parish of Auldearn, viz., Belgeam's Croft, otherwise called the Smiddie lands, and Bellsacre, both below the village of Auldearn, which he held of the Crown, for the annual payment of "six horse's shoes made of iron." The number of shoes was increased to twelve when the property, after going to the Cummings, came back to the provost's son. His first wife was Isabel Cumming, daughter of William Cumming of the Bught, descended from the Altyre family. In 1589 Provost John went to Aberdeen, and subscribed the "band in defence of the true religion and his Majesty's Government." On his return, his wife being dead, he married a lady who had had four husbands—Elizabeth Rose. She was a daughter of the Black Baron, and consequently a first cousin of the provost. Her husbands were successively Urquhart of Cromarty, Munro of Foulis, Cumming of Earnside, and M'Culloch of Plaids. The provost having deposited his papers in the tower of Kilravock, summoned his clansmen, the Roses of Ardclach, and led an expedition against the Munroes and Sinclairs, who sought to deprive his wife of her just dues and rents as Lady Foulis. He had afterwards to find heavy caution for his deeds against his wife's former connexions. After a bitter and protracted quarrel, the provost found that his marriage was illegal, and it was dissolved, whereupon Lady Foulis consoled herself with a sixth husband—William Gordon of Broadland. It is remarkable to find that Lady Foulis could not write. For over forty years John Rose was provost of Nairn, and ruled the town with a firm hand.

The Roses were not the only disturbers of the peace. The Mackintoshes were only too glad of any excuse for a raid. Colin Campbell of Clunes set forth his grievances against them in a petition still extant. He states that William Mackintosh of Essich, and some twenty other persons, with a great number of Clan Chattan, and broken Highlandmen thereabout, to the number of 200 persons, being all armed with bows, dorlupes, two-handed swords, dirks, hagbuts, dagis, pistols, and other forbidden weapons, in deadly feud against the complainer, his kith and friends, upon the first day of September, 1599, came early in the morning, about six o'clock, to the lands of Dunachtane and to a barn where he was, with certain of his friends, lying in their beds for the time, expecting no harm, and there besieged him for five hours, together with divers shots of hagbuts and pistols in at them, together with their arrows, and compelled him and his said company to surrender, with their weapons, into their merciless hands. The Mackintoshes promised faithfully to do them no harm, except to disarm them, but they slew his companions with their dirks, and took from Colin his sword and his purse containing one hundred pounds of gold, also a stand of cloth worth forty pounds, his horse and his gear worth a hundred pounds more. After putting violent hands on Colin, they kept him captive, carried him the first night to Kyllachie in Strathern, where they held him captive two days, thereafter they carried him to Borlum, and thereafter up and down the country to divers houses, and thereafter back again to Kyllachie, the space of fifteen days altogether, every hour threatening him with present death, until for fear of his life, he was compelled to subscribe to them such unreasonable bonds and conditions as they presented to him, tending to his great hurt.

Two months previously William Mackintosh in Urlathurst and some thirty broken Highlandmen, all armed, came to the lands of Easter and Wester Banchories, Dales, Terphogreene, Drynachan, and Meikle and Little Cullechar (all in the Streens). There he sorned, reived, and oppressed the tenants, and cut down 276 young growing trees of the wood of Easter Banchrie, called Torgarve, which he transported partly with his own men and horses and partly by Calder's men and horses, whom he compelled to do the same, to his lands and steading of Urlathurst. Lachlan Mackintosh, their chief, was cautioner for his clansmen for this latter action to the extent of 10,000 merks.

The excuse given for this conduct of the Mackintoshes is that they were incensed at the Campbells on account of Sir Donald Campbell, Dean of Lismore (a brother of the Laird of Calder), having presumed to marry the widow of the Laird of Mackintosh. Colin himself, who was so badly used, had married a daughter of Lachlan Mackintosh of Corryborough, and was thus drawn into a closer connection with Clan Chattan than he found desirable for his comfort.

The truth appears to be that the absence of the Thane of Cawdor at that time encouraged depredations on the property. Cawdor Castle was deserted, and its roofs and walls were becoming dilapidated. John of Cawdor, the grandson of Lady Muriel, found Argyllshire a sphere more suited for his ambition. Having married Mary, a sister of Dame Annas Keith, now Countess of Argyll, he was left by the Earl of Argyll one of the guardians of his son and administrators of his vast property. Several trustees had been appointed, but Cawdor and Campbell of Ardkinglass contrived to get all the power into their own hands—Cawdor, after the death of the countess, having charge of the heir, and Ardkinglass of the household. On the death of the latter, his son, who expected to be received into the same position, became excessively jealous of Cawdor's influence with young Argyll. He is said to have used the arts of witchcraft to gain the young Earl's affections, but in vain. He then entered into a plot, the mysteries of which have never been unravelled. One night, as the Thane of Cawdor was at Knepoch in Lorn, he was shot dead by three bullets fired through a window from a hagbut. The assassins were at once seized. They were two poor natives, who confessed they had been employed to do the deed by young Campbell of Ardkinglass. He was arrested, and being threatened with torture, confessed his own complicity, but averred that a bond for the deed had been entered into by the Earl of Huntly, the Earl of Glencairn, Lord Maxwell, the Earl of Morton, Campbell of Glenurchy, and other leading nobles of the time. The country at the time was ringing with indignation against Huntly for the murder of the Bonnie Earl of Moray at Donnibristle, and the belief was widespread that this was the first act in a new and terrible conspiracy by these nobles at the time high in favour with King James VI. to exterminate the house of Argyll. The young Earl of Argyll shared this view, and loudly demanded of the King that these nobles be brought to trial. Ardkinglass, however, soon afterwards recalled his statement implicating these nobles, and declared that he alone was concerned. This confession he repeated before a solemn assembly of the ministers of Glasgow. A suspicious feature in the proceedings is that although he was ostensibly at the King's instance arraigned for trial, when at length the case was called, none of the King's advocates appeared to prosecute, the diet was deserted, and he was liberated.

Margaret Campbell, the daughter of the murdered thane, had married a Celtic chieftain, Sir James Macdonald of the Isles. He was a remarkable character, engaged in the most sanguinary and bloody affairs on the west coast, but he was no mere unlettered savage—he had literary tastes and made himself a favourite in the best society of the time. His lawless conquests had brought him under the displeasure of the Crown, and he had to stand his trial at Edinburgh. Popular passion was aroused against him, and all men forsook him. The advocate assigned him dared not undertake his defence, and the only support he had was that of his brave wife, who stood beside him at the bar. He eventually made his escape from this country to Spain, and his last note before quitting the country was addressed to a friend begging him to befriend his wife. He subsequently found favour at the court in England.

It was probably through this connection that John Campbell of Cawdor, when he came of age, had his thoughts turned to the acquisition of Islay—an island which was believed to be of fabulous fertility and abounding in lead mines. His brother-in-law's father, the old chief of Islay, granted to the Thane of Cawdor a renunciation of his rights for six thousand merks, and after much negotiation with the Government, Sir John fitted out a military expedition for the purpose of conquering the island and capturing its castles of Duniveg and Lochgorme. The Government furnished him with 200 English troops and six cannon, in addition to his own followers. The expedition was completely successful. The rebellious subjects of Islay were subdued, and John of Calder ruled as a despotic island king. But the prize he had coveted and won proved a very costly acquisition. A heavy rent was extorted by the Government ; presents and largesses had to be made to those who had assisted him ; his visit to the English court, and the extravagant state he kept up, required much more money than Islay could produce. Twice a year immense droves of cattle were sent into England to be turned into cash. But still expenses could not be met. He meditated selling off the Cawdor estates in the north, but stopped short of that, burdening them, however, to the last penny with wadsets. Previous to this the barony of Ferintosh, which had come to the family through Mariot Sutherland of Dunbeath, who married Thane William, son of the builder of Cawdor Castle, was sold to Lord Lovat for £44,000. Durris and Borlum, etc., were purchased as an offset. But now Dunmaglass, the earliest acquisition of the Calders, was feued out to the M'Gillivrays, and wadsets were laid upon every available acre of land. Even the household plenishing of the castle was not spared. Sir John resigned the estate into his son John's hands, as advised by a meeting of his friends, but financial embarrassments increased. His son married a daughter of the eccentric Urquhart, Laird of Cromarty, and the marriage turned out most unhappy. A series of misfortunes befell the house of Cawdor in rapid succession. The fiar or young laird who ruled in Islay turned morose and misanthropic, and was at length declared insane and placed in confinement. Happily his brother Colin who was appointed tutor was a man of capacity and business tact. He set himself to retrieve the fallen fortunes of the house of Cawdor, and though the times were unsettled and unprosperous, he succeeded in putting matters into a better condition, and even found sufficient funds for repairing and enlarging the castle of Cawdor. The young heir attending Glasgow University was seized by the plague and died at Irvine, whither he had been removed; his grandfather, Sir John, died; and his unfortunate father, the fiar, followed a few years later, leaving the whole possessions of Cawdor to devolve on Hugh, the tutor's eldest son.

The Government took various steps to strengthen the arm of the law, and suppress private feuds and clan raids. In 1574 the old statute requiring the holding of wappinshaws was re-enacted, and in the county of Nairn the carrying out of the provisions of the Act was entrusted to Hucheon Rose of Kilravock, with the Sheriff Principals and deputies. An Act of Parliament for the purpose of suppressing the robberies and plundering carried on by " broken men," and " thieves and lymmaris of the Hielands," was passed in 1587, the year in which James VI. came of age. It required all noblemen and gentlemen who had estates in the neighbourhood of the Highlands, who had been accustomed either from fear or corrupt motives to harbour or protect disorderly and turbulent men, to give bail to the King that they would not do so in future. In this Act, amongst those enumerated are the Laird of Cawdor, Sheriff of Nairn, and Mackintosh. In 1594 the former Act not having been effectual, another Act was passed against the " thieves and lymmaris " who infested certain counties, and Nairn is mentioned as one. Circuit courts by the judges of the College of Justice, assisted by commissioners chosen from amongst the proprietors in the different counties, were set up for the trial of offenders, and seven commissioners were ordered to be selected from the county of Nairn. In the same year it was ordained that 200 officers of arms, and no more, should be appointed for the whole kingdom, and two were to be chosen from the county of Nairn.

For their own protection, the proprietors in the district sought and obtained grants of baronage, which gave them jurisdiction over offenders within the bounds of their own possessions, and established rights of defence against aggressors from outside. In this way several baronies were created.

Kilravock had long been a barony, and in 1600 the town of Geddes was erected by charter into a burgh of barony, with the power of creating bailies and burgesses, and of selling wine, ale, and all other merchandise whatsoever.

In 1623, by a charter from the Great Seal, the thanedom of Calder and the barony of Durris (which had been recently acquired from Mark Dunbar) were erected into a barony, called Campbeltown, with power to create bailies, constables, sergeants, and other officers, also liberty to buy and sell within the freedom, and to have a town-house and market cross, and to hold a weekly market on Wednesday and an annual fair on 15th July. The baron bailie of Cawdor exercised some functions down to a recent date, but the intention of forming a town was never carried into effect further than the erection of the present village.

A few years afterwards there was a similar attempt made to establish a burgh of Moyness. By a charter in 1635 in favour of John Grant of Logie, Moyness, Broadland, and Auldearn were erected into the barony of Moyness, with a weekly market on Saturday and an annual fair at Christmas. Previous to this the lands of Kinsteary and Brightmony, possessed by the Sutherlands of Duffus, formed part of the barony of Duffus, whilst Budgate at Cawdor was declared to be in the barony of Ardclach. A proprietor generally succeeded in getting all his lands, wherever situated, included in one barony, convenient for his exclusive jurisdiction, and it was in this way that certain parts of one county were held to be for all public purposes in another county, and described as " detached portions " of it.

Amidst all this turmoil it was only in the royal burghs that any settled industry flourished, and any regular enforcement of law and order was maintained. They were really centres of civilisation and organised trade, defective enough, no doubt, according to modern ideas, but in their constitutions and laws exhibiting features of social life and industrial organization far ahead of what prevailed in the country districts. The town of Nairn had enjoyed the privileges and immunities of a royal burgh for centuries, but its original charter had been destroyed in the depredations of the " Irish rebels," and on 16th October, 1589, a new charter was granted by King James VI., which was ratified by an Act of Parliament in 1597. The King was at Inverness about the year

1589, and passed through Nairn.   It was probably on that occasion he was struck with a feature of the population of the burgh, namely, that it was divided into two sections, one speaking English and the other Gaelic—a circumstance about which in after years he is credited with having made a joke to his English courtiers, that he had " a toun in Scotland—the toun of Nairn—so big that the people at the one end did not understand the language spoken by those at the other end."   It is frequently represented that it was the fishermen who spoke Gaelic and the other inhabitants English. But this is a mistake.   It was a colony of Gaelic-speaking High-landers who had congregated at the west end of the town, and dwelt apart.   The fishermen and the bulk of the inhabitants spoke English, and had no great love for the Highlanders, their language, or their practices.   The burgh records abound with expressions of contempt for " broken Hie'landmen," disturbing the peace of the burgh in time of market and other occasions.

The comparative prosperity which prevailed in the burgh, where all sorts of trades were carried on, appears to have excited the jealousy of the landed proprietors.   Some of them secured pro-perties within the burgh, and found it to their benefit to share in the trade, especially in corn, salmon, and herrings, and no doubt the attempts to start similar towns in the country arose to some extent from seeing the advantages exemplified in the burghs.

CHAPTER XII

COVENANTING TIMES

The earlier changes from Presbyterianism to Episcopacy do not appear to have excited any popular feeling in the district, but there can be little doubt that the great bulk of the people were Puritans from the beginning.

Some changes had taken place in the county of Nairn in the years immediately preceding Covenanting times.

The gentle family of Falconer of Lethen, probably sick of the feuds of their neighbours, sold the lands of Lethen and retired to their paternal estates in the south. They had occupied Lethen from before the year 1295. A pass is preserved at Kilravock which was granted by the Earl of Huntly charging all and sundry " the Queen's officers and subjects, burgh as well as landward, to abstain from molesting or interfering with Alexander Falconer of Halkertoun, his wife, bairns, and family, either in their bodies or goods, in their passing, removing, or returning to and from the north parts of the realm." The final " flitting " took place in 1600. A tablet in the old choir of Auldearn Church, over against the Lethen tomb, preserves the record of their Nairnshire habitation. It runs—" The Sepulchre of the Honourable and Ancient the Laird of Halkerstown and Leatin and Dunearn and his familie. Blised . ar . the . dead . which . de . in . the . Lord. Hencefurth . is . laid . up . for . me . a . Crown . of . Righteousness. O . death . where . is . thy . sting, . O . grave . where . is . thy . victory." It is undated. An old stone built into the wall near it bears a shield with three stars, two at the head and one at the foot of the figure of a hawk, and beneath are the letters " W.F." The base of the tomb is ornamented with capitals and devices.

The new proprietor of Lethen was John Grant of Freuchy, who had by this time become one of the most extensive landowners in the north. He built a large house at Lethen. No detailed description of this building has been preserved, but from various incidental references to it, the house of Lethen appears to have been a place of great strength. The Grants retained Lethen for some thirty-four years, but on the accession of Sir John at his father's death, he sold it to Alexander Brodie, in 1634.

This Alexander Brodie, the first of Lethen, was the second son of David, the thirteenth Laird of Brodie. David his father had made a curious marriage—he married Janet Hay of Lochloy, who was a younger sister of his own stepmother. Her mother was one of the Sutherlands of Duffus. Old David Brodie had had his fair share of the trials of the time, having run some risk from siding with the Earl of Huntly against the Earl of Moray, when they were at deadly feud, but he managed during his long life to accumulate a good deal of wealth, and when he died his family of six sons nearly all made purchases of land and became the founders of families of substance.

Alexander, the second son, was not left dependent upon his father's means, but went in early life to Edinburgh to push his fortune. He became a burgess of the city, and married a grandchild of the Provost of Edinburgh, Alexander Clerk of Balbirnie. His marriage connexion brought him into close contact with Thomas, Lord Bruce of Kinloss, who was his wife's cousin-german, and he was appointed chamberlain of the ecclesiastical lands and revenues in the north which Bruce had obtained.

Alexander Brodie's first purchase was a portion of Kinloss. He next advanced a thousand merks to James, Earl of Moray, as a wadset on Kinnudie, and he bought the lands of Pitgavenie from Alexander Hay of Kinnudie, and the lands of East Grange and Little Earnside from Patrick Dunbar. In the year 1634 he bought the lands and barony of Lethen, including the feu-duties of Clune, for 105,000 merks (£7,500 sterling). His purchases did not stop there. In 1643 he bought the whole abbey lands of Kinloss, with the abbey itself, and the mass of superiorities which belonged to the abbey in the counties of Inverness, Ross, Banff, Aberdeen,

Moray, and Nairn, from Thomas Bruce, now Earl of Elgin. He was besides banker for many of the needy lairds of his day, and at a later time advanced considerable sums to the Government. The family of Brodie of Lethen at its outset was thus of consideration in the district, equalling, if it did not exceed, the old house of Brodie in the extent of its possessions. Alexander of Lethen, on the death of his eldest brother David, the thirteenth Laird of Brodie, succeeded to the management of the Brodie estates as tutor to his brother's children. He lived through the stormy Covenanting times, and warmly espoused, as will be seen, the cause of the Puritans. He married as his second wife Margaret Grant, cousin of the Laird of Grant.

Alexander, the young Laird of Brodie, Lethen's nephew, who became Lord Brodie, had been sent into England when eleven years old for his education. He returned in 1632 on his father's death, and by special dispensation from the Lords of Council was declared of age (he was but nineteen). He was served heir to the estates in 1636. While yet a minor, he married Elizabeth Innes, widow of John Urquhart, of Craigston, Tutor of Cromarty, and daughter of Sir Robert Innes of Innes, by Lady Grizzel Stewart, daughter of James, the Bonnie Earl of Moray. This worthy lady's influence over the young laird deepened his religious tendency, and confirmed in him his bias towards Puritanism. His wife, who was the delight of his eyes, died suddenly at an early age, leaving him with one son and one daughter. Brodie had hitherto taken little part in public affairs, but he now joined his neighbours in resisting the attempt of King Charles I. and his minister Laud to impose the obnoxious Service Book on the Church of Scotland.

The Laird of Brodie and Brodie of Lethen, as might be expected, signed the National Covenant. David Hay of Lochloy also adhibited his name. David had had rather an adventurous career. He was the second son, and in the year 1600 succeeded his brother John. A letter of his has been preserved which gives a curious account of the upbringing of a Nairnshire laird in those early days. He says that in his minority, being under the government of Walter and Alexander Hay of Kinnudie, then his curators, he was transported from the county of Moray to Lothian for his education at the schools there. He remained there until the year of the Plague. He was left desolate, until Sir Alexander Hay, Clerk of the Register, at the earnest entreaty of Sir Alexander Hay of Fosterseat, removed him to Whittingeham, where he was lovingly entertained for a year. The origin of the Hays of Fosterseat may be thus traced. John of Lochloy, the hero of the breach of promise case, was succeeded by his son William, of Lochloy, Dallas, and Park, who was succeeded by his son John in 1480. John's eldest son, William, succeeded him, and marrying Katherine Urquhart of Cromarty, had John, who married Isobel Dunbar in 1554 and died in 1563. This John left several sons—John, who succeeded him, David and Alexander of Foynesfield, and George, who, dying before 1600, left a son Alexander, who married Catherine Skene, and became Sir Alexander Hay of Fosterseat. The Hays of Kinfauns, of Wariston, of Easter Kennet, of Mondon, of Woodcockdale in Kirkcudbright, and of Carriber, can all be traced to the Hays of Lochloy.

It happened that when young Lochloy came on a visit to Sir Alexander Hay at Kelso, he was just starting for London, and invited the young laird to accompany him, and (writes young Lochloy) " transported me with horse and abulments effeiring to my rank with him towards the said city of London, to the effect that I might see and understand good manners and fashions." Lochloy's expenses in London for breakfast, dinner, supper, and bed, " conform to the order of England," were 36s. Scots per day, his horse 6d., hay 6d., oats 2d., and bread 14s. Scots. He remained in London from September till March, and thereafter till his marriage. His kinsman, Sir Alexander, defrayed all his expenses, and when troubles arose with his uncles and cousins of Kinnudie and Foynesfield in regard to count and reckoning during his minority, his cousin of Fosterseat helped him most lovingly to redeem his property, and to recover his woods, which were, he says, " the pleasure of my estate." David married Marie Rose of Kilravock and had a numerous family.

All the leading men in the county of Nairn were staunch Presbyterians, and at the time were nearly all connected with each other by marriage.

Colin, the Tutor of Cawdor, was married to Elizabeth, sister of the young Laird of Brodie. She became the mother of the next Thane of Cawdor. Colin was a member of the Glasgow Assembly which abolished the bishops, and he warmly espoused the Presbyterian cause.

Hugh, Baron of Kilravock, succeeded his father, William the peaceful baron, in 1611. He married Magdalen Fraser, of Strichen, and was one of the gentlemen who met the commissioners at Inverness for the signing of the Covenant in 1638. He took an active part along with his kinsmen and followers in opposing a party of Huntly's men who had come to take possession of the castle of Inverness, and under command of his father-in-law, Fraser of Strichen, he assisted in the blockade and capture of the stronghold. He was also one of the gentlemen of quality who took part in the Trot of Turriff, as that somewhat inglorious episode is called.

One of the most remarkable men of the time in the district was the provost of Nairn. John of Dunearn, " the bold resolute provost," was succeeded in the provostship by Patrick his son. Patrick possessed the lands of Broadley, but he died without issue, and his property went to John, fourth son of Kilravock. To the office of provost was elected William Rose, the second son of the peaceful baron. William is first styled of Fleenas, but he afterwards acquired the property of Clava. He married a daughter of Chisholm of Cromlix. He it was who built the first bridge of Nairn, and he did so at his own expense. It was, for the time, a magnificent structure, of many arches, with a splendid high pillared gateway, richly carved and ornamented. When it was finished, a tablet was placed on it bearing the following inscription : " Guliemus Rose de Clava, non est salus nisi in Christ. Soli Deo Gloria. 1631." He also built a bridge over the river Nairn at Cantray at his own expense. The site of the present town and county buildings appears also to have been a gift from Clava, as an entry occurs in the burgh records in 1669, giving a new charter " to the merchant booth under the Council-house," in respect it was sufficiently known that Hugh Rose of Clava, his ancestors and predecessors, had undoubted right to the same, " because the ground upon which the tolbooth is built was given by them of their own private patrimony." The Provost of Nairn was a member of the Glasgow Assembly of 1638, and voted for deposing the bishops. The Assembly appointed Mr. John Hay, minister of Rafford, and Mr. David Dunbar, minister of Edinkillie, with William Rose, the Provost of Nairn, to communicate the sentence of deposition to Bishop Guthrie of Moray, which they did on their return at his palace of Spynie. The bishop's answer was to fortify Spynie Castle and lay in a store of gunpowder. He was the only one of the Scottish bishops who did not flee the country, and he ultimately was prevailed upon to surrender his palace peaceably and go into private life in another part of the country.

Mr. David Dunbar belonged to the family of Dunbar of Boath. The Boath family are descended from David Dunbar, Dean of Moray, of the Durris branch of the Dunbars. A stone in the choir of the church of Auldearn bears the inscription—" Heir lyis ane honorable man, Maister David Dumbar, Dean of Murray, quha departit on the 10 day of Februar, 1556 years, and Alexander Dumbar of Both, his sone, quha diet ye 13 of February, 1664, D.D., m.o., A.D.B.H." Underneath the inscription are two shields, on one of which are three diamond-shaped figures and a lion rampant; the other shield bears three small shields. The armorial bearings of the family now exhibit a lion rampant within a bordure charged with eight roses. Along the edge of the stone is inscribed in two lines—" Whaso fearis ye Lord it sal go weil with him and he sal find favor at ye last. The eyes of ye Lord in everi place behold ye evil and ye good." Mr. David Dunbar was the second son of James Dunbar of Boath, and became minister of Nairn in 1638. A monumental stone above the west door of Nairn parish church records in Latin that he " with the highest character for fidelity, discharged during twenty years the duties of pastor in the church of Nairn, and died in peace in the Lord, 22nd February, 1660."

The Laird of Brodie, Brodie of Lethen, Hay of Lochloy, Kinnaird of Culbin, the Baron of Kilravock, the Laird of Innes, the Laird of Grant, and others subscribed the Covenant. The commissioners visited the burgh of Nairn, and it is recorded that the people came forward most willingly, the magistrates being very zealous in the cause. Colin, the tutor of Cawdor, was also a strong Covenanter, and when the assembly of the kirk met in Glasgow in November, Colin the tutor was there. The minister of Rafford, Mr. Thomas Hay, was a member of the Lochloy family, and received the thanks of the assembly for an able work he had written, entitled " A Censure of the Service Book." William Falconer, minister of Dyke, was a member of the committee appointed to enquire into the conduct of the bishops. The minister of Auldearn at the time was Mr. John Brodie, an uncle of the Laird of Brodie and a strong Puritan. He succeeded Thomas Dunbar, his maternal grandfather, who was appointed minister of Nairn in 1590. In the following year he was transferred to Auldearn and died about 1623.

These were the leading men in the district when the troubles arose in connection with Laud's attempt to impose a liturgy. There was much excitement of committees and some marching and manoeuvring of armed men, but there was no fighting in Moray at this time. The pacification was arranged, and the Covenanting camp formed at Elgin was broken up.

An incident about the end of the year 1640 shows the young Laird of Brodie as exceedingly zealous in his hatred of everything that savoured of popery and idolatry, according to his view. Service had been discontinued in Elgin Cathedral many years before, but a carved screen which divided the church from the chancel, on which were paintings of the Crucifixion and the Day of Judgment, was destroyed by Brodie, his brother-in-law, the young Laird of Innes, and the parish minister of Elgin.

The year 1645 was a memorable year in the history of Nairnshire. Montrose had broken with the Covenanters, and had taken up the cause of King Charles I. when it was at its lowest ebb. In the month of February of that year he made one of his sudden dashes into the northern Highlands, and after winning the battle of Inverlochy, appeared on the borders of Moray. The Earl of Seaforth was at the head of the Covenanting committee assembled at Elgin, and so great was the terror of an invasion of Moray by Montrose that a deputation of the leading men went to beseech him to spare the district. Seaforth, with his son-in-law, the Laird

of Grant, his brother Mackenzie of Pluscardine, and Sir Robert
Gordon actually went over to Montrose's side.   The same absolute
unanimity did not prevail as at the time when the Covenanters of
Moray first took the field.   Sympathy for the King existed to
some extent, and probably Seaforth and others thought they might
be Royalists and Covenanters at the same time.   Whatever passed
between Montrose and the deputation, he did not grant their
request, but sent out bands of his men to burn, pillage, and waste
the country.   They went down to Culbin at the seaside—the
Laird of Culbin had been one of the deputation—and burned and
plundered the still fair domain.   Grangehill (now Dalvey) belonging to Ninian Dunbar, was set on fire and pillaged.

Montrose appears to have been in some doubt as to whether he
should risk a battle with Hurry, but General Baillie, the commander-in-chief of the Covenanting army, being on his rear, he
resolved to meet Hurry's attack, which he understood was now
determined upon.   According to Royalist authorities, Montrose
had with him only 1500 foot and 250 horse, but this is evidently
an under-statement.   Montrose made Boath his headquarters, and
a well near the house is known to this day as Montrose's well.
His position was a strong one, and in setting his forces in array, he
took full advantage of the natural defences of the ground.   He
resolved to put into execution a plan of battle which was boldly
conceived.   It was in effect to throw the main strength of his
forces into the left wing, and to fight with no proper centre or
right wing.   He stationed Lord Lewis Gordon with his cavalry
towards the south, approaching Newmill, on the extremity of the
left wing.   His infantry under his own command were drawn up
along the ridge, on the top of which the road now passes, the troops
being placed a few yards back from that line on the broken ground
of the Kinsteary park, and thus partially concealed from view of
the enemy.   A hollow in the park is said to be the place where the
cavalry were stationed until brought into action.

The village at that time occupied a somewhat different position
from what it does now.   The turnpike road, forming the main
street of the present village, had then no existence.   The village
ran north and south, instead of as at present, east and west.   The

Boath road which intersects the village gives the general lie of the hamlet. The houses occupied the slope, with their gardens and crofts running down to the flat ground bounded by the burn. The mill and its croft were in the same position as now. The brew-house (afterwards a granary) occupied the site of the present village hall. It now seems to have been in John Belgeam's lands, between the old smith's toft and croft, at the mouth of the narrow ravine, that Montrose placed the Royal standard, and stationed his Major-General, Alexander Macdonald, generally known as M'Coll or Colkitto. The foot of the village was protected by some turf dykes answering the purpose of temporary ramparts, behind which were put a few men. Contemporary accounts state that Montrose placed a few picked musketeers, with some cannon, on " the height directly in front of the village." As the main part of the village clustered below the church-yard, the height in front of the village must be the old Castle Hill (or Doocot hill, as it is now called), though it might now be more accurately described as on the right front flank. No skilful general in a disposition of his forces would neglect to avail himself of the advantages of this knoll, which would be very difficult to scale. It is in fact a fort of considerable strength, with remnants of earthwork ramparts of some height, which half-a-dozen men could hold against a formidable attack, and tradition states that this is what actually occurred. Having thus set his army in position, Montrose waited the arrival of the Covenanters. One change took place, according to the Clanranald MS. When Macdonald was ordering his troops and arranging his defences by placing brushwood in front, a gentleman came to him with a message from Lord Gordon, in these words—" Allaster Macdonald, I have heard that there was a bond of friendship between our fore-fathers not to strike a blow against each other, whatever quarrel might be between them and the rest of Scotland, and none excelled them in deeds of honour ; therefore, let us now renew that bond by exchanging foot soldiers, on this the first day of my doing battle for my King—send me your foot soldiers and take mine." Mac-donald, whose vanity was flattered, at once agreed, and ordered ninety of his veterans, " tried in many a battle," to join his noble friend, who in return sent three hundred of his foot, brought from

Strathbogie and the other northern possessions of Huntly. They were inexperienced levies, which Lord Lewis Gordon was only too glad to get rid of. Macdonald was left with only fifty veteran troops, and he placed twenty-five in front and twenty-five in rear of the Gordon recruits, to keep them from running away.

The plan of battle was skilfully laid, whether it was designed by Montrose himself, or as some suppose, by his Major-General, Macdonald. His object was to draw the best fighting regiments of the Covenanters to attack Macdonald and the phantom centre in the village, while he would swoop down with the left wing as soon as they were engaged.

The courtly Montrose, with the air of courage and command characteristic of him, as he paced the paved terrace beside the churchyard, with the whole Covenanting force in view, so much superior to his own, must have felt the desperate character of the venture he was about to make, and probably steeled his heart with the sentiment of the couplet he wrote when a youth—

" He either fears his fate too much or his deserts are small,
    That dares not put it to the touch, to gain or lose it all."

Distinguished in appearance as Montrose was, the rival commander, General Hurry, was the handsomer man of the two. Hurry is described as a robust, tall, stately fellow, with a long cut in his cheek, which, however, did not mar his aspect. He was a brave soldier, but as ready to draw his sword for the cause of the Royalists as for that of the Covenant.

The army of the Covenanters, which had concentrated at Inverness, now moved forward. It was immensely superior in every respect to Montrose's ragged little force. It numbered 3500 foot and 400 horse, all well equipped. Major Drummond led the van with the horse. The gallant Campbell of Lawers rode at the head of a body of veteran soldiers of the Estates. The Earl of Seaforth brought the Mackenzies to the field, albeit somewhat unwillingly. Lawrie, Loudon, and Buchanan had command of regiments of the garrison and Estates troops. The Earl of Findlater had also a command. The Earl of Sutherland came with his clansmen. Lovat brought the Frasers, Kilravock the Roses, while the Brodies,

Inneses, Calders, and other Moray and Nairn clansmen followed their respective chiefs, and all hurried forward to Auldearn.

On Friday morning, 9th May, the battle was fought. It began shortly before noon. The army of the Covenanters appeared on the scene from behind Kinnudie. Hurry seems from the way in which he prepared for the attack to have had a pretty accurate idea of the general disposition of Montrose's troops, though probably ignorant of the relative strength of its ostensible divisions. He drew his forces up in three divisions, answering to those of Montrose. The engagement began by Loudon and Laurie, with their trained veterans, supported by some horse, being despatched to attack Macdonald's position on the north of the village. They followed the line of the Kinnudie Burn and in a few minutes were in front of Macdonald's quarters. The horse could not charge him, as the ground was broken and boggy, and he had the protection of the burn and the enclosures, with the brushwood he had heaped up in front of his position. Shots were exchanged, and the cannon on the hill fired an occasional ball. The combatants came so near to each other that the Covenanters taunted the Major-General with the cowardice of fighting under cover. Macdonald's Highland blood was roused by these taunts, and although strictly enjoined by Montrose not to leave his defences, but to keep the enemy occupied, he boldly sallied forth at the head of his men to give them battle in the open. A fierce fight now ensued—the like of it, says one who was present, had never been seen in the low country. But Macdonald's raw Gordon Highlanders would not fight. Whenever they heard the sough of an arrow or the whistle of a ball, they ducked their heads. Their officers had actually to shoot some of them to prevent a general flight. Macdonald was forced to fall back, but he fought his ground step by step. Defending his body with a large target, he resisted single-handed the assaults of the enemy. The pikemen were so close upon him as to fix their spears in his target. These he cut off with his broadsword by threes and fours at a stroke. He was the last man to leave the field and seek the protection of the enclosures. When he had just reached the garden gate, Hay of Kinnudie, a tall powerful man, uncle of young Hay of Lochloy, pressed him hard (so local tradition runs), but he called out to him, " I'll not deceive you, my men are coming up behind you." Hay turned round, and Macdonald seizing his advantage, cut him down with one sweep of his broadsword. Another minute and Macdonald's own sword was shivered to pieces. His brother-in-law, Davidson of Ardnacross, flew to his side, and handed him his sword. He saved Macdonald's life, but lost his own, for he fell mortally wounded in the very act. Macdonald at last got within the enclosure, but some of the enemy got in at the same time. Ranald Mackinnon of Mull, seeing the pikemen about to enter, stood boldly a few paces in front of the entrance, his shield in his left hand and his gun in his other hand, presented at them. Some bowmen coming up let fly their arrows with deadly effect among the retreating Gordon soldiers, and rushed past Ranald, and one of them turning round, shot him in the face, the arrow penetrating one cheek and appearing out at the other. The Clanranald chronicler, who relates the incident, says that Ranald, throwing away his gun and stretching out his shield to save himself from the pikes, attempted to draw his sword, but it would not come ; he tried it again, and the cross hilt twisted about ; a third time he made the attempt, using his shield-hand to hold the sheath, and succeeded, but at the expense of five pike wounds in his breast. In this state he gained the entrance to the garden, closely followed by one of the enemy, but as the latter bowed his head under the gate, Macdonald, who had been watching the passage at arms, with one swoop of his claymore severed the head from the body, the head falling between Ranald's legs and the body in the doorway. Macdonald's next act was to cut away the arrow that stuck in the young man's cheek and restored him speech. The Covenanters who had got inside the garden were speedily despatched and the entrance once more secured. Seventeen of Macdonald's officers lay wounded and many of the Gordon soldiers were slain in the desperate affray.

Montrose watched the fighting from the churchyard. When he saw Macdonald in his folly leave his well-protected position and go out to the open he must have foreseen the result. Mortified at having had his plans frustrated by this rash movement, he rode off to take command of the left wing to the south of the village. He was followed a few minutes later by an orderly, who whispered to him, " Macdonald is completely routed ! " It was a critical moment. If the tidings of the disaster on the right reached the troops under his command, the day would be lost. He immediately shouted to Lord Gordon, " Macdonald is gaining the victory single-handed ! Come, come, my Lord Gordon, shall he carry all before him and leave no laurels for the house of Huntly ! Charge ! "

The two divisions of the Covenanting force had meanwhile drawn slowly forward from Kinnudie. The main body, consisting principally of Seaforth's men, advanced towards the mill, partly on the high ground and partly on the fields below. The other division, composed of the Frasers and Sutherland men, crossed over the rough boggy land more to the south. Some firing had taken place, but a general advance in line had not yet been made. Just about the moment when Montrose ordered the charge of his cavalry, Drummond with his horse was commanded to advance and open the battle. He made one charge, but for some inexplicable reason, immediately wheeled round, broke through the ranks of the infantry supports behind him, and made off. Had there been no suspicion of treachery, this sudden movement might have been due to the discovery of the alarming strength of the enemy. It was then that Montrose's charge was made. It fell upon the already broken ranks of the wing before them. The Frasers and Sutherland men stood their ground. But the horse swept through them like a whirlwind. They fell thickly, mown down like grass. Montrose's infantry came on, and utterly defeated them. " Give no quarter ! " shouted Montrose, and scarcely a man of the whole division but was slain.

The Seaforth men on the high ground, seeing Drummond's horse in full retreat and their right wing overborne, instead of going to their aid, turned and fled, without striking a blow or firing a shot. Those in the plain below remained for a little time irresolute, not knowing what to do, but seeing their comrades in retreat, they followed the example and took to flight. There were, however, a few brilliant exceptions. Rory M'Lennan, the Kintail bannerman, tried to retain his kinsmen. He fastened the staff of the standard of the Mackenzies in the ground and protected it with his two-handed sword. Beside him stood three others—his own brother, Malcolm Macrae, and Duncan MacIan Oig. They were speedily cut down by Lord Gordon's men. Captain Bernard Mackenzie, who had with him a company of his men from Chanonry, on seeing the rout, declared that he and his kinsmen would remain on the field while the standard of the Mackenzies floated, and remain they did, until they were cut down on the spot where they stood. Two men of some note among the Mackenzies refused to fly. They were Mackenzie of Kernsary, cousin-german to Seaforth, and Donald Bayne, a brother of Tulloch, and Seaforth's chamberlain in the Lewis. The reason assigned for their remaining, however, detracts from their credit, as it is said they were too heavy and stout to run.

Having swept the south field clear, Lord Gordon's horse, followed by Montrose and his Irish infantry, crossed over to attack Loudon and Lawrie's regiments. Macdonald, seeing his friends approaching, came out of his lair once more, and revenged his former repulse by a fierce onslaught upon his opponents. The combined attack fell disastrously upon the devoted regiments. They were outnumbered and annihilated. Campbell of Lawers, and Sir John and Gideon Murray were slain. Alexander Drummond of Meedhope, the last of his house, along with many other brave officers, fell with his regiment. On the other side, young Napier of Merchistown greatly distinguished himself.

Montrose's victory was complete. He had crushed a splendid army, superior in all respects to his own. He now followed up the victory by inflicting terrible punishment. Every fugitive overtaken was slain—no prisoners were made.

Sixteen colours, the whole baggage, ammunition, and money fell into the hands of the victors. While the Covenanters left nearly two thousand men dead on the field, Montrose's loss was comparatively slight. Those who fell in the shock of the two wings on the south were buried in trenches in a piece of waste land, which has since been planted, and is known as the Dead Men's Wood. The men who were slain in front of Macdonald's position were buried in the hollow below the churchyard wall at the north-west corner, probably a part of the Smith's croft. Near the door of the present church a slab marks the place where Captain Bernard Mackenzie was buried, and bears the following inscription—" Here lyeth Captaine Bernard Mackenzie, who in defence of his Religion and Country, fechting, diet at Aulderne, 9th May, 1645." A stone in the church commemorates the death of three other Covenanting officers. It was originally built into the steeple, but on the demolition of that erection it was removed by the late Rev. Wm. Barclay, minister of the parish, to the choir, where it stood, much wasted, until it was replaced by Sir Thomas D. Brodie with a new monument. The inscription runs—" This monument is erected by Sir Robert Innes, younger of that Ilk, in memorie of Alexander Drummond of Meedhope, Sir John Murray, and Maister Gideon Murray, who lyes here intered, who fighting valiantly in defence of their Religion, King, and native Country, died at Aulderne, 9th May, 1645." Montrose set fire to a part of the village, and then fell back towards Elgin. General Hurry and the Covenanting leaders made their escape to Inverness, where Major Drummond was tried by court-martial, and shot, for the bad handling of the cavalry. Allegations of treachery were made against him, and he confessed that he had spoken to the enemy after the sign of battle was given. The popular belief is that Hurry and the Earl of Seaforth fought to lose and not to win at Auldearn, and the fact that they both went over to Montrose's side shortly after the disaster confirmed the popular impression. There is, however, no conclusive evidence of such a plot. A few years later, Montrose and Hurry passed south, bound as prisoners, and were executed together.

Nairnshire again soon afterwards felt the scourge of war. Lord Huntly and his sons entered the county with a force of two thousand horse and foot and besieged the strong house of Lethen. For no less than twelve weeks the Gordons sat before Lethen and tried hard to take it. Its natural position does not afford it any great protection. It stands on a terrace of the hill-side, facing the south, and its garden in front slopes down to the burn. The small stream, however, could be easily crossed, and the house must have depended for its security on the height and stoutness of its walls.   It was strongly garrisoned, and its defenders appear to have given a good account of themselves against the Gordons, many of the latter being killed.   Enraged and disappointed, the Marquis of Huntly utterly burned and wasted the lands of Lethen, on which, it is stated, there were some eight score persons, and he left not ten of them upon the lands.   He pillaged and burned Lethen's house at Kinloss, lifting the hearth-stones in search of valuables.   Unfortunately he discovered the family charter chest with its writs and papers concealed beneath the fireplace, and its contents were immediately destroyed.   So long as the ammunition lasted, the Lethen people held out bravely.   The laird himself and all his friends in the district (excepting the Laird of Brodie, who was with the garrison at Inverness) were shut up in the beleaguered fortress. Day after day, during those twelve weeks, they were sustained by the hope of troops coming to their relief from Inverness or Darnaway.   Secret messengers at dead of night had been despatched to tell their friends of their straits, and again and again tidings were brought that the soldiers were on their way.   But none came, and famine stared them in the face.   The plucky little garrison at length lost heart.   They reluctantly resolved to capitulate, and with the object of getting the best conditions they could from the Marquis of Huntly, Mr. Joseph Brodie, the minister of Auldearn, was deputed to open parley with the enemy.   Huntly stipulated that a bond of money should be made payable to him in case Lethen and his friends did not conform to His Majesty's service.   This done, Huntly raised the siege, and took his departure.

About half a year later the Highlanders made a raid on Lethen, and took away all that was left on the ground.   Brodie of Lethen at this time represented the county of Nairn in Parliament, and he represented his losses to the Estates, estimating them £95,000 Scots.   The Parliament granted him £10,000 for his subsistence and the support of the garrison in his house, and he proceeded to replenish his lands with stock ; but he had no sooner done so than the enemy " for his refusal to concur in the late unlawful engagement " " did eat up and destroy his haill corn, and plundered of new again his haill nolt and bestial, and left the land in a worse condition nor it was before." Such are the statements set forth in an Act of Parliament dated 25th March, 1649.

For the next thirty or more years the most prominent person connected with Nairnshire was the Laird of Brodie. He, too, had suffered severely in those troubled times. "We fell before the wild Irishes six times without interruption," he says in his diary; " my house and my mains and my bigging was burnt to the ground and my estate made desolate and no place left me nor means to subsist." A man of devout religious feelings, Alexander Brodie of Brodie impressed his contemporaries no less by his earnestness in the cause of civil and religious freedom than by his great abilities and sound judgment. He was drawn away from his secluded heritage of Brodie to the seat of government at Edinburgh, and as a representative of the county of Elgin in the Parliament, and a member of the General Assembly of the Kirk, he occupied the position of one of the foremost men of the day, and had some considerable hand in shaping the history of the time. Although he had no special training as a lawyer he was made a judge of the Court of Session, and was thereafter styled Lord Brodie.

The execution of Charles I. having taken place, the thoughts of the Scottish leaders turned towards his son. Charles II. was proclaimed King of Great Britain, and if only he would give satisfaction to the kingdom " in these things that concern the security of Religion, the Union betwixt the Kingdoms, and the good and peace of this Kingdom, according to the National Covenant and the Solemn League and Covenant," he would at once be admitted to the exercise of his royal power. Lord Brodie was appointed by Parliament one of the five commissioners to proceed to Holland and treat with the young King. They found Charles at The Hague, but he was buoyed up with the hopes of winning the crown by the sword independently of the Parliament and unfettered by their engagements, and therefore refused the overtures made to him by Lord Brodie and his fellow commissioners. Their negotiations failed, but next year (21st February, 1650), Lord Brodie, the Earl of Cassillis, Lord Lothian, Sir John Smith, Alexander Jaffray, Provost of Aberdeen, and George Wynrame were commissioned to treat with the King, who was represented to be in a more tractable mood. His visions of military success had by this time vanished. The commissioners met Charles at Breda, but found him in so reckless a mood—he was prepared to sign anything without the least appearance of a sense of the responsibility of what he was undertaking—that some of the commissioners hesitated to proceed further. Lord Brodie and Jaffray objected to the King being made to swear to a covenant which they knew he hated in his heart. Brodie appears to have suggested as a compromise that the assent of Charles might be taken by word of mouth. Both he and Jaffray were outvoted, and the King was ready to sign anything to secure Scotland. Lord Brodie's position among the commissioners is shown by the circumstance that the drawing up of the papers was entrusted to him on behalf of the Estates. In his feelings of compassion for the young King, he appears to have omitted some things, and softened down others, contained in the Parliament's instructions, but upon debate next morning these were restored to their original severity. Lord Brodie returned with the papers signed by the King, and received the thanks of the Scottish Parliament. There had been some difficulty about the expenses, and as the Parliament had no public credit abroad, Lord Brodie became surety for a large share of the 100,000 merks borrowed in Holland, and was never repaid, though he made frequent application. He was deputed by the Parliament along with certain others, "to repair and congratulate his Majesty's happy arrival in the Kingdom," and while he probably still had lingering doubts as to the wisdom of the whole transaction, he shared in the enthusiasm which prevailed in the nation at the King's coming. He appears to have conceived a strong personal liking for the young King, and Charles as a mark of esteem for him, presented him with a portrait of his father, Charles I., by Vandyke, which still hangs in the drawing-room at Brodie Castle.

In the national events which rapidly followed the crowning of the King at Scone, Lord Brodie took an active part. The English army under Cromwell entered Scotland, and there was a call to arms. From Nairnshire Brodie of Lethen marched south with a contingent. He was present at the conflict at Eastwick, and commanded a troop with some credit at the disastrous battle of Dunbar.

Lord Brodie gave the Estates pecuniary assistance, lent them a considerable sum when the troops were at Stirling, greatly in want of money, immediately after the battle of Dunbar, and was elected Commissary-General to the Army in October, 1650. He was superseded as a Lord of Session by Cromwell's English judges, and being strongly averse to the English rule he resolved, "in the strength of the Lord to eschew and avoid employment under Cromwell." He was summoned to London to treat with the Commonwealth for a Union of the two Kingdoms, and repeated offers were made to him by Cromwell of important positions in the administration of affairs in Scotland, but contrary to the advice of his most trusted friends, he declined all offers until the death of the Protector, when he went back to his post at the Court of Justice.

In common with other parts of the country, the district of Moray and Nairn felt the beneficial effects of Cromwell's firm administration. His government was not popular, but the people soon learned to respect it. Order was restored, and industry revived. Detachments of the soldiers of the English Commonwealth were stationed at Elgin, Darnaway, and Inverness. Sometimes parties of them were billeted at Nairn and Lethen. The Laird of Cawdor had sufficient influence to procure an order from General Monk exempting Cawdor Castle from occupation by the troops. The officers mixed freely with the people, and sometimes preached to them on Sundays. The Laird of Brodie mentions his sitting up late of nights discussing points of theology and the principles of religious toleration with certain of the major-generals, colonels, and cornets of Cromwell's Ironsides, some of whom "exercised with him"—namely, conducted family worship in his house. Brodie's views were somewhat enlarged by this intercourse, but he still stuck to the Westminster Confession of Faith as the only true system of theology and church polity. General Monk addressed letters to the magistrates of Nairn, and two of these communications have been preserved.

Cromwell built a great citadel at Inverness, the ruins of which, called Cromwell's Fort, still exist. The officers entrusted with the work ruthlessly dismantled the disused Catholic edifices in the district for building materials for it, and in this way the beautiful old abbey of Kinloss was dismantled.   It belonged to the Laird of Lethen, and the local presbytery appointed a deputation to wait upon Lethen to ask him to save the chapter house in which religious ordinances had been conducted since the Reformation.   Lethen replied that it was against his will that these stones of Kinloss were taken away, and he promised to go to Inverness and do his best to preserve the remainder.   He gave £100 towards the new church and half the glebe.   But only fragments of the noble structure were spared.

Once only was the peace of the county broken.   The Earl of Glencairn in 1654 made an expedition into the Highlands in favour of Charles II.   He entered Moray on 10th January, and on the same day despatched letters to Lord Brodie demanding money.   Brodie was in great straits whether to comply or refuse. Happily for him, a party of English troops turned up unexpectedly at Darnaway, and he was safe.   The river Findhorn came down in great flood, and Glencairn on his way to Lethen was unable to cross it.   Lord Brodie found matter for thankfulness in " the Lord's ridding these in Nairnshire out of perplexity."   But it was only a reprieve, not a deliverance, for the Laird of Lethen.   Two days later Glencairn and his forces forded the river, and once more Lethen House was besieged.   The barns wherein were stored the corn for the year were burned, and the houses given to the flames. An illustration of the religious feeling of the times is afforded by the way in which the Brodies were affected by this calamity.   The last day of January was set apart as a solemn day of humiliation, and the various branches of the family met at Lethen.   " They met," says Hugh Miller, " in that dreary season amid the blackened and wasted walls, when every streamlet was swollen into a river, and the winds howled amid the roofless and darkened turrets, but to what intent ?   In the simple language of the Brodie diary it was —' to come under a new, firm, inviolable covenant with God that they should be His and He theirs.' "   The covenants and fasts, the self-introspection and diary-writing of the time, were but outward manifestations of the strong earnest religious spirit that prevailed.

The restoration of Charles II. to the English throne was followed shortly afterwards by the re-enactment of Episcopacy in
Scotland.   Bishoprics were revived, and Presbyterianism, in name
at least, was abolished.   No changes of any consequences were,
however, introduced into the services or the ritual of the churches.
Along with questions as to whether the Prelatic or Presbyterian
form of church government was the more scriptural came the
principle of the spiritual independence of the Church, and the whole
movement turned upon the question, " Is the Church supreme
within its own domain, or is it to be subject in spiritual matters to
the King ? "   The watchword of the evangelical party of the time
was " For Christ's Crown and Covenant."   It happened that the
Presbyterian Church of Scotland had been greatly weakened by
internal divisions some time previous to this.   The General
Assembly, before it was suppressed by Cromwell, had been torn
by two factions—one the Resolutioners and the other the Protesters.   The dispute arose out of what is known as the Duke's
Engagement—all who had taken part in Hamilton's expedition in
favour of Charles I. being regarded by the Protesters as malignants
and unworthy to be admitted to civil office in the country.   The
Baron of Kilravock, who took part at the battle of Auldearn, was
one of those sought to be proscribed for having accompanied
the Duke into England.   Lord Brodie had some sympathy with
the views of the Protesters, but he considered they went too far.
He, however, joined his two uncles, John Brodie of Auldearn and
Joseph Brodie of Forres, Hugh Campbell of Auchindoune, and
some others, at a meeting of the Synod of Moray, in protesting
against the legality of the election of the members of the Assembly
in 1651.   It went no further.   He kept himself aloof from the
Protesters as a party, though in friendly intercourse with Samuel
Rutherford and the other leaders.   But now when Episcopacy was
restored, nine years after the event, Sir Ludovick Gordon, Lord
Brodie, Brodie of Lethen, Patrick Campbell of Boath, Hugh Campbell of Auchindoun, and several others, were suspended by the synod
for their well-nigh forgotten protest.   They were specially exempted from the Act of Indemnification, and heavy fines were
imposed on them.   One of the bailies of Nairn, John Tulloch,

was fined at the same time. This was but the first step in the new persecution. Ministers who did not conform to the new order of things, and receive fresh induction to their charges by the hands of the new bishops, were ejected from their benefices, and forbidden to reside within twenty miles of their churches. The old spirit of independence burned rather low at this time amongst the clergy of Moray and Nairn, and nearly all conformed. It was quite different with the laity. The old Presbyterian families sought to have as little to do as possible with the renegade " curates," as they were called. They despised both the men and their preaching, and they looked upon them as having broken their solemn vows. That was the view taken by the most intelligent people in the district. The Rev. Harry Forbes, minister of Auldearn, after some hesitation gave up his church rather than conform, and retired to Nairn. Poor man, he seemed to be in great straits as regards his worldly circumstances, and all the efforts of Denoon, the burgh officer, and the magistrates were needed to make him pay his merchants' accounts. Mr. James Urquhart, minister of Kinloss, was ejected from his charge for refusing to recognise the bishops, and took up his residence in Penick in the parish of Auldearn. He was connected with the Brodies by marriage.

Nairnshire became the asylum for the exiled Nonconformist ministers of the north. They were a band of able men, and their preaching made a powerful impression, especially in the country districts. The people deserted the parish churches for the ministrations of the Covenanting clergy, and Sabbath after Sabbath meetings were held at some private house or in some sheltered ravine. Besides the ejected minister of Kinloss, there were in this movement Thomas Hogg of Kiltearn, John M'Killican, James Ross, Hugh Anderson of Cromarty, Thomas Urquhart of Essil, Colin M'Culloch of Ardersier, and later on James Fraser of Brea.

It became a question whether it was not sinful to hear the curates, and many absented themselves entirely from the church services. The Government passed Acts against conventicles in house or in field, and it behoved the lairds to be careful how they gave their presence at such meetings. As a rule they abstained from the open-air meetings, but the Nonconformist ministers were received as welcome guests and honoured friends at every house in the district, save at Darnaway Castle, the earl being a sworn enemy to them. The ladies evinced stronger attachment to the cause of religious liberty than even their husbands. The baron of Kilravock was friendly enough, but his wife, the lady of Kilravock, was an enthusiastic supporter of the persecuted ministers. She was a daughter of the laird of Innes, and her religion took the form of charity to the poor and succour to the distressed. Colin, the Tutor of Cawdor, had by this time been removed from this earthly scene, but his son Hugh reigned in his stead, having succeeded as nearest male heir to the Cawdor estates. Like his father, Sir Hugh was a strong Presbyterian, and the harsh treatment of the Earl of Argyll, the head of his race, embittered his feelings against the Government. He retained the hereditary office of sheriff of the county of Nairn, and stretched his powers to the utmost limit to afford protection to the Nonconformists. His wife, Lady Henrietta Stewart, daughter of the third Earl of Moray, still more ardently espoused the cause of the oppressed ministers, and had scruples about hearing prayers by her chaplain because he had been licensed by a bishop. She preferred the hearty services held at Penick by conscientious men to the lifeless devotions of the curates. The Lethen family were on the closest terms of intimacy with the Presbyterian ministers, and Lethen House was one of the centres of hospitality for the refugees. For some time it afforded protection for a distinguished Covenanter from the south—George Pringle of Torwoodlee. He had married the laird of Lethen's only daughter Janet, and according to Wodrow the historian, he was a gentleman of a fine spirit and singularly religious, of a masculine presence and eloquence, " and the representative of a family that had the honour and happiness to be among the first who publicly owned and stood up for our holy Reformation." Wodrow speaks warmly in praise of his wife—" I cannot forbear to mention," he says, " the heroic spirit of his lady, who, in most of all the parts of his trials, gave him an account of their approach, and this not to affright or deter him from suffering for his country's interest, but to arm and prepare him for what he was to undergo. She bore all her difficulties with unexampled serenity and evenness of temper, one evidence of which was, when the harpies of that time came and seized her estate, set her lands and rummaged her house, her only son lay upon her hand despaired of by the physicians and her husband in hazard of a public death for his firm adherence to the good cause, she showed such contentment and acquiescence under all these complicated disasters as is rarely to be found ; and in her darkest night rejoiced in the faith and hope of those days she lived to see after the Revolution. She was a daughter of Brodie of Lethen, in the north of Scotland, a name very well known for a staunch adherence to their country's interest." The lady in her youth had been one of the little garrison at Lethen which stood a twelve weeks' siege by the Marquis of Huntly.

The Hays of Lochloy and Park were ardent Covenanters, and famous religious gatherings were wont to be held at one or other of the places belonging to them—Penick, Park, Inshoch, or Knockoudie. Thomas Hogg married a sister of Hay of Lochloy, and the marriage was celebrated at Inshoch. Lord Brodie, though abstaining personally from joining in the popular gatherings in order not to give his enemies a hold upon him, rejoiced in the movement, and found a warm seconder in his son's young wife, Lady Mary Ker, daughter of the Earl of Lothian, who had sub-scribed the Covenant on the eve of her marriage. Lady Mary had a great dislike to the clergy who had conformed, and a strong admiration for the men who had sacrificed their positions for conscience' sake. Parliament might pass Acts of Parliament ordering every one to attend the parish church, but Lady Mary declined to sit under the ministrations of Mr. William Falconer of Dyke, who had conformed, and went as often as she could to hear Hogg, McKillican, and other outed ministers.

It is not always the most conspicuous figures who do the greatest amount of service in such movements, and in this case a devout woman in humble life, but of superior intelligence and education, who lived at what was called the Bridge-end of Inshoch and sup-ported herself by teaching sewing, was a chief agent in maintaining the struggle for independence in religious matters. Her name was Margaret Collace, and she had the ear of all the good ladies in the county. When Lord Brodie was disposed to compromise matters by going occasionally to the parish church, she reminded him that in matters of principle no compromise is admissible. Lilias Dunbar also took an active part in connection with this movement. She was a ward of Sir Hugh Campbell, and had been brought up by Lady Duffus. Coming under the preaching of Thomas Hogg she was led to take a deep interest in spiritual matters. Her marriage with young Campbell of Torrich, who was also a relative of the Cawdor family, being descended from the fifth son of Sir John and Lady Muriel, brought them into collision with the civil power. They had been married by a Nonconformist minister—an unpardonable offence in the eyes of the rulers of the time.

If justice could be done to all those who suffered for the cause of religious liberty, the name of Alexander Dunbar, the young schoolmaster of Auldearn, would be placed in the forefront. He was a most zealous Covenanter, and enjoyed the respect of Lord Brodie and others. He had been for a time tutor at Kilravock, and having decided to enter the ministry he took up his abode at Brodie Castle, and served as chaplain there for several years. He was ultimately licensed, but when the dark days of cruel persecution came the young teacher was sent a prisoner to the Bass Rock.

Up to this time somewhat considerable liberty had been enjoyed, and fines and warnings were the only weapons wielded; but an event happened which drew down the ire of the ruling powers. Professor Macdonald, in his " Covenanters of Moray and Ross," thus describes a memorable scene—" Standing at the door of the Free Church manse of Auldearn and looking south, you have before you the steep gorse-covered side of the Hill of the Arr. The rugged slope is furrowed by several torrent courses. One of these, somewhat deeper and wider than the others, with a mass of gray boulder shutting it in at the lower end, you observe above the farmhouse of Dalmore. This ravine is still known as Hogg's Strype. To this sheltered hollow Hogg retired with the congregation, which had grown too large for the dwelling and barns of Knockoudie. There for many a Sabbath, with the granite boulder as his pulpit, and the blue sky as his canopy, he preached the Word with power. This was defying the Act against conventicles with a witness; for the Act was peculiarly stringent with respect to meetings in the fields. But the outed minister of Kiltearn determined to take a still bolder step. Why should the flock that gathered around him be for years denied the privilege of communicating with their Lord, and with one another, in the Sacrament of the Supper ? The Strype became the scene of one of the most solemn of those open-air celebrations of the Supper, once so common, but now confined to the Gaelic-speaking districts of the north. A considerable number of the devout from a wide circuit of country—some all the way from Easter Ross—joined in the sacred ordinance. The occasion was marked by signal tokens of the Lord's presence, and ' the communicants,' we are told, ' returned to their habitations with joy unspeakable.' "

Soon afterwards Thomas Hogg, M'Killican, and Thomas Urquhart of Essil, were apprehended and thrown into prison in Forres, but through influence they were liberated after a few months' confinement. Nothing daunted, they proceeded to assert their right to administer religious ordinances, and formed themselves into a presbytery, which came to be known as the Field Presbytery of Moray. Young Fraser of Brea, a distinguished theologian and scholar, and Robert Gillespie, a son of the leader of the Scottish Commissioners at the famous Westminster Assembly, received ordination at their hands either at Inshoch or the Park. This was an assertion of independence which the Church Courts could not brook, and the machinery of the law was set in motion to stamp out the ecclesiastical rebellion. Troopers were sent into the district to put down " conventicles," as they were called ; proclamation was made at the market cross and kirk doors forbidding all persons to hold intercourse with the " rebels " ; and the Nonconformist ministers were ultimately hunted down. Thomas Hogg, James Fraser of Brea, M'Killican, and others were sent to the Bass, where they were kept in confinement for several years. Liberated for a short time, they were again imprisoned—some in Blackness castle, others banished the country.

The Test—a repudiation of the Covenant and an acknowledgment of the King as the sole head of the Church—was ordered to be rigorously enforced in Moray and Nairn. Hugh Rose, the minister of Nairn, who had up to this retained his benefice, without declaring himself, was induced to sign it and undergo fresh induction at the hands of the Bishop of Moray. The minister of Auldearn, John Cumming, had the courage to repudiate it, though he held office under the bishop for some years, and retired from his charge. Seven of his fellow-ministers in the Diocese or Synod of Moray followed suit. The first Bishop of Moray under the new Episcopal regime had been Murdoch Mackenzie, who was intensely disliked for his tyranny. He was succeeded by a man of a different stamp—Colin Falconer of Downduff. Colin was a descendant of the family of Falconer of Lethen and Hawkertown. When the old family took its departure from the district, a branch stayed on at the small property of Downduff, touching Lethen lands on the banks of the Findhorn. Bishop Colin Falconer was of an eminently conciliatory disposition, but had often perforce to act an unpopular part in the troubles of the times. The two subsequent bishops were Nairnshire men—the one, strangely enough, descended of the strong Presbyterian family of Hay of Park, the other of the Roses of Insch, a branch of the Roses of Kilravock.

On the last day of the year 1680 the Nairn Town Council met in the Tolbooth. The business was the subscribing of the Test. The minute of the proceedings records that—" The magistrates of the said burgh having seriously taken to their consideration the Act of Parliament dated the last day of August last bypast, intituled an Act anent Religion and the Test, and also having seriously considered the oath and bond thereto subjoined, they solemnly did take and subscribe the same, and ordained the principal by them subscribed to be recorded in the Burrow Court books of the said burgh, and a real and authentic extract thereof to be extracted under the hand of the Clerk of Court, and to be reported to his Majesty's Privy Council betwixt and the first day of March next to come, and that conforme to the tenor and contents of the said Act of Parliament." It is signed by John Rose, provost ; J. Rose, bailie ; Hugh Rose, bailie ; J. Rose, bailie ; Isat Angus, bailie ; George Household, treasurer ; William Rose, clerk ; Thomas M'Phaill, fiscal ; J. Rose, councillor ; William Tulloch ;

Alex. Ore, councillor; Hugh Wilson, councillor; A. L. R., councillor.

A grave crisis arose. The Government appointed a commission consisting of the Earls of Kintore and Errol, and Sir George Munro, to try all persons guilty of attending "conventicles" and entertaining vagrant preachers. The commissioners on their arrival at Elgin erected a gallows, and proceeded to summon some two hundred and fifty suspected delinquents. These belonged to every class of society. Lord Brodie was dead by this time, but his son James, now the Laird of Brodie, was more averse even than his father had been to "keeping his own parish church." He was examined before the commission. So was Lady Mary Ker, his wife, who confessed to "three years withdrawing and more," after old Brodie's death. The Laird of Brodie was fined £24,000 Scots. The first Laird of Lethen died in 1672, but his son had followed in his father's footsteps as regards the church. Two years previously Hugh Campbell of Cawdor, as Sheriff of Nairn, was ordered by the Privy Council to summon Lethen before him at the court of Nairn. Sir Hugh, with characteristic kindness, went up to Lethen and took his deposition there, making his report as mild as he possibly could. The commission now fined him for his own and his wife's misdeeds in hearing vagrant preachers in his own house and not keeping the kirk, in the sum of £40,000 Scots. His son-in-law, Ludovick Grant of Grant, was fined £42,000, his wife (Lethen's daughter) having been a chief offender in this matter. Lethen's brother, David Brodie of Pitgavenie, was fined £18,722, and imprisoned in Blackness. Another brother, James Brodie of Kinloss, was fined 200 merks Scots. His cousin, Francis Brodie of Milton, was fined £10,000, and Francis Brodie of Windiehills, 5,000 merks. Mr. Campbell of Torrich fled to the north of Ireland, and experienced great kindness from the Presbyterians there. His wife, Lilias Dunbar, stood her trial before the commission and refused to promise "to keep the kirk" in future, and she was sentenced to be banished the country. John Montford, described as chamberlain to Hay of Park, refusing to keep the kirk, was sentenced to be imprisoned in the prison of Elgin. A sepulchral monument with Latin inscription in the Auldearn churchyard to

John Montford, notary public, his wife, Magdalene Matthew, and their children Alexander, Elizabeth, Mary, Jane, Margaret, and Hugh Montford, probably relates to the chamberlain of Park, who was thus dealt with. One John Montford was a burgess in Nairn in 1715.

The commission's work was cut short by the intelligence of the King's death, and some of their sentences were never carried out. The fines, however, were extorted in the case of the Lairds of Brodie and Lethen. This brought the family of Lethen to the verge of ruin. Lethen was denounced rebel in 1687, and the official receivers proceeded to lead an adjudication of the estate. Poor Lethen died in the following year, and was spared the humiliation of witnessing his home on the sweet burnside of Lethen in the possession of strangers. He left no son, and his brother David of Pitgavenie succeeded to the estate, and after some years got the fine mitigated and the property relieved. Lethen's daughter Janet, who had married Ludovick Grant of Freuchie, became mother of Sir James Grant of Grant, and one of her daughters became wife of Simon, Lord Lovat. Francis William, 10th Earl of Seafield, and James, 5th Earl of Fife, were both great-great-grandsons of this Janet Brodie, Lady Grant.

Lord Brodie's position has already been referred to. The " Diary " he wrote presents only the subjective side of his religious character. When he made a visit to the south he was welcomed in the best society of the time. In 1654 he was presented with the freedom of the City of Glasgow. In 1661 he went on a mission to London about his own and his neighbours' private affairs, and experienced all the bitterness and disappointment of a suppliant at court. He was specially concerned in getting the Argyll estates restored to Lord Lorne. There he met Sharp and Leighton and had frequent interviews with the Earls of Lauderdale, Middleton, Glencairn, and other high officers of State. He was permitted an interview with King Charles II., and kissed hands, but very little success attended his stay at court, which extended over ten months. He died on 17th April, 1680. His son James continues the " Diary," and exhibits the same disposition and character as his father. He died in 1708, two days after his wife,

Lady Mary Ker, and their bodies were borne to the family tomb in one carriage—" they were lovely and pleasant in their lives, and in their death they were not divided." They had nine daughters, but no son, and the Brodie estates went to George Brodie of Asliesk, who was both nephew and son-in-law to the deceased laird.

Old Bailie Tulloch of Nairn appears to have been an interesting character. He was a wealthy merchant, and the hand of his daughter was sought for by more than one suitor on the look-out for a rich wife. The chief of the Tulloch family in Moray was Tulloch of Tanachie (now called Invererne), and with the view doubtless of the old merchant's gear helping to maintain the decaying glories of the ancient house, young Tanachie made a desperate effort to secure the prize. The old bailie was a Covenanter, while the Tanachie Tullochs were on the other side in Church and State politics, and rather suspected of leanings to Popery. On the 11th of June, 1684, old Tanachie and his son John, and the scapegrace Lord Doune, son of Lord Moray, after a bout of drinking, drove into Nairn during the night time and carried off the young lady. She was engaged, it appears, to Bishop Colin Falconer's son, and the Laird of Brodie says there was a great talk in the country about the abduction. The Tullochs of Tanachie were compelled to restore the lady to her father's house. On the hereditary Sheriff of Moray declining the Test, Lord Doune had been made Sheriff Principal, and he appointed Tulloch of Tanachie his deputy—a precious pair of sheriffs !

The Revolution Settlement put an end to the persecution, and the outed ministers who survived were restored to their charges. Mr. Alexander Dunbar was liberated from the prison of the Bass, and became minister of Auldearn. Mr. James Urquhart went back to his flock at Kinloss. Thomas Hogg returned to Kiltearn. Fraser of Brea settled at Culross, his only daughter and heiress marrying the laird of Kilravock.

The struggle had lasted twenty-eight years. The principles contended for by the Covenanters had triumphed, and once more were embodied in the constitution of the Church of Scotland. The church had regained its independence.

CHAPTER XIII

FROM THE REVOLUTION TO THE RISING OF 1715

THE great sand-drift which overwhelmed the estate of Culbin took place in the autumn of the year 1694. Previous to this, however, it is recorded that storms and tempests of unusual violence had occurred, the sea making encroachments on the land and carrying away houses. Great floods in the rivers are also mentioned. On 11th April, in the year 1663, Lord Brodie records, " I heard that Nairn was in danger to be quite lost by the sand and by the water." The report was exaggerated, but no doubt circumstances of exceptional severity had occurred to give rise to it. The grand bridge erected by Clava was injured by the flood, and was not repaired until 1669. As a precaution against sand-drift, the Town Council of Nairn issued about this time orders forbidding any one cutting turf at the seaside. The order was from time to time renewed, showing that the sand-drift had become a source of trouble and alarm. The sea in its inroads had cut into the flat shore, stripping it of its covering of turf, and leaving large areas of sand exposed to the action of the wind. The waves had also cast up and deposited large quantities of sand along the margin of the beach, and the westerly wind, catching up the sand, sent it in streams over the arable land for some distance inland, forming in some places isolated hills and in other places continuous ranges of mounds. The great sand-drift can be traced from Ardersier to Nairn, and thence from the mouth of the river Nairn to the mouth of the Findhorn. Two immense hills of blown sand formed on the flat marsh land below Mavistown, and from these the sand

spread eastward in a desolating stream. On reaching the cultivated land of Culbin it overran the fields and pastures. According to tradition, the estate with its mansion-house, orchard, farm
houses, and biggings was overwhelmed in one night of awful drift.
The truth appears to be that one terrible storm completed the work
of destruction which had been going on gradually for some years
before. It was in the autumn of 1694 that these lands were
finally overwhelmed. The storm came suddenly and with short
warning. The drift, like a mighty river, came on steadily and
ruthlessly, grasping field after field, and burying everything in a
tomb of sand. Whatever obstructed its progress became the
nucleus of a sand mound. In terrible gusts the wind carried the
sand amongst the dwelling-houses, sparing neither the hut of the
cottar nor the mansion of the laird. The splendid orchard, the
beautiful lawn, all shared the same fate. The people fled for their
lives, and on returning next morning when the wind had subsided,
were met with nothing but a sea of sand. Not a vestige, not a
trace of their houses was to be seen. They lay buried under the
avalanche.

The desolating and destructive effects of the sand-drift, notwithstanding recent efforts made to recover portions of the land
by planting and other means, remain visible to this day, and the
marks of the ploughshare where the fields were cultivated, and are
now from time to time exposed, can still be seen. The sand
occupies an area of three thousand six hundred acres by actual
measurement, extending four or five miles along the shore and two
miles from the sea inland. The rental of the estate in the year
1694, before its destruction, was £2720 Scots, 640 bolls wheat,
640 bolls bear, 640 bolls oats, and 640 bolls oatmeal besides salmon
fishings. The estate was divided into sixteen farms, apparently of
uniform size. Some of the farms bore such names as Dalpottie,
Laik, Sandifield, Culbin, Middlebin, Earnhill, etc. An old
formula in the district for wishing one to go to a remote region
was " Gang to Dalpottie ! " When the estate was thus overwhelmed, Alexander Kinnaird was in possession. His grandfather,
Walter Kinnaird, received a charter from Charles I. in 1642, and
Thomas, his father, was served heir in 1677. The family had

been all along of good standing. Thomas Kinnaird was married to Anna Rose, widow of Hugh Rose of Kilravock. She was a sister of Lord Forbes, and had been brought up with her father in Germany, he having been an officer in the Swedish Army. Alexander Kinnaird applied to the Scottish Parliament to be relieved of the payment of cess or land tax, setting forth " that the best three parts of his estate of Culbin, by an inevitable fatality, were quite ruined and destroyed, occasioned by vast heaps of sand which had over-blown the same, so that there was not a vestige to be seen of the manor place of Culbin, yards, orchards, and mains thereof, and which within these twenty years were as considerable as many in the county of Moray," while the small area which yet remained uncovered was exposed to the like hazard with the sand daily gaining ground thereon. Kinnaird pleaded exemption on the ground that such an occurrence had no parallel in Scotland. All the Government appears to have done was to pass an Act with special reference to the circumstances which had occurred, prohibiting the pulling or cutting of bent grass, to which cause the Act assigns the sand-drift. The family had been in embarrassed circumstances previous to the loss of their lands, and James, Laird of Brodie, who, however, was engaged in a lawsuit with them, gives a very bad account of their goings-on. The people of the district regarded so singular an occurrence as a judgment. The place was sold to the Duffs, was acquired afterwards by the Grants, and now belongs to Grant of Glenmorriston. The last Kinnaird, with the few hundred pounds he got from the sale, embarked in the Darien Expedition, and perished among the adventurers on the Isthmus. His widow lived to an advanced age, and her son by Kinnaird, through the good offices of a kinsman of Kilravock, got a commission in the army, rose to the rank of Major, and died unmarried, the old family thus coming to an end with the destruction of their estate.

Sir Hugh Campbell of Cawdor was one of the notable men of the period in which he lived. He set himself to redeem the diminished fortunes of his house, and by great prudence, sagacity, and energy succeeded in a great measure, in spite of the drain of that costly acquisition Islay. Sir Hugh loved his home at Cawdor, and spent money freely in making additions to the castle and in planting and laying out the grounds. The Cawdor Castle of the present day, with only some trifling changes, is the castle as it came from Sir Hugh's hands. He liked to hear the sound of the mason's hammer and to see the foresters at work. He took the farm of Auchindoune into his own hands, and with the assistance of his neighbours and tenants, had it ploughed and sown, every rig of it, for the first time. He also added considerably to the estate. He purchased Meikle Urchany and Lynemore from the Hays, and Moyness and Crachies from James Grant of Moyness; while he re-acquired Fleenasmore from the Campbells of Moy. Blackhills, Leylands, and Boghole also came into the titles of Cawdor in Sir Hugh's time, although a good many wadsets still remained unredeemed over these and other portions of the estates. Lady Henrietta Stewart, his wife, procured for her state-bedroom, from the looms of Arras, tapestry with scriptural scenes, namely, events in the life of Noah and Abraham, the destruction of the Cities of the Plain, and the passage of the Red Sea. These acquisitions cost (including freight from Flanders to Leith and thence to Findhorn) £483 7s. 6d. The tapestry still remains in the state-bedroom.

Sir Hugh was a strict Presbyterian, and held strong views in favour of the repetition of the Lord's Prayer in the services of the Church. He wrote a book on the subject, and entered into a warm controversy with the learned divines of the time. On being taunted with lukewarmness, he was able to say—" Since ever I came to the age of a man I made it my business to do every honest minister of the Gospel all the good offices and service that was in my power, as I could find occasion; and God honoured me so much that I relieved many honest ministers out of prison, kept more from trouble, and was an instrument to save the lives of several who were pious, eminently pious and knowing beyond many of their brethren, such as Mr. William Guthrie, Mr. William Veitch, and several others; and I can say I spared neither my pains nor what credit I had with any who governed the State, nor my fortune nor my purse. I ventured these and my office and life too, to save honest people, who walked according to their light without flying to extremities and taking arms against the King and

Government; so that all the time from 1662 to the late Revolution there was not one man paid a fine in the shire of Nairn except two or three."

Sir Hugh had also a project for establishing a system of free education. " I hope you will not discourage me and the people," he wrote to a member of Presbytery, " from the great and good design I have still of settling eight or ten schools, which shall be so placed that all the poor people in the parish shall have their children taught to read the Bible without the least expense, and even the tenants have their children taught for very little. I have three of the schools set up already, and will settle the rest as soon as I can get masters or mistresses to teach them."

Sir Hugh was much troubled by the depredations of the Highland reivers. Writing to the laird of Park, who was at Edinburgh in June, 1691, Sir Hugh gives a lively picture of the times in Nairnshire. He had been at Inshoch, tending a daughter of Park's who had been taken seriously ill with sore throat, and he continues —" Just upon the back of this there came two or three parties of Hielanders, one of them carried away a great many cattle out of Aitnoch, and carried away above ane hundred head of cattle. The party was strong, betwixt fifty and three score. The people were secure and without fear, hearing there was four and five hundred of them in Ross whom Sir James Leslie and Balnagown were pursuing; in short, they were surprised and the cattle were carried into Lochaber. The next party fell upon my lands in the muir and braes of Altherg, when I was at Inshoch, and carried such cattle as they found right away—about thirty head and four piece of horse. The third party fell upon my lands of Boath, but then I was at home, and sent my son Archie and the lightest lads I had after them. They were overtaken in the braes of Stratherrick and brought back. One of their boys was likewise caught and brought prisoner. And just as this letter is a-writing I have advertisement from several friends of the brae of Strathnairn that there is a party of five or six score Lochaber men passed by them, who is like may make an onset this night somewhere in our braes. If we knew where, we would endeavour to buckle a touch with them. However, I am just about convening the county, and will do what we can to find them out." His neighbour Kilravock bought off the reivers by paying blackmail.

According to the traditional stories of the district, Sir Hugh had a notorious cattle reiver among his own tenants—one Callum Beg. Sir Walter Scott in his novel of Waverley introduces " Callum Beg " as the page of Fergus M'Ivor, but the Nairnshire Callum Beg was a totally different sort of character. He dwelt in a remote part of Nairnshire known as the Streens, on the north bank of the Findhorn. Callum Beg's house was situated a few hundred yards above the present suspension bridge at Banchor. The spot is very wild and rugged, and, when the river is in flood, the noise of the rushing water sounds like thunder. Such was the scene in which the dauntless spirit of Callum Beg was nursed, and it was here that he devised his deeds of robbery, which made his name the terror of the district. From his upland retreat he made periodical descents on the lowlands, uplifting the very pick of the cattle. There appears to have been some kind of fascination in the character of the bold robber. He was a giant in strength, and could carry a weight of booty slung over his shoulders which would crush any ordinary man. His immediate neighbours always spoke of him as that " honest man Callum Beg ! " Perhaps in their case it may be accounted for by the fact that Callum never " killed a beast " but he shared it with his friends. He was a great favourite of the laird of Cawdor, who got him out of many a scrape. As a retainer, he attended his lordship on his hunting expeditions on the moors, and enjoyed his closest friendship. On one occasion the laird was greatly annoyed, a day or two before setting out for a week's stay at the Streens, at the loss of the prime bullock of his herd at Cawdor Castle. It had been stolen over-night, and the thief had not been discovered. Each day as the laird sat down to lunch with Callum he began to lament the loss of the " fine mert " that had been stolen. At last Callum could stand it no longer. " Laird ! " said Callum, " ye need na mak' sae much din about it, for ye have had your ain share of the beast ! " Callum had been dining the laird off his stolen bullock.

Callum came down to pay his rent one day, and the laird said that as the night was so stormy he had better remain and share the bed with the grieve. During the night Callum got up, selected a nice fat mert, drove the beast across the hills to Banchor, and was back again before the grieve awoke. Next day there was a great noise about the beast that had been stolen, but the grieve would not allow any one to hint a suspicion that it had been taken by " that honest man Callum Beg ! "

Callum Beg often turned up at the cattle markets, and was regarded with a suspicious eye. One day he went to Forres market and spied a nice little cow. He could easily " lift " the cow, but owing to a marked peculiarity, he was afraid of detection. The cow in fact wanted the tail. Callum, however, was equal to the occasion. Next morning in broad daylight he was seen driving a cow from Forres towards Nairn. At the Findhorn bridge he was met by the owner of the lost cow. " That's my beast ! " exclaimed the man. " Had your beast a tail like that ? " asked Callum. The poor man had to admit that his little cow was minus a tail. So Callum drove off in triumph. He had cut off the tail of another animal during the night and had fastened it on to the crofter's cow.

The story is told how Callum was one day brought before the laird, having been caught with stolen property in his possession, namely, a good fat sheep. Having a kindness for Callum, notwithstanding his evil doings, the laird did not know well how to act. At length he ordered the culprit and the sheep to be put into the " donjon keep " of the castle, at the same time giving directions that the people who lodged the complaint should be amply regaled with bread and ale. While the latter were indulging in this repast, the laird slipt out and enquired of Callum if he had a good knife. Being answered in the affirmative—" then," said he, " I shall send your customers for your wedder." Callum took the hint and killed the sheep. He cut it into small morsels and threw the whole out of an aperture in the dungeon, constructed rather for air than for light, at the outside of which there was a pack of hounds, by whom the sheep was speedily devoured. Time having been allowed for the accomplishment of this feat, the laird took his chair of state, and summoned that " obdurate thief," Callum Beg, into his presence together with the stolen property and the witnesses. The door of the cell was forthwith opened and Callum brought out, but not a vestige of the sheep could be found.   Upon this hint the justice spake, charging the witnesses with conspiring against that honest man Callum Beg, and accordingly set the prisoner free.

Callum, however, was not always so fortunate.   On one occasion he fell into the hands of the laird of Kilravock, and was committed to durance vile.   His natural chief, the Thane of Cawdor, hearing of the jeopardy in which Callum was placed, repaired to the mansion of his friend on the first day of the new year, and seated himself on the great stair in front of the castle.   The usual greetings having passed, the Laird of Cawdor was invited into the house ; but he replied that he had a new-year's gift to ask, and unless it were granted he would not enter the house or partake of his neighbour's hospitality.   " I shall grant you every favour in my power," replied Kilravock, " but the life of Callum Beg."   " That," rejoined the other, " is the very request I came to make, and, being denied, it is unnecessary for me to stay."   The laird accordingly departed, and Callum Beg was—hanged.   In the nineteenth century a skeleton was dug up in the district with a rope round its neck, which the country people identified as the body of Callum Beg.

Sir Hugh Campbell took a keen interest in public affairs, and in 1705, when the question of the union of the two kingdoms of Scotland and England was being discussed, Sir Hugh in a letter to Hugh Rose of Kilravock, who represented the county of Nairn in the Scottish Parliament, expressed his strong disapproval of the proposed incorporating union.   " I received," he writes, " a packet of prints for which I thank you.   According as you desired, I have called for all the freeholders in the shire that they might advise you in the matter of the union.   I told you my thoughts of it before you went south, in short, all of us are of the same mind, and although we be very desirous to live in love and friendship with the rich and wise and good people of England, yet we desire not to be incorporated into one kingdom with them, since we are sensible that cannot be without loss of honour and interest.   We have had the honour of being a kingdom and a free people governed by our own laws for more than two thousand years.   We have had a hundred and eleven kings before our present gracious Queen, whom God long preserve, an honour which few kingdoms in

Christendom can pretend to, and for point of interest it's evident
and capable of a full demonstration, that poverty and being under-
valued by all nations in the world, even by the English themselves,
would be a consequence of an incorporated union, but a federal
union and free trade would certainly be an advantage, and it's a
wonder that a free trade was not established betwixt them when
we came first to be under the same king." He adds—" I shall not
enlarge, only assure you that I know not a man in this or Inverness-
shire who is for the incorporate union, and if any had been at the
pains you might have got an address against it subscribed by every
man that can write his name."

The laird of Kilravock was of the same mind as his correspondent, and was one of the eighty-two members who voted
against incorporating the two kingdoms into one. He joined the
party favourable to a federal union. In taking this stand, however,
he had no sympathy with the Jacobites who wished to bring back
the Stewart dynasty to the throne. When the union was concluded
Kilravock was named by the Parliament one of the commissioners
to represent Scotland in the first Parliament of Great Britain.

Sir Hugh Campbell was still alive when the Jacobite Rising of
1715 occurred. His eldest son, Sir Alexander, had married
Elizabeth Lort, the heiress of Stackpole Court, Pembrokeshire,
and thus formed the first connection of the Campbells of Cawdor
with Wales. Sir Alexander predeceased his father, and his eldest
son Gilbert dying young, the second son, John, became heir. The
old laird appears to have entertained a strong affection for another
grandson, Duncan Campbell, son of Sir Archibald of Clunas.
This Duncan Campbell mixed a good deal in Jacobite society, and
came fresh from a visit he had paid to the Earl of Breadalbane to
see his grandfather, Sir Hugh, at Cawdor. Lord Breadalbane,
representing a younger branch of the Campbells, contrary to the
traditions of the family, separated himself from his chief, the Earl
of Argyll, who, as of yore, adhered to the Protestant succession.
The old Thane of Cawdor received overtures to join in the proposed rebellion and acceded. The Earl of Mar issued a proclamation to the effect that " our rightful and natural King, James
the VIII., by the grace of God (who is now coming to relieve us

of our oppression) having been pleased to instrust me with the direction of his affairs and the command of his forces in this his ancient kingdom, therefore let all his faithful and loving subjects and lovers of their country, with all possible speed put themselves into arms." He wrote to the Laird of Calder as a sympathiser, requesting him in His Majesty's name, to raise his men, friends, and following, with their best arms, and to order his grandchild, Duncan Campbell, younger of Clunas, to march his men in the shires of Inverness, Moray, and Nairn, to join the Mackenzies and Macphersons and the King's forces, who were ordered to march through Perthshire towards Stirling.

Sir Hugh entertained the design, and granted the following mandate to his loving grandchild, Duncan Campbell, younger of Clunas—"Since I am not able to take the field myself, these are therefore empowering you to do everything which I might do myself, and that with all possible expedition." Four days later (September 23) he renewed his commands to the young man, and authorised him to draw out his whole following in his north country estate, with their best clothes and arms, and three days' provisions, in order to be in readiness to march with all expedition to the King's standard, and if possible to encamp at Auldearn the following night. There seems to be little doubt but that the Cawdor tenants, with Duncan of Clunas at their head, joined the "Standard on the Braes of Mar." Old Sir Hugh's conduct in this matter is inexplicable. His son, Sir Archibald of Clunas, was a strong supporter of the House of Hanover, and all the laird's former principles and actions would have rendered any suspicion of disloyalty on his part improbable. Perhaps his feeling against the union of the two kingdoms, and the influence of his favourite grandson, may have perverted his judgment.

Another Nairnshire laird, Hugh Rose of Clava, was also induced to join the rising. His connection by marriage with the Earl Marischal accounts for his action. The Roses of Clava had considerable means, but no great following. Clava's joining the Jacobite party must have been a sudden resolve, as on 14th February of the same year he was appointed the delegate of the Nairn Town Council to vote at Fortrose for a member of Parliament to represent the

Inverness burghs, and only a supposed loyalist would have been chosen.

A letter preserved amongst the State Papers from " A Gentleman in Moray " (who does not sign his name) to Captain John Brodie at Edinburgh, gives the following account of the state of the district :—" Sir, Knowing that you are a friend of Brodie's and that he cannot write himself, being defending his own house, I must acquaint you in the first place my Lord Huntly sent him a civil letter demanding his horse and arms, and that the lairds of Alter and Tannachy Tulloch would give receipt therefore, to return the same within six months, or the highest value for them in case they were not returned within the six months. But in case of his refusal, under the highest threats of military execution, as that of battering down his house, razeing his tenents, burning their cornes, and killing their persons. Brodie returned ane very civil answer, that he had no arms but those were necessary for preserving his family in such a time of confusion, and horses only sufficient for himself and servants, and therefore begged to be excused. Upon which he got a second letter from my Lord Huntly, assuring him of protection to himself, family, and tenents provided he would comply with his first demands of surrendering his horses, arms, and ammunition, which occasioned Brodie to return ane other answer to his lordship, importing that he had already laid his account with the worst, and therefore resolved rather to suffer in so good a cause than to be ane abettor or ane assister any manner of way to the rebels, whereupon Huntly searched all the country over for cannon, but found none but those of two pounders, or three at most, and for want of big cannon, notwithstanding that his lordship had gathered all the cannon ball he found in the country, and of his having received a sudden message from the Earl of Mar to join him, he gave over the project. Notwithstanding likewise that they had ane engineer who had viewed the house, his lordship used all the stratagems imaginable to bring Brodie to a complyance by sending the good lairds of Dunbar of Grange, Dipple, Tannachy, and Altyre to converse with him, thinking to frighten him into his Lo'p. measures by reason of his youth. He admitted all of them to commune with him but Alter, and notwithstanding of all their amusing stories and threats, he stood firm and still does to his great applause in this country. Tho', on the other hand, to their disgrace, most of the gentlemen in Moray have surrendered their horse and arms—such as the lairds of Innes, Dunbar of Thunderton, Pitgavenie, Mackintosh of Blervy, and many more. But the garrisoned houses, such as Culloden, Kilraick, and Brodie give out that they'll defend them to the utmost of their power. Huntly is gone with all his vassals and followers, which are a great many, to join Mar, and his retinue of gentlemen from this country are Sir Robert Gordon, Cluny, his curator, Alter, Sir Thomas Calder, Tannachy, Innes, and Dunkinty, and with a troup of horse from Elgin, and this besyd many less conspicuous people." The plucky young Laird of Brodie was James, son of George Brodie of Asliesk, who was served heir to his father in the Brodie estate only a few months before this occurrence. He afterwards sat in Parliament for the county of Elgin.

At the outset of the troubles in 1715, the Baron of Kilravock took care to have his castle of Kilravock well fortified. Bands of Highlanders were roving up and down the country, burning houses and pillaging right and left. They knew better than to attack the castle, but as Kilravock had a " town house " in Nairn, there was some apprehension lest the Highlanders should seek revenge on him by attacking and burning the town of Nairn. Kilravock the younger was provost of Nairn at the time, and the magistrates and burgesses, like their provost, were loyal to the House of Hanover, and hostile to the Stewarts. As early as 26th August of the previous year (1714) there was a meeting of the Town Council, when a letter was presented from the Lords of Justiciary and Exchequer, conveying the intelligence of the serious illness of Queen Anne, and an order from the Privy Council requiring the authorities to look to the defences of the place, and prevent any disturbance of the public peace within their jurisdiction. In obedience to this command, a night-guard of selected burgesses was formed, and a council of war established to see to the arms and ammunition being in readiness. One of the magistrates at the time was James Falconer of Blackhills, and in the absence of the chief magistrate on affairs of state, the duties of local leader were undertaken by him, and he proved equal to the occasion.

In the early part of the year 1715 there was a good deal of political excitement, and as summer advanced the state of the country became once more alarming. On 2nd August the magistrates ordained by tuck of drum a muster of the whole inhabitants in order to know the strength of the place and how they were armed. Arthur Rose (a son of the Lady of Culbin by her first husband), who had been a foreign trader and had just got back from servitude amongst the Turks—a hero of strange adventures —was there in his Turkish dress, stimulating the martial ardour of the townsmen. The old list of captains of the guard was revised, and the night-watch of twenty was once more set, each captain being responsible for his twenty men. Every " armedless " burgess (to quote the curious expression of the records) was to be fined £5. It appears there was a scarcity of powder and lead, and a committee was authorised to " search and secure " all the ammunition in the burgh and to divide it amongst the respective captains of companies.

On 12th September news reached Nairn of the Rising and of the town of Inverness, with its two garrisons, being in the hands of the rebels. " There being fears that this place " (that is Nairn) " may be assaulted "—so runs the official record of the day— " the Council appoint the guard to be punctually kept by all the respective captains under the highest peril, and one of the guards to be despatched express to Kilravock for further intelligence, and to learn if those Highlanders be like to come further east ! " Such is the quaint entry in the Council's records.

If the " guardsman " from the town of Nairn happened to be at Kilravock on a certain morning about that time, he would see a strange trio arriving. There was much company at Kilravock. The castle and town of Inverness, it was too true, were in the hands of the Highlanders, and Mackenzie of Coul, with his clansmen held the castle for " James VIII." The Stewart flag floated from the bartizan of the Tolbooth, and the great body of the inhabitants had declared for the Stewarts. The leading loyalists in the country had assembled at Kilravock to concert measures, when the strange

trio referred to presented themselves at the castle door. The one
was recognised as Duncan Forbes of Culloden, the Lord Advocate,
a welcome guest; but who were the two others? Simon, Lord
Lovat, was one, and his erratic kinsman Major Fraser—" Major
Cracks," he was afterwards nicknamed by old Lovat—was the
other. The two worthies had just come from France—Lovat
disguised as the Major's servant.

At Leith they had foregathered with Duncan Forbes of Culloden, and taking passage in a small boat, had landed at Fraserburgh.
An out-of-the-way place surely, but they were not an hour at the
inn before they were nearly detected by Lord Saltoun. Lovat in
his young days had all but hanged Lord Saltoun's father—he had
erected the gallows for the purpose—and had now no wish to meet
his son. The Major, however, was equal to the occasion. While
Lovat kept to his room above, the Major met Lord Saltoun in the
inn parlour below—told him they were Highland drovers returning
from the southern markets—drank no end of drams with his lordship. In the end, on the faith of the Major's lies and under the
influence of much whisky, Saltoun provided horses to carry
them the rest of the journey.   .

And here they were on Saltoun's Portsoy nags at Kilravock.
The queerest of mortals, Major Fraser was devoted to Lovat, and
his object in bringing him home was to set him up as chief of
the Frasers, and to lead them to join the standard, not of the
Chevalier but of the King. Lovat was really a Catholic and a
Jacobite, but he fell in with the Major's plan to take the Protestant
and Hanoverian side, as it promised to turn out for his immediate
advantage. It must have been a merry party, but Major Fraser
had other work still to do. Kilravock told Lovat that some 300
of the Frasers in Stratherrick were waiting for the word of their
chief to come down to join them. On hearing this, the Major
started off that same night—a wild night it was—and by daylight
he was addressing his clansmen. " But," asked the Frasers, " has
the Government given Lord Lovat a pardon?" " To be sure,"
said the Major, telling a downright falsehood, " and has promised
him his estates if you join him." Whereupon stoups of whisky
went round to the health of the King, who had given their chief

peace. Next day they went to Culloden, met Kilravock and his 400 men, Culloden with his 200, and the others, numbering 1300 men. And they then marched upon Inverness.

A plan of operations was settled. It was agreed to blockade the town and force the garrison to surrender by starving it, to avoid needless bloodshed. The Frasers invested the town on the north side; Kilravock, Culloden, and the Grants on the east and south sides.

This leisurely proceeding did not suit two parties concerned. Major Fraser whispered to Lovat—" Now is your chance to distinguish yourself, be the first to attack, and you will gain credit with the Government and dispel their suspicions." Lovat saw the advantage, left his position and closed in upon Inverness with his troops. The consequence was that the garrison betook themselves to the Tolbooth.

Arthur Rose was equally impatient. He proposed to seize the garrison now in the Tolbooth by stratagem. He got Rose of Blackhills, now in command of a detachment of the Roses, to give him a party to enter the town during the darkness of night and seize the Tolbooth. The contemporary history states that his guide led him all right until the top of the lower staircase was reached. He then called to the guard to open the door, which they did, and the guide entered, followed by Arthur Rose, with sword and pistol. Just as Arthur was entering, the treacherous guide shouted, " He is an enemy! an enemy!" Bullets whizzed through the passage, Arthur fell back, shot through the body, and the iron door was closed upon him, crushing him against the stone wall. He was carried down by his friends to a house in the town, where he died in a few hours.

Kilravock's anger was roused to the highest pitch at this tragic end of his favourite brother, and he sent a message to the governor that unless he surrendered both garrisons within an hour he would reduce the town to ashes and take the governor dead or alive. The governor, Sir John Mackenzie (who was married to an aunt of Kilravock's), begged for mercy, surrendered the place, and he and his clansmen slunk down to the quay and embarked in boats for the Ross-shire side of the Firth.

Poor Arthur Rose, who met with so untimely an end, had had a most adventurous career. The family historian relates that in a voyage to the Levant, Arthur was taken by Algerine pirates. "He was kept for some time prisoner in Algiers, but upon notice given to the British Consul at Grand Cairo in Egypt, he was purchased from these barbarians, and kept in the consul's own company till he was ransomed in the year 1714." A portrait of him in his Turkish dress is preserved at Kilravock. Arthur is described as a brave resolute man, without fear of danger.

The abortive Rebellion was crushed at Sheriffmuir on the same day as the town of Inverness was taken. A brother of Arthur Rose, Colonel Alexander Rose, who had served under the Duke of Marlborough, distinguished himself on the Hanoverian side at Sheriffmuir, while two cousins, one the son of Archbishop Rose of St. Andrews, and the other of Bishop Rose of Edinburgh, were taken prisoners on the other side.

The day of reckoning with those who had taken up arms against King George speedily arrived. Duncan Campbell of Clunas was banished the country, and for several years resided in Paris. There, prosecuting his studies, he had a brother Hugh, who was a Jacobite. Major Fraser in his search for Lovat had met him, and received much kindness from him. Hugh Rose of Clava surrendered to the Justices of the Peace at Nairn, and through the influence of his kinsman Kilravock, was pardoned. Sir Hugh of Calder would certainly have suffered in his estate, if not in his person, for the part he had taken, but he was prostrated by illness and died on Sunday, 11th March, of the following year. He had reached the age of seventy-seven. One of his last acts was to write a touching letter to his grandson John, his heir, urging him to use all his endeavours, sparing no pains or money, to prevent Mackintosh of Kyllachie, a neighbour, being sent to prison for taking part in the Rising, for a close imprisonment, he says, will certainly destroy him, considering the circumstances of his age and health. Sir Hugh appears to have regretted the Rising, for he speaks of Kyllachie having been prevailed upon by "his children and other worse counsellors to go with a number of his kindred where he went."

The obsequies of Sir Hugh Campbell were observed with great

state. It was a typical Highland funeral. All the great men in the north attended. From Sunday, 11th March, till Thursday, 29th, the body lay in state, and open house was kept at Cawdor Castle. The body was placed in two coffins—the coffins costing £110 13s. 4d. Refreshments were ordered on a large scale. Bailie John Finlay, Forres, supplied brandy to the amount of £40 ; Bailie John Roy in Forres, supplied claret to the value of £25 4s. A still larger account was incurred to James Cuthbert, merchant. It included " 22 pints of brandy at 48s. per pint," 6 dozen pipes and 3 lb. cut tobacco, currants, raisins, cinnamon, and other spices which, with a few etceteras, amounted to £407 8s. 4d. To make sure that there would be enough liquor, a quantity of claret was ordered from Bailie Cattanach of Aberdeen, costing £82 6s., and a local merchant, John Fraser in Clunas, supplied " waters " to the value of £35—probably smuggled whisky. Besides the Clunas waters, home-brewed ale of sixteen bolls and a half of bere was consumed between the date of death and interment. The feast was on a scale corresponding with the drink. A cow, an ox, five kids, two wedders, eggs, geese, ducks, turkeys, pigs, and moorfowl, costing £55 15s., were consumed. Five bolls of flour were used, and the baker and cook who dressed the meat for the entertainment got between them £39 12s. The hearse was magnificently furnished. A painter in Forres, William Ker, furnished two escutcheons, which must have been of an elaborate character, as they cost £100 each. The hearse had eight branches and there were four mortheads. The horses were decorated with little escutcheons and thanes, and two dozen knops, coloured and gilded, were used. The undertaker's account alone came to about £400. The minister of Calder, Mr. John Calder, got a new set of mournings for the occasion, costing within a trifle of £30. The domestic chaplain was content with £20 for mournings. The sum total of the expenses of this great funeral was £1647 16s. 4d.

The cortege had but a short distance to go. In former times the family buried at the ancient church of Barevan, but a new departure was made in this respect, and the remains of the worthy old laird were interred at the church of Cawdor. The spectacle must have been a most imposing one. All the gentlemen of quality came on horseback, and they vied with each other in the splendour of their mounts. Simon, Lord Lovat, and his hench-man, Major Fraser, were there, carrying it grandly amongst their compeers—no finer horses were to be observed than those upon which the chief of the Frasers and his leading clansmen rode. Their horses were vastly admired, especially a handsome bay mare, until someone whispered that they had not been come by honestly. It turned out that the horses—some nine in number—had actually been stolen from the stables of Sir Archibald Dunbar of Thunderton a few weeks before by the Frasers. A lawsuit followed. Three of the horses were returned, but the decreet for the remaining six was unpaid when old Simon's estates were forfeited. Lord Lovat, however, meanwhile treated such matters loftily, and appeared shortly afterwards as a fortunate bridegroom, marrying, with the approval of the Earl of Argyll and Lord Lorn, a daughter of the Laird of Grant by his wife Janet Brodie of Lethen. She had been brought up in the strictest school of Puritanism, and was now transferred to the somewhat peculiar atmosphere of Castle Downie.

CHAPTER XIV

THE BURGH OF NAIRN

ALTHOUGH the rebels in the Rising of 1715 did not attack Nairn, as its magistrates feared, the town suffered a considerable loss, not by the Jacobites but by the Royalists. The Tolbooth or townhouse, which was also the prison, was burnt in the year 1716 " by His Majesty's forces when they kept guard." The Tolbooth does not appear to have been at any time a very formidable structure. About the year 1667 it was badly in need of repair, and the Town Council despatched some of the magistrates to bring timber from Rothiemurchus for its reconstruction. It must then have got a mere patch up, for in 1670, a poor Covenanting preacher, Thomas Ross, sent a petition to the Privy Council representing that the Tolbooth of the burgh of Nairn was very insufficient, and not able, from want of roof and repairs, to shelter him from the rain and storm, so that his life was in hazard. The Privy Council must have known that his report was true, as they ordered his removal from the prison of Nairn to that of Tain. It was probably this old prison which the Dunbars of Tarbet and Dunphail broke open, and liberated therefrom a kinsman of theirs who had been imprisoned for smuggling. The escapade cost them dearly, for the fine imposed upon old Dunbar compelled his son some years later to sell off his little property to discharge the burden. From various references to the Tolbooth in the burgh records, it appears to have had an outside stair leading to the council chamber and the prison. The basement was used for merchandise, and a little booth was constructed under the staircase. The Tolbooth had a steeple, which was furnished with two bells, and in the year 1707

243

the magistrates parted with one of the bells to the parish kirk, which had none. The bell they retained was encircled near the top with the following inscription—" Di Deus nobis quis contra nos. 1699." It survived the hand of time down to comparatively recent years, and is described in 1843 as being a beautifully cast bell, of silvery tones, ornamented with flower wreaths and other embellishments. About that time it was sold, along with another and larger bell, bearing the date 1769, to Messrs Bartlett of Birmingham, when a new bell was purchased. The rebuilding of the Tolbooth was too much for the finance of the burgh. Ten years afterwards it is recorded that " the place is altogether useless." Application was made to the Privy Council for aid, but no assistance was given. An appeal was addressed to the Synod of Moray, and a collection for it and the bridge, which was also in disrepair, was recommended to be made in all the churches within the bounds ; but a sum of £34 was all that was received from that source. One Highland kirk session—that of Alvie—voted " saxpence " for the bridge ! Duncan Forbes, the Lord Advocate, who represented the Inverness burghs, gave a contribution of thirty guineas towards the object. In the year 1715, the Council in forwarding a commission to the provost (who was in Edinburgh) to represent the burgh at the Convention of Burghs, sent him instructions to procure a committee of the burghs " to make cognition of the state of the burgh and to see if there can be any contribution had for repairing and perfecting the tolbooth, or if any assistance can be had for contributing to our harbour ! " Some small contribution appears to have been given, but it was some twenty years after this before the town was in a position partially to rebuild the edifice.

The imperial land tax, known as stent, pressed very heavily on the smaller burghs. It had to be collected monthly, and if the town got into arrears of payment, which Nairn unfortunately often did, troops were quartered upon the inhabitants until it was paid. In the year of the Jacobite Rising there were troops thus quartered on the place. Stentmasters were regularly appointed to collect the tax, but it was badly paid. In addition, the burgh had to pay eque and missive dues to the Convention of Burghs, and defray the expense of a commissioner to Edinburgh.

In 1659, William Murray, late bailie, was appointed commissioner to the Convention of Burghs summoned by General Monk, and was offered " for his expenses for himself and his ain horse twa merks and halfe in the day." The bailie, however, " absolutely refusing to go," was fined twenty merks in terms of the Act " anent any member that should refuse to goe any journey, after writing past." In the following year Robert Baine, burgess, was appointed commissioner to attend at Edinburgh on 2nd July, " his horse being hyred to him for 20 merks Scots, and for his ain expenses he is to have 24s. Scots every day during his absence." In November of the same year Rose of Broadley was sent to Edinburgh to attend the convention, and was allowed 14s. per day for himself, his horse, and his servant each, the allowance being increased on account of its being the winter season. A few years later the allowance mentioned is a crown per day.

The earliest " Cite Roll of the Burrow Roodes within the Burghe of Nairne " occurs on the fly-leaf of the Council's oldest minute book extant, which begins 16th November, 1657. The roll is not dated, but appears to have been drawn up in that, or the beginning of the following, year. The entries (except one or two which were added) are in the handwriting of William Man, who was town clerk at the time, and received instructions to prepare the roll. It shows that the total number of roods within the burgh was 309½, of which 107 belonged to Rose of Clava, and 80 to Rose of Broadley.

When the Rev. Hugh Rose was ordained assistant and successor to the Rev. David Dunbar in the year 1659, it was found necessary to rebuild the manse, and the extent of land belonging to the burgh of Nairn liable for the assessment is stated to be " twelve ploughs " —a ploughgate of land being 104 acres.

In 1712 the Convention of Burghs insisted upon the Town Council making up a proper valuation, and the committee appointed for that purpose on 24th June of that year gave in its valuation as follows :—The tenements of the burgh extend to £456 9s. ; the real rent of mill, fishing, and burgage lands to £1334 13s. 4d. Scots.

A revaluation was made on November 4th, 1714, when the committee reported " that the whole lands of ye said burgh extends to 300 bolls victual, which, according to the sheriff fiars, at £3 per boll, and with deduction of the tiends, extend to £900 Scots, and that the real rent of the tenements and houses of the said burgh liable in payment of cess and in use of payment amounts to £430 Scots."

In addition to these dues, the burgh had to make a contribution of men and money to the militia. The quota in 1680 was eight men and a half man, fitted out and supplied with arms. With so small a rent roll, the taxes came to be very oppressive. Accordingly, in the year 1726, the Council sought the aid of their representative in Parliament, Mr. Duncan Forbes of Culloden, Lord Advocate, and presented the following memorial to him :—" 16th October, 1726—The Council being met in order to draw a memorial to the Right Honourable His Majesty's Advocate, Duncan Forbes, Esquire, their representative in Parliament, concerning several matters relating to the interest of the town which want to be adverted to without loss of time, the Council think proper there be a memorial accordingly drawn up of the several particulars, following, viz. :—Concerning the eques and missive dues, to find out a way to get the town discharged of them. *Item*, to endeavour to get all the advantages possible by the encouragement allowed for the fishery, sowing of hemp and lint, and to get the encouragement of a spinning school. *Item*, to get a fund for rebuilding the town house and tolbooth, the same being now altogether useless, having been burnt in the year 1716 by His Majesty's Forces when they kept guard therein, and ordain the said proposals in a short note to be put into the advocate's hands."

The reference to the fishing industry relates to certain Acts passed by the Legislature for the encouragement of the herring fishery. Something had, however, been done previous to this. In 1712 a company was established at Nairn for carrying on the herring fishery. On 9th April of that year the Herring Company at Nairn constituted Hugh Rose of Clava, one of their number, "sole manager for providing materials," instructing him to have casks and salt and other materials necessary lodged at Nairn betwixt this date and the middle of July, sufficient for making 120 lasts of herrings. The herring shoals apparently made their appearance about the same time as they do now. A "last" is ten crans. During that and the following year mention is made of 167 lasts having been cured.

On 26th August, 1720, the Town Council being convened in order to consider an Act of the late Convention of Burghs anent erecting a fishery trade, gave instructions to their clerk to make up a return asked for, and appointed the second day of September ensuing for their next meeting, ordaining the officer to intimate to the haill burgesses to meet and give attendance when called same day. The meeting did not take place till 21st September, but having then convened " for the above affair of a fishery trade, and having called all the burgesses and ordered the clerk to keep a note of such as are to subscribe with their sums in order to be inserted in the Council book, when they all come in, the same was accordingly done on the 26th September. The Council having called all the burgesses willing to enter the Fishery Company, and having made lists ordain the same, with certificate and what further is required, to be sent to Edinburgh, conform to the Act of Convention of Royal Burghs, and letters sent to the burgh relative thereto, to be transmitted in due form." There is no further mention of the affairs of the company in the burgh records, until 20th June, 1729, when Bailie Robert Sutherland petitioned the Council to be appointed cure and wreckmaster of herrings, conform to a letter from the secretary of the commissioners and trustees appointed for improving the fisheries and manufactures in Scotland, and the Council thereupon nominated the said Robert Sutherland cure and wreckmaster.

The salmon fishing appears to have been of very considerable importance from a very early time, and the Brodies and Roses had corff houses and stores at the shore at Nairn. The salmon were exported in exchange for lime, salt, and other commodities. The fishing was by net and coble, or stell fishing, and the right to fish the river Nairn was, at one time at least, divided amongst the proprietors by days. The burgh also had a right of salmon fishing in the Nairn.

In 1684 a contract is recorded in the sheriff books between John Hay of Lochloy and James Dunbar, younger of Boath, according to which the former binds and obliges himself to deliver to the latter 300 bolls good sufficient French salt free of all public dues and burdens, whereof 200 bolls at Nairn and what he desired of the whole number at Findhorn, were to be measured by James Calder of Muirtown's ordinary measure for giving out of salt. Failing to deliver the salt, Hay is to pay £6 Scots for each undelivered boll.   The prospects of trade in Nairn were so good in the year 1712 that Alexander Falconer of Blackhills petitioned the Council to feu out to him " a piece of useless ground be-east Broadley's corff-house, that he might have the convenience of building some fishers' houses for accommodating some seamen who might labour a boat or yoale for his son's use, whom he designed to settle amongst them for following merchandise, and for building a corff-house for the convenience of washing his fish in the neighbouring fresh water."   The petition concludes that " others might be induced by his example to feu more of the said barren ground which yielded nothing to the town and might tend to the ornament of the place, the increase of the common good, and the furtherance of trade."   The Council thought the desire of the petition reasonable, and agreed to give off the feu, measuring one hundred feet in breadth, and about one hundred and ten feet in length, at 20s. Scots of a yearly feu duty.

The laird of Clava, though engaged in the local trade himself, had higher ambitions for his son.   An indenture is recorded in the book of the burgh sasines dated 6th June, 1671, betwixt Hugh Rose of Clava and John Rose, merchant burgess of Aberdeen, whereby Clava's third son, David, is to be apprenticed to his kinsman in Aberdeen, in the trade, employment, and occupation of a merchant for the space of five years.   The premium paid down was £1000, and it is stipulated that the master shall not conceal any part or point of the said calling from him as he shall answer to God, and shall furnish him with bed and board and good and sufficient clothing, and further " that he shall during the three last years of his prenticeship send the said David, his said prentice, every year at least once for a foreign voyage beyond seas, in such business and affairs of merchandise belonging to the said John Rose, as may give the said David insight in dealing and bargainings of the said nature." David is taken bound to abstain from carding, night walking, and bad company.

The Town Council took a somewhat selfish interest in the fishers and their white fish. "Complaint having been made," the records of October 22nd, 1711, state "that the fishers carry out their fish to the country and oblige the inhabitants to go down to their houses to buy their fish at their houses, to the great prejudice of the town in hindering the country people to frequent it, do therefore appoint that all fishers henceforth be obliged to sell none of their fish till they come to the cross with them, and in respect it is suggested that all the fishers threaten to make their fish dear in contempt of this Act, and that they may presume to go into the country after the town refuses to buy their fish, do therefore appoint that the said fishers shall not exact above forty pennies for the score of their greatest haddocks, twenty pence for the score of the middle size, and sixteen pennies Scots for the smallest fish, and that the said fishers be obliged to stay at the cross with their fish at least three hours unless they sell sooner, and in case the said fishers out of contempt of this Act, refrain going to sea, it is recommended to the bailies to see this Act put in execution by imprisoning or fining those fishers in case of refusal to follow their employment conform to use and wont, and for further prosecution of this good and necessary Act, they thought fit to constitute David Taylor another officer, who, in conjunction with William Chisholm, is to see the said Act put in due execution at the discretion and orders of the said bailies, and to search the said fishers' houses, and in case of concealing the said best fish, to confiscate the same for use of the poor, and fine them day by day as they find occasion."

Flax was grown extensively in the lower lands of the county, especially in the neighbourhood of Nairn. As early as 1660 the Council issued an order, as a precaution against fire, forbidding the drying of lint in houses within the burgh. An Act of Parliament in 1686 ordained that no person should be buried in any shirt, sheet, or anything else except in plain linen, and within eight days of burial the relatives of the deceased person were obliged to declare on oath before the parish minister that the rule had been complied

with.   Another Act was passed ordaining that for the same
end no lint should be exported from the kingdom, and rules were
promulgated enjoining a uniform breadth of the cloth produced.
In 1720 Nairn Town Council issued an order for putting in force
the Acts anent linen.   The flax crop required all the attention of
a garden plant, and consequently gave employment to a great many
hands, young and old.   The plant when ripe was pulled up, and
laid out in handfuls to be sun dried.   It was then " rippled," and
the seed laid aside for winter food, along with grain, for the cattle.
The iron combs for rippling are still to be found about old farm
houses.   One of these combs used in the district is preserved in
Nairn Museum.   The stalks were put in sheaves and then steeped
in pools, stagnant water being preferred.   A favourite place at
Nairn for steeping the lint was where the water collected in pools
along the links of Nairn and the Seabank lands, and the name
" Lint Pots " was applied to the ground below the modern mansions
of Invernairne and Firthside.   After the lint had been scutched,
it was handed over to skilled hands to be " heckled "—*i.e.* the finer
spinning lint to be separated from the coarser tow.   A worthy
man of respectable position who died some years ago in Nairn
was familiarly known as " Davie Heckler," having in his younger
days been engaged in the work of " heckling."   When finished,
the lint was handed over to the women to be spun.   The Government encouraged the trade by bounties.   A prominent member of
Nairn Town Council about 1770 was òne Walter Dallas, who is
sometimes designated " weaver," but at other times styled " linen
manufacturer."   He was a descendant of the old family of Dallas
of Cantray, and when the family estates were sold off, he betook
himself to this industry.   The weavers, who appear also to have
engaged in the linen manufacture, were a numerous class of
tradesmen in the burgh.   There are few specimens of the old
home-made linen now in existence, but the industry was at one
time of considerable local importance.

The Town Council were invested with very extensive powers,
and the magistrates had authority over all matters civil and criminal
within the burgh.   Early in the year 1657 they took cognisance
of offences usually regarded as coming within the ecclesiastical

domain, and two cases of immorality are mentioned in which the Burgh Court imposed fines. At a later time, however, they declined to consider even cases of defamation of character, handing the parties over to be dealt with by the kirk session. They had under their royal charter the right of " pit and gallows," and administered capital punishment. The gallows stood at the west end of the town, somewhere in the neighbourhood of Lodgehill, and the road leading to it was called the Gallowgate. The record is preserved of the trial of John Smith *alias* John Williamson, " a stranger vagabond," who had got work from George Household the cooper. A series of housebreakings had occurred. In one case the exact amount of the money stolen was known. Suspicion pointed to Smith as the robber. When apprehended he was found to have 400 shillings and a half-crown in a black bag. The fiscal, Macphail, noticed that this was exactly one-third of the sum stolen, and came to the conclusion that Smith must have had two accomplices, who had each got an equal share. Smith admitted that this was the case, implicating two young men of the town, and the three were placed on trial before John Rose of Broadley, provost, John Tulloch, John Inglis, and John Wilson, bailies. The first act of court was significant of the gravity with which the offence was regarded by the magistrates—John M'Donnachie Roy was sworn in as Dempster of Court. The fiscal stated his case, mentioning that when the prisoner was searched a " testificate " from one John Finlayson, parish of Urquhart, in Ross, was found in his possession, stating his name to be Donald M'Gown, his back bore marks of scourging, and his shoulder had been branded with a hot iron. The fiscal wished to make out that the prisoner was none other than a notorious robber, David Williamson, who had recently broken out of Elgin prison. A jury consisting of the leading burgesses was empanelled, and they brought in a verdict of guilty on the principal counts of the indictment—to two of which he had indeed pled guilty ; but they did not consider the evidence of identification sufficient to prove that he was the Elgin robber. The record of court sets forth that the judges having taken the said verdict to their serious consideration, and having found the inquest to have convicted, and the panel guilty of five criminal points of

law, " do find him GUILTY OF DEATH, and by the mouth of John
M'Donnachie Roy, their dempster of court, sentence and ordain
the said John Smith, panel, to be hanged at the public place of
execution till he be dead, by the hand of the public executioner,
upon Friday next ensuing, and also declared all his goods escheat
and ordained the same to be inbrought." The fiscal moved for a
verdict against his two accomplices, but the jury refused to convict
them, on the ground that Smith had withdrawn that part of his
confession, now stating that he had no accomplices. The fiscal
maintained that he had evidence that the prisoner had been tam-
pered with while in jail, in particular that the two young men went
to the jail door during the silence of night and begged of him not
to tell upon them—hence the withdrawal of that part of the confession. The magistrates took the same merciful view as the jury,
but in order to vindicate law and authority, liberated them on heavy
bail to come up when cited.

A few years later an entry occurs indicating that another execution had taken place, at which all the inhabitants had been ordered
to attend with arms. For failing to do so John Macdonald,
burgess, was fined £5.

It was the duty of the burgh magistrates to carry out the capital
sentences pronounced by the sheriff court. In the year 1742
Murdoch Mackenzie, who appears to have been the leader of a
band of reivers from Lochaber, was convicted by the sheriff and
jury of the theft of two mares, and was sentenced to be hanged.
Murdoch, it is stated, did not understand the English language.
It happened that there was no hangman in Nairn, and the Council
dispatched a messenger post haste to Inverness to see if the authorities would lend their executioner for the occasion. The answer
brought back was that they would, provided a sufficient guard was
sent to convey him from Inverness to Nairn. This having been
done, the execution was duly carried out on the 21st day of January,
1743.

The punishments inflicted for minor offences were severe.
Two domestic servants at Broadley, for the theft of butter, cheese,
and other commodities, were sentenced " to be kairted and scourged
openly, from one end of the street to the other on ane market day,

and thereafter to be banished furth of the town." Two women
found guilty of the reset were exempted from punishment on their
husbands giving their carts and acting as scourgers to the chief
delinquents. On 6th March, 1660, a dishonest weaver, Donald
M'James, at the Mill, for stealing six pounds weight of yarn of a
plaiding web which he did weave for Donald Gow and Alexander
M'Glashan, and for taking double woff to said web, was sentenced
to pay to the party wronged the price of the yarn at 5s. per pound,
and a fine of 30s., and " to stand ane marcat day in tyme of open
marcat in the jougs and ane clew of yarn in his arms." Janet
Gow, for stealing kail and hens, divers and sundry times, was fined
£5 Scots, and ordained " to stand in the collar on ane marcat day
from seven hours in the morning to eleven hours, and to be put in
the blackhole till such time as she should pay the fine." William
Hendrie, found guilty of stealing corn, was fined " in ane merk
and ordained to stand in the collar for the space of four hours."
Custen Clunas for stealing a Holland band or leather belt, was
ordered to restore the goods, pay a fine of £2 to the treasurer, and
stand in the jougs on Friday next in time of market. Magdalen
Rose, for opening certain parcels left in her master's house, and
stealing " a great quantity of indigo, alme, anest seeds, and ginger "
got as an option to corporal punishment " to leave the burgh
absolutelie and no to trouble the samen any more." Janet Simson,
servant to Beatrix Thomson, spouse to William Murray, late bailie,
was charged with having divers times " gone to two puncheons of
wyne and drunken ane great quantitie of the samen, being about
the value of £40 Scots money, and that she had stolen ane pair of
plaids worth £4 Scots, and stollen her butter." She confessed to
the charges, and was sentenced " to be scourged publicly ane mercat
day from one end of the toune to the t'other and her ears to be
nailed to the tron, and thereafter proclamation to be made that she
was banished, and any one who should receive her within the town
or territories thereof should pay £10 Scots." For threatening a
bailie with a drawn sword, Hugheon Tulloch was ordained to
stand two several markets days in the stocks, with his head and
arms fast therein, with a paper about his head and a naked sword
about his neck and an officer beside him.

Some of the sheriff court sentences were quite as severe. On 16th April, 1742, William Mackay in Fleenas was charged with having stolen a grey mare. He was found guilty, and adjudged to be carried from the Tolbooth of Nairn, under a sure guard and his hands tied, to the Bridge of Nairn, and there to be bared to the body, and by the hands of the common hangman then to receive on his naked back the number of twelve stripes, and from thence with the hangman at his back to be brought to the Tron of Nairn and his right ear affixed to the Tron with a nail, and in that situation to remain for the space of two minutes, and then at that place to the like number of twelve stripes, and from thence to the Dial and there to receive the like number of stripes, and from thence to the Gallow-hill of Nairn, and there to receive the like number of twelve stripes by the hands of the said hangman, and for ever to be banished the shire and territories thereof, under the pain of whipping the first Monday of each month after his return in manner and at the time and places convenient.

On 29th September, 1743, Margaret Davidson, was convicted before Sheriff Depute Patrick Clark, of theft. The poor wretch appeared from the testimony of witnesses to have been a " common thief," and had been " jougged " and afterwards imprisoned in the jail of Cawdor for a considerable time. The sentence now was that she was to remain in sure ward in the Tolbooth of Nairn from that date (29th September) till Friday, the 11th day of November next to come, and that day betwixt the hours of two and three afternoon brought from prison to the Tron of Nairn, and her right ear affixed to the Tron by the hands of the common hangman and then to be by him cut off, and the town's iron put upon her left cheek by the hands of the said hangman until the skin be burnt, and immediately thereafter to be carried to the bridge of Nairn under a sure guard and the hangman at her back, and there and then to be stript to the middle, and when so stripped to receive six strokes upon the back with a whip from the hangman, the like number at the cross of Nairn, the like number at the Horologe Stone, and the like number at the foot of the Gallows, and from thence to be banished never again to be seen within the shire under the pain of death.

Complaints having been made regarding people stealing pease, the sheriff issued the following curious order—" Considering that it is the duty of all judges to curb such pernicious and destructive practices, and as in time coming the sheriff intends without respect of persons to put the laws in execution upon the first complaint, but wanting previously to advertise the lieges of his intention in order to obviate and remove any defence and to render transgressors excuseless, the said sheriff hereby discharges all and sundry persons, old or young, from stealing, away carrying, pulling and destroying of pease, before or after reaping, without the special consent of the owner or proprietor, with certification to such as shall be seized in the act, or against whom legal evidence shall be brought, they shall be holden and obliged to stand in the pillory within the town of Nairn in the juggs, bared to the britch, with a bale of pease about their middle and a paper on their breast with these words—' Here I stand for pease stealing ! ' This Act to be published at the mercat cross and read at the door of the several parish churches within the county upon Sabbath day next after divine service. Given at Nairn the 10th August, 1745 years. DA. CUMYNG, Shf."

The old cross of Nairn stood in the centre of the street. It was a built structure of stone and lime, requiring to be pointed and harled. In 1757, amongst the public works reported by the Council as having been carried out that summer, was the " removing the old ruinous cross," and " building a new one." The Horologe Stone or Dial appears to have stood about the corner of Leopold Street. When the Council were improving the street in 1757, they considered the necessity of making an addition thereto " from the Horologe Stone westward to the end of the town." The old sun dial on the top of the pillar which goes by the name of the cross at the present day, is probably the Horologe Stone so frequently referred to in the records.

The Council exercised the right of appointing a minister, and on one occasion went pretty far afield. On 21st April, 1729, having considered " the want of a minister for the burgh and parish, and that it's necessary there be one nominated and presented to the presbytery before the elapsing of the six months from the demise of

Mr. George Dunbar, late incumbent, and having considered the fitness and good qualifications of Mr. Lachlan Rose, minister of the gospel at Rukewood Hall in Essex of England, the Council therefore do unanimously agree that the said Mr. Lachlan Rose be presented and called to the said paroch, and that his settlement therein be prosecuted and followed furth according to laws in such cases, and appoint Bailie Alexander Falconer, John Rose, younger of Blackhills, James Rose of Hunterbog, and Alexander Rose, clerk, as a quorum of their number in name of the town and Council to prosecute the same according to the usual form."

The call to Mr. Lachlan Rose was not accepted. The Council met in February of the following year to consider " making choice of another minister for this paroch in respect Mr. Lachlan Rose, to whom a call had been given, had declared his being unable to accept of that call. After thinking fully thereof, they unanimously agree that Mr. Alexander Rose, probationer, now in the Synod of Ross, is a person fit to be called to the said charge, and that the Magistrates and Council are to concur in using all the ordinary ways for obtaining him settled as minister of this place." The Council had the satisfaction of seeing him ordained their minister in July following.

The Council also was concerned with the appointment of a schoolmaster. In 1751 the following resolution was passed— " That this burgh is at a considerable loss by the school continuing so long vacant, though a presentation was some time ago signed by the whole heritors recommending Mr. James Rose, present school-master at Croy, to that office, which Mr. James Rose was cast by the reverend Presbytery of Forres as insufficient for the charge of our school, notwithstanding of his having past trial with appro-bation some years ago before the Presbytery of Inverness—this be-haviour of the Presbytery of Forres would induce us to believe that our school is likely to continue long enough vacant did the settlement thereof depend upon them solely !—we do therefore in confirmation of our former opinion and in conjunction with the heritors of this parish who did formerly unanimously nominate the said Mr. James Rose, appoint him schoolmaster of this place, and we recommend to the Reverend Alex. Rose, our minister, and the kirk session, to appoint the said Mr. James Rose their session clerk, with the hail privileges and emoluments thereto pertaining."

The earliest medical practitioner mentioned as settled in Nairn is one Dr. Savage, who flourished about the year 1670, and whose sons gave trouble to the magistrates by fighting. In the next generation a very humane doctor was in the place, as appears from the following minute, dated 1st August, 1721—"There being a petition given in by William M'Phail, chirurgeon and burgess, craving a piece of waste ground at the back of the houses and kiln belonging to and possessed by the petitioner on the south side of the burgh, near and adjoining the river, with the Laird of Calder's land on the east, might be granted to him by charter for an herb garden for the use of the poor, it being absolutely necessary, and the said ground being quite useless." The Council appointed a committee to visit the piece of ground, and doubtless granted it.

The Town Council consisted of seventeen members—including Provost, three Bailies, Dean of Guild and Treasurer. The Council elected the provost and magistrates annually, and the " old Council did elect the new." The provostship was confined for centuries to one family and its branches. The Roses of Kilravock, Dunearn, Broadley, Clava, and Newton furnished the provosts of Nairn in unbroken succession down to 1750, and then an exception was made in favour only of Kilravock's brother-in-law !

In one official document—a writ authorising an election of Parliament—the chief magistrate is addressed as " the Lord Provost of Nairn." On 13th May, 1734, the Council, " taking into consideration that there is a precept from the Sheriff Principal of the Sheriffdom of Nairn, in obedience to a writ from His Majesty's Chancellary delivered to My Lord Provost, for choosing a delegate for this burgh to meet with the other delegates and commissioners of this district and class of burghs at Forres, being the presiding burgh, in order to elect a member of Parliament in the ensuing Parliament of Great Britain, which is to be held at Westminster, the 13th day of June next, the Council appoint Thursday next, the 17th, for the Council to meet in order to choose a delegate for the above purpose." The Council promptly accepted the title of " Lord Provost " for their chief magistrate, and in making out the commission, it runs in favour of " Hugh Rose of Geddes, Esquire, Lord Provost of the Burgh ! " Something unpleasant, however, occurred at the election in March of the following year, for the Council met on the 29th of that month " in order to write a letter to My Lord Advocate and Hugh Rose of Kilravock, Esquire, concerning the indignity done the town at the election of a member of Parliament upon the 17th current." Next year another parliamentary vacancy occurred, in consequence of the resignation of " Duncan Forbes, Esq., lately chosen member for them, and who since the said election hath accepted the office of Lord President of the College of Justice."

The river appears to have had a trick of running away from the town. It is a small stream in summer, but in an autumn flood or a winter's spate it comes down in great volume. In 1720 the Council, considering the advantage it would be to cause the river to run in a straight channel, appointed three leading townsmen to begin with a body of forty-eight men each under their charge, with spades and shovels, and to continue till the work be done. In January, 1734, a minute states that " the Council taking into consideration the loss the burgh received by the water or river of Nairn running to the *westward* of the town, they therefore recommend to the magistrates of the burgh to take the proper measures of rectifying the same, and that it be gone about without loss of time." The river had evidently resumed its ancient channel along the Links. The next mention of the river is that it had escaped to the east. In 1737 the magistrates, with as many of the councillors as could attend, were appointed to see how the run of the water could be put right. In March of the following year the Council had information " of an instrument of interruption to be taken against the town and heritors of the fishing upon the river of this place, to hinder the water (which lately broke out on the bounds of the laird of Brodie) being brought back to the property and bounds of the burgh where it formerly ran, and that application may be made to the Lords of Session for procuring a warrant to stop the bringing back the said water ; therefore the Council order the clerk to write to Hugh Rose of Geddes, Esquire, one of their number, who is now at Edinburgh, to take proper care no such warrant be obtained, and to do what may be necessary for the town and heritors' interest in the said matter." The Council did not succeed in preventing the laird of Brodie taking the threatened action. Interim interdict or suspension was granted to Brodie, and on June 20th the Council sent up some of its papers to Edinburgh to prove the town's rights. The papers sent were King James VI.'s confirmation charter of 1598, the Parliament's ratification of the same in 1661, and a decreet arbitral betwixt the burgh of Nairn and John Hay of Lochloy determining their marches, dated at King's Steps the 6th and 7th days of August, 1574. A long litigation ensued. The burgh applied to the Convention of Royal Burghs for assistance to prosecute the cause at law, " it being thought absolutely necessary for the interest of the town that the run should be on its own property." A map of the burgh lands, prepared by order of the Court of Session in connection with another law process in the year 1777, shows the river flowing into the sea beyond King's Steps quarries, with a large store-house on its west bank. It was not till 1820 that the river was finally brought back to its present channel.

The regulation of the liquor traffic engaged a good deal of the attention of the Town Council, and a series of enactments appears in the burgh books. Their spirit may be described as an effort to secure ale of good quality, and plenty of it, at a cheap price. In 1663 the Council passed a resolution that " considering the great plenty of victual wherewith the Lord in his goodness has been pleased to bless the land this year, by which means the ale and beer in all neighbouring and adjacent places is sold at a lower rate than in this place hereto," it is ordained that no brewer shall presume upon any pretext whatever, to take above 7d. Scots for the pint of ale, and 2d. for the pint of beer. The enactment provides that what persons please, for the better accommodation of gentlemen passengers and others, to brew good and sufficient ale or beer esteemed by the cunnisters to be worth more, the same will be taken into consideration.

The cunnisters were a committee of ale tasters or testers appointed by the Council, with authority to set the price upon such ale and beer as should be brewed within the town, according to its

worth.   When any insufficient drink was found the brewers were
to be fined one shilling sterling.   According to an old burgh law
the cunnisters were required to stand in the middle of the street
and call upon the publican to bring out his liquor to be tested—a
rule wisely providing that the duty be performed in public under
the eye of their fellow-burgesses.   It is expressly stated that the
cunnisters appointed in Nairn " to take tryall of the ale or beer,
once, twice, or thrice in the week," are " honest conscientious
men ! "   In 1659 an Act of the magistrates was passed that all
brewers within the burgh, being stallengers, should pay hereafter
yearly 40s. Scots as stallenger's money.   In the same year it was
ordained that " all brewers of acquavitie within the town should
keep acquavitie of every breust for the use of the inhabitants within
the town and for passengers and strangers, under the pain of con-
fiscation of a pint of acquavitie, or the price thereof, how-so-often
as they should be found contravening."   Soon afterwards John
Rose, burgess of Nairn, was accused of deforcing the officers and
exacting prices for his ale more than the cunnisters allowed, and
was fined 2s. 6d.   The brewers were divided into two classes—
innkeepers and stallengers.   On 6th October, 1658, William
Murray, John Gordon, Hughone Rose, John Glass, Alexander
M'Phail, and John Rose, brewers in Nairn, voluntarily obliged
themselves to keep honest bed and buird to gentlemen and strangers
when they came to their houses, under the penalty of half-a-crown.
The stallengers were an inferior class.   On one occasion, a publican who had forfeited the liberty to sell on his premises, was
allowed to be a stallenger, that is, to sell in an open stall or booth.
There appears to have been no restriction at first as to the number
of persons engaged in the traffic, provided they were burgesses ;
but after the passing of a new Act of Parliament, they had to apply
to the magistrates, who gave them licence to sell for one year only.
Thus, in 1756, two of the bailies met to admit and license proper
persons duly qualified for retailing ale, beer, etc., in terms of the
late Act of Parliament, and did " admit, license, and allow the
persons following, viz. :—Mrs. Christian Sutherland, Mrs. Grizell
Miller, George Grant, James Taylor, John Rose, weaver, and
John Mackay, and none other person or persons within the burgh

to retail ale, beer, etc., and that for one year commencing upon the 26th day of October, 1756."

The Council had to maintain constant vigilance against the introduction of malt from the country, and passed various enactments requiring all country malt to be measured by the town's firlot, paying certain charges therefor. The regulations of the trade of the burgh were numerous and excessively strict. No man could open a shop or engage in trade unless he were previously admitted a freeman burgess and guild brother. Unfree traders were constantly being prosecuted. It was necessary that a merchant burgess should take up house within the burgh. John Wilson, Auldearn, thought he could enjoy the privilege of being a burgess of Nairn with residence at Auldearn, but he was peremptorily ordered to take up house and keep open shop within the burgh on pain of forfeiting his freedom. Auldearn butchers were absolutely prohibited from exercising their trade outside the burgh of Nairn. The right to kill beasts and prepare the hides was a strictly burghal privilege. Country people were allowed to slaughter cattle for their own use. This was the defence pled by the Auldearn people.

Whilst preserving a monopoly of trade in the burgh, the town did all it could to enhance the importance of its markets. These were held at Michaelmas. Leather merchants were bound to exhibit a certain quantity of leather in open booth. Shoemakers required to have ready for sale several dozen pairs of shoes, which they must show at the market stalls. Two markets were held, and they appear to have been attended by a large concourse of people. One of the never-failing duties of the magistrates, a day or two before the fair, was to appoint a guard of twenty men to keep the peace of the market. The merchandise proper was confined to the booths on the High Street. Agricultural produce was sold at the Shambles Yard (now the site of the Congregational Church). The cattle were exposed for sale at the Links, and there was a horse-wynd somewhere in the neighbourhood of Bridge Street and Harbour Street. The fair was really a business occasion, and the bulk of the commodities exposed were products of local industry—leather, dressed and tanned, homespun cloth, plaidings,

hose, and other materials for the wearing apparel of the times.
The small crofters in the uplands brought wooden tubs, cogs, and
churns—at least these latter were features of the market in the
beginning of the nineteenth century. The tolls of the market
were let for about £8 or £10, each booth or stall-holder paying a
few pence. The " Michael markets "—there were latterly three
of them, the middle one being the " big market "—were the great
annual events in the burgh for centuries. There was also a
weekly market held on Fridays, at which fleshers were bound to
present carcases for sale, with hide, etc., uncut.

Amongst other monopolies of trade was the manufacture of
snuff—the exclusive right of manufacture being regularly let along
with the common good by the burgh, and generally fetching about
£8 or £10. A waulkmill was erected by John Cumming, and no
person was allowed to follow the trade of a dyer unless specially
licensed by him. Makers of linen cloth had to give caution that
the material they manufactured was in accordance with statutory
requirements. The smith was a town officer, appointed by the
magistrates. He had also a monopoly, but the difficulty seemed
rather to be to find sufficient work for him. In 1750 it was stated
that one John Falconer, in Moyness, was qualified for the trade, and
as the town was much in need of such a craftsman he was appointed.
The former smith had a croft from the town, called the Smith's
Croft, now forming part of the property of the Hermitage. The
smith had to do all the Town Council's work without payment, and
his charges to the public were fixed—" penny work " covering a
variety of small iron-making and mending. Falconer had great
difficulty in making a livelihood. There were a gunsmith and a
wigmaker in Nairn in 1720. The wigmaker was in that year
admitted a burgess on the ground that " there was none other of
his employment in town, and that it was absolutely necessary there
should be one such." In consideration of his mean circumstances
he was admitted gratis.

The town required a gunsmith and sword-maker. The gunsmith was granted a feu at a nominal rent for his greater encouragement. The sword-maker was an incorrigible character, and he
and his wife were ultimately banished the town. The following

entry (reproduced with its original orthography) applies to the sword-maker and his wife—" 9th Aprile, 1658.—That day in refference to the former Acts enacted anent swearing and such lyke, the said Huchone Tulloch in Nairn and Margaret Russell, his spouse, being dyvers and severall tymes found cursers, swerars, and turbulent personnes, and formerlie ordainet to be banished for sick lyke offences, nevertheless in houpes of amendiement has bein hitherto spaired, yet the fornamed persones ar so far from amendiement that they ar altogidder become worss, and lyklie to become worser, as by the pntt. given in against them appears." Therefore the judge gives them the option of standing in the jougs or leaving the town by the next Sunday night.

A feature of the times was the great number of vagrants resorting to the burgh. In 1658 the magistrates enacted that no " strange vagabonds " should be harboured within the town or territories thereof, " except crepill, blynd, and almes deides." Some fifteen years later it was found necessary to put into execution this and other laws made against strange vagabonds, beggars, and their resetters and lodgers " by reason of great multitudes of such persons resorting to this place," and the Council authorised and empowered the scourger to imprison all such vagabonds and to take notice of the places where they lodged, that those receiving them might be punished and fined.

One advantage Nairn had was its possession of a good moss about two miles westward of the town. Each burgess and resident inhabitant had a right to a lair in the moss. Many and grievous were the disputes by neighbours as to the quantity of peats each was entitled to bring home, and the difficulties of the Town Council increased as the moss became worked out. In the year 1772 the Council "anxiously recommend to the inhabitants the use of coals, that the moss may be no more than a secondary aid to their firing, at least till it shall increase, which may happen in a few years."

Tea was sold by John Ore, merchant in Nairn, in the year 1733, at £3 12s. per lb. It came into use as a beverage in the burgh long before it extended to the country districts.

An old custom in Nairn was the morning and evening calls— the one to work and the other to rest. On 21st October, 1717, the Council ordered " the drummer to beat the taptow and revelzie daily, as also the officer to ring the bell."

A favourite resort for the youth of the town was the Nairn mill, when it happened to be under the charge of a good-natured miller. The Council, on 10th September, 1660, minute that " there was a complaint given in against the miller that he did harbour so monie litill ones in the mill, whilk did great prejudice by stealling of honest men's victuall in the night and day, the said John being summendit did compear and did hereby enact himselfe that he should have non such in or about the myline, only except almes deids and fatherless and motherless bairns," under pains and penalties.

When a funeral took place the inhabitants were summoned by the officer to attend. They had become remiss in this duty, and the Council, on 6th November, 1660, ordained, as there was " ane great slyghting of not keeping comon burialls after advertisement, that every burgess inhabitant within the toune, he being tymouslie advertised by the officer, if he should absent himself he is to pay one shilling sterling *toties quoties*, without reason shewn to Provost or Bailies present and leave asked and obtained." A similar enactment was passed in regard to the " whole commonaltie within the toune and territories thereof," the fine to be 6s. Scots. It was a standing order that when the provost and bailies went from home to attend a funeral a certain number of the burgesses were to accompany them on horseback as a guard of honour.

There appears to have been no lack of public spirit amongst the burgesses and inhabitants in those early days. It showed itself in the readiness to make voluntary contributions towards public improvements, and especially in giving personal service, with horse, spades, and barrows. The ambition of the town was to have the High Street—its only street—paved from end to end, and the inhabitants in relays assisted in the work. It was found desirable to enclose by a dyke the ground called the Calfward, lying between the parish church and the Millroad, and the inhabitants in sets, under the provost and bailies, performed the work. It also became necessary to divert the river into a temporary channel in order to repair the bridge of Nairn, and again the inhabitants turned out with spades and barrows.

The great antiquity of the burgh of Nairn is undoubted. Lachlan Shaw, the historian of Moray, states that he found mention of it as early as 1006. It originally owed whatever importance it possessed to its garrison. The King's House, however, fell into decay, and although attempts were made to establish various industries in the place, none of them assumed any great proportions, and the more enterprising and adventurous amongst successive generations sought a wider field in military service and mercantile pursuits in other lands.

CHAPTER XV

FROM THE RISING TO THE REBELLION

THE period between the Rising of 1715 and the Rebellion of 1745 was not marked by any public events of special note in Nairnshire, but the history of the leading men in the district is interesting.

Although the head of the house of Cawdor—Sir Hugh Campbell's grandson John—no longer made Cawdor Castle his residence, the old place was well looked after by Sir Archibald Campbell of Clunas and Budgate, who acted as manager of the estates for commissioners during the earlier years of the young laird of Cawdor. At his own expense Sir Archibald formed plantations near the castle, planted trees on the banks of the Cawdor Burn, laid out a handsome garden, which even in his day grew all " sorts of fruit that are to be found in Scotland," and enclosed it with a lime and stone dyke ten feet high, besides planting hedges and enclosing nearly twenty acres to the east of the deer park—improvements that are visible to this day. The deer park at that time contained some eighteen red deer.

Sir Archibald was made Sheriff-Principal of Nairnshire, holding the office as a life appointment, and took an active part in the business of the county. He had been knighted by the Duke of Argyll, and was strongly attached to the House of Hanover. He frequently held the Sheriff Courts at Cawdor, and granted decreets and passed sentences there, ignoring so far the claim of the burgh to be the seat of the head court. He married Anna, only daughter of Duncan Macpherson of Cluny, and had ten of a family. His eldest son Duncan, who had been for some years in exile in consequence of the part he took in the Rising of 1715, returned to this country and took up his abode for a time at Delnies and afterwards at Clunas.   He had married Katherine, daughter of Trotter of Morton Hall, and a daughter Elizabeth was born to them in Rome in the year 1724.   She was their only child, and grew up in their home in Delnies and Clunas one of the most beautiful and accomplished ladies of the time.   She had many suitors, and old beaux, like Lord Lovat, paid her courtly compliments, but according to tradition, she favoured young M'Gillivray of Dunmaglass—the fairest, handsomest youth in the Highlands.   The romance of their lives, as will be seen later, ended in the tragedy of Culloden Moor.   Judging from the frank way in which Lord Lovat confided in him, Duncan Campbell still cherished Jacobite sympathies, and the family historian says that he was a man " of great intelligence, some accomplishments, with a dash of affected peevishness and humour."   He wisely left politics alone, however, and busied himself when at Clunas with hunting on the moor and fruit-growing, attributing the occasional failure of his crop to his Siberian situation.   The second son, Hugh, who received his education in Paris, was a good deal with his cousin, the laird of Calder, in Wales, and when his father, Sir Archibald, began to grow valetudinarian, as the phrase of the day went, he was appointed factor on the Cawdor estates in the north.   Sir Archibald settled the property of Budgate on his fourth son Colin, who studied medicine and took up practice as a doctor in Inverness, whence his fame as a physician extended throughout the north.   Dr. Colin Campbell married a sister of Duncan Forbes of Culloden, then Lord Advocate, and had a family of several children.   He was called upon to attend the Countess of Moray at Darnaway Castle, caught her fever, and died at Darnaway.   A tombstone in the enclosure in the old church of Barevan records his death.   His son succeeded to Budgate, became a surgeon, and married a daughter of Duff of Drummuir.   Their daughter married Colonel John Baillie of Dunain, and the wadset of Budgate was redeemed in her time by Cawdor.

In 1735, Sir Archibald Campbell, as sheriff-principal, appointed Robert Donaldson of Arr his sheriff-depute.   His predecessor had been David Cuthbert of Draikies.   Robert Donaldson and his wife, Katherine Brodie, took part in one of the Covenanting family meetings in 1654, and he is frequently mentioned subsequently by James Brodie in his diary, in connection with business matters.   His second son, Alexander, who inherited some money under the marriage contract of Alexander Urquhart, then of Kinnudie, and Bessie Hay, his grandmother, went furth the kingdom in 1684—his father advancing him money in lieu of his rights under the will.   Some years later he reappeared as Major Alexander Donaldson, late of the 76th Regiment, and had the freedom of the burgh of Nairn bestowed upon him.   Subsequently he became Colonel of the West Lowland Fencibles.   The Robert Donaldson who was appointed sheriff-depute appears to have been the eldest son.   He held office until 1740, and was a leading man in the district.   At the time when Robert Donaldson was appointed sheriff-depute, Thomas Brodie, writer in Edinburgh, received the post of sheriff-clerk, and to make the monopoly of offices complete in the family, George Donaldson was appointed sheriff-clerk depute.   He was also for a time town-clerk of Nairn.   His son Robert Donaldson was apprenticed to Thomas Brodie, and admitted a Writer to the Signet on 26th June, 1769, becoming a freehold voter in the county of Nairn a few years later, on Lethen and Cawdor qualifications.   He married, April 1767, Helen, only daughter of John Grant, W.S.

Thomas Brodie, sheriff-clerk of Nairn, became a Writer to the Signet, and a well-known member of the legal profession in those days in Edinburgh.   The present family of Brodie of Lethen is descended from him.   David Brodie of Pitgavenie, who succeeded his brother, the second laird of Lethen, and saved the estates from forfeiture, left a son Alexander Brodie (known as Dunearn) who succeeded to the Lethen estates.   He had married, before he came into possession, Sophia Campbell, fifth daughter of Sir Hugh Campbell (by Lady Henrietta Stewart), and had a numerous family. Alexander was the eldest, and Thomas, the above-mentioned Writer to the Signet, the second son.   In 1732 he gave up Lethen to his eldest son Alexander, and built a house at Brightmony, where he and his wife, Sophia Campbell, spent their remaining years.   He was not a very old man when he retired, but he made way for the young laird, who was ambitious to have a seat in Parliament. After a keen contest, young Lethen was elected Member of Parliament for Nairnshire in 1735.

The young laird of Brodie, who defended Brodie Castle so valiantly against Huntly in the Rising of 1715, died in the year 1720, and was succeeded by his immediately younger brother, Alexander Brodie, who in room of his deceased brother was elected Member of Parliament for Elgin. His youngest sister Anne married George Munro of Novar.

Some years previous to this the good old family of Hay of Lochloy went down. Pecuniary embarrassments, partly due to fines for nonconformity, pressed heavily on the family. The sheriff court books of Nairn are crowded with bonds registered against the estate of John Hay of Lochloy, by his procurator John Dallas, burgess of Nairn. He appears to have borrowed money freely from all sorts and conditions of people. Amongst others, old Bailie Tulloch advanced him considerable sums, and the bailie's daughter Anna, who had been abducted by the Tullochs of Tannachie, but was now happily married to her first lover, Alexander Falconer, the bishop's son, ranked for payment. The lairds of Brodie, Lethen, Clava, and Boath were large creditors. Hay of Lochloy sold Kilhill to James Dunbar, younger of Boath, for £600. He was due him £3500. Newton of Park came into possession of the laird of Brodie about this time. William Hay, while younger of Lochloy, in 1686 sold the wood of Lochloy, and the father let the salmon fishings on a long lease, with the mansion house. But all these expedients did not avert the crash. The estates, which had been in the family since the days of Baliol and Bruce, if not earlier, were exposed to judicial sale in 1710.

The desire for acquiring land amounted at this time almost to a passion. Kilravock and Calder entered into a compact previous to the sale, one of the conditions of which was—" We are by any means to be the highest bidders, cost what it will," and they arranged to divide the property—the portion lying east of the kirk of Auldearn to belong to the one, and the portion west of the kirk to the other, according as they might choose. This curious compact was drawn up by a man who afterwards became famous—Duncan

Forbes, the Lord Advocate, and subsequently Lord President. Two merchants at Inverness, who had made some money, attended the sale, and were aghast at the style of bidding. The price not only covered the value of the land but also the debts of the family. Kilravock had fortified himself by getting a promise of the money he might want for the purchase from Duff of Dipple, the ancestor of the Duke of Fife, and as security he granted him a bond over Muirtown near Findhorn, an estate which he had recently purchased from his brother-in-law, Innes of Muirtown, who had fallen into financial difficulties. This is not the only banking transaction Kilravock had with the Duffs of Braco. William, Lord Braco, was a freeholder, having a right to vote in the county of Nairn in virtue of a Kilravock property qualification down to 1747, when his claim was purged and paid. The laird of Brodie was exceedingly annoyed when he found that Calder and Kilravock kept the estate of Lochloy to themselves, but a few years later he got Inshoch and Lochloy proper (with its moss, which he much desired), and these lands have since continued in the possession of the family of Brodie of Brodie. The last of the old family of Lochloy was Colonel William Hay. Hugh Hay of Park continued a freeholder in virtue of his possession of Park, Newton of Park, Bognafouran, etc., but in the year 1755 these lands passed into the hands of Sir Alexander Grant of Dalvey. A tablet with an elaborate Latin dedication to the Hays of Lochloy still exists in the old choir of the church of Auldearn, but during some repairs of the wall it appears to have been found necessary to reduce the size of the monument, which was done by slipping out the middle portion containing several lines of the elegy, and this was built into an outside wall, along with a fragment turned upside down !

Sir Archibald Campbell, the sheriff of Nairn, did not live to witness the Rebellion. He died in 1744. Charles Robertson of Urchany succeeded to the office of depute sheriff on the demise of Robert Donaldson, but it was again vacant in 1742, and Patrick Clark, surgeon in Nairn, was appointed. He had acted as sheriff-substitute on several occasions, and now received the salaried appointment. It was he who passed the ferocious sentence of branding in the Sheriff Court in 1743. On the death of Sir Archibald, John Campbell of Calder, as hereditary sheriff, resumed the office of high sheriff, and appointed his kinsman Alexander Campbell of Delnies to be his depute. The laird of Calder had by this time attained to considerable eminence in the political world. He had a seat in Parliament, was for some years a Lord of the Admiralty, and became a Lord of the Treasury in 1746.

The laird of Brodie, who retained his seat for Elginshire, was now Lord Lyon of Scotland. Thomas Brodie (Lethen's brother), the Writer to the Signet, was Depute Lord Lyon. Duncan Forbes of Culloden (Kilravock's brother-in-law) was Lord President of the Session, and exerted himself to the utmost to prevent his northern countrymen joining the Jacobite Rebellion.

In the burgh of Nairn, between the years 1729 and 1736 (with one year's exception), the chief magistrate was a military man of some renown—Colonel Alexander Rose (brother of the unfortunate Arthur), who has already been mentioned as having greatly distinguished himself at Sheriffmuir on the Royalist side. He is described as Colonel Rose of Lord Londonderry's Regiment. It was he who gave a start in life to the young laird of Culbin after the ruin of that house. He was a half-brother of the old baron, and resided in the Kilravock " town-house," as the building which stood on the north side of High Street (now Macgillivray's Buildings) was called. It had been enlarged and repaired, and a handsome outside stair erected, and when all was finished in 1722, a slab was placed in front bearing the following inscription :

> " Omnia terrena per vices sunt aliena ;
> Nunc mea nunc hujus, post mortem nescio cujus ;
> Nulli certa domus."

Of which a translation is given thus :—

> " All terrene things by turns we see
> Become another's property ;
> Mine now, must be another's soon,
> I know not whose, when I am gone ;
> An earthly house is bound to none."

The stone with its inscription still remains in the renovated building, and one room of a back wing, with fine oak panelling, is still preserved intact.   From a return a few years later, it appears that the original building had fourteen windows.   Colonel Rose had passed away before the Rebellion, and the laird of Kilravock was once more Provost of Nairn.   The only recorded official act the magistrates performed was to appoint a quartermaster for disposing of the troops halting in the town—their first visitors being the army of Sir John Cope, when he hurried from Inverness to embark at Aberdeen for the south.   His troops lay at Merryton, to the east of Nairn, for a day, and Lady Dunbar's tenants refused to pay their next year's rents in consequence of the damage their crops had sustained from the soldiers.   A curious reminiscence of the visit of Sir John Cope is preserved.   A fisherman's wife presented her husband with a son on the morning of Sir John Cope's arrival, and the child was christened John Cope.   The child's descendants still bear the name of Main Cope or Coup.

Prince Charles Edward landed from a French frigate at Moidart in the Hebrides on 19th July, 1745, and raised his standard at Glenfinnan on 20th August.   Cameron of Lochiel joined him, and was followed by several other Highland chiefs.   His force amounted to only fifteen hundred men, but in his march southward it swelled into an army.   Charles entered Edinburgh in triumph, and his father was proclaimed " James the Eighth " at the Market Cross.   On 21st September he fought the battle of Prestonpans, completely routing Sir John Cope and his army.   He continued his march with an army augmented to 6000 men, as far as Derby, which he reached on 4th December, and intended proceeding onward to London.   But the support he calculated upon from the Catholics and Jacobites of the north of England failed him.   Three English armies were on the move against him.   In these circumstances he deemed retreat to the Highlands advisable, and fell back rapidly on Glasgow.   Reinforced there by several thousand men, he at Falkirk attacked and defeated General Hawley's army, which had followed him from England.   Many of the Highlanders after the victory made off to the mountains with their booty, and Charles marched the remainder of his troops northwards to Inverness.   He arrived there on 16th February, and additional clansmen joined him.   The district between the Spey and the Ness was now in his hands, and the Highlanders pillaged and robbed friend and foe indiscriminately. During part of the month of March the Prince was at Gordon Castle and Elgin, where he was overtaken by severe illness, but he returned early in April to Inverness. He left a force under Lord John Drummond to dispute the passage across the Spey of the Hanoverian army which was in pursuit of him, and, if that failed, to harass it on its march.

The Duke of Cumberland remained at Aberdeen till 8th April, his progress northward having been stopped by the flooded state of the Spey. Having forded the Spey on the 12th the army resumed its march, passed through Elgin on Sunday the 13th, and halted at the Moss of Alves. Next day the march was resumed. Ray, in his " History of the Rebellion "—he was a volunteer officer in the Royalist Army—mentions that they were obliged to ford the Findhorn, " a broad and deep river." " From this to Nairn," continues Ray, " is a very moorish country ; to the left of which we perceived a body of the rebels at a mile distant, on which we drew up ; but perceiving they did not advance, we fell into marching order until we came within half-a-mile of them, and then, observing that they did not form but kept in a moving posture, the Duke of Kingston's horse, with four companies of the Campbells, were ordered to advance ; on this the rebels fled, and being pursued by some volunteers, we had a fine hunting-match after them. We took some prisoners, of whom I had the good fortune to get two, the one a Fraser, who could speak no English, and had not the sense to stand when shot at until he was cut twice in the head ; the other was a Montrose man called Sanders Stewart (heard of him on my return, that he served an apprenticeship to a barber there), he told me that the rebels were 5000 the day we crossed the Spey, under the command of Lord John Drummond, and that the Chevalier and the rest of his army were then at Inverness. After I had got these two fellows held together with my horse collar they proved very troublesome to drive, and I had above two miles over a moor to go with them to our army, who were then encamped at Nairn, which before I entered I had occasion to go through that wing of our army where the old Buffs were pitching, and my prisoners were condemned to various deaths by the Old

Buffs' wives. I delivered my prisoners to the guard, and in the evening went and dressed the wounded Highlander. By this time the quarters were all taken up, so that I did not go to bed the two nights the army lay there."

Lord John Drummond had fallen back as the Royalist army advanced, but at Nairn he made a stand with a large party of men. They barricaded the bridge, and as Kingston's horse advanced, they fired upon them. The troopers and some detachments of infantry then began a regular assault on the bridge. Shots were exchanged and a brisk fire kept up, but as the main body of the Royalist army had now made its appearance, Drummond drew off his men and fled precipitately towards Inverness.

Lord Albemarle, commander of one of the divisions, writing from Nairn on 15th April to the Duke of Richmond, thus alludes to the incident at Nairn bridge—" The rebels might with ease and no danger to themselves have disputed the passage of every one. At this town [Nairn] whether insolence in them or whether they did not expect us so soon I can't tell, we heard they proposed waiting for us. The Duke immediately sent the cavalry forward, who not only drove them out of it, but four miles beyond, where, having taken a few prisoners, they were forced to stop for want of the foot coming up in time to sustain them. This body of theirs, consisting of about four thousand, retired to Inverness, to meet and fight us on our march thither, but I don't believe it."

The entry of the Duke of Cumberland's army into Nairn must have been an imposing sight. His forces numbered about 7000 infantry and 2000 horse. The Old Buffs, as Ray mentions, bivouacked on the east bank of the river. A portion of the troops was lodged in the town, but the main body marched out to Balblair where they formed a camp. The Duke of Cumberland took up his abode in Kilravock's town-house, already described. The next largest house was the manse. The minister at the time was Mr. Alexander Rose. Clava's house (now the Caledonian Hotel) was also occupied by the officers. Bailie Kenneth Sutherland had a pretty large house on the High Street, and Mr. John Falconer and Mr. George Grant came next with houses of some size. These were all occupied by officers. The Tolbooth was also made of use

for sleeping accommodation. The whole town was thronged with
the military, and guards patrolled the street from the bridge to the
Horologe Stone.

The Duke of Cumberland gave orders that the troops should
rest next day, and it being his Royal Highness's birthday, the army
celebrated the occasion with great rejoicings. The centre of the
camp was the house of Balblair, a gaunt old building belonging to
Rose of Clava—the only gentleman of Jacobite proclivities in the
district. The house stands on a slight eminence, and the tents
were pitched on the slopes around it, a line of guards being posted
westward along the ridge as far as Kildrummie and eastward to
the town. In the town and at Balblair the mirth and revelry ran
high, but at ten o'clock lights were ordered out, and all betook
themselves to rest, to be refreshed for an early start in the morning.

On the evening of the 14th Prince Charles moved from Inverness to Culloden. Here he was joined by the party under Lord
John Drummond which had retreated from Nairn, and, expecting
the Royalists to advance, drew up his army in order of battle on
the moor. Lord George Murray, with the trained eye of a soldier,
saw the advantages which the level field would give to regular
troops, and strongly urged that the Highland army should cross
the river Nairn and take up a position on the slopes and heights
on the south, with the mountainous region behind to retire upon.
But his advice, though supported by most of the Highland chiefs,
was rejected by the Prince, probably because it would leave Inverness exposed.

On the Tuesday Prince Charles rode out to survey the field.
About two o'clock he sent an officer to Kilravock Castle to inform
the laird that he would dine with him that day. He arrived about
three and was received with all respect, though Kilravock was on
the opposite side. The Prince charmed his host and hostess by his
affability. He asked to see their three children, kissed each of
them and praised their beauty. Observing a famous old violin,
he begged the laird to play a tune. Kilravock, who was a good
performer, played an Italian minuet, remarking, " That, if I mistake not, is a favourite of your Royal Highness." " That it is a
favourite of mine, Mr. Rose, is certain, but how you came to know

that it is so I am quite at a loss to guess." "That, sir," replied Mr. Rose, "may serve to show you that whatever people of your rank may do or say is sure to be remarked." "I thank you," said the Prince, "for your observation." The Prince walked out with the laird to see his trees. Observing the people busy planting, the Prince remarked "How happy you must be, Mr. Rose, in being thus peacefully engaged, when the whole country around you is in a stir." The Prince, Mr. Hay his secretary, and Mr. and Mrs. Rose dined together in what is now the parlour of the old castle, while forty of the Prince's attendants dined in a large hall adjoining. The short passage between the two rooms was guarded by two of the Prince's officers with drawn swords while he was at dinner. When the cloth was removed, Kilravock proposed to the Prince that he should allow these gentlemen to go to dinner, adding, "Your Royal Highness may be satisfied that you are perfectly safe in this house." To which he replied, "I know, sir, that I am safe here; you can desire them to go to dinner." Some joking followed at the expense of the Prince's secretary, who expressed a wish to see a huge china bowl, capable of containing sixteen bottles of liquor, filled. It was promptly filled with whisky punch, and the Prince in gay humour insisted that Mr. Hay, since he had challenged the bowl, should stay to see it out. He took but one glass, and then accompanied his master back to Culloden.

On the return of the Prince from Kilravock, Lord George Murray suggested that instead of waiting for the advance of the Royalist army, they should attack the camp at Nairn after nightfall. This bold scheme pleased the Prince, but when the troops assembled in the evening it was found that they had no bread and were in a half-famished state. Several officers advised giving up the night march, but the Prince gave peremptory orders, and the expedition set out for Nairn, marching in two columns. The first, composed of the clans, was led by Lord George Murray, the second, consisting chiefly of Lowland regiments, by the Earl of Perth. The Prince, with his staff, was between the two columns. The plan was boldly conceived. The first column had orders to cross the river about three miles from Nairn, and then lower down re-cross and attack the English army in flank and rear. The second column was to make its attack from the west, keeping as near as possible to the coast road. This would have brought the one division out at the Nairn Moor (now Tradespark), and the other at Broadley or Firhall. But the night was dark, the road was rough, and the men were exhausted for want of food, so that the march was slow. At two o'clock in the morning, when the attack was to have been delivered, the advance column had only reached Knockanbuie ("the Yellow Knoll"), about three miles from Balblair. The leaders called a halt, held a consultation and decided it was too late to make the attack. Lord George Murray thereupon gave the order to retrace their steps. The roll of a distant drum indicated that the English were on the alert. The Prince, who was in the rear, was very angry when he learned that the retreat had been ordered, and military critics are of opinion that Lord George Murray's judgment was at fault in having so readily given up a plan of battle, which, whether carried out at night or in daylight, was vastly better than retiring again to the level plain of Culloden Moor, which now became the scene of the final stand.

On the morning of the 16th, whilst the Highland army was once more getting into position on Culloden Moor, several ladies rode on to the field. One of these was Miss Elizabeth Campbell of Clunas, the lovely daughter of Duncan Campbell. She was specially interested in the gallant leader of the Clan Mackintosh. Lady Anne Mackintosh, whose husband, the chief of the Mackintoshes, was on the Hanoverian side, and at the time was with Loudon's Regiment in the Black Isle, called out the clan in favour of the Prince, to whom she was devotedly attached, and had asked Duncan Mackintosh of Castle Leathers, who was residing at the time at Daviot, to lead the clansmen. He was highly pleased at this mark of honour (says the writer of a manuscript of the time, quoted by Mr. Fraser-Mackintosh), but in the meantime Macgillivray of Dunmaglass sent a message to her ladyship that the Macgillivrays would not follow her banner unless the chief command was entrusted to him. The lady, fearful of losing so important an ally, made a polite excuse to her relative, Duncan Mackintosh, importing that she had been compelled to place

Macgillivray over him.   He, indignant at what he justly conceived
an affront, retired to his own home and vowed he would not take
part with one or the other.   Mackintosh at the time was engaged
to be married to Miss Dallas of Cantray, whose brother was a
strong Jacobite and had raised a regiment for the Prince.   " Miss
Dallas of Cantray carries the bell of fine ladies," wrote a swain of
the period to a friend in the south ; " I shall see her before I leave
the country."   She subsequently consoled Castle Leathers for his
disappointment in not being allowed to lead his clan.   Macgillivray
of Dunmaglass was the *beau ideal* of a Highland chief.   He was
of gigantic stature, strong limbed, and of huge strength, and yet
there was a feminine delicacy about his features that was very
remarkable.   An old man who had seen him described him thus
—" He was a clean purty man, he stood six feet two in his stocking
soles, his hair was red and his skin white as milk."   Such was the
hero to whom Elizabeth Campbell had come to say a parting word
on the morning of the battle.

Meanwhile the Royalist camp at Nairn was quickly aroused.
The Duke of Cumberland had information from his spies that an
attack at Nairn had been intended, though he did not expect that
it would take the form of a night surprise.   The soldiers the night
before had received a liberal allowance of brandy, biscuit, and cheese,
but the Duke took care to see that when they retired to rest each
man's accoutrements should lie at his side in case of a hurried call,
and, to make sure there would be no disorder or confusion, he left
his quarters at Nairn and slept at Balblair in the midst of the camp.
A hurried meal was made, the tents were struck, and the troops
formed into three divisions of four regiments each, commanded
respectively by Huske, Sempill, and Mordaunt, with a column of
artillery on one hand and a column of horse on the other.   Just
before leaving Balblair Cumberland rode along the parallel divisions,
and the general orders of the day, threatening immediate death to
deserters or defaulters in action, were read at the head of each
regiment.   It was five o'clock when the march began, and by nine
o'clock they were passing Kilravock.

When the Duke came up with his troops, Kilravock was at the
gate to receive him.   " So I understand you had my cousin, Charles,

here yesterday?" "Yes, please your Royal Highness," replied Kilravock; "not having an armed force, I could not prevent him." "You did perfectly right," said the Duke, "and I entirely approve of your conduct." So saying he rode on to the moor of Culloden to meet his cousin.

An unpublished letter by James Granger, surgeon's mate in Pultney's Regiment, to his brother William in London, gives the following account of the march and the engagement, which, though strongly biased in favour of the Royalists, has the interest and merit of being the description of an eye-witness—

"On the morning of the 16th we decamped by break of day from Nairn and were in sight of the enemy by eleven, who were drawn up in one very long line across Culloden Moor. Upon this our advanced guard came back, the army was in an instant marshalled in order of battle. The cavalry was equally divided on the flanks, the Campbells were posted at a little distance from the left of the front line, and orders were sent to the ba-men, women, etc., forbidding them to come within a mile of the rear. These material points thus settled, we continued our march, and about 12 were come so near them that I could observe their right wing to be composed of the Clans, the left of the French, and their centre of the Lowlanders. Where their cavalry was I could not see. The ground on which they stood was plain, and the field seemed every way adapted to decide the fate of the Rebellion. Here the whole army fixed bayonets, and renewed their priming, while our nine piece of cannon were planted at regular distances in the front of the first line. The Duke says a battle without cannon is like dancing without music—his ears were soon gratified with that martial music. For the Rebels now welcomed us to the plain from a battery on their right, but they fired too high and the balls whizzed over the Corps de Reserve. The compliment was returned forthwith by a complete round from our Artillery, but to better purpose; most of the shots took effect and laid numbers of them sprawling on the ground. The cannon gave our men infinite spirits. The enemy renewed their charge not only from their first battery but from two others to their left. They only made our gunners fire the faster, and really complimented the enemy at least twenty for one. The wind drove the smoke in the teeth of the enemy; their batteries were silenced in the space of eight minutes, and their line partly raked. The thunder of our cannon was perpetual, and if they had stood still much longer where they were, our matrosses would have done the business. This they were sensible of. Their whole line advanced forward to attack our first line in the order they were drawn up.

"The Clans rather flew than marched, consequently our left was not only soonest but hottest engaged, for nothing could be more furious than their onset, which no troops but these, headed by our magnanimous hero, could have withstood. Yet not a regiment was broke, not a soul deserted his colours, true, indeed, their small arms did little execution, but they seemed determined to make amends for this by their broadswords, had not the regiments they attacked prevented them by a very brisk and heavy fire—we had some hundreds of them breathless on the ground. This ruder reception (perhaps) than they expected did not, however, dispirit the Clans. They rallied, and before our left (viz., Barrels, Monroes, and the Highlanders), could load, came again like lions to the charge, sword in hand, but the claymores would make no impression against the bayonet charged breast high. Our men stood like a wall, shoulder to shoulder. Here, however, Lord Robert Ker was killed and Lieut.-Colonel Rich lost his left hand. More officers than these must have fallen had not the battalions in the centre of our line, viz., Scots Fusiliers and Cholmondeley's, before whom the Lowlanders began precipitately to fly almost without attacking, turned part of their fire against the Clans, and with such success that but few of them had leisure to return from the attack."

So runs the letter of Surgeon Granger.

The charge of the Highlanders was, however, more formidable than this Royalist account represents it. Galled by the fire of the artillery, there were murmurs for the charge, but minute after minute sped, and no order was given. The Prince and his staff occupied an eminence a little distance behind the two lines, and Lord George Murray waited for his order. But no order came. Unknown to him, young Maclauchlan, the Prince's aide-de-camp, had been struck by a cannon ball on his way to the front, and lay dead on the field with the Prince's order in his pocket. The Mackintoshes in the centre, who had been exposed to the hottest fire of the artillery, could stand it no longer, and with Dunmaglass at their head, they rushed forward to engage the enemy. Lord George Murray called on the Athole men, Camerons, Stuarts, Frasers, and Macleans to follow him. The charge became general along the whole line, except on the left, where the Macdonalds, offended at not being placed on the right, refused to move. Onward rushed the devoted Highlanders in face of a blinding hailstorm, in face of the deadly grape-shot from the cannon, and the volleys of bullets from a thousand muskets—into the smoke and fire they plunged, and madly flung themselves on the solid wall of glistening bayonets. The shock broke the first line of the Royalists, but like a spent wave, the onward motion had exhausted itself, and not a man reached the second line. The Highlanders lay in piles three and four deep.

Surgeon Granger's narrative at this point goes on to say—

"The confusion of the enemy was now pretty universal, only the French as they marched more orderly so they were only come now within musket shot of our right. At the beginning of the action our regiment, Pultney's, was advanced from the Corps de Reserve and posted on the right of the Royals, an honour for which we were indebted to the Duke of Cumberland, and here it was that we not only regained our character, but were particularly complimented by his Royal Highness. But what could they or any other troops have done ? The Royals and our regiment were ready and eager to engage, and not a man of either the 2nd or Corps de Reserve had discharged. They (the French), however, made a show to charge and flank us, but after a fire (not like the French) they followed the example of their mountainous friends and made with all the swiftness their feet could carry them towards the town. Our regiment did not miss this opportunity, and with one good volley made numbers of them bite the ground.

"The whole field on their side was one continued scene of slaughter and dismay. They flew scattered in little clusters everywhere, but most made after the Pretender to the mountains. Our

cannon again thundered.   Our light horse and dragoons who had
never been engaged were sent after them and did terrible execution
—many they took prisoners, but more they killed, for the pursuit
lasted four miles beyond Inverness.

" In the field were taken ten 6-pounders.   Whilst His Royal
Highness advanced at the head of the infantry towards Inverness
he was met by an officer from the Brigades who surrendered themselves prisoners of war in town.   Inverness was immediately taken
possession of by a regiment, where they found six more field pieces,
and our royal conqueror entered the place about 4 o'clock.

" Immediately upon flight of the enemy, I rode over the field of
battle.   You may be sure it gave me infinite joy to see those who
threatened ruin to our glorious constitution of Church and State
dead in the field, which joy was not a little augmented by observing
how very few, not twenty of our men, were killed.   As the Campbells were on the left, and therefore in the hottest of the action,
they lost two captains—that is the sum of the slain.   That of the
enemy cannot certainly be known, for we daily find dead bodies,
six, eight miles from the place—it is conjectured to amount to
1800.   Our men have got a great deal of booty.   The Pretender's
coach and Boger's are taken.   On the coach was painted the
Welsh arms and below ' Prince Charles ' in letters of gold.   We
have between 2000 and 3000 prisoners.   Amongst several of distinction are Earls Kilmarnock, Cromarty, and their sons ;   Lord
Drummond, Glenbucket, Stewart of Ardshiel, Appin, etc.   They
mustered 8350 the day before the battle, as was found in an officer's
pocket ;   it would have been ended fatal to us, had we given way,
for their Prince gave orders to spare neither man, woman, or child,
and so confident was he of success that in the same orders he forbad
any man to stir from his rank to plunder till after the pursuit."

The carnage which ensued has for ever dimmed the lustre of
the feat of arms achieved by the Royalist Army.   The wounded
on the field were butchered as if in sport.   Prisoners were shot
down in batches, and in some cases houses were fired and the
refugees roasted alive.   The shocking atrocities exceeded the
bounds of civilised warfare, and have made the name of Cumberland infamous for ever among the Highlanders.

Prince Charles witnessed the destruction of his army from a hillock still marked by a tree, and when he saw all was lost, he rode off accompanied by one or two members of his staff, crossing the river Nairn at the ford at Faillie. His subsequent wanderings and escape to France belong to general history. The Royalist forces pushed on to Inverness, leaving the dead unburied and the dying uncared for. The night which succeeded the battle was intensely cold, and many of the poor soldiers in whom life still lingered made the night hideous by groans and cries for water—that last solace of a wounded soldier. During the night some of them extricated themselves from among the corpses of their companions piled in the ditch and dragged themselves to a little well close by. Here, next morning, was found the body of Macgillivray of Dunmaglass. According to the tradition of the country, Dunmaglass was one of the gallant band who broke through the front line of the defence, and was last seen fighting with his broadsword in rear of the enemy's cannon. He cut down a dozen of his assailants before he was overpowered and laid low. He was left for dead, but according to the current story he was one of the miserable sufferers who lingered on during the night and who crept to the well, and a touch of deepest pathos is imparted to the circumstance inasmuch as it is said that he, commiserating the sufferings of a wounded lad, summoned up his remaining strength and carried him to the well, and then fell back and expired. Whilst the rank and file of the clansmen were buried in trenches according to their tartans, the body of Macgillivray of Dunmaglass was borne by the country people, amidst great lamentations, to the churchyard of Petty and there decently interred. There was grief that morning in many a Highland home, but in none was it more poignant and distressful than in the old house of Clunas, where the fair Elizabeth Campbell mourned the fate of her lover. She survived his death but two short years, dying of a broken heart, and a stone still marks her grave in the enclosure in Barevan churchyard.

The Duke of Cumberland remained in the north for some time after. At Inverness he met Lord President Forbes, who pled hard for mercy for his misguided countrymen. Writing to the Duke of Newcastle on 30th April, His Royal Highness remarks " that the affair is now almost over with regard to the military operations, but Jacobite rebellious principle is so rooted in the nation's mind that this generation must be pretty well wore out before this country will be quiet. . . . Lord President has just joined me, and as yet we are vastly fond of one another, but I fear it won't last, as he is as arrant Highland mad as Lord Stair or Crawford. He wishes for lenity if it can be with safety, which he thinks, but I don't, for they really think that when once they are dispersed it is of no worse consequence than a London mob, and but yesterday a Sir William Gordon wrote to one of the officers to complain that his house has been plundered whilst he was out *following his duty* (as he is pleased to call the Rebellion). They are now dispersed all over the kingdom at their own homes, and nobody meddles with them except I send the military force after them. I have got the Lord President to direct Sir E. Fawkener in the drawing up of a proclamation which I shall take the liberty to publish in His Majesty's name, requiring of all civil magistrates to exert themselves in order that these dispersed Rebels may be brought to justice, but as one-half of the magistracy have been either aiders or abettors to this Rebellion, and the others dare not act through fear of offending the Chiefs, or of hanging their own cousins, I hope for little from them." On President Forbes remonstrating with His Royal Highness in regard to the barbarities committed by the soldiery in burning houses, plundering, and murdering, reminding him they were breaking the laws of the country, he replied with an oath, "The laws! I'll make a brigade give laws!" and he was heard at Inverness to allude to the president as "that old woman who talked to me about humanity." In another letter, Cumberland says—"I am sorry to leave this country in the condition it is in, for all the good that we have done has been a little *blood-letting*! which has only weakened the madness but not at all cured, and I tremble for fear that this vile spot may still be the ruin of this Island and of our Family."

Many of the fugitives died from exhaustion on the lone hill sides. A Culloden soldier's grave on a moor, now planted, near the ford on the Muckle Burn at Keppernach, Ardclach, is still preserved, though covered merely by loose stones.

Local tradition has it that a concealed chamber in the roof of

one of the wings of Cawdor Castle was the hiding place of Lord
Lovat.   It is called " Lovat's Hole."   Tradition, however, is at
fault, for old Simon was in hiding at Gorthlick near Foyers when
the battle was fought, and then fled to the west coast, where he was
captured, sent to the Tower of London, and executed, as were also
Lords Balmerino and Kilmarnock.   It has been suggested that
Lovat may have been in hiding at Cawdor from Lord Loudon's
troops some months before the battle.   There is, however, one
argument against the " Hole " having ever been used by Lovat
which seems pretty conclusive.   Old Lovat had become so stout
that it was a physical impossibility he could have been squeezed
into so narrow a space.   On the window of the place is scratched
the word " Overcome," with the date " 1685."   James Fraser of
Brea, the Covenanting preacher, was in hiding that year in Nairnshire, and as he was a favourite of Sir Hugh Campbell, he may
have been concealed in this secret recess, the name " Fraser's Hole "
becoming a century later " Lovat's Hole."

Lord Lovat and his kinsman Major Fraser, who brought him
from France, had quarrelled some years before the Rebellion, and
the Major consistently supported the Whigs and got some employment from Cumberland in connection with the Lovat estates.   He
spent the later years of his life at Inshoch, near Auldearn, with his
son Robert (who was for a time factor for the laird of Brodie),
and died at the age of ninety-two.   The Major's portrait hangs in
Inverness Town Hall.

Although the Rebellion was totally suppressed within the next
few weeks, the town of Nairn was kept in a state of commotion
for some time by the presence of large bodies of military.   Four
battalions which had been despatched from London about the end
of March did not arrive in the Moray Firth till the 6th of May.
They had been tossed about in the North Sea, and terrible disease
had broken out amongst them.   A fever of a malignant type prevailed, which was believed at the time to be the dreaded yellow
fever, brought from India by some of the troops.   Houghton's
regiment, amongst others, rested at Nairn on its way to Inverness,
and several of its officers and men were suffering from fever.   A
young officer, Captain Robert Nisbit, unable to proceed with his

regiment, was taken into the house of Dr. Clark, the sheriff-substitute, and one of the leading men in the place. Nisbit belonged to the knightly family of Nisbit of Dirlton, in Haddington. He was carefully nursed by the doctor and his wife, a daughter of Rose of Broadley, but he died. His remains were interred in Dr. Clark's burying-place in Nairn churchyard, and a tombstone there bears the inscription : " Here lies the body of Captain Robert Nisbit, of Brigadier Houghton's Regiment, who died May 19, 1746, aged 26 years." Dr. Clark, the young officer's host, caught the fever, died a few days afterwards, and was interred in the same grave, but the tablet to his memory has disappeared. Strangely enough, some twenty years later, a young officer in Montgomerie's Highlanders (the old 77th), Lieutenant Lachlan R. Grant, son of Sir Patrick Grant of Rothiemurchus, died in the same house, then the residence of Dr. Forbes, who had married Dr. Clark's widow —the lady who had nursed Nisbit in his illness. Young Grant of Rothiemurchus was buried in the same grave, and the following inscription was added to the tablet—" As also here lies Lieutenant Lach. R. Grant, of Colonel Archibald Montgomerie's Highland Regiment, son of the Laird of Rothiemurchus, aged 25 years, and died November, 1767." It is probable that Dr. Clark at the time occupied Firhall, which belonged to the Grants of Rothiemurchus. The forest of Rothiemurchus had yielded considerable wealth to the family, and, desiring a winter residence in a less severe climate than their paternal home, they built a house at Nairn, which they called Firhall, because it was built with money got for the firs, and with wood brought from their forest.

On 18th August, 1746, the Town Council received notice " that four companies belonging to the Royal Irish are to be lodged in this town for winter quarters," and accordingly " they have, after billeting the private men, made out such a form of accommodating the officers, and fixed on a place for an hospital in case of sick among them, of which, according to directions in writing, the clerk is to make out a copy and deliver the same to the commanding officer for disposing of the officers under his command." At the same time the council directed the bailies and a quorum of the council to meet and make out such a stent upon the inhabitants of all ranks as would be sufficient for defraying the expense of coal and candle to the guard. On 2nd September the four companies arrived, and the records state that " in consideration that the troops now lying in town will want fire and candle for their guard room, do hereby empower the Collector of Cess of the burgh, to collect, conform to the roll of the inhabitants in his hands, in such proportion from each as shall be appointed by the following committee hereby appointed, namely, Bailie Robert Sutherland, Mr. William Inglis, and Hugh Robertson, bailies, and the clerk to attend, whatever other councillors please to be present and vote, the collector to keep exact accompt of disbursements upon the said subject to be given into the council against the first of October, the peats to be given in by order of the magistrates and to be gotten from the town and territories and an account kept of it in like manner, to ascertain from whom they are got and what number of loads ; as also the commanding officer here, having made a demand for coal and candle to an hospital in which he has some sick people, the bailies above named are to enquire what is law and common practice in the like case and to direct accordingly ; likewise as to the blankets required for the people lodged in town, the council find that all houses here are mostly taken up and given to their respective lodgers what bed clothes they say they can afford, so this must be referred to the meeting of the justices that they may judge and interpose their authority for providing what clothes the town cannot serve the troops with from the county, and a copy of this day's minute to be given to the commanding officer, subscribed by the clerk."

The Act forbidding the wearing of the Highland dress was duly enforced in Nairnshire, although most of its inhabitants had been loyal to King George. The sheriff-substitute of Nairn (James Rose of Brea) issued an order the 27th day of December, 1748, to the effect that, considering that the late Acts of Parliament made anent " restraining the Highland garb have with respect to the plaids and philabeg, or little kilt, taken place and commenced the 25th day of this month, and apprehending that many of the lieges may be brought to punishment by reason of their not being duly apprised of the same, for remeid thereof ordains publication and intimation to be made at the Mercat Cross of Nairn on a mercat day, and at the several parish churches of the shire upon Sunday next, and recommends to the several ministers to cause their respective precentors read the proclamation to be issued immediately after divine service, that all persons may be duly cautioned of their danger in case they trespass." The Act was disregarded by so many that the sheriff considered it necessary to issue a second proclamation a few months later to be published at the cross in the burgh, and at the parish kirk doors, and also to be read at the close of divine service, the ministers being recommended seriously to exhort their regular congregations to the due observance and performance of these Acts.

The laird of Calder, residing at the time in Wales, heard of the dissatisfaction the abolition of the Highland dress had caused among his tenants at Cawdor, and he wrote to his factor suggesting that they should wear canvas knickerbockers in lieu of the tartan kilts— " I have thought that the poor Highlanders who are distressed by wearing breeches might be very agreeably accommodated by wearing wide trousers, like seamen, made of canvas or the like. Nankeen might be for the more genteel. But I would have the cut as short as the philabeg, and then they would be almost as good and yet be lawful." Very sensible ; but how little does the laird of Calder understand the Highland character !

The state of feeling produced by these and other harsh and insulting measures must have inevitably led to another and perhaps more formidable rebellion, as soon as the natural elements gathered strength, had it not been for two causes which worked for peace and reconciliation, namely, the abolition of heritable jurisdictions and the raising of Highland regiments for the King.

CHAPTER XVI

THE LAST HEREDITARY SHERIFF

JOHN CAMPBELL of Calder was the last hereditary Sheriff of Nairn. The Act abolishing the heritable jurisdictions was passed in 1747. The holders of these offices were called upon to lodge any claims they might have to compensation, and these claims were investigated and reported on by the Court of Session. In only sixteen cases were the claims of the hereditary sheriffs held to be proved. One of the sixteen was that of the Sheriff of Nairn, but the change from the Calders to the Campbells had to a certain extent affected its monetary value. The laird of Calder claimed £3000 as compensation for the abolition of the sheriffship and £500 for the abolition of the office of Constable of the King's Castle at Nairn. For the former he was awarded £2000, but for the latter he got nothing, as the place was in ruins. The ground of the old castle still bears the name of the Constabulary, or Constabulary Garden. On it Lord Cawdor in recent years built a handsome house.

After the resignation of Alexander Campbell of Delnies, who had for some time the management of the Cawdor property, John Campbell of Calder sent north a Welsh factor, Mr. Valentine White, to attend to his interests. Valentine White resided at Polenach and afterwards at Brackla, and the correspondence kept up between laird and factor furnishes some interesting information regarding Nairnshire in those days. John Campbell, the laird of Calder, parted with the expensive acquisition of Islay and also sold off Muckairn, but, though seldom visiting Cawdor, he had great affection for the old place. Late in life—he died in 1777—he wrote—" If my grandson sees with my eyes, nothing done here

[Stackpole Court] will make him insensible to the natural beauties of Calder, or slight that ancient, honourable, and agreeable seat of the family. It would be tedious and fruitless to give the reasons why I have resided so little, and not laid out money at Calder, but I can truly say want of love or liking to the place was none of them. With the same money I might have made Calder exceed this place in everything except being farther north and the high rocks by the sea, which are indeed a great natural beauty."

The laird of Calder in his Welsh home, was, however, kept informed of everything that was passing in Nairnshire. Valentine wrote him that he had received, in the autumn of 1773, a visit from two distinguished strangers, namely, Dr. Samuel Johnson and James Boswell. He met them at tea in the manse of Cawdor. Their host, the minister, was the Rev. Kenneth Macaulay (grand-uncle of Lord Macaulay). Previous to his settlement at Cawdor, he had been minister at Ardnamurchan, and was the author of " A History of St. Kilda "—a work which procured him this visit of Dr. Johnson. Valentine asked the strangers to his house, and gave them a letter of introduction to Mr. Ferne, master of stores at Fort George. Boswell in his Journal records their meeting with Valentine White and getting the letter of introduction. " He showed the letter to me," says Boswell; " it recommended two celebrated gentlemen; no less than Dr. Johnson, author of his Dictionary, and Mr. Boswell, known at Edinburgh by the name of Paoli "—a compliment to Boswell's admiration of the Corsican hero. " He said," continues Boswell, " he hoped I had no objection to what he had written; if I had he would alter it. I thought it was a pity to check his effusions, and acquiesced, taking care, however, to seal the letter, that it might not appear that I had read it." In commenting on the news, the laird of Calder gives his personal opinion of the two distinguished visitors. " The weakness of Mr. Boswell," he writes, " in regard to the foolish and absurd stories which abound in the Highlands, and indeed in all very remote and lonely places, amazes me. Mr. Johnson is a learned and ingenious man, and his Dictionary a useful book; but there are some things in it which, I fancy, he now wishes were not there. For instance the articles on ' oats ' and ' excise,' which are both silly and impertinent; and I observed two or three things in Mr. Boswell's books which I thought wrong; but no man is or can be without failings." Johnson and Boswell spent a night in the inn at Nairn, and the great lexicographer records that the place was "in a state of miserable decay, and for aught he knew, might have still a Lord Provost!" "At Nairn," says Dr. Johnson, "we may fix the verge of the Highlands; for here I first saw peat fires, and first heard the Erse language." He was attracted by a girl he saw industriously working her spinning wheel and singing a Gaelic song.

Valentine White informed the laird of all that was doing in ecclesiastical matters. Calder disliked immensely the "high flyers"—the evangelical party of the time. On the subject of popular election in the Church he had strong opinions. "I think," he wrote, "the popular calls, concurrent in a presentation, are very absurd things, and the gentlemen by giving in to them increase the pride and insolence of the clergy, and encourage a turbulent disposition in the common people. True national religion is the best thing in the world, but superstition and enthusiasm are two of the worst and most mischievous. They usurp the name of religion, but are in reality the greatest enemies to it and to the peace of the world. They are the engines of wicked hypocrites to work their ends and bad purposes, and to govern and mislead the weak and well meaning." Like most men in his position, the laird of Calder misunderstood the real character of these religious revivals. They are reactions from deadness and formality in religion, and impart fresh vigour and life to the Church.

Valentine White did not find the tenantry of Cawdor very well satisfied when he arrived amongst them. Unpopular changes had been introduced in regard to their holdings by Sir Archibald Campbell and his son. Sir Archibald in his report to the Commissioners in 1725, wrote—"The tenants upon the Cawdor estate being numerous and generally poor, refuse to take leases at the present rent, and their houses are all of faile." He could think of no other way for bettering or improving the estate than "if the Commissioners incline to give him a nineteen years' lease thereof, he will transmit his proposals whereby he will be enabled to find more substantial tenants, fewer in number, and instead of heightening their rents or taking entries, he will take them bound to build their houses in stone, enlarge their gardens, and plant about their several possessions." This was the state of things Valentine White found, and he was at a loss what to do. Evictions were not to be thought of, and yet there was absolute need of consolidation of holdings in order that the tenants might be comfortable, and new methods of cultivation introduced to improve the estate. He wrote to the laird that he had consulted the laird of Lethen, and Calder wrote back—" Lethen's information and advice will certainly be of great use to you, and you will take some pains calmly to reason with the people and show and convince them of their past mistakes, and how much better it will be for themselves in many things to follow new methods. I don't say that all will be capable, or can be made willing, to hearken to good advice and instruction; that is more than can be expected in any country; but I am satisfied you will find many that will be persuaded to hearken to reason, and, when they hear it, may be made to understand it, and then they will follow it. Great allowance must be made for the pre-judices of education and old habits."

All men will honour John Campbell for the sentiments contained in the following letter of his to his factor—" You were extremely in the right in choosing to make labourers of the poor people in the country. And indeed there can be no improvement made about Calder which will please or oblige me so much as improving the poor people by teaching them industry and such work as is proper for the country. I hate to hear the people of any country thought below the rest of mankind because they are untaught. There was a time when the inhabitants of the politest parts of England were at least as rude and ignorant as any Highlanders; and those who in their pride despise the inhabitants of remote, ill-cultivated countries, might have been among the worst of their people. It must cost time and trouble to teach the ignorant what they never learned, and to *unteach* them, if I may use such a word, what they have learned wrong, but the time is well spent, and the trouble will afford great pleasure to an honest, benevolent mind."

At a later period he writes—" It grieves me to hear of so much sickness among my poor tenants. I wish I had sooner thought of sending Dr. James's book and powders, which I really believe will be of great service if the people will be persuaded to follow the directions. In this country many people, I believe, are killed in fevers by keeping them too hot, not letting any air come to them, heaping clothes upon them, and letting numbers of people come into their room and talk to them, whereas they should be kept as quiet as can be, the air cool, etc."

Cattle disease broke out in 1770, and the laird wrote to his factor—" I am extremely sorry to hear that the distemper among the cattle is broken out so near our country. Its being in the air I think a groundless imagination. But from what happened in Greenwich Park when the like distemper was in England, I am satisfied it may be carried by dogs in their hair, and that being near the ground, and they apt to tumble on the ground, the dogs infect the grass."

The factor consulted him on the subject of hedges, indicating a preference for whin hedges. The laird does not much fancy them, but he yields the point. " My objection to whin hedges was that I thought frost would kill them, but after what you say, I can only prefer hawthorns for their beauty." He recommends constant clipping and pruning. " Hawthorns," he adds, " are very beautiful as standard trees, though not large ; and I should fancy some here and there in your whin hedges, pruned up above the top of the whins, would have a pleasing effect and not hurt the hedges."

The wasteful and slovenly method of covering roofs with sods or divots, the laird of Calder could not abide. He wrote—" No tack or lease to be given without a clause to prevent cutting of divots for covering of buildings. Straw, I know, is scarce, but broom or heather may be had. It is true it will take a little more trouble to cover with than with divots, but if even the poorest tenants spent a little more of their time in taking care of their houses and other proper work, instead of lying a great part of the day idle upon the side of a brae, it would be better for themselves as well as for their landlords." The sting in the tail of the letter was probably required at the time. The laird was fond of having his own ideas in the matter of planting carried out, but he showed consideration for the feelings of his neighbours—" Remember," he

There was evidently an intention to create a series of rural villages along the cultivated land between Delnies and Ardersier, and places are marked out and named as Frasertown, Campbeltown (of Delnies), Cuthbertown, etc. The " Cadger's Road," leading from Delnies in the direction of Kildrummie, indicates that the Delnies fishers took their fish to the country and not to the town. A hill to the south of Easter Delnies was named " Tomintoul." The ridge running east and west was called the Drum of Nairn.

After the Rebellion of 1745, the Government wished to build a fort to overawe the Highlanders, and selected as the site a fishing village called Blacktown, belonging to Calder, at the point or sand-spit below Ardersier. These lands, as formerly mentioned, belonged in early times to the Order of the Knights Templar. Calder now disposed of part of them to the Government, the inhabitants of Blacktown were removed to the nearest point beyond the Government ground, and the new locality was called Campbell-town, in honour of the superior of the soil—making the third village of that name. The Government also acquired the neighbouring farm of Hillhead, in proximity to the garrison, which was named Fort George in honour of George II. The Government sold this farm of Hillhead in 1833 to Mr. Archibald, Edinburgh, whose representative sold it again to Mr. Orr Ewing. In 1792 the rental was £50 ; it is now over £500. The building of Fort George was begun in 1747, and cost £160,000 ere it was finished.

CHAPTER XVII

POLITICAL HISTORY

THE system of parliamentary representation began, properly speaking, in the year 1681. Previous to that time, all barons were required to give personal attendance at the parliaments. The barons regarded it as a burden rather than a privilege, and sought relief and obtained it so far as to be allowed to combine in sending two or more " wise men " of their number from each sheriffdom. Hence arose the custom of payment of members. Sir Hugh Campbell's bill against the eighteen poor heritors of Nairnshire in 1673 for attendance at four sessions of Parliament amounted to £1785, not including his own share, which would probably be a fourth more. In the course of the seventeenth century more value began to be attached to a seat in Parliament, and various Acts were passed defining the qualifications of those who had a right to vote for Commissioners to Parliament.

In 1681 an Act was passed declaring that none should have a vote but those who were publicly infeft in property or superiority, or in possession of a forty shilling land of Old Extent holden of the King, or in lands liable in public burdens for four hundred pounds of valued rent, or wadsetters (bond-holders in possession of the rents of the land), apparent heirs to deceased predecessors, and husbands in right of their wives. These constituted the county freeholders entitled to vote, down to the passing of the Reform Bill of 1832.

The burghs each sent one or more commissioners to the Convention of Royal Burghs.

When the Rolls of Parliament were called previous to the Union, Nairnshire stood twentieth among the counties, taking precedence, of Cromarty, Argyll, Forfar, Banff, Kirkcudbright, Sutherland, Caithness, Elgin, Orkney, Clackmannan, Ross, and Kinross.

After the Treaty of Union an Act was passed which ordained that thirty of the forty-five representatives in the British Parliament allocated to Scotland should be chosen by the shires, one for every shire, excepting the shires of Nairn and Cromarty, which should choose by turns (Nairn having the first election), and the shires of Bute and Caithness, and Clackmannan and Ross, which were similarly bracketed. It thus happened that at each alternative Parliament the county of Nairn had no representative. The burgh of Nairn was grouped with Inverness, Forres, and Fortrose. The Town Councils of each burgh elected a delegate, and these delegates elected the Member of Parliament, the election taking place in each burgh by turn, which was called for that time the presiding burgh.

The first Member of Parliament for Nairnshire after the Union was Hugh Rose of Kilravock—the baron who afterwards took such an active part against the Jacobites in the Rising of 1715. He had at the time of the Union been a commissioner of the shire, and was nominated as its representative to the United Parliament of Great Britain. When it came to be Cromarty's turn to elect in 1710, that county returned Sir Kenneth Mackenzie of Cromarty, and with little variation continued the representation in the laird of Cromarty's family in subsequent parliaments.

The first contest of which there is any particular account was in 1735, when Alexander Brodie of Lethen was chosen member for Nairnshire. His opponent was James Brodie of Spynie. The contest lay between the interests of Calder and Lethen on the one side, and that of the Brodies of Brodie on the other. The number of voters on the roll was eleven. According to James Brodie of Spynie there ought to have been more, but the sheriff-clerk, Mr. Robert Donaldson, had made up a " packed roll "—he had left out some unfavourable to Lethen's side. However that may be, the sheriff-principal (Sir Archibald Campbell of Clunas) declared Lethen duly elected. The laird of Spynie petitioned the House of Commons against his return, and raised an action in the Court of Session in regard to the disputed points relative to the making up of the roll, but the election was sustained by the House of Commons, and the litigation in the courts came to nought. When the barons or freeholders met in 1742 the heat generated by the election had not subsided, and there was a renewal of the fight. Every claim was keenly contested. It was the fixed rule of procedure that the last member of Parliament present should receive the roll of freemen from the sheriff and should call it. Mr. Brodie objected to Lethen doing so, but the custom depended on statute, and Lethen called the roll. When it came to electing a preses of the meeting, however, Alexander Brodie, Lord Lyon, was chosen. The majority this time was the other way, and several names were added and expunged by the Lord Lyon's party, in spite of Lethen's opposition. It was, however, the turn of Cromarty to elect for this Parliament, so there was nothing at stake. When the next election came round, in the year 1747, peace had been made up, and John Campbell of Calder (whose letters to his factor have been given) was unanimously elected member for the shire of Nairn. He had been a Lord of the Admiralty in 1736, and served in the Ministry of Pelham in 1746, as a Lord of the Treasury. He sat for Nairnshire till 1754, when it became the turn of Cromarty to elect.

At Brodie's death the office of Lord Lyon was gifted to John Campbell, second son of the laird of Calder, and Alexander Campbell, his brother, who became conjunct Lords Lyon, with retention to the longest liver. Alexander became a lieut.-colonel in the army, and left the duties to be performed by his brother John, who assumed the name of Hooke in addition to that of Campbell—John Campbell Hooke becoming a well known personage in political circles.

John Campbell of Calder was then proposed for the Inverness burghs. The representation of these burghs was practically in the hands of Culloden and Kilravock. The Forbeses were provosts of Inverness, and the Roses of Nairn. Kilravock also exercised a controlling influence in Fortrose, and Forbes usually followed suit. Duncan Forbes of Culloden represented the Inverness burghs from 1722 till 1737, when he was appointed Lord President of the Court of Session. In 1747 Alexander Brodie of Brodie, Lord Lyon, was elected.   Inverness was the presiding burgh on that occasion, and the Nairn Town Council deputed Hugh Rose, younger of Kilravock (or Geddes, as he was called), to represent the burgh of Nairn at the election.   Brodie died on 9th March, 1754, in London, of heart disease.

The election of John Campbell of Calder in 1754 was attended by great excitement.   Nairn was the presiding burgh, and an armed mob seized the town.   The minutes of the council (written in a shaky hand indicative of the excitement of George Donaldson, the town clerk) give a graphic account of the circumstance—" At and within the dwelling-house of Hugh Rose of Kilravock, Esq., in the Burrow of Nairn, and in the hall of the said house, the thirty day of Aprile, 1754 years, betwixt the hours of eleven and one of the clock, the said day in presence of Hugh Robertson, bailie, Nathaniel Leitch, Dean of Guild, Hugh Rose of Kilraick, Esq., James Rose of Brea, Lewis Rose, Esq., Alexander Campbell of Delnies, David Falconer of Grieshop, and Alexander Douglas, wright, common councillors of the said burgh.   The council, considering that for these several days past there has been a tumultuous assembling of armed men in this town, who having upon last Lord's Day, commonly called Sunday, got possession of the Court-house and Tolbooth of this place, forcibly and contumelously keepit the same, and without any known reason have frequently refused access to the Sheriff-Substitute of this county when demanding the same in an agreeable manner, in order to hold courts and administer justice.   As also considering that the mob, armed as above, have frequently thrown stones at, and threatened to stab and shoot any persons who should attempt to enter the said Tolbooth or walk upon the outer stair thereof—they particularly did yesterday, the twenty-ninth instant, menace the said Hugh Rose of Kilraick, and swear that they would shoot him with a pistol one of them had then in his hand if he offered to move one step further towards the Tolbooth, where the said Hugh Rose was then intending to go, and at the stair-foot of which he was then standing ; as also did catch hold of Alexander Dunbar of Boath, Sheriff-Substitute of the County, by the breast, and did threaten and abuse him, both yesterday and this day, and when he demanded access, as said is, the mob from the steeple of the prison threw stones at the said Sheriff and others present with him, notwithstanding of the Mob Act, it being publicly and audibly read at the stair of the said Tolbooth in presence and by appointment of the said Sheriff, and the mob desired to dismiss under the certification and penalty mentioned in the said Act. And further, considering that the said mob is still in possession of the said Tolbooth and the doors shut, notwithstanding of the hour appointed to meet for the election of the delegate being past, as appears by an instrument of protest taken in the street opposite the door of the said Tolbooth, under the hand of a notary and witnesses. Therefore and in order to prevent any bad consequences from the said tumultuous mob, them or any of them, did and do hereby agree to hold this meeting for choosing the Commissioner or Delegate in consequence of the appointment of the twenty-sixth current, at the said house of Hugh Rose of Kilraick, within the burgh of Nairn, being the most secure and convenient place for that purpose." They proceeded to the election according to the usual forms, and " the vote being put, Doctor Joshua Mackenzie, son-in-law of the said Hugh Rose of Kilraick, was by the whole members present, being a majority of the Town Council of the said Burgh, unani- mously elected and chosen Commissioner or Delegate of the said Burgh of Nairn."

On the 9th of May following, the delegates met within the tolbooth without obstruction or molestation. They unanimously elected John Campbell of Calder. Doctor Joshua Mackenzie, the delegate of Nairn, was the father of Henry Mackenzie, the author of the " Man of Feeling." He had married Kilravock's daughter Margaret.

Sir Alexander Grant of Dalvey was chosen for the Inverness burghs in 1761. He was engaged in extensive foreign business, and had made a large fortune. He purchased the property of Grangehill belonging to the Dunbars, and changed its name to Dalvey, which it has since retained. Sir Alexander also acquired the property of Park in Nairnshire from the old family of Hay which, like the Dunbars of Grangehill, decayed about this time. He also acquired lands in the burgh of Fortrose. Sir Alexander was made a burgess of Nairn, and was on very friendly terms with the magistrates, but on his purchasing James Rose of Clava's property, they had a violent dispute with him about the boundaries of Balblair, which ended in an expensive lawsuit carried on for years by his brother Sir Ludovick, who succeeded him. The Grants had misfortunes in business, and had to part with their property in this district. Sir Alexander Grant, at a later day Principal of Edinburgh University, represented the baronetcy.

Colonel Hector Munro of Novar, the distinguished Indian officer, was elected member for the Inverness burghs in 1768. On his return from India he purchased from Rose of Kilravock the property of Muirtown at Findhorn (a part of which still belongs to Munro-Ferguson of Novar), and with it secured the representation of the burghs. His relative, Sir Harry Munro of Foulis, was appointed the delegate of Nairn to attend the election at Fortrose. Colonel Hector Munro had cultivated the good graces of the Nairn Town Council by becoming a member of the council some years before, and he continued a member for several years, eventually becoming Provost of Nairn as well as member for the Inverness burghs. A few weeks after his first election to Parliament, he presented the town with a clock for the steeple, which the Edinburgh clock-maker guaranteed to be " as good a clock as is in Scotland for its size." Novar was knighted and continued to represent the Inverness burghs till 1802, having been returned to six parliaments successively. Sir Hector's re-election to the Parliament of 1780 took place at Nairn, when " Alexander Munro, Esq., his Majesty's Consul General to Spain," was appointed the Nairn delegate, the council testifying that " he was a man fearing God, and of the true Protestant religion now publicly professed and authorised by the laws of the realm."

On the retirement of Sir Hector Munro in 1802, the representation of the Inverness burghs passed to the Gordon-Cummings. Sir Alexander Penrose Cumming-Gordon, son and heir of Cumming of Altyre, was elected in 1802, but accepted the Chiltern Hundreds in the following year. His brother, George Cumming of London, who had been in the naval service of the East India Company, and afterwards settled in London as a merchant, succeeded him in the representation of the burghs. In 1806 he made way for the Hon. Colonel Francis William Grant of Grant, who, however, stood in the following year for Elginshire, which he represented without a break until 1837. He became Earl of Seafield in 1840.

Mr. Peter Baillie of Dochfour represented the burghs from 1807 till 1811. Following the precedent of Novar, he became a member of the Nairn Town Council, but seldom attended its meetings.

In 1811 Charles Grant of Glenelg became member for the Inverness burghs, and sat till 1818, when he stood for Inverness-shire and was elected. He held high office in successive governments, and on his elevation to the peerage took the title of Lord Glenelg. Mr. George Cumming of London again came forward in 1818 and was elected, remaining until 1826. Sir Robert Grant, a brother of Lord Glenelg, succeeded him, and sat for the burghs from 1826 till 1830. He married a daughter of Sir David Davidson of Cantray. Sir Robert Grant became Governor of Bombay, and occupied a distinguished position amongst the public men of the time. He was succeeded by Colonel John Baillie of the Leys.

To return to the county representation. While John Campbell, the old laird of Calder, represented the Inverness burghs, his eldest son Pryse Campbell sat for the county of Nairn. He was unanimously elected in 1761. In the previous Parliament he represented Inverness-shire. Valentine White, the factor for Cawdor, acted as his procurator in the election proceedings at Nairn. On 4th December, 1766, Pryse Campbell sought re-election in consequence of having accepted office in the Ministry as a Lord of the Treasury. Two years later he died—his death happening on 4th December, 1768, the second anniversary of his re-election. A new Parliament having to be elected in that year, Cromartyshire had the choice of the representative, and, departing from the traditional custom, elected a stranger—William Pulteney —who sat till the Parliament expired in 1774. Mr. Pulteney was really a Johnstone of Dumfries, but having married the heiress of Daniel Pulteney, first cousin of William, Earl of Bath, he assumed the name of Pulteney and dropped that of Johnstone. He was a man of enormous wealth, commonly reputed to be one of the richest subjects in Great Britain. He hoped to be retained for Nairnshire when it came to be its turn to elect, and with that view he acquired an electoral qualification as a freeholder of two davochs of land at Auldearn. His procurator was Hugh Rose of Aitnoch, who was the liferenter of the two davochs, Mr. Pulteney being only entitled to exercise the vote in the absence of the liferenter. Thus Hugh Rose began to manufacture votes in the county in the interests apparently of Mr. Pulteney, among others claiming being the Earl of Fife, George Ross of Pitkery, and John Ross, advocate. The two first claims were rejected. The other side added Captain John Fraser, late captain of a company in the 48th Regiment of Foot, on a liferent qualification on Kilravock property, Henry Mackenzie, attorney in exchequer, "The Man of Feeling," on a vote for Coulmony, etc. Two years previously Kilravock had created four additional votes on his property, in addition to his own and his son's vote. These new voters were Mr. Lewis Rose, Captain William Rose, Captain Hugh Rose of Brea, and Mr. Alexander Rose in Flemington. They held in liferent. The manufacture of one of these faggot votes led to a change in the destination of the property in a later generation. It is curious to find one of the great ecclesiastical leaders in Scotland at this time —Principal Hill of St. Andrews—holding a fictitious vote in Nairnshire. He qualified on the liferent of the superiority of Balmakeith. During the twenty years he held the qualification he, however, voted only once.

The election, for which there was so much preparation, took place on the 25th October, 1774. There were nineteen voters on the roll, and thirteen voted. The contest lay between Cosmo Gordon of Cluny and Mr. Pulteney, and of that number eleven voted for Gordon, and two—Rose of Aitnoch and Mr. John Ross —for Pulteney. The Gordons of Cluny had by this time acquired the property of Kinsteary, formerly a possession of the Sutherlands. Mr. Pulteney soon afterwards relinquished his faggot vote in Nairnshire, having found a seat in England. He died in 1805, and was buried in Westminster Abbey. His daughter was created Countess of Bath.

Mr. Cosmo Gordon was made a Baron of Her Majesty's Exchequer in Scotland in 1777, and resigned as member for Nairnshire. The Whig compiler of the " Confidential Report on the Political State of Scotland " at that period, remarks about the Gordons— " Baron Gordon was made a Judge by Lord North, and is attached to Campbell of Calder, and his brother Charles Gordon made a Clerk of Session by Dundas and the Duke of Gordon. They have a good estate and interest. As the Baron has no children Charles is the heir-presumptive, and will be much directed by the Baron. They are both men of character and abilities."

Baron Gordon presided at the election of his successor on 18th April of that year. John Campbell, younger of Calder (his grand-father was still alive, but died a few months later), was unanimously elected, and represented the county of Nairn till the close of the Parliament in 1780, when, it being Cromarty's turn to elect, he sought and obtained a seat in Wales, which he retained until raised to the peerage as Baron Cawdor of Castlemartin in 1796—the first laird of Calder who became a peer.

In 1784 the minute of election of a member for the county of Nairn records that Captain Alexander Campbell, of the late 75th Regiment of Foot, was elected and chosen to be their representative by those present (except James Brodie of Brodie, who voted for himself). Captain Campbell's death in the following year caused a vacancy, when the candidates were Mr. Alexander Brodie, now returned from Madras, and Captain George Campbell, of the Orpheus frigate, a brother of John Campbell of Calder. Brodie, the Indian nabob, was elected by a majority of one—the votes being 9 to 8. He was a man of considerable wealth, and purchased the estate of Arnhall in Kincardine. He was presented with the free-dom of the city of Edinburgh, and married a daughter of the Hon. James Wemyss of Wemyss Castle by Lady Elizabeth Suther-land, daughter of the seventeenth Earl of Sutherland. His only daughter and heiress, Elizabeth Brodie, became Duchess of Gordon, having married in 1813 George, last Duke of Gordon. In the following Parliament, Cromarty having the choice of the member, Alexander Brodie stood for the Elgin burghs, and was elected. He was a great friend of Henry Dundas, who administered affairs in Scotland.

B.H.N.   U

When the county of Nairn in 1796 was again called upon to elect, they unanimously chose Colonel Henry Frederick Campbell, of the First Regiment of Guards, and re-elected him in 1806. He was a cousin of Lord Cawdor, and served with distinction in Holland and the Peninsula, being made a General and a K.C.B. Sir Henry retired in 1808.

In 1812 Hugh Rose of Kilravock was elected member for the county, but in the following year accepted the Chiltern Hundreds.

In 1813 the county of Nairn returned as its member one of the most distinguished men of the time—Sir James Mackintosh, the statesman and philosopher. Sir James was descended of the family of Mackintosh of Kyllachie. The fame he had acquired by his great work the "Vindiciae Gallicae" had reached the north, and the Cawdor family, always friendly to the house of Kyllachie, made interest for him and got him the seat. On the occasion of his election he came to Nairn, and revisited the scenes of his youth. Sir James is said to have been a pupil at the Nairn parish school, but this is doubtful. He received part of his early education at the old grammar school at Fortrose. Sir James continued to represent the county of Nairn till the dissolution in 1818, when Cromarty once more elected the member.

In 1820 Admiral George Pryse Campbell, R.N., son of Lord Cawdor, was elected, and represented Nairnshire till the dissolution of 1826. He was again elected in 1830, and sat till 1831.

Major Cumming Bruce was member for the Inverness burghs during the agitation immediately preceding the passing of the Reform Act of 1832. His election in 1831 took place at Nairn. Captain Rose of Kilravock presided at the election, and the provosts of the other burghs were present—namely, Provost Robertson for Inverness, Provost Gordon for Forres, and Provost Macfarquhar for Fortrose. According to a contemporary account, Captain Rose proposed the Major's election "in a very neat and appropriate manner." The election was unanimous, and after the Major had returned thanks, he invited the commissioners and his friends to a dinner in Richardson's Hotel. It was the last political dinner under the old regime. When next the Major sought re-election, he had to fight for his seat under the extended franchise.

There were several meetings for reform in the burgh of Nairn, and a great trades demonstration took place. On the last night of the year 1831, a large anti-slavery meeting of the inhabitants was held in the Secession Church. " The night was intensely cold," says the newspaper account, " but there were many people from the country present." Mr. Robert Falconer occupied the chair, and addresses were delivered by Mr. Isaac Ketchen, Mr. Mackintosh, Millbank, Dr. Smith, Rev. James Mein, Secession minister, Mr. Henry Mackenzie, Mr. Cant, and Mr. Cameron. Resolutions were passed calling upon the Government to abolish slavery in the British Dominions, and to use its influence with the nations of Europe and America for the entire extinction of the slave trade. The petition was forwarded to Mr. Joseph Hume, M.P. Shortly afterwards another meeting was held in favour of the passing of the Reform Bill, when Mr. Ketchen and the other leading Reformers gave addresses, and a petition was drawn up and copies were ordered to be forwarded to the Earl of Cawdor, Lord Brougham, and Mr. Joseph Hume. It is apparent from the numerous petitions sent to him by the burgesses of Nairn that Mr. Joseph Hume was the popular politician of the day.

By the Reform Act of 1832 Nairnshire was combined with the county of Elgin in the election of a member. The first member returned by the united votes of the combined counties was Colonel Francis William Grant, who retained the seat till 1840, when he became Earl of Seafield. He was succeeded in the representation by Major Cumming Bruce of Dunphail, who sat in seven parliaments, extending over the period from 1840 till 1868. Major Cumming Bruce was a strong Conservative. The Duffs made several efforts to defeat him, but failed. The leading Whig or Liberal family in the county of Nairn was that of Brodie of Lethen.

When Major Cumming Bruce retired, he was succeeded without a contest by the Hon. James Grant, who sat till 1874, when, after a keen fight, the seat was gained by Lord Macduff for the Liberals.

On the death of his father in 1879 Lord Macduff became Earl of Fife. He was created Duke of Fife in 1889, on the occasion of his marriage with Princess Louise of Wales. The bye-election which followed on the elevation of Lord Macduff to the Upper

House was keenly contested.   Sir George Macpherson Grant of Ballindalloch was the Liberal candidate, and Brodie of Brodie the Conservative.   Both gentlemen were personally very popular, and the election turned almost exclusively on the Eastern question, then occupying public attention.   Sir George won by a majority of 56 votes.   At the General Election of 1885 a three-cornered fight took place.   The extension of household suffrage had enfranchised a large class of new voters in the counties.   Brodie again entered the field as Conservative candidate against Sir George as the Liberal, while Mr. C. W. Anderson, Q.C., appealed to the Radical voters. Sir George was returned at the top of the poll by a majority of 56, receiving 1612 votes.   Brodie polled 1556 votes, and Mr. Anderson 1435.   At the General Election of 1886 the split had occurred in the Liberal Party over the question of Home Rule for Ireland, and Sir George, though receiving as a Liberal Unionist the support of most of the Conservatives, was defeated by Mr. Anderson by a majority of 119.   The numbers were: Mr. Anderson, 1991 ; Sir George, 1872.   Mr. Anderson having gone to Natal and settled there, the early resignation of his seat was looked for, and the Conservatives and Liberal Unionists adopted Brodie of Brodie as their candidate.   Brodie's health, however, gave way, and he had to seek alleviation of his suffering by travelling on the Continent.   Mr. Anderson's unexpected death in Africa in 1889 necessitated an election, and Brodie being still unwell, retired. The Unionists selected Mr. C. B. Logan, W.S., and the Radicals adopted Mr. Seymour Keay.   Mr. Keay was returned by a majority of 529.   Whilst the contest was in progress intelligence came of the death of Brodie of Brodie.   At the General Election of 1892 Mr. Keay was opposed by Sir William Cameron Gull, but was again returned, by a majority of 545.   The result of these last two elections showed that the sympathies of the great body of the electors enfranchised under the Act of 1885—notably the fishermen and farm servants—were with the Radical section of the Liberal party.

Later members for the constituency of Moray and Nairn were Mr. John E. Sutherland and Mr. John E. Gordon.

Resuming the history of the representation of the Inverness

burghs, Colonel John Baillie of Leys, as already stated, succeeded Sir Robert Grant in 1830 at the election caused by the death of King George IV. Colonel Baillie had a most interesting career. His father was Dr. George Baillie of Inverness, who was the grandson of the first possessor of Mid Leys, and his mother was a sister of Colonel John Baillie of Dunain. He was intended for the profession of law, but ran away from the law office in Edinburgh where he had been serving as an apprentice. A friend in England procured him a commission as Ensign, and he went to India. He had a brilliant record as a soldier, and came home in 1822 with an ample fortune, out of which he built Leys Castle. Colonel Baillie was a Whig, and voted for the Reform Bill, which established a £10 household qualification in the burghs and enfranchised leaseholders and copyholders of £50 and upwards in counties. The Bill having been thrown out, Earl Grey's Ministry appealed to the country in 1831. Colonel Baillie's pronounced Liberalism had apparently given offence to the managers of the representation of the Inverness burghs, and Major Cumming Bruce was elected in his stead. The Reform Bill having passed the House of Commons, and the House of Lords having offered it no further opposition, it became law, and a dissolution of Parliament followed.

The first election under the extended franchise took place in the month of December of 1832. No fewer than four candidates stood for the Inverness burghs, namely, Colonel Baillie, Mr. Stewart of Belladrum, Major Cumming Bruce and Mr. Fraser of Torbreck. The candidature of Mr. Fraser was regarded somewhat as a farce, and the contest really lay between the three first-named. The electors had the choice of three shades of politics— Major Cumming Bruce representing the uncompromising Tory, Colonel Baillie the Whig, and Stewart of Belladrum the Radical. There was extraordinary excitement at the time. It was of course open voting, and feeling ran very high. Colonel Baillie was returned at the top of the poll with 250 votes, Stewart of Belladrum came next with 243, Major Cumming Bruce polled 142, and Fraser of Torbreck 6. Poor Colonel Baillie did not live long to enjoy his parliamentary honours. He died of influenza in April of the following year (1833), leaving Leys Castle uncompleted.

At the election which followed, Major Cumming Bruce again came forward to do battle for his party, and Stewart of Belladrum stood as the accepted Liberal candidate. The bulk of the Whigs voted for the Major in preference to Belladrum, and he was returned by a majority of 66, the numbers being—Major Cumming Bruce, 358 ; Stewart, 292.

In 1834 another keen contest took place. Major Cumming Bruce was opposed by Mr. Edward Ellice of Invergarry, in the Whig interest. Young Ellice was a strong opponent, and was very popular, especially with the numerous class of non-electors, but Major Cumming Bruce's supporters stuck to him, and he was returned again, but only by the narrow majority of 4. The numbers were—Cumming Bruce, 344 ; Edward Ellice, 340. The electors in Forres warmly espoused the cause of the Major, their friend and near neighbour, which saved his seat. Apparently Major Cumming Bruce accepted the vote as a warning to remove, and he did not stand again for the Inverness burghs, but a few years later re-entered Parliament for the counties of Elgin and Nairn. Mr. Ellice was returned for the St. Andrews burghs at the next election, and sat for the constituency for forty-three years continuously, becoming one of the most influential private members of the House of Commons. He died in 1880.

At the General Election in 1837 on the death of King William, and the accession of Queen Victoria, the seat was contested by Mr. Roderick M'Leod of Cadboll in the Liberal interest, against Mackenzie of Scatwell, Conservative, who was defeated by 19 votes. Young Cadboll accepted the Chiltern Hundreds in 1840, and in the election which followed there was a keen fight between Mr. J. Fraser, Cromarty House, and Mr. James Morrison, a London merchant, head of the great drapery firm of Morrison, Dillon and Coy. Mr. Morrison was returned by a majority of 46, the numbers being—Morrison, 353 ; Fraser, 307.

A General Election took place in the following year (1841) and Mr. Morrison was unopposed. Morrison made lavish promises, few of which he ever fulfilled. He was a millionaire, but some years before his death he believed he was a poor man, and insisted upon his relatives contributing £1 a week towards his support.

The elections over the country had gone against the Whigs, and Sir Robert Peel took office at the head of the opposite party (who adopted for the first time the name of Conservatives) with a majority of over a hundred. It was a very strong government, but it split up over the repeal of the Corn Laws, and the Whigs returned to power under Lord John Russell.

At the election of 1847 Mr. Alexander Matheson of Ardross came forward as a supporter of Lord John Russell. He was opposed by Mr. Hartley Kennedy, a London merchant, as an independent candidate, but Mr. Matheson was returned by a majority of 81, having polled 280 votes as against 199 for Kennedy. Mr. Matheson held the seat for the next five parliaments—a period extending from 1847 till 1868. During that time he was unsuccessfully opposed on two occasions by Mr. Campbell of Monzie. Mr. Matheson, although not a great speaker, was a most useful member, and was largely instrumental in opening up the north by means of railways. On retiring from the Inverness burghs in 1868 he was elected for Ross-shire, and was created a baronet in 1882.

Mr. Mackintosh of Raigmore succeeded Mr. Alexander Matheson of Ardross in 1868 without a contest, but was defeated by Mr. Charles Fraser Mackintosh of Drummond in 1874. Mr. Fraser Mackintosh retained the seat until 1885, when he stood for Inverness-shire. The Liberal Association invited three candidates to address the constituency—Mr. W. S. B. M'Laren, manufacturer, Mr. J. Macdonnell, barrister, and Mr. R. B. Finlay, Queen's Counsel. The Association chose Mr. M'Laren, and Mr. Macdonnell retired, but a large body of the electors declined to accept the association's nomination, and invited Mr. Finlay to come forward. He did so, and won by 163 votes. Mr. Finlay voted against the Home Rule Bill in 1886, and at the General Election which followed he was opposed by Sir Robert Peel, as the Gladstonian candidate. He defeated Sir Robert by 273 votes, and during the succeeding Parliament he supported the Unionist Government with conspicuous ability. In 1892 he was opposed by Mr. Gilbert Beith, Gladstonian candidate, who was returned by a majority of 53. Mr. (now Viscount) Finlay in 1887 purchased the property of Newton, near Nairn.

At the subsequent election in 1895 Mr. Finlay recovered the seat from Mr. Gilbert Beith, and held it till 1906, when he was defeated by Mr. J. Annan Bryce.

After the transference of the burgh of Nairn to the county constituency of Moray and Nairn, in 1918, the representative was Sir Archibald Williamson. Following him, at the election in November 1922, Mr. T. Maule Guthrie, as Coalition candidate, defeated Mr. James Scott, Liberal. At the election in the following year Mr. Guthrie was in turn defeated by Captain the Hon. James Stuart, Unionist, youngest son of the Earl of Moray, who retained the seat at the election in 1924 against Mr. Benjamin Skene Mackay, the Socialist candidate.

CHAPTER XVIII

AFTER THE REBELLION OF 1745

DURING the fifteen or twenty years immediately succeeding the Rebellion of 1745, the district of Nairn, in common with the Highlands generally, appears to have been in a very deplorable condition. A memorial presented to the Convention of Burghs by the Town Council of Nairn in the year 1751 gives a very vivid, but perhaps overdrawn, picture of the impoverished state of the burgh. The council being distrained by diligence for arrears of missive dues at the instance of George Irvine of Newton as executor to his father (who had been agent for the Royal Burghs for several years), the council prayed the convention in Edinburgh to make a visitation of the burgh with the view of ascertaining its true condition, and granting relief. The memorial sets forth that " the common good of the burgh is so inconsiderable that, *communibus annis*, it will scarce amount to £50 Scots, which is not sufficient to pay the town's servants, support the windows of the court house, and defray the charge of coal and candle to the military and other measures necessary for their guards, who in the winter season are constantly quartered here and are daily passing and repassing, and have been so since the year 1715 ; that several of the treasurers of this burgh have broke and gone off with the town's revenue, small as it is, without accounting for several years, and some of them died bankrupt, considerably in arrear to the town ; that by reason of the smallness of the common good the burgh is not able to send a commissioner to the convention to represent their grievances, and the small trifle it is possessed of is expended annually as aforesaid and not sufficient even to answer those ends ; that the

King's House, public streets and harbour are all decayed and in a ruinous state, which is a considerable loss to the place, and trade also decayed, as are a great part of the biggings within the burgh ; that Kilraick, the present provost, when last a member of the convention (which is not many years ago) applied for relief of the claim of missive dues then, in consideration of the extreme poverty of the place, and having scarce any such thing as trade stirring amongst us, to which the convention was pleased to give a favourable answer, and surely had not the troubles happening in the country intervened, application had been long ere now made for relief and redress of these grievances and for assistance from the Royal Burghs." On 3rd July, 1751, after due consideration of the foregoing memorial, the convention appointed the burghs of Inverness, Forres, and Elgin to inquire into the state of the burgh of Nairn. Accordingly on 20th December of that year, Bailie John Mackintosh, delegate from Inverness, Alexander Brodie of Brodie, Lord Lyon, delegate from Forres, and Alexander Brodie, Esq., delegate from Elgin, visited Nairn, and reported to the convention that they according to the evidence laid before them, found " that all the public good or revenue of the burgh of Nairn consisted of shore dues, one public market, and a calfward or piece of grass, which three articles have been set annually by public roup from the year 1740 at £40, £60, £70, and £80, all Scots money, and for one year, viz., 1742, at £99 like money ; that they have likewise two acres of land and a house belonging to it which has been always given to their clerk and is his only salary ; that there are some trifling feu duties payable to the town, so small that they have not been exacted within memory ; that the same is reported to us for we have seen no evidence of it, and is also reported that there is no feu duties expressed in any charter or holding, but use and wont ; that from the year 1711 to 1740 the said articles have been much lower, some years at £20 and one year at £19 Scots money ; that we find the tolbooth or town house to be very insufficient and wants reparation ; and that the streets are in very bad order and much want to be causewayed ; that we find all the town treasurers preceding the year 1745 are dead and are told some of them died in the town's debt." The merchants in town appeared similarly depressed.

The state of matters was very different from that of a generation or two before, when one Nairn bailie, Hugh Robertson, gave a loan of five thousand pounds sterling to Lord Strathnaver, and another, Bailie Tulloch, made large advances to the neighbouring lairds.

When the Government under Pitt conceived the idea of raising regiments in the Highlands for service under the Crown, a new interest in life was created for the Highlanders. The experiment succeeded beyond all expectation. Regiment succeeded regiment. Government nominated certain prominent men as officers, and each officer secured his commission on bringing a quota of men to the field. Recruiting went on in the lowlands of Moray and Nairn as well as in the upland districts, and the proximity of Nairn to Fort George, the headquarters of the new levies, brought it into contact with the excitement of the new recruiting.

One of the earliest regiments raised in the north was that of the Fraser Highlanders. Government appointed the Hon. Simon Fraser (son of Lord Lovat), who had been, like his father, involved in the recent Rebellion, to raise a battalion on the forfeited estates of the family. Simon Fraser was to be Lieut.-Colonel Commandant. He raised 700 men. The next in command was Major James Clephane, whose sister had married Rose of Kilravock. Major Clephane had already seen much hard fighting. He had been an officer in a Scottish regiment in the Dutch war, and was taken prisoner at Sluys in May, 1747, and carried off to Dijon in Burgundy. His friends had him exchanged for another prisoner, and shortly afterwards he was put in command of Stewart's Regiment at the garrison of Tournay. Tired of Holland, he transferred to the British army, and received a commission in the Fraser Highlanders, on condition of his raising a company and undertaking to serve with the troops in North America. Arthur Rose, an uncle of the baron of Kilravock, who had also been in the Dutch service, assisted the Major greatly in the recruiting, and was appointed a lieutenant in the regiment. The business of recruiting for the Fraser Highlanders went on merrily in the earlier months of the year 1757. The ladies even took part in it, and one young lady writes to a friend—" I am happy to say I have made out my man!" meaning that she had won a recruit. The Major wrote to his brother that since he came north he had not been twenty-four hours at one time in one place—"one day at Inverness, next day return to Kilravock, and a third day at Nairn, and so on alternately, and often reviewing my recruits, and Kilravock and I engaging good men and dismissing worse." The Major's success is shown by the following minute of the Nairn Town Council—"20th April, 1757.—Whilst the council had under consideration the condition of the streets a letter was laid before them from James Clephane, Esq., First Major to the Second Battalion of Fraser Highlanders, directed to Mr. Alexander Ore of Knockoudie, treasurer of the burgh, wherein was inclosed five guineas gifted by that worthy gentleman, brother to Mrs. Elizabeth Clephane, Lady Kilravock, and freeman burgess and guild brother, as a token of his friendship, for being applied towards repairing the street. The which letter being read, the council in testimony of the high value they set on his friendship and of their due esteem and sincere affection for him do appoint and ordain their clerk to record said letter in the council book and lodge the original among the town's papers."

Major Clephane's letter is as follows—" Sir, I could not think of leaving this country without desiring you as treasurer to return my most sincere thanks to the magistrates and Town Council of your good town of Nairn and to all the honest inhabitants of it for the repeated marks of their friendship ever since I had the good fortune to be acquainted with them, but just now in a more particular manner for their activity and cheerfulness in assisting me in the recruiting of my company, when the assistance of real friends was so necessary to perform so great a work in so short a time, in which I own they have exerted themselves in a very remarkable manner towards me, and although my power be but small, consequently, as I can assure all of you, far below my inclinations to be of use or service to your town, yet I hope the magistrates and council will be so good as accept of my small mite here enclosed to you as treasurer towards assisting to repair the street at the west end of the town of Nairn, when the magistrates think proper to cause it to be repaired, where I yet hope to be merry with my friends after doing my duty to my King and country.—I am, sir, your obedt. humble servt.,   JAMES CLEPHANE."

Major Clephane was able to send off to Glasgow a company of 124 recruits, raised (he wrote to his brother) " by my worthy friend Kilravock and a few other friends, without any assistance from Colonel Fraser or his officers,"—" as good hearty young fellows as are to be seen in many regiments, and all as willingly and cheerfully engaged as is possible for any men to be." Arthur Rose went to Canada with him. The regiment was soon in the thick of the fighting. Arthur Rose was wounded, and wrote home to his grand-nephew—" I am sorry I can't accompany you with the fiddle any more, my left hand being rendered useless. The many battles, sieges, and skirmishes we have had fell heavier on us than any other regiment, having thirteen officers killed between Louisburg and Quebec, and a great number of men, among whom is poor Sandy Rose of Littletown." He expressed longings to be home again, to kill some muir fowl on the muirs about Coulmony or a fox in the mickle park or birkenward. But he appears never to have returned. At the conclusion of the war, a large number of the men, instead of returning home, procured leave to remain in Canada, and several lads from Nairnshire were amongst those who settled there.

Major Clephane came back to be merry with his friends in Nairn. He sold out of the army in 1760, and three years later he was elected a member of Nairn Town Council. In 1765 he was unanimously elected Provost of Nairn, which office he held for several years. He revived the custom of making honorary burgesses, which had declined during the dull times, and he never missed an opportunity of merry-making. His name occurs for the last time as a signatory to the appointment of Sir Henry Munro of Foulis as the burgh's representative at the parliamentary election in 1780. The village of Clephantown, near Kilravock, preserves the name of the Clephanes.

Two years after the embodying of the Fraser Highlanders, a regiment of Gordon Highlanders was raised by the Duchess of Gordon and her sons. Several of the officers belonged to Moray and Nairn, and a number of young men joined them. The second

Major was Hector Munro of Novar. He had been engaged in capturing the fugitive Jacobite chiefs in the Highlands. Alexander Duff, who had succeeded to the property of Culbin, was a captain; and young M'Gillivray of Dunmaglass, Ludovick Grant of Knockando, Archibald Dunbar, son of Dunbar of Northfield, and Duncan Macpherson also held commissions in the Gordon Highlanders, or old 89th. The regiment proceeded to India, and Major Hector Munro greatly distinguished himself. His career was most brilliant, and he was ultimately promoted to the rank of Major-General and made a K.C.B. The regiment served in India for four years, and when it was sent home and reduced, it returned with every officer it started with, excepting one, who had been promoted to another regiment, and not a man was brought to the halberts or deserted duty during the four years. The regiment was reduced in 1765.

A sensational incident occurred on the occasion of Novar's first return from India. As he was passing through the wilds of Badenoch, on his way to Inverness, he was beset by highwaymen, who attempted to rob him. The band was led by a scapegrace son of a Highland laird—Mackintosh of Borlum. Young Borlum fled the country. Three of his kinsmen concerned in the affair were convicted and hanged at Inverness for the crime. It was the last incident of the kind in the Highlands.

Whilst engaged in official duties at Fort George, Colonel Hector Munro appears to have been a good deal about Nairn and its district. In 1767 he was elected a member of Nairn Town Council— Major Clephane being provost. He was present at a meeting of council in the following year, and was annually elected to the office of councillor for many years. He is usually described as " absent," but the town clerk duly gives effect to the various distinctions won by this gallant soldier on the plains of India. He held the appointment of Governor of Fort George, and reviewed the successive regiments sent abroad from the north. Sir Hector (as elsewhere stated) was elected M.P. for the Inverness burghs, and made a gift of a town clock to the burgh of Nairn. He still kept up his connection with the place, and while serving in Parliament accepted the office of Provost of Nairn. A handsome portrait of this distinguished man is preserved in the Town Hall of Inverness. He died in 1806. Sir Hector had acquired a vast fortune, and expended £70,000 in building Novar House and laying out the garden, which latter alone is said to have cost £10,000.

In 1772 the Lovat property was restored to Colonel Simon Fraser, and in 1775 he was commissioned to raise another regiment of two battalions. He had six chiefs of clans amongst his officers, including Mackintosh of Mackintosh, Cluny, and Lochiel. They raised in all 2340 men. Colonel Simon Fraser, apparently on a recruiting expedition, was in Nairn early in 1776, and at a later meeting of the Nairn Town Council, Major-General Simon Fraser of Lovat was elected a Town Councillor. He continued one of the seventeen members of that body till his death in 1782.

Captain William Rose of the Earl of Sutherland's Regiment (second son of Kilravock) was admitted a burgess of Nairn on 2nd September, 1761. This Fencible regiment is said to have been the handsomest body of men under arms in Scotland. Captain Rose brought with him a quota of recruits from this district, mostly Roses and Frasers.

A prominent figure in Nairnshire at this time was Captain John Fraser in Geddes. He appears to have been a relative of Rose of Kilravock, and on his retirement from the army, having served with distinction in the 48th Regiment of Foot, he turned his attention to farming. He gave up the farm of Holme, however, after a short trial, and during the remainder of his life resided at Geddes. He appears as a freehold voter in the county of Nairn in 1774, and was a most regular attender at all the meetings of the barons. He also became a member of the Town Council, and acted for a time as town treasurer. Captain Fraser died about the year 1809.

Major Alexander Donaldson, of the Arr family, formerly referred to, was admitted a freeholder at the same time as Captain Fraser. Donaldson was at that time Major in the 76th Regiment or Macdonald Highlanders. Previous to this, he had served with the Black Watch in many a hard-fought battle. He joined the 2nd battalion of the 42nd as ensign in 1758, and for nineteen years, during one of the most heroic periods of the regiment's

history, he was its adjutant and a captain.   He is mentioned by
Colonel Stewart, in his history of the Highland Regiments, in
terms of high praise.   When the Macdonald Highlanders were
raised in the year 1778, they were, after being inspected at Inverness, immediately afterwards marched to Fort George under the
command of Major Donaldson.   The regiment remained for
twelve months at Fort George under the training of Major
Donaldson, " an officer," says Stewart, " admirably calculated to
command and train a body of young Highlanders."   An unfortunate incident in the history of the regiment happened on their
removal to the south to embark for foreign service.   They muti-
nied at Burntisland.   Each company gave in a written statement,
complaining of the non-performance by the Government of
promises made to them, accompanied by a declaration that until
their claims were satisfactorily settled they would not embark.
They requested that Lord Macdonald, the chief of the regiment,
should be sent to see justice done them.   Not having received a
satisfactory answer, they marched away in a body and took possession of a hill above the town of Burntisland, continuing firm to
their purpose, but abstaining from all violence.   There they remained for some days, sending into town for provisions, which they
paid for out of their own pockets.   " It happened fortunately,"
says Stewart, " that the regiment was at that time commanded by
Major Donaldson, an officer of great experience and not less firm
than conciliatory."   Born in the Highlands he understood perfectly the peculiar habits and dispositions of his countrymen.
Aided by the paymaster, an investigation took place, and every
man's claim was clearly made out.   When Lord Macdonald came
on the scene, he paid out of his own pocket the money claimed by
and justly due to the soldiers, and when all was settled they embarked with the greatest alacrity.   Major Donaldson, however,
did not accompany the regiment.   His state of health did not allow
of his going to America again, and he sold his commission to the
Hon. Major Needham, who afterwards rose to the rank of Lieut.-
General.   Major Donaldson received the appointment of Colonel
in the West Lowland Fencibles, no doubt through the influence
of the Campbells of Cawdor, to which house the Donaldsons were

warmly attached. Colonel Donaldson died about the year 1796. Captain Alexander Donaldson, of the 36th Regiment (apparently his son), qualified in October 1779 as a county voter on a Cawdor qualification—the superiority of Clunas—formerly held by Major Donaldson.

In addition to the recruiting for the regular army, a movement was set on foot in Scotland for the establishment of a local force. Stewart states that previous to the peace of 1801 the Volunteers in the Highlands and Islands exceeded 11,500 men. When the war recommenced, some 13,000 volunteers were embodied and placed in corps. Nairn had a regiment of 200, whilst Moray raised only 150, Banff 80, and Aberdeen 120. Inverness-shire, however, had four regiments, numbering in the aggregate nearly 2000 men, commanded by Culloden, Lovat, Glengarry, and Lochiel.

The early volunteer movement collapsed through the parsimony of the government of the day. At a meeting of freeholders of the county on 9th November, 1806, the thanks of the meeting were accorded to the battalion of Volunteer Infantry serving for the county, for the alacrity with which they enrolled themselves in the defence of the country, the zeal which they uniformly mani-fested in the discharge of their duty, and the high state of discipline and improvement which they had attained. At the same time, it was recorded " that the members comprising the meeting, and the county in general, are decidedly of opinion that though the battalion early and unanimously agreed to continue their services under every privation and discouragement, yet the reduction of their allowances is highly prejudicial, and must in the end prove destructive of the volunteer service." The minute goes on to say " that without a design to contemn or arraign the measures of the Government, this meeting candidly declare their opinion that unless the former allowances are continued, the volunteer service must dwindle to insignificance." The meeting directed that a copy of the above resolutions be transmitted to Lord Spencer and to Colonel Camp-bell, the member for the county. With a view to the formation of public opinion on the subject the press was called in, for the clerk was instructed to have the resolutions published in the " Edinburgh Evening Courant and Advertiser " and in the " Aberdeen Journal." But nothing came of it, and in a short time the anticipations of the meeting were realized.

Nearly fifty years before this an agitation had arisen for establishing a militia force on the same footing as in England. Apprehension of a French invasion was the active cause. In February 1760 a letter from the Lord Provost of Edinburgh (George Drummond) was submitted to Nairn Town Council urging them to support the annual committee of the Convention of Royal Burghs in having a militia established, " which recommendation his lordship enforced by mentioning the well known fact that during the greatest part of last summer all the burghs situated upon the seacoast of Scotland continued under the justest apprehension of being insulted or even destroyed by Captain Thurst's (French) Squadron." The council returned a warm approval of the proposal. Two years later both the freeholders of the county and the members of the Town Council of Nairn petitioned Parliament in favour of the establishment of such a force. In the minute of the Town Council, dated 11th February, 1762, it is declared that the council were unanimously of opinion that " the safety and honour of this country depend much on obtaining at the present juncture an extension of the Militia Laws to Scotland." The Local Militia was not established till 1808.

The Nairnshire Regiment of Local Militia was formed in the year 1808. The pay-list for the three months ending December 1808, shows that Hugh Rose of Kilravock was Commandant; David Davidson, Major; Benjamin Coates, Adjutant; and James Murray, Quartermaster. The pay of the Adjutant and Quartermaster was 6s. per day. The non-commissioned officers were— Sergeant-Major George Gowans; Sergeants Alexander Falconer, James Mackintosh, Duncan Smith, and Daniel Fraser; Drummers William Laing and Hugh Rose. Their pay was at the rate of 1s. 6d. per day. An account for " Breast Plates of Nairnshire Militia 1811 " gives the following details—15 corporals' plates, 8 drummers' plates, 258 privates' at 2s. each, £28 2s. Lieutenant-Colonel Rose certified that the above number of breast plates was furnished for the regiment by his direction and was necessary to complete the equipment of the regiment, and Major-General Leslie gave a certificate to the effect that he had inspected the breast plates, and that the supply was necessary to complete the equipment of the regiment as directed by the King's Regulations. One pleasant glimpse is afforded of this old Regiment of Militia. Mrs. Elizabeth Rose of Kilravock records in her Diary—" June 4, 1810—Morning, up early, drest to go to Nairn, and after an early breakfast Mrs. R. and I set out with the children.   Alighted at the Inn, and in about an hour after, accompanied by the Lord-Lieutenant (Brodie) and my son [Kilravock], the Sheriff and the Rev. Mr. Paterson, proceeded to the Links, where the Regiment of Local Militia were drawn up, and their colours being properly placed, Mr. Paterson, the chaplain (in his pontificals), proceeded to consecrate them, which he did in a most sublime, appropriate address to the Almighty, in which he alluded to the late disturbances in London, exhorting them to maintain our happy condition by resisting both internal and external foes.   Brodie then, taking the colours in his hand, addresst the Colonel and the Regiment, exhorting them to maintain the character they had already acquired, defending their country and families, and what was perhaps as dear as all else to a soldier, their honour ; he then delivered the colours to the Colonel, who, calling out the Ensigns, addresst them and the rest in a spirited manly voice, reminding them that though not called on as their fellow soldiers of the line to oppose our inveterate foe in foreign countries, to them was committed the arduous charge of defending their native country from invasion, and he trusted they would under these banners defend all that was dear to them to the last drop of their blood.   He then presented the colours to the Ensigns, and afterwards ordering the Regiment to present arms, he marched them into town, where they fired three volleys, a *feu de joie* on the King's birthday."   One of the Ensigns was Mr. James Grant, who a few years later became parish minister.   The day, it appears, from a story still current, was very windy, and Ensign Grant had some difficulty in keeping the colours flying aright.   He was provoked into the use of a choleric word.   It nearly lost him the kirk, for an old gossip who overheard it, treasured it up, and repeated the expression to the presbytery before his settlement. The minister of Ardersier, Mr. Pryse Campbell, came to the rescue, and suggested that the woman must have been entirely mistaken—the young minister could have *stappit* the water, but never the wind! The colours of the regiment, consecrated on the occasion, are still preserved at Kilravock, and the old drum is also in existence.

A distinguished man of letters, Mr. Henry Mackenzie, was about this time much associated with the county and burgh of Nairn. His father, Dr. Joshua Mackenzie, had married Margaret Rose, sister of the Laird of Kilravock. The marriage took place at Coulmony in 1747, and the ceremony was performed by Mr. Barron, minister of Ardclach. The Mackenzies frequently resided at Coulmony. Their son Henry was intended for the legal profession and went to London to pursue his law studies. He became a strong supporter of Pitt's Ministry, and was rewarded with the appointment of Crown Attorney in the Court of Exchequer in Scotland. He regularly spent the summer vacation in Nairnshire, and composed poetical inscriptions for walks at Coulmony, specimens of which are preserved in the Kilravock Papers. In the year 1771 he published his novel "The Man of Feeling," which had extraordinary popularity, and made the author famous. He became one of the leaders of literary society in the metropolis of Scotland, and in contemporary opinion was "among the last of the illustrious men who made the literature of the eighteenth century famous"—an estimate, however, not confirmed by later critics. His novel is written in the vein of false sentimentality made popular by Sterne and Richardson. Professor Henry Morley in his edition of "The Man of Feeling" cruelly prefixes an index to the "Weepings not including the Chokings" which occur in the work. Although his works of fiction are now unread, Henry Mackenzie did good service in his day as chairman of the Highland Society in investigating the Ossian controversy, and he also has the credit of being the first man of literary eminence who recognised the poetical genius of Robert Burns. It is curious to find the author of "The Man of Feeling" acting as a Town Councillor in Nairn. He was elected to that office on 30th September, 1776, in the very plenitude of his fame. Previous to the business of electing members on the occasion, Cosmo Gordon of Cluny, Lord Gordonston ; Dr. John Alves of Inverness ; James Fraser of Gortulig, Writer to the Signet; William Ballantyne at Balloan, William Fraser, Surgeon in the East India Company's Service; and Lieutenant Hugh Lawson, R.N., were received burgesses and guild brethren of the burgh with the usual powers. Lewis Rose of Coulmony—the "Will Wimple" of the Kilravock family—was provost, and the laird of Kilravock, Rose of Holme, Sutherland of Kinstearie, Captain Hugh Rose of Brea, Bailie Ore of Knockoudie, and other members of the retiring council, were present. Some vacancies having occurred, Henry Mackenzie, styled "Attorney in the Court of Exchequer," was elected a councillor, as were also James Fraser of Gortulig, W.S. ; Dr. John Alves, physician in Inverness ; and William Ballantine, Supervisor of Customs. Unlike some others, Henry Mackenzie, though absent from the first meeting, gave frequent attendance at the meetings of the Town Council, and on more than one occasion rendered useful service in connection with business matters of the town in Edinburgh.

In the year 1783 there was a great flood in the river Nairn which, according to the burgh records, swept away a considerable part of the bridge at the lower end of the town. The Town Council met on 13th August of that year to consider what was to be done. Henry Mackenzie was present at the meeting, when it was resolved that "masons, wrights, and artists" should be employed to make estimates of a temporary bridge, and Mackenzie was "earnestly recommended" to open such subscriptions and make such applications in Edinburgh and other places as he saw proper.

The appointment of non-resident persons as members of the Town Council had become a great scandal. The council in the year Henry Mackenzie entered was constituted as follows :—

> HUGH ROSE of Kilravock.
> MAJOR GENERAL SIMON FRASER of Lovat.
> COLONEL HECTOR MUNRO of Novar.
> LEWIS ROSE of Coulmony.
> CAPTAIN HUGH ROSE of Brea.
> ALEXANDER ROSE in Flemington.
> HUGH ROSE of Aitnoch.

ALEXANDER BAILLIE of Dochfour.
MR. HUGH FALCONAR, Merchant in Nairn.
MR. DAVID FALCONAR there.
ALEXANDER ORE of Knockoudie.
CAPTAIN JOHN FRASER in Geddes.
JAMES FRASER of Gortulig, W.S.
HENRY MACKENZIE, Attorney in the Court of Exchequer.
DR. JOHN ALVES, Physician in Inverness.
WILLIAM BALLENTINE at Balloan.
ROBERT GLASS, Shoemaker in Nairn.

Of the seventeen members three only were townsmen. The system was fruitful of many evils and abuses in the administration of burgh affairs, and was utterly indefensible. The position was sought for purely political ends. As the times advanced, municipal reform began to be demanded, and a reforming party sprang up in the burgh of Nairn.

The legality of the election of Novar as provost, gallant soldier though he was, was challenged, and the question whether non-resident persons could hold office as magistrates was raised in the Court of Session and carried eventually to the House of Lords.

A weaver named David Bremner was the leader of the reformers at the time. On 17th September, 1782, the town clerk reported to the council that on the previous day a petition had been lodged with him by David Bremner, weaver in Nairn, and subscribed by him and a number of the inhabitants, praying the Town Council upon the day of the election to choose and appoint the whole of the magistrates and councillors for the ensuing year out of the inhabitants of the burgh, such persons as may appear to them to be disinterested in their principles, independent in their way of life, and disengaged from every other public charge. David Bremner was called in, and adhered to the petition. The council adjourned consideration of it to another meeting. When they met, Henry Mackenzie was present as a member of council, and his hand may be recognised in the courteous but evasive answer given to the petitioners :—" The council being this day met to deliberate upon the petition presented to the council upon 17th current, and being extremely concerned that by the death of their late worthy provost and eldest magistrate since the annual election in the year 1781, it has been yet impossible to supply their place, which the council would otherwise have willingly done, though they believe every attention has been paid to the town's business by those remaining in office, and as nothing can be a more desirable object to them than the appointment of proper magistrates and councillors at the ensuing election, they trust that their choice will fall upon persons every way well qualified for the discharge of their respective offices, and to support and promote the interest and welfare of the burgh and its inhabitants." The petitioners were of course dissatisfied, and as the meeting was breaking up they took a protest against the finding. Two days later was the appointed day of the election. Bailie Alexander Rose, the presiding magistrate at last meeting, was absent, "refusing to attend, though repeatedly requested by the council, and walking at the stairfoot of the tolbooth when the council met." The clerk reported that a petition had that morning been lodged with him, in name of Robert Forbes and others, of the same nature and tendency with that presented to and considered by the council at their last meeting. The council unanimously resolved to adhere to their former answer, and proceeded to the election. The list of the council was worse than any former one. The town clerk resigned apparently in order to become a bailie, and there was but one other genuine burgh resident amongst the seventeen elected. Baillie of Dochfour, who was present at the meeting, retired at this time, but the new members added to the old council were Benjamin Dunbar of Hempriggs, Captain George Brodie, John Rose of Househill, David Davidson of Cantray, George Mackenzie of Inchcoulter, and Peter M'Arthur, tacksman of Polneach. William Rose of Montcoffer was added in the following year. The council elected Sir Hector Munro of Novar their provost. The reformers raised the question of the legality of Novar's election, he being non-resident. Public agitation came to a head in the following year, and a riot ensued. Bailie Hay and Bailie Rose informed the council that on Monday, 25th August last, while they and the other magistrates were in the exercise of their duty, "a set of ill disposed and disorderly persons assembled in the street, interrupted them in the course of their duty, violently assaulted Robert Glass, Dean of Guild, and afterwards used the most sanguinary threats against some of the peaceable inhabitants, putting them in terror of their lives and properties." John Nicolson, tanner, son of Charles Nicolson, was the ringleader of the mob. A precognition of the facts was laid before James Brodie of Brodie, one of Her Majesty's Justices of the Peace. The council, considering that such proceedings were subversive of all government and good order, and destructive of the peace and freedom of the community, unanimously resolved to take steps to bring the said John Nicolson and others therein concerned to condign punishment by a prosecution in a competent court.

The reformers still harassed the council. At the next meeting a petition was lodged, subscribed by Robert Forbes, Alexander Dunbar, Charles Nicolson, Robert Falconer, Hugh Rose, David Bremner, Alexander Falconer, William Alexander, and Alexander Kinnaird, demanding that a regular statement of the town's accounts be exhibited. These were the parties who had raised the question of declarator in the Court of Session. The council, while considering the demand captious and calculated to give trouble, recommend the treasurer to furnish the petitioners with copies of the accounts.

The decision of the House of Lords in the Nairn case was to the effect that it was not necessary the provost should be resident, but it was so as regards the other magistrates. The decision having thus virtually gone against the reformers, the old system was carried on without abatement until, in 1833, the great measure of municipal reform was passed, which began a new era in municipal government.

Henry Mackenzie was not the only literary man during this period who had intimate relations with Nairnshire. Some years before, Dr. Clephane, whose sister married Kilravock the younger (usually styled " Geddes "), was an occasional visitor, and kept up a correspondence with the family of Kilravock. Whilst Major Clephane was a type of the rollicking soldier of the day, Dr. Clephane was a representative of the educated Scot abroad. He was a man of learning, a physician and traveller, the associate of the eminent men of the day both in this country and on the Continent. David Hume was one of his most intimate friends. He had studied under Boerhaave, and could claim the best known artists, musicians, and litterateurs in Europe as intimate acquaintances and friends. Dr. Clephane's opportunities for becoming acquainted with the Continental savants arose partly from his being employed as the travelling tutor or companion to young English noblemen doing the grand tour, then necessary to a polite education. Mr. Cosmo Innes states that Dr. Clephane's letters in the Kilravock charter chest have really supplied the materials of the literary history of Scotland, and were largely used by Hill Burton in his Life of Hume. Dr. Clephane made his friends in Nairnshire acquainted with the great personages in the circles in which he moved. He had a sympathetic audience.

Young Geddes, his brother-in-law, was himself a man of scholarly attainments. He was an accomplished linguist, and was recognised as one of the best Greek scholars in the kingdom. His friendship was cultivated by the most distinguished literary men in Scotland. Professor Moor of Glasgow consulted him about difficulties which met him in editing an edition of Homer's *Iliad*, and young Kilravock pointed out some errors in the text as printed. Lord Kaimes wrote to him familiarly, and brought a number of kindred friends on a visit to him. James Ferguson, the self-taught astronomer, wrote telling him of the new inventions he was engaged upon, and sent him as a present a kind of perpetual pocket almanack, showing the changes of the moon. They were evidently on very friendly terms—Ferguson expressing a desire to hear from him how he and his worthy lady and family were, and Mrs. Ferguson joining in good wishes. While maintaining the closest connection with the learned men of the day, young Kilravock's ambition was satisfied with his avocations in planting and improving his land at Geddes, and the only office he ever solicited or accepted was that of Sheriff of Ross—a post that had, previous to the abolition of heritable jurisdictions, been almost invariably held by some member of the family for many generations back. His letters to his correspondents are exceedingly clever and racy. He was a pure Whig in politics. Some seven years after the battle of Culloden, he wrote to a friend that he did not think he could wish for a more effectual punishment to all Jacobites than that they had their James or Charles to govern them on some spot of this globe far distant from us. "Sure I am," he adds, "they'd soon tire of it, and heartily wish to be back to Britain and live again under that King and Government they have so often endeavoured to distress." No wise man, he remarks, would wish to live under absolute monarchy.

His daughter Elizabeth inherited much of her father's literary and musical tastes, and was a voluminous correspondent, a painstaking diarist, and a most extensive reader. Authors were her heroes and musicians her friends. Henry Mackenzie, her cousin, sent her the proof-sheets of "The Man of Feeling" to read, and she sat down and made a copy of each chapter as it came to hand. Her father's literary friends indulged and gratified the young lady by sending her occasional letters. Mr. Cosmo Innes excuses the severely religious tone of her private journal on the ground that it was the habit of the time merely to record pious reflections, and says she was really the leader of all cheerful amusements, the humorous story-teller, the clever mimic, the very soul of society. In early youth she was the centre of a little circle of ladies of kindred spirit—the Russels of Earlsmill, the Brodies of Lethen, and the Grants of Castle Grant. As she grew up, and circumstances as romantic and singular as ever happened a heroine of fiction, fell to her lot, she became the most interesting personage in Nairnshire, the central figure in its society, the moving spirit in all that was worthy and good.

Taking up residence with her father at Kilravock some time before the death of his father in 1755, she spent her youth and young womanhood amidst the lovely scenery of the ancient seat of the Roses. "I was fostered like a hot-bed plant in the lap of ease and indulgence for the first twenty years and more of my life, surrounded by a constant succession of persons agreeable to me." Such is her own description of her early circumstances. But sorrow after sorrow followed in rapid succession. She lost her favourite brother and her devoted father within one month—the dreary November of the year 1772. The brother who succeeded made an unequal marriage, and on his bringing home the handsome girl, Jane Fraser, whom he had made his wife, Elizabeth and her gentle-born mother, heart-broken, left the castle, as they thought, for ever, and betook themselves to the gloomy town-house at Nairn, with its commonplace surroundings. Elizabeth detested Nairn at this time—" a place," she says, " where not a bud or blossom marks the change of seasons." The description, of course, could apply only to the outlook to the High Street from the narrow windows of her dwelling. Her imprisonment was mitigated somewhat by an occasional change of residence to Firhall, where her spirits revived and her literary correspondence and studies were resumed. She was, however, not destined to waste her life in vain regrets. A singular chain of circumstances presently developed. Her early friend and companion, Margaret Russell, had some years previously married Elizabeth's cousin, Hugh Rose of Broadley. To identify this Hugh Rose it is necessary to go back in the family genealogy to the fifteenth baron, who, as formerly mentioned, married as his second wife the heiress of Fraser of Brea, the Covenanting preacher. The baron settled the property of Brea on James, the eldest son of this marriage, to the exclusion of his eldest son by his first wife.

James Rose of Brea, as he was called, was Sheriff-Substitute of Nairn, and took a prominent part in all the affairs of the town and county during his lifetime. He sold the estate of Brea and married Margaret, heiress of James Rose of Broadley, a near kinsman. It was his son Hugh who married Margaret Russell. When a youth, Hugh Rose of Broadley entered the army, was assisted by Dr. Clephane, and became a captain in the 57th Regiment, but his tastes lay in another direction, and he retired from the army and studied medicine. Having graduated in medicine, he set up in practice in Forres. His mother, Lady Brea, as she was still called, and his sisters, resided at Meikle Kildrummie. Dr. Rose had a wadset over Kildrummie, and got a lease of the lands for thirty-eight years, beginning in the year after the wadset should be redeemed. He also feued the Smith's Croft from the Nairn Town Council, adding to it the eighth part of the Grieshop, lying contiguous, which he also possessed. The lands there had the curious names of Overmoor, Crocodales, Wallace Butts, and the Little Acre. He also purchased from Hugh Robertson of Ardulzie the burgh property now known as Rosebank, originally acquired by

Hugh Rose of Geddes, the Greek scholar.   He was a man of substance, and like the rest of the Roses, literary and musical in his
tastes.   Margaret Russell, his young and beautiful wife, did not
live long.   In the year 1777 Dr. Rose of Broadley was left a
widower, with a son James, and two daughters, Margaret and
Rachel—all of tender years.   He looked out for a second wife,
and his choice fell upon Elizabeth Rose, his cousin and the friend
of his first wife.   There was no family at Kilravock Castle and
Dr. Rose was the nearest male heir of the line, whilst Elizabeth
was the nearest heir whatsoever.   With some reluctance, though
not from any want of regard for him, Elizabeth accepted him as
her husband, and they were married in 1778.   Two brief years of
married life were all that were in store for Elizabeth.   Dr. Rose
was seized with fever in Forres, and died 1st November, 1780.
In February following his widow gave birth to a posthumous child
—a son.   Two years later, the baron of Kilravock died, leaving
no issue.   His widow, Jane Fraser, who had been a great favourite
with Jane, the gay Duchess of Gordon, the Queen of the North,
and succeeded in asserting her position in a fashionable but fast
set, retired into obscurity, but an old tombstone at Geddes, erected
by a faithful servant, records that she lived till she was ninety years
of age.

An important question of succession now arose.   There was no
doubt that, issue of the last baron having failed, the nearest male
heir of line was Dr. Rose of Broadley, whilst it was equally clear
that Mrs. Elizabeth was the nearest heir whatsoever, and the question the courts had to decide was whether it was Dr. Rose's first
born son James by Margaret Russell, or his second wife Elizabeth
Rose and her son, who were entitled to the estates.   Litigation
was at once entered upon.   It was the great *cause célèbre* of the
time.   The Rev. James Rose of Ockham, near Reply, in Surrey,
as uncle and tutor to the children of the first marriage, took up
their cause, and Mr. Francis Russell, of Westfield, advocate, as
tutor dative, pursued it still more actively.   Poor Mrs. Elizabeth
records that she entered on the contest to maintain her rights of
succession " without friends or means against a powerful opposition."   She was a brave woman, and was animated and sustained

all through the prolonged litigation by the feeling that she was seeking to preserve the ancient heritage to the rightful heir. In 1783 the Court of Session decided practically in her favour, to the great joy of the district. When the tidings of the decision arrived, there were bonfires, dancing, and general rejoicing at Nairn and Kilravock. The case was appealed to the House of Lords, but four years later the decision in her favour was confirmed. The old lands and barony of Kilravock became hers, but Geddes, which stood on a different footing, fell to James Rose, as nearest male heir. It turned out that in creating a faggot vote on Kilravock barony for his brother Lewis, the old laird, her father, had—whether intentionally or not is not clear—made the property to revert on his brother's death to himself " or his nearest heirs whatsoever in fee." The fortunate clause enabled Mrs. Elizabeth, with her son and her mother, to return to the home of her forefathers, where for the remainder of her life she ruled and reigned, not only as mistress of Kilravock, but as queen of Nairnshire.

In the autumn of 1787 the poet Burns paid a visit to Kilravock, and breakfasted with the two ladies. He had a letter of introduction from Henry Mackenzie. Burns records in his diary— " Old Mrs. Rose, sterling sense, warm heart, strong passions, and honest pride, all in an uncommon degree. Mrs. Rose, junr., a little milder than the mother—this perhaps owing to her being younger." Burns, accompanied by Mrs. Elizabeth Rose and Mrs. Grant, the wife of the minister of Cawdor, went over to Kildrummie, where old Lady Brea still resided. The poet there met two young ladies—" Miss Rose, who sang two Gaelic songs, beautiful and lovely—Miss Sophia Brodie, most agreeable and amiable—both of them gentle, mild, the sweetest creatures on earth, and happiness be with them ! " Elizabeth Rose and Burns afterwards corresponded. " There was," he says in one of his letters, " something in my reception at Kilravock so different from the cold obsequious dancing school bow of politeness, that it almost got into my head that friendship had occupied her ground without the intermediate march of acquaintance. I wish I could transcribe, or rather transfuse into language, the glow of my heart when I read your letter. My ready fancy, with colours more mellow than life itself, painted the beautiful wild scenery of Kilravock, the venerable grandeur of the castle, the spreading woods; the winding river, gladly leaving his unsightly heathery source and lingering with apparent delight as he passes the fairy walk at the bottom of the garden; your late distressful anxieties; your present enjoyments; your dear little angel, the pride of your hopes; my aged friend, venerable in worth and years—you cannot imagine, Madam, how much such feelings delight me, they are my dearest proofs of my own immortality." Burns was at this time assisting a friend in a collection of Scottish songs, set to their proper tunes, and as a small mark of his grateful remembrance, he presented Mrs. Rose with a copy as far as it was printed. He added " 'The Man of Feeling,' that first of men, has promised to transmit it by the first opportunity." " When you see the ' two fair spirits of the hill ' at Kildrummie, tell them " (says Burns) " I have done myself the honour of setting myself down as one of their admirers for at least twenty years to come, consequently they must look upon me as an acquaintance for the same period." The one lady, Miss Rose, was the daughter of the house, sister of the late Dr. Rose; the other, Miss Sophia Brodie, became the wife of Mr. Dunbar Brodie of Burgie, and inherited Lethen. Amongst the Gaelic pieces with which Burns was entertained, it would be interesting to know if the old composition, " The Baron of Kilravock," was one. The old tune has been preserved, but the words are awanting.

Burns was probably received in what was known as " Miss Brodie's Room," and if he glanced at the books in the library he must have been considerably astonished at finding in a farm house in Nairnshire such a collection of high class literature. An inventory taken a few years before his visit shows that the library at Kildrummie included Pope's Letters, the Tatler, the works of Milton, Shenstone, Prior, and Dryden, Voltaire, twenty-one volumes, Horace, Virgil, Juvenal, Terence, and Tacitus, the History of the Caesars and the Life of Cicero, Parner's and Roscommon's Poems, the Life of Rosilli, Butler's Hudibras, the Devil on Sticks, a French New Testament, Select Plays, Entertaining Fabulists, and Mackenzie's Meditations, with seventy pamphlets and a volume of Jocular Songs.

The poet Burns also visited the town of Nairn. In coming from Strathspey he had crossed to Kilravock by way of the bridge of Dulsie and General Wade's road. His visit to Kilravock over, he proceeded to Inverness and went to see the Falls of Foyers.

For more than half a century Mrs. Elizabeth Rose maintained her social supremacy. In her later years she formed a link between several generations. No stranger of note visited the district without being entertained by her. Veteran soldiers returning from active service had, on arrival, to report themselves at Kilravock. Young men leaving the district called upon her, some to receive advice and assistance, others to get letters of introduction. Was not George Rose of the Treasury her kinsman, and Commissioner Rose of the Customs her most obliging friend? Mrs. Rose attended the parish kirk either at Croy or Cawdor, and she counted all the Highland ministers of note at the time as her particular friends—an invitation to dinner at Kilravock invariably followed the preaching of a good sermon at Croy. Amidst all the business and social cares of her life, she never lost her early love of literature. The names of the books she read were carefully noted in her diary each day, and the periodical arrival of the box of books from Isaac Forsyth's, the Elgin bookseller, or a parcel of latest literature from Edinburgh, gave her infinite pleasure. The reading of books and the planting of trees may be said to have formed the passion of her life. But her busy useful career drew to a close in the year 1813. In November of that year she died and was buried at Geddes, her funeral being the greatest gathering of the kind witnessed in the district. In accordance with directions in her will, the coffin, resting apart on birch trees cut in Kilravock wood, was borne by the tenants to the family tomb in the old chapel at Geddes. Thus passed off the scene one of the most remarkable women of her time in the north of Scotland.

CHAPTER XIX

LANDS AND LANDOWNERS

Towards the close of the eighteenth century several changes took place in the ownership of lands in Nairnshire.

The old family of Sutherland of Kinsteary had to part with their estate, which had been possessed by them for centuries. James Sutherland of Kinsteary had become involved in cautionary obligations for Sir James Calder of Muirtown. Rose of Kilravock, the brother-in-law of the laird of Muirtown, purchased that estate from the trustees appointed, and the purchase price being insufficient to clear off its owner's debts, James Sutherland was held to his obligations. Financial ruin came upon him in consequence. The estate of Kinsteary, after being in sequestration for some years, was judicially sold by the Court of Session, and was purchased by Mr. Cosmo Gordon for £4200—a price equal to about three years' rental of the property at the present time. In a memorial for James Sutherland of Kinsteary (December 1763) it is stated " that when this price, with the rents during the sequestration, shall be applied towards the paying off the creditors' debts in the ranking, if the creditors content themselves with the payment of their principal sums and annual rents without accumulations, there is reason to hope that some small reversion may be recovered to the heir." Creditors are hard to deal with, and James Sutherland had to seek employment in the Excise. His name was struck off the roll of barons and freeholders of the county on 1st October, 1772, by reason of his having denuded himself of the lands and titles upon which he had formerly claimed, in favour of Mr. Cosmo Gordon. A tablet in the west gable of the church of Auldearn preserves the record of the old connection with the district. The dedication runs—" This is the burial place of James Sutherland of Kinstearie, second son to the Laird of Duffus, and Magdalene Falconer, daughter to the Laird of Halcartown, his spouse, and their posteritie. Builded 1624." The armorial bearings show the three stars of the old Moravia family, with the boar's head, representing the Chisholm connection of the Sutherlands, whilst the lady has the three stars and the falcon of the Falconers of Lethen and Hawkerton—now represented by the Earls of Kintore.

Mr. Cosmo Gordon, who acquired Kinsteary on the decline of the Sutherlands, was a son of John Gordon, who had been factor to the third Duke of Gordon, and had amassed a great deal of wealth as tacksman of the salmon fishings of the Spey. He belonged to Strathawn in Glenlivet. There is evidence that the Gordons of Strathawn were descended from the old Gordons of Cluny (Seton-Gordons) who had, among other possessions in the north, lands in Nairnshire in early times, as formerly mentioned. The property of Cluny had passed out of the first Gordon family to the Gordons of Gordonstown, and it was probably ambition to re-acquire the early heritage of the old Gordons that induced John Gordon, the wealthy factor, to invest his savings in the princely domain of Cluny, though a hundred years had run since his ancestors had possessed it. Cosmo Gordon, some few years after purchasing Kinsteary, became member of Parliament for Nairnshire, which office he resigned on being made a Baron of Exchequer. He was latterly styled Baron Gordon. He was a keen politician, and manufactured numerous votes out of his property in Nairnshire. Two of his brothers, Charles and Alexander, made great fortunes in the West Indies, and both of them were freehold voters in the county of Nairn. They were the principal owners of the island of Tobago, in the West Indies, and Alexander is designated in the register of voters as of Bellmount, Tobago. The Gordons, on the failure of Sir Ludovick Grant of Dalvey, acquired the properties of Mid-Fleenas, Kinnudie, Park, Knocknagillan, Bognafouran, Foynesfield, the Newmill, etc., which remains with the family. Baron Cosmo Gordon was succeeded by his brother Charles, styled " of Braid," a property near Edinburgh, where he resided. He intro-

underwritten, viz., all and whole the towns and lands of Cantray-down, Dellagramich, and Drumtenval, with houses, biggings," etc., " lying within the parish of Croy, barony of Clava, and shire of Nairn ; as also all and whole the towns and lands of Clava or Clavalg and Dalcroy with the pertinents thereof, the town and lands of Drumore and universal pertinents thereof, with the sucken, sequels, knaveships, fishings, services, and whole other pertinents of the said lands lying within the parish of Croy, barony of Clavalg and shire of Nairn, with power of erecting and building mills upon the said lands, and of receiving the emoluments thereof in manner mentioned in the late and original rights of the same, which lands and ancient barony, together with certain other lands, were lately erected in one barony called the barony of Clava." The Roses of Clava also owned Balblair and properties in the burgh of Nairn.

The family connections of the Roses of Clava were widespread. The wife of William of Clava, the Provost of Nairn, who built the Nairn Bridge, was a daughter of Chisholm of Comar. Their eldest son Hugh married Elizabeth Sutherland of Duffus, and their daughter Anna went down to preside in the now lost mansion-house of Culbin as wife to Alexander Kinnaird, whilst their daughter Margaret crossed over from Balblair to grace her cousin's house of Broadley. Alexander, the next laird of Clava, had for his first wife a daughter of Sir Robert Innes of Innes (by whom he had no family), and for his second wife the widow of Gordon of Cluny (Gordonstown family). She was a daughter of Mackenzie of Coul, her mother being a daughter of Chisholm of Comar. Clava's eldest son Hugh married a daughter of Irvine of Crimond, and several daughters made good marriages. Bishop Colin Falconer married Lilias Rose of Clava. The Roses of Tarlogie trace their descent to the Clava Roses. Baptisms in those days were occasions of great family gatherings, and the baptismal register of the parish of Nairn preserves the record of the principal guests at the baptisms of several of the children of Hugh Rose of Clava. On August 29, 1708, there was the baptism of a son, apparently the third. James Dunbar, the Sheriff of Moray, was there, and the boy was named James. The company included Roses from Coulmony, Broadley, and Culless, who were set down as witnesses. In December of the following year a daughter was baptised Anna, but it was thought sufficient to have her baptism authenticated by the names of James Rose, the town clerk of Nairn, and John Rose of Newton. On July 27, 1711, there was a great gathering on similar business. William, Lord Strathnaver, was the principal guest, and the boy was named William. The connection with the Sutherland family began with the first laird of Clava. There were present also William Mackenzie of Belmaduthy, who had married Clava's sister Margaret, and several Roses. The next child being a daughter and baptized Margaret, the occasion was sufficiently honoured by the presence of John Rose of Broadley and the Town Clerk of Nairn; but on January 15, 1715—the date is significant—William, Earl Marischal, was the principal guest and witness, and the child was baptized William. The Earl Marischal was engaged in Jacobite intrigues at this time, and it was doubtless through the Earl's influence that Clava was led to join the Rising of 1715, a few months later. Through the influence of friends his property was ultimately restored to him, but it was heavily burdened. Two more children were born to him. In 1718 a son was baptized Robert, the witnesses on the occasion being Sir Robert Gordon of Gordonstown and Robert Innes of Innes; in 1721 a daughter was baptized Isabel, and her godmother was Lady Crimond (Irvine of Crimond), who was present along with " Lady Crimond, younger." Hugh Rose, the eldest son and younger of Clava, married Frances Macleod of Cadboll, and died before his father, leaving a daughter Janet, who married Charles Robertson of Kindeace—the family from which the Right Hon. W. E. Gladstone descended. Clava, the younger, appears also to have left an infant son. Old Clava died in 1741, and his third son James claimed the property as a creditor. His sister Ann, who had married her cousin, Hugh Rose of Coulmony, had an action with her brother James, in which she says—" The affairs of Clava's family went into disorder by the precipitate action of the pursuer in the character of being a creditor, and the defender, a widow with a family of young children, did not know what course to take for obtaining justice, as her brother's heir (i.e., young Clava's child) was an infant, and the pursuer would take no concern for him in his affairs.　Indeed he swept away the brother's executry and attached the estate by a judicial sale upon some debts he acquired right to."　This James, who is thus represented as an unjust man, married Margaret, daughter of Alexander Irvine of Drum.　He is said to have been a shipbuilder at Gothenburg. He sold the Clava estates to Sir Alexander Grant of Dalvey, and they were re-sold by Sir Ludovick Grant to David Davidson, who also acquired the estate of Cantray, and passed on these properties to his descendants.

The family of Brodie of Brodie had also its vicissitudes.　Going back for the sake of genealogical clearness, Lord Brodie was succeeded by his son James, who, dying in 1708, left nine daughters but no son.　His fifth daughter married George Brodie of Asliesk, her father's cousin-german, and he succeeded to the Brodie estates as nearest male heir.　His father, Joseph Brodie, was the youngest son of old David Brodie of Brodie, and the youngest brother of Lord Brodie.

George Brodie lived to enjoy his new property for but seven years.　His eldest son James succeeded him, but five years later there was again mourning at Brodie Castle for the death of the laird.　James was succeeded by his immediate younger brother, Alexander, who became Lord Lyon of Scotland.　The prosperity of the family greatly increased during the Lord Lyon's reign, but on his death in 1760 the estates descended to his son Alexander, who was barely of age at the time.　He lived but a few years after his succession, and, as he died unmarried, there was once more a break in the direct descent.　The nearest male heir was James Brodie of Spynie.　His grandfather was James Brodie of Whitehill (the immediate younger brother of Joseph Brodie of Asliesk), who had married Margaret Brodie, one of the ten daughters of James Brodie of Brodie, and had purchased the lands of Spynie from Douglas of Spynie.　James Brodie of Spynie, the grandson, who now became laird of Brodie, was thus a second cousin of the last laird.　He had qualified as an advocate, and became sheriff-depute first of Sutherland and Caithness, and afterwards of Moray and Nairn. He was an active politician, but did not enter Parliament.　He had eight children, and died in 1756.　His eldest son James succeeded him. Alexander, the third son, went to India, made a great fortune, and, returning to this country, resided at Thunderton House, at Elgin, and afterwards acquired the property of Arnhall and the Burn in Kincardine. His daughter became Duchess of Gordon—the " good Duchess " who made Huntly Lodge a centre of religious influence. Two of the daughters (namely, of the late laird) married ministers. Elizabeth married the Rev. Mr. Ketchen, minister of the Secession Church at Nairn. Margaret married the Rev. Mr. Calder, and attained the age of ninety-two years.

James Brodie of Brodie married, in 1767, Lady Margaret Duff, youngest daughter of William, first Earl of Fife. The couple appear to have eloped. A letter is preserved of Lord Fife, Lady Margaret's brother, who, writing to a friend under date 12th March, 1767, says—" I am informed Mr. Brodie and Lady Margaret have stole a marriage. I wonder neither the one nor the other chose to drop me a little civil note. However, their want of discretion gives me no pain. I wish they may pass a happy life together." They had a family of two sons and three daughters. Though Brodie of Brodie had inherited a considerable estate, his style of living in London ultimately exhausted his resources, and financial embarrassment came upon his house. The whole estates were exposed to judicial sale in 1774. The Earl of Fife, Brodie's brother-in-law, came to the rescue, and bought them in for £31,500 sterling. The purchase, it was understood, was a family arrangement with Brodie, under which he was to redeem the property when able. Lord Fife re-settled all the properties on the west side of the Findhorn on the laird of Brodie and his heirs, but retained all the properties on the east side of the Findhorn. Kineddar, Grieship, Brounsernick, and Coltfield he sold to various purchasers, the prices amounting in the aggregate to nearly £20,000, whilst the lands of Monaughty, Asliesk, and Spynie were added to the Fife estates—a very remunerative transaction as far as the Earl of Fife was concerned. The laird of Brodie was thus shorn of considerably more than half of his possessions. He learned wisdom in the school of adversity, and applied himself diligently to improving the remainder of his property. He was a good botanist and

naturalist, and made a collection of the plants in the district.   His
list was published in the " Zoologist," and the herbarium itself was
a century later in possession of a gentleman in Edinburgh.   The
older relics of the family at Brodie Castle were carried away to
Dunvegan Castle in Skye.   Mrs. M'Leod of Dunvegan, Emilia
Brodie, a daughter of the Lord Lyon, was heir of line, and although
she renounced her right to the unentailed property in consequence
of the debts with which it was burdened, she removed all the effects
in the house, except an old clock and some pictures.

A tragic event occurred at Brodie Castle on the night of Friday,
24th February, 1786.   On Thursday, 23rd February, the laird
of Brodie and two friends, Major Munro and Captain Fraser,
went to the Nairn Assembly—a fashionable ball of the district.
They returned next day to Brodie Castle, and found Lady Margaret Brodie in good spirits, full of fun and drollery, which she
kept up the whole day.   In the evening she played at cards with
her husband and the guests, and then sat down to supper.   As the
gentlemen were sleepy after the previous night's gaiety, and were
to hunt early next morning near Nairn, the party broke up about
eleven o'clock.   Brodie accompanied Lady Margaret to her bedroom, and saw to her fire, which was burning brightly.   Her
daughter, Charlotte, a little girl, who slept with her, was already
in bed, and her maid was in attendance.   Lady Margaret, however,
sat down to read.   The maid, who usually sat with her until she
went to bed, complaining of being unwell, was told by Lady Margaret she need not wait, and left after laying out her nightdress.
Brodie showed the gentlemen to their bedrooms, and then retiring
to his own room immediately above Lady Margaret's, went to bed
and immediately fell asleep.   All these particulars are furnished by
letters written by friends at the time.

About an hour later agonising screams rang through the stillness
of the house, proceeding from Lady Margaret's bedroom.   The
butler and the footman, who alone of the inmates had not retired
for the night, ran up stairs, and finding flames and smoke issuing
from the bedroom, raised their cries, but having lost their presence
of mind, made no attempt to save Lady Margaret.   A letter by
Mr. A. P. Cumming to Miss Urquhart of Meldrum, describes the

harrowing scene that followed. Brodie, awakened by the dismal shrieks from below, "rushed naked down stairs and in the passage from her dressing-room to her bed-chamber was met by the flames. At the risk of his life and being burnt in the hand and leg, he pushed forward and sought the dear unfortunate in vain—suffocation and flame drove him to the passage to recover his breath. Frantic, he again pushed in, for the whole room to the very cornice and furniture was in a blaze, and in his second attempt he found the lovely sufferer extended on the floor. He thinks then he felt her heart beat once; she was all on fire. He carried her to the dressing-room and rolled her in the carpet, but ere this her soul had fled." "From the most minute investigations," continues the writer, "it appears she immediately sent away her maid and sat down before a large fire with a volume of Dodd's Works, that she fell asleep and that a peat fell on her petticoats, which set her in a blaze. She must have run to the bed, to which she communicated it, for it was at the foot of it she was found. Her sufferings could not have been long, as her piercing cries preceded suffocation. Her child Charlotte, who was her bedfellow, escaped downstairs, nobody knows how." Miss Tulloch, who supplied the Earl of Fife at his request with a full account of the particulars of the melancholy occurrence, confirmed the above details. She mentioned that the child was awake when Lady Margaret came to her room, and spoke several times to her mother, desiring her to come to bed; but she must have fallen asleep during the time Lady Margaret was sitting by the fire. "There is every reason to hope," continues Lord Fife's correspondent, "that she did not suffer so much as at first people were apt to imagine, as it is supposed the fright and terror had soon deprived her of the power of screaming out, but she certainly had made an attempt to get at the bed, perhaps with an intention to wake the child, and had fallen down probably in a faint at the bedside, by which means the curtains, bed, and bedclothes were set on fire. Either her fall or the light of the flames seems to have awoke the child, who got up in a fright, and not seeing her mother, and perceiving her own danger from the flames, got into a dark closet at the head of the bed and endeavoured to shut the door after her, but providentially for her-

self and the rest of the family it would not shut. She then, with
some difficulty, got past the flames, opened the room door, and ran
out calling upon her papa." It was at that moment the butler and
his fellow-servant came upstairs. Miss Tulloch mentions further
that when Brodie came down he was soon followed by the two
gentlemen who were in the house. The servants said Lady Margaret was gone, but Brodie " caught her out of the flames as soon as
the thickness of the smoke allowed him to discover in what part of
the room she was. The scene then may be imagined, but is too
terrible to describe ; but everybody says a few minutes more would
have made it impossible for any of the family above stairs to have
been saved from suffocation, and the flames were beginning to
communicate to Mr. Brodie's room above ; but the short space of
time in which the dreadful accident happened not being more than
an hour from the time poor Lady Margaret left the dining room,
prevented any bad consequences to the house and family."

The poor laird was overwhelmed with grief. " My poor
friend's distress," writes Mr. Cumming, " beggars description.
At first he was torpid and as it were benumbed with grief—the
second day he got some relief from tears, he is now again worse, it
seems to enter his soul—he refuses all sustenance, gets no rest, and
seems to wish to follow her." At five o'clock on the Friday morning Brodie despatched a note to Major the Hon. Lewis Duff at
Rothiemay acquainting him of the dreadful catastrophe that had
occurred, and asking him or his brother Arthur to " hurry immediately to your truly afflicted and miserable.—J. BRODIE." The
Hon. Arthur Duff came to Brodie immediately, and in a letter to
Lord Fife detailing the circumstances, mentioned that Lady
Margaret had a custom of reading at night after going to her own
room, and had once before set fire to her clothes, which made
Brodie order her maid never to leave her till her candle was
extinguished. " Unfortunately, the girl was that night ill, and
having been ten years in her service Lady Margaret's humanity
was too much interested to allow her to sit up further." He adds,
" I neither had nor have any suspicion but that the whole catastrophe was purely accidental." The latter remark was probably
made in reference to some idle and cruel gossip about the accident,

based only on the circumstance that Brodie and Lord Fife were not on friendly terms at the time. A portrait of Lady Margaret, the colour much faded, still exists at Brodie. She is represented with her forefinger at her mouth, as if she were imposing silence.

Brodie in later years had also to bear the sorrow of losing his eldest son James, who was in the Civil Service of the East India Company on the Madras establishment, and was drowned by the upsetting of a boat on 14th October, 1801, near the Bar of St. Thome River at Madras. The body was recovered, and taken to the house of Major Jones (father of Mrs. Augustus Clarke of Achareidh), in whose care were the sons of the notorious Tippoo Sahib. A handsome residence near Madras, which belonged to Brodie, bears the name of Brodie Castle. The connection of the Brodies with Madras at that time was very prominent. It began with Alexander Brodie of Arnhall (father of the Duchess of Gordon), and was continued by various members of the family, who served in that presidency in civil and military capacities. The second son, William Douglas Brodie, who had been Consul at Malaga, died at Madras in 1826, and in the same year his nephew George Brodie, who had entered the Madras Cavalry, also died there. William Brodie, eldest son of James Brodie who was drowned, succeeded to the estates on the death of his grandfather in 1824. He was also for some time at Madras. One of his sisters, Jane, married Francis Whitworth Russell of the Bengal Civil Service; another sister, Charlotte, married Edward Humphrey Woodcock of the Madras Civil Service; a third sister, Isabella, married Captain Archibald Erskine Patullo of the Madras Cavalry, who greatly distinguished himself in the Crimea and fell mortally wounded at the assault on the Redan; and a fourth, Louisa, married Hugh Calveley Cotton of the Madras Engineers.

William Brodie of Brodie was Lord-Lieutenant of Nairnshire for nearly fifty years. His singularly courteous, courtly manner, his witty, wise sayings, and generous disposition, made him a great favourite in society in London, to which he was much drawn, but latterly he loved to dwell among his own people at Brodie, where he spent many happy years. In early manhood he married Elizabeth Baillie, third daughter of Colonel Hugh Baillie of

Tarradale and Redcastle, M.P.—a lady of remarkable accomplishments and distinguished character. Of their four sons, George, the eldest, who was in the navy, died during his father's lifetime; Caithness, the third son, survives; William, the youngest son, died from the effects of a carriage accident which happened near the Church of England Chapel at Nairn in 1865. Hugh Fife Ashley Brodie, the second son, on the death of his father in 1873, succeeded to the estates. He had married, on 1st January, 1863, Lady Eleanor Moreton, daughter of Henry George, second Earl of Ducie. Hugh Brodie of Brodie shed fresh lustre on the old house of Brodie. He was a man of chivalrous character, an eloquent speaker, fond of music and art, a keen sportsman, and a patron of all manly sports. Though not destined to enter Parliament, where his abilities would have gained him distinction, he exercised a unique influence in the district, his character inspiring admiration and affection among all classes. Brodie was nobly sustained in his high ideals of life and duty by Lady Eleanor Brodie. His death at the age of forty-nine was regarded as a public calamity. He died on 20th September, 1889, at Glion, Switzerland, whither he had gone for the benefit of his health, in company of his brother Caithness. His remains were conveyed to Brodie Castle, and laid in the tomb of his ancestors at the church of Dyke. Lady Eleanor Brodie survived her husband for many years, took a leading part in the benevolent enterprises of the county, and was lamented by rich and poor at her death in 1925. Hugh Brodie left a numerous family, and was succeeded by his eldest son Ian. For some three years the new laird held a commission in the Scots Guards. He served with Lord Lovat's Scouts in the South African War, where he was wounded and received the D.S.O., and in the Dardanelles, Egypt, and Palestine in the Great War, when he was mentioned in despatches and won the Military Cross. In 1905 he married Violet, only child of the late Colonel Montague Hope, younger of Luffness, by whom he has two sons living, and he is Lord-Lieutenant of the county of Nairn. His brother Alastair was killed at Magersfontein in the South African War, and his brother Douglas was killed and his brother Duncan twice wounded in France.

Few changes have taken place at Brodie Castle in recent times. The house has from time to time been added to, but the older part with its narrow door and corner turrets is preserved intact. The massive pillars in the entrance hall form a quaint feature of the interior. The basement is mainly occupied by the library, which contains a very good collection of books. The dining room has a richly-carved ceiling, the work of an Italian artist. There are several good paintings, and amongst the curiosities preserved are Guy Fawkes's lantern, Queen Adelaide's coronation robes, and collections of objects of interest which belonged to the Duchess of Gordon. The Duchess's valuable cabinet of minerals, bequeathed to William Brodie of Brodie, was presented by him to the Nairn Museum. Brodie Castle, with its stately avenues of trees, its spacious lawn, and placid lake, resembles some old English manor in its rich luxuriance and quiet beauty.

The Brodies of Lethen, in later years, have had an interesting history. Alexander Brodie, who represented the county of Nairn in Parliament from 1735 till 1741, was an outstanding figure of his time. His brother, Charles Brodie of Ardersier, and he embarked in some bold commercial enterprises, and Charles established a considerable trade between Inverness and Holland and other Continental countries. Their speculations consisted chiefly in the export of corn, and the importation of Continental commodities. Charles Brodie was the first merchant who introduced coals into the north. The Crawfords and Halliburtons of Leith and Rotterdam, well known shippers of the time, were their correspondents. Alexander, the laird of Lethen, had strong literary inclinations, and was minded to found a great library at Lethen. He set about it in a very ingenious and original way. He drew up a catalogue containing every book he would like to have in his library, and then proceeded to buy such books as were on his list as he found opportunity, but when he died he had only secured six hundred and five volumes. He entailed the estates on his children, whom failing on the heirs of Thomas Brodie, the Lord Lyon Depute, whom failing on some collateral branches of the family. His eldest son Alexander succeeded him, but died at the age of fifteen, a few months after his father. The second son, John, who succeeded, died at Nice, where he had gone for the benefit of his health, three years later. He was only sixteen years of age. The estates now devolved on the eldest daughter, Anne. She was about eighteen years of age on her accession, and was assisted in the management of the property by Mr. Duncan Campbell, tacksman of Fornighty, as factor—a situation he held under her father. Miss Anne Brodie was a remarkably active lady. Though much sought after, she did not marry. She showed her interest in the welfare of her tenants by establishing a spinning school. It is to Miss Anne that Lethen House owes its west wing, and also the grand staircase. The estate of Coulmony, long the summer resort of the Roses of Kilravock, was purchased by her apparently in lieu of the lands and fishings of Kinloss, which she sold to Forbes of Echt. Anne Brodie died in October 1805, in the fifty-first year of her age. Her sister Sophia—one of the " fair spirits of the hill " so much admired by Burns—succeeded to the estate. Some nine years before this Sophia had become the wife of Lewis Dunbar of Grange, afterwards of Burgie. He was her cousin, his mother having been a daughter of Anne Brodie, wife of Alexander Campbell of Delnies. On succeeding to the Lethen estates Sophia took the name of Dunbar Brodie of Lethen and Burgie, and her husband changed his name to the same effect. A fine portrait of this worthy lady is preserved at Lethen House. During her husband's lifetime she resided at Burgie. The castle of Burgie, now in ruins, appears to have been a fine old place. Patrick Gordon in his " Britaine's Distemper," in defending Huntly's conduct in spending nearly three months besieging Lethen House, says that " Burgie, Moyness, and Are " were " the three best houses in Murray, except Darnaway and Spynie, and had he been master of Spynie, as he was of those three, he would have been master of Murray." Lethen, it would appear from the context, is meant by the Arr. In 1808 Mrs. Dunbar Brodie sold the part of the lands of Coulmony on the south side of the Findhorn to Major (afterwards Sir) James Cunningham. These lands now form the estate of Glenferness. Sir James Cunningham died before he had completed the building of Glenferness House, and the property was sold to John Dougal of Ratho Park, who again parted with it to the Earl of Leven and Melville, in whose family's possession the estate remains.

On the death of Mrs. Dunbar Brodie without issue, the succession to Lethen reverted to the heirs of Thomas Brodie, the Lord Lyon Depute. The heir of line was James Campbell Brodie, grandson of the Lyon Depute. His father held an appointment in the House of Lords in connection with the journals of the House. He had four sons and four daughters—James the eldest, who succeeded to Lethen, Thomas, who became a Colonel in the East India Company's service, David, an Indian officer who died young, and John Clerk Brodie of Idvies, who was successively Crown Agent for Scotland under successive Liberal administrations, and latterly held the office of Principal Keeper of the General Register of Sasines and other important offices. His son, Thomas Dawson Brodie, who was made a baronet in 1892, took a very active and kindly interest in Nairnshire, befriending its institutions and promoting its prosperity both by his means and his personal efforts.

James Campbell Brodie, who succeeded to the Lethen and Coulmony estates, set about improving the property. He was a man of much activity, of great conscientiousness, and of very enlightened views. He took a leading part in all the public events of the time in the district, and the value of the estate was greatly enhanced by his judicious administration. He died in the year 1857 at the age of fifty-six years, having been the chief Whig landlord in the county in his day. He left two sons—Thomas Stewart Brodie, who succeeded him, and James Campbell Brodie. Thomas Brodie died in 1865, in his twenty-ninth year, and left a family of four daughters but no son. He was succeeded by his brother James Campbell Brodie, who added considerably to the house of Lethen and greatly improved its grounds. He married, in 1869, Fanny Sophia Constance Wood, third daughter of Edward Thomas Wedgwood of Watlands. Mr. J. C. J. Brodie of Lethen was Lord-Lieutenant of Nairnshire, and was of a most amiable and kindly disposition. He died at Madeira on 25th February, 1880. Mrs. Brodie, during the minority of her eldest son, Alastair (born 1876), maintained the best traditions of the house of Lethen.

Alastair Brodie of Lethen died in January 1908, and was succeeded by his brother, Captain Ewen J. Brodie. The latter had joined the Cameron Highlanders during the Boer War, and was with the Mounted Infantry in South Africa. On the outbreak of the Great War in 1914 he left for the front with the Cameron Highlanders, and after taking part in the fierce fighting round Ypres was killed while repulsing a German attack on 11th November. By his marriage with Miss Stirling of Fairburn he left two sons, David and Peter, and a daughter, Helen. Of his sisters, Constance married in 1898 the Hon. Montague Waldegrave, son of Lord Radstock, and Sophia married in 1908 Alwyn Parker, C.B., C.M.G., of the Diplomatic Service. The fine old beeches, which shelter the mansion from the east wind, still stand hoar with age, and one of them, a veritable family tree, bears in its bark the signatures of successive generations of the family.

The Dunbars of Boath, while suffering considerable pecuniary losses through the financial embarrassment of their neighbours in the end of the eighteenth century, held their own, and added from time to time to their paternal property. Their earlier history has already been narrated.

Alexander Dunbar of Boath was one of the barons of the county of Nairn in 1735. His son, Alexander Dunbar, succeeded about 1740. Political feeling running high between the lairds of Brodie and the lairds of Lethen, young Dunbar of Boath was objected to by Lethen at the meeting of freeholders in 1743 as not having lodged a claim for enrolment two months before the meeting, as required by statute. Boath replied that he was an apparent-heir, his father's name standing on the roll, and therefore he did not require to lodge a claim—a well-established rule which the meeting recognised. At the meeting in 1747, in order to avoid any exceptions to his title as a freeholder, he produced a special retour in his favour as heir to the deceased Alexander Dunbar, his father, dated 19th September, 1740, infefting him in all and haill the lands and barony of Boath, Boathill, and Quarter of Little Penick, and others therein mentioned. He married Janet Brodie, daughter of James Brodie of Whitehill, and on 23rd April, 1755, was appointed Sheriff-Substitute of Nairnshire by James Brodie of Spynie (afterwards of Brodie), who himself was that day at Auldearn commissioned as Sheriff Depute of Elgin and Nairn. The laird of Boath was a most upright judge, and during a period of considerable popular excitement and disturbance, administered justice firmly and impartially in the court at Nairn. He had three sons and two daughters. His second son James was an eminent scholar, received the degree of LL.D., and was appointed Professor of Philosophy at Aberdeen University. The third son William became a Writer to the Signet, and year after year was appointed the representative elder of the Nairn Town Council to the General Assembly. He was a distinguished member of the legal profession in Edinburgh. A faggot vote was created for him in Nairnshire, but being a conscientious man " he would not swear "—namely, take the trust oath that the qualification was genuine, and he renounced. He was in the Calder interest in the county, and usually came down from Edinburgh to attend the making up of the electoral roll. One of the sheriff's daughters, Magdalen, married Lieutenant Fordyce, of the Royal Navy, but he died in early life, leaving two daughters, Emilia and Elizabeth, whose right to a sum of £1250, invested in the Brodie estate, was established by their mother and their uncle, the Writer to the Signet. The second daughter, Marjory, married Alexander Dunbar, Nairn. The old laird of Boath, having died in the year 1774, was succeeded by his son Alexander. Curiously enough, when the latter claimed enrolment as a freeholder, he was objected to, as his father had been before him. The objectors were Kilravock, Rose of Brea, and Charles Gordon, and by a majority his claim was rejected and he was kept off the roll for several years. The grounds of objection are not recorded, but it was probably a claim of the Gordons of Kinsteary to the superiority of two davochs of land lying in the village of Auldearn, namely, Belgeam's lands and the Smiddy Croft, which are also in the Boath titles. The description of the Boath property is interesting on account of the old place names at Auldearn which it preserves. The first subject specified is the town and lands of " Pitwhin," mentioned in early charters, and its pertinents of Broombank, etc. The next is " the acres of arable land called in the original writs Belgeam's or Smiddy lands "—(another writ

gives it the additional *alias* of the "Card's Croft")—sometime
belonging to Alexander Urquhart formerly of Kinnudie, afterwards of Newhall; also the Mill Acre of Auldearn, with a piece
of barren or uncultivated land belonging thereto; likewise the
acres of land lying in the fields called Cloggan's and Tobacco lands,
with the privilege of building houses on any part of the said lands.
There is no explanation of how the latter subject came by the
name of Tobacco lands :—it is stated to have formerly belonged
heritably to Alexander, Lord Duffus.   In addition to these there
are the Broadlands, the pertinents of which are called Roan and
Castlehill—both names survive—"the said lands of Broadlands,
with the burgh of barony into which the said lands of Broadlands
of Auldearn were created, with the weekly market and free yearly
markets, particularly the free yearly market called St. Colm's Fair,
held upon the 9th of June yearly—all of which are united and
incorporated into one whole and free barony, called the barony of
Boath; and in like manner, the town and lands of Boathill, with
the stone house and other houses and biggings, etc., gardens,
orchards, meadows, mills of the same; also the fourth part of
Little Penick and the lands of Brewlands, with the multures and
sequels of the said lands of Boathill, Fynesfield, Dean's Acre of
Auldearn, and lands of Penick aforesaid." The mill called the
Mill of Boath is also referred to.   Alexander Dunbar, who succeeded in 1774, married Jane, daughter of Alexander Burnett of
Kemnay, Aberdeenshire.   An entry in the Council Books dated
28th September, 1772, records the admission as honorary burgesses
of James Dunbar, Professor in Aberdeen, George Burnett of
Kemnay, and Alexander Burnett, younger.   They were doubtless
on a visit to the lady of Boath at the time.   Her husband died in
1787, and in the absence of the young laird, who went to India,
matters were looked after by his uncle the professor.   He applied
for enrolment of his nephew at the Michaelmas meeting following
as a freeholder of the county, and in the application is styled Dr.
James Dunbar.   The second son, George, graduated in medicine,
and went to India also, where he died unmarried.   James entered
the Royal Navy; William found a grave in Jamaica; and Peter
became an officer in the East India Service; Helen, the only

daughter, remained unmarried with her widowed mother. The old lady died 9th November, 1805, and a tablet in the old choir of Auldearn runs thus—"Sacred to the memory of Jean Burnett, widow of Alexander Dunbar, Esq., of Boath, a person of singular accomplishments, of understanding, and of the most active benevolence, whose exemplary regard to all the tender charities of life was exalted by piety, adorned by elegance, and regulated by the soundest discernment." The epitaph, though stilted in language, truthfully describes the good lady of Boath. Her daughter Helen belonged to the literary circle of which Mrs. Elizabeth Rose of Kilravock was the centre. Though of a younger generation, Miss Dunbar was drawn to the old Lady Kilravock by kindred tastes. Mrs. Grant of Laggan, who was then writing her charming " Letters from the Mountains," was also a most intimate friend. Many of Mrs. Grant's letters and poems were addressed to her. Miss Dunbar also made the acquaintance and secured the friendship of Hugh Miller, the Cromarty geologist, then unknown to fame. He had only published a small volume of poems. Hugh Miller was induced to make two visits to Boath, and in his work " My Schools and Schoolmasters," he paid a very graceful tribute to his hostess and her literary friends. " Miss Dunbar belonged," he declared, " to a type of literary lady now well-nigh passed away, but of which I find frequent trace in the epistolary literature of last century. The class comes before us in elegant and tasteful letters, indicative of minds imbued with literature, though mayhap not ambitious of authorship, and that show what ornaments their writers must have proved of the society to which they belonged, and what delight they must have given to the circles in which they more immediately moved." Hugh Miller found that the central figure of the interesting group had been Mrs. Elizabeth Rose—" a lady of a singularly fine mind, though a little touched mayhap by the prevailing sentimentalism of the age." He had perused portions of her journals, and a copy of one of them was in his possession. " My friend, Miss Dunbar," he says, " was at this time considerably advanced in life, and her health far from good. She possessed, however, a singular buoyancy of spirits, which years and frequent illness had failed to depress ; and her interest and enjoyment in

nature and in books remained as high as when, long before, her
friend Mrs. Grant [of Laggan] had addressed her as

> Helen, by every sympathy allied,
> By love of virtue and by love of song,
> Compassionate in youth and beauty's pride."

Hugh Miller mentions that Miss Dunbar wrote pleasingly and
with great facility in both prose and verse, and he gives the opening
stanza of a light *jeu d'esprit* on a young naval officer engaged in a
lady-killing expedition in Cromarty—the gay and gallant first
lieutenant of the ship of which her brother, Sir James, was captain.
" I greatly enjoyed my visits to this genial hearted and accomplished
lady," says the geologist. A tablet in the choir of Auldearn church
records that Helen Dunbar died 29th June, 1835, aged 60 years.

Alexander Dunbar, the laird of Boath, had returned to this
country after pretty long residence in India. He was still in the
prime of life, but he fell ill, and after years of suffering died unmarried on 29th August, 1808.

His brother, Captain James Dunbar of the Royal Navy, succeeded. He was knighted in the year 1810, and came home for
a short stay. Mrs. Elizabeth Rose, in her diary, records meeting
him and finding him a most pleasant, excellent man. In February
1814 he married Helen Coull of Ashgrove, Elgin, a niece of Sir
Archibald Dunbar of Northfield. On 10th September of the
same year he was created a baronet of the United Kingdom. Sir
James had established himself as a great favourite in the town and
county of Nairn by this time, and there was much rejoicing over
the distinction conferred upon him. He purchased several properties lying between Nairn and Auldearn. In addition to the old
barony of Boath and lands about Auldearn, the farms of Auchnacloich, Camperdown, Balmakerdach (a burgh feu), Balmakeith,
Merryton, the Broadhill, and others, belonged by this time to
Boath. The house at the west corner of Bridge Street was the
Boath town-house in olden times. The first Sir James was a
great land improver and built a new mansion at Boath, in lieu of
" the great stane house " of former days. He died 5th January,
1836, aged sixty-five. Two sons, Peter and Ernest, aged 8 and
11 years respectively, died in the month of February of the previous

year. He left two sons, Frederick William and James Alexander, and two daughters, Jane and Helen, the former marrying Arthur Grant of Bogton, Forres, and the latter Captain Duncan Milne of the 24th Regiment.

Sir Frederick succeeded his father, but died in 1851, and his brother James became baronet and laird of Boath. Like his father, James was an officer in the Royal Navy, but soon after succeeding he retired from the service. On 3rd May, 1854, Sir James was married at Stoke Church, Devonport, to Miss Louisa Pemble, third daughter of the late Lieut.-Colonel Parsons, C.M.G. From the time they came to reside at Boath House, a few years after their marriage, Sir James and Lady Dunbar closely identified themselves with the interests and institutions of the district. Sir James's independent character and conscientious discharge of duty won for him great respect. He formed one of the group of very remarkable men who took the lead in public matters in Nairnshire during the latter part of the century. He died 7th October, 1883. A deserved tribute to his memory was the erection at Auldearn of a " Dunbar Memorial Hall." Lady Dunbar, who was associated with her husband in his good work, continued for another quarter of a century to assist in every worthy cause. Sir James left two sons—Alexander and Frederick, and one daughter Nina, who married the Rev. James Bonallo, minister of Auldearn, and for public service during the Great War was awarded the M.B.E. Sir Alexander attained his majority in 1891, but was accidentally drowned in the river Nairn in 1900. His brother, Sir Frederick, disposed of Boath to Rear-Admiral Sir Heathcote Grant, K.C.M.G., a distinguished naval officer whose services included the defence of the Falkland Islands after the action off Coronel in 1914, operations against the Turkish defences of the Dardanelles, Gallipoli, and the Gulf of Smyrna, and the duties of Senior Naval Officer at Gilbraltar during the last year of the Great War. Admiral Grant, who is a son of Captain John Grant of Glenmorriston, married in 1899 Ethel, daughter of Andrew Knowles Swinton, Old Hall, Lancashire, and has a family of four sons and three daughters.

Debrett gives the armorial bearings of the family of Dunbar of

Boath as—Gules, a lion rampant, argent, within a bordure of the last, charged with eight roses of the first.   Crest—A dexter hand paume, proper, reaching to two earl's coronets, tied together: motto, " Sub spe "—(Under hope.)

The Cawdor family continued to make their estates in Wales their home, and the old castle of Cawdor was seldom visited. John Campbell succeeded his grandfather, the last hereditary sheriff. His history is particulary interesting.   Unlike his father and grandfather, who had married heiresses, the young laird of Calder married for love—and love at first sight.   According to Lord Robert Seymour, a contemporary, young John Campbell had been waiting in Grosvenor Place one morning for a sale to begin at Tattersall's, when he saw a beautiful young lady at a window.   He continued walking up and down the street looking at the lady, and though word was sent him that the sale had begun he would not be drawn away whilst the young lady was visible.   He was informed by Mr. Tattersall that the lady he so much admired was the daughter of Lord Carlisle—at the time a very poor and distressed nobleman.   Next day the laird of Calder got a friend to introduce him, and without loss of time made proposals, was accepted by Lady Caroline Howard, and in order to avoid any unnecessary delay in the making of marriage settlements, gave her father *carte blanche* in that matter.   It turned out a most happy marriage.

In the year 1796 John Campbell, laird of Calder, was created " Baron Cawdor of Castlemartin "—a place in Wales.   In the following year he greatly distinguished himself by his spirited conduct in opposing an invasion of the French in Wales.   Early in February of the year 1799 some fourteen hundred French troops sailed from Brest, burned some British merchant ships at sea, and landed on the coast of Pembroke.   The French army had been largely recruited from amongst the criminal classes let loose from prison on condition that they joined the expedition.   They expected the country people to rise and join them, but not finding them willing to do so, they began to pillage the inhabitants.   Information of their landing was speedily brought to Lord Cawdor, who was colonel of the local militia, and without waiting for reinforcements, his lordship at the head of a detachment of the militia, along with the peasantry armed with pikes and scythes, immediately attacked the Frenchmen, and compelled them to surrender. It is stated that the Welsh women in a large body came on the field during the action, and the Frenchmen seeing them with their high hats and red jackets thought they were additional reinforcements of regular troops, against whom they had no chance. The despatch which Lord Cawdor sent to the Home Secretary (the Duke of Portland) giving information of what had taken place, was published in a special London Gazette, and evoked great rejoicing throughout the country. Lord Cawdor wrote—" Fishguard Friday, February 1797.—My Lord—In consequence of having received information, on Wednesday night at eleven o'clock, that three large ships of war and a lugger had anchored in a small roadsted upon the coast in the neighbourhood of this town, I proceeded immediately with a detachment of the Cardigan Militia and all the provincial force I could collect to the place. I soon gained positive intelligence they had disembarked about 1200 men but no cannon. Upon the night's setting in, a French officer, whom I found to be second in command, came in with a letter, a copy of which I have the honour to enclose to your Grace, together with my answer, in consequence of which they determined to surrender themselves prisoners of war, and accordingly laid down their arms this day at two o'clock. I cannot at the moment inform your Grace of the exact number of prisoners, but I believe it to be their whole force. It is my intention to march them this night to Haverfordwest, where I shall make the best distribution in my power. The frigates, corvette, and lugger got under weigh yesterday evening and were this morning entirely out of sight. The fatigue we have experienced will, I trust, excuse me to your Grace for not giving a more particular detail, but my anxiety to do justice to the officers and men I had the honour to command will induce me to attend your Grace with as little delay as possible to state their merits and at the same time to give you every information in my power upon this subject. The spirit of loyalty which has pervaded all ranks throughout this country is infinitely beyond what I can express."

Lord Cawdor, in his communications with the enemy, declined to treat upon any terms short of the surrender of the whole force as prisoners of war, and the Frenchmen had to accept his terms. Lord Cawdor received great credit for his gallant conduct. The Cawdor tenants in Nairnshire heard the news of their laird's patriotic services through a letter which James Macpherson of Ardersier, the factor, received from an officer in Lord Cawdor's cavalry. The letter gives some further particulars. It appears that the remainder of the French prisoners taken by Lord Cawdor were on the 4th March safely lodged on board ship, and that the papers found on the officers contained directions from the French Government to destroy and lay waste the country wherever they went, and, when joined by the inhabitants, to put them in front in case any attack should be made on them, and if they did not do their duty, to bayonet them. The factor remarks, in writing these particulars to his ground officer, that this invasion was a great surprise to the people of that country, and as there were very few troops that could be collected in a moment, the country was in great danger.

Lord Cawdor gave a series of entertainments at Cawdor Castle in the autumn of 1810, and in October of that year a picnic party, the first on record, was given at the Hermitage—a well known romantic spot on Cawdor Burn—at which the leading people of the district were present. Old Mrs. Elizabeth Rose mentions in her diary that her son and his young wife had gone to it and returned late. The season of the year at which it took place seems a little advanced for an *al fresco* entertainment, but the weather may have been exceptionally fine.

Lord Cawdor died at Bath in 1821, and was succeeded by his son, John Frederick, who was created Earl Cawdor and Viscount Emlyn in 1827. The Earl married Lady Elizabeth Thynne, daughter of the second Marquis of Bath. Previous to his going to the Upper House, he had represented Carmarthen in the House of Commons, whilst his brother, George Pryse Campbell, the rear-admiral, represented Nairnshire.

Earl Cawdor carried on the work of improvement begun a generation or two before. The tenants in his father's time had signed a petition in which they embodied their grievances, the principal being the want of leases by the smaller tenants. Mrs. Elizabeth Rose records having made a copy of the petition in 1810 —as it might be useful to her. Earl Cawdor was as anxious as his tenants to improve the agricultural condition of the estate, and he gave them leases with encouragement to undertake reclamation of waste land. He had, like his grandfather, a strong affection for the old castle, and whilst of necessity having to add to the accommodation, he took care to preserve intact every feature of its antiquity, even to the old furniture and wall-hangings. The Earl had very decided literary and scientific tastes, and was a member of many learned societies. His lordship placed all the papers in the charter-room of Cawdor at the disposal of the Spalding Club, of the council of which he was long a member, and a collection selected therefrom was edited by Mr. Cosmo Innes, and published at the earl's expense, under the title of the " Book of the Thanes of Cawdor," forming a most valuable contribution to the history of Scotland, as well as to local genealogy. Lord Cawdor had a large family—1st, John Frederick Vaughan, who succeeded him on his death in 1860 ; 2nd, Archibald George, who became a clergyman and married Charlotte Henrietta Howard, second daughter of the Hon. Henry Howard, Dean of Lichfield ; 3rd, Colonel Henry Walter of the Coldstream Guards ; 4th, Lady Emily Caroline, who married Octavius Duncombe, M.P. ; 5th, Lady Georgina Isabella, who married Balfour of Balbirnie ; 6th, Lady Elizabeth Lucy, who married the Earl of Desart ; and 7th, Lady Louisa, who married the Earl of Ellesmere. Lord Cawdor was very fond of planting, and very averse to cutting—a taste shared by his factor, Alexander Stables, and by that factor's son, William A. Stables, who succeeded him.

The " Hawthorn Tree " continues to flourish. The second Earl married the Hon. Sarah Mary Cavendish, and had three sons and four daughters and numerous grandchildren. He represented Carmarthen in Parliament from 1841 to 1846, and was afterwards Lord-Lieutenant of the county.

Earl Cawdor's second son, Ronald, a youth of great promise, fell in the Zulu War. General Wood was clearing the Zlobani mountain. Ronald rushed forward, in advance of his men, to the mouth of a cave where some of the enemy had established themselves, and was shot dead. A tablet in Cawdor parish church records the sad event. The eldest daughter, Lady Victoria, married Colonel Lambton; the second daughter, Lady Muriel married Sir Courtenay Boyle; and the youngest daughter, Lady Rachel, married Mr. E. S. Howard of Greystock. Lady Evelyn, the third daughter, died unmarried. Lord Cawdor himself died in 1898, and was succeeded by his eldest son, Frederick Archibald Vaughan Campbell.

The third Earl Cawdor manifested a great attachment to Cawdor, and resided a portion of each year at the old castle. In his relations towards his tenantry, he acted pretty much on the good old principles laid down by the old laird of Calder in his letters to Valentine White, and regarded the people on his estates as his personal friends—very much as if they were a large family of which he happened to be the head. As Viscount Emlyn he represented Carmarthenshire in Parliament from 1874 till 1885; he was chairman of the Great Western Railway Company from 1895 till 1905, became First Lord of the Admiralty in 1905, and was an A.D.C. to King Edward. He died in 1911. His son, Hugh Frederick Vaughan Campbell, the fourth Earl, held the title only for a short time. He married a great-granddaughter of the second Marquis of Bath, and died in 1913. His eldest son, John Duncan Vaughan Campbell, the fifth Earl, born 17th May, 1900, served as a junior officer in the Royal Navy during the Great War. In 1924 he accompanied Captain F. Kingdon Ward on his exploring expedition through Tibet and the Himalayas, and contributed two chapters to his book, "The Riddle of the Tsangpo Gorges," in which many of the illustrations are from photographs taken by Lord Cawdor.

The Roses of Kilravock, though shorn of a large portion of their possessions by the decision of the House of Lords, which gave James Rose the ancient barony of Geddes and other lands long the heritage of the family, had still the barony of Kilravock and its old tower. Hugh Rose, Mrs. Elizabeth's son, married, first, Katherine Baillie of Budgate. Her father was Colonel John Baillie of

Dunain, and her mother was Isabella, daughter of Dr. Archibald Campbell of Clunas, who had a wadset over Budgate. The lady was married to the young laird of Kilravock when she was eighteen years of age. The marriage took place at the old house of Budgate, still in occupancy, and now belonging to Lord Cawdor. Kilravock, as already mentioned, became Colonel of the Nairnshire Militia, and took an active part in public affairs. Amongst other duties which fell to his lot was the conveyance to prison of Gillan, a man who had been convicted at the Circuit Court of the murder of a little girl near Elgin. Old Mrs. Rose records in her diary 15th November, 1810—" My mind much distressed by hearing the particulars of the wretched Gillan's execution which my son and Mr. F. had witnessed yesterday." The crime had excited great horror, but no sooner was the execution over than the hatred of the people turned upon the poor executioner, who had been brought from Inverness to perform the duty. He fled for his life from the Elgin mob, only to be barbarously murdered by the populace at Forres—happily the last instance of the kind. The balls at Nairn, reviews at Fort George, the races at Inverness, the Fort, and Delnies, farmers' dinners and ploughing matches, hunting in the woods of Kilravock (where the sport is varied by killing an occasional fox and polecat), with due attendance at public meetings, formed the ordinary avocations of the young laird.

Hugh Rose succeeded to the estate on his mother's death in 1815. He had three sons and four daughters by his first wife. The eldest daughter Isabella—the object of old Mrs. Rose's fond affections—curiously enough, relinked the friends of a former generation. She married Cosmo Innes, whose mother was Euphemia Russell, of Earlsmill, the devoted friend and correspondent of Elizabeth Rose, Isabella's grandmother. Cosmo Innes, the eminent legal antiquarian and historian, and one of the most brilliant conversationalists of his day, died in 1874. Mrs. Innes survived till 1891, dying at Newton, Nairn, the residence of her son-in-law, Mr. R. B. Finlay. Another of Hugh Rose's daughters, Elizabeth, married Peter Grant of Corrimony, and their daughter, Isabella Baillie, married the Rev. Hugh Francis Rose of Holme Rose. On the death of his first wife, Kilravock married

Catherine Mackintosh of Farr, by whom he had five sons and three daughters. He was succeeded by his eldest son Hugh, who entered the Civil Service of the East India Company, and went to Bengal immediately after his father's death. He resembled his grandmother, Mrs. Elizabeth Rose, in mental qualities as well as in her family enthusiasm and passionate attachment to the old place, "endeared to him," says Cosmo Innes, "not only as the inheritance of his forefathers, but as the scene of youthful rural sports in which he took great delight." He died in India in the prime of life in 1847. He was succeeded by his brother, John Baillie Rose. John entered the British Army while quite a youth. He joined the 55th Regiment of Foot in April 1826, and served with his regiment in the Chinese War at Chun Kaing Foo. In 1851 he was promoted to brevet rank of Major. His regiment was in the second division at the battle of the Alma and in the thick of the fight. He received a severe wound about three o'clock in the afternoon, and was carried to the rear. Surgeon Blake found that a bullet had penetrated his chest. Kilravock was fully aware of his danger, and, awakening after a short sleep, desired the surgeon to send word home that the last name on his lips was that of his dear wife. Major Rose's death was lamented by the whole regiment, and he was interred side by side with Captain Shaw, another officer of the regiment, who fell on the same day. Major Rose was married to Ellen Phyllis Pattinson, daughter of Richard Pattinson of Montreal, and left no family.

The succession now devolved on James Rose, eldest son of the second marriage. He had entered the military service of the East India Company, and remaining in India for some years after the death of his brother, he went through the Indian Mutiny. On retiring, Major James Rose took up his residence at Kilravock Castle. He became Lord-Lieutenant of Nairnshire in 1890; and, after a busy and useful life in connection with the county, and on his estate, he died in his eighty-ninth year, on March 30th, 1909. Of his two daughters the elder, Catherine, married the late Rev. A. F. Pope. They had four sons and one daughter, Muriel. The eldest son, Harold, served with distinction in the 118th Heavy Battery R.A. during most of the Great War, and was killed just before its conclusion by an enemy bomb. He was awarded the M.C. and bar for his gallant conduct on two occasions. The second son, James, I.C.S., is at present Commissioner of Excise in Central India. He served with the Indian Army in India during the War. The third son, now Commander C. Y. Pope of the Royal Australian Navy, when Lieutenant, navigated the Australian cruiser, " Sydney," to her famous encounter off Cocos Islands with the German raider Emden, in which the latter vessel was destroyed. Hugh, the youngest son, was accidentally killed while climbing in the Pyrenees at the age of 23. Muriel married the Rev. W. T. Stubbs, son of the late Bishop of Oxford. Major Rose's younger daughter, Elizabeth, married Sheriff Ronald Baillie, eldest son of the late Colonel Duncan Baillie, Royal Horse Guards, of Lochloy. They have two daughters. Of Major Rose's two sons, the younger, John, joined the 98th North Stafford-shire Regiment, rose to the rank of captain, and died in Cairo of fever at the close of the Dongola campaign of 1896. The elder, Hugh, 24th in succession, joined the 1st Battalion The Black Watch, 42nd, in 1884, and served in it continuously for thirty years, during the last four of which he commanded the battalion. He took part in the Nile River Campaign of 1884-85, and in the South African War 1901-02. In the Great War he served with Headquarters III. Corps in France for nearly four years, and was in part of the retreat from Mons, being awarded a C.M.G. and mentioned four times in despatches. He married, in 1920, Ruth Guillemard, eldest daughter of the late W. G. Guillemard, of Malverley, E. Woodhay, Hampshire. She served from 1915 to 1919 as a V.A.D. nurse in military hospitals at home and in France, and in hospital ships in the Mediterranean. They have issue, Hugh, born November 26th, 1921, and two daughters, Elizabeth and Madeleine.

In 1926 a notable addition was made to the south face of the castle, in harmony with the old building, yet embodying many modern improvements to the interior, while restoring some parts of the latter to their original state of two hundred, or more, years ago. The old tower of Kilravock, in its picturesque situation, remains as beautiful as it was when the poet Burns visited and described it.

The " gooseberry bush " on the very top of the tower—the traditional emblem of the family's prosperity—still sends forth fresh buds at the touch of spring. The rooms of the old castle are kept intact, and the family relics and writs, of which there is great wealth, are preserved as a sacred inheritance. With the single exception of Elizabeth Rose's succession, the estates have descended in an unbroken line from the first baron in the thirteenth century to the present laird of Kilravock, who is the twenty-fourth in succession—a genealogy perhaps unique in Scotland. Kilravock is chief of the Roses.

The family of Rose of Holme branched off in the fifteenth century from Kilravock. John Rose of Holme was admitted, apparently for the first time, a freeholder entitled to vote in the county of Nairn in the year 1783. As the lands of Holme lie mainly in Inverness-shire, he qualified on the lands of Wester Bracklie and others, and his name was retained until 1803, before which time he had died. John Rose of Holme took a great interest in Nairn burgh affairs, and was elected a magistrate. He was succeeded by Colonel Rose, whose only son was killed by a fall from a horse in 1815. Colonel Rose, who had a command in the East India Company's Cavalry, had two daughters, one of whom, Charlotte, married Sir John Fox Burgoyne, K.C.B., and the other, Grace, married William Mackintosh, first of Geddes. The Colonel was succeeded by his brother, Major (afterwards Sir John) Rose. Sir John had a distinguished military career. In the year 1797 he was appointed an Ensign in the East India Company's Bengal Army. He was present during the whole siege and capture of Seringapatam, for his services at which he received a gold medal. After the fall of the fortress, Lieutenant Rose served under the Duke of Wellington (then Colonel Wellesley) at the taking of several forts in the Mysore and Bednore countries. In 1800 he volunteered for the expedition to Egypt, and served under Sir David Baird, and then joined the expedition against the Portuguese settlements of Demann. In the following year he was with the Bombay Army in Guzerat. In 1803 he served under General Lake at the battle of Delhi and the reduction of several fortresses. At the capture of Agra he commanded his own regiment of

Sepoys, when he was severely wounded, and half of his regiment were either killed or wounded in taking the batteries. In the same year he was also present at the siege and capture of Gwalior. Upon this occasion he received the thanks of the Commander-in-Chief. In the year 1804, when the fortress of Delhi was besieged by a great native army and 130 guns, Lieutenant Rose commanded a sortie upon the enemy's breaching batteries, inflicting severe loss upon them, and rendered their guns unserviceable. For this gallant exploit he was again thanked in general orders. In 1805 he was present with General Lake when he pursued Holkar through the Punjab. Major Rose was in Nairnshire 1810-11, and Mrs. Elizabeth Rose, who had a great liking for the brave soldier, records in her diary, apparently with great glee, on 21st February, 1811— " Went in the carriage with my son to see the old ladies and the new church (at Nairn). Heard of Major Rose's marriage with Miss Lily Fraser ! " Lilias Fraser was a daughter of James Fraser of Culduthel. The marriage took place on the 16th February, 1811. Major Rose returned to India a few years after his marriage, and was actively engaged until 1823, when he finally returned to this country, having served in eight campaigns, three expeditions, four great sieges, assisted at the capture of eight forts, and taken part in two great battles, and numerous minor engagements. In recognition of his valour and distinguished services he was created a Knight Commander of the Bath in 1837. On retiring (his brother being still alive), Lieut.-General Sir John Rose purchased the residential property of Castlehill, Inverness.

Sir John was a keen politician and a reformer, and threw himself with great ardour into the political struggle which preceded the passing of the Reform Bill of 1832. He took an active part in the elections in Inverness county and burgh, and while regarded as a great acquisition to the popular side, he was made a not infrequent subject of political squib and pasquinade by the opposite party. He was no hectoring, roystering soldier, but really a quiet-mannered sensible man. On the death of his elder brother, Colonel Rose, in 1836, Sir John succeeded to the Holme Rose property, which he greatly improved. In particular he enhanced the charming situation of the house by judicious planting and laying out of the grounds. He died in 1852.

Sir John Rose left two daughters. One became Mrs. Oliver Jackson, the other Mrs. Pallisser. His youngest son, Henry Francis Rose, served in the Civil Service of the East India Company, and on retiring took up his residence for a time at Heathmount, at Geddes, and afterwards purchased lands adjoining the Grieshop, near Nairn, where he built a residence and to which he gave the name of Ruallan. He married a daughter of James Augustus Grant of Viewfield, Nairn, and left a son, Henry Augustus Nugent, now of Ruallan, and three daughters, Lilias, Mary, and Alice.

Sir John Rose was succeeded in the Holme Rose estate by his eldest son, John Nugent Rose, C.B., Bengal Civil Service, who married Anne Margaret, daughter of Colonel Wray Palliser, of Derryluskan and Comragh, Ireland, and died without issue. He was succeeded by his brother, the Rev. Hugh Francis Rose. The new laird was educated at Cambridge and took orders in the Church of England, becoming Rector of Homersfield and St. Cross, Suffolk. He retired, however, and took up his abode at Holme Rose. He married Isabella Baillie, daughter of Peter Grant of Corrimony, Inverness-shire. Mr. Rose's kindly humorous disposition—his conversation overflowed with joke and witty sayings—made him a great favourite. He died in 1890, leaving two sons, Hugh Francis, now of Holme Rose, and John Baillie, Major in the Seaforth Highlanders, as well as one daughter, Millicent, who married Major Hugh Graham Lang of the Seaforth Highlanders.

The Dallases of Cantray lost their property some time after the battle of Culloden. Going back on their genealogy for a generation or two prior to that time, we find John Dallas of Cantray, in 1662, taking part in the trial of Isobel Gowdie, a reputed witch, at Auldearn. He was then Sheriff-Depute of the county of Nairn. He was succeeded by his son Alexander, who married Isobel, daughter of James Dallas of North Newton, and granddaughter of George Dallas of St. Martin's. His daughter Anna, a great beauty in her day, married Duncan Mackintosh of Castleleather, and was the mother of Angus Mackintosh, who in 1827 succeeded his brother Alexander as chief of Clan Chattan.   Alexander Dallas was succeeded by his eldest son James, who was out in the Rising of 1715, joined in the Rebellion of 1745, and was killed at the battle of Culloden.   He married Margaret Hamilton, and left an only son, William, a minor, who afterwards married Stewart, daughter of Sir George Mackenzie of Coul.   William Dallas parted with the property in 1767, and died abroad, leaving four daughters.   The male line was now represented by Walter Dallas, who had settled in Nairn as a weaver and linen manufacturer, and is frequently mentioned in connection with the Town Council, of which he was a member.   His sons were well educated, and two of them went abroad, dying in Jamaica without issue. One, James, died at Nairn.   Alexander Dallas, Walter's second son, went to London and engaged in business as a merchant, and when the young Nairnshire lairds of his generation visited London, they frequently put up at his house at Great Towerhill.   He married Cordelia Phipps, daughter of a London solicitor, and had one daughter, Elizabeth.   He returned to Nairn (his brother James being then alive), and took a great interest in all religious matters.   He died in 1849.   His daughter Elizabeth, usually known as little Miss Dallas, was a very enthusiastic member of the Free Church.   She lived in Church Street, with the Cantray-Dallas arms above the door of her house, an old thatched dwelling —a quaint personage full of traditional lore and pride of ancestry.

The family of George Dallas of St. Martins claims now to be the main line of the Dallases.   George Dallas of St. Martins was a well known lawyer in his day, and a book he wrote, usually called " St. Martin's Styles," is still a work of reference in the legal profession in Scotland.   His son sold St. Martins and purchased the property of North Newton in Stirlingshire.   He was twice married, and after his death litigation arose among his family as to the succession to the property.   William, the youngest son, appears in possession, having apparently bought off the other claimants, and his grandson was Thomas Yorke Dallas-Yorke of Walmsgate, Lincolnshire, whose only daughter, Winifred, married the sixth Duke of Portland.   The fair Duchess of Portland's claim to be the nearest heir of the old line is ungallantly called in question by some of the genealogists, but they have not agreed amongst themselves as to who is better entitled to the family honour.

There are numerous families of Dallases in America, and one branch has risen to great distinction. They trace their descent from James Dallas, the eldest son of the second marriage of James Dallas of North Newton, who was the son of George Dallas of St. Martins, who was the son of William Dallas of Budgate, 1617. The family originally settled in Jamaica, but emigrated to Philadelphia in 1783. James Dallas became Secretary of the Treasury in the Cabinet of President James Madison. He was also Secretary for War, and effected the reduction of the army of the war of 1812 to a peace footing. He was an eminent lawyer, and was approached to become a candidate for the presidency of the United States. This he declined, on the ground that he shared the feeling that none but native-born citizens should hold that exalted position. His third son, Alexander James, was Commodore in the United States Navy, and in the action with the " Little Belt," fired the first gun in the war of 1812 with the mother country. His first wife's brother was Major-General George Gordon Meade, the victor of the battle of Gettysburg in the Civil War. Commodore Dallas's son by his first wife was Colonel A. J. Dallas of the United States Army. His second wife was connected with the Washington family, and the second son by that marriage, George Mifflin Dallas, became the American Ambassador to Russia, afterwards to the Court of St. James, and finally was appointed Vice-President of the United States. He died in 1864, and his descendants occupy high stations in the public service and learned professions. Commodore Dallas's daughter, Sophia, married Richard Bach, whose mother was Sally Franklin, daughter of Benjamin Franklin. Sophia Dallas (who thus became Mrs. Bach) was one of the most intellectual women in the States, and was the friend and adviser of the greatest American statesmen of her day. The learned Professor Bach of Philadelphia was her son. The ramifications of the family are widespread. The Nairnshire origin of the family is a cherished tradition among the members of this American branch.

David Davidson purchased the estate of Dallas of Cantray, and also acquired the property of the Roses of Clava from Sir Ludovick

Grant of Dalvey. He was admitted a freeholder of the county of Nairn in respect of the Clava property on 18th June, 1796, " but only as a fiar, and having right to vote in the absence of the life-renter of the said lands," viz., Sir Ludovick Grant, who had retained the superiority. David Davidson died in 1804. His son, David Davidson of Cantray, claimed enrolment at the Michaelmas meeting in 1809. He was represented by Æneas M'Bean, W.S., and his claim was admitted, but " only as fiar." He married Margaret Rose, daughter of Dr. Rose of Broadley by his first wife, Margaret Russell, and was knighted in 1812. The Davidsons had considerable wealth, and led the fashion in the district in extravagant living. Margaret Davidson of Cantray married Robert Grant, M.P., brother of Lord Glenelg, who afterwards became Governor of Bombay and a K.C.B., and their son was Sir Charles Grant, of Indian Civil Service fame. Sir Robert died in 1838, and his widow in 1848 married Lord Joceline Percy, brother of the Duke of Northumberland. Sir David Davidson died in 1817, and was succeeded by his son David, who died in 1824. Hugh Cochrane Davidson succeeded. Like his neighbour, Sir John Rose of Holme Rose, he was a Liberal, and was one of the leading speakers at a banquet given to General Duff, the defeated candidate for Moray and Nairn in 1841. He married an Irish lady, Maria Grogan. He died in 1846, and was succeeded by his son Hugh, who was a short time in the army, and afterwards studied law. Hugh Davidson of Cantray took a leading part in the public affairs of the counties of Inverness and Nairn, and was convener of the county of Inverness at the time of his death in 1889. He was a very able business man, and an excellent public speaker. He left a son Hugh and a daughter Clara. This son, Hugh Davidson of Cantray, was a captain in the Seaforth Highlanders, and married Miss Hugonin, Kinmylies.

The Campbells of Delnies, closely related to the Brodies of Lethen, were at one time a flourishing house, but have ceased for many years to have any lands in Nairnshire. Delnies was held by them for several generations under wadset of the laird of Cawdor. Alexander Campbell of Delnies, eldest son of Colin Campbell of Delnies and Mary Duff, second daughter of Adam Duff of Drummuir, married Ann Brodie of Lethen on 9th April, 1730. He was sheriff of the county of Nairn under the hereditary sheriff, and retired on the abolition of heritable jurisdictions. His eldest son, Alexander Campbell, was Sheriff-Substitute of Inverness-shire, and married in 1777 Katharine Baillie, widow of Alexander Mackenzie of Flowerburn, and daughter, by the second marriage, of William Baillie of Rosehall, in Ross-shire. Alexander Campbell, the Sheriff-Substitute of Inverness, had a lease of the farm of Delnies after the wadset had been redeemed. When the tack had nearly expired he became anxious about its renewal, and resolved to seek a personal interview with the laird of Calder in London. It was a serious journey, and the sheriff, according to custom, made his will and arranged his affairs before setting out. Arrived in London, he appeared in the full dress of a Highland sheriff of the period—broad-skirted coat, breeches with knee buckles of silver, large silver buckles in his square-toed shoes, cocked hat, and powdered queue hanging behind, and his gold-headed official staff in his hand. He lost no time in finding the residence of the laird, and was fortunate in getting an immediate interview, when he told the laird the object of his mission. After hearing all, the laird said—" Well, Mr. Campbell, you shall have the lease of the farm of Delnies renewed, and that, too, more favourably than before." On hearing this, the worthy sheriff politely and gratefully returned thanks. Thereafter he was invited to lunch, and was introduced to Lady Caroline, the laird's wife, who had never been in Scotland. She was much taken with his courtly demeanour and quaint but stately appearance, and privately inquired of her husband who the gentleman was. The laird replied—" One of my Scottish tenants." Lady Caroline, much surprised, said—" Indeed ! Then I suppose all the Scottish farmers are gentlemen ! " The laird gaily replied —" And that they are ! " The tenant of Delnies, having succeeded beyond all his expectations, returned a happy man, and never wearied of telling his neighbours of the hospitality and kindness shown him by his laird and the beautiful Lady Caroline. The sheriff was a good sportsman, and rode to hounds along with the neighbouring lairds. Horse-racing had become the fashionable pastime in the district, and a racecourse was established at Delnies.

Mrs. Elizabeth Rose, in her diary records on 1st October, 1810, that her son, Kilravock, and his wife and family had gone to the horse-races at Delnies. The course would no doubt be along the level sea-margin or carse beyond the fishing village of Delnies. The tradition is that half the lairds in the county were well-nigh ruined by over-devotion to the turf, and the Delnies races, like the Fort George and Inverness race meetings, were given up. Sheriff Campbell had a son, Pryse John Campbell, born at Inverness, in 1778, and a daughter, Anne, born at Inverness in 1779.

Old Alexander Campbell of Delnies, the Sheriff of Nairn, had, besides Alexander, the Sheriff-Substitute of Inverness, above referred to, a son Colin who went to Jamaica, also John, Sophia, and Pryse Campbell. Sophia married Joseph Dunbar of Grange. It was their son Lewis who married Sophia Brodie of Lethen.

The Forbeses of Culloden appear on the roll of freeholders in the county of Nairn in virtue of their lands of Ferintosh, a detached part of Nairnshire, situated in Ross-shire. The claim of Arthur Forbes came before the barons on 22nd December, 1785, when they were assembled to elect a member of Parliament. The candidates were Alexander Brodie of Madras, representing the Dundas administration, and Captain Campbell, late of the Orpheus frigate, in the Whig interest. Culloden was known to be favourable to Mr. Brodie's election, and the Calder party, in the Whig interest, strongly opposed his admission. The grounds of objection are not stated, but on a vote being taken Arthur Forbes was enrolled by a majority of one—the numbers being 8 to 7—and his name was continued thereafter on the roll. On 6th October, 1803, a claim was lodged by Duncan George Forbes of Culloden, stating " that he is the only lawful son and apparent heir of the now deceased Arthur Forbes of Culloden, Esquire, who stood heritably infeft and seized in all and whole the lands and barony of Ferintosh or Thainland, called in the ancient infeftments thereof Kinkel Fraser " (of which a detailed description is given), all as contained in the original charter granted under the Great Seal in favour of Arthur Forbes, his grandfather, of date the 22nd January, 1697. In enumerating the ecclesiastical properties of the united churches and parishes of Logie and Urquhart, these churches and parishes are expressly stated to lie within the thanedom of Calder and sheriff-dom of Nairn, and, by annexation, within the diocese of Ross. The claim was admitted. In more recent times, Forbes of Culloden was admitted as a Commissioner of Supply in virtue of those parts of his lands lying in the parishes of Croy, Daviot, and Dunlichty, within the shire of Nairn. Mr. Duncan Forbes was convener of the Commissioners of Supply of the County of Nairn. By buying up the mills of Nairn and removing the weir or intack there he greatly improved the Nairn as a salmon river.

James Rose of Geddes, who divided the inheritance with Elizabeth Rose, did not long retain the property which had come to him. He was admitted a baron and freeholder at the Michaelmas meeting in 1797, in virtue of his being infeft in the lands of Easter Geddes, called Allanhall and Chapeltown, with the burgh barony of the same. In October 1801 the court found that he had denuded himself of his property of Geddes in favour of William Mackintosh of Geddes. Captivated by the beauty of Peggy Duncan of Morriston, young Geddes made his first plunge into matrimonial life. He married her on 8th May, 1802, and she bore him three daughters, but he was a widower a few years later, and on 2nd April, 1811, married Elizabeth, fourth daughter of David Hunter of Blackness. His connection with this district ceased thereafter.

After the lapse of centuries the Mackintoshes thus reappeared in the neighbourhood of Rait. " The eldest cadet of the house of Mackintosh " (says Mr. Fraser-Mackintosh) " was that of Rothiemurchus, and the second Kyllachy. From Kyllachy springs Holme, Farr, and Dalmigavie. The next is Balnespick; and of the others—Borlum, Aberarder, Corrybrough, are descended of younger sons of Lachlan Mor Mackintosh of Mackintosh, who died in 1606. Raigmore, Drummond, and Geddes are cadets of Borlum."

William Mackintosh, who purchased Geddes, had made a fortune in India. He married a sister of Sir John Rose of Holme Rose, who survived him, and was succeeded about 1814 by his nephew, William Mackintosh, sometimes styled Dr. Mackintosh from his having been in the medical service of the East India

Company. This William Mackintosh of Geddes kept up a large establishment, and Geddes House, which had been rebuilt, became a centre of great hospitality and festivity. He married, first, a daughter of Mackintosh of Balnespick and niece of Sir Æneas Mackintosh of Mackintosh, chief of Clan Chattan, by whom he had four sons. His youngest son John (by his second wife Jane Jolly) was the " Earnest Student " of Dr. Norman MacLeod's well-known biography. John Mackintosh was much attached to Geddes, the scene of his early youth. In his wanderings amongst the scenery of Switzerland and Italy, he can see nothing finer than the view from the Hill of Urchany. His letters abound in descriptions of the scenery of Nairnshire, and a passage in his diary in which he relates the incident of a stolen visit from the south to his father's grave is singularly pathetic in its character and remarkably graphic and truthful to the minutest touch of local colouring. It was the last time he visited Nairnshire. He had been a student at Cambridge when the Disruption of the Church of Scotland occurred, and though the bias of family connections and associations drew him the other way, he joined the Free Church from conscientious conviction. He was a favourite student of Dr. Chalmers, and assisted Chalmers in the work of founding the territorial mission of the West Port in Edinburgh. While studying in Germany, he fell ill, and died of consumption. " Bury me beside Chalmers," was his dying request and it was complied with. Dr. Norman MacLeod, whose large-hearted, generous spirit is nowhere more evident than in his " Memorials of John Mackintosh," was a frequent visitor at Geddes, and married a sister of " The Earnest Student." Another sister married Sir William Gordon Cumming of Altyre. The estate of Geddes descended to George Mackintosh, the eldest son of the first marriage. He was for many years convener of the county of Nairn. On his death (his only son William Alfred Bruce having predeceased him), the property passed to his daughter Anna Agnew, and she married Mr. John Walker, who assumed the name of Mackintosh-Walker. On the death of Mr. Mackintosh-Walker in December 1907, he was succeeded by his only son, Thomas Charles Bruce, LL.B. (Cantab.), barrister-at-law, and a Deputy-Lieutenant for Nairnshire, who acted as Vice-Lieutenant during the absence of the Lord-Lieutenant in the Great War. He married Marianne, daughter of the Rev. J. C. Gardner, Fluke Hall, Lancashire, and has, with three daughters, two sons—Charlie Algernon, late captain Cameron Highlanders, and John Ronald, now captain Seaforth Highlanders, who in the Great War earned the Military Cross, with bar.

Another family of Mackintoshes of some fortune settled at Torrich in the beginning of the century. Dr. John Mackintosh, who had been in the West Indies, resided for a time at Brightmony, and then removed to Torrich. He owned the Grove near Nairn for some years, and also acquired Firhall, but remained at Torrich. He married a daughter of the Rev. Alexander Grant, minister of Cawdor.

Another of the minister's daughters married Captain William Fraser of Fort George, who had seen considerable service in Batavia and the East, and who, settling down at Brackla, ultimately became the proprietor of the distillery, which had been erected there in 1812 by a small company of local gentlemen, of which he was one. In carrying on the distillery, he was succeeded by his son Robert, who married Mary Gordon, daughter of Robert Gordon of Croughly, and niece of Lieut.-General Gordon of Lochdhu. Robert Fraser's only son, William, predeceased him. One of his four daughters became Mrs. Jerdeine, and another Mrs. Colin Campbell. He was convener of the county previous to the election of 1892, when he retired.

The minister of Cawdor's son, George Grant, became a merchant in Liverpool, and was the " Grant " of the firm of Messrs. Grant, Gladstone & Coy.—the " Gladstone " being the father of the Right Hon. W. E. Gladstone. Captain William Fraser's eldest son, George, entered his granduncle's office in Liverpool, and had as a fellow-clerk Mr. Gladstone's son William. George Fraser and young Gladstone were great friends. The latter, on one occasion, arranged to spend a part of his holidays at Brackla, having doubtless heard much from his fellow-clerk about Cawdor and its romantic surroundings, but the arrangement fell through, and the death of George Fraser soon after broke the connection. Captain

William Fraser's daughter married Alexander Mackintosh, son of John Mackintosh, Torrich. He went to India, and had two sons, William and Ernest, and a daughter Nellie. William became a Lieut.-Colonel in the Royal Artillery, and Ernest a merchant in Calcutta. William, a younger son of John Mackintosh, Torrich, devoted himself to missionary work, and was for many years a missionary in Tangier, Morocco. He married a daughter of Mr. Seeley, the London publisher.

The property of Achareidh was given off by the Town Council on 20th September, 1791, to Captain John Fraser. It was then called Nairn Grove, and consisted of the lands in the more immediate neighbourhood of the house, still marked by boundary walls. Captain Fraser did not retain it long, and it was purchased from him by William Ross and his spouse in 1794. A family of Macfarlanes came into possession in 1807, but four years later it was purchased by Captain Andrew Fraser. He only held it for six months, when it was acquired by Colonel Alex. Mair, in command at Fort George. It was customary for officers at the Fort to reside, for the sake of their families, at convenient places outside the garrison, and in this way several of the smaller properties in the neighbourhood passed into the hands of military officers. Dr. John Mackintosh was the next proprietor of the Grove, and he sold it in 1825 to John Stuart of Belladrum. In 1828 Stuart parted with it to Robert Gordon, whose son John succeeded to it in 1835. He sold it in 1839 to Augustus Clarke, who changed the name to Achareidh ("The Cleared Field"). The small property of Wester Newton and Moor of Newton, which had been feued to David Davidson of Cantray at the same time as the Grove was given off by the Town Council, namely, in 1791, changed hands in 1832. In consequence of the financial embarrassment of the affairs of Sir David Davidson, his trustee Thomas Mackenzie, W.S., sold Wester Newton to John Grant, who left it to Miss Mary Grant. She sold it in 1835 to Dr. John Grant, who sold it in 1855 to Augustus Clarke, and along with the Alton lands acquired from the Sheriff Falconar, it was added to Achareidh. Mr. Clarke died in 1886. He was of scientific tastes, and for a series of years kept meteorological observations of considerable value. He habitually wore the Highland dress, and was a striking figure at all public assemblies during his generation. He took a warm interest in all religious and social improvement. He was succeeded by his eldest son, Lieut.-Colonel Montague Clarke, late of the 50th Regiment, who served in the Crimea, and was wounded and taken prisoner at the trenches before Sebastopol. He afterwards served in the East, and in the New Zealand War. Colonel Clarke was elected convener of the county of Nairn in 1892. At his death in 1902 he was succeeded by his brother, Mr. Hastings A. Clarke. The latter, who was born at Nairn in 1842, went to Ceylon at the age of 18, but finally returned in 1896. He took a warm interest in the welfare of Nairn, and was a J.P., D.L., and county councillor. Just before his death in 1908 he rebuilt a considerable portion of the house at Achareidh. In 1880 he married Rachel Eleanor Jane, second daughter of Andrew Stewart, J.P., D.L., of Auchluncart, Banffshire, by whom he had a family of five sons. It was the third and eldest surviving of them who succeeded him. Major A. C. Keir S. Clarke served during the South African War in 1901 with the 3rd (Militia) Battalion Royal West Kent Regiment, and he served in the Indian Army with the 15th Lancers from 1903 till 1922, when he retired. During the Great War he served in France in 1914 and 1915, and in Mesopotamia from 1916 till 1918. He was wounded in France in 1915 and was awarded the M.C. and twice mentioned in despatches. In 1926 he married Maud Ursula Sealy, second daughter of Mr. W. Sealy Fisher of Wirksworth, Derbyshire. His next surviving brother, Major Alister H. S. Clarke, served with the 7th Seaforths in France from 1915 till 1918, and was wounded twice and awarded the M.C. His youngest brother, Ian H. S. Clarke, served in the Indian Army with the 57th (Wilde's) Rifles.

The estate of Lochdhu is made up of a number of small properties, the largest of which were Janefield and Mosshall. The Ores of Knockoudie were proprietors of lands there at one time, and in 1777 secured from the Town Council a lease for five nineteen years of seventeen acres of moorland lying to the west of the Black Loch. Colonel William Mackintosh of Millbank, who was a great land improver, drained a large part of the moss land,

and planted the sides of the open ditches with willows, forming regular squares, but they have not been preserved. His resources becoming exhausted, he was unable to reap the benefit of the skill and energy he had expended on Janefield and other lands in his possession, and the property passed into the hands of trustees. Lieut.-General W. A. Gordon, who had acquired the house of the Ores of Knockoudie in Nairn, the old name of which was Nairn Lodge, became the next owner. General Gordon belonged to the same stock as the present Gordons of Cluny, and came of the family of Gordons of Croughly. He served with the 26th Regiment, was Lieutenant in the 92nd in 1799, and Captain in 1801, and latterly served with the 50th Regiment. He served at the Helder, at Malta and Gibraltar, at Walcheren, in the Peninsula, and in France till the end of the Napoleonic War. He was wounded at Vittoria and Helleta, and particularly distinguished himself in command of the advanced battalion at the passage of the Nive, where he was wounded and had his horse shot under him. For this he got the rank of Major, a gold medal, and the thanks of Lord Hill. At the crossing of the Nive at daybreak the native guide, whose duty it was to point out the ford, disappeared almost the instant he entered the water; the soldiers, supposing that he had acted treacherously, became alarmed, and hesitated as to entering. At this juncture Gordon, laying hold of two soldiers, rushed forward with them, and plunged into the water, calling out in Gaelic " Highlanders, shoulder to shoulder ! " The effect was electric. The whole of the men immediately followed, and the passage of the river was effected in the face of a galling and destructive fire from the enemy, who lined the opposite bank. Gordon was afterwards created a C.B., and appointed Colonel of the 54th Regiment. On retiring from the army General Gordon settled down to farming at Inverlochy, on Avenside, which, however, he gave up after a time and came to Nairn. The veteran soldier was for many years a prominent townsman, and lived to see his five stalwart sons enter the army. It was he who changed the name of Janefield to Lochdhu. Before the drainage operations of Colonel Mackintosh, a loch existed near the present house. It was called the Black Loch, and is shown on old maps as of considerable extent, its overflow feeding the Alton Burn, which before entering the sea spread along the carse land for about a mile westward, and also bore the name of the Black Loch. General Gordon gave the property the Gaelic synonym, "Lochdhu." Both the lochs, at the moss lands and on the sea margin, have been drained off. The General died in 1856, and his family in 1860 sold the property to Robert Anderson, a practical agriculturist. This new laird, following up extensive improvements on the neighbouring farm of Meikle Kildrummie, of which he was the tenant, put an entirely new aspect on the place, converting the mossy and moorish lands into well cultivated arable fields. He built a commodious house at Lochdhu, erected a new steading, and enclosed the lands with substantial stone dykes. He added to the estate from time to time, the burgh lands of Moss-side, a large portion of the Grieship, and the property of Broadley, all lying contiguous. His only son died abroad, and his daughter, marrying Mr. D. A. Stewart, transferred the ownership to that name.

Newton, or Easter Newton, as it was sometimes designated, was a possession of a branch of the Roses of Kilravock. "John Rose of Newton, Provost of Nairn," is a familiar entry in the burgh records. The property reverted to the Roses of Kilravock on the failure of the line of John Rose of Newton, but was sold by Kilravock about 1780 to Hugh Falconar, a representative of a family long connected with Nairn. The first of the name mentioned is Robert Falconar at Inshoch and Mavistown. He was probably descended from the Falconars of Kincorth, and naturally enough married Elizabeth Kinnaird of Culbin, the daughter of a near neighbour. This Robert Falconar had several sons. John, the eldest, purchased the estate of Easter Draikies at Inverness, on the decline of the Cuthberts, and his son Hugh, who married Jean Dunbar, retained Draikies, and being a very enterprising man, entered into large contracts for cutting timber, keeping his bank account with Forbes & Coy. of London. At the time of his death in 1782 he was engaged in cutting an extensive tract of wood belonging to The Chisholm in Strathglass. A letter of his written in 1780 states that he had sustained severe loss by a great flood in the river, which occurred on 6th or 7th March of that year. An inventory in the Nairn Sheriff Court books refers to his son John as a student residing in Nairn, a minor, and his curators as Robert Falconar of Nairn, and Alexander Mackintosh of Aberarder. John Falconar became the British Consul at Leghorn, and carried on a large mercantile business. He was a claimant for the Aberarder estate when old Provost Mackintosh of Inverness obtained possession. Robert Falconar of Inshoch's second son, Robert, died in 1776 and left a son, still another Robert, who married a daughter of Alexander Inglis, Sheriff-Substitute of Nairn, and succeeded his father-in-law in that office. His son Alexander Falconar, succeeded to the office of Sheriff-Substitute, and was the last resident sheriff in Nairn. He married Agnes, daughter of the Rev. Dr. Macdonald of Ferintosh, the " Apostle of the North." Hugh Falconar, the third son of Falconar of Inshoch, was a merchant in Nairn, and like his brother of Draikies, engaged in some extensive speculations. It was he who purchased Newton from Kilravock, and was the first to improve and enclose the lands. He died in 1786. A daughter married James Smith of Gorskieneuk, and from her are numerous descendants. Major James Falconar, his brother, was the last of the Falconars of Newton.

Dr. Peter Macarthur, who had been in India, was the next possessor. He had also a lease of some lands at Moss-side, and a road leading to the Moss is known as " The Doctor's Road," having been made by him. He had been for some time tenant of Delnies previous to purchasing Newton, and belonged to the family of Macarthur of Polneach.

About the year 1840 Harry Robertson, who had been in business in the West Indies, purchased Newton. He took an active part in all religious and temperance work, threw himself with great ardour into the conflict which preceded the Disruption, and became a liberal supporter and leading elder of the Free Church. He removed in 1873 to Fortrose, where he died. His only surviving daughter married Mr. Walter Arres, Fodderty.

In 1872 Colonel William Fraser purchased Newton from Mr. Robertson. Colonel Fraser's ancestor was the second son of the fourth Lord Lovat. The early heritage of the family was Guisachan, to which was added on the death of the third son the property of Culbokie, from which the family thence took their territorial designation. Culbokie is situated in close proximity to Ferintosh, a detached portion of Nairnshire, and in 1607 when the Thane of Cawdor, Sir John Campbell, sold the barony of Ferintosh to Simon Lord Lovat for £44,000 Scots, one of Lovat's cautioners was Huchon Fraser of Culbokie. Young William Fraser of Culbokie, along with the Master of Lovat, led the Frasers at Culloden, and having escaped after the battle to the fastnesses of Strathglass, was hid there by the tenantry. In revenge the Duke of Cumberland's troops burned down the house of Guisachan over the head of his father, a very old man, who had taken no part in the affair of 1745. The second son, John, was an officer in the Fraser Highlanders, and was at the taking of Quebec in 1759. When Major Clephane (Kilravock's brother-in-law, who became Provost of Nairn) was about to leave Canada for home, he generously procured a command for John Fraser, Culbokie's son. Captain John married and settled in Canada, as did also his brother Simon, who, going out West on an adventurous expedition, became known to fame as the discoverer of the Fraser River, which was called after him. Colonel William Fraser, the purchaser of Newton, sold the estate of Guisachan to Sir Dudley Coutts Marjoribanks (afterwards Lord Tweedmouth), and purchased the estate of Kilmuir in Skye. On the Newton estate he erected the present very handsome residence, incorporating with it the old house and greatly improving the grounds. Colonel Fraser took a very great interest in Nairn and its institutions, particularly in the local Artillery Volunteers, of which he held the command for many years, latterly becoming Colonel Commanding the Highland Artillery. In 1887 Newton was acquired by Mr. R. B. Finlay, Q.C., one of the most distinguished lawyers at the English Bar, who had a family connection with the county through his wife, the youngest daughter of Cosmo Innes and a granddaughter of Rose of Kilravock. From 1885 till 1892 and from 1895 till 1906 Mr. Finlay was M.P. for the Inverness burghs. He was Solicitor-General from 1895 till 1900, Attorney-General from 1900 till 1906, and Lord Chancellor from 1916 till 1918. He was chosen Lord Rector of Edinburgh University in 1902, and represented Edinburgh and St. Andrews Universities in Parliament from 1910 till 1916. He was knighted in 1895, created a baron in 1916, and made a viscount in 1919. He was appointed a member of the Permanent Court of Arbitration at The Hague in 1920, and a member of the International Court of Justice established by the League of Nations Assembly in 1921. His only son, the Hon. Sir William Finlay, K.B.E., a well-known K.C. and Judge, married in 1903 Beatrice, daughter of Edward Kirkpatrick Hall, Kevin, Nairn. Lord Finlay has been a generous friend to Nairn Golf Club, the new club-house as well as the Newton ground being given to the club in free occupancy. Indeed, much of the present-day popularity of Nairn has been owed to the vogue set by Lord Finlay and his friends.

The lands of Seabank, adjoining Newton, were acquired by William Grigor, Elgin, from the trustees of Robert Young, of Palmercross, Elgin, to whom they had come from the Rev. Ludovick Grant of Boyndie, Banff. Mr. Grigor early saw the advantages of the Seabank lands for feuing purposes, and declined tempting offers to sell out. The property of Viewfield lying to the east of it belonged to James Augustus Grant, who had been a judge at Guzerat in India. He was for many years Convener of the County of Nairn, and a handsome portrait of him, painted by Colvin Smith, R.S.A., and presented by a number of friends during his lifetime, hangs in the Nairn Sheriff Court-room. He married a daughter of Colonel Mackintosh of Millbank, by whom he had one son, John, who died in infancy, and seven daughters, the eldest of whom, Eliza, widow of Major General Eneas Shirreff, succeeded him at Viewfield, and left the property to her nephew, Henry Augustus Nugent Rose of Ruallan, only son of her youngest sister, who is the present proprietor. The lands to the west of Viewfield were sold at Mr. Grant's death for feuing purposes, and a large number of villas and residences have been built on these lands—the largest being Firthside, built by the late Lord Thurlow, and Invernairne, built by Dr. Grigor and afterwards the property of Mr. A. T. Lawrence, Lord Trevethin, and called Castella Mare.

The lands of Seabank originally extended southward to the Gallowgate, the road which branched off the High Street at Ivybank. The name Ivybank is of comparatively modern date. It was originally Seabank, and a cottage in its vicinity bears the name of Seabank Cottage. Ivybank became the residence of Captain Gordon of Revack—a brother of General Gordon of Lochdhu. Captain Gordon served in the Peninsular War with the 92nd, of which he was long the paymaster, and was present at the battle of Waterloo. He was of a singularly quiet, amiable disposition, so that it was said of him that he never made an enemy or lost a friend. His first wife was Miss Knight, whose beauty was celebrated in Strathspey in the popular song, " The Bonnie Wife of Revack." After her death he married a daughter of Major John Grant of Auchterblair, and sister of Field-Marshal Sir Patrick Grant. Captain Gordon died, aged ninety years, on 8th April, 1867. He was survived by three sons and three daughters, but they did not retain Ivybank. The property then passed into the hands of Colonel Bethune, and after him to his son, Duncan Norfolk Bethune, who died in 1926. He disposed of it to the County Education Authority, which demolished the old house in 1927 to make room for extensions to the Academy.

About the beginning of the century there was a re-allocation of the burgh lands in the neighbourhood of the town. They had been held in run-rig, and when an improved system of cultivation came in, it was found necessary to assign each proprietor his burgh roods contiguously. The Glebe was defined to march with View-field on the one side and the Skateraw on the other. Viewfield, or the lands so designed, was in this division allotted to the Earl of Findlater and Seafield. In a plan of the town lands made at that time, Kingillie, probably originally part of the Skateraw, is shown as it now is. It received its name of Kingillie from a Captain Fraser, who adopted the name from Kingillie in Inverness-shire— a possession of the Frasers. It was purchased by General Ketchen (a son of the minister of the Secession Church, Nairn), who had been Colonel of Artillery in the East India Company's service, and had been long in command of the Artillery in the Madras Presidency. General Ketchen was succeeded by his brother Isaac. His three sons entered the army. James, the eldest son, died a Major in the Indian Army ; the second son was Major-General Isaac Ketchen, R.A. ; William, the youngest, at his death in 1890, was Colonel-Commanding the Nair Brigade in Trivandrum, Travancore, and was a very distinguished officer. The Maharajah erected a monument to his memory. The property of Kingillie was purchased by David Anderson, a native of Nairn, who had been in business in Demerara. He died in 1891. Mrs. Anderson afterwards married William Lightbody, a retired Glasgow West India merchant, and dying in 1896, left it in his possession. Mr. Lightbody settled in Nairn, and as an honorary sheriff took an active and highly useful part in public affairs. He died in 1928.

Firhall, long the possession of the Grants of Rothiemurchus, passed into other hands about the end of the eighteenth century, and was purchased by Captain Troup, who married John Rose of Holme's daughter Jane. They had four sons, brought up at Firhall, all of whom entered the military service of the East India Company. Hugh retired as General; Colin became Brigadier General; Robert had command of the 2nd Oude Local Infantry; Captain John Rose Troup married an Indian lady of great wealth, and in remembrance of his early days in Nairn left a sum of £2000 for the indigent poor, and £2000 to Nairn Academy. A sister of Mrs. Troup of Firhall married the Rev. Dr. Cormack of Stowe, and their son, Sir John Rose Cormack, was physician to the British Embassy, and greatly distinguished himself at the siege of Paris in 1871 by his humane efforts to succour the distressed and wounded. In recognition of his services he was knighted by Queen Victoria. Colin Rose Troup, who was with Stanley in his expedition for the relief of Emin Pasha, and was left with Major Bartelot in the ill-fated rear detachment, was a grandson of Captain Troup of Firhall.

Firhall was purchased by John Mackintosh, Torrich, but he sold it in 1843 to Angus Cameron, late of the North West and Hon. Hudson Bay Coy.'s service, who, under his uncle, Æneas Cameron, was one of the leading pioneers of Canadian settlement and progress. Mr. Cameron was greatly respected in Nairn, and many young men belonging to the district owed their first appointment in the Hudson Bay Company to his influence. Dr. James Angus Cameron succeeded his father at Firhall in 1877 and, after practising in Nairn and at Bawtry, Yorkshire, was appointed in 1890 Medical Officer of Health for the combined counties of Banff,

Moray, and Nairn.   He retired from his public appointments in
1917, and died at Firhall in 1924.   Dr. Cameron married a
daughter of Mr. Skinner Drumin, Glenlivet, who predeceased
him in 1921.   He was succeeded by his eldest son, Lieut.-Colonel
Angus Cameron, who, after serving in the Cameron Highlanders,
joined the Egyptian Army in 1899, and remained in that service
and that of the Sudan Government until he retired in 1921.   He
married Florence Muriel, daughter of Major H. C. H. Allanby
of Balblair, in 1923.   Dr. Cameron's younger son, Hamish, went
to Ceylon, where he engaged in tea and rubber planting, and his
two daughters married Captain Mark Burns-Lindow and Mr. A.
G. R. Mackenzie respectively.

Broadley, in ancient times the residence of the branch of the
Roses known as " the Provost of Nairn's family," was purchased
by Captain Grant, Congash, factor for Strathspey.   It occupied a
charming situation, and the house, though unpretentious, had a
famous fruit garden.   A mill was erected at Broadley in Dr.
James Rose's time, and was known as the Newmill.   The mill
lade at the riverside can still be traced.   When the Rev. James
Grant was minister of Nairn he became tenant of Broadley, and
resided there for several months each summer.

The adjacent lands of Grieship have a somewhat interesting
history.   Originally belonging to the burgh, they are found at an
early time in the possession of the Thanes of Cawdor, then of old
Bailie Tulloch, probably under wadset.   His daughter, who was
abducted by the Tullochs of Tannachy, and afterwards married
William Falconer, the third son of Colin Falconer, Bishop of
Moray, inherited the Grieship lands.   She was succeeded by her
eldest son Alexander, who was senior bailie in charge of the burgh
of Nairn when the Rising of 1715 occurred.   He was succeeded
by his brother David, who from all accounts was a very energetic
and somewhat eccentric personage, and was known among his
contemporaries as " The Admiral."   He owned an eighth part of
the salmon fishings of the river Nairn, and according to an entry
in the Sheriff Court books in 1766, possessed the property " lying
immediately to the east of Kilravock's great stonehouse in the
burgh, and bounded on the east by the tenements belonging to

Broadley "—a description answering to Falconer's Lane. "The Admiral" married Isabella Dunbar. His daughter Emilia, "a beautiful and accomplished woman," according to a memorandum in the handwriting of Robert Falconar, the Sheriff-Substitute of Nairn, died unmarried, and this branch of the family became extinct. The old sheriff adds—"Another of the sons of the Bishop of Moray was the father of Mrs. Innes of Instellie, with whom I had the pleasure of passing an evening in my father's house in the year 1769. She was nearly related to a daughter of the family of Clava, who was married to Mr. Hugh Falconar, my uncle. Mrs. Innes was at this time accompanied by Mr. David Falconer, 'The Admiral,' and a young lady of the name of M'Kenzie, her grand-daughter." Sir Hugh Innes, Bart., M.P., Lochalsh, the grandson of Mrs. Innes, erected a monument to his ancestor, Bishop Colin Falconer, at Elgin Cathedral. He died unmarried in 1831. It would appear from an entry in the burgh records that the Falconers parted with the Grieship to Patrick Grant of Rothiemurchus—in 1769, the council finding that the latter had for several years past held the lands of Grieship in non-entry.

The Grieship lands were purchased by Captain Grant of Congash, who left Broadley to his relative, Grant of the Aird in Strathspey, and the Grieship to the Rev. Mr. Stewart of Dalvey. Both properties in succession were purchased by Robert Anderson of Lochdhu, already mentioned.

Househill and Crook were held of the burgh of Nairn by the Roses of Kilravock, and were sold by Hugh Rose of Kilravock about the year 1780 to Hugh Robertson, merchant in Nairn. The property came from the Robertsons to a nephew, Lieut.-Colonel Hugh Robertson Murray, H.E.I.C.S., who had acquired Lodge-hill, and was sold by him to Colonel J. A. Grant, son of the Rev. James Grant, minister of Nairn. Colonel Grant served in the Sikh War and the Indian Mutiny, and was wounded at the relief of Lucknow. After the suppression of the Mutiny, Grant joined Captain Speke in the expedition to discover the sources of the Nile. The record of their wonderful march into the interior, and their discovery of the Victoria Nyanza, forms one of the most interesting chapters of African travel. For some time before they emerged from the Dark Continent by way of Khartoum, nearly all hope of their return had been given up. Sir Roderick Murchison almost alone believed in their safety. The news of their reappearance was hailed with joy throughout the length and breadth of the land. When the travellers came home they were lionised in London, and received marks of distinction from the King of the Belgians, King Victor Emmanuel of Italy, and other European potentates. Grant was made a Civil Companion of the Bath by Queen Victoria. On returning to his native town Captain Grant was presented with the freedom of the burgh, and with a piece of silver plate by the county. His mother being resident at Dingwall (her daughter had married the Rev. Dr. Mackenzie of Ferintosh), Captain Grant took up his abode there, and wrote the account of his African travels, " A Walk Across Africa," the title of which was suggested by a remark of Lord Palmerston in greeting him, " You have had a long walk, sir." Whilst he was engaged on the work, news came of the death of Captain Speke, who had been accidentally killed when out shooting by his gun going off. Captain Grant married Miss Laurie, niece of Sir Peter Laurie, Lord Mayor of London. After his marriage he went back to India, but returned after a few years' further service. When the Abyssinian Expedition of 1868 was dispatched, Captain Grant, at the urgent request of the Government, joined the Intelligence Department, and rendered valuable service to the expedition. On his return from Africa he received the Star of India. He purchased Househill in 1872 and resided there when in the North. He kept up his connection with African travellers and geographers, and was a prominent member of the Royal Geographical Society. He was a warm friend of Stanley, and used to say—" If you ever hear any unfavourable remark about Stanley, don't believe it ! Stanley is one of the best of men." Colonel Grant died at Househill on 11th February, 1892, and the coffin was borne shoulder-high to the Nairn Cemetery by a detachment of the 78th Highlanders—his old regiment—preceded by the pipers playing " The Flowers of the Forest "—a simple but touching ceremony. An interesting biography of Colonel Grant appeared in Blackwood's Magazine for April 1892. He left two sons and three daughters. His eldest son, James Augustus, following in the footsteps of his father, was with Joseph Thomson in his expedition to Mashonaland when his father died. At the General Election of 1892, he stood as a candidate in the Unionist interest for the Elgin burghs, and made a good though unsuccessful fight. He also contested Banffshire at the bye-election in 1893, and reduced the majority, but was defeated by 771 votes. In recognition of the valuable services he rendered during the Great War he was created a baronet. He is now (1927) M.P. for Derbyshire South. The second son, Alister, adopted the army as a career, and fell in the South African War.

Millbank, a burgh heritage, belonged in early times to various proprietors. Kilravock, Calder, Rose of Belivat, and others, had roods " in the Millbank." Dr. Forbes, surgeon in Nairn, became heritable proprietor of the consolidated property, and the Earl of Findlater had a parcel of land lying to the south of it. The original kirk glebe was in this quarter. Millfield was also carved out of it. Millbank, as at present bounded, along with " the field between the roads "—a description still recognisable—was purchased by Colonel William Mackintosh, who was succeeded by his son William—both of them, father and son, were great land improvers, but some of the speculations of the latter turned out badly. The trustees sold the property to Colonel Alexander Findlay—a native of the district, who had risen in the army. His son, Alexander Findlay, also a Colonel, succeeded him, and became a very prominent citizen of Nairn. He farmed for a time Balblair, Lochdhu, and other lands in the neighbourhood. He was Provost of Nairn for many years, and was the first Commandant of the Nairn Artillery Volunteers. The house was occupied for a period by the Rev. Dr. Edwin Wrenford as a boarding school for boys. The property was purchased by Mr. John Howden of Inverness on the decease of Colonel Findlay, and is now (1927) in the possession of Mr. R. L. Mackintosh of Inshes, Inverness.

The property of Larkfield was originally the Smith's Croft of the burgh. The blacksmith of the town held it from the Town Council as part of his emoluments. Occasionally other arrangements were made, and in the year 1662 William Man, town clerk

of Nairn, held it on tack.   It was, however, usually let along with
the other subjects of the Common Good of the burgh.   On 27th
September, 1779, Dr. Hugh Rose of Brea asked for and obtained
a feu of the Smith's Acre, " as presently occupied by Alexander
Clark, blacksmith," the price being fixed at 20s. per Scots acre.
In 1813 a feu charter for the ground was granted to his son, who
is designated James Rose of Flemington.   In the same year Rose
sold it to Colonel Alexander Mair, and three years later it was
purchased by Mrs. Grace or Grizel Grant, relict of the deceased
Major John Grant, Auchindoune.   A good house was built, the
grounds laid out and enclosed, and the name changed to Larkfield.
Mrs. Grant left the property to her daughters, Jane and Eliza
Grant, and it was bequeathed by the latter, the last survivor, in
1860 to Dr. John Grigor, a medical practitioner of eminence in
Nairn, as a mark of esteem.   Dr. Grigor, who had established a
practice at Rome, resided, on retiring, at Larkfield.   He did much
to bring the burgh of Nairn into notice as a health resort, and took
a leading part for many years in developing its attractions.   He
was a man of cultivated tastes, widely known both for his professional skill and his interest in antiquarian research.   He was
the means of establishing a local museum, and at his death in 1886
he left £1000 for the Nairn Literary Institute, with which the
museum was connected, and also bequests for university medical
bursaries, free scholarships at Nairn Academy, and for the poor.
His fellow-citizens and other friends erected a bronze statue on the
High Street to his memory, the work of Mr. J. Hutchison, the
well-known sculptor.   At Mrs. Grigor's demise Larkfield went
to Dr. Grigor's nephew, Mr. Clement Gordon, Banff, from whom
it was purchased by Dr. H. W. Mann—the property thus reverting
to one of the same name as its holder over two hundred years before.
The family of the name of Mann has been very prominently
associated with the town of Nairn for many generations, members
of it holding official positions in the burgh and taking a leading
part in its affairs.   Dr. Mann followed in the footsteps of his
ancestors in this respect, and was for some time Provost of Nairn.
The property afterwards passed into possession of Mr. A. M.
Mackintosh, author of the History of the Mackintoshes and Clan

Chattan, a monograph on Mackintosh of Borlum, and other highly interesting and valuable literary works. Mr. Mackintosh changed the name of the property to The Hermitage.

Any notice of lands and land owners in Nairnshire would be incomplete without mention of the Baillies of Lochloy. The chivalrous old knights of Lochloy have happily been succeeded by a family of distinction. The Baillies as a clan trace descent from Baillie of Lamington, who married the daughter of Sir William Wallace, the Scottish patriot. The branch to which the Baillies of Lochloy belong is the family of Redcastle. Colonel Hugh Smith Baillie and General Duncan Baillie were younger sons of Colonel Hugh Baillie of Redcastle and Tarradale. After residing for some time at Househill, General Baillie built a handsome mansion at Lochloy on a long lease, and his brother, who married Viscountess Glentworth, usually resided there also. General Baillie married Anna Burnaby (sister of Colonel Frederick Burnaby of military renown, and niece of Lady Glentworth). On retiring from the Royal Horse Guards, he took up permanent abode at Lochloy, and settled down to the enjoyment of country life. He was devoted to Nairnshire, and maintained friendly intercourse with all ranks and classes. No public gathering was considered complete without his handsome genial presence, and every institution felt his kindly influence. He was warmly attached to his nephew, the laird of Brodie, and admired his brilliant qualities. When the first County Council was formed in 1890 General Baillie was elected convener, but he died before completing his first year of office. He left a family of sons and daughters. The eldest son, Ronald, O.B.E., joined the Scottish Bar, was appointed Sheriff-Substitute of Roxburghshire in 1897 and married Elizabeth, M.B.E., younger daughter of Major Rose of Kilravock. The second, Captain Alan, joined the Seaforth Highlanders and, after seeing considerable active service in India, was severely wounded at the battle of Atbara in the Sudan in 1898, and died of his wounds. The third son, Captain Ian, served with the 4th Camerons in the Great War, and died of wounds received at the battle of Festubert in 1915. The fourth son, Colonel Duncan Baillie, C.M.G., D.S.O., commanded the Lovat Scouts through-

out the War, and the fifth son, Colonel Hugh Baillie, D.S.O.,
served on the staff during the War and thereafter commanded the
1st Seaforth Highlanders.   Mrs. Baillie and her daughters continue
to reside at Lochloy, which was acquired by the family a number
of years ago.

CHAPTER XX

ECCLESIASTICAL HISTORY

ALTHOUGH Presbyterianism was restored as the national form of church government in Scotland by the Revolution Settlement in 1690, the organisation of the Church in many parts of the country was for a long period thereafter exceedingly defective. The Episcopal ministers who conformed to the extent of taking the oath of allegiance to the civil power were allowed to retain their benefices during their lives. It thus happened that in one parish the minister might be an Episcopalian and in the adjoining parish a Presbyterian. The form of worship in the two probably did not differ very materially, but a marked distinction existed in the spirit in which the work was performed.

It was not till 1702 that a Synod of Moray was revived, the Presbyterian ministers being so few in number that they were content to have one Presbytery for the whole diocese of Moray. The parishes of Auldearn, Ardclach, and Nairn formed part of the Presbytery of Forres by a later arrangement, and it was not until 1773 that they were finally erected into the Presbytery of Nairn, along with Cawdor and Croy taken from Inverness, and Ardersier from Chanonry—the six parishes which now form the Nairn Presbytery.

The church of Nairn in ancient times stood on the west side of the Constabulary Gardens, or Castlehill, some little distance back from the High Street. There is no record of the date when it was removed to the site on the bank of the river, but probably the change took place soon after the Reformation. In the year 1658 there is a reference in the burgh records evidently to the building of a new church.   It is stated there that the trades of Nairn had agreed voluntarily to contribute £30 Scots—a large sum in those days—towards the erection of a trades gallery in the church.   The only ecclesiastical relic preserved is a small handbell bearing the name " NARN "—evidently, from the spelling and the form of the letters, of a pretty old date.

The Rev. Hugh Rose, minister of Nairn, whose literary labours have made his name better known than that of any of his contemporaries, did not live to witness the Revolution.   He died in 1686.   He was the eldest son of David Rose of Earlsmill, fifth son of William, the eleventh baron of Kilravock.   David Rose had a wadset of Termet in the parish of Petty and of Earlsmill. He assigned Earlsmill to Hugh, minister of Nairn, but Lord Moray redeemed it in 1667, and David made provision for his son by giving him the wadset of Termet instead.   Hugh was intended for the legal profession, and for that purpose studied at Leyden, having for his companion there Sir George Mackenzie of legal fame, who, it is said, knowing his extraordinary abilities as a lawyer, expressed great surprise on hearing that his fellow-student had abandoned law for divinity.   In the intervals of study for the pulpit in the years 1683-4, the minister drew up a History of the Family of Kilravock of great interest and value.   It was edited and supplemented by Mr. Cosmo Innes, and published by the Spalding Club in 1848. The old minister was laid aside by illness for several years before his death, and being debarred from preaching, he employed himself in writing a series of " Meditations on Several Interesting Subjects," which was published in 1762 by an Inverness bookseller. The little volume shows the minister of Nairn to have been a pious, scholarly man of the type of Leighton.

The minister in possession when Presbyterianism was re-established was George Dunbar.   He had been schoolmaster at Auldearn, and graduated at Aberdeen University.   He conformed to Episcopacy, and was ordained to the church of Dallas in 1682. In 1687 he was translated to Nairn, being presented by the Dean of Moray.   He did not preach in Gaelic.   Retaining his benefice under the new ecclesiastical order, he died in 1728, aged about seventy-six years.

The next minister was Alexander Rose, licentiate, who was appointed by the unanimous call of the magistrates of the burgh of Nairn. In his time a curious question of discipline arose. At the Commission of the General Assembly in August 1739 a representation was read from the Synod of Moray and Presbytery of Forres respecting Robert Main, skipper of a fishing boat at Nairn, and five other seamen, his crew, who had given offence to the session of Tarbet in Ross-shire by setting to sea from a harbour in that parish on a Sabbath morning. They had expressed their willingness to remove the offence by submitting to the discipline of the Church, but the magistrates of Nairn had by their authority discharged their compearance. Hugh Rose of Clava was Provost of Nairn at the time, and he had pretty strong Jacobite-Episcopalian sympathies, which may account for the unusual proceeding of the magistrates interposing between the ecclesiastical courts and the subjects of discipline. The Commission, however, found the representation incompetent, not containing information as to whither the said seamen went, what they did at sea after they went out, etc., and therefore could give no advice until a more distinct account of the case be laid before them. No further mention of the case occurs in the church records. Alexander Rose married Elizabeth Ross in 1753, and died in 1757. It is recorded in Scott's " Fasti " that his pecuniary affairs were left in such a state as to cause loss to many, and to give occasion to much unfavourable reflection, yet his memory was cherished, as he introduced the preaching of Gaelic to the congregation.

His successor, Patrick Dunbar, was a native of Auldearn, and on his being presented by Brodie of Brodie, who now claimed the right of patronage, his settlement was opposed before the Presbytery on account of his lacking the Gaelic; but the Presbytery were of opinion that Gaelic was not necessary to the minister of Nairn, and he was accordingly ordained on 12th April, 1759. He married Elizabeth Davidson, and died in 1787, having been minister of Nairn for twenty-nine years.

John Morrison succeeded in the following year. He was a native of Mortlach, and had been schoolmaster of Nigg in Ross-shire. He could preach in Gaelic, which he probably learned in

Ross-shire, and the Gaelic service, to the joy of the Highlanders, was resumed. He married Jean Grant. In 1789 the Presbytery ordained the heritors to pay the sum of £56 8s. 7½d. for repairing the kirk, manse, offices, and garden wall. In 1797 a visitation of the kirk took place; it was found sufficient, but the Presbytery authorised the minister to get any necessary repairs on the ecclesiastical buildings done at the expense of the heritors. In 1805 the heritors were assessed for £71. A serious panic arose in the church in the year 1808, from an alarm that the galleries were giving way, and some of the worshippers jumped from the loft to the floor. It was a false alarm, but the Presbytery on 23rd November, 1808, declared the building to be insufficient, and on 4th May of the following year it was resolved to erect a new church to accommodate from 900 to 1000. The amount levied on the heritors for the new church was £1357. The smallness of the sum was probably due to the circumstance that the foundation walls and materials of the old edifice were used in the building of the new church. The stone vaults in the interior of the old church were, according to common report, merely covered with sand and floored over. The rule for assessing the heritors for their proportions of the stipend and expense of repairs was a rental prepared in 1805 for apportioning the expense of supporting the wives and families of militiamen; but when the new church was built the assessment was laid upon the burgh heritors and feuars, as well as the heritors of the landward parish, and several refusing to pay, the decreet was enforced against them by legal process. In the old church the magistrates and Town Council had a loft for themselves, but in the new church no such accommodation was claimed or provided. The church was finished early in the year 1810. There was much debate amongst the heritors regarding the allocation of the seats, but Mrs. Elizabeth Rose of Kilravock records in her diary that her son Kilravock, with Cantray and others, returned to dinner in the evening from a meeting at Nairn regarding the allocation, all highly pleased at the arrangements, except the laird of Boath. Mrs. Rose herself made a special journey in her old age to see the grand new church. It was, however, a very plain structure which the heritors had erected, and being seated for only 900, it was quite inadequate for the population of the burgh and landward parish. It provided only sixty sittings for fisher people—thirty for the fishers of Nairn and thirty for those of Delnies. Mr. Morrison died in 1814, in the thirtieth year of his ministry.

James Grant, son of the Rev. Alexander Grant of Cawdor, who succeeded, was a graduate of Aberdeen University and King's College. Some objections were raised to his settlement, but they were fallen from at the bar of the Assembly, and he was ordained minister of Nairn, 13th July, 1815. He married Christian Mackintosh, and had three sons and one daughter. The distinguished career of his son, Colonel James A. Grant, has already been described. Mr. Grant was minister when the Disruption occurred.

The church of Auldearn stands on the same spot as it did when it was the Deanery of Moray in ancient times, but the present edifice bears the comparatively recent date of 1757. The choir— an unroofed portion still devoted to sepulture—is of much older date, and its windows bear traces of the Gothic architecture of the more ancient structure of which it formed a part. According to tradition the old church was struck by lightning and partially destroyed by fire. In 1640 John Hay of Lochloy, by his last will and testament, left his body to be buried in the burial place " of his forbears within the quier of Auldearn," and ordained " ane loft to be biggit within the kirk of Auldearn on the north side thereof with the timber gotten of the Chanonrie Kirk of Elgin." Lord Brodie, in his time, had much trouble of mind concerning the spiritual condition of Auldearn. Writing in 1671, he says—" I desire to be affected with the withered and dry state of Dyke and Auldearn. Oh! does there fall any rain upon them ! "

The last Dean of Moray was Thomas Keay. It was men like Keay who deepened the dislike of the people to prelacy. He was a thoroughly bad character, in fact a notorious drunkard. One ecclesiastical authority says he was " expelled " from Auldearn, another that he " deserted his charge." He afterwards intruded at Crimmond. His successor—the first Presbyterian minister after the Revolution—was of a very different stamp. The saintly, heroic schoolmaster of Auldearn, Alexander Dunbar, who had been a prisoner on the Bass Rock for twelve months, now occupied the pulpit.   No tablet at the place perpetuates his memory, but in other days he would have been canonised.   He was inducted to Auldearn in 1689, and attended the meetings of the General Assembly in 1690 and 1692.   He was twice married, first, to Margaret Meldrum, who died 29th September, 1689, and secondly to Beatrix Fowler, who survived him.   His confinement in the Bass prison had weakened his health, never very strong, and after an illness of three years he died on 29th October, 1707, aged about sixty-seven.   He left a sum of money to buy two large silver cups for communion, though these are not now in existence.   He was succeeded by David Henderson, of whom nothing particular is recorded.   He died, after a ministry of sixteen years, in 1725, and was succeeded by James Winchester, who had been chaplain to the baron of Kilravock, and afterwards presented by Brodie of Lethen to the kirk of Rafford.   He remained in Auldearn for five years, and then accepted a presentation to St. Giles Church, Elgin, whence a few years later he was translated to Jedburgh.   On his leaving Elgin, the kirk of St. Giles once more took away the minister of Auldearn—Alexander Irvine, who had been brought from St. Andrews to Auldearn.   He had two daughters—Mary, who married James Gray, minister of Lanark, and Sophia, who married John Wood, minister of Rosemarkie.

A strong antipathy existed in the minds of the kirk session of Auldearn towards Highlanders.   They passed a series of severe enactments against them.   The first begins in September 29, 1728, when Winchester was minister.   It runs as follows—" The Session agreed that intimation be made to the congregation that they be cautious in harbouring strangers in their families, and receive none without clear certificates relating to their behaviour." On February 27, 1732, " intimation was this day made from the pulpit according to the appointment of a former session, to masters of families, etc., within the parish, warning them against receiving servants or subtenants, who understood not the English language." Irvine, the St. Andrews man, was the minister at the time.   As the Whitsunday term was drawing near it was thought desirable to renew the injunction, and accordingly on May 14, 1732, " the session appointed that next Lord's Day from the pulpit all masters and heads of families in this parish be exhorted to enquire for testimonials from such strangers as are in their service." Again, on October 29, 1732, "it was recommended to the elders to take care that no servants be received in their corners without sufficient testimonials, and the minister was desired to make intimation of the same from the pulpit next Lord's Day." Finally, on May 19th, 1735, "the elders were desired to inspect their respective districts about servants not understanding the English language, and to do what they could to hinder their reception." A happy day dawned for the Highlanders in the district when Irvine quitted his post, and Daniel Munro, himself a Gaelic speaker, was installed as minister of Auldearn. This happened in the year following the date of the last edict of the session, on 23rd September, 1736. Munro was a very powerful evangelical preacher. He laboured in Auldearn for some nine years. At Tain, where he had occasion to preach, the people were vastly taken with him, and having knowledge of his high repute for faithfulness and godliness, they lost not a day in moving for a call to him. The magistrates generously undertook to bear all expense. The call was given, and Daniel Munro, to the sorrow of the people of Auldearn, accepted it. He may have heard what happened to his predecessor at Tain, recently deceased. He had been minister of Tarbat, and declined the call to Tain, but a number of the Tain parishioners went down to Tarbat and, entering the church, went straight to the pulpit and carried him off bodily.

A very unhappy period followed in the history of the parish of Auldearn. The patron, Brodie of Brodie, presented Thomas Gordon from Cabrach, but his settlement was opposed. The presentee was unpopular, and was not allowed to be settled till 12th February, 1747, nearly two years after his presentation. A number of the parishioners seceded, and formed the nucleus of the Secession church at Boghole. Thomas Gordon turned out, however, to be a man who could look after his own affairs and the parishioners' rights as well. It is to him that the parish owes the present church. He compelled the heritors to pull down the old church, which had fallen into a ruinous state, and to erect a new edifice, which bears the date 1757, the tenth year of his ministry.

He had no hesitation in suing the Laird of Brodie, his patron, and other heritors, in the Sheriff Court of Nairn, as the records show. He lived to the age of eighty-five, during forty-six years of which he was minister of Auldearn. A tombstone in the old choir bears the following inscription—" To the memory of the Rev. Thomas Gordon, who was 8 years minister of the Gospel at Cabrach, and 46 at Auldearn. A man of exemplary piety, the strictest integrity, and remarkable for the extent of his erudition. After a life devoted to the duties of his sacred function, he was summoned to his reward, 25th November, A.D., 1793, aged 85 years."

John Paterson, a native of Morayshire, the next minister, was admitted in 1794. It was he who dedicated the colours of the Nairnshire Militia in 1810 on the links of Nairn " in full pontificals." He was a very scholarly man, and according to Scott's Fasti, " eminently possessed the virtues of candour, benevolence, and unsullied integrity." The stories preserved of him, however, show him to have been a " muscular Christian," who rather shocked the Seceders of the time by his candour of speech and unconventionality of conduct. He died at the comparatively early age of forty-two.

Of quite a different type was his successor, William Barclay. He was a fervid evangelical preacher, a keen theologian, devoted to pastoral duties, and at the same time something of a doctor, lawyer, and mechanic. Many who formerly worshipped in the church at Auldearn but had gone over to the Secession church at Boghole, returned in his time to the old fold. In his report in the New Statistical Account, Barclay states that there is scarcely a child in the parish between six and fifteen years of age who cannot read. There might be from twelve to fourteen persons above fifteen who could not read. He was, in short, a model parish minister. His influence in the parish was probably all the greater from the circumstance that he was connected by marriage with the laird of Lethen, who was of a kindred spirit. Barclay was minister of Auldearn when the Disruption took place.

Ardclach for many years after the Reformation had scant provision for religious services. At one time it was a vicarage, under the patronage of the parson of Rafford as sub-chantor of Moray, and it was afterwards united to the kirk of Edinkillie. Efforts were made to have it erected into an independent parish, and in the hope of this being done, Donald Macpherson, a graduate of St. Andrews, accepted the charge. He was forced, however, to leave it and accept a call to Cawdor, " as he had no means to live by." John Balfour, who must have been a man of some courage, undertook in 1642 the duties of the charge. The Assembly had in the previous year agreed to erect it into a separate parish, but the matter lay with the Scottish Parliament, and it was not till 1650 that the parish of Ardclach as it now exists was constituted. It was one of the charges established by decreet of Platt, as it was called, and in order to make it sufficient for the sustenance of the minister, a portion of Auldearn parish was annexed to it, viz., " the lands of Lethenbar, Fornighty, Fleenasnagael, Achamore, and Achavelgin, belonging to Alexander Brodie of Lethen ; and Middle Fleenas and Achnatone, belonging to William Rose of Clava, and Hugh Rose, fiar thereof."

In 1680 Patrick Grant, brother of the laird of Grant, was appointed minister of Ardclach, and for thirty-six years served in that office. He was succeeded in 1716 by John Duncanson, who was translated to Petty in 1728. His successor was William Barron, an eminent Hebrew scholar, a good preacher, and a most agreeable person. His friendship was much cultivated by the learned men who made visits to Coulmony as guests of the barons of Kilravock. He married Jean Grant, had sixteen children, and died 17th August, 1784.

A very eccentric person named William Shaw, from Arran, next found his way into the Ardclach pulpit. He quarrelled with many of his parishioners, and became so unpopular that, after less than a twelvemonth's residence, he quitted his charge and went off to London. Before settling at Ardclach, he had published an Analysis of the Gaelic Language, and having compiled a Dictionary of the Gaelic Language, went to London in order to get it published. He made the acquaintance of Dr. Samuel Johnson, and through him got an incumbency in the Church of England worth £200 a year. His Gaelic Dictionary, published by subscription, was found to be so valueless that many of the subscribers refused to pay for it, but were compelled by decreet of the Court of Session to do so, the judges taking a lenient view of the performance not coming up to the prospectus. Dr. Samuel Johnson's favour for him was due to his having taken the same side in the controversy regarding the authenticity of Macpherson's " Ossian."

Donald Mitchell, the next minister, was a native of Cromarty. He had been minister of the Little Church of Elgin, and was presented by Miss Brodie of Lethen from her knowledge of his character and ministerial gifts. He was admitted to Ardclach in 1781, and laboured with great faithfulness for thirty-seven years. On 8th April, 1810, the year before his death, Mrs. Elizabeth Rose of Kilravock, in her diary records hearing him preach at Croy—" a very fine sermon "—and gives notes of his discourse. His parishioners erected a handsome monument over his grave. Of his six sons and two daughters, Donald became the first Scottish missionary to India. He had attended the University of Aberdeen with a view to entering the ministry, but relinquished that purpose on finding he could not conscientiously sign the Confession of Faith. He got an appointment in the East India Company's service, sailed for India in 1811, and remained there for nine years. While stationed at Surat he met with two missionaries of the London Missionary Society, whose preaching and conversation led him to a complete change of view. He now became ardent to enter on Christian work, and resigned his commission in the Bombay Army. Returning to his native land, he finished his theological training, and offered his services to the Scottish Missionary Society. The Presbytery of Nairn met at Nairn, and licensed and ordained him—setting him forth as the first Scottish missionary to India. He arrived in India in 1822, and settled at Bankot, on the Savitri river, in the Presidency of Bombay. There he opened schools for the natives and taught them to read the gospels in Marathi. He was, however, after less than a year's service, laid low by fever, and died on the way to Satara for change of air. He was buried in a field a short distance beyond the village of Poladhpur, where the mango trees to this day overshadow his tomb. A marble tablet thus records the death of the heroic pioneer missionary—" In memory of Rev. Donald Mitchell, first missionary of the Scottish Missionary Society in India. He left the Bombay Army, of which he was a commissioned officer, to become a preacher of the Gospel to the benighted inhabitants of this country, but he was removed from the chosen sphere of this work of faith within the first year of his ministerial services. He died at this village on the 20th November, 1823."

The minister of Ardclach's second son, James Errol Mitchell, was unfortunately born deaf and dumb and blind. As he grew up to manhood, he developed a remarkable degree of intelligence, mainly through the abnormal development of the senses of touch, taste, and smell. His case excited great interest amongst scientific men, and formed the subject of a paper by Professor Dugald Stewart of Edinburgh. He reached a good old age, and died about the year 1869 at Nairn, where he was long a familiar figure. Lewis, another son of the minister of Ardclach, became a lieutenant in the Royal Navy. The Rev. R. A. Mitchell, Free Gilcomston Church, Aberdeen, was his son.

The parish church of Ardclach occupies a peculiar position. It is situated on a low haugh on the left side of the river Findhorn, about the centre of the parish. To reach it, there is a precipitous descent from each bank of the river. The tradition is that the site was adopted as a compromise—the party on each side claiming to have the church on its own side of the water, but ultimately agreeing to its being at the water edge on the north side. The records show that the church was built in 1626, rebuilt in 1762, again rebuilt in 1839, and renovated in 1892. As it would be of no use ringing the church-bell in its low-lying situation, the belfry is perched on the top of a hill north of the church, and is consequently said to be the highest bell-tower in Scotland. This old tower, however, was probably erected originally as a watch-house. One of the traditions regarding it is that the watchers rang the bell the moment they observed the Highland reivers coming down the pass of the Streens on foraging expeditions. The inhabitants of Ardclach for miles around had thus timely warning of the approach of the enemy. The cattle-lifters were so annoyed that their plans were frustrated by the ringing of the bell, whose sound was carried to the utmost corner of the parish, that they resolved to

steal the bell.   The boldest robber of the gang succeeded in cutting
it down, and threw it into the river Findhorn.   The construction
of the building, and the dungeon and shot-holes, lent colour to the
surmise that it was originally a watch-tower, but the ecclesiastical
records show that it was also used as a church prison, several defaulters having been committed by the session to the kirk steeple
for a term of imprisonment.

Mitchell was succeeded in Ardclach by Hugh Macbean, a
native of Inverness-shire, who was admitted in 1812.   He wrote
an excellent description of the parish for the New Statistical Account,
and was minister when the Disruption occurred.   His son, Æneas
Macbean, was a well-known Writer to the Signet in Edinburgh.

The church at Cawdor was erected in 1619, according to tradition, by the laird of Calder in fulfilment of a vow he made when in
danger of shipwreck in coming from Islay.   In the report furnished
by Sir Archibald Campbell of Clunas to the commissioners on the
Cawdor estate in 1725, it is stated—" As to the church of Calder,
which was built by Sir Hugh Campbell's grandfather, Sir John,
being the only heritor except Rose of Holme, a small heritor, the
roof thereof is entirely rott and many of the slate fallen off, never
being repaired since the erection thereof, except three or four
couples furnished in Sir Hugh's time, when the pricket or top of
the steeple was by storm blown over and broke these couples;
needs to be immediately repaired, and will cost double the money
if it is delayed another year.   The Sacrament not being administered for the years 1722-25, Sir Archibald has retained the element
money, which being yearly £50 Scots, amounts to £150, and
proposes that the said sum be applied in the first place towards
the repair which he shall finish as effectually and frugally as possible.   The families new burial place which lies under that part
betwixt the steeple and the body of the church is much abused and
like to go to ruin altogether, by the insufficient roof of the church;
and the old burial place, called Barrivan, of the Thanes and all the
Campbells of Calder who died in the north preceding Sir Hugh's
time, where formerly the old kirk of Calder was, likewise needs to
be repaired, which Sir Archibald conceives may be done for £10
sterling, which he expects the commissioners will comply with, for

the honour and memory of the family." A relic of the olden time when church discipline was enforced by corporal punishment is preserved in a very complete state, namely, the jougs.

The last minister who preached in the old church of Barevan was Andrew Balfour, who had been minister of Nairn down to 1601, and who occupied the new church of Cawdor till his death in 1625. He was succeeded by Gilbert Anderson, who was translated to Cromarty in 1641. Donald Macpherson, who had been starved out of Ardclach, was admitted to Cawdor in the following year. He shared to the full the prevalent belief in witchcraft, and in 1643 a complaint was made to the Privy Council against him and the Tutor of Cawdor for "waking a woman, the space of twenty days naked, with nothing on her but sackcloth, under a charge of witchcraft," whom their lordships ordered to be liberated. Donald Macpherson's services were sought for by Ardersier, but he remained at Cawdor, and died there in 1686, aged about seventy-two years.

Lauchlan M'Bean was minister of Cawdor when the Revolution Act was passed, having been ordained in 1687. He had been schoolmaster of Nairn, and is mentioned as having been admitted as a burgess of the burgh. He was a worthless character, and had to demit his office. He intruded at Ardersier in 1695, but was deposed in 1706 for immorality. He was succeeded at Cawdor by James Chapman, son of an Inverness merchant, who was translated to Cromdale in 1702.

John Calder, chaplain to Sir James Calder in Muirtown, was the next minister of Cawdor. He was the ancestor of a race of eminent ministers in the north, and was a Gaelic preacher of some note. He died in 1717.

Lachlan Shaw, the historian of Moray, laboured at Cawdor from 1719 till 1734. It was during his pastorate here that he collected the materials for his History, and put them into shape for the press. He also wrote a continuation of Rose's Genealogy of the Family of Kilravock, and the description of Moray in Pennant's Tour. As he was on intimate terms with the laird of Calder, he had access to all the family muniments in the district. Shaw gives a deplorable account of the state of religion in the remoter parts of the Highlands, and he himself on more than one occasion received very rough treatment at the hands of parishioners who had no desire to be brought under the government and discipline of the Presbyterian Kirk. He removed to Elgin in 1744, and was minister there until 1774, when he retired. His History appeared in the following year, and two years later the worthy old man died, greatly venerated, at the age of ninety-one. A slab of Peterhead granite has been placed in the chancel of Elgin Cathedral to his memory. He was twice married, and had a large family, some of his descendants migrating to America. A grandson, Lachlan Donaldson, was sometime Mayor of the City of St. John, New Brunswick, and placed a memorial window in the parish church to the author of the " History of Moray."

Patrick Grant, the next minister, was ordained at Cawdor in 1735, and was translated to Urray in 1749. He became Moderator of the General Assembly in 1778, having a few years previously been made a Doctor of Divinity by the University of Aberdeen. Dr. Patrick Grant was a learned man, and his point of view of the questions of his time is indicated by the title of a sermon he published in 1779—" The Spirit of Moderation in Religion Recommended."

Daniel Brodie, connected with the Brodies of Lethen, took the place of Patrick Grant. He had been minister of Ardersier for some years before. He married Margaret Rose, and died in his forty-seventh year, in 1771.

In 1772 Kenneth M'Aulay was translated from Ardnamurchan to Cawdor. His entertainment of Dr. Samuel Johnson and Boswell at the manse of Cawdor has been already related. Copies of his History of St. Kilda are now scarce. M'Aulay was pleased with the situation of his charge, but was dissatisfied with the amount of his stipend. The minister of Calder, with the exception of his brother of Ardclach, had the smallest stipend in the Presbytery. It amounted to only £56 14s. 5½d., whereas the stipend of Auldearn was £82; Nairn, £76; Croy, £75; and Petty the same, with a good glebe. M'Aulay said he would be content if it were raised to an equality with that of his fellow presbyters, and the laird of Calder, on the representation of

Valentine White, his factor, increased it to that extent. As already stated, the minister was grand-uncle to Lord Macaulay.

He died in 1779, and was succeeded by Alexander Grant, who had been minister of the parishes of Daviot and Dunlichty, an unruly charge, which he had succeeded in reducing to order and decency. Alexander Grant was a son of George Grant, minister of Kirkmichael, of whom it is related that he had twenty-one children, sixteen of whom came to maturity, and although he had a stipend of only £47 sterling he contrived to leave each of his children the sum of £100. The minister of Cawdor had three sons— Alexander, James who became minister of Nairn, and George who was a partner in the firm of " Grant, Gladstone & Coy.," merchants in Liverpool. The old minister died in 1828 in his 85th year.

Alexander Fraser, son of the Rev. Donald Fraser of Kirkhill, succeeded. On his father's death in 1837 he was translated to his native parish. He was a chaplain in the army in the Crimea, and was greatly respected by all classes. The minister at the Disruption was Simon Fraser M'Lauchlan, who had been translated from Snizort to Cawdor in 1837.

The minister of Croy at the time of the Revolution was Hugh Fraser, a native of Aberdeenshire. He was an Episcopalian, but stayed on. Like so many of the other " Curates," he was a man of disreputable character. While Keay, the Dean of Auldearn, was a drunkard, and M'Bean, the minister of Cawdor, an immoral person, the minister of Croy was accused of bigamy. He was deposed by the Commission of Assembly in 1700. The writer of the Statistical Account gives a frightful picture of the demoralisation of the parish. " There were fightings at lykewakes, fightings even at church, sad immorality, and attempts at compassing death by charms and spells. One parishioner is recorded as having in 1748, on the death of his mother on a Sunday evening, gathered together some neighbours, got up a dance, and continued the orgies till next day. For this the shameless reveller had to stand publicly and penitentially in the church for six consecutive Sundays." By the time the particular instance mentioned occurred, James Calder, translated from Ardersier, must have been minister of Croy. His predecessor, Farquhar Beton or Bethune, was usually spoken of as " the worthy Mr. Bethune," but he suffered long from ill health. He was a great genealogist, and married a daughter of John Rose of Newton, Provost of Nairn. It took a whole generation, however, to civilise the people of Croy.

James Calder is described as possessing gentle manners, great humility, extensive charity, and fervent piety, with labour unwearied, and his compositions from the pulpit were remarkable for genius, taste, and judgment, so that his services were rewarded with uncommon success. The eulogium on his tombstone is supported by the testimony of oral tradition, and his published diary shows him to have been a man of intense spirituality. He married a daughter of Thomas Inglis, minister of Resolis—one of the Inglises of Nairn—and had three sons in the ministry—at Rosskeen, Urquhart, and Croy. His son Hugh succeeded him at Croy in 1778, and laboured there with much success till a few years before his death, when he had to employ an assistant. One of his assistants was Mr. Carment. Another was his son Alexander —a youth of great promise, whose illness and death at an early age are mentioned in sympathetic terms in Mrs. Elizabeth Rose of Kilravock's unpublished diary in 1810. The minister himself died in 1822. A brighter picture of the social state of the people could then be given. Mr. Sage of Resolis says the parish of Croy at the beginning of his ministry, from various associations in his mind connected with it, was to him at least a " Holy Land." " In that part of the north," he says, " I met with a goodly number of men bearing the name of Christ who were certainly among the most eminent Christians I ever had the privilege to meet during my life and ministry. Their names are engraved upon my most vivid and affectionate remembrances of the past. These were Hugh Macdonald at Campbeltown; his senior in years and grace, John Macnishie, and his son Donald, who lived at Milton of Connage; John Munro at Croy; Angus Ross, catechist of Nairn; Hugh Clunas at Ardclach; William Sinclair at Auldearn; John Fraser, catechist both of Ardersier and Petty, and many others. I was first introduced to this Christian circle in 1822, during the vacancy at Croy caused by the death of Mr. Hugh Calder."

Lord Cawdor next made an unpopular presentation, and serious disturbances occurred. When the presentee, Alexander Campbell, minister of Dores, made his appearance in the parish to preach, he along with his friends was met by a mob, refused admittance to the church, and assaulted. The military had to be used to enforce his settlement. Several of the rioters were tried before the High Court of Justiciary, and four of them sentenced to terms of imprisonment, which, to his credit, Campbell used his influence to get shortened. He was minister when the Disruption occurred.

Ardersier was not added to the Presbytery of Nairn till 1773. The transference from Chanonry to Nairn Presbytery was mainly brought about by Walter Morrison, the minister at that time. The laird of Calder, John Campbell, claimed the right of patronage, and in his self-complacent manner communicated to Valentine White his views on ecclesiastical affairs in Ardersier. " Enclosed is an answer," he wrote, " to the Presbytery of Chanonry to let them know that they are misinformed as to the necessity of the Erse language in Ardersier parish. The sooner the Erse and Welsh languages are worn out of use among the common people the better. I am told Mr. Morrison is not one of the enthusiastic tribe, which is what I would chiefly guard against." The laird of Calder was correctly informed regarding Walter Morrison—he was known amongst his contemporaries as " the Witty Walter." The chaplaincy of Fort George was also instituted as a function of the minister of Ardersier in Morrison's time. He died in 1780.

Pryce Campbell, who was ordained to the charge in 1781, was a younger brother of Duncan Campbell, factor for Lethen. Pryce was a man of extraordinary physical endurance in his earlier days. It is told of him that on one occasion he left Fornighty on foot to attend his classes at Aberdeen University, and was just entering the Granite City when he recollected that he had left a class-book at home, value 7s. 6d. Money was scarce in those days, and he immediately turned and went back to Fornighty for his book. The inmates were all asleep, but by raising a window he got hold of the book in question without disturbing the family, and then proceeded to Aberdeen, where he arrived in time for the opening exercises of the session, having done the double journey without a single break or rest. It was his frequent practice in the course of

the session to leave Aberdeen on Friday evening, proceed to Fornighty, and return in time for his classes on Monday, performing
the journey on foot. He and Mr. Mitchell of Ardclach married two
sisters. During his later years he was unable from failing strength
to overtake all the duties of his office, but with his old spirit of
dogged endurance, he struggled on. When, at last, on complaints
reaching the General Assembly in 1835, he was enjoined to desist
from the exercise of his ministry, he was over eighty years of age.
John Matheson was appointed his colleague and successor. A
daughter of Pryce Campbell married Mr. Young, Hillhead, and
Matheson, the young minister, married their daughter Grace.
Another of Campbell's daughters, Jane, married James Clark,
Dalnahegleish, and their daughter married John M'Killican,
Piperhill, afterwards of Achagour, of whom were the M'Killicans
of Achagour. A son, Robert Calder Campbell, became a Major
in the East India Company's service, and was the author of " Lays
from the East." Pryce Campbell died in 1840, aged 86 years.
Matheson was minister when the Disruption occurred. His only
surviving son was Colonel John Matheson of the Royal Engineers,
latterly at the War Office.

The united parishes of Moy and Dalarossie, though joined to
the Presbytery of Inverness, were territorially in Nairnshire. At
the Revolution the curate, Alexander Cumin, though a Jacobite,
continued undisturbed, and remained in possession till his death.
His successor, James Leslie, was a man of great muscular
power. He hailed from Ardclach, and appears to have been one
of the Leslies of Drumlochan—a family who have been in possession of this small upland farm for nearly three centuries. It is
of him the story is told that, finding it impossible to get an audience
to hear him preach, the parishioners being engaged in the pastime
of putting the stone, he challenged the best of them at the game,
making it a condition, however, that should he beat them they
should all attend church, to which they agreed. The minister
threw off his coat, took up the heavy stone, and distanced all of
them. He thus won the respect of his parishioners, and speedily
worked a remarkable change amongst them. He married Janet
Robertson, widow of Alexander Rose of Holme Rose, and died in

1766. Patronage having been restored, Hugh Rose of Kilravock exercised his right, and made a bad selection. He presented James Mackintosh, schoolmaster and session clerk of Cawdor, who had been a missionary in Strathdearn, and who was deposed for immorality in 1787. His successor was William M'Bean, but after four years' service he accepted a call to Alves. M'Bean's successor was Hugh Mackay, and on his death James M'Lachlan was presented by William Mackintosh of Geddes. The right of patronage was carried, on the division of the Kilravock inheritance, by the laird of Geddes. James M'Lachlan was a conspicuous figure in the troublous times preceding the Disruption. He was one of the leaders of the anti-patronage party in the Highlands, and for the part he took at the settlement of an obnoxious presentee at Kiltarlity, he was rebuked at the bar of the Assembly in 1824. Mr. James Grant, the minister of Nairn, was mixed up with the proceedings at Kiltarlity, but was on the other side, having been appointed a commissioner by the Synod to assist the Presbytery. M'Lachlan had two sons—Simon, who became minister of Cawdor, and Thomas, who succeeded his father. Thomas M'Lachlan came out at the Disruption, and became minister of the Free Church at Dores. He afterwards was minister of Free St. Columba's (Gaelic charge) in Edinburgh, and did eminent literary work as a Celtic scholar, besides earning distinction as a minister of the church.

The parishes of Daviot and Dunlichty, in the patronage of the laird of Calder, have had a curious history. The first minister presented after the introduction of patronage was Alexander Rose, a natural son of William Rose of Clava. William got a presentation to the better living of Alves from the Earl of Moray, but the Presbytery of Inverness would not allow him to accept it, and continued him at Daviot "in respect of the Gaelic language." He died in 1664, and was succeeded as Episcopal curate by Alexander Fraser, descended from the family of Fruid in Tweeddale. Alexander, however, developed strong Presbyterian tendencies, and was deposed in 1672 for "deserting his charge," which really meant in his case that he did not confine his ministrations to his own parish. In the summer of 1675 he was found preaching among the Nonconformists in Moray and Ross, to the great displeasure of the bishops. He became chaplain to the family of Ludovick Grant of Grant, whose wife was a Brodie of Lethen, and both she and her husband were zealous Covenanters. Driven from that position, Alexander Fraser took up his abode at Croy. Meanwhile, the kirks of Daviot and Dunlichty were supplied by Michael Fraser, as curate. Fraser was an artist, and was enjoined by the Synod in 1675, in all time coming " to abstaine from all limning and painting, quhich hes diverted him from his ministerial employments." At the Revolution the artist-minister of Daviot and Dunlichty held on to his benefice, and also continued his limning and painting. He was for forty-five years the minister of the parish, surviving until 1726. When Lachlan Shaw, the historian of Moray, then minister of Cawdor, went to declare the church vacant in that year, he was unable to discharge the duty in consequence of the people carrying off the key of the kirk, and behaving so rudely that he could not worship even in the churchyard. Accustomed to the easy-going ways of the former regime, the Highlanders wanted no Whig ministers, as they called the Presbyterian clergy from the lowlands, amongst them. It was not until Alexander Grant of Kirkmichael took them in hand that any real impression was made.

The Secession Church took its rise in this district from very small beginnings, but received an accession of strength through the unpopular presentation of Thomas Gordon from Cabrach to the parish of Auldearn in the year 1747. Many of the men who originally formed the body were descendants, in spirit at least, of the old Covenanters. A touch of romance was imparted to their first meetings. They met in a cave—a deep rocky recess on the left bank of the Muckle Burn—called " Rob Roy's Cave," near Whitemire. They afterwards met in summer in the courtyard of the old ruined castle of Moyness, and in winter descended into the vault beneath. They were united with the Seceders in Morayshire under the designation of " The United Congregations of Elgin and Boghole," and they shared the ministrations of the first missionary, Alexander Troup, whose field of labour embraced the counties of Moray, Nairn, and Ross. Troup and the majority

of those to whom he ministered became anti-burghers, when the
" Breach " occurred in 1747. The dispute referred to the meaning of the terms of the oath exacted in 1745 from all persons
becoming burgesses in the principal cities. The one party held
that the terms of the oath implied approval of the alleged corrup-
tions of the Established Church, and therefore that all persons
taking the oath should be excluded from the communion of the
Secession Church. The other party viewed the terms of the oath
as merely indicating the approval of the national religion in its
Presbyterian form as against prelacy and popery, and therefore held
that forbearance should be exercised. The Seceders of Boghole
were thus in favour of toleration. In 1753 a small church was
built by the congregation at Boghole, where Troup continued to
conduct services every alternate Sunday till the year 1753, when
he accepted a call to Perth. The Boghole congregation was then
disjoined from Elgin, and elected Henry Clark from Abernethy as
their minister. He continued their minister for forty-six years,
dying in the year 1809. His son became a surgeon in the Royal
Navy, and was lost in the wreck of the Villette on the coast of
Sweden.

During Henry Clark's time a portion of the congregation resident
in and about Nairn decided to build a separate church at Nairn for
themselves, but to continue united with the congregation of Boghole under the pastorate of Clark. The church they built was
near the foot of Castle Lane—probably on the actual site of the
old church of Nairn. In 1769, however, three elders and sixty-
one members of the Boghole congregation resident near Nairn,
applied to the General Associate Presbytery of Perth to be disjoined from Boghole and formed into a separate congregation, on
the understanding that public worship was to be conducted in
Gaelic only. The congregation of Boghole strongly objected to
this, on the ground that the preaching of Gaelic at Nairn would
affect the attendance at Boghole. A compromise was agreed
upon—the preaching of Gaelic must not come nearer than Balblair, a mile to the west of Nairn. Here the Gaelic-speaking
people worshipped in the open air for about a year. The Boghole
congregation was still dissatisfied, and the Highlanders, having to

move a mile further away, settled at Howford, and built a church there in the year 1777, containing 500 sittings. A young probationer named Alexander Howison, from Logiealmond, who had, apparently against his will, been sent by the anti-burgher Synod hither and thither to learn Gaelic, was appointed to take charge of the Gaelic congregation at Nairn, but the young man utterly failed to learn the Gaelic tongue, and the Highlanders who met at Howford were treated to an English discourse when they expected a Gaelic sermon.   Howison's Gaelic was said to be more unintelligible than his English to the natives.   He was ordained minister of Howford in 1780, in the expectation that his Gaelic might improve, but latterly gave up the attempt to speak Gaelic, and confined himself to English.   The Boghole congregation brought his conduct before the Synod, and the Howford case, in many puzzling aspects, came before the Synod year after year.   The difficulty was ultimately solved by Howison resigning his charge in 1792, and returning to Perthshire, where he succeeded in obtaining a charge—the congregation of Auchtergaven—more adapted to his talents.   The Gaelic charge at Howford came to an end in 1795, but the edifice—a low, thatched, turf building— remained a picturesque object near the Howford Bridge until quite recently.   The " manse " disappeared only in 1892.

The ministers of the three secession churches in Nairnshire came together in connection with a remarkable occurrence.   Mr. Isaac Ketchen, a native of Alloa, was in 1780 ordained minister of the Nairn congregation which met in the Castle Lane church. The ordination took place in the open air.   It was early in April, and instead of meeting in the low-roofed church, the people gathered in the Constabulary park, the garden of the old Castle of Nairn, where the formalities of ordination were gone through—a unique occurrence in ecclesiastical procedure.   The memorable event which brought the three Seceder ministers together took place six years later.   On 30th November, 1786, the Nairn congregation met in the old church, and, repeating the solemn procedure common in the Covenanting communities of a former century, swore to the Covenants.   What led to their doing so at this particular time does not appear, but the act may be taken as an indication of the spirit of the congregation. They first swore to the National Covenant, then to the Solemn League and Covenant, and then to the Acknowledgment of Sins, and forty-one members, male and female, came forward and signed these documents. The deed was attested by the signatures of the Rev. Isaac Ketchen, minister of Nairn, the Rev. Henry Clark of Boghole, the Rev. Alexander Howison of Howford, and the Rev. William Bennett of Forres. It was probably the last covenanting meeting of the kind in Scotland.

These old Seceder ministers were scholarly men, well trained in theology, and deeply imbued with the Puritan spirit. Isaac Ketchen—staid, circumspect gentleman though he was—fell in love with the laird of Brodie's daughter Margaret, and won her affections, and they were married quietly at Forres. The event caused a sensation at the time, but the minister's wife accommodated herself to the humble manse, with its multifarious duties, to the entire satisfaction of the congregation. One Sabbath evening in March 1796, ominous creaks were heard by the congregation among the rafters just as the service was about to commence. The minister recommended the congregation to disperse as orderly and quietly as possible, which they did. The roof soon afterwards gave way, and next morning the church was in ruins. It was rebuilt in the same year, and continued to be occupied till 1816, when, the accommodation being inadequate for the congregation, a new church was built on the High Street opposite the County Buildings. The foundation stone was laid by Mrs. Ketchen. In the diary of Mrs. Elizabeth Rose of Kilravock there are frequent references to Mrs. Ketchen, who appears to have been a favourite with the old lady. In the year 1810 Mr. Ketchen and his son Isaac made a call at Kilravock on the occasion of the young man setting out for London. His brother James had already entered the army, and carried with him throughout life the religious spirit imbibed in the old Seceder manse. Ketchen had the long ministry of forty years. He died in 1820. Mrs. Ketchen survived him for some years.

In 1820, a few months after Ketchen's death, the two sections of the Secession Church in Scotland came together, and the Nairn congregation concurred. In 1822 the Rev. James Mein, a native of Jedburgh, was ordained minister, and as exemplifying the kindly relations between the Church people and the Seceders, the parish minister, Mr. Grant, gave the parish church for the ordination services. Mein laboured with great success in Nairn, making a deep impression, especially amongst the seafaring population, the majority of whom by this time had joined his church. He died in 1841, and was succeeded by the Rev. John Bisset, from Arbroath. Bisset was a notable preacher—a stalwart man of striking appearance and dark rugged countenance, he might have stood for a picture of John Knox.

In the year 1851 the church on High Street was vacated in favour of a new church erected at Leopold Street. The foundation stone was laid by General James Ketchen, son of the former minister. In 1876 Henry J. S. Turnbull was elected colleague and successor, but died after a pastorate of little more than a year and a half. G. K. Heughan succeeded, and after a ministry of ten years accepted a call to Pollokshaws. Rev. James Macmillan, who was ordained to the charge in 1890, declined a·call to Pollok Street Church, Glasgow, in 1893. In his time a new hall was erected in connection with the church. Since the union with the Free Church, the ministers of Nairn Rosebank United Free Church, as this congregation is now called, have been—Rev. Geo. Erskine Nicol, ordained 1897—Rev. David Ross, M.A., ordained in 1905—Rev. James Macleod, 1917, and Rev. William King, inducted in 1922.

After the death of Henry Clark in 1809 the Boghole congregation was without a minister for six years. In 1815 David Anderson was settled over it, but resigned in consequence of some disagreements, went to America, and died of apoplexy on a public street in Philadelphia in 1841. The congregation called as his successor James Morison, whose theological views, known as "Morisonianism," were much discussed throughout Scotland. Morison, who became the virtual founder of the Evangelical Union, declined the call of Boghole, as also did Andrew Gardiner. In 1842 John Whyte was ordained minister of Boghole, or Moyness, as it was then and is now called. Mr. Whyte, after some forty years of ministry, retired from active duties, and Mr. J. Ker was appointed colleague and successor. Mr. Whyte's jubilee as senior minister was celebrated in 1892.

A small body of Seceders was formed into a congregation at Campbeltown, Ardersier, in 1843. Lady Anderson, wife of the Governor of Fort George, though an Episcopalian herself, gave liberal assistance to the congregation. Their first minister was William Main, who was ordained in 1852, and died in 1871. He was succeeded by Robert Primrose Douglas from Lockerbie, and he again by Alexander A. Robertson. A new church was built shortly after Mr. Robertson's settlement. As colleague and successor to Mr. Robertson, Rev. Wm. Gray was ordained in 1925. He was translated to Avon Bridge, 1927.

It does not appear that George Whitfield ever visited the district of Moray and Nairn, but John Wesley undoubtedly did. With provoking brevity, Mrs. Elizabeth Rose in the year 1810 has the following entry—" Heard Mr. Wesley preach." She does not say whether it was at Nairn or at Croy. Probably it was at Nairn, from the old stone stairs in front of the town-house, that the great preacher held forth. He did not, however, succeed in establishing a congregation.

Towards the close of the eighteenth century two laymen preached from the flight of steps in front of Nairn Jail. The Churchmen and Seceders of the time as a rule regarded lay-preaching as an alarming and dangerous innovation. A few persons in the town and county sympathised, however, with the lay preachers in their mission. Other lay preachers from time to time followed, and they were cordially welcomed by the small band of sympathisers. This led to the formation among these sympathisers of a meeting for prayer held at each other's houses. They had not originally the remotest intention of forming a church or congregation, but " The Society for Propagating the Gospel at Home," having sent several preachers to the north, who visited Nairn in the course of their itinerancy, it was found necessary to have some suitable place at which to hold their services. A piece of ground on the north side of King Street was acquired for this purpose in May 1801, and also the house behind, which had been erected some short time before. The title to the property was made out in the names of " Lewis M'Ilvain, in Golford ; Hugh Cameron, *alias* M'Phatrick at Newton of Park ; David Rose at Allanaha ; Hugh Rose, James Wallace, and Alexander Nicol, weavers in Nairn, as trustees and managers for a congregation, established or about to be established in the town and county of Nairn." For some time afterwards they met for worship in the house, and, when weather permitted, outside, the preacher being in a box made for the purpose. In March 1802 they obtained the services of one Ferguson, who laboured for about two years as an unordained preacher. In an account of the congregation, it is related that Ferguson travelled on foot from Edinburgh to Nairn, and that on the day on which he was expected one or two of the brethren went to meet him. At a short distance from the town they met one whom they knew to be a stranger, " he had a staff, an umbrella, and a small bundle." The brethren accosted the stranger with the question, " Art thou he that should come, or look we for another ? " The question sufficed to convince Ferguson he was now amongst his friends, and they entered the town in company. The Haldanes interested themselves in the erection of the church at Nairn, and Robert Haldane gave £400 on loan, which with a sum of £130 raised by voluntary contributions, sufficed for the erection of the modest building. It was called the Independent Chapel, and the object in view in its erection was "that it will be open to all evangelical ministers of the Gospel who may be pleased to officiate in it." Some time later the supporters formed themselves into a Congregational Church. Ferguson was succeeded in 1803 by one Mackay, who, however, resigned in 1804. The first pastorate of importance was that of James Dewar. He was a native of Breadalbane, of a devoted evangelical spirit, entirely in harmony with the feelings of his little flock, and was ordained in July 1806, at which time the church was regularly formed. The number of members composing the church was seventeen. Serious financial embarrassments overtook the little congregation. Mr. Haldane called up his money, now amounting, with accumulated interest, to £500, and the property was about to be sold, when Mr. Dewar undertook to see Mr. Haldane, whom he had known in early life. The sum of £250 had been subscribed by friends, and on Dewar candidly telling Haldane that only half the sum they owed could be paid, he frankly forgave the rest. The congregation now plucked up courage, and the cause amongst them prospered. Dewar preached three English sermons and one Gaelic sermon every Sabbath. He opened the first Sabbath School in Nairn. Each summer, in company with his brother, he made wide tours throughout the Highlands, travelling on foot and preaching wherever he went. It was no uncommon thing for him to walk forty miles in a day and preach three or four sermons in addition. These journeys were undertaken every year till within a year or two of his death. Dewar's simple, earnest character dispelled any prejudice that existed against the missioners, as they were called, and he lived in terms of friendship with Seceder and Churchman alike. When the parish church was being rebuilt in 1810 the congregation held their services in the Independent chapel. In 1818 there was a religious revival in Nairn, and one still more marked in 1842. The Congregational chapel was the centre of the work, and union meetings for prayer were held daily, morning and evening, for several weeks, when the chapel was generally filled. In December 1842 Dewar died, to the great sorrow of his congregation and regret of the community. He was succeeded by John Gillies, who was ordained in 1844, but resigned in the following year. The congregation was once more restored to prosperity by the settlement of James Howie, who laboured amongst them for eleven years, on the lines laid down by Dewar. In 1857, however, he accepted a call to a church in Adelaide. He was succeeded by Mr. Ingram, who, however, demitted the charge after a short pastorate. The Rev. James Johnstone was settled in 1859, and he was minister when the new chapel at Crescent Road was built. The foundation stone was laid by Dr. Grigor in 1861. Johnstone, in 1870, accepted a call to Glasgow, where he died. The Rev. Robert Day and the Rev. Charles Whyte were next ministers in succession, and after a pastorate of a few years each, they both accepted charges in New South Wales, where they attained distinction as preachers. J. W. Thornton, the next pastor, died in 1889, and was succeeded by the Rev. G. Currie Martin, B.D., who left for Reigate in 1895. He was followed successively by Frederick J. Japp, who left for Coatbridge in 1901, George Scanlan who left for Falkirk in 1904, James Ross who went to Findhorn in 1918, Æneas Anderson who went to Hawick in 1922, and Donald McIntosh who left for Aberdeen in 1927. The Rev. James Stewart, B.D., was translated from St. Andrews in 1928.

The Disruption of the Church of Scotland in 1843 was preceded by much controversy and agitation in Nairnshire. The leading laymen in the county associated with it were Forbes of Culloden and Brodie of Lethen. The members of Nairn Presbytery identified with the non-intrusion party were Barclay of Auldearn, M'Lachlan of Cawdor, and Mathieson of Ardersier. The Presbytery was thus equally divided. In the town and parish of Nairn, Mr. Robertson of Newton, Sheriff Falconar, Dr. Bayne of Firhall, Bailie John Donaldson, Bailie J. Malcolm, and others, anticipated the Disruption by commencing the building of a church in 1842. As far back as 1839, when Dr. Chalmers paid a visit to Nairn in connection with the Church Endowment Fund, the necessity for erecting an additional parish church was recognised. A movement was set on foot for building a new church, but those interested in it being almost entirely composed of those favourable to the abolition of patronage, about a year before the Disruption they dropped the intention of connecting it with the Church of Scotland, and proceeded with it on an independent footing. When the Disruption took place, they adhered to the Free Church, and the third Sabbath after the Disruption they entered into possession of the new building, then all but finished. Hence, with the exception of Dr. Candlish's brick church in Edinburgh, it was the first Free Church opened in Scotland. The first minister elected was Alexander Mackenzie, who was ordained in November of the Disruption year. A school was also built, which was called the Free Church Institution, and was carried on with conspicuous success by Mr. Graham, afterwards of the Normal School, Donald M'Leod, afterwards of Rothesay Academy, and William Rait. It ceased when the national system of education was introduced. The church completed at the Disruption served the congregation till 1882, when a handsome new church was erected on High

Street at a cost of £8000. Mackenzie accepted a call to Free Tolbooth, Edinburgh, in 1873. He was succeeded by Murdoch Macdonald, who published a little work entitled "The Covenanters of Moray and Ross." He accepted the charge of the Presbyterian Church in Toorak, Melbourne, and afterwards became Professor of Theology in the Presbyterian College of Victoria. Professor Macdonald was succeeded at Nairn by Alexander Lee (formerly of Lybster), in the earlier period of whose ministry the new church was erected. Lee took a prominent position in the church. A Gaelic service was maintained at the beginning, but the numbers attending it gradually fell off. The congregation is one of the largest in the north. In the year 1891 three ministers of the Nairn congregation were present at a meeting in the church, and Professor Macdonald, who was home on a visit from Australia, received an address of welcome. In 1895 Mr. Lee retired in order to take up secretarial work for the General Assembly of the Free Church in Edinburgh, and was succeeded by the Rev. John Martin, who was minister at the time of the union of the Free and United Presbyterian Churches. The congregation then took the name of Nairn Free High Church. Mr. Martin was succeeded by the Rev. John S. Macdonald in 1901, the Rev. Robert Wilson, M.A., in 1910, the Rev. John G. Smart, M.A., in 1917, and the Rev. J. M. Little in 1921.

The effects of the Disruption of the Church of Scotland were more strikingly visible in the country parishes than in the town of Nairn, where a portion only had hived off from the overgrown congregation. The Rev. Simon M'Lachlan, minister of Cawdor, who adhered to the Protest, intimated to his congregation on the Sabbath immediately subsequent to the Disruption that it was not his intention to officiate again in the parish church, and for some time thereafter he preached to very large audiences from a tent at the corner of the wood at Newton of Budgate. All the elders in Cawdor church signed the Deed of Demission, and were constituted into a kirk session of the Free Church. The Sacrament was dispensed on Sabbath, 23rd July, at Cawdor in the open air. The English-speaking congregation was estimated at 1000, and the Gaelic congregation at from 3000 to 4000, people attending from all parts of the district. Probably these numbers are an over-estimate, but the assemblage was undoubtedly the largest which ever met at one time in the county for religious worship. Lord Cawdor was averse to granting a site for a church, not expecting the movement to be permanent, but he allowed the adherents of the Free Church to erect a temporary wooden building for public worship, and ultimately, though after considerable delay, gave the site of the present U.F. Church for a permanent building. Mr. M'Lachlan continued to minister to the congregation till 1877, when he retired to Nairn to spend the evening of his days. He was a strikingly handsome figure, and his discourses were marked by extreme simplicity of language and beauty of thought. Mr. John Macpherson was elected colleague and successor. Mr. M'Lachlan died in 1881, and Mr. Macpherson in 1884. Mr. John George M'Neill, formerly of Portnahaven, Islay, was then appointed. He was recognised as a Gaelic scholar of repute, and did a good deal of literary work in that connection for the Free Church. Since the Union the ministers of Cawdor United Free Church, as it is now called, have been the Rev. John Macdonald Rose, M.A., inducted in 1910, and the Rev. John Rose, M.A., inducted in 1918.

In the parish of Croy, the minister, Mr. Campbell, did not secede. He having been inducted at the point of the bayonet, most of the parishioners of Croy retained but a very loose connection with the church, and those adhering to the Free Church attended for a time at Cawdor and Ardersier. Mr. Sage of Resolis, however, offered to conduct services at Croy once a month, and the Presbytery accepted his offer. These services were conducted in a huge gravel pit, with a tent for the preacher, and eventually the congregation was constituted. Mr. Adam G. M'Leod, a native of Sutherlandshire, was the first minister. He accepted a call to Greenock, but not liking his new sphere, returned to Croy before the vacancy was filled up, and was minister there till his death in 1892. He was succeeded by Mr. Malcolm M'Leod, a native of Lewis.

In Ardersier, Mr. Matheson gave up his charge. On the Sabbath after the Disruption he preached at Milton of Connage to a large congregation.   Captain Shaw, the tenant, a man of some influence, was a warm supporter.   Mr. Matheson continued service there for several Sabbaths.   A site for a church was ultimately got, from one of the feuars, in the village of Campbeltown, but the first dispensation of the Sacrament took place in the open air at one of the farms in the neighbourhood.   The Rev. Dr. M'Farlan, of Greenock, one of the leaders of the Free Church, assisted on the occasion, and services in English and Gaelic were conducted.   Mr. Matheson died in 1850, and was succeeded by Mr. Alexander Cameron, who previously had a charge in Canada.   In 1887 Mr. Duncan M'Leod was elected minister of the congregation, having formerly been minister at Fortingall, Perthshire.

In Auldearn Mr. Barclay preached for the last time in the parish church on 4th June.   On the following Sabbath he conducted divine service in the space in front of the Innes School. All the elders adhered to the Free Church.   The congregation lost no time in setting about building a church.   No site nearer the village than Dalmore could be obtained, but ground there was given by Brodie of Lethen, who also contributed towards the erection of the church.   On 19th July the foundation stone was laid by the laird of Lethen.   The communion was dispensed in the open air on Sabbath, 27th August, when it was estimated that over 2000 persons were present.   The summer of 1843 being exceptionally fine, these out-of-door gatherings were attended with very little discomfort.   Barclay, after a laborious pastorate, died in 1857.   W. G. Forrester, who succeeded him, was a very eloquent preacher.   He was succeeded in 1886 by John M'Neill, formerly of Oban.   Since the Union the ministers have been Rev. D. M. Johnston, B.D., 1921, and Rev. Peter Chapman, inducted 1926.

In Ardclach Mr. M'Bean retained his charge at the Disruption. For some time previously, however, most of the elders and principal families had deserted the services of the parish church for the ministrations of a young missionary of the Secession Church—a Mr. Handyside, who subsequently went to America and died there. The missionary usually preached within the precincts of one of the farm houses in the parish.   When the Disruption occurred the entire session joined the Free Church.   A site for a church was granted by Brodie of Lethen at the Crask, about a mile and a half from the parish church. Adam M'Leod, who was elected minister, was rather noted for his quaint peculiar sayings. He was a very accomplished Hebrew scholar. He died in 1872, and was succeeded by Alexander Macdonald, one of several brothers ministers in the Free Church. Since the Union the ministers have been Rev. John A. Sutherland, M.A., ordained 1909, and Rev. William Adam, M.A., inducted 1927.

On the union of the United Presbyterian and the Free Churches of Scotland in 1900 a minority of members of the Free Church remained apart, and in Nairnshire eventually erected new churches at Ardersier, Cawdor, and Nairn itself. At Ardersier the ministers have been Rev. James Mackay, inducted 1907, Rev. Kenneth C. M'Lennan 1925-27; at Cawdor Rev. T. A. McElphatric 1906, and Rev. William Martin 1911; and at Nairn Rev. Robert M. Knox, inducted 1910, Rev. John Calvin Mackay, M.A., 1915, and Rev. D. M'Kenzie, M.A. (Hons.) 1921.

The Presbytery of the Established Church met on 6th June, 1843, and took steps to fill up the vacancies caused by the ministers who had demitted. Mr. Grant intimated the vacancy at Auldearn on the following Sabbath. Mr. Grant's remarks on the occasion illustrate the feelings of those who remained in the Church of Scotland. " In the course of his address he stated that it was his painful duty—a duty which he had most reluctantly undertaken by command of the Assembly—to intimate that Mr. Barclay was no longer the minister of the parish. He expressed the hope that Mr. Barclay, for whom he had the highest esteem, might yet be re-admitted into the church, at which no man would more heartily rejoice than he would. The difficulties of the Church, in his opinion, were due to the Veto Act. Though this was doubtless a time of darkness, he had no fear for the Church." On 10th August the Presbytery sustained a call, signed by thirty parishioners, to the Rev. Charles Fowler, assistant and successor at St. Monance. He was presented by Brodie of Brodie on the recommendation of the Rev. Dr. Cook. Fowler was inducted on 21st September, 1843, but died at Nairn on 2nd November, of consumption, having been but five weeks minister of Auldearn. Though but twenty-seven years of age, he was an eloquent preacher, with a brilliant record as a scholar, and his premature death caused much sorrow. He was succeeded by James Reid, who was minister thereafter for thirty years. He married Mary Skene, Skenepark—member of a family connected with Nairnshire for a long period —and died in 1873, at the age of seventy-one. He was succeeded by the Rev. James Bonallo, son of the Rev. David Bonallo, of Blackford, Perthshire, and Mr. Bonallo was succeeded in 1926 by the Rev. George M'William, from Clepington Parish Church, Dundee.

In Ardclach parish church Mr. M'Bean, who died in 1851, was succeeded by Colin Mackenzie, from Fort William—a kindly, hospitable man, who did much to soften the asperities of ecclesiastical feeling. He was succeeded by the Rev. David Miller, B.D., who faithfully ministered to his flock till his death in 1916, when he was succeeded by the Rev. Robert Kerr, who had been assistant in St. John's parish, Edinburgh.

The parish church of Cawdor was closed for several Sabbaths after the Disruption, but George Campbell was ordained in December 1843. He was succeeded by Lewis Macpherson in 1845, who died in 1876, when Thomas Fraser was translated from Portgordon to Cawdor. Mr. Fraser resigned in 1909, and was succeeded by the Rev. Alexander Hay Forbes, who accepted a call to Methil in 1927. Rev. Wm. Metcalfe, from Caterham, Surrey, was inducted to the charge in February, 1928.

Mr. Campbell of Croy was succeeded by Thomas Fraser in 1853. Fraser was an accomplished botanist, and contributed lists of the flora of the parish of Croy to northern scientific societies. He died in 1885, and was succeeded by the Rev. John Grant, from Cromdale. Mr. Grant died in 1890, and was succeeded by the Rev. Charles Fraser, B.D.

In Ardersier parish church the following have been the ministers —Simon Fraser ordained in 21st December, 1843; William Forsyth elected in 1846; Evan Ross elected in 1853; and John Paton ordained to the charge in 1884. In 1920 Mr. Paton was followed by the Rev. William M. Graham, from the West Kirk, Greenock.

In the parish church of Nairn Mr. Grant, after the long ministry
of thirty-seven years, died in 1853, and was succeeded by James
Burns.   Previous to the induction of Burns, the question of resuming the Gaelic service, which had latterly been discontinued
by Grant, was raised, and Mr. Ross of Ardersier took an appeal in
favour of a Gaelic service.   Motions were made in the Assembly
by Principal Lee and Dr. Robertson, and a resolution was adopted
remitting the matter back to the Presbytery to receive and report
for the Assembly's consideration any objections to the discon-
tinuance of Gaelic that might be made, but when the time came
none was tendered.   Mr. Burns was unanimously elected.   In
1893 the congregation proceeded to build a new church, by voluntary subscription, at the south corner of Seabank Road, at an
estimated cost of £8000.   Four years later Mr. Burns died, after
the long ministry of forty-five years.   He was succeeded by the
Rev. William R. Pirie, D.D., translated from Keith, in whose
time the present handsome church was completed.

The old Episcopal Church party died out entirely in Nairnshire,
but about 1840 some families of English origin or connection,
settling in the district, were desirous of having a place of worship
of their own denomination.   Bishop Low and Bishop Ewing
interested themselves in the matter, but those in the district specially
concerned objected to being connected with the Scottish communion, desiring instead to be placed under the jurisdiction of the
Church of England, in the same manner as consulate chapels
abroad.   Differences on theological and ecclesiastical questions
existed.   Accordingly in 1845 a Church of England chapel, near
the bridge, was built by subscription.   William Brodie of Brodie,
Mr. Clark of Achareidh, and Mrs. Campbell, lessee of Kilravock
Castle, were the principal supporters of the chapel.   The first incumbent was Mr. Hitchcock.   He was succeeded by Mr. Roberts.
Mr. Brasby, who died at Nairn, was the third minister in succession,
and he was succeeded by the Rev. Dr. Edwin Wrenford, who
removed in 1879.   The congregation enjoyed a fair measure of
prosperity, but there was continual controversy between its members and those of the Scottish Episcopal Church as to its position
and standing.   After Dr. Wrenford's departure services were dis-

continued. Bishop Eden, having at the outset failed to effect a reconciliation, started a mission in 1853 in connection with the Scottish Episcopal Church. The Rev. John Comper (afterwards of Aberdeen) was the priest in charge. In 1854 a regular congregation was formed, with the Rev. Charles M. Keith as rector, and in 1857 a chapel, dedicated to St. Columba, was erected at Queen Street, as well as a manse and school. In 1864 the Rev. William West, who published an edition of the works of Leighton, was settled over the congregation. He removed in 1879, and was succeeded in 1880 by the Rev. H. E. Mackenzie-Hughes, who was followed successively by the Rev. J. M. Fergus in 1896, the Rev. P. F. Young in 1921, and the Rev. J. M. Ballard in 1924. Most of those connected with the Church of England chapel joined the communion, and the church was afterwards enlarged.

A Roman Catholic congregation was established about the year 1857. A large body of crofters from the Island of Barra, removed, it was said, by Colonel Gordon of Cluny, came to Nairn and settled there. They were Roman Catholics in religion, were purely Gaelic-speaking, and were exceedingly poor; but the men found work as labourers, and the women and children made a living by cutting and selling firewood. Occasional services were held, and in 1864 a chapel, dedicated to St. Mary, was erected in Academy Street. The first priest was the Rev. Donald Mackenzie, Beauly, who was succeeded by the Rev. A. Bisset. Next came the Rev. John Rodger, who died in 1920. He was followed by the Rev. Michael Barrett, O.S.B., and the Rev. Martin Wall, O.S.B., who were succeeded in 1922 by the Rev. James Anton, the present incumbent.

A Convent of the Sacred Heart was established in 1891. The congregation in 1893 numbered about 200. The incumbent officiates each Sunday at Fort George.

CHAPTER XXI

BURGH HISTORY—CONCLUSION

TOWARDS the close of the eighteenth century there was an enormous rush from the North to the West Indies. Sir Alexander Grant of Dalvey, from his intimate relations politically and otherwise with the burgh and county of Nairn, interested himself in obtaining situations for young men belonging to the place in mercantile houses with a West Indian connection. Roses, Brodies, Falconers, Inglises, Mackintoshes, Campbells, and Frasers from Nairnshire were to be found in every part of the West Indies. One of the earliest and most successful planters was Samuel Falconer, grandson of Bishop Colin Falconer, and brother of " The Admiral " of Nairn Grieship. Leaving Jamaica with a fortune about the year 1760, Samuel Falconer returned to Nairn, and no deserving lad applied to him in vain for a start in life. Some acquired wealth, but a greater number found graves. Amongst those who went out was Mark Campbell, a nephew of Sheriff Inglis of Nairn. He succeeded well, and along with a partner purchased an estate in the island of St. Vincent. The original deed of conveyance from the Charribes is still in existence. The native chiefs signed with a cross. In 1791 Mark Campbell was struck down by fever, and made his will. His thoughts reverted to a certain young lady in Nairn—his pretty cousin Amelia Inglis, and he left her a handsome annuity. He left his share of the estate to his partner. As an indication of the view of a West Indian planter at the time regarding slavery, Mark Campbell requested his executor " to endeavour to make free my housekeeper Petoneé and her daughter Margarate," leaving it to him to assist Petoneé and her daughter as he chooses. Mark

Campbell died on 2nd December, 1791. When the crash came in West Indian affairs some years later, Miss Amelia's annuity was lost. These were but examples of the ups and downs of fortune of the time.

The means of education in Nairn for equipping young men for a mercantile career were at that time excellent. The earliest burgh school of which there is any record was situate in Church Street, but in the year 1762 the council decided to give a new site. The minute of the council of date 13th April, 1762, runs as follows—" The Council met, and taking into their serious consideration that the building of a school-house with some accommodation for lodgings to a master is to be soon set about, which being a matter of great public utility, justly merits the attention and encouragement of the magistrates and Town Council, therefore in order to the better executing of the same they not only unanimously agree that the sum of five pounds sterling be given out of the town's common good towards defraying the expense thereof over and above as an addition to the heritors their different proportions, which sum is hereby ordered to be forthwith paid by the treasurer to Mr. Robert Davidson, the schoolmaster, for the above purpose upon his receipt, but also for rendering said school-house more agreeable, wholesome, and commodious both for master and scholars, hereby unanimously give as much ground as will be necessary for building the same on, with a proper area in front, of and upon the easter part of that particate or piece of ground of a triangular form, belonging to the Town Council, lying at the wester end thereof, 'twixt the Gallowgate and Kildrummie gate ; and the stance of the old school being thought sufficiently fit for a house and school-room to a schoolmistress for teaching sewing and other necessary branches of education, the Council resolve to employ the said old stance to that use how soon a fund necessary for executing the same in a proper manner can be established." The subscriptions to the girls' school came in slowly, and it was some time before the institution was established. It continued to flourish down to about 1860, mainly supported by the Town Council. Other establishments having sprung up, it was discontinued.

The parish school reached its greatest fame under John Straith. His celebrity as a teacher drew pupils from all parts of the country. The writer of the article in " Ree's Cyclopaedia " about 1800 says—" In the town is an excellent school, in which the number of scholars is seldom under 100, parents sending thither children from all parts of the country, and frequently even from England. Every branch of study now in repute at the universities is taught here to perfection ; and several of the most distinguished characters for science and literature in Great Britain first rose to comparative eminence in the provincial school of Nairn." The writer appears to have been indebted for his information to the Rev. Mr. Morrison, the parish minister.

Straith is mentioned in the burgh records, 3rd October, 1774, as having been admitted a burgess, along with Peter Withraw (from his name he may be judged to be a schoolmaster), Robert Falconer, junior, and Hugh Kinnaird, land surveyor. Straith was a teacher in Nairn for over forty years. He became a member of the Town Council, and was for many years senior bailie of the burgh.

Following the usual custom in Nairn, many of his pupils went abroad, but in the beginning of the nineteenth century the goal of youthful ambition was an appointment in London. So numerous were the Nairnshire lads at that time in London that they formed a London-Nairnshire Society. The society was started in 1808, and continued in existence till 1821. The first meeting was held at " The George and Vulture Tavern," St. Michael's Alley, Cornhill, London. The names of seven of those present are recorded, viz., James Dunbar, John M'Lean, John Storm, James Grant, Peter Campbell, George Skene, and Isaac Ketchen. These exiles met (as set forth in the minute-book) " influenced by a sincere attachment to their native county—a desire to keep up friendly fellowship with their schoolfellows and other friends from that part of the country, and reflecting on the difficulties which from circumstances naturally prevent the wished-for sociality in London" —they therefore met to consult as to the best method of forming a society to commemorate " the days of other years." The meeting came to the conclusion that the best method of satisfying their desire for social intercourse was to have an annual dinner. To this dinner all the residents in London, "who have been, are, or may be connected with the county by birth, education, or residence, were invited," and each member might introduce a friend. The first anniversary dinner was held at " The George and Vulture " on 10th November, 1809. The number attending was fourteen, and besides those mentioned at the first meeting there were present Alexander Dallas, John Rose, Arthur Geddes, John Davidson, Samuel Falconer, with Dr. Cumming of Forres and Mr. Kincaid as guests. The membership continuing to increase, it was found necessary to draw up rules and regulations, with office-bearers to be annually elected. The first president nominated was John Innes—" the great Mr. Innes," as he used to be called, in whose memory the Innes School at Auldearn some years later was founded. He was a partner in the house of Fairley, Bonham & Co., of Indian connection, and had a seat in Parliament for several years. The inscription on the tablet at the Innes School runs as follows—" To perpetuate the memory of a man of worth, and for the education of infants in his native parish, this building was erected by the friends of John Innes, Esquire, of Broad Street Buildings, London, who was born at Auldearn, the 25th December, 1767, and died in London the 24th November, 1838." Barclay, in his account of the parish, remarks that it was to the extensive influence of Innes, and his unwearied benevolence to his countrymen, that the rise of many a private fortune may be traced. Financial reverses overtook the great merchant ere his death, but when he accepted the presidency of the London-Nairnshire Society he was one of the most influential men in mercantile circles in the metropolis. Charles Mann (spelt " Man," the old form) was appointed depute chairman, and presided in the following year. Later on the names of William, Christopher, Henry, and John Man are met with, all active members of the society. Their connection with the family of the name in Nairn cannot be traced. One of the rules of the meeting was that the chair should be taken at five o'clock p.m., and that the meeting be " considered as dissolved at eleven "—a phrase which meant, it appears, not that the company should then separate, but that each member was to pay for what he ordered after that hour. Some friends had been ordering supper in addition to dinner, but as the dinner ticket was only 25s. it would not cover that extravagance. The seventh rule, directed against extravagance, now reads curiously—" That neither claret, madeira, or other expensive wines be introduced at table ! " The Nairnshire meeting did not begin and end in conviviality. At the sixth anniversary the subject of having a pier at Nairn was mooted. A subscription was started among friends in London, and the London subscriptions amounted to £300. John Innes gave twenty guineas, Alexander Brodie, South Audley Street (the Indian nabob) gave a like sum. Hugh Macintosh, the millionaire contractor, who had left the sweet hamlet of Balloan, at Cawdor, some thirty or forty years before, with his shovel on his shoulder, gave twenty guineas. His nephew, David Macintosh, gave a modest five guineas—he was yet to be the owner of the broad acres of Havering Park in Essex.

At the eighth meeting, Sir James Mackintosh, the statesman, was to have presided, but was detained at the last moment. Sir James Mackintosh had a twofold connection with Nairnshire—he represented the county of Nairn in Parliament, and had several family ties with the district. Talk of early schooldays at the dinner led to recollections of their schoolmaster, and a resolution was drawn up expressing regret " that no distinguishing monument had been erected in the churchyard of Nairn to perpetuate the rare virtues of their lamented honest schoolmaster, the late Mr. Straith, who for a period of forty years had laboured with the utmost zeal for the benefit of many rising generations, and it was resolved to open a subscription by those members who were educated by Mr. Straith for the purpose of getting a suitable tablet prepared and sent down to be erected in the new church lately built there." The proposal was taken up with great enthusiasm, and by next meeting the treasurer reported that he had received sixty-eight guineas for the tablet. Amongst others, the minister of the Scots Kirk of Rotterdam sent £5. He was an Auldearn man—a son of Alexander Mackintosh, Dalmore, and now a D.D., in charge of the Presbyterian congregation at Rotterdam. The proposal took a wider scope. Instead of a tablet in the parish church of Nairn, it was decided to erect a pillar (as it was called) in front of the parish school. Isaac Ketchen, who was the secretary of the London-Nairnshire Society, being at Nairn for his holidays, carried out the arrangements. Sir Thomas Dick Lauder of Relugas furnished the sketch, and the foundation stone was laid on 15th April, 1816, in presence of the sheriff-substitute, the magistrates, and principal inhabitants of the burgh. The great demonstration was reserved for the inauguration of the monument. On 28th May the pillar was completed and the tablet inserted into its front. The day " was celebrated as a solemn commemoration." The procession was formed at Richardson's Inn, and proceeded in the following order—" Three Town Officers—Band of Inverness-shire Militia —The Vice-Lieutenant and the Sheriff-Substitute—The Burgh Magistrates and Dean of Guild—The three Town Clergy— Mr. John Straith and Major Macdonald as representatives of Mr. Straith—The Secretary of the Nairnshire Meeting and Captain Rose, R.N., a subscriber to the monument—Mr. David Miller, a subscriber, etc.—The Master, Architect, and the Brethren of the Nairn St. Ninian Operative Lodge, two and two —Mr. Simpson, schoolmaster, etc.—The Latin Scholars, two and two—·The English Scholars, two and two—The Scholars of Mr. Straith, two and two, according to seniority—The other friends of the late Mr. Straith—The Visitors closed the procession." Arrived at the monument, and a semi-circle having been formed, the secretary, Isaac Ketchen, addressed the meeting in an enthusiastic speech, explaining that the motive which had led the Nairnshire Meeting to the erection of this monument was the desire to establish a token of gratitude for the benefits received, and to awaken interest and emulation in the minds and hearts of teachers and pupils in Nairn for generations to come. The procession, with colours hoisted (they had before been reversed), after walking round the monument and schoolhouse, returned to the inn, where the party afterwards dined together and patriotic speeches were made. The total cost of the monument was £118. Ketchen's idea was that the " Commemoration of Straith " would be held as an anniversary, and " tend hereafter to encourage the whole community to place the seminaries of education in Nairn in a position worthy

of what the Grammar School once was." " Straith's Commemoration Day " has fallen into oblivion, and the monument
inaugurated with so much enthusiasm is sometimes threatened with
removal as an eye-sore ! The tablet bears the following inscription—" 1815. Erected by the members of the Nairnshire Meeting, London, scholars of the late Mr. John Straith, 40 years
schoolmaster in this town. Nat. 1732. Ob. 1807. Quis est
nostrum liberaliter educatus . cui non eductor, cui non magister
sum atque doctor . cui non locus . ille mutus, ubi ipse altus aut
doctus est, cum grata recordatione in mente versatur." (Who is
there of us liberally educated, to whom I am not a guide, a teacher,
an instructor, in whose thoughts there does not dwell with grateful
recollection that quiet place where he himself has been reared or
taught ?)

After Straith's time, the reputation of Nairn parish school was
not maintained, and on 13th January, 1830, a number of the
leading citizens met and resolved to establish an academy for the
better education of the youth of the place. Within a short time
sums of money in the form of shares were subscribed to the amount
of over £600, and Theodore Allan was elected the first teacher.
The pupils of the Academy for the first half year of the existence of
the institution met in the news-room in the County Buildings.
The new institution found a good friend in Captain James Rose,
of the Royal Navy. Captain Rose was one of the largest subscribers from the first ; then he gave half of his garden for a site
for the school, doubled his subscription of one hundred guineas,
and, money for prizes being scarce, he bestowed the Turkish gold
medal awarded to him for his services in the war in Egypt, as a
medal for the dux of the school. Finally, he made the Academy
directors his residuary legatees, bequeathing his whole estate to
them at his wife's death, which happened in 1850. Captain Rose
was a son of James Rose of Lochiehills, by Magdalen Dunbar of
Kilflett, and was descended from the Roses of Belivat. He had
seen a good deal of service, and had risen to the rank of commander.
He was made a Knight of the Swedish Order of the Sword for his
gallantry at Gluckstadt, and received the gold medal for Egypt in
1801. The old sailor had lost a hand, but an iron hook which

supplied its place did wonderful service.   He was a genuine type
of the old tar, and his yarns of sea-fights and storms, told with great
animation, made him a most interesting personage in Nairn.   His
great desire was to benefit the youth of the place by giving them a
good start in life by means of a superior education.   Captain Rose
died 15th December, 1840.   The institution, which had been
called originally the Nairn Academy was, in honour of its chief
benefactor, re-named in 1841 Rose's Academical Institution.
The school hours were conducive to habits of early rising.   In
1832, when the school was opened under Mr. Allan, the directors
fixed the hours of teaching as—from seven till nine a.m., from ten
a.m. till one p.m., and from three till five p.m.

The new Academy speedily became a little nursery for officers
for the army.   The two veteran soldiers, General Gordon and
Captain Gordon, Ivybank—the one a hero of the Nive, the other
of Waterloo—were familiar figures in the place.   The two Grants
of Auchterblair, William and Patrick, brothers of the second Mrs.
Gordon of Ivybank, became Nairn lads by residence.   William,
who, curiously enough, married a daughter of Captain Gordon by
his first wife, was at home from India in 1837, and became one of
the *pro indiviso* proprietors of the Academy in room of his mother.
Returning to India, he became Assistant Adjutant-General to the
unfortunate expedition to Afghanistan in 1841, and was massacred
in the retreat from Kabul.   His brother Patrick had to vindicate
his memory from some unjust aspersions cast by Lady Sale in her
Letters published in England, and the testimony of his fellow-
officers proved that it was General Elphinstone and not young
Captain Grant who was the cause of the vacillation complained of.
A strange story became current in Nairn some years afterwards to
the effect that Captain Grant was still alive—a prisoner among the
Afghans.   His young wife resided usually at Ivybank, and his
mother at Duntroon Cottage, Queen Street, and for many years
they hoped against hope that the report might prove true, but there
never was any confirmation of it.   Patrick Grant (Mrs. Grant in
Duntroon's youngest son) had entered upon that splendid career
which in later years culminated in his being made a Field-Marshal.
Sir Hugh Rose, descended from the Roses of Earlsmill—his ancestor

was a brother of the Rev. Hugh Rose, minister of Nairn—had begun those brilliant achievements in India which earned him his great military renown, and which were finally rewarded, like those of his countryman, Sir Patrick Grant, with the Field-Marshal's baton, and a peerage in addition. Both Sir Patrick Grant and Lord Strathnairn accepted the freedom of the burgh of Nairn on retiring from their Indian career. A youth of great promise, Alick Rose, son of Sir John Rose of Holme Rose, was the pioneer of the younger lads who went out to the Indian Army. In November 1841 the camp at which he was stationed at Kohisthan was attacked, and desperate fighting ensued. All the European officers except Ensign Rose were killed. He took command, and endeavoured with the handful of men remaining to cut his way through the besiegers. He fought with desperate courage, hand to hand, keeping his little band of Ghurkas close together, and, charging the enemy with the bayonet, drove into the mass like a wedge. The Ghurkas broke the lines and got through, but young Rose received a fatal wound and died shortly afterwards. The Ghurkas carried his lifeless body with them, but had to abandon it to save themselves from the enemy in pursuit. It was many months ere the Ghurkas reached the nearest British encampment, and they wept bitterly as they told the sad fate of their young commander. He fought like a young lion, they said.

A few years later a quota of Nairn Academy boys managed to get commissions, and followed each other to India. Five of General Gordon's sons went out one after the other. Two sons of Captain Gordon of Ivybank followed their cousins. Two of the parish minister's sons, Alexander and James Augustus Grant, joined them. Three of the Kilravock boys—James, Wellington, and Arthur—were in India when the Mutiny broke out. George G. Mackenzie, son of Roderick Mackenzie of Nairn, was already a captain in the Madras Army, and from working sums in the Nairn Academy, was set to manage the military finances of the Presidency. Two of Dr. Bayne's sons joined their school comrades. A little incident which happened at school sent away another youth, who was destined to achieve distinction in the army. One of the smallest boys for his age, but the pluckiest in the school, was Herbert Macpherson. He was a class-fellow of James A. Grant, Wellington Rose, and Arthur Mitchell. Arthur Mitchell, the best scholar in the school, had the distinction of receiving the prize for good conduct, unanimously voted him by his fellow-scholars. Herbert Macpherson, for loading and firing a cannon, which brought down part of the Academy wall and frightened the lieges, was cheered by his schoolmates, who shouted "Well done, Bertie!" Both of them—the quiet scholar and the budding artilleryman—were in later years knighted by Queen Victoria for the distinction they earned in their respective walks of life. Herbert Macpherson's career illustrates the difficulties that beset the path of an aspirant without fortune or favour for a military cadetship at this time. Herbert's grandfather was James Macpherson of Ardersier, factor to Lord Cawdor. Two of the factor's sons had raised the quota of recruits for the 78th Highlanders which entitled them to commissions in that regiment when it was embodied. They both served with it in all the great wars in which it was employed, and Duncan, the eldest, became its colonel. On retiring from the army, he went back to the parental home at Ardersier, the farm of which his father had long occupied. He married a daughter of Duncan Campbell of Fornighty, factor for Lethen, whose wife was a daughter of Mackintosh of Kyllachie and a sister of Sir James Mackintosh, the statesman. Colonel Macpherson was, however, not rich enough to buy a commission for his son Herbert, and the War Office authorities had apparently forgotten the services of the Macphersons of Ardersier in the early days of the 78th Highlanders. Having thus neither money nor influence to procure a commission, Herbert was, much against his will, sent to London to a merchant's office as clerk. The junior clerk, however, managed to get a glimpse of the *Times* occasionally, and he read one morning that his father's old regiment, the 78th, had been attacked by cholera at Sciende with appalling loss. He walked over to the War Office and asked to see the Adjutant-General, Lord Fitzroy Somerset (afterwards Lord Raglan). An interview was granted, and the youth stated his request—it was for a commission in the 78th. "Do you know," asked his Lordship, "what has happened to that regiment?" "I do," said

Macpherson, " but it was my father's regiment." The pluck of the youth in wanting to go out to a situation of such deadly peril excited the admiration of the Adjutant-General, and he immediately granted him an Ensign's commission in the 78th. This was in February 1845. He left immediately for India, and was soon in the midst of active service in the Persian War. When the Indian Mutiny broke out, the 78th, arriving at Calcutta, was at once sent on under Sir Henry Havelock to the relief of Lucknow. There Macpherson won the proud honour of the Victoria Cross. When Lord Beaconsfield, twenty years later, brought the Indian troops to Malta, Colonel Macpherson was assigned a divisional command. He was with Sir Samuel Browne in the advance into Afghanistan, and commanded a brigade under General Roberts in the march to Cabul. It is recorded that when Roberts was forced to take shelter in the cantonments of Sherpore, Macpherson with his brigade, consisting of Ghurkas and the 92nd Highlanders, supported by a body of cavalry, by a rapid dash intercepted the junction of the two bodies of Afghans, and thereby saved the army from disaster. He and his brigade performed other great achievements. He was with General Roberts in the great march from Cabul to Candahar, and in the final battle he and his Ghurkas and Highlanders bore the principal part. For his services in the campaign he was created a K.C.B. When the Egyptian Expedition of 1880 was undertaken, Sir Herbert Macpherson was appointed Commander of the Indian troops sent to join the forces of Sir Garnet Wolseley. After the battle of Tel-el-Kebir, in which he took part, his brigade was sent in hot haste to Zagazig, where he arrived at three in the afternoon, having marched thirty miles through the desert in a blazing sun. He arrived at the railway station in the nick of time. Five trains with armed men were about to start for Cairo. On Sir Herbert's approach with thirty Indian troopers they surrendered. Next day Sir Herbert had the proud triumph of entering and taking possession of the city of Cairo. For this exploit he was awarded the thanks of both Houses of Parliament and received many coveted decorations.

After the Egyptian War, General Sir Herbert Macpherson came north on a visit to his own country, and was presented with the freedom of the burgh of Nairn. On being asked if he remembered the incident of the firing of the cannon at the Academy, " I should think so," he replied. " I have got the summons to the court tied up with my first commission, and when passing the sheriff's house to-day I expected every minute to see him coming out to seize me." Sir Herbert returned to India, and became Commander-in-Chief of the Madras Army. He died in Burmah from fever in October 1886.

Another youth, who sat on the same form with Herbert Macpherson, also distinguished himself, and his last exploit and sad end were much talked of at the time. Wellington Rose was the first to scale the walls of Gwalior and to plant the British flag on its ramparts. The feat was warmly cheered, and his kinsman, Sir Hugh Rose (afterwards Lord Strathnairn), used to relate that he had mentally resolved to recommend the plucky lad for the Victoria Cross for what he had done, when a moment later a fakir was observed stealing up behind him, who levelled his pistol at him, although by this time the fort had capitulated. Poor Wellington Rose was mortally wounded. His brother Arthur died from the effects of excessive fatigue a fortnight later. There are now no survivors of the youthful band who entered the Indian Army. Colonel J. A. Grant of the Nile, one of the Academy lads, died in 1892, and Lieut.-General William R. Gordon (third son of General Gordon of Lochdhu), died at Gordonville, Nairn, on 15th June, 1893—his four brothers had predeceased him. The record of the great majority may be summed up in the words " Died in India," though several attained high rank and distinction.

The Academy had a succession of able teachers. Theodore Allan got a kirk, and his place was taken by the Rev. James B. Brichan as classical master, and by William Welsh as English master. Their appointments were made on 27th November, 1838, but Welsh resigned in August 1839. The school was carried on by Brichan with an assistant, but in December 1840 Brichan resigned. There were two candidates for the office—Basil Bell of Edinburgh and James Petrie—the latter was appointed by a majority. Petrie was an able teacher, and along with his brother, as assistant, did good work. The emoluments, however, were small, and in order to increase them and make the Academy a well-equipped school, the heritors agreed to discontinue teaching in the parish school, and to pay the parochial schoolmaster's salary due by them to the Academy. Even this augmentation did not serve to retain Petrie's services, and in 1847 he resigned. A most unfortunate dispute arose as to the appointment of a successor. Two candidates were proposed—the one, John M'Gregor of Invergordon, was supported by the Dissenters, and the other, John Marshall, Arbroath, by the Churchmen. Technical objections were raised as to mandates and rights of voters, the power of the heritors, and so forth, and on the final division both parties claimed a majority. The chairman ruled that Marshall had been appointed. Instead of the other party accepting this ruling, they took possession of the Academy and installed their candidate, M'Gregor, as teacher. Excitement ran very high, and ultimately the dispute was carried to the Court of Session by the Church party. In both the Outer and Inner Houses the judges decided against the Dissenters, who were cast in heavy expenses. So far as the Academy was concerned its usefulness was crippled. The children of the Dissenters were marched out with M'Gregor at their head and Isaac Ketchen in command. Few of them ever returned. M'Gregor taught for a year or two in the Free Church Institution without any conspicuous success.

The Parish School was re-opened, and the Sessional and Monitory schools being in existence, the attendance at the Academy was often exceedingly meagre. In 1850 F. Farries was appointed headmaster of the Academy, but he resigned in 1855. The Academy recovered some of its lost ground under William Falconer, who was appointed in 1856, and was rector until 1879, when he died. Meanwhile, by various benefactions, the Academy under his charge greatly improved its position. In 1861 Captain John Rose Troup left a sum of £2000, the interest of which went to increase the salary of the headmaster. Legacies from D. Mackenzie, bookseller (who was for many years its treasurer); from Dr. Grigor; from William Dick, town clerk, and others, increased the endowments. A proposal was made before the Endowed Schools Commission to have the Academy put under the School Board, but the commission held that this could not be legally done. They granted a new constitution so far as the governing body was concerned, leaving two life-members to represent the old proprietors, while the remainder were elected by the School Boards of town and parish, the County Council, and Town Council. In 1893 a scheme was drawn up and accepted by all parties, constituting the Academy a secondary school for the town and county, the Burgh School Board agreeing to transfer all their pupils above Standard V. to the Academy, along with Kenneth Macrae, the headmaster of the Church Street School. Macrae was the first teacher under the School Board in the new school built in Church Street, and had earned a good reputation as a successful teacher. He became English master in the Academy, which, with Alexander Lobban as rector, became once more a school of note in the country. Mr. Lobban, on retiring, was succeeded in 1920 by Mr. J. Mathewson Milne, D.Litt.

The municipal history of the burgh from the latter part of the eighteenth century down to the passing of the Municipal Reform Act of 1834 is a record mainly of financial embarrassment and difficulty. The system of electing non-residents as members of the Council had mischievous results, whilst the custom of restricting trade to freemen burgesses, who paid very high fees of admission, hindered any development of trade.

Sir Hector Munro of Novar continued Provost of Nairn till 1785, when, as there was no Rose of Kilravock at the time available, Henry Mackenzie, "The Man of Feeling," was elected. An amusing incident is recorded in connection with Henry Mackenzie's election, which appears not to have been too popular with a section of the community. As he, along with John Fraser of Geddes, a councillor of the burgh, was coming up the street in order to attend their duty at the meeting of the Council on the day of the election, they were met (so the record runs) by John Nicolson, tanner in Nairn, Brian Battersby, shoemaker, and others, who under pretence of speaking to Fraser, carried him into the shop of Robert Falconer, merchant, where he was surrounded by several others who declared in Mackenzie's presence that they would not allow him to depart, but would even detain him by violence if necessary till their pretended business with him was finished. The Council despatched the town officer, with two others, to serve him with a copy of citation to attend his duty, but the messengers were compelled by a number of the inhabitants to carry back the summons to the Council undelivered. Henry Mackenzie, however, was elected without Fraser's vote and in spite of a protest lodged against the validity of his election. The minutes when he was present are usually in his handwriting. He retained office until 1788, when Lewis Alexander Grant, yr. of Grant, was elected provost. Henry Mackenzie was married to Penuel Grant, daughter of Sir Ludovick Grant of Grant, and aunt of the young provost. The Earl of Findlater had by this time become the principal heritor in the burgh of Nairn by buying up a number of properties. Lewis Grant, Provost of Nairn, was heir to the Earl of Findlater's estates, and succeeded him as Earl of Seafield in 1811. The Council was swamped by non-resident members favourable to the Grant interest in politics. The provost attended only on very special occasions, and the business was carried on by the two or three resident members. Charles Robertson of Kindace, who resided in Nairn, was made senior bailie, and was the young Laird of Grant's substitute. In 1791 James Grant of Corriemony, an advocate, was made provost, and when he had served a term, another Grant was found for the post in the person of Major John Grant, tenant of Auchindoune. He was the father of the Misses Grant of Larkfield. The Cummings, seeing how well the Grants had managed the burgh, began to take an interest in it, and Mr. (afterwards Sir) A. P. Gordon-Cumming became provost. A parliamentary election coming round, he was appointed the Nairn delegate, and Forres, in the person of Sir Archibald Dunbar of Northfield, supporting him, he was elected member by his own casting vote. Sir Alexander Penrose Gordon-Cumming was a notable man in his day, of striking appearance and strong character. He resembled his grandson of the same name, who when in full Highland dress, must have been a brave-looking gentleman. "The coat," says Lady Middleton, his daughter, "was velvet, garnet-coloured, and gold-laced, the garters were gold, rich lace was worn at the neck and falling over the wrists, and among the gold and velvet belts hung the enamel powder-horn and stuck the inlaid pistols once the property of King James VI. (I. of England)." For the next fifteen years the Gordon-Cummings, either personally or by their friendly deputy Sir Archibald Dunbar, retained the provostship in the family. Sir Archibald was a brother-in-law of Sir A. P. Gordon-Cumming, and to do him justice he was a most regular attender at the Council meetings. From 1818 till the passing of the Reform Bill of 1832 Major Cumming Bruce and Sir William Gordon-Cumming were alternately Provosts of Nairn.

On one occasion Sir William had to do the honours to Royalty. His Royal Highness Prince Leopold of Saxe-Coburg, on a visit to the north in the autumn of 1819, was presented with the freedom of the burgh of Nairn, being created, admitted, and received a freeman burgess and guild brother thereof, " with all the powers and privileges thereto pertaining, and that for the high respect which the Magistrates and Council have for His Royal Highness the said Prince Leopold." The burgess ticket was signed by Sir William as Provost on 2nd September, 1819. In honour of the event a new street was named Leopold Street. It formerly went by the name of the " Pole Road," from a signboard hoisted on a pole, bearing a direction to travellers that this was the road to Inverness.

Several expensive works were undertaken during the civic reign of the Gordon-Cummings. The building of a new jail was forced on the burgh, and the Council had to contribute the sum of £695 as their proportion of the expense. The construction of a harbour at Nairn was long talked of, and ultimately a number of gentlemen came forward with subscriptions. The London-Nairnshire Club, as already stated, gave donations amounting to £300, and the Parliamentary Commissioners for Highland roads and bridges promised support. A plan was got from Mr. Gibb of Aberdeen, which, however, was set aside for a more expensive scheme by Telford, the famous engineer. The laird of Brodie, in compensation for loss he might sustain to the salmon fishings, had to be paid a substantial sum ere he would allow the course of the river to be diverted into the harbour channel. Altogether, a sum of over £5500 was expended. In the course of the work Telford's plan was modified without his authority or the advice of any competent engineer. The Highland Road Commissioners gave a grant of £1862, and the Convention of Royal Burghs £400. The works had been begun by certain members of the Town Council and others in their private capacity, but a stoppage being imminent the Council stepped in and became responsible for the expense. To meet the cost of the harbour and the other improvements they had from time to time to sell off large tracts of land in the immediate neighbourhood of the town, realizing £3478. Amongst the properties sold were the Muir of Crook, extending to about 40 acres, Whinnyknowe, the Elsherach, the Hempholes (below Viewfield), Mosshall, and a large number of feus and feu-duties. A strong feeling existed in the burgh that sufficient publicity had not been given to insure a fair price, and in 1823 an information was filed in Exchequer at the instance of certain burgesses against the magistrates on the ground that the statutory provisions had not been complied with in bringing these lands to sale. The Government Commissioners who reported on the affairs of the burgh in 1834, were satisfied that no undue advantage was taken, but added that instead of defending their conduct in this action, " the magistrates thought proper to meet the action by a technical objection to the title of the plaintiffs. Their objection was sustained, but this proceeding tended to destroy the confidence of the burgesses in the administrators of the common good, and to spread very widely the belief of their malversation." Sir William Gordon-Cumming claimed to have advanced from the year 1816 sums amounting to £2835, for which he charged 5 per cent. interest (at settlement modified to 4 per cent.), and it was chiefly to meet this debt to Sir William that the burgh lands and heritages were sold. When the commissioners made their investigation the balance due to him had been reduced to £240.

All might have been well if it had not been for the disastrous floods of 1829, described by Sir Thomas Dick Lauder. The 3rd of August of that year was a stormy day. Rain fell incessantly, with a heavy gale from the north. The river Nairn rose nine feet above its ordinary level as measured below the bridge. Two stone bulwarks eleven feet high stood immediately below the bridge on the left bank. One of these gave way, and the flood made a breach through it, endangering the safety of the lower part of the town. A little lower down the water rebounded to the other side and cut away a portion of the Maggot or Salt Marsh. The flood also undermined the foundation of the pier. What the flood of the 3rd began, the still greater flood of the 27th completed. It carried away one of the arches of the bridge and damaged the whole fabric. The stone embankments below the bridge were now entirely demolished. The east pier was completely broken down and a gap made in the west pier. The schooner, " Mariner of Sutherland," broke away from her moorings and was wrecked in the harbour. " The harbour," says Sir Thomas, " presented a truly lamentable sight." " Nothing," he adds, " could be more cheerless and depressing than the view of the harbour looking seaward, with its defences entirely gone, and every successive surge washing down fresh portions of the raw banks, the hull of the wrecked vessel lying in the throat of the channel, and at every stroke of the tide spouting up the water into the air through some hole in her timbers. One very remarkable feature in the surrounding scene was a fishing hut, about twelve feet long, standing in the middle of the river on a bench constructed of four posts with bearers stretched between them at top and bottom, and covered, roof and all, without side planks. While the bridge, the pier, the vessel, nay, the very rocks, were yielding to the furious force of the deluge, this ark stood unmoved in the midst of the waters of both floods uninjured." The damage to the harbour alone was estimated at £2500. For twenty years afterwards it remained in a dilapidated condition. The bridge had practically to be rebuilt.

The passing of the Reform Bill put an end to the packing of the Council by strangers, and in 1832 the lairds, their factors, and friends withdrew, leaving the townsmen to manage the burgh affairs. The Reform party in the burgh carried everything before it, and the old Tory party did not put in appearance. The first election took place on 5th November, 1833. A list of seventeen candidates had been previously arranged, and when the polling took place their supporters met to elect them. The retiring provost, W. Robertson of Househill, was the presiding officer, and Adam Davidson, who had been appointed town clerk in 1827, conducted the proceedings. The election was by open voting, and the seventeen were unanimously elected, each receiving 39 votes. The following were those elected—

1. James Anderson in Nairn.
2. Robert Cameron, shoemaker.
3. Arthur Cant, residing at Millfield.
4. William Donaldson, merchant.
5. Alexander Falconer, salmon fisher.
6. Donald Fraser, merchant.
7. William Gordon, tinsmith.
8. Alexander Hay, spirit dealer.
9. Isaac Ketchen, residing in Nairn.
10. William Mackintosh, Esq. of Millbank.
11. William M'Lean, merchant.
12. John M'Watt, mason.
13. John Malcolm, baker and merchant.
14. James Simpson, shoemaker.
15. Robert Simpson, grocer.
16. John Smith, surgeon in Nairn.
17. John Smith, merchant.

Provost Robertson then retired. At a subsequent meeting Isaac Ketchen, the leader of the Reformers, was elected provost, William M'Lean, senior bailie, William Donaldson, second bailie, and John Smith, third bailie. For several years there was no contest, and very little change in the composition of the Council. It went vigorously to work in looking after municipal matters, and applied to the Convention of Burghs, the Fishery Board, and the Treasury for a grant to aid in constructing a new harbour. Joseph Mitchell, C.E., advised the abandonment of the existing site, and suggested the construction of a new harbour at a cost of £4000 at the west corner of the links. Among its advantages, he reported that a harbour there would have a greater depth of water—some fourteen or fifteen feet—would be founded on rock, and would be free from silt. No immediate outside aid being received, however, the Council were content to patch up the old pier.

Provost Ketchen's love of political demonstrations was gratified on the occasion of the arrival at Nairn of Lord Brougham, the

Lord Chancellor, who had been on a visit to Dunrobin Castle. On 9th September the whole community was early astir. Lord Brougham was to arrive that day. The Provost, Magistrates, and Council, with a large concourse of the inhabitants, went out to the western confines of the burgh to await the arrival of his lordship's carriage. On its approach there was great cheering. Lord Brougham alighted, and was conducted with great state to the Town Hall, where he was presented with the freedom of the burgh, his burgess ticket setting forth that this honour was conferred upon him " because of their high respect for his Lordship as a pre-eminently distinguished statesman and scholar, who has long proved himself the powerful advocate of Liberal principles, civil and religious, who has signally aided in carrying into effect the great and healing measures of Parliamentary, Municipal, and Judicial Reform, Negro Emancipation, the opening of India and China to native and British enterprise, and numerous other improvements, conducive to the stability of the Throne, and the happiness of the people, and who, notwithstanding a life of more than ordinarily anxious public and professional exertion, holds the most conspicuous station as the promoter of Literature and Science." Lord Brougham, in reply, made a speech in which he " handsomely acknowledged the honour done him by the Magistrates and Council of Nairn." Having feted the Liberal Lord Chancellor, Provost Ketchen found an opportunity of paying a little compliment to the Premier, Earl Grey, in the person of his son, the Hon. Charles Grey, M.P., who was Lieut.-Colonel of the Highland Light Infantry. Happening to pass through Nairn on his way to Fort George, Colonel Grey was presented with the freedom of the burgh, but declined a public dinner. When Earl Grey came to Scotland in September 1834 the Nairn Town Council sent an address of welcome to him at the great Edinburgh Festival. It was with feelings of indignation and anger that Provost Ketchen and the Nairn Town Council heard a few months later of the dismissal of the Whig Ministry, and the instalment of the Duke of Wellington at the head of a Conservative administration. The Council addressed a strongly-worded remonstrance to the King for having so changed his Cabinet, with a request that

His Majesty should instantly remove his new councillors in the interest of peace and good government. Two questions of an ecclesiastical character gave rise to the first, and for a long period the only, divisions in the Council. The one was the subject of electing a representative elder to the General Assembly. On the first occasion Provost Ketchen failed to carry his motion refusing to elect, being defeated by a majority of six, but in subsequent years he was more successful. On his retirement from the Council, the custom of electing a representative elder was resumed. The other burning question was in regard to the ringing of the town bell on Sunday to suit the evening service of the Seceder congregation, the Church people maintaining that it was illegal to do so, and ultimately it was discontinued. Provost Ketchen retired from the provostship in 1836, but still continued to take a prominent part in public affairs. He did good service in connection with the founding of the Town and County Hospital in 1852. Dr. Smith was the next provost. He was greatly esteemed in Nairn, and when he died suddenly in office, his funeral was conducted with more than ordinary circumstances, over fifteen hundred people attending it. A monument was erected in Nairn churchyard, which sets forth his private benevolence and public spirit. He was succeeded by Dr. Falconer. In 1839 John Wilson was elected provost, and for the next fifteen years he was the energetic head of the Council, devising and carrying out extensive improvements. Provost Wilson was a builder and was engaged in large undertakings.

With the freer municipal life, a spirit of local enterprise sprang up. The shipping trade was developed. Large tracts of wood were cut down. A ready market was found for fir props in the north of England collieries, and the larger trees were manufactured into railway sleepers for the south. Shipbuilding was started, and several handsome schooners were launched from the yards at the shore. The timber was obtained from the neighbouring estates, and the vessels were named after members of the families from whose property the wood came. There was thus the " Sir William Cumming " from the Altyre woods, the " Lady Louisa Stuart " from Darnaway Forest, the " Countess of Cawdor " from the

Cawdor woods, and so on. The leading shipowners of the time were Bailie Mackenzie, Hugh Mann, William Dallas, and Hugh and John Mackintosh. Hugh Mann sent his two younger brothers, Peter and David, to look after his business at Sunderland, and they ultimately became leading merchants in Seaham. Alexander Mann, another brother, developed the salmon fishing. Robert Anderson engaged in exporting agricultural produce. William Dallas conceived the bold idea of establishing a trade between the Moray Firth and Australia, and despatched the " Countess of Cawdor " from Inverness and Cromarty with emigrants and a cargo of oatmeal—the venture, however, turned out badly, mainly through mismanagement at the Colonial end. One Nairn vessel, " The Lady Campbell," was fitted out for the seal fishing, but met with misfortunes. " The John and Margaret," " The Millert," " The Mary," " The Nairnshire," " The Janes," " The Margaret and Elizabeth," " The Hydee," " Christina," " John and Madby," and other vessels were also owned in Nairn. A hardy race of seamen was thus bred at the port. The smacks which sailed regularly between Inverness and Leith and London with passengers were superseded by a line of steamers which made Nairn bay a place of call. Fish-curing was carried on, and pretty extensive cooperages and ropeworks were established. Visions of making Nairn an important maritime port were constantly before the minds of its citizens. The trade of Strathspey and the district lying between was finding its way to Nairn for transport, whilst a passenger traffic from Ross-shire was developing. Renewed efforts were made to extend the harbour—first one pier and then another being erected at great cost. But an unlooked for change occurred, which revolutionised the entire prospects of the place.

In early times the riding post to Aberdeen was the only regular means of communication with the south. The post was superseded by the stage coach about the year 1805. The coaches became popular institutions. " The Mail," " The Defiance," and " The Star " were familiar names, associated with travellers and the outer world. The arrival of the coach from the south was heralded by the blowing of the guard's horn as the bridge was approached, and the four horses entered the town at a rapid pace. If it carried the Royal mails, it drew up for a moment at the corner of Bridge Street, near to which was the Post Office, and then with a crack of the whip the horses sped up the brae, and were halted in front of the new hotel, known as Anderson's. The guard having seen to his passengers' refreshment, and the driver to his horses being properly baited and new relays provided, an adjournment was made to the courtyard of the stabling, where there was a skittle alley, and the favourite game of knocking the nine-pins down was engaged in. The letters, few as they were, were kept at the Post Office till the following morning, and some time during the forenoon of that day an elderly woman leisurely went round with them, having them rolled up in her apron.

On 21st September, 1854, the first turf of the Inverness and Nairn Railway was cut by the Countess of Seafield. There was a great demonstration on the occasion at Inverness, and the Provost and Magistrates of Nairn were assigned a prominent position at the ceremony. The cost of the fifteen and a half miles of railway was £65,000, or a little more than £4000 per mile. James Falshaw (in conjunction with Mr. Brassey) was the contractor, and during the carrying out of the work and for several years afterwards resided at Nairn. He became a member of the Town Council, and was understood to have an ambition to be provost, but was only elected a bailie. The city of Edinburgh, however, made him its Lord Provost, and Queen Victoria conferred a baronetcy upon him. The Inverness and Nairn Railway was opened on 5th November, 1855. It was connected in 1858 with the Aberdeen Junction Railway, and afterwards was absorbed in the system of the Highland Railway, which in turn has become part of the London, Midland & Scottish Railway. A strenuous effort was made to make Nairn instead of Forres the starting point of the Perth extension, and if this had been carried out there would have been no need for the construction of the Carr Bridge line.

Few of the smaller towns in the north have benefited so much by the opening up of the country by railway communication as Nairn has done. Its prosperity dates from that development. A new direction was given to the enterprise of its citizens. It was then seen that the future progress of the town depended upon its development as a sea-bathing place. In its dry bracing climate, its pure air, its light porous subsoil, and·its excellent bathing beach, it possessed great natural advantages as a health resort, and during recent years these have been enhanced by the introduction of a good water supply, a very complete system of drainage, and the establishment of facilities for bathing. The old thatched houses with gable-ends to the High Street have been replaced by handsome buildings and smart-looking shops. New streets have been formed and built upon. Numerous villas have sprung up in and around the town, and, with many comfortable and first class hotels and boarding houses, afford accommodation for visitors. A large indoor swimming bath and other bathing establishments have become attractions to the place. Progress in other matters has kept pace. Many of these improvements are due to the initiative of Dr. Grigor, whose statue adorns the High Street. He was ably seconded by Mr. William Leslie, for fifteen years Provost of Nairn.

The town got a fresh start with the introduction of golf. The game is not new in Nairn. In 1672 Lord Brodie records his playing golf at Burgie, and expresses the hope that its attractions may not be a snare to him. An entry in the Nairn Town Council Records brings golf-playing still nearer. On 10th June, 1797, it is stated that the magistrates had met that day to roup the grass of the Links for three years, and one of the conditions is " that the set now to be made shall not prohibit the gentlemen of the town or others from playing golff or walking on the whole links at pleasure, or in passing to and from any part of the sea-shore." The minute is signed by John Straith as senior bailie, and it is permissible to suppose that the famous schoolmaster may have taught his pupils golf as well as Latinity. The modern golf course lies about half a mile west of the town links proper, and extends to Delnies—a three-mile course of eighteen holes. Another very sporting course of eighteen holes has more recently been laid out to the east of the river, and named the Dunbar Course after its donor, the late Sir Alexander Dunbar of Boath. Its intention is to provide more ample facilities for the artisans of the town.

The Town Links still remains one of the features of the place. It is the popular resort and recreation ground, where cricket and other games are played. The old game of " bools," as it was called, which used to be played on the links, has died out. It was immensely popular in olden times, and was principally played by the fishermen in frosty weather.

Although the railways prevented the development of the trade at the port of Nairn, the fishing industry continued to increase. After the herring fishing at Nairn was given up, the Nairn boats went each season about the beginning of July to Portmahomack, where for many years they had prosperous seasons. A very fine class of decked boats was latterly introduced, and the fishermen now prosecute the herring fishing mostly at Fraserburgh from July to September, and at Yarmouth from September to December. At the beginning of the year they prosecute the white fishing from Nairn, going down to Smith's Bank, at the entrance of the Moray Firth. About the end of March the boats proceed to Kinsale in Ireland, and on the first of May to the West Coast of Scotland. The introduction of trawl fishing in the last quarter of the nineteenth century seriously threatened the prosperity of the Nairn industry; but the Government stepped in and protected the local fishing grounds by forbidding the use of the trawl in the Moray Firth, and the fishermen themselves rose to the emergency by adopting steam drifters and auxiliary motor power which enabled them to go further afield. A remarkable change in the social habits of the fishing population has taken place. Two-thirds of the fishermen are total abstainers, and they have a beautiful hall of their own for social and religious meetings, with a library and reading-room.

Nairn harbour has had an unfortunate history. Extensions of the wooden piers were made from time to time, but the work had no stability. Afterwards, by the employment of concrete, more permanence was attained. In 1893 an extension of the east breakwater was carried out, a sum of £1000 being raised by means of a bazaar, and the Council contributing £1200. It was built of concrete, and gave greater safety to boats and shipping within the harbour. Unfortunately, being built upon sand, the concrete piers themselves in time were undermined and broken by the wash of the river and the winter gales. After much agitation, and amid no little difference of opinion, powers were obtained in 1927 to repair the harbour and construct a drifter shelter at an estimated cost of £47,000.

The first newspaper in Nairn was started in 1841. There had been much cogitating amongst the leading men interested as to what should be the name of the paper. It was regarded as a happy inspiration that Sheriff Falconer, whilst shaving, should have hit upon calling the paper " The Mirror." Its editor and proprietor was Charles M'Watt, who had been a pupil of Straith's, and afterwards graduated at Aberdeen. It was published once a month at first and then once a fortnight. In 1853 the " Nairnshire Telegraph " was established as a weekly paper by James Wilson, and in 1854 the " Mirror " and " Telegraph " were combined under his management. M'Watt, who had been in delicate health, died soon afterwards. His son, Daniel M'Watt, attained a good position in Barrie, Ontario, Canada. About the year 1864 James Wilson went to China, his uncle, Alexander Wilson, being in business in Hong Kong. He set up the plant of a newspaper in Shanghai, but died before the first number appeared. His cousin, Hugh Wilson, remained in charge of the " Telegraph " for some years, but eventually sought a wider field. Along with his brothers, James and John Wilson, he established the Edinburgh " Evening News." Patrick Rose Smith, a licentiate of the Church of Scotland, and a man of literary ability, was for a time connected with the " Telegraph," but went to London, where he did work for the " Athenaeum " and other literary papers. He was a personal friend of George Macdonald, the novelist, who showed him much kindness. David Law of Edinburgh was the next editor. He was afterwards sub-editor of the " Bombay Gazette," and, having passed as a barrister in London, was assigned an important position on the staff of the " Times," which he retained until his death. Patrick R. Smith, nephew of James Wilson, carried on the " Telegraph " for some years, but accepted a post on the " North China Herald." After a few years he returned to London, and passed as a barrister. He was for a time employed in literary work by Herbert Spencer, the philosopher. He went back to Hong Kong, where he received a legal appointment, but died soon after. The " Telegraph " was acquired in 1869 by George Bain, who carried it on till his death in 1926. Throughout his long life Mr. Bain was untiring in his efforts to further the interests of Nairn. Since his death the paper has been carried on by his executrix. Many of the young men brought up in the office have taken good positions. Among them may be mentioned Mr. Hugh Mackintosh, sometime editor of the " Weekly Irish Times," Mr. John Mitchell of Dublin, Mr. Donald M'Leod of the " Kirkintilloch Herald," and Mr. Alexander Urquhart of the " Dundee Courier and Advertiser."

The Nairn Literary Institute has done a great deal to promote an interest in scientific and literary subjects, and papers of permanent value have been contributed on local subjects. Dr. Cruickshank drew up a list of the " Place Names in the District," Mr. H. T. Donaldson described " The Castles of Nairnshire," and Mr. Wm. Laing, town clerk, wrote on the subject of old social customs in the burgh of Nairn, while Mr. George Bain conducted the members on many excursions of exploration to the Culbin Sands and other places of interest, besides delivering a number of exceedingly interesting and instructive lectures on historical places in Nairn and neighbourhood. His work as curator of the museum for many years was highly appreciated, and to him the Institute owes a deep debt of gratitude. A good deal of miscellaneous work has been done by other members. The museum of the Institute is much hampered for space. It has a valuable collection of minerals, which belonged to the late Duchess of Gordon. A library and reading-room are maintained in connection with the Institute.

Beyond the ordinary trades, no special industries have developed in Nairn. As of yore, young men both in town and county seek employment elsewhere. The military service now attracts very few. Mercantile careers in India and Ceylon are more favoured by those of the class who used to aspire to commissions in the army. Agriculturists seek homes in the colonies and the United States, and mechanics and merchants betake themselves to Glasgow. A

Glasgow-Nairnshire Society, established in 1876, numbered several hundred natives of Nairn, and its annual re-union has been for many years a gathering of much interest. Nairn men abroad continue to make their mark, and are to be found occupying positions of importance in all parts of the world. Amongst the best known have been Duncan Macarthur of Winnipeg, Gilbert Fraser, the British Consul at New York, William M'Bean of the same city, the Squairs and Macqueens of Chicago, the Hon. John Macintosh of Sydney, James Simpson of Port Elizabeth, Alexander Hector at Capetown, John Macdonald of Brisbane, the Wallaces of Ballarat, James Mackillican of Calcutta, the Smiths of Hong Kong, and the Clarkes of Shanghai and Ceylon. Attachment to Nairn and Nairnshire continues to be a marked characteristic of Nairn men wherever their lot is cast.

CHAPTER XXII

GENERAL FEATURES OF THE COUNTY

NAIRNSHIRE presents several interesting geological features. Its configuration may be described as consisting of three platforms or divisions. The first consists of a fertile belt of land extending from the shore inland for a few miles, at an average height of from 80 to 120 feet above sea level. The river Nairn in its approach to the sea passes through the centre of this plain. The soil within the area is light, with a subsoil of pure white sand, or sand and gravel. The underlying rock is the Old Red Sandstone, which forms the basin or cup of the Moray Firth. Along the shore, at King's Steps and Newton, the sandstone is quarried for building purposes. It yields fossils characteristic of the upper division of the Old Red Sandstone. The stone is often " keel-marked," that is, pitted with nodules of greenish clay, which crumble when exposed to the air. In the Newton quarry some remarkable specimens of sun-cracks have been found, showing that the rock was deposited in shallow water. Dr. Malcolmson, in the year 1832, called attention to the marked difference between the lithological character and organic remains of these beds and the sandstones exposed in the higher ground, and his view has been confirmed by Dr. Archibald Geikie and Mr. John Horne of the Geographical Survey, who found in addition an unconformity between the deposits.

The second or middle division of the county gradually attains to an altitude of 600 feet, as it extends southwards. The Hill of Urchany and the Lethen Bar are its highest elevations. The lands are mostly under cultivation or covered with thriving woods, interspersed with patches of whin and peat mosses. The Muckle Burn and its contributaries drain this middle area. A mass of granite occurs on the border line between the first and second platforms, extending from Rait to Kinsteary. The junction of the granite with the Old Red Sandstone is exposed near the Geddes Burn. The granite has been quarried at Newton of Park. It is of a reddish colour, and when polished has a beautiful appearance from the large pink crystals of orthoclase felspar contained in it. The presence of this crystal is so marked as to give it a distinctive character, unmistakable either in the rough boulders carried into other districts or in polished slabs and obelisks. The natural surface of the granite rock near Newton shows fine examples of striation, the ice-markings indicating that the direction of the ice-flow was east with a slight southerly inclination. The rock surfaces behind Rait Castle afford further examples of ice-scratching in the same direction. On the west border of the county the glaciated surfaces, however, incline from the east point rather to the north, indicating that the direction of the ice-flow was deflected on approaching the plains of Nairn and Moray from ENE. to ESE. The enormous deposits of boulder clays, sands, and gravels have left few rock surfaces exposed. Mr. Horne, in his survey, found in certain parts of the county two distinct boulder clays separated by an important series of inter-glacial sands, gravels, and finely laminated clays.

Over the middle and lower districts occur numerous travelled boulders composed of a conglomerate rock, studded with pink quartzite. The boulder on Culloden Moor, known as the Cumberland Stone, is an example. A huge boulder called " Tomriach," at Croygorston, on the south side of the river Nairn, is the most remarkable, and is said to be the second largest boulder in Scotland. Its dimensions are—Length 35 feet, circumference 92 feet, breadth about 20 feet, height 13 feet, estimated weight 560 tons. A boulder south of Cawdor Castle, two at the westerly base of the Hill of the Ord, and several on its shoulders and easterly slopes, are further examples. The parent rock from which they appear to have been derived occurs on the heights of Strathdearn, about thirty miles south-westward. The lie of the boulders, along with the circumstance that some striated blocks of the Red Sandstone have been carried into the purely metamorphic rock area, further indicates that the ice-sheet was compelled to move eastward along the slopes of the hills.

A remarkable kame of sand and shingle exists on the low ground about a mile to the west of Nairn. It begins at Meikle Kildrummie, and extends to Flemington, near Fort George, a distance of over three miles. The ridge at the east end rises to the height of 100 feet above sea level, and at the western to 140 feet. It is now for the most part covered with a scanty herbage, and towards the western end houses have been built upon it. Similar kames, but of less extent, exist on the moorlands in the upper division of the county.

The discovery was made by Mr. James Fraser, C.E., Inverness, of the existence of a shell bed on the farm of Drumore of Clava, at an elevation of 500 feet above sea level. Arctic shells had been found previously in a bed of blue clay in the ninety-feet terrace on the Fort George road. The British Association in 1892 appointed a committee to investigate the questions connected with the Clava shell-bed. The shells are found to be very little injured, which favours the theory of a marine deposit at the place, but the general opinion is that they were carried and deposited by ice.

Much interest was excited by the discovery of a fossil fish-bed at Lethenbar and the Clune by Dr. Malcolmson about the year 1820. The limestone nodules which contain the fossils were being quarried and burned for lime. Specimens of the old Red Sandstone fishes from Lethenbar have found their way into nearly every museum in the country. The plates in Agassiz's great work on the Old Red Sandstone fishes were taken from specimens obtained from Lethenbar. The quarries have now been closed, but specimens are found in a cutting in the Lethen Burn. A fairly good collection of these fossil fish, collected by Mr. W. A. Stables, and presented by Earl Cawdor, is in the Nairn Museum. Similar nodules have turned up on the farm of Knockloam, on the Cawdor estate, and Mr. Wallace, Inverness, has found the fish-bed extending underneath the river Nairn at Nairnside, in the parish of Croy.

The third or upper division of the county is a typical Highland district, stretching southward in wild moorland and flanked by lofty hills almost attaining the altitude of mountains. The highest peak of the range is over 2000 feet, and the average height is from 1200 to 1500 feet. The boundary at the south extends to within a mile and a half of Dava Station. The rock is metamorphic and crystalline. Lochindorb and Lochan Tutach lie in a corner touching the boundary line. The river Findhorn passes through this division, and has a course of nineteen miles through Nairnshire. It enters the county near the centre of the south-western end, and flows across towards the north-east, passing into Morayshire at Downduff. Its entrance through the narrow defile at Pollochaig is peculiarly gloomy. The Streens, through which it flows, is a very picturesque region. At Drynachan, Earl Cawdor has a lodge convenient for the moors and the fishing on the Findhorn. At Dulsie the river bends into a narrow rocky channel, across which General Wade threw a bridge of a single arch, which still carries the road down a very perilous declivity. The river scenery from Dulsie Bridge is very grand. Perhaps the most romantic part is the reach at Ferness. The Findhorn passes Coulmony, and then makes its exit in fleck and foam from the county of Nairn through the narrow pass of Randolph's Leap, below Downduff. The Rhilean and Leonach burns, joining their waters above Lynemore, where there is a lovely cascade, fall into the Findhorn a little above Dulsie. The burn of Tomlachlan, also on the south side, has a diversified course, and falls into the Findhorn above Glenferness. A little stream on the left bank of the river has a very pretty fall called Altnara. It is in the Dulsie wood, close to the public road between Daltra and Dulsie.

The river Nairn takes its rise in Inverness-shire at a height of 2500 feet above the sea level, and about ten miles east of the point where the river Foyers enters Loch Ness. The Nairn has a course of 38 miles, measuring its windings; in a straight line from source to mouth it measures 30½ miles. Of these, 18 miles are in Inverness-shire. It passes through a very wild and rugged channel, flanked on the south-east side by bare hills, rising to the height of from 1500 to 2000 feet. At one point it comes to within three

miles of the river Findhorn, and it has been estimated that a rise
of 80 feet would send the water of the Findhorn down the channel
of the Nairn. It is supposed by geologists that this actually
occurred, the blocking up of the Pass of Pollochaig by ice causing
an overflow into Loch Moy, which raised it to a level—a few feet
would do it—sufficient to send its water down the Nairn valley.
As the glen widens, beautiful haugh farms are found along its
course, and richly-wooded knolls and hills slope down towards the
stream. The name of Strathnairn is now exclusively applied to
this upper region. From its source to Daviot the river scenery is
very wild, and the extraordinary evidences of glacial action, and
the remarkable cuttings made by the stream, have attracted the
attention and study of geologists. Several important papers on the
subject of its geology have appeared in the Transactions of the
Inverness Field Club. After passing on to the Old Red Sandstone
at Daviot, the river has a comparatively peaceful flow to its mouth
at the town of Nairn.

The interesting discovery was made a number of years ago that
gold exists in the river Nairn. A labourer, a native of the district,
who had been at the gold-diggings at Kildonan, in Sutherlandshire,
in 1869, detected among the river-sand near the mouth of the
Daltulich Burn, at its junction with the Nairn, some particles of
gold. He set to work with the usual process of " washing," and
got a quantity sufficient to make a finger-ring. Further investigation by some scientific gentlemen in Inverness confirmed the
discovery, but they found that the gold was in such small quantities
that it would not repay the labour of searching for it. No syste-
matic investigation has yet, however, been made. It is not improbable that amongst the deposits of sand, the washings of the
detritus of the primary and crystalline rocks, the auriferous ore
may some day be found in greater abundance.

About 13,000 acres of the county of Nairn were, prior to the War,
under wood. The Thanes of Cawdor had a fondness for planting,
and the old oakwood south of the castle is a remnant of their love
of forestry. Early in the nineteenth century the work of planting
was undertaken on a large scale on the Cawdor estate. When
Alexander Black entered upon his work as forester in 1825, the

number of acres under wood on the Cawdor estate was 2156. A memorandum in his own handwriting shows that between 1825 and 1854, both inclusive, he planted 4130 acres additional, raising the total of the woods on the estates to 6286 acres. The description of the principal trees planted is of interest. Scots Fir came first, with 13,204,700 trees, Larch numbered 486,090; Oaks, 390,380; Spruce, 29,060; Black Austrian Pine, 684; Hanganae, 290; Pinus cembra, 60; Corsican Pine, 40; Deodars, 6; Sycamores, 2320; Elm, 2200; Ash, 860; Horse Chestnuts, 262; Birch, 200; Norway Maple, 150; Walnut, 54; Spanish Chestnut, 54; Limes, 40—total, 14,117,450. Mr. Black, who lived to a good old age, had the rare experience of cutting down woods, of full-grown timber, which he had himself planted. A nursery for trees was formed at Cawdor, and from time to time new plantations are formed. On the Kilravock, Lethen, and Brodie estates large areas have also been planted, and some magnificent trees surround these residences. Next to the Darnaway Forest, the Low Wood, or Black Forest, as it is sometimes called, is the largest. It extends along the seaside from Maviston Sandhills to the Culbin Sands, and the plants were put down amongst the sand-drift. A detailed account of the work and its remarkable results has been given by Mr. J. Grigor, of Forres.

From the diversified nature of the physical features of the county, the botany of the district, as might be expected, is rich and varied. Lists of the plants found were contributed to "The Flora of Moray" by W. A. Stables, Sheriff Falconer, Mr. Brichan, and others. The Rev. Thomas Fraser of Croy compiled a list of the plants in the parish of Croy, which has been published, and Robert Thomson of Ardclach made a valuable collection of the plants found in that upland parish. The Nairn Literary Institute, which had excellent botanists in Mr. Lobban and Dr. Cruickshank, has also done some work in this department. The *Monotropa hypopitus* was found by Mr. Stables at Cawdor, this being its first recorded station in Scotland. The *Gagea lutea* existed for some time at Blackhills, in the parish of Auldearn, but the rare bulb was inadvertently ploughed up. The *Listera Nidusavis* appears (and disappears) at Cawdor. The *Linnea Borealis* has been found in

Dulsie Wood by Mr. Thomson. The oyster plant grows abundantly at the sea-shore some four miles to the east of Nairn. The profuse abundance of the white Campion on the waysides and waste places, and the *Trientalis Europœa* and *Lysimachia nemorum* in the woodlands strikes a stranger as remarkable. The links and carse lands have their own flora. The whin everywhere abounds, and in the early summer imparts a rich glow of golden colour to the landscape. Amongst the ferns are the green and black spleenworts, the fragile oak and beech ferns, the adder tongue and moonwort, *Blechnum spicant*, *Adiantum Nigrum*, the *P. aculeatum*, *angulare*, and *Lonchitis*. The bulrush and reed-grass grow magnificently at the Loch of Leetie.

The fauna of Nairnshire has been described by St. John, the sportsman. He resided for some years at Nairn, and made daily excursions along the shore to Lochloy and other parts of the coast, watching the sea-fowl. In the uplands foxes were, until recent times, occasionally met with. The polecat is not yet extinct. Weasels and stoats are common. In 1892 a colony of fifty or sixty stoats appeared below Delnies. The otter frequents the Muckleburn and the Findhorn. Roedeer are common in the upper districts, and are found also in cover on the coast. Squirrels are very numerous, and do immense injury to the young plantations. The brown hare is not now so common, but mountain or white hares are very numerous. The mole and water vole are to be found all over the lower district. Seals frequent the coast, but are rarely shot. The rabbit, introduced early last century, swarms everywhere. Amongst birds the shrike and sand-grouse are visitants. The cross-bill has established himself along the valley of the Nairn. Starlings have increased in vast flocks. The magpie is still met with, but is less common. The jackdaw, carrion crow, and hooded-crow are familiar residents, whilst the rooks are so troublesome to the farmer that an association was formed for the purpose of destroying them. Rookeries exist at Kinsteary and Culloden. Owls are less common than they were. A bittern was shot at Coulmony about 1890. Wild duck are common on the lower marsh lands, and snipe in the uplands. Pheasants (preserved) and partridge are abundant. Quail, ptarmigan, and grouse afford sport on the upland moors, of which Cawdor and Dunearn are the most extensive. Of the hawk species, the common buzzard, the kestrel, and the sparrow-hawk are met with at the Findhorn Valley. An occasional heron appears on the Findhorn, but since the old heronry at St. John's Meads was deserted, the birds do not appear to breed there. A pair or two of swans usually maintain kingship amidst the multitude of seafowl on Lochloy and the Cran Loch. The river Nairn is a fair trouting stream. The salmon and grilse pass to the upper reaches of the Nairn, and good fishing is obtained in the autumn at Holme Rose and Culloden. The Loch of Belivat was stocked with trout by Sir Thomas Brodie. Lochindorb produces a small trout. Loch-an-Tutach is a better trouting sheet of water. The Nairn Angling Association exercises the right of fishing within the burgh boundaries for both salmon and trout, but the fishing on the Nairn upper reaches is preserved.

Although historically unauthentic, the scenes of Shakespeare's " Macbeth " laid in Nairnshire are regarded as places of interest. The " Blasted Heath " where Macbeth met the witches lies on the eastern boundary of the county, and the mound is pointed out around which the witches danced hand-in-hand. The Hardmuir has now in large part been planted or cultivated, but a stretch remaining of the peat-moss, lying to the north-west towards Inshoch, gives an idea of the dreary, weird character of the old " Blasted Heath." Cawdor Castle has attractions of its own sufficient for the lover of old castellated buildings, but the Shakespearean association of the Thane of Cawdor with the Tragedy of Macbeth invests it with additional interest.

Superstitions still exist, though they are fast losing their hold. A belief in omens, fairies, and witches lingers on in the remoter districts and among the older people. When Henry Irving and Ellen Terry visited the Blasted Heath, in the summer of 1887, Irving enquired of the driver whether there were still any witches, and he was much mystified with the answer he got, that they had disappeared " at the time of the flood." The driver meant the great Moray Flood of 1829. It was a not uncommon custom in the district to date events as occurring so many years before or

who allowed the weed to get into seed on their farms. A year or two later it was reported that some fields, particularly in the neighbourhood of Calder, were very bad, and as the society was determined to get rid of the weed they resolved to impose a penalty of half-a-guinea for each plant found in full blossom on any member's farm. In 1806 a committee reported that considerable exertions had been made to cut down and root out the noxious weed, and they hoped by perseverance in these endeavours to extirpate it. The local opinion was that the weed had been introduced by the Duke of Cumberland's provender train, hence the origin of the opprobrious term applied to it. It has now been practically exterminated.

The first formal discussion on an agricultural question took place at the meeting in 1807, when the subject was the best method of applying lime to the land. The finding of the meeting was that the most advantageous mode of using lime is by spreading it on lea one year previous to the lea being broken up, and they were the more confirmed in this opinion from an experiment made on the Mains of Kilravock. At the following meeting the subject discussed was whether oxen or horses are the most advantageous to be used for husbandry in this county, and the finding was that in light soils or where long draughts were necessary, horses were preferable ; upon other lands, where stiff soil intervenes, oxen were the more useful ; but upon the whole, it is the general opinion that a judicious use or distribution of both horses and oxen suitable to the particular cases of the farms and the nearer an equilibrium, was the most advantageous for the county. In the year 1808 the first ploughing match in connection with the Highland Society took place at Broadley. In 1810 the society, finding the great benefit derived from lime, gave an order for 2200 bolls of lime to Mr. Dempster, and at the same time the members joined together to purchase coal. Quantities amounting to 720 barrels were ordered to be delivered at Fort George, and 897 barrels at Nairn. It was specified that South Moor Main coals of the best quality were to be supplied, and the price was to be 2s. 4d. per barrel. The practice of ordering coal was kept up regularly for many years. Samples of wheat, barley, and oats were produced at the meeting on 7th February, 1815. It was resolved to petition Parliament in favour of such alteration in the corn laws as would enable the British farmer to meet foreign grain in the home market.   At the May meeting, on the suggestion of George Macandrew, it was agreed to take steps for establishing a savings bank in each parish.

In the year 1819 a show of young cattle was held at Clephanton, where cattle trysts had been established.   The first prize was won by a heifer belonging to Alexander Stables, Cawdor Castle, the second by Kilravock, and the third by Mr. Macandrew, Torrich.   It was resolved in future to hold all cattle shows at Nairn, but the change was not finally made till a much more recent time.   In 1820 it was agreed to open the competition in cattle to all practical farmers in the county, whether they were members of the society or not.   One of the most active members of the society in its earlier years was George Macandrew, Torrich (grandfather of Sir Henry Macandrew of Inverness), and on his retiring from the society in the year 1821 the compliment was paid of electing him an honorary member.   His son, John Macandrew, who established an important law firm in Inverness, married a daughter of James Macpherson of Ardersier.   The old family burying place of the Macandrews is at Ardclach churchyard.

The society encouraged the starting of a steamboat in 1826, and in 1832 established at Nairn a weekly corn market and an annual hiring market for farm servants.   Alexander Stables, factor for Lord Cawdor, was for many years secretary of the society, and was succeeded by his son, William A. Stables, W. D. Penny, parochial schoolmaster, John Joss, Budgate, and Capt. A. J. Mackintosh, who was appointed in 1902.   The society for the first fifty years of its existence seldom exceeded twenty members. In 1892 the membership was 120, with an income of £222, which was expended mainly in premiums at exhibitions of stock, grain, grass seeds, and roots.   The society has now over 200 members, and continues in a flourishing condition, its annual show of cattle, horses, etc., being looked upon as one of the principal local events of the year.

In the early part of the century attention was chiefly devoted to the reclamation of land, and a vast tract of country was brought under cultivation.   Many farms doubled and even trebled the extent of their arable acreage. The most extensive improvements made by a single tenant on one farm were effected by John Rose, of Leonach, on the braes and haughs of the river Nairn, near Clava and Culloden Moor. Above 300 acres were improved by him, and his sons brought the number up to 400 acres. James Macpherson, a most enterprising man, who had a passion for improving land, brought into cultivation a large extent of waste ground on the farms of Drumore and Assich on the Cantray estate, Clunas on the Cawdor estate, and Dulsie on the Lethen estate. He was assisted by his brother, Angus Macpherson, in the improvements on the Cantray farms. These improvements paid during the period from 1860 to 1880. In the year 1869 Angus Macpherson entered on his own account on a tack of Cantray-doune, agreeing to bring into cultivation 170 acres. In the year 1888 he had improved 130 acres, and asked his landlord to relieve him of the condition to improve the remainder, on account of the change in the times having rendered it impossible to improve the land profitably. By this time land-improving had practically ceased in the county, and all the leading agriculturists gave evidence to the effect that the land in question could not be improved except at a loss, and that in fact the best of subjects would not now pay the cost of labour. The case was carried to the Court of Session, and the Supreme Court held that a bargain was a bargain, and that the conditions of the lease must be fulfilled. The tenant had in consequence to surrender his farm. This notable case illustrates the change which took place in agricultural industry during the eighties of the nineteenth century. It became a question whether a good deal of the land brought under cultivation would not under the altered circumstances be more profitable as out-runs of natural pasture. The "clod," as it is locally called, of the lighter lands appeared to be pretty much worn out, and was every year, except during very favourable seasons, throwing a lighter crop. Wheat up to the year 1860 was grown on all the better class lands in Nairnshire, but its cultivation had by 1892 practically ceased. A very fine sample of wheat used to be produced, as is shown by the fact that the first prize was awarded at the great International Exhibition in London in 1852, to a sample sent from

Piperhill in the Cawdor valley (as also the first prize for ryegrass seed). But the crop of wheat was too light to be remunerative at the lower prices. Barley, at the end of the century, became the staple crop, and except in adverse seasons the grain, both in weight and quality, keeps up to the ordinary standard. The wintering of sheep by Highland flockmasters, and the letting to them of turnips not required for the stock of the farm, is a common custom. The improvement of stock has kept pace with the general advancement in the country. Mainly through the influence of Earl Cawdor's stud, the breed of horses was vastly improved, and the Clydesdales exhibited at the annual local agricultural show are most creditable specimens. The breed of sheep was also improved.

Brackla Distillery was built in the year 1812. Captain William Fraser, whose property it became, carried on the work with much energy and success, and secured the Royal patronage. The distillery became a great convenience to the farmers, whose barley was taken on the spot instead of having to be transported to the ports of Inverness and Findhorn. Captain Fraser was succeeded by his son, Robert Fraser, who was born in the year in which the distillery started. Mr. Fraser continued proprietor of the distillery till the eighties, when it was acquired by a firm of Edinburgh distillers. Under the management of Mr. Walter C. Newbigging the business was greatly extended, and with the new machinery introduced, the annual output was more than doubled. It was 70,000 gallons in 1892. The make is pure Highland malt. Peats are extensively used in the heating of the plates. Both water and steam-power are used, and the barley consumed is, as far as possible, home-grown.

Amongst the most energetic and successful agriculturists in Nairnshire was Robert Anderson of Lochdhu. Brought up on his father's small farm of Cooperhill, Darnaway, Anderson became a leading corn merchant and agricultural judge in the north. His first considerable venture in farming was his tenancy of Meikle Kildrummie, on an improving lease. He brought under cultivation about 350 acres. His improvements on that farm were the astonishment of the country. They paid him, however, and through his indomitable energy in business he was able to purchase the property of Lochdhu, and to add to it various other lands, such as Grieship, Broadley, and Nairn Moss. For considerably over half a century he was the leading agriculturist in the county of Nairn, and was regarded as the father of modern improvements in farming. His services to his agricultural friends were recognised on one occasion by their presenting him with a piece of silver plate and 600 sovereigns, and on another occasion with a life-sized portrait of himself.

What the Farming Society did for husbandry in general, the several Horticultural and Industrial societies did for the minor departments of rural industry. As an index to the social state of the district, these district exhibitions showed a very decided revival of industrial art and increased attention to the amenities and comforts of rural life. Wood-carving, as a home-industry for young men, became highly popular.

An experiment in land cultivation in connection with the burgh of Nairn is interesting from its economic results. A movement originated amongst the townspeople about the year 1769 for allotments of land. A Trades Society was formed, and an application was made to the Council for a long lease of " the uncultivated moorish ground belonging to the community lying to the west of the Auldton Burn or strype that runs down from the Moss of Nairn." A few years later the Council granted a lease of about 141 Scots acres for a term of five nineteen years at an annual rent of £5 sterling for the first nineteen years, £10 for the second nineteen, £15 for the third, £20 for the fourth, and £25 for the fifth and last nineteen years. The experiment was only a very partial success. The lands were brought under cultivation, but, with one or two exceptions, the houses erected (which fell to the town on expiry of the lease) were miserably poor, and the land was starved towards the close of the lease. The Trades Society had virtually become defunct, but its treasurer managed to gather the amount of rent from sub-tenants. In 1889 the lease expired, and the Town Council resumed possession of its property. A new scheme was then started. The lands were disposed of, along with such houses as existed, as perpetual feus, to the highest bidder at a public sale on the ground, the purchaser having the option of redeeming one-half the capitalised feu-duty, or of erecting sufficient buildings in security. The former course generally was adopted. The effect was most satisfactory. The best land was taken up, comfortable cottages were erected, the land was well laboured, and an industrious community was settled upon it. The average feu-duty was about £4 an acre, half of which was commuted by capital payment. Not a single feuar failed, although there were a good many changes amongst the tenants who rented the unfeued ground. Market gardening and the letting of the cottages as summer quarters no doubt aided the experiment, but it demonstrated the superiority of feuing over leasing.

A further experiment may be mentioned. When drainage was introduced into the burgh the disposal of the sewage became a serious question. It was happily solved by establishing a sewage-irrigation farm on a piece of waste land on the east side of the harbour. The land was worked by three shifts, and gave in ordinary seasons five crops of ryegrass each year, leaving a substantial surplus of profit.

The meteorological statistics show that the climate of Nairn is singularly dry and temperate. The average rainfall is about 20 inches, as recorded at the station of the London Meteorological Society at Delnies, 82 feet above mean sea-level. A rain-gauge kept at Budgate of Cawdor (about 200 feet above sea-level) gives a slightly higher rainfall. The observations for the lower district generally go to prove that the rainfall in Nairn is the smallest in Scotland. This is due in a large measure to the peculiar position of the district, occupying the centre of a semi-circle formed by the neighbouring hills. The heavy rain-clouds follow the hill ranges, leaving the plain dry or but slightly watered. The mean annual temperature is 45·86°. The prevailing winds are southerly and westerly, except during the months of March, April, and part of May, when they are northerly and easterly. The east wind brings the heaviest rainfall, and a north-east gale is the most severely felt. The healthiness of the district is established by the vital statistics and the official reports of the Medical Officer, which show that diseases of a zymotic type are infrequent. A convalescent home for the northern counties has been built at Tradespark, near Nairn, and is maintained by voluntary contributions. The town and county maintain a general hospital at Nairn, which has proved a most useful institution. Gifted to the community by the late Mr. Alexander Mann, Guayaquil, a worthy son of Nairn, the buildings were opened for occupation by the late Earl Cawdor, First Lord of the Admiralty, in August, 1906. The hospital is supported almost entirely by voluntary effort. An up-to-date installation of X-ray apparatus and an electric lighting system are about to be introduced which will make the hospital one of the best equipped voluntary hospitals of its size in Scotland. Cases of infectious disease are at present treated in the old hospital at Lodgehill Road, but a proposal for the erection of a more com-‑ modious building is engaging the attention of the authorities.

Smuggling was exceedingly common throughout the upland district previous to the erection of the Brackla Distillery, and the illicit trade was carried on with little concealment. The occa- sional prosecutions had no effect. One of the last cases tried at Nairn came before the Justice of Peace Court, when two of the justices on the bench privately admitted that they regularly sold their barley to the smuggler, and were in the custom of giving him orders for illicit spirits. To obviate the scandal of punishing men they were privately encouraging to break the law, they became promoters of the new distillery. It is a circumstance of some interest that in the county of Nairn (excluding the burgh) there is not, and has not been for some forty years, a single place licensed for the sale of spirits. Formerly there were half-a-dozen. One hostelry still exists, but is restricted to a wine-and-beer licence.

Banking facilities at Nairn were unknown till the year 1829, when the National Bank of Scotland established a branch there under Æneas Grant. Previous to this, someone rather better off than his neighbours used to give small loans to his friends, whilst in some cases the laird or the factor took charge of the savings of the tenants and allowed them interest. Rents were at first wholly and afterwards partly paid in kind, the grain being stored in granaries and the cattle gathered together when the droves were made up for the south. In the year 1783 an inventory of the estate of Alexander Fraser of Little Aitnoch is recorded in the

Sheriff Court books in favour of his eldest son, Simon, which exhibits an elaborate system of loans in the form of bills drawn for various sums and for different periods. Over a hundred and sixty of these bill transactions are included as assets. Private banking, however, gave way before the facilities of the ordinary banks. Mr. Grant was succeeded in the National Bank by the late J. D. Lamb. The British Linen Company's Bank established a branch under Adam Davidson in 1836, and the Caledonian Bank followed in 1838. These three banks occupied the field till 1879, when the Royal Bank established an agency. The North of Scotland Bank opened a branch in 1898. No change has taken place since then, except that in 1907 the Caledonian Bank was merged in the Bank of Scotland.

The Boundary Commission of 1891 have, as regards the area of rating for County Council purposes, lopped off all the detached portions of Nairnshire, and at the western end for the same purpose the boundary has been altered considerably, to the disadvantage of Nairnshire. The Nairn County Council agreed to the line originally drawn by the commissioners, but Inverness-shire appealed against it, and prevailed. For parliamentary purposes, however, the boundaries remain unaltered. The total area of Nairnshire is, in round figures, 200 square miles. From the town of Nairn at the north to Cairn Glass at the south is 17½ miles, and the mean breadth from east to west is about 11 miles. The total acreage is 125,918, of which about 25,000 acres are under crop or grass, 13,000 under wood, and 2000 under permanent pasture. The remainder is classed as waste, heath, or moorland. Nairnshire ranks amongst the counties of Scotland as the thirtieth in area, thirty-second in population, and thirty-third in valuation. In 1781 the real rent for the whole county was given at £8000 ; in 1811 the gross rental was stated at £11,726 ; in 1815 the annual value of the assessed property was £12,324 ; the valuation given in the Lands Valuation Roll for 1892-93 was £37,160 ; and the valuation for 1926-27, including the railway, was £41,581.

CHAPTER XXIII

LATER YEARS

Since the first edition of the " History of Nairnshire " appeared in 1893 great changes have taken place, and the country has lived through the most tremendous conflict the world has ever seen. Men and institutions have been put to the test as they never had been before, and, if Nairnshire has not come unscathed through the ordeal, it can still hold its head high, for its wounds are all honourable wounds, and its sons, may of whom sleep their last sleep on our far-flung battlefields, proved themselves everywhere without fear and without reproach.

One change that has been gradual, but not the less far-reaching, is the extraordinary revival in road transport by reason of the development of the motor car. Thousands of people every year, who might never have made their way so far into the north, now travel through the county, visiting its places of interest, and spending a holiday, long or short, in the town of Nairn. Where one or two horse-drawn vehicles per hour might formerly be seen upon a stretch of road, one may now count a dozen motor cars, half of them carrying visitors from far afield. To this cause may be attributed not a little of the increased popularity of the town of Nairn as a summer resort during the last thirty years.

Another maker of that popularity has undoubtedly been the development and excellence of the golf links which lie along the coast of the Moray Firth within half a mile of Nairn. Much of the amenity of these links has been owed to the public spirit of neighbouring lairds, like Earl Cawdor, Viscount Finlay of Nairn, and Colonel Clarke of Achareidh, whose example has also helped to make them a favourite resort of people of influence and fashion.

476

The course itself is one of the finest in the country. The greens have the reputation of being fast and difficult, and special interest and variety characterise nearly every hole. During the early years of the new century the constantly growing vogue of the golf links brought about a considerable extension of Nairn, through the building of many new houses of the better class, and several new fashionable hotels, between the western end of the town and the sea. The great European conflict of 1914-1918 stopped development for a time, but whenever the country fully recovers from the shock and impoverishment of the Great War, that development is certain to be resumed.

Still another attraction was added to Nairn when the Town Council, on behalf of the inhabitants, in 1923 acquired the fishings in the Nairn from the harbour to Howford Bridge. An Angling Association was formed, which rents the stretch of water from the Council, protects it against unfair fishing, and issues permits to anglers.

The outstanding event of these years, however, beside which everything else sinks to insignificance, alike for Nairn and for the whole country, has been the cataclysm brought about by Germany's ambition to dominate the world. Nairnshire, as may be seen in the pages of this History, has always looked to the army as a career for its sons. When the Great War, therefore, broke out in August 1914, most of the county families had members who were immediately engaged at the battle front. The rest of the young men at once came forward gallantly, and in a few months well-nigh every household, from castle to cottage, had one or more brave lads somewhere in the fighting line. Of these a heavy proportion never came back, and more than one family saw its fairest hopes perish, and its line come to an end, with the fall of its sons. When the war at last was over, and the Nairnshire War Memorial, in the form of a Pillar of Victory, was unveiled in the county town by Brodie of Brodie, D.S.O., M.C., there were inscribed on it two hundred and eighty-nine names of the fallen of all ranks and from all the parishes. These included members of the houses of Cawdor and Brodie, Lethen and Loch-loy, sons, sometimes two or three of the same family, from the mansions of Nairn, lads from offices and banks, skippers and sea-men from the fishing fleet, ploughmen from the farm lands, and artisans and shopmen from town and village. Every class and calling was represented on the roll of honoured dead.

At the unveiling of the Memorial on Sunday, 15th January, 1922, there was an extremely fine turn-out of Nairnshire officers and men who had served in the war, and a special place in the area fronting the monument was occupied by the relatives of the fallen. Nairn, town and county, had good reason to feel that it had played its part effectively in the greatest conflict of all time.

The names of the fallen inscribed on the War Memorial will be found in Appendix II.

A very notable occasion in the more recent history of the county was the visit paid to the town of Nairn by the Prince of Wales on Wednesday, 22nd August, 1923. Royalty had paid no official visit to the town since the Duke of Cumberland passed through on his way to the battle of Culloden in 1746. The chief purpose of the coming of His Royal Highness was to help the project of the Nairn branch of the Seaforth Highlanders' Association for setting up a club in the town, for the benefit of local ex-Seaforths and men from the Depot, Fort George, who make their way there in considerable numbers. Nairn was *en fête* on the occasion, and the Prince, after inspecting the War Memorial, graciously per-formed the ceremony of opening a bazaar organised to raise funds for the club. Needless to say, the enterprise was entirely successful, and the Seaforth Highlanders' Club is now an established institution in Nairn.

Two other events may be recorded here, which were thought at the time to presage possible future developments to the town. On 8th August, 1913, Captain Dawes, flying from Montrose, made the first aeroplane landing at Nairn, and in February, 1916, after the extinction of shipbuilding in the place for half a century, the first steam drifter built at Nairn harbour was launched by Mr. George Walker, boat-builder. Neither of the hoped-for develop-ments, however, has yet materialized. Shipbuilding at Nairn has since comprised only small fishing yawls; and the town has not yet had its means of access increased by any service of air liners.

APPENDIX I

LIST OF PROVOSTS OF NAIRN

1450—JOHN ROSE of Broadley.
    —DAVID ROSE of Broadley.
    —JOHN ROSE of Broadley.
    —PATRICK ROSE of Broadley.
1620—WILLIAM ROSE of Clava.
1657—HUGH ROSE of Clava.
1658—JOHN ROSE, yr. of Broadley.
1659—JOHN ROSE, elder, of Broadley.
1660 HUGH ROSE of Clava.
1661—JOHN ROSE, yr. of Broadley.
1662—HUGH ROSE, yr. of Clava.
1663—JOHN ROSE of Broadley.
1664—WILLIAM ROSE, brother germane to John Rose of Broadley.
1665—WILLIAM ROSE, re-elected.
1666—JOHN ROSE of Broadley.
1667—HUGH ROSE of Clava.
1668—JOHN ROSE of Broadley.
1669—JOHN ROSE, re-elected.
1670—HUGH ROSE of Clava.
1671—WILLIAM ROSE of Newton.
1672—HUGH ROSE of Clava.
1683—ALEX. ROSE of Clava.
1695—   Do   do.
    —HUGH ROSE of Clava.
1712—HUGH ROSE, younger of Kilravock.
1721—HUGH ROSE, elder of Kilravock.
1723—HUGH ROSE, younger of Kilravock.
1725—HUGH ROSE of Clava.
1729—Colonel ALEXANDER ROSE.
1733—HUGH ROSE of Geddes (styled Lord Provost).
1734—Colonel ALEXANDER ROSE.
1737—HUGH ROSE of Clava.
1740—LEWIS ROSE of Coulmony.

1743—HUGH ROSE of Kilravock.
1746—LEWIS ROSE of Coulmony.
1748—HUGH ROSE of Kilravock.
1751—HUGH ROSE of Geddes.
1754—HUGH ROSE of Kilravock.
1757—LEWIS ROSE of Coulmony.
1759—HUGH ROSE of Kilravock.
1761—HUGH ROSE of Geddes.
1765—Major JAMES CLEPHANE.
1768—HUGH ROSE of Geddes.
1773—Capt. JOHN ROSE of Brea.
1775—LEWIS ROSE of Coulmony.
1777—HUGH ROSE of Kilravock.
1782—Sir HECTOR MUNRO of Novar.
1785—HENRY MACKENZIE, Author of the " Man of Feeling.'
1788—LEWIS GRANT, yr. of Coulmony.
1791—JAMES GRANT of Corriemony.
1794—Major JOHN GRANT of Auchindoune.
1797—ALEX. PENROSE CUMMING-GORDON of Altyre.
1800—Sir ARCHIBALD DUNBAR of Northfield.
1803—ALEX. PENROSE CUMMING-GORDON.
1804—Sir ALEX. PENROSE CUMMING-GORDON.
1806—Sir ARCHIBALD DUNBAR of Northfield.
1809—Sir WILLIAM GORDON-CUMMING, Bart. of Altyre and Gordonston.
1812—Sir ARCHIBALD DUNBAR of Northfield.
1815—CHARLES LENOX-CUMMING of Roseisle.
1817—Sir ARCHIBALD DUNBAR of Northfield.
1818—Sir WILLIAM GORDON GORDON-CUMMING.
1821—C. L. CUMMING BRUCE of Roseisle.
1822—Sir WILLIAM GORDON GORDON-CUMMING.
1825—C. L. CUMMING BRUCE.
1828—Sir WILLIAM GORDON GORDON-CUMMING.
1831—C. L. CUMMING BRUCE.
1832—WILLIAM ROBERTSON of Househill.
1833—ISAAC KETCHEN.
1836—Dr. JOHN SMITH.
1838—ROBERT FALCONER, Surgeon.
1839—JOHN WILSON.
1854—Colonel ALEXANDER FINDLAY.
1860—Dr. JOHN GRIGOR.
1861—Capt. RODERICK MACKENZIE, I.N.
1862—Colonel FINDLAY.
1866—ALEXANDER MANN.
1869—C. B. MACKINTOSH.
1872—WILLIAM LESLIE.
1887—HUGH MACKINTOSH.

1890—Dr. H. W. MANN.
1892—ALEXANDER GORDON.
1896—HARRY TULLOH DONALDSON.
1898—WILLIAM DALLAS.
1905—ALEXANDER MACKINTOSH.
1911—KENNETH MACRAE.
1924—JOHN FLETCHER.

APPENDIX II

PARISH OF ARDCLACH.

Name and Rank.	Unit.
Capt. Ewen James Brodie of Lethen -	1st Cameron Hrs.
Lieut. James Macdonald, M.C. -	72nd Canadian Battalion.
Lnc.-Cpl. James Anderson - -	6th Cameron Hrs.
Lnc.-Cpl. Alexander McQuibban -	7th Cameron Hrs.
Lnc.-Corpl. William F. Main - -	1st Cameron Hrs.
Pte. John Black - - - -	1st Seaforth Hrs.
Pte. Alexander Clark - - -	6th Cameron Hrs.
Pte. Peter Clark - - - -	Royal Fusiliers.
Gunner Hugh Mackintosh Forbes -	Australian Machine Gun Corps.
Pte. Donald Mackenzie - - -	7th Cameron Hrs.
Pte. Alexander McRonald - -	5th Cameron Hrs.
Gunner Norman McLee - - -	Royal Garrison Artillery.
Pte. Alexander Martin - - -	1st Seaforth Hrs.
Pte. Fred Masson - - - -	2nd Gordon Hrs.
Trimmer William B. Mitchell -	Royal Naval Reserve.
Pte. Alexander Moir - - -	1/4 Cameron Hrs.
Pte. John Stephen - - - -	4th Cameron Hrs.

PARISH OF AULDEARN.

Captain Ian Henry Baillie - -	4th Cameron Hrs.
Captain Douglas E. Brodie - -	1st Cameron Hrs.
Srgt.-Mjr. Hugh Mackenzie, M.M. -	8th Canadians.
Sergt. Gilbert Falconer - -	4th Cameron Hrs.
Sergt. Alexander Ross - - -	8th Canadians.
Sergt. James Bonallo Smith - -	4th Cameron Hrs.
Corpl. John Duff - - - -	4th Cameron Hrs.
Corpl. Alexander Fraser - -	Seaforth Hrs.
Corpl. Daniel Fraser - - -	4th Cameron Hrs.
Corpl. Ian MacGregor - - -	Motor Machine Gun Service.

PARISH OF AULDEARN—*contd.*

NAME AND RANK.	UNIT.
Corpl. ALEXANDER MACKENZIE -	4th Cameron Hrs.
Lnc.-Corpl. DONALD MACKENZIE	4th Cameron Hrs.
Lnc.-Corpl. WILLIAM SHAW -	2nd Seaforth Hrs.
Lnc.-Corpl. JAMES R. SINCLAIR -	1st Seaforth Hrs.
Lnc.-Corpl. JAMES STRONACH -	4th Cameron Hrs.
Lnc.-Corpl. JAMES TULLOCH -	1st Seaforth Hrs.
Lnc.-Corpl. JOHN TULLOCH -	Seaforth Hrs.
Pte. JOHN JAMES ANDERSON -	4th Cameron Hrs.
Pte. ADAM CAMERON -	4th Cameron Hrs.
Pte. DONALD CAMERON -	2nd Seaforth Hrs.
Pte. JAMES KYD CAMERON -	7th Seaforth Hrs.
Pte. ALEXANDER CAMPBELL -	1st Scots Guards.
Pte. WILLIAM FRASER -	4th Cameron Hrs.
Pte. PETER FRASER -	4th Cameron Hrs.
Pte. JOHN GRANT -	5th Cameron Hrs.
Trooper JOHN MACGREGOR GRANT -	Lovat Scouts.
Pte. HAROLD ILES -	2nd Seaforth Hrs.
Pte. GEORGE JAMES -	4th Cameron Hrs.
Pte. MALCOLM LAMONT -	4th Cameron Hrs.
Pte. WILLIAM MACBEAN -	Seaforth Hrs.
Pte. JAMES MACBEAN -	Canadians.
Pte. ALEXANDER MACDONALD -	Seaforth Hrs.
Pte. DONALD MacDOUGALL -	1/7 Gordon Hrs.
Pte. PETER MACDOUGALL -	85th Canadians.
Pte. WILLIAM MACKENZIE -	Seaforth Hrs.
Pte. ROGER MACKENZIE -	Seaforth Hrs.
Pte. ROBERT MACKINTOSH -	6th Seaforth Hrs.
Pte. THOMAS MACQUEEN -	2nd Seaforth Hrs.
Pte. ALEXANDER MACRAE -	Seaforth Hrs.
Pte. ALEXANDER MARTIN -	Seaforth Hrs.
Pte. EDWIN MASSON -	Royal Engineers.
Pte. ROBERT MASSON -	Canadians.
Pte. JAMES C. NICHOLSON -	4th Cameron Hrs.
Pte. JOHN SELLAR -	South Africans.
Pte. DUNCAN SMITH -	4th Cameron Hrs.
Pte. JAMES SMITH -	4th Cameron Hrs.
Pte. JOHN STEPHEN -	6th Seaforth Hrs.
Pte. DONALD SUTHERLAND -	4th Cameron Hrs.
Pte. DUNCAN THOMSON -	Seaforth Hrs.
Pte. ALEXANDER TULLOCH -	Seaforth Hrs.
Pte. WILLIAM TULLOCH -	Seaforth Hrs.
Pte. ALEXANDER J. WATSON -	9th Gordon Hrs.

PARISH OF CAWDOR.

NAME AND RANK.	UNIT.
Lieut.-Col. The Hon. ERIC CAMPBELL, D.S.O.	Seaforth Hrs.
Capt. CHARLES C. K. CAMPBELL -	Cameron Hrs.
Sergt.-Major JAMES BRUCE, D.C.M. -	Gordon Hrs.
Sergt. JOHN MACPHERSON - - -	Australians.
Corpl. ALEXANDER FRASER - -	Cameron Hrs.
Corpl. WILLIAM MACGREGOR - -	Cameron Hrs.
Corpl. ROBERT MACKENZIE - -	Machine Gun Corps.
Corpl. KENNETH ROSS - - -	Scots Guards.
Lnc.-Corpl. DUNCAN A. CLARK - -	Cameron Hrs.
Lnc.-Corpl. JOHN HOSSACK - -	4th Cameron Hrs.
Lnc.-Corpl. WILLIAM ROSS - -	Seaforth Hrs.
Lnc.-Corpl. KENNETH URQUHART -	4th Gordon Hrs.
Pte. ADAM CAMERON - - -	Cameron Hrs.
Pte. ROBERT S. CHAPMAN - - -	Black Watch.
Pte. JOHN C. DOUGLAS - - -	Cameron Hrs.
Pte. ALEXANDER FALCONER - -	Seaforth Hrs.
Pte. JOHN FRASER - - - -	Gordon Hrs.
Pte. ALEXANDER MACDONALD - -	Cameron Hrs.
Pte. JOHN MCINTOSH - - -	Cameron Hrs.
Pte. DUNCAN D. MCLEOD - -	Australians.
Pte. ANGUS MCRITCHIE - - -	Seaforth Hrs.
Gunner EBENEZER K. MORRISON -	Royal Garrison Artillery.
Pte. DAVID ROSS - - - -	Cameron Hrs.
Pte. SIMON ROSS - - - -	Seaforth Hrs.
Pte. DONALD RUSSELL - - -	Australians.
Pte. THOMAS RUSSELL - - -	Scots Guards.
Gunner PETER SHAW - - -	Canadian Field Artillery.
Pte. ARCHIBALD SMITH - - -	Cameron Hrs.
Pte. ANDREW VASS - - - -	1st Camerons.
Pte. JOHN WATSON - - - -	Royal Scots.

PARISH OF CROY.

Capt. H. E. POPE, M.C. (bar) - -	R.G.A.
Lieut. JAMES KENNEDY - - -	Cameron Hrs.
Sergt. JAMES ADAM - - - -	K.O.S.B.
Sergt. DAVID MACGREGOR - -	Scots Guards.
Sergt. RODERICK MCLENNAN -	Gordon Hrs.
Corpl. DONALD MATHIESON -	Cameron Hrs.
Lnc.-Corpl. JAMES MATHIESON -	Cameron Hrs.
Lnc.-Corpl. PETER MACDONALD -	Cameron Hrs.
Lnc.-Corpl. ALEXANDER WEBSTER -	Seaforth Hrs.

PARISH OF CROY—*contd.*

NAME AND RANK.	UNIT.
Lnc.-Corpl. ROBERT WEBSTER - -	Cameron Hrs.
Pte. PETER LOWE - - - -	Cameron Hrs.
Pte. Duncan McGILLIVRAY -	Cameron Hrs.
Pte. RODERICK McKECHNIE -	Seaforth Hrs.
Pte. ALEXANDER McKENZIE -	Seaforth Hrs.
Pte. JOHN McLEAN - - -	Cameron Hrs.
Pte. KENNETH McLEAN - -	Gordon Hrs.
Trooper DUNCAN McLENNAN -	Lovat Scouts.
Pte. JOHN A. McLENNAN - -	Cameron Hrs.
Pte. JOHN WILLIAM WALLACE -	Highland Light Infantry.

PARISH OF NAIRN

(Including Burgh of Nairn).

Sister ISOBEL MARION MACKINTOSH -	Royal Red Cross.
Commander FITZROY HALL -	Royal Navy.
Major JOHN MACLEAN MACANDREW -	Recruiting Officer.
Capt. KENNETH MACKAY, M.C. -	6th Gordon Hrs.
Capt. DONALD MACLEOD MACKENZIE -	H.M. Transport Service.
Lieut. JOHN BAIN - - -	Canadian Machine Gun Corps.
Lieut. MALCOLM GILBERT S. BLANE -	5th Cameron Hrs.
Lieut. IAN H. S. CLARKE - -	Indian Army, 57th Rifles.
Lieut. IAN CLARK - - -	Seaforth Hrs.
Lieut. PETER GORDON - -	King's Royal Rifles.
Lieut. J. E. K. HALL - -	South Wales Borderers.
Lieut. JAMES M. LAING - -	Machine Gun Corps.
Lieut. IAN MACLEAN MACANDREW -	1st Seaforth Hrs.
Lieut. JAMES L. MACKINTOSH -	Indian Army.
Lieut. ROBERT McLEAN - -	Royal Engineers.
Lieut. ALEX. DAVID MANN -	1/6 Seaforth Hrs.
Lieut. CHARLES B. ROBERTSON -	Royal Field Artillery.
Lieut. IAN S. ROBERTSON - -	7th Cameron Hrs.
Lieut. WILLIAM A. WHITELAW -	3rd A. & S. Hrs.
Lieut. ROBERT H. L. WHITELAW	Household Battalion.
Lieut. GEOFFREY L. WHITELAW	Household Battalion
Lieut. C. G. GORDON WILSON -	Scottish Rifles.
Skipper JOHN BARRON - -	Royal Naval Reserve.
Skipper WILLIAM DAVIDSON -	H.M.D. Greatheart.
Skipper JAMES McINTOSH -	M.M.R.
Skipper RODERICK RALPH, D.S.C. -	Royal Naval Reserve.
Q.-M.-Sergt. DONALD CAMPBELL -	Royal Field Artillery.
Q.-M.-Sergt. JAMES INNES (Mons Star)	1st Seaforth Hrs.

PARISH OF NAIRN—*contd.*

NAME AND RANK.	UNIT.
Q.-M.-Sergt. D. MATHIESON - -	Seaforth Hrs.
Sergt. COLIN BAIN - - - -	Seaforth Hrs.
Sergt. WILLIAM SMITH DOUGLAS -	Cameron Hrs.
Sergt. ALEXANDER JOHNSTON - -	1/4 Cameron Hrs.
Sergt. C. MACLEAN - - -	5th Seaforth Hrs.
Sergt. GEORGE SIMPSON MACRAE -	Black Watch.
Sergt. D. MAIR - - - -	4th Cameron Hrs.
Sergt. W. D. NOBLE - - -	1st Seaforth Hrs.
Sergt. JOHN PATIENCE - - -	Cameron Hrs.
Sergt. W. J. REID, D.C.M. - -	Scottish Rifles.
L.-Sergt. ROBERT MERCER MCARTHUR, D.C.M. - - - -	5th Royal Scots.
Corpl. JOHN BARRON - - -	245th S.B., R.G.A.
Corpl. A. M. BAILLIE - - -	Sherwood Foresters.
Petty-Officer WILLIAM MAIN DUGGIE	Royal Naval Reserve.
Corpl. DONALD FRASER - - -	Royal Defence Corps.
Corpl. CHARLES FRASER - - -	1st Royal Scots Fusiliers.
Corpl. DAVID JOHN FRASER - -	Cameron Hrs.
Corpl. JAMES GORDON - - -	1st Seaforth Hrs.
Corpl. RICHARD GRANT - - -	47th Canadians.
Corpl. DUNCAN MACGREGOR - -	6th Seaforth Hrs.
Corpl. JAMES MACGREGOR - -	1st Cameron Hrs.
Corpl. K. MCHATTIE - - -	2nd Cameron Hrs.
Corpl. J. MACKAY - - - -	2nd Seaforth Hrs.
Corpl. J. M'KECHNIE - - -	Canadians.
Corpl. THOMAS MACKENZIE - -	4th Cameron Hrs.
Corpl. ALEXANDER MACKINNON - -	1st Seaforth Hrs.
Corpl. JOHN MCNEIL - - -	1st Seaforth Hrs.
Corpl. H. MONTGOMERY - - -	1st Highland Light Infantry.
Corpl. RODERICK S. MUNRO - -	1st Seaforth Hrs.
Corpl. J. B. ROBERTSON - - -	Cameron Hrs.
Corpl. WILLIAM R. SHAW - - -	R.A.M.C.
Lnc.-Corpl. JAMES J. ALEXANDER -	4th Cameron Hrs.
Lnc.-Corpl. ROBERT INNES - -	Army Service Corps.
Lnc.-Corpl. WILLIAM MACBEAN -	1st Seaforth Hrs.
Lnc.-Corpl. ARCHIBALD C. MCDONALD	1/6 Seaforth Hrs.
Lnc.-Corpl. A. R. MACDONELL - -	Seaforth Hrs.
Lnc.-Corpl. JAMES MCINTOSH - -	7th Cameron Hrs.
Lnc.-Corpl. JOHN MCNEIL - -	1/4 Cameron Hrs.
Lnc.-Corpl. JAMES MACMILLAN -	Australians.
Lnc.-Corpl. DONALD C. MELVEN -	1/4 Cameron Hrs.
Lnc.-Corpl. ERNEST A. K. MILLER -	18th Canadian Infantry Brigade.
Lnc.-Corpl. PATRICK N. ROSE - -	3rd South African Infantry.

PARISH OF NAIRN—*contd.*

NAME AND RANK.	UNIT.
Lnc.-Corpl. WILLIAM ROSS	2nd Australians.
Lnc.-Corpl. A. SPENCE	Australians.
Lnc.-Corpl. HARRY A. STUART	Northumberland Fusiliers.
Engineman WILLIAM ALLAN	H.M.D. Greatheart.
Pte. A. ALLAN	Scots Fusiliers.
Seaman JOHN BARRON	Naval Transport Service.
Pte. HUGH BARRON	Army Service Corps.
Pte. JAMES BARRON	16th Canadian Scottish.
Pte. JAMES MAIN BOCHEL	Canadian Engineers.
Pte. J. CAMERON	Cameron Hrs.
Pte. WILLIAM DUNBAR CAMERON	Tyneside Scottish.
Pte. DONALD CAMPBELL	15th Royal Scots.
Pte. HUGH CAMPBELL	1st Life Guards.
Pte. JAMES CAMPBELL	43rd Canadians.
Pte. JAMES PETRIE CAMPBELL	1/6 Seaforth Hrs.
Pte. JOHN STUART CASSELS	94th Canadians.
Trooper A. CLARK	5th Dragoon Guards.
Pte. JOHN GRIGOR CLARK	New Zealanders.
Pte. STUART MACDONALD CLARK	New Zealanders.
Stoker JOHN CURRIE COPE	H.M.S. Cornwall.
Pte. JAMES DILLON	7th Seaforth Hrs.
Pte. WILLIAM DUFFUS	6th Seaforth Hrs.
Pte. DONALD DOUGLAS	1st Canadians.
Sen. Rigger WILLIAM MAIN DUGGIE	Royal Naval Reserve.
Seaman JOHN FINDLAY	Patrol Service.
Seaman ROBERT FINLAYSON	H.M.D. Greatheart.
Stoker J. FLETCHER	H.M.S. Indefatigable.
Pte. DAVID FORBES	Cameron Hrs.
Pte. A. J. FRASER	7th Cameron Hrs.
Pte. P. FRASER	2nd Seaforth Hrs.
Rifleman CHARLES D. FRASER	8th King's Royal Rifles.
Pte. W. J. MORGAN FRASER	2nd Seaforth Hrs.
Pte. ALEXANDER FRASER	7th Cameron Hrs.
Pte. ALEXANDER FRASER	7th Cameron Hrs.
Pte. PETER FRASER	29th Canadians.
Pte. PETER FRASER	1st Seaforth Hrs.
Pte. WILLIAM FRASER	Australians.
Pte. JOHN FORSYTH	1st Gordon Hrs.
Gunner NORMAN GILZEAN	R.H.A.
Seaman JAMES GRANT	Patrol Service.
Pte. JOHN C. GRANT	Highland Light Infantry.
Pte. W. GRANT	1st Seaforth Hrs.
Pte. JOHN GRANT	Cameron Hrs.

PARISH OF NAIRN—*contd.*

NAME AND RANK.	UNIT.
Pte. JAMES GRANT - - - -	Cameron Hrs.
Bandsman ROBERT GREEN -	Highland Light Infantry.
Driver JOHN HARROW - -	2/1 Battery Inverness R.H.A.
Pte. R. M. K. HEUGHAN - -	6th Gordon Hrs.
Seaman W. JAMIESON - -	Patrol Service.
Pte. JOHN W. LAMB - -	8th Canadians.
Pte. ROBERT T. V. LAPHAM -	5th Cameron Hrs.
Pte. ALEXANDER McBAIN - -	Machine Gun Corps.
Pte. PETER McBAIN - -	15th Royal Scots.
Pte. ALEXANDER McCULLOCH -	32nd Australians.
Pte. ALEXANDER MACDONALD -	5th Cameron Hrs.
Gunner W. H. MACDONALD -	3rd Siege Battery, R.G.A.
Pte. ARCHIBALD E. MACDONALD -	4th Canadian Vet. Section.
Pte. HARRY MACDONALD - -	2nd Cameron Hrs.
Pte. WILLIAM MACDONALD -	2nd Seaforth Hrs.
Pte. ANGUS MACGILLIVRAY -	3rd Seaforth Hrs.
Pte. JOHN McINTOSH - -	2nd Seaforth Hrs.
Pte. JAMES McINTYRE - -	Black Watch.
Pte. WILLIAM MACKAY - -	Cameron Hrs.
Pte. ALEXANDER MACKENZIE -	4th Cameron Hrs.
Pte. DUNCAN MACKENZIE - -	5th Seaforth Hrs.
Pte. JOHN MACKENZIE -	7th Seaforth Hrs.
Pte. JOHN ANGUS PAUL McKILLOP -	7th Cameron Hrs.
Pte. ALASTAIR MACKINTOSH -	2nd Seaforth Hrs.
Pte. ALEXANDER MACKINTOSH -	10th L.S. Battalion Cameron Hrs.
Pte. ALEXANDER MACKINTOSH -	Royal Scots.
Pte. JOHN MACKINTOSH - -	4th Cameron Hrs.
Pte. P. MACLACHLAN - -	Scottish Rifles.
Pte. JOHN MACLENNAN - -	Seaforth Hrs.
Pte. W. MACLENNAN - -	Canadians.
Pte. ALEXANDER McLEAN -	2nd Seaforth Hrs.
Pte. DONALD McLEAN - -	5th Black Watch.
Pte. ALEXANDER McNEIL -	7th Cameron Hrs.
Pte. MURDOCH McNEIL - -	2nd Seaforth Hrs.
Gunner A. MACRAE - -	Glamorgans.
Gunner D. BAIN MACRAE -	Warwicks.
Seaman Gunner DAVID MAIN -	H.M.T. Drumtochty.
Engineer ISAAC MAIN - -	Royal Naval Reserve.
Pte. D. MAIN - - - -	Highland Light Infantry.
Pte. THOMAS MARTIN - -	2nd Scottish Rifles.
Pte. JAMES MASSON - - -	1st Cameronians.
Second Hand JOHN M. MAIN -	H.M.T. Bradford.
Pte. HUGH W. MELVEN - -	15th Royal Scots.

PARISH OF NAIRN—*contd.*

NAME AND RANK.	UNIT.
Pte. Francis A. Millar - - -	1st Royal Scots Fusiliers.
Pte. James Fraser Mills - - -	Seaforth Hrs.
Pte. Donald Morgan - - -	6th Seaforth Hrs.
Pte. James S. Munro - - -	4th Cameron Hrs.
Pte. W. Nicholson - - - -	1st Seaforth Hrs.
Pte. D. Noble - - - -	2nd Seaforth Hrs.
Pte. Alexander Noble - - -	Canadians.
Pte. James Petrie - - - -	Seaforth Hrs.
Second Hand George Ralph - -	Patrol Service.
Signalman R. A. W. Rankine - -	H.M.S. Defence.
Pte. Alastair Reid - - - -	Scots Guards.
Pte. J. Reid - - - - -	Black Watch.
Pte. Alexander Riddell - - -	Canadians.
Pte. John Ross - - - -	Highland Light Infantry.
Pte. George Ross - - - -	5th Black Watch.
Pte. Gordon Ross - - - -	Seaforth Hrs.
Pte. John Ross - - - -	2nd Seaforth Hrs.
Trumpeter Thomas George Ross -	Inverness R.H.A.
Pte. William Ross - - - -	Canadians.
Pte. Alastair Scott - - -	7th Cameron Hrs.
Pte. Alexander Shaw - - -	7th Gordon Hrs.
Pte. J. Shearer - - - -	A. & S. Hrs.
Pte. David Christie Sinclair - -	6th Manchesters.
Pte. James Sim - - - -	4th Cameron Hrs.
Pte. T. Maclean Smith - - -	Motor Transport
Pte. Duncan Smith - - -	1/4 Cameron Hrs.
Pte. James Smith - - - -	Australians.
Pte. Albert Edward Stewart - -	Labour Battalion.
Seaman J. Storm - - - -	H.M.D. Greatheart.
Pte. John Urquhart - - -	15th Royal Scots.
Pte. C. Williamson - - -	Seaforth Hrs.

INDEX

491